As German as Kafka

IDENTITY AND SINGULARITY IN GERMAN
LITERATURE AROUND 1900 AND 2000

As German as Kafka

IDENTITY AND SINGULARITY IN GERMAN
LITERATURE AROUND 1900 AND 2000

Lene Rock

Leuven University Press

Published with the support of the
KU Leuven Fund for Fair Open Access

Published in 2019 by Leuven University Press / Presses Universitaires de Louvain / Universitaire Pers Leuven. Minderbroedersstraat 4, B-3000 Leuven (Belgium).

© Lene Rock, 2019

This book is published under a Creative Commons Attribution Non-Commercial Non-Derivative 4.0 Licence.

Further details about Creative Commons licenses are available at
http://creativecommons.org/licenses/
Attribution should include the following information:
Lene Rock, *As German as Kafka: Identity and Singularity in German Literature around 1900 and 2000.* Leuven, Leuven University Press. (CC BY-NC-ND 4.0)

ISBN 978 94 6270 178 6 (Paperback)
ISBN 978 94 6166 284 2 (ePDF)
ISBN 978 94 6166 285 9 (ePUB)
https://doi.org/10.11116/9789461662842
D/2019/1869/49
NUR: 617

Layout: Friedemann Vervoort
Cover design: Anton Lecock

CONTENTS

Acknowledgements	9
Introduction	11

Chapter 1
Constitutive outsiders — 31

1.1	Ambivalences of *Kultur* and *Aufklärung*	31
	Constructions of German identity	32
	Kultur versus *Zivilisation*	34
1.2	"Trapped by the image of a rejected self"—Jews in Germany, German Jews	38
	Emancipation and acculturation (1770–1880)	38
	Modern anti-Semitism and Jewish dissimilation (1880–1933)	41
	The ambivalence of assimilation	50
1.3	A reluctant country of immigration	52
	From emigration to immigration	52
	Kultur in the aftermath of non-policy: *MultiKulti—Leitkultur—*'Deutschland schafft sich ab'	54
1.4	Literature, identity, and singularity	63

Chapter 2
Aesthetes between identity and opposition 67

2.1 The authenticity paradox—Writing between identity and opposition 67

2.2 The aesthete's retreat: Arthur Schnitzler's *Fräulein Else* (1924) versus Navid Kermani's *Kurzmitteilung* (2007) 74
    The 'value' of cultural difference: Arthur Schnitzler and Navid Kermani 74
    A conflict of codes: 'aesthetics of opposition' versus 'aesthetics of identity' 79

2.3 The aesthete's awakening: Beer-Hofmann's *Der Tod Georgs* (1900) versus Zaimoglu's *Liebesbrand* (2008) 102
    Jewish aesthete and romantic rebel: Richard Beer-Hofmann and Feridun Zaimoglu 102
    Realitätsablehnung & experiences of finitude 109
    Aesthetics of becoming—The ambivalent rhetoric of blood 122

Conclusion 140

Chapter 3
City dwellers between difference and indifference 143

3.1 Images of the city: emancipatory visions and spatialized difference 143
    Berlin: image of an unsettled national identity 144
    Indifference to difference 146
    The city as a site of Jewish self-definition 148
    Urban stereotype and spatialized difference 149

3.2 The failure of exemplarity—'Figures of immanence':Ludwig Jacobowski's *Werther, der Jude* (1892) versus Terézia Mora's *Alle Tage* (2004) 151
    Exemplarity, identification, alienation 151
    'Figures of immanence': the atomic individual versus the *Leerstelle* 155
    Metropolitan milieus: 'the law of the proper' versus *Verletzbarkeit* 163

3.3 Disoriented city dwellers—Figures of 'distanced proximity': Franz Hessel's *Spazieren in Berlin* (1929) versus Emine Sevgi Özdamar's "Der Hof im Spiegel" (2001) 170
    Reading the city 171
    Disoriented/dis-Oriented city dwellers 180

Conclusion 197

Chapter 4
Family heroes between myth and storytelling — 199

   4.1 Writing in the shadow of an empire — 199

   4.2 Family heroes redefined: Joseph Roth's *Radetzkymarsch* (1932) versus Dimitré Dinev's *Engelszungen* (2003) — 208
        Storytellers between empires and nations: Joseph Roth and Dimitré Dinev — 208
        "Listening to the same story"—Heroic grandfathers and the power of fiction — 212
        "Against the confines of the image"—Un-/antiheroic grandsons and the power of storytelling — 234

   4.3 "Diaspora's children"—Heroics of endurance and hope: Joseph Roth's *Hiob* (1930) versus Zsuzsa Bánk's *Der Schwimmer* (2002) — 251
        Between East and West—Between pathos and hope: Joseph Roth and Zsuzsa Bánk — 251
        Communities of violence—Communities of silence — 257
        Allowing something to be said—Hope emerging from silence — 269

   Conclusion — 284

Conclusion
The fallibility of *Bildung* — 285

Notes — 289
    Introduction — 289
    Chapter 1: Constitutive outsiders — 294
    Chapter 2: Aesthetes between identity and opposition — 308
    Chapter 3. City dwellers between difference and indifference — 321
    Chapter 4. Family heroes between myth and storytelling — 330
    Conclusion: The fallibility of *Bildung* — 343

Bibliography — 345

ACKNOWLEDGEMENTS

This study would never have made its way out of the labyrinth without the indispensable support from a great many individuals. My sincere gratitude goes out to Anke Gilleir, for her meticulous readings, her unwavering confidence, her intellectual generosity, and for arousing my interest in this highly relevant topic; to Vivian Liska, for reminding me of the potential dangers in historical comparison; to Bart Philipsen, for encouraging me to explore the writings of Jean-Luc Nancy. I also wish to thank the Research Foundation Flanders for allowing me to conduct my research in a comfortable manner; Leuven University Press, KU Leuven Libraries, and the KU Leuven Fund for Fair Open Access for the realization of this publication. And finally, I would like to thank my office mates Benedicte and Debbie; my friends Hanne and Isa; my parents-in-law, my *Geschwister*, my parents, and most of all Bert, Noor, and Tess.

INTRODUCTION[1]

"What is Enlightenment at the beginning of the 21st century? [Was ist Aufklärung am Beginn des 21. Jahrhunderts?]"[2] In his plea for a Europe beyond the national paradigm, the German sociologist Ulrich Beck argues that an embrace of Enlightenment values is more urgent than ever. Europe, he argues, suffers from a paradox: "Whoever thinks of Europe as a large nation [...] awakens the national primal fears of Europeans: either Europe or the European nations—a third option is simply impossible [Wer Europa als Großnation denkt [...] weckt die nationalen Urängste der Europäer: entweder Europa, oder die europäischen Nationen—ein Drittes ist ausgeschlossen]." Yet in order to allay the fears of member states, "that with their approval of the European Constitution they commit cultural suicide [dass sie mit ihrer Zustimmung zur Europäischen Verfassung kulturellen Selbstmord begehen]," they must step outside of a national concept of Europe, and rethink it from a cosmopolitan perspective—"a Europe of differences, of acknowledged national particularities [das Europa der Differenz, der anerkannten nationalen Partikularitäten]."[3] Beck rephrases Kant's *sapere aude* in terms of the courage to acknowledge religious, cultural, and national pluralism and to strive for equality despite those differences:

> Have the courage to engage your 'cosmopolitan view', i.e. to profess your multiple identities: to connect the lifestyles born of language, skin color, nationality, or religion with the awareness that in the radical precariousness of the world everyone is equal and everyone is different.
>
> [Habe den Mut, dich deines 'kosmopolitischen Blickes' zu bedienen, das heißt, dich zu deinen vielfältigen Identitäten zu bekennen: die aus Sprache, Hautfarbe, Nationalität oder Religion erwachsenen Lebensformen mit dem Bewusstsein zu verbinden, dass in der radikalen Unsicherheit der Welt alle gleich sind und jeder anders ist.][4]

Beck revisits the Enlightened foundations of the European project in a context of radical global insecurity. At the onset of the twenty-first century the effects of decades-long globalization processes and migration waves are evident in the increasingly diversified ethnic, cultural, and religious makeup of Western societies. Yet the apparent triumph of 'the global' over 'the local' is only one aspect of that *Unsicherheit*. Europe today bears the traces of a fundamental tension of modernity: alongside globalizing tendencies and transnational cultural processes, it has also witnessed the resurgence of nationalism and particularism. In the light of European ideological history, this is a "remarkable reversal, a most unexpected turn of events," according to Stuart Hall.[5] Both the liberal and the Marxist paths of modernization "implied that the attachment to the local and the particular would gradually give way to more universalistic and cosmopolitan or international values and identities; that nationalism and ethnicity were archaic forms of attachment—the sorts of thing that would be 'melted' away by the revolutionizing force of modernity."[6] Instead, "the intensification of worldwide relations," which affect "distant localities in such a way that local happenings are shaped by events occurring many miles away and vice versa,"[7] seems to go hand in hand with its opposite: the insistence on the local and the particular.

That tension is especially evident in Germany, a country that—unlike Britain or France—has a very limited colonial history, and struggles to this day with its status as a country of immigration, even if it houses a 'minority' of 17 million people with migration backgrounds.[8] The presence of that minority of millions is—in part—the long-term effect of an economic globalization process initiated with foreign recruitment agreements between the 1950s and the 1970s. Since then, and with renewed intensity after the 9/11 attacks, the visibility of religious and cultural difference in German society has been the topic of heated debate. Any debate about the 'Other' is indirectly a demarcation of one's own identity. Indeed, the intensity of the *Leitkultur* debate (2000/2001) illustrates how Germany struggles to define itself as an inclusive *Einwanderungsland* and instead continues to adhere to national concepts of culture and identity, as the more recent successes of *Alternative für Deutschland* confirm. In other words, Germany, like Europe, is affected deeply by that modern tension between the global and the local, the universal and the particular.

How, then, does *Aufklärung* fit the German context? Over the last couple of years, the debate on immigration and integration has been fueled by a perhaps familiar but in fact oversimplifying distinction between defenders of Western civilization and the perceived opponents of its secular, Enlightened foundations. The debate recently flared to new heights as thousands of people marched the streets of Dresden, protesting the 'Islamisierung des Abendlandes'. Yet although the current debate feels urgent and unique, it is not entirely without historical precedent. Both at the beginning and at the end of the twentieth century, Germany witnessed polarizing discourses on identity, culture, and nationhood. In these debates, two groups of people were increasingly considered as outsiders of 'the' German nation: at the beginning of the twentieth century they were Jews; at the end of the twentieth century they were immigrants. There needs to be no argument about the differences between both historical periods. Jews have had a longer presence on German 'soil' than many so-called authentic Germans. And there is the caesura of the Shoah, the irredeemable cut through the history of civilization that is often banalized in discussions about exclusion. Yet these crucial differences should not obscure the long history of Jews in Germany before the *Shoah*, nor the valuable insights that their history may offer.

The social position of German Jews, among whom many strongly identified with the Enlightenment project, puts the frequent references to *Aufklärung* today in an interesting historical perspective. German Jews around 1900 and new German citizens around 2000 found themselves in comparable paradoxical positions. Despite the emphasis on their perceived cultural or racial incompatibility, heightened by increasingly explicit anti-Semitic or xenophobic sentiment, the society German Jews and 'new' Germans live in continues to insist on adaptation, assimilation, and integration. This paradox reveals a more fundamental contradiction at the heart of the German integration debate. The apparent conflict between *Aufklärung* and its opponents seems to cover a tendency to functionalize Enlightened values in the promotion of an exclusive German identity. The belief in an inclusive society of equals that informs assimilation and integration processes then hits a wall: outsiders are promised access, but when they obtain the key, the locks appear to have been changed.

This investigation compares literary endeavors by German Jews and by 'new' Germans who find themselves caught in that social paradox, in which, despite the broken promise of inclusion and the insistence on differences, assimilation and integration continue to be required by host societies. At both ends of the twentieth century, authors and artists were and are sensitive to various questions of cultural identity—of normativity, coercion, exclusion, assimilation, or hybridity—many of which have been disclosed and digested in a fascinating diversity of artistic modes. While history has proven that art and literature are vulnerable to ideological cooptation, to instrumentalization in identity formation or national(istic) programs, many literary texts can be regarded to function as a particular kind of "social imaginary" as well. As a highly subtle form of art it communicates the ways "people imagine their social existence, how they fit together with others, […] the expectations that are normally met, and the deeper normative notions and images that underlie these expectations."[9] As such, it may add more nuance to the public debate. Whereas 'cultural identity' is often used as a static description of an individual's life, or of the experience of collectivities, many literary texts fathom and expose irritating and insolvable complexities that are missing from the debate and from its conviction of 'common sense'. Nevertheless, the literary endeavors of German Jews and new Germans are confronted with an *Identitätszwang* that deeply affects their self-perception as writers and their role as intellectuals. They are expected to account for, represent, mediate, or reject their perceived cultural difference through fiction, or to take a stand in political and social matters that involve their minority position. As a result, they are torn between the allure of artistic autonomy and the fear of losing social relevance as intellectuals. By comparing a selected number of literary texts, this study reveals comparable tensions manifesting themselves in the two periods and show some remarkable common patterns in the variegated responses to that imperative of identity. A range of issues related to the 'politics' of literature will be addressed. How does literature intervene in the debate on culture, identity, and difference? Does it subvert, question, or resist the assumptions that govern the discussion? Or does it withdraw from it altogether, taking position on a side stage instead? How does it resist the myth-making on which nations founded themselves? And, finally, can literature imagine a way out of the dead end that the Enlightened promise seems to have reached?

The title may have fooled the reader: this is not a study on Franz Kafka. It is, nevertheless, an investigation into the intricate connection between literature and identity that Kafka has come to represent—almost to the point of commonplace. The title refers to a quote by the Iranian-German writer and intellectual Navid Kermani. In an interview for the magazine *Literaturen,* four "not quite German writers [nicht ganz deutsche Autoren]"[10]—Kermani, Terézia Mora, Imran Ayata, and Wladimir Kaminer—are asked about the 'added value' of cultural difference to their writing. To the interviewer's suggestion that they are not "German authors […] in the sense of Goethe or Thomas Mann [deutsche Autoren […] im Sinne von Goethe oder Thomas Mann]," Kermani responds that he considers himself "German rather in the sense of Kafka [deutsch eher im Sinne von Kafka],"[11] even if he finds national designations irrelevant in a literary context. His Kafka reference at first seems to indicate a strong identification with the German literary canon, from which the interviewer apparently excludes him. Yet Kermani's response is also, especially, an ironic reminder of the cultural heterogeneity of that national canon. For Kafka was, of course, not a German. First, he was an Austrian living in the multiethnic, multilingual Austro-Hungarian conglomerate. After the triumph of nationalist differences in the First World War, he became a Czech who belonged to a German-speaking Jewish elite in Bohemia surrounded by strong Czech and (now minority) German nationalist sentiments. The designation 'German' thus hardly captures the linguistic, cultural, and national complexity that Kermani's Kafka reference evokes. Precisely that heterogeneity is the reason why his comparison makes sense—the historical analogy is not merely anecdotal. At both ends of the twentieth century German-Jewish writers and writers from non-German backgrounds were and are well aware of how the multiplicity of their national, cultural, or religious identities affects their writing and their reception as 'not quite German' writers.

This study investigates that historical analogy by comparative close reading of a selection of texts. The comparison demonstrates that in a context of intense identity discourses and perceived threat to 'German' values, many literary texts seem to re-enter into an implicit dialogue with the Enlightenment, a dialogue that does not involve a return to but a re-evaluation of its premise: *Bildung*—the humanistic ideal of self-cultivation—and the insistence on autonomy as the precondition of a society of equal individuals. The different literary texts reveal a wavering confidence in Enlightened individualism, while at the same time drawing contours of unexpected, tentative, and ephemeral forms of intimacy. The distinctly relational individuals engendered by fleeting forms of connection resist the embrace of collective identities. Instead, the texts imagine a variety of fragile senses of community in defiance of the monolithic rhetoric of otherness and incompatibility that characterizes the *communis opinio*.

The comparison builds a bridge between two productive fields of study that have remained largely unrelated: *interkulturelle Germanistik* and German-Jewish studies. German-Jewish studies focus on the relations between European Jewish communities and German-speaking society from a broad historical, social, and cultural perspective. Exemplary would be Arno Herzig's *Jüdische Geschichte in Deutschland. Von den Anfängen bis zur Gegenwart* (2002).[12] These investigations analyze, among other themes and periods, the *Haskalah*—the

Jewish Enlightenment of the eighteenth century—as do for example Shmuel Feiner and David Sorkin in *New Perspectives on the Haskalah* (2001);[13] the Jewish acculturation process, as investigated by Shulamit Volkov in *Das jüdische Projekt der Moderne* (2001);[14] the history of anti-Semitism and anti-Semitic rhetorics in the German public debate, which Marcel Stoetzler analyzes in *The State, the Nation, and the Jews* (2008);[15] and the Holocaust and postwar European history. The study of German-Jewish literature within that framework is rich and variegated. Its scope ranges from encyclopedic works on German-Jewish authors such as Sander Gilman's and Jack Zipes' *Yale Companion to Jewish Writing and Thought in German Culture* (1997) and Andreas B. Kilcher's *Metzler Lexikon der deutsch-jüdischen Literatur* (2000),[16] to studies of more specific cultural contexts such as Cultural Zionism, of which Mark Gelber's *Melancholy Pride: Nation, Race, and Gender in the German Literature of Cultural Zionism* (2000) is a revealing investigation,[17] to analyses from a gender perspective, like Barbara Hahn's *Die Jüdin Pallas Athene* (2002).[18]

Interkulturelle Germanistik deals with a far more limited historical period. It developed as a subfield of *Germanistik* only after the emergence of so-called guest workers' literature in the 1980s,[19] but it has widened its scope. A standard work is Carmine Chiellino's *Interkulturelle Literatur in Deutschland* (2000).[20] From an institutional point of view, *interkulturelle Germanistik* reveals conspicuous contrasts between the theoretical approaches of German Studies in the United States or Britain and of the *Germanistik* 'intra muros', where postcolonial theory and 'minority writing' have only recently started shifting away from the margins of literary study. In German studies, 'new' German literatures and theoretical concepts of the representation of cultural identity have been central research topics, as in for instance Leslie Adelson's *The Turkish Turn* (2005) and Tom Cheesman's *Cosmopolite Fictions* (2005).[21] In German studies, these 'new' literatures are also studied from a wider perspective that includes them in the whole of contemporary German literature, as in Lyn Marven's and Stuart Taberner's *Emerging German-Language Novelists of the Twenty-First Century* (2011)[22] and of gender studies, as illustrated by Brigid Haines' and Margaret Littler's *Contemporary Women's Writing in German: Changing the Subject* (2004).[23]

Despite their different foci, German-Jewish studies and *interkulturelle Germanistik* address issues of cultural identity in a German(-language) context. They engage with questions of cultural difference, adaptation, and exchange; they investigate mechanisms of subjection and exclusion, stereotype and prejudice; and they reflect on the power relations between so-called minority and majority groups. Yet a comparison between them has rarely been made.

A few recent contributions have already pointed out interesting parallels between German-Jewish writing around 1900 and contemporary 'literature of migration'. In *Beyond the Mother Tongue* (2012), Yasemin Yildiz investigates "the postmonolingual condition" and the impact of the "monolingual paradigm" from a historical perspective, focusing on the writings of Kafka, Emine Sevgi Özdamar, Yoko Tawada, and Feridun Zaimoglu.[24] Liesbeth Minnaard, in *New Germans, New Dutch* (2008), points out that a "trialogue" between Germans, Jews, and Turks—or other minorities—may be a valuable approach in debates on identity. The concept of triangulation may break away from the problematic and limiting situation in which, implicitly, "the position of all other minorities in Germany is measured and negotiated in relation to [the] German-Jewish trauma."[25] An approach that takes into account multiple relations—historically or comparatively—may "achieve a more differentiated reflection of (xenophobic, anti-Semitic or racist) structures of Othering and discrimination."[26] Minnaard demonstrates that such a comparative approach between Dutch and German minority literatures is fruitful. As I aim to illustrate, a *historical* comparison as well yields interesting parallels between writers from different periods who all acutely sensed and addressed the vexed issue of 'belonging'.

Any historical comparison warrants caution. A juxtaposition of German-Jewish literature and contemporary 'literature of migration' must remain aware of the implications of the comparative process itself. On a fundamental *historical* level, it should be noted that Nazism and the *Shoah* constitute a moment of incommensurability between German Jews and 'new German citizens'. The comparability of anti-Semitism and what is commonly referred to as 'islamophobia',[27] is, to say the least, up for debate. The anti-Semitic discourse that led to the Holocaust is deeply rooted in European and German history, and from that historical perspective bears only limited resemblance to the anti-Islamic sentiments that flared to new heights after the 9/11 attacks. The danger in commonplace analogies such as "Gestern die Juden, heute die Muslime"[28] resides in the abstraction—and potentially banalization—of very specific, different historical contexts. Therefore, the present selection of German-Jewish texts is limited to the period before 1933. Hitler's rise to power marks the moment when anti-Semitism becomes official state ideology, and any ground for comparison is lost. Even so, while it is difficult to blank out the course of history from our contemporary perspective on pre-war German-Jewish relations, it would be a loss—from both historical and literary perspectives—if that 'teleological awareness' made it impossible to look for parallels in a past that preceded the *Shoah*. The observation that, at both ends of the twentieth century, a considerable group of writers were confronted with a hostile climate and addressed issues of identity, exclusion, or community, should be food for thought.

From a *literary* perspective, it could be argued that "the comparison of the cultural expressions of different languages, nations, peoples in practice seems always constrained by an invisible binary bind in which comparison must end either by accentuating differences or by subsuming them under some overarching unity."[29] Armed with that awareness, the literary analyses in this study consistently take into account the historical contexts of individual texts. Although inspired by a comparable social paradox, the comparison will be executed primarily on a thematic level. The close readings are clustered around similar themes and motifs: the artist and the aesthete, the metropolitan experience, and (post-) imperial forms of (anti-) heroism. These clusters support an approach to coercive mechanisms of assimilation, compliance, stereotype, and collective identity, leading to an argument about the modern individual. In other words, the present investigation aims to acquire more insight into the 'politics' of literature against the background of historical and social realities.

A methodological concern involves the delineation of the object of study. When I refer to 'German-Jewish literature' or 'intercultural literature', I do so with reservation, in the awareness that the study of minority writing involves a typical and inevitable paradox. It brings down a corpus of texts to a common denominator—usually the author's Jewish or non-German origins. Yet even a brief glance at the field uncovers an aesthetic, thematic, and generic variety that defies such categorization. A strict biographical delineation reduces writers and their works to their 'ethnic' belonging. As such, it reproduces and reinforces the differences and power relations that these texts often seem to challenge. By designating a separate status to minority writers, their outsider position is once more confirmed in terms of their artistic endeavors.

That paradox has visibly affected the two fields of study. In an essay on the question "What is 'German-Jewish literature'? [Was ist 'deutsch-jüdische Literatur'?]," Andreas B. Kilcher remarks that, despite considerable critical interest in German-Jewish writing, 'German-Jewish literature' as a descriptive category for a long time lacked a clear conceptual, terminological, and methodological foundation.[30] He points out the problems associated with a strictly biographical delineation. It might seem like an unproblematic method at first—"In order to determine the corpus of this literature, therefore, there would be little more to do than to compile a corresponding list of authors and works. [Um das Korpus dieser Literatur zu bestimmen, bliebe folglich nicht mehr zu tun, als eine entsprechende Autoren- und Werkliste zu erstellen.]"[31] But the danger resides in the assumption that Jewish identity is objectifiable and visible as a literary feature, which potentially leads to the instrumentalization and disregard of aesthetic qualities.[32] The only 'fact' that can be determined and researched, according to Kilcher, is not an aspect of literature itself but the many variegated interpretations of and discourses about German-Jewish literature.[33] I am however convinced that it is also valuable to scrutinize individual texts, since close reading uncovers a far more variegated palette of meanings and interpretations than a strict focus on the ideological or poetological positions of authors.

The *interkulturelle Germanistik* has encountered a similar problem in defining its object of investigation, as reflected by ongoing terminological confusion.[34] Over the years, literature from 'non-ethnic' German writers has been designated as *Gastarbeiterliteratur*,[35] which emphasizes the social position of the authors; *Ausländerliteratur*,[36] which extends the scope beyond the realm of foreign workers; *Migrantenliteratur, Migrationsliteratur*,[37] 'literature of migration,'[38] and 'literature of settlement,'[39] which all reflect the authors' recent German residence. Having gained currency in the course of the 1990s, the term 'intercultural literature'[40] focuses on cultural exchanges within German society, acknowledging that, in a globalized, multiethnic, and multicultural society, cultural identities are not determined by a fixed set of features.

The evolving terminology at first seems to mirror a thematic transformation within this literature, which, broadly speaking, has exchanged its initially oppositional character for increasing aesthetic self-awareness. The changing terms, though, are also evidence of how this highly heterogeneous literature resists categorization, as well as challenges dominant concepts of identity and culture. Increasing awareness of how specific designations may reproduce power relations has contributed to a reluctance to fixate and determine the body of texts. This literature is now often received as a challenge to the concept of national identities

> as a form of writing after the dissolution of fixed national cultural concepts after the demise of the East/West power blocs, as a literature beyond the bourgeois concept with its background in nationalism and imperialism, as a literature that subverts the opposites of 'foreign' and 'own', native and foreign, as a literature of hybridity and patchwork identities [...]. In other words, a literature that permits the experience of the illusion of a homogeneous cultural identity as well as of non-bipolar and hierarchical encounters with the foreign, articulates the foreign, and undermines the fixation of the foreign.

[als Form des Schreibens nach der Auflösung von festen nationalen Kulturbegriffen nach dem Ende der ost/westlichen Machtblöcke, als Literatur jenseits eines bürgerlichen Literaturbegriffs mit seinem Hintergrund in Nationalismus und Imperialismus, als Literatur, die die Gegensätze von 'Fremd' und 'Eigen', Einheimischem und Fremdem unterläuft, als eine Literatur der Hybridität und der Patchwork-Identitäten [...]. Eine Literatur also, die zum einen die Illusion einer homogenen kulturellen Identität als auch nicht-bipolare und hierarchische Begegnungen mit dem Fremden erfahrbar macht, die Fremdheit artikuliert und die Festschreibung von Fremdheit unterläuft].[41]

However, that 'intercultural' focus—described above in terms of postcolonial hybridity *and* of a binary of *Eigen-* and *Fremdheit*—has yielded very different, even conflicting, interpretations. The study of 'literature of migration' has been the domain of two schools of thought.[42] The German-based *interkulturelle Germanistik* has adopted a predominantly hermeneutic paradigm that 'reads' interculturality as an exchange between German and non-German cultures, and is founded on "the central principle of 'understanding' the foreign, of insight into the foreign culture [die leitende Idee eines 'Verstehens' des Fremden, einer Einfühlung in die fremde Kultur]."[43] In anglophone German studies, this literature is usually approached from postcolonial perspectives, which chart the social and political power relations represented or subverted by literature. They reject the notion of clearly defined cultural entities—and thus any distinction between *eigen* and *fremd*. Instead, the latter school of thought "attend[s] to the unsettling of all identities [...], and indeed see[s] any attribution of identity as essentializing and exclusive."[44] The postcolonial perspective has gradually entered the scope of the German-based school,[45] even if there remains some skepticism towards its method and concepts. Volker C. Dörr characterizes the gradual evolution towards the Anglo-American model as follows—by his own admission "overly trenchantly [überpointiert]":

While in the 1980s it was still a question of how guest worker literature could assist its German reader in understanding a foreign culture from the (hierarchically higher) point of view of his own culture, and in doing so learn something about the foreign view of his 'own' culture— or possibly even *through* the foreign view *about* his own culture—today things are as complicated as they have ever been: The understanding that cultures are not self-contained homogeneous essences, 'not completely isolated and compartmentalized entities,' but rather that they are 'reciprocal interactions of different, even antagonistic cultures and subcultures' 'within' cultures, has become widely accepted.

[Ging es noch in den 1980er Jahren darum, wie Gastarbeiterliteratur ihrem deutschen Leser dabei helfen kann, eine fremde Kultur vom (hierarchisch höheren) Standpunkt seiner eigenen Kultur aus zu verstehen und dabei etwas über den fremden Blick auf seine 'eigene' Kultur zu erfahren—oder womöglich sogar *durch* den fremden Blick *über* seine eigene Kultur—, so gelten die Dinge heute als so kompliziert, wie sie wohl immer schon gewesen sind: Weitgehend durchgesetzt haben sich die Einsichten, dass Kulturen keine in sich abgeschlossenen homogenen Wesenheiten, "keine von einander völlig isolierten und sich abschottenden Gebilde sind," sondern dass es sich um ein "wechselseitiges Ineinanderwirken verschiedener, auch antagonistischer Kulturen und Teilkulturen" "in" den Kulturen handelt [...]].[46]

The skepticism of the *Inlandsgermanistik* towards concepts of 'hybridity' and 'third space'[47] is possibly related to the idea that a (post)colonial paradigm does not entirely fit the German situation since the 1980s—and not just because the story of labor migration is not a colonial relation *strictu senso*.[48] The reluctance can also be attributed to the fact that for a long time, Germany has not recognized its own status as a country of immigration—unlike for instance Canada and the United States, where the postcolonial approach has been long established as a valid method for describing minority writing.

Even though a postcolonial perspective has been embraced gradually by the *interkulturelle Germanistik*, Dörr formulates a crucial reservation about the way it has been applied, pointing out that the concept of hybridity itself may be vulnerable to re-essentialization. Homi K. Bhabha emphasizes that "the importance of hybridity is not to be able to trace two original moments from which the third space emerges," and that hybridity itself is "the 'third space' which enables other positions to emerge."[49] Hybridity is, in other words, not the mixed result of two pre-existing substances. However, the concept has often been applied that way, leading to an inadvertent but problematic sequence:

And so, implicitly, the idea returns that the source of the hybrid culture consists of two cultures as self-contained homogeneous entities. The notion of hybridity thus leads to (re-)essentializations. [...] It also leads to the re-essentialization of the hybrid third itself, for the hybrid is by no means always understood in a differential way [...]. The special thing about German-Turkish migrants, then, is not just that their culture is a mixture of 'the' German and 'the' Turkish; there is also 'the' hybrid migrant culture.

[[U]nausgesprochen kehrt dann die Vorstellung wieder, dasjenige, aus dem die eine hybride Kultur gemischt sei, seien eben doch zwei Kulturen als in sich abgeschlossene homogene Wesenheiten. Die Vorstellung der Hybridität verleitet also zu (Re-) Essentialisierungen. [...] Sie verleitet auch zur Re-Essentialisierung des hybriden Dritten selbst, denn keineswegs immer wird das Hybride dann differentiell verstanden [...]. Dann erscheint als das Besondere etwa der deutsch-türkischen Migranten nicht nur, dass ihre Kultur aus 'dem' Deutschen und 'dem' Türkischen gemischt ist; es gibt dann auch gleich 'die' hybride Migrantenkultur.][50]

The danger of re-essentializing hybridity may explain why, both in German-Jewish Studies and in research on intercultural literature, there have emerged tendencies to move away from descriptions of identity in reference to an implicit scale between 'Germanness' and 'non-Germanness'. My approach joins more recent attempts to study minority writing beyond cultural binaries. Both fields of study exhibit an increasing weariness with such binaries, since they unduly imply that one's very personal and subjective experience, one's self-definition, can be explained entirely in reference to a polarity of (non-) Germanness. In other words, such binaries do not do justice to the complexities of historical intercultural processes, and most certainly not to the variegated literary responses to them.

In the field of intercultural literature, particularly the "two-worlds paradigm"[51] has grown contested. In a series of articles, as well as in her seminal *The Turkish Turn*,[52] Leslie A. Adelson criticizes the trope for its implied reference to two delineated cultures—a concept that hinders the development of new insights and perspectives on literature: "'Between Two Worlds' is the place customarily reserved for these authors and their texts on the cultural maps of our time, but the trope of 'betweenness' often functions like a reservation designed to contain, restrain, and impede new knowledge, not enable it."[53] The popular descriptive metaphor of an existence 'on a bridge between two cultures' was voluntarily adopted by early migrant writers,[54] but its borrowing by literary critics has had a "regressive effect" on the reception of more complex explorations of identity formation.[55] The paradigm has become "a cultural fable" that "exerts the enormous gravitational pull of a black hole in spite of its historical obsolescence."[56] In other words, the insights and aesthetic complexity of this 'literature of migration' warrant more subtle approaches than a perhaps satisfying but imprecise metaphor can deliver.

In research on German-Jewish literature it is the contested notion of *assimilation* that has given way to alternative approaches. The term implies that, in the process of emancipation, German Jews gradually abandoned all aspects of their Jewish heritage in order to integrate into German society. But that one-sided evolution of a minority dissolving into 'mainstream' culture has long been revealed as an inadequate description.[57] Still, German-Jewish authors are often investigated in reference to their position on the ideological spectrum between dissimilation and assimilation. However, neither in the lived experience of German Jews, nor in their writings, do the two poles emerge as mutually exclusive. As for instance Jonathan Skolnik argues in the context of German-Jewish historical fiction,

> the Jewish embrace of German-language culture also took on forms which encompassed a different relation between 'Jewish past' and 'German fiction', one that makes necessary a different view of integration and acculturation. By imagining, indeed reinventing Jewish history through German-language historical novels, German Jews asserted their own unique identity as they integrated into larger narratives of German and European history. [...] Dissimilation is the crystallization of a new form of Jewish identity and distinctiveness that occurs as part of the dynamic of acculturation and alongside the phenomenon of assimilation.[58]

In the same vein, Scott Spector argues that, even if it allows nuance, the imagined spectrum between absolute Jewish identification at one end, and complete appropriation of German identity at the other, is inadequate and deceptive.[59] "The distinctions between 'spontaneous' and 'acquired' cultural character, accidental adaptation and essential adoption, or stable essence and assimilatory appearance are all themselves powerfully ideological instruments of segregation, rather than descriptors of a cultural condition."[60] Instead, Spector pleads for studying history and literature by shifting focus from assimilatory identity to subjective experiences—especially their inconsistencies and surprising contradictions. Vivian Liska addresses a similar issue in her investigation into "uncommon communities" in German-Jewish literature.[61] Her study resists the "widespread practice in cultural studies and political theory that invokes literary texts only to subsume them under pre-existing concepts and categories [...]." Instead, she sets out to illustrate "the complex, conflicting, and polyvalent, multi-interpretable relations to communities [...]."[62] Discussing instances of ambivalence toward collectivities and the Jewish community in particular, she investigates how the undecided position of German-Jewish authors, between insider and outsider, engenders unusual affiliations that challenge the conventional foundation of community on principles of sameness and identity.[63]

Taking into consideration the insights from both fields, this investigation charts instances of *inbetweenness* that do not emerge from a binary of identities. Rather, any inbetweenness on the part of the examined authors and texts can be attributed to a particular *literary* sensitivity, which enhances their reflection on issues of cultural identity. They are not primarily positioned 'in-between two cultures' but on a field of tensions between identity and opposition, between difference and indifference, between myth and storytelling. The selected texts—even if the selection is neither exhaustive nor entirely representative—reflect the variety of authors' biographies, ideological affiliations, and poetological views, as well as the stylistic, thematic, and generic responses to the imperative of identity in both periods. I argue that the selected literary works are not primarily stories of identity but, rather, of *singularity*. They evoke a gradual erosion of the Enlightened individual in the course of various assimilation processes. At the moment when assimilatory desire sees its Enlightened foundations crumbling, a vulnerable and relational individual emerges, as well as forms of connection that resist being claimed by any form of collective identity. As the present texts show, the way out of such expired individualism can be inspired by storytelling, by adopting and cultivating an aesthetic or hermeneutic distance towards reality. Indeed, many protagonists are performers, spectators, readers, and storytellers. From a metatextual perspective, then, they reflect the potential of the arts to imagine alternative forms of community, beyond the imperative to self-identify as 'German', 'Jewish', or anything 'in-between'.

The emergence of these tentative forms of community is reminiscent of the philosophy of Jean-Luc Nancy (1940–) and of his notion of 'being singular plural' in particular. Nancy, whose work is influenced by Heidegger, Bataille, and Derrida, has reconceptualized community in non-identitarian terms. One of the main questions in his writing is how—in the light of the violent implications of collective identity witnessed during the twentieth century—we can still think and speak of a plural 'we', without transforming it into an essential, substantial, and exclusive identity.[64] In *The Inoperative Community* (1991) and in *Being Singular Plural* (2000),[65] Nancy calls into question traditional and modern communitarian impulses, as well as the individualism supported by Enlightened modernity. Written against the backdrop of a disintegrating Soviet Union, of the violent culmination of ethnic particularism in the Balkan conflict, and of advancing neoliberalism, Nancy's seminal texts convey a pronounced sensitivity to the coercive, potentially destructive nature of hypostatized community, as well as to the instrumentalization of the subject in economic, political, or ideological narratives. Nancy criticizes the mythical "longing for an original community"[66] at the heart of Western political thought. He proposes an alternative notion of community, one that resists "any communion or fusion based on a unified, institutionalized, and exclusionary common ground, a sharply defined goal, and a clear conceptualization of itself."[67] Whereas commonly notions of community are predicated on exterior definition, or on a well-defined common purpose, Nancy proposes 'being-with' instead—a connection relying on shared exposure that does not heed the "communal desire for a closed and undivided social identity."[68] It implies the radical, mutual openness of singular beings, who as a result are in a constant state of change, and thus resist the static notion of community as a fusion of pre-existing individuals.

Nancy does not offer a concrete methodology for literary analysis. Nevertheless, his philosophical insights allow for uncovering the intricate way in which literary texts are concerned with community, prejudice, and myth-making. They make the reader more attuned to subtle, often unspoken aspects of cultural identity. Due to the extended scope of his work, I will limit my—inevitably abbreviated and simplified—introduction to his writing to the concepts relevant to the literary analyses in the upcoming chapters: 'being singular plural', community as a resistance to 'immanence', and the 'interruption of myth'.

Rejecting a Cartesian-Kantian model of the subject "as an active, synthesizing individual" that is "present to itself,"[69] Nancy argues that the notion of an absolute individual, independent from or in control of the outside world, is at odds with its existential interrelatedness. For the 'subject' only ever experiences itself as a singular being by 'being outside of itself', in the mutual exposure to another singular being. Nancy describes this exposure—which is fleeting and must always be experienced anew—as a moment of sharing and 'being singular plural'—a community that serves no other purpose, an 'inoperative community'. In other words, no singular being exists *before* the experience of community. This non-identitarian, non-foundational community emerges as a resistance to *immanence*. In Nancy's writing, *immanence* denotes the destructive desire for a closed social identity that fueled the conflicts of the European twentieth century—from the nationalisms leading to the First World War, to Nazism, to the Balkan conflict of the 1990s. Immanentism is present in communities or nations who try to defend 'their identity' from 'external' influence, so that they remain "united around their undivided selfhood, culture or values."[70] Immanentism was also at work in former socialist regimes, which considered the communist ideal as the final destination of humanity. In these cases, immanentism denotes the desire for a perfectly transparent self-identity, found in the people united as one to achieve a common goal: to remove all alienation of the capitalist way of life, so as to create a society that is "harmoniously present with itself."[71] Nancy is critical of the fusional self-perception of societies, nations, or communities, and particularly the mechanism of myth-making at work in them. Communities found and identify themselves through an "apparently coherent fictional narrative and then (and this turns the fiction into a myth), simultaneously, [...] erase and obliterate this very fictional gesture in order to suggest the naturalness and ontological essentiality of the imagined community."[72] Myth creates the illusion of full transparency and "pure identification"[73] within the community, which implies that every 'member' mirrors and represents the community's origin, destiny, identity: "In myth [...] existences are not offered in their singularity: but the characteristics of particularity contribute to the system of the 'exemplary life' in which nothing holds back, where nothing remains within a singular limit, where, on the contrary, everything is communicated and set up for identification."[74] Nancy reserves a particular role for literature in the exposure, or 'interruption', of these myths. As opposed to the mythic story of community, which relies on pure identification, exemplarity, and heroism, literature instead "unworks" the myth. Literature "incompletes it instead of completing it, and suspends the completion of the heroic-mythic figure."[75] In other words, literary texts convey images of a singularity of being that myths of identity and community fail to represent.

Nancy's notions of 'being singular plural', 'resistance to immanence', and the literary 'interruption of myth' have inspired the scope and the selection of texts at hand. The selection represents only a portion of the texts examined in preceding research. In a dialogue with Nancy's theory, which described and confirmed some of the tendencies uncovered by my initial readings, the body of texts has been limited to three thematic clusters, each dealing with various aspects of identity, community, prejudice, exclusion, and assimilation, and which furthermore illustrate the ambivalences of *Aufklärung* in a variety of ways. The selection is the result of the historical comparison, as it reflects similar patterns and thematic preferences in both periods: the position of the artist, the metropolitan experience, and the myths of empires. Due to a vast body of texts dealing with identity issues, many potential comparisons have fallen outside the scope of this investigation. For instance, travel literature (fictional or documentary) warrants further investigation. It would be interesting to compare for instance Joseph Roth's *Juden auf Wanderschaft* (1927), Alfred Döblin's *Reise in Polen* (1925), Ilja Trojanow's *Der Weltensammler* (2006), Navid Kermani's *Ausnahmezustand* (2013) and Else Lasker-Schüler's *Das Hebräerland* (1937). A comparison of literary reflections on war experiences at both ends of the century could be revealing as well, with stories about the Balkan conflict, such as Saša Stanišić's *Wie der Soldat das Grammophon repariert* (2006) and about the First World War, such as Arnold Zweig's *Der Streit um den Sergeanten Grischa* (1927). Issues of multilingualism associated with cultural identity or migration are present in texts from both periods as well. Contemporary texts like Marica Bodrozić's *Sterne erben, Sterne färben* (2007) or Özdamar's *Mutterzunge* (1990) can be read with an eye to the role of Yiddish in Kafka's or Roth's writings or Fritz Mauthner's thoughts on the *Sprachkrise* around 1900. Yet the selected works bring forward literary themes crucial to each period and illustrate several aspects of the modern experience at both ends of the century from a variety of perspectives.

The literary analyses of Chapters 2 to 4 are clustered around three types of 'individuals'—the aesthete, the city dweller, and the family hero. These thematic clusters reflect a scaling implicit in Nancy's thought. The immanentism of radical individualism as exhibited by the aesthete is analyzed in Chapter 2. Chapter 3 presents the metropolitan experience as a moment of recalibration in which the radical individual is confronted with fleeting forms of intimacy. Chapter 4 investigates imperial myths and the immanentism of the 'collective individual'. All these protagonists represent faltering narratives of assimilation and Enlightenment. At the same time, they are spectators, city readers and storytellers who are able to discern and produce communities and singularities beyond familiar identities, and beyond the myths that have shaped their existence.

Chapter 1 offers a historical introduction into the discursive and sociohistorical contexts of German-Jewish literature around 1900 and 'literature of migration' around 2000. Both periods are characterized by a (discursive) conflation of the notions *Kultur* and *Zivilisation*. On the one hand, the insistence on integration and assimilation—emancipation processes that emphasize individual improvement and self-realization—suggests that German society is founded on an Enlightened promise of inclusion. However, in both periods that promise becomes problematically entangled in an exclusionary notion of *Kultur*. Especially when *Aufklärung* is invoked as a 'German' value—a cultural achievement rather than an ongoing process to be realized by individuals— the principles of freedom, pluralism, and tolerance become an instrument of exclusionary language. This leads to a paradoxical position of German Jews and new German citizens, who are expected to integrate, though they continue to be singled out as 'Others'.

Chapter 2 investigates the erosion of assimilation narratives through the lens of the aesthete. It compares two texts from the *Wiener Moderne*—Arthur Schnitzler's *Fräulein Else* (1924) and Richard Beer-Hofmann's *Der Tod Georgs* (1900)—to Navid Kermani's *Kurzmitteilung* (2007) and Feridun Zaimoglu's *Liebesbrand* (2008).[76] In *Fräulein Else* and in *Kurzmitteilung*, the aesthetes fashion themselves as images to behold, as works of art. Their self-performance is partially motivated by an assimilatory drive, which in both cases reaches a dead end. The two novels contain a critique of radical assimilation as a process of self-aestheticization culminating in self-commodification and destructive isolation. The other two novels start from that dead end and outline the aesthete's 'conversion' to undecided, tentative forms of community. The (semi-) aesthetes in *Der Tod Georgs* and in *Liebesbrand* suffer from a 'perceptive disorder' symptomatic of their submission to idealism, both in an everyday and in a philosophical sense. At the same time, their disorder allows them to recover a sense of connection to the world—in discovering a forgotten (Jewish) heritage, or in finding 'ordinary' love and a 'kinship without obligation'. On a metafictional level, these variations on the aesthete illustrate that the oppositional character of art is not necessarily found in the explicit thematization of identity issues yet resides precisely in its aesthetic, mediated, and anti-mimetic nature.

Chapter 3 examines the metropolitan experience as a moment of recalibration for the autonomous, Enlightened individual. The chapter compares Ludwig Jacobowski's *Werther, der Jude* (1892) and Franz Hessel's *Spazieren in Berlin* (1929) to Terézia Mora's *Alle Tage* (2006) and Emine Sevgi Özdamar's story "Der Hof im Spiegel" (2001).[77] These stories feature the city as an ambivalent space that exposes the futility of emancipatory effort, yet where the erosion of individualism also engenders vulnerability and connection. This recalibration finds expression in two themes. Firstly, in a comparison of Jacobowski's and Mora's novels, I discuss two 'failed' individuals in the light of a confrontation between *Bildung* and pervasive stereotype. Secondly, in a comparison of Özdamar's story and Hessel's reflections, I will focus on experiences of labyrinthine disorientation/dis-Orientation and on the adoption of hermeneutic distance. These strategies allow the individual to define itself not in terms of autonomy, but of relationality and proximity. The four city dwellers illustrate that neither radical individualism nor collectivism can lay claim to the city. Rather, the city space enables a resistance to *immanence*.

Chapter 4 examines the workings of imperial myths and their demise through the lens of the family hero. Four family (hi)stories relate the decline of the Austro-Hungarian Empire and of the Bulgarian and Hungarian socialist regimes. A comparison of Joseph Roth's (post-) imperial writing and two instances of the 'Eastern turn' in contemporary literature deals with imperial myths losing their hold, as people resist and subvert the regimes' tendencies toward de-individualization. In the comparison of Joseph Roth's famous novel on the imperial past *Radetzkymarsch* (1932) and Dimitré Dinev's (post-) communist family saga *Engelszungen* (2003), the family motif highlights the illusory nature of imperial unity.[78] The intertwining narratives of family and imperial history expose the fissures in the smooth surface of imperial myth. By way of contrast to these novels' past orientation, the disintegrated families in Roth's *Hiob* (1930) and Zsuzsa Bánk's *Der Schwimmer* (2002) recover a future-oriented perspective.[79] Featuring nomadic and diasporic families, the novels seem to reflect a sense of vanishing (comm)unity. Yet against the background of failed revolution and insistent modernity, the families' experiences of *Heimatlosigkeit* provide the condition for transformation in terms of a new, postcommunist temporality (in *Der Schwimmer*) or a renewed religious experience (in *Hiob*). On a metafictional level, the four novels in this chapter convey the redemptive potential of art and storytelling. They are presented as strategies of subversion, of emancipation from the 'collective individual', of connection and endurance, whenever confidence in modern progress starts wavering. In other words, connecting singular beings, art and storytelling 'interrupt' the oppressive myths of imperial authority.

CHAPTER 1

CONSTITUTIVE OUTSIDERS

1.1 Ambivalences of *Kultur* and *Aufklärung*

In the past few decades, the German debate on immigration and integration has revolved around highly symbolic issues such as the *Kopftuchstreit*, the contested notion of *Leitkultur*, the perceived *Islamisierung des Abendlandes* or the commotion about *Parallelgesellschaften*. Yet no matter what particular issue is at stake, they all refer to a familiar but in fact oversimplifying distinction between Western secularism versus non-Western religious 'otherness', i.e. fundamentalism—or between the advocates of *Aufklärung* and those who resist or even seek to destroy its modern premise of autonomy and self-determination. This stark rhetorical contrast continues to fuel public debate and imbues it with a sense of urgency and unicity. It is, however, not entirely without historical precedent. The example of German Jews and their "romance with *Bildung*"[1] puts references to *Aufklärung* in recent debates in an interesting perspective. By the turn of the twentieth century, Jews in Germany had reached a turning point in a decades-long process of secularization and emancipation. During the *Haskalah*, or Jewish Enlightenment, they had internalized the ideal of *Bildung* and were to a large degree acculturated into German society. When from the 1880s onwards migration waves of evidently religious *Ostjuden* fueled increasingly explicit anti-Semitic sentiment, the assimilated *Westjuden* became the subject of intense public debates as well.

This chapter outlines the historical and discursive contexts of German Jews around 1900, who became "trapped by the image of a rejected self,"[2] and 'new' German citizens around 2000, who live in a reluctant country of immigration. There are considerable differences between these two historical minorities—in terms of their sociocultural position, language, and number, and especially in terms of their cultural histories and diasporic memory. Yet they seem to share a paradoxical position in identity discourses: despite the mainstream insistence on their adaptation, integration, or assimilation, their perceived incompatibility remains the subject of heated public debate. This first chapter section outlines the main elements that contribute to that position on the 'constitutive outside' of the nation.

Constructions of German identity

Since its birth as a 'belated' nation, then as an armed and aggressive nation, later as a divided and then reunified nation, Germany has a turbulent history of reimagining, reinventing, and reconfiguring national identity. These constructions have, in general, proceeded *ex negativo*, through the production of what Stuart Hall calls "frontier-effects" resulting from the creation of a "constitutive outside"—a discursively generated "excess" from which the nation differentiates itself for the purpose of homogenizing and sustaining its proper identity.[3] The many historical ruptures and ideological transformations that have shaped German history have been accompanied by reconfigurations of this 'outside', which has been construed as the historical, the ideological, the non-German Other.[4]

This pattern can be traced back to the German nation-building process.[5] The nineteenth-century Franco-German wars had established the image of a shared enemy, which consolidated feelings of community and Germanness among the confederated states.[6] Around the turn of the twentieth century, German identity took shape in a multivalent discourse with nationalist-cultural, religious, and racial or *völkisch* components, which defined 'Germanness' in terms of membership in the *Volks-* or *Kulturnation*, in terms of a shared Christian heritage, or in terms of a biological 'essence'.[7] Especially German Jews were, despite their lawful citizenship and their social and cultural integration, considered as religious, racial, and national Others. Under National Socialism, these multiple discourses were violently reduced to the all-encompassing notion of an innate racial purity.

After Nazism and the destruction of the German, and European, Jewish Other, any confident sense of Germanness had become suspect, if not impossible—"As a medium for integration and stability, the nation has turned into a source of insecurity. It no longer feels at home in its homeland. [Die Nation als Medium von Integration und Stabilität hat sich verkehrt in eine Quelle von Verunsicherung. Die Heimat ist unheimlich geworden.]"[8] The two German states articulated their postwar identities by creating a historical and ideological Other. Emphatically they dissociated themselves from the Nazi past and mutually attributed the role of ideological outsider to the other Germany. Although the —more or less—successful reconstruction of the states and the *Wirtschaftswunder* in the Federal Republic of Germany provided opportunities for positive national identification, the considerable contribution of foreign laborers to this boom became a source of negative identification. The economic crisis of the mid-1960s shook the new German self-confidence. One of its side-effects was that the initial solution of labor migration gradually turned into a 'Turkish problem.'[9]

The relatively sudden *Wende* and reunification of 1989/1990 marked a new phase in the history of German national identity. More than forty years of separation had left both sides of the former wall uncertain as to its 'common' identity, which allowed an ethnic argument to enter the debates. As Liesbeth Minnaard states: "After the *Wende* the dominant (political) discourse expected (indigenous) Germans to identify with the 'myth' of a shared, ethnoculturally defined Germanness."[10] The obvious political and personal arguments for a common identification—democracy and economic success—failed to work, and soon an old bias of Western self-definition appeared in the initial euphoria of unification. The process of reunification, "in which East Germany was the de facto second-class partner," was joined by anti-foreign sentiments, as it "relegated 'foreigners' to a third-class position in the symbolic hierarchy of this new Germany."[11] The increasingly xenophobic climate, as illustrated by several acts of violence in the early 1990s (in Hoyerswerda, Rostock, Mölln, and Solingen), was, according to Andreas Huyssen, the result of "the displacement onto the non-Germans of forty years of an inner-German hostility where another kind of foreign body was identified as the source of most problems: the other Germany."[12] Huyssen's statement is relevant still, even if the German 'constitutive outside' is no longer occupied by *Gastarbeiter* offspring alone. Since the events of September 11, 2001, the presence of Muslims in Germany has been perceived increasingly as suspicious. Over the past few decades, a self-confident, positive German identification as a pluralist country has grown entangled with the notion of an 'outside' of 'Islamic threat' within society.

A comparison of German Jews around 1900 and new Germans around 2000 reveals their similar positions as 'constitutive outsiders', i.e. as groups constructed and perceived as such in the process of German self-definition, or at least in the wishful fantasies of German national identity. The 'excess' of their presence (to remain consistent with Hall's terminology) finds different expressions at both ends of the twentieth century, although it seems to inspire a similar rhetoric. The presence of Jews was perceived as threatening, ironically due to their 'excessive', and therefore invisible, adaptation to 'German' society. Non-ethnic Germans, by contrast, embody "too much diversity,"[13] which in political discourse is often translated in terms of the "failure of multiculturalism."[14] Despite different degrees of 'visibility', the discursive mechanisms are largely the same and reveal remarkable rhetorical overlap. The myth of 'race' that inspired early twentieth-century anti-Semitic discourse[15] is not all that different from the contemporary myth of 'culture',[16] which, as Christopher Douglas argues, suffers from an "unacknowledged turn to race,"[17] and perpetuates some of its essentializing aspects.[18] As Alana Lentin observes as well, the continuity between racial and cultural rhetorics of difference consists of a current "culturalization of politics" that "bears similarities to the idea that 'race is all' that came to dominate European politics in the nineteenth century."[19] To a similar effect as 'race', 'culture' establishes a framework that explains and justifies differences in cultural terms, even if these differences originate in inequality, exploitation, or injustice. In other words, the word 'culture' has become a descriptor of collectivities that proves as static as the phantasmagoric naturalization of the Other that dominated a century ago.

Kultur versus Zivilisation

The notion of *Kultur*—a common language, history, heritage and value system—had been crucial to the development of a German nation-state and national identity. The German self-definition as a *Kulturnation*—rather than a *Staatsnation*[20]—turned out problematic for the Jewish minority, which strongly identified with German culture but was not considered a part of it, especially when, in the course of the nineteenth century, the German nation increasingly articulated itself in ethnic-racial terms, as well as the unique expression of a German *Volksgeist*.[21] More recently, Sigrid Weigel has detected a rekindled interest in the *Kulturnation*, which—in contrast to the impersonal *Verfassungspatriotismus* of the reunified country—fosters "an emotional attachment to the nation [...] without inciting xenophobic nationalism [eine emotionale Bindung an die Nation [...], ohne einen xenophoben Nationalismus zu schüren]."[22] But the rediscovery of a 'national' cultural heritage still warrants caution: "When understood as property, cultural heritage still becomes an argument of cultural standards legitimized by origin—quite different from tradition, which can be understood as the inhomogeneous whole of culture [...]. [Als Besitz begriffen, gerät das kulturelle Erbe dennoch zum Argument kultureller Normen, die durch Herkunft legitimiert sind—ganz anders als die Überlieferung, die sich als das inhomogene Ganze der Kultur verstehen lässt [...]]."[23] Weigel points out that the national literary tradition is traversed by "phantoms and revenants [Phantome und Wiedergänger]" that remind the reader of the heterogeneous origins of the nation.[24]

The potentially exclusivist nature of *Kultur* and the allure of the derivative *Kulturnation* have been analyzed in detail by Norbert Elias,[25] who distinguishes the German usage of (Romantic) *Kultur* from (Enlightened) *Zivilisation*. In British and French contexts, the two terms have historically evolved into near-synonyms for the opposite of 'primitivism', but in the German context they are quite distinct. According to Elias, *Kultur* is an exclusionary notion, produced and defined by a local community. *Zivilisation* involves a universal and cosmopolitan view of society, in which the *individual*, rather than the shared characteristics of a (national) community, becomes the reference point for inclusion. "To a certain extent," Elias argues, "the concept of civilization plays down the national differences between peoples; it emphasizes what is common to all human beings, or—in the view of its bearers—should be."[26] From this perspective, any individual can participate in society, as long as they are willing to accept values that are deemed universal. By contrast, Elias continues, "the German concept of *Kultur* places special stress on national difference and the particular identity of groups."[27] Elias attributes the allure of *Kultur* to Germany's history as a "belated nation-state [verspäteter Nationalstaat]:"[28] "[T]he concept of *Kultur* mirrors the self-consciousness of a nation which had constantly to seek out and constitute its boundaries anew, in a political as well as a spiritual sense, and again and again had to ask itself: 'What really is our identity?'"[29] The distinction between *Kultur* and *Zivilisation* is however not always clear-cut. When the inherently dynamic process of *Zivilisation* is reduced to its result, it can become an instrument of superiority and exclusivity. When "nations consider the *process* of civilization as completed within their own societies," Elias remarks, "they see themselves as bearers of an existing or finished civilization to others, as standard-bearers of expanding civilization."[30] In such cases, the result of 'civilization' can become incorporated into the static 'cultural' heritage of a nation. Arguably, such a conflation of the notions *Kultur* and *Zivilisation* has entered the German debates around 2000, where inclusionary and exclusionary notions of culture have been used interchangeably.[31] The result is a paradoxical situation, where immigrants are expected to integrate—implying an inclusive notion of society—yet continue to be portrayed as 'Others' who do not share the Enlightened tradition that warrants the autonomy of the subject. Especially when *Aufklärung* is invoked as a 'German' value—a cultural achievement rather than an ongoing process to be realized by single individuals—its principles of freedom, pluralism, and tolerance can become an instrument of exclusionary rhetoric.

In his essay collection *Deutschsein: Eine Aufklärungsschrift* (2011), the Turkish-German writer Zafer Şenocak pleads for a deliberate and careful engagement with *Aufklärung*.[32] Reiterating Elias' observations, he criticizes the fact that in current integration debates, Germany cultivates "a sensibility for its own body [ein Gefühl für den eigenen Körper]," and continues to support a delimiting notion of *Kultur*:

> Germany's *Leitkultur* as a democratic, pluralistic country is not about wheat beer and roast pork, but about the values of a constitutional state that guarantees its citizens freedom and human rights. These values are much better preserved universally than in a national identity program. The concept of civilization with its universal claim continues to find no emotional grounds that resonate in Germany.
>
> [Es geht bei der Leitkultur Deutschlands als demokratischem, pluralistischem Land nicht um Hefeweizen und Schweinebraten, sondern um die Werte eines Rechtsstaates, der seinen Bürgern Freiheit und Menschenrechte garantiert. Diese Werte sind viel besser universell aufgehoben als in einem nationalen Identitätsprogramm. Der Zivilisationsbegriff mit seinem universellem Anspruch findet in Deutschland nach wie vor keinen emotionalen Resonanzboden.][33]

According to Şenocak, an intensified Enlightened focus on *individuals*, rather than cultural collectivities, could be a valuable approach in integration debates. Recalling the violent consequences of nationalism and collectivism witnessed throughout the twentieth century, he emphasizes the danger in thinking about society and culture in terms of homogenized clusters: "If not individuals but instead ethnic and cultural templates determine thought patterns, and these thought patterns inscribe a constant and unchangeable otherness, then a breach of civilization occurs. [Wenn nicht Individuen, sondern ethnische und kulturelle Schablonen die Denkmuster bestimmen und diese Denkmuster eine stetige und unveränderbare Andersartigkeit festschreiben, dann tritt ein Zivilisationsbruch ein.]"³⁴ Şenocak attributes the country's reluctant attitude towards *Aufklärung* to a confounded historical awareness: it reserves "a secluded space for memory [...] so as not to let them encounter the manifold voices from outside [einen abgeschlossenen Raum für die Erinnerungen [...], um sie nicht in Berührung kommen zu lassen mit den vielfältigen Stimmen von draußen]."³⁵ As a result of this blind spot, the integration debate has come to resemble a self-involved monologue:

> In the integration debates we are dealing with a Germany curiously lacking history. As if this country had no experience whatsoever with migration, with immigration and emigration, with cultural debates about German identity. The emancipation and assimilation of German Jews, the expulsion of Germans from Eastern Europe were accompanied by vehement identity debates, which are part of the German cultural self-image. If today we are referring to the Judeo-Christian heritage of German culture, Muslim integration can only be accomplished if this heritage is extracted from the Sunday speeches and perceived not only as part of the culture of remembrance, but also as a horizon of experience. Jewish emancipation as a consequence of the Enlightenment is one of the greatest heydays of the human experience of civilization. But to what extent is it still present today?
>
> [So haben wir es in den Integrationsdebatten mit einem seltsam geschichtslosen Deutschland zu tun. Als hätte dieses Land keinerlei Erfahrung mit Migration, mit Ein- und Auswanderung, mit kulturellen Debatten um die deutsche Identität. Die Emanzipation und Assimilation der deutschen Juden, die Vertreibung der Deutschen aus Osteuropa wurden von heftigen Identitätsdebatten begleitet, die Teil des deutschen kulturellen Selbstverständnisses sind. Wenn heute vom jüdisch-christlichen Erbe deutscher Kultur die Rede ist, kann eine muslimische Integration nur dann gestaltet werden, wenn dieses Erbe aus den Sonntagsreden ausgepackt wird und nicht nur als Teil der Erinnerungskultur, sondern auch als Erfahrungshorizont wahrgenommen wird. [...] Die jüdische Emanzipation als eine Folge der Aufklärung gehört zu den größten Blütezeiten der menschlichen Zivilisationserfahrung. Wie weit ist sie aber heute noch gegenwärtig?]³⁶

Şenocak suggests that, in the current integration debate, the emancipation history of German Jews rarely serves as an illustration of successful *Aufklärung*, because people can only think of it "in terms of its catastrophic end [von ihrem katastrophalen Ende her]."³⁷ While it is true that German-Jewish history is one of a confident adoption of Enlightenment principles, it was not simply a *Blütezeit*. Especially relevant to debates today is a conflict between, or conflation of, *Kultur* and *Aufklärung* that determined pre-war German-Jewish relations. Already in the decades before the German-Jewish *Beziehungsgeschichte* came to a disastrous end, it had become clear that the adoption of *Aufklärung* did not guarantee inclusion and did not deliver on its promise of countering anti-Semitic prejudice. Whereas the Jews envisioned a modern society of equal individuals, and nurtured an inclusive, cosmopolitan conception of *Bildung*, the status attached to it however "soon became a monopoly of a caste rather than accessible to anyone willing and able to participate in the process of self-cultivation."[38] *Bildung* became an instrument in the construction of a compelling German identity, an identity cultivated in terms of a German *Kulturnation*.[39] The story of German-Jewish emancipation is, in other words, also a story of gradual disillusionment with *Aufklärung*.

The following chapter sections outline the individual historical contexts of German Jews on the one hand and new Germans on the other, as well as discuss in greater detail the impact of their position as constitutive outsiders of the German *Kulturnation*. In both periods, symptomatic of the conflation of *Kultur* and *Aufklärung* is the remarkably similar rhetoric of "liberals who [want] to assert their antiliberal opinion."[40]

1.2 "Trapped by the image of a rejected self"[41] Jews in Germany, German Jews

Emancipation and acculturation (1770–1880)

A portrait of Jews in Germany between 1770 and 1933 inevitably revolves around their transforming relationship to Judaism, to modernity, and to the history and culture of non-Jewish civil society. Over more than a century, from the 1770s to the 1890s, many European Jewish communities were engaged in the *Haskalah*, the Jewish chapter of European Enlightenment. Although it was a diversified movement, more nuanced than a simple dichotomy between modernization and orthodoxy suggests,[42] the *Haskalah* is generally considered to be the intellectual foundation of Jewish secularization and political emancipation. The Reform Movement of Moses Mendelssohn (1729—1786), later David Friedländer (1750—1834), and Abraham Geiger (1810—1874) strove for a synthesis of traditional and reformed worship, advocating a Jewish religion of reason reconcilable with Enlightenment ideals, such as civic equality and the separation of church and state.[43] Hoping to overcome Jewish isolation and cultural arrears, which had originated in their exclusion from professional life, they found no contradiction in simultaneous Jewish ceremony and German citizenship, or even Christian practices like baptism. These first beginnings of acculturation were advanced further by Napoleonic equality laws in 1806, which allowed a certain degree of political and economic participation. These were the seeds of an "inner-Jewish turn [innerjüdische Wende]."[44] Efforts to gain equal rights unified and strengthened, and in 1871, with the foundation of the German nation-state, equality and religious freedom were constitutionalized.

As mutually dependent conditions of a social agreement, Jewish political emancipation was inextricably bound up with efforts of cultural assimilation. Their strong identification with the ethic of *Bildung*[45] was motivated by its fundamentally humanistic, ahistorical, and inclusive character. It promised to bring forth a community of equals: every individual, irrespective of religion, culture, or descent, could access the process of self-education and German cultural heritage. Perceiving the absence of common historical roots as an obstacle to integration, they believed that the ideal of *Bildung* enabled a dissociation from the ghetto past, yet also the chance of "transcending a German past,"[46] so that "Jew [could] meet German on equal terms."[47] In their eagerness to internalize the ideal, *Bildung* came to be their "secular religion."[48] By the 1870s, the Jews had become members of the German *Bildungsbürgertum* as passionate participants in cultural life. Their support for cultural innovation and avant-gardism could even be considered as "disproportionate"[49]—an acculturative overcompensation[50] for the absence of common historical ground.[51]

Jewish acculturation coincided with remarkable social mobility and urbanization. Whereas the majority of Jews in Germany at the beginning of the nineteenth century had lived on the fringes, by the 1870s more than sixty percent had become part of the (upper) middle class, with twenty percent of them living in large cities (versus only 4,8 percent of population in general).[52] Such rapid urbanization and *embourgoisement* could not be observed for society as a whole, which indicates relative social seclusion. Shulamit Volkov indeed recognizes German Jewry at the end of the nineteenth century as a separate cultural system, a "third sphere"[53] that had developed throughout the century as a complex network of public, private, and educational institutions, and in which the internalization of dominant German values had in fact contributed to a process of "negative integration."[54] Similarly, David Sorkin has argued that the Jewish *Bürgertum* was a subculture emerging from a "parallel associational life" after the model of the

German associations from which they were excluded.[55] Clearly, Jewish efforts to become full members of society did not simply resolve their minority status, but instead redefined its characteristics, redirecting them into a position relying on both German and Jewish cultures.

The incongruence between their rapid sociocultural advancement and their apparent relative seclusion suggests that an assessment only in terms of their degree of 'assimilation' remains inadequate. Obviously, the reality of German-Jewish relations was more ambiguous and nuanced than the bipolarity of the term accounts for.[56] The validity of the term has been a subject of controversy, and its ambivalent interpretations vary according to the historiographical and ideological perspective from which German-Jewish relations are assessed. Already from the onset of its currency around the 1870s, the term covered a range of meanings,[57] and represented both narrow and broad views on the Jewish self-positioning vis-à-vis German culture and society.[58] In a broad understanding, assimilation eventually leads to the dissolution of Jewish particularity as a precondition of political equality.[59] The narrow interpretation was the more current one, held by liberal Jews and taken up by most German-Jewish historiography.[60] The condition is articulated differently: the internalization of German cultural values would bring about social acceptance, characterized by tolerance towards the (continued) presence of a Jewish collective identity.

However, their successful acculturation did not lead to social acceptance. Due to the catastrophic culmination of anti-Semitism, and the "negative verdict" history has cast on German-Jewish relations,[61] 'assimilation' as a descriptive category is subject to the "fallacy of retrospective judgment."[62] The inherently dynamic process of assimilation is easily mistaken for a teleological development towards an inevitable outcome of (self-) destruction. Gershom Scholem has denounced the German-Jewish dialogue as a myth, arguing that the illusion that assimilation would bring acceptance "was one of the factors that retarded, disturbed, and eventually brought to a gruesome end the [dialectical] process."[63] However, as Paul Mendes-Flohr counters

> although it may be possible for historians to explain by the wisdom of hindsight the logical consequence of events leading to the advent of the Third Reich and the crazed schemes it was to institute, it is epistemologically erroneous to assume that contemporaries could—not to say, should—have had the same knowledge that historians have at their disposal.[64]

For the same reason, the opposite view—a portrayal of pre-war German-Jewish relations as a fruitful cultural 'symbiosis'—is equally fallacious: it is "pre-eminently a post-Second World War construct [...] expressing an idealized image of a world brutally disrupted by Hitler."[65] Both extremes give an undeserved impression of acculturating German Jews as either naive or willfully ignorant about their increasingly hostile surroundings. Perhaps more accurately, the "undeniable reality" of German Jews should be seen as defined by the problem "as how to preserve Jewish cultural memory and identity while passionately and creatively embracing another culture."[66]

Modern anti-Semitism and Jewish dissimilation (1880–1933)

Rather than participants in a history of emancipation and assimilation, German Jews should be considered as a minority,[67] a community that negotiates with and asserts itself within larger society but is characterized by a very vivid internal dialogue and a dynamic of its own. Volkov focuses on "neither the assimilatory forces in the development of the Jewish community in Germany [...] nor the repelling forces of an anti-Semitic host society," but on "forces from within, which were drawing German Jews back together again even despite themselves."[68] Volkov's perspective uncovers a dialectical relation between internal and external, seemingly contradictory developments within the Jewish community—more specifically: how assimilatory efforts eventually produced the trend of Jewish dissimilation and cultural reassertion that emerged around the 1890s.

'Race' and modern anti-Semitism

Primary catalyst of dissimilation trends was the increasingly tangible anti-Semitic climate. From around the 1880s, a modernized and racially inspired anti-Semitism found programmatic expression in the establishment of explicitly anti-Jewish political parties.[69] The rise of political anti-Semitism is generally associated with increasing anti-modern sentiments and considered a reaction against the social advancement of secularized Jewry into the core domains of modern society, finance, politics, press, and culture. More fundamentally, the rise of racial anti-Semitism harks back to the political function of 'race' as a tool in the consolidation of modern state power. Rejecting the relatively common assumption that racism is a psychological, individualized "aberration of the European norm of democracy,"[70] Lentin explains how an essentialist and exclusionary notion like 'race' could be embraced by democratic nation-states.

The Enlightenment project itself was based on a "Janus-faced universalism"[71] that allowed the racialization of difference to emerge:

> Both the emancipation of the European Jews and the anti-slavery of the Enlightenment radicals brought with them a concomitant drive to uniformisation that, paradoxically, made more obvious the difference between human groups previously kept apart. The persistence of domination, this time under the guise of assimilation or the 'mission of civilisation', created the conditions for the racialisation of Jews or blacks that, despite initial intentions to the contrary, focused on hierarchies of progress that, due to the primacy of scientific rationalization, saw the concept of 'race' as the principal reason for their existence.[72]

In reference to Étienne Balibar,[73] Lentin argues that 'race' assisted state nationalism in creating a fantasy of political and cultural homogeneity. 'Race' intervened as a tool to produce the "mythical ethnicity"[74] necessary to maintain the nation's unity: it naturalized differences and inequality between populations and, in doing so, drew a demarcation line between them.

The politicization of anti-Semitism in the 1880s had a distinctive yet contradictory racial aspect to it. The Jewish assimilation project—which relied on the barter of citizenship and equality in exchange for cultural adaptation— was indeed a response to the state's drive to uniformity. Yet the resulting relative integration of Jews into bourgeois society seems at odds with the increasingly political dimensions of anti-Jewish sentiment. Founders and advocates of modern, racial anti-Semitism—Wilhelm Marr (1819–1904), Adolf Stöcker (1835–1909), and Eugen Dühring (1833–1921)—translated the *Judenfrage*[75] from a religious question to a "question of race, morals, and culture [Racen-, Sitten- und Culturfrage],"[76] opposing the so-called *Verjudung* of society. At first sight, they reacted against the perceived 'disproportionate' influence of Jews in pivotal positions. Remarkable in the anti-Semitic rhetoric, however, is a sinister contradiction between a demand for assimilation and its strong conviction about the fundamental, biological otherness of Jews. The actual threat, as Dühring argues, is not Jewish acculturation per se, but an invisible Jewish 'essence' seeping—or being 'injected'—into German society:[77]

> A Jewish question would exist […] even if all Jews had turned their backs on their religion and joined one of our prevailing churches. […] The baptized Jews are those who, without impediment, penetrate all the

passages of social and political life the furthest. [...] [The] interspersion of racial Jewry into the joints and crevices of our national dwellings must, the more complete it becomes, lead increasingly to backlash. It is impossible for a close encounter to gain traction without our simultaneous realization of how incompatible with our best instincts is the *inoculation* of the traits of the Jewish race into our living conditions.

[Eine Judenfrage würde [...] auch existieren, wenn alle Juden ihre Religion den Rücken gekehrt und zu einer bei uns vorherrschenden Kirchen herübergetreten wären. [...] Gerade die getauften Juden sind diejenigen, die ohne Hindernisse am weitesten in alle Canäle der Gesellschaft und des politischen Gemeinlebens eindringen. [...] [Die] Einstreuung von Racenjudenthum in die Fugen und Spalten unserer nationalen Behausungen muss, je vollständiger sie wird, umsomehr zu einer Rückwirkung führen. Es ist unmöglich, dass eine nahe Berührung platzgreife, ohne dass sich bei uns zugleich die Erkenntnis einfinde, wie unverträglich mit unseren besten Trieben die *Einimpfung* der Eigenschaften der Judenrace in unsere Zustände ist.][78]

Dühring compares 'Jewishness' and even complete secularization to a disease that spreads itself invisibly and therefore all the more dangerously. Still, the metaphor of inoculation does not produce the intended effect. The injection of a foreign element, a disease, eventually leads to immunity or tolerance to the once foreign element. The inoculation image thus contradicts the anti-Semitic claim that German and Jewish cultures are mutually unassimilable. In other words, even when articulated in modernized and scientific imagery, the paradox of anti-Semitic prejudice remained the same: the Jew was either too assimilated or not assimilated enough.

Rhetorical inconsistencies like these betray an incoherent fear of a Jewish menace, a fear that has been associated with social changes wrought by the modernization process.[79] Anti-modern sentiments rooted in the social and economic decline of *Modernisierungsverlierer*[80] were directed at the Jews. Ironically, their successful acculturation and secularization made them all the more visible as *Jewish* "representatives of modernity and secularism."[81] Accordingly, anti-Jewish stereotypes were no longer inspired by a religious distinction between Judaism and Christianity, but by economic and national arguments instead— "The Jew was now no longer the anti-Christ, the one condemned by God, but the profiteer, the racketeer, the bankrupt, the sworn enemy, a danger to the economic and political existence of Germany and the Germans themselves. [Der Jude war jetzt nicht mehr der Anti-Christ, der von Gott Verdammte, sondern der Wucherer, der Preistreiber, der Bankrotteur, der Todfeind, eine

Gefahr für die wirtschaftliche und politische Existenz Deutschlands und der Deutschen schlechthin.]"[82] Before it entered political programs, anti-Semitism resembled a "cultural code,"[83] a symbolic language that subsumed anti-modern, anti-liberal, right-wing sympathies. 'Anti-Semitism' was a populist term coined in a lower-middle class milieu,[84] but it soon became *salonfähig* among middle-class intellectuals as well. The at the time reputable historian and politician Heinrich von Treitschke (1834—1896) contributed significantly to making it intellectually and politically acceptable, when he published the essay "Unsere Aussichten" in 1879.[85] The text calls for complete assimilation and the abandonment of Jewish specificity but does so in a peculiar manner: [86]

> What we demand from our Israelite fellow citizens is straightforward: they are to become Germans, to consider themselves quite simply to be Germans—without prejudice to their faith and their ancient sacred memory, which is venerable to us all; for we do not want the millennia of Germanic morality to be succeeded by an age of German-Jewish mixed culture.
>
> [Was wir von unseren Israelitischen Mitbürgern zu fordern haben, ist einfach: sie sollen Deutsche werden, sich schlicht und recht als Deutsche fühlen—unbeschadet ihres Glaubens und ihrer alten heiligen Erinnerungen, die uns alle ehrwürdig sind; denn wir wollen nicht, daß auf die Jahrtausende germanischer Gesittung ein Zeitalter deutsch-jüdischer Mischcultur folge.][87]

Initially, Treitschke articulates his demand for assimilation in terms of Jewish self-perception as Germans or as a matter of citizenship—in any case regardless of religious affiliation, and apparently assuming that it is *possible* to become German. This would correspond to the liberal barter of emancipation in exchange for assimilation. But then he suggests that it is a matter of culture, religion, and memory after all: 'feeling German' cannot be reconciled with an inalienable Jewish identity and will result in an unwanted mixed culture. In a contradictory rhetoric resembling Dühring's, Treitschke's 'liberal' proposal that Jews become Germans is paired with the conviction of Jewish unassimilability. Treitschke's piece garnered attention especially because of his ambivalent political stance. As a leading German liberal who now expressed sympathy for anti-Semitic attempts to revoke Jewish emancipation, he now remarkably took a stand against one of the pillars of the liberal program. Such ambivalence, as Marcel Stoetzler observes, is characteristic of racialized state nationalism:

> In the period of the consolidation of the German nation-state, most National Liberals tended to subordinate a rather diffuse feeling of antipathy toward Jews to the larger objective, national unity. [...] [What] prompted him to transform his latent, as it were acceptable, dislike of Jews—the 'normal' antisemitism that has been described as a 'cultural code'—into a virulent and 'political' endorsement of antisemitism?[88]

Even if Treitschke does not explicitly invoke the notion of 'race', he is convinced of an immutable Jewish difference threatening the precarious unity of the new state, its society, and its national culture.[89]

Treitschke's statements elicited a vigorous press debate among politicians and leading academics that lasted until 1881. The *Berliner Antisemitismusstreit* concerned "the ways in which national culture was understood to mediate between state, society, and individual in the modern context."[90] Because it addressed the conditions of Jewish (non-) belonging to the German nation as well, however, the debate became a platform for anti-Semitism to acquire a politically mainstream position. Yet the historical significance of this sinister debate is not primarily related to its content. Rather, the various argumentations on the *Judenfrage* all relied on an implicit consensus on the suitability of the nation-state as a form of government for liberal society, based on national culture as a necessary means of consolidation.[91] The dispute, in other words, reveals the contradictory conflation of liberal and nationalist tendencies in the 'nation-form':[92] when liberal society takes the shape of a national state, it requires conformity with a static national culture and loses the idea of liberty.[93] It is due to this ambivalence that Treitschke's antiliberal liberalism could thrive—and becomes relevant to the situation around 2000 as well.[94] As I will illustrate in the section on Germany as a reluctant country of immigration, a similar discordance between liberal state and national culture is evident there as well.

Jewish dissimilation & the *Ostjude* as a mirror image

Surely, the persistent negative portrayal of German Jews drew them together as a community, but a sense of *Trotzjudentum* alone was not the only factor to set a dissimilation process in motion. Volkov illustrates how a community of successful and educated Jews provided a counter-image for positive Jewish identification.[95] Paradoxically, their success at internalizing modern and secular values made full assimilation more difficult, since such "social attraction among the likes"[96] shifted the focus of identification back to within the Jewish community itself.[97]

From the 1880s onwards, a wave of orthodox Jews from Eastern Europe dispersed westward in the wake of pogroms and poverty. Their immigration into Germany and Austria not only irked anti-Semites like Treitschke, it also enhanced the already heightened self-awareness of westernized Jews. As it forced German Jews to reassess their position, the immigration wave initiated a deliberate dissimilatory course.[98] By 1910, these *Ostjuden* constituted up to eleven percent of Jewry, but they remained largely isolated.[99] German Jews received the *Ostjuden* with an "uneasy alliance" of "protective and dissociative modes."[100] Their response is especially revealing with regard to their self-perception as *both* Germans and Jews. On the one hand, they were concerned that the arrival of a destitute Jewry would jeopardize their hard-won status in German society, especially at a moment when they already found themselves in a tight spot. On the other, their presence elicited a sense of inherited responsibility. It appealed to their liberal, humanist, and philanthropic ideals, but at the same time their philanthropy contained an element of superiority, which confirmed the distance between them and their Eastern 'brothers'.[101]

Their ambivalence towards the sudden reality of Eastern Jewish immigration was related to the mythologized status that the *Ostjude* had achieved in the minds of modernized Jews. Steven Aschheim demonstrates in great detail how the Eastern Jew functioned as an "inverted image"[102] of transforming German Jews. During the acculturation process, re-creations and recontextualizations of the caricature of the ghetto Jew portrayed the exact antithesis of what modern Jews aspired: "[L]ocked in narrow Talmudic worlds, unproductive itinerants, boorish and dirty, still speaking the despised *Jargon*, they were identical with *Unbildung*, the incarnation of the Jewish past which German Jews had rejected and transcended."[103] Even so, as a mirror image, it continued to register their self-perception. With the first signs of dissimilation, the inverted ideal of the *Ostjude* underwent ideological reevaluation. From an object of dissociation, it transformed into one of identification. Gradually, for some, it became the glorifying image of "Jewish authenticity" and of "the unfragmented self" of the Jewish people.[104] As such, the *Ostjude* reflected a fundamental revision of the relation between Eastern and Western Jews: no longer one of patronizing philanthropy but one between equals in a Jewish nation.

Zionism & Cultural Zionism

The image of the *Ostjude* "reflected the complex and contradictory face of German Jewry itself"[105] and, consequently, not the reality of Eastern Jewish immigrants. Although a positive view on Eastern Jewry was indispensable to the formation of a national self-understanding, the idealizing symbol of the *Ostjude* was primarily a matter of rhetoric and pragmatism in the service of political goals. The recruitment of immigrants for the Zionist cause was qualified as a liberation from ghetto misery and actually resembled the patronizing stance that they criticized in assimilationists.[106] In their rejection of the ghetto, the ideology of Zionist pioneers Theodor Herzl (1860–1904) and Max Nordau (1849–1923) bore the impress of the assimilated environments where they had grown up.[107] That liberal continuity in political Zionism was one of the causes for the emergence of Cultural Zionism, which advocated the Jewish nation in terms of reviving the Jewish spirit, language, and cultural history.

As a worldwide movement that aspired to represent the entire Jewish people, Zionism was from its onset a "tapestry of powers,"[108] comprising various political, religious, and cultural positions that envisioned the Jewish nation or state differently. Herzl's Zionism was established as a political movement in 1897, at the first Zionist congress in Basel, one year after the publication of his pamphlet *Der Judenstaat* (1896).[109] The solution to the *Judenfrage*, according to Herzl, was the restoration of a Jewish state. His view is conventionally considered the Western-civic strain of Zionism, in contrast to the Eastern-ethnic movement that developed in the 1880s in the wake of pogroms against Russian Jews.[110] Eastern Jews who adopted Zionism did so to distance themselves from their ghetto past, though they favored the continuity of the Jewish spirit. Because of their close affinity with Jewish cultural roots, they resisted the Western Zionist strain, which, they believed, was moving towards a loss of Jewishness, rather than towards its positive assertion.

Achad Ha'am (1856–1927), for instance, founder of Cultural Zionism, fiercely denounced the continuation of liberalism in Herzl's utopia *Altneuland* (1902),[111] calling it an instance of "mechanical mimicry, devoid of any national character, pervaded by the scent of that 'serfdom in the midst of freedom', which is a hallmark of the occidental *Golus* [mechanisches Nachäffen, ohne jegliche nationale Eigenheit, von dem Duft jener 'Knechtschaft mitten in der Freiheit' durchweht, die ein Kennzeichen des abendländischen Golus bildet]."[112] Instead, he advocated the awakening of Jewish consciousness and a common cultural tradition. This, too, required an "intellectual national center [geistiges nationales Zentrum]," which however was not to be regarded as a "refuge for Jewry, but for Judaism [Zufluchtsstätte für die Judenheit, sondern für das Judentum]"[113]—a spiritual rather than a geographical refuge. Ha'am's ideas influenced the Austrian-Jewish philosopher Martin Buber (1878–1965), who laid the groundwork for a "Jüdische Renaissance."[114] Mysticism and the Hasidic tradition were his sources of inspiration for a Jewish revival. The Jewish "resurrection from half to to full life [Auferstehung aus halbem Leben zu ganzem]"[115] should complement the Zionist political project towards an all-encompassing national consciousness. The short-lived but innovative *jungjüdische Bewegung* in turn-of-the-century Vienna and Berlin heeded Buber's call. The movement gave expression to his idea in new forms of physical and youth culture,[116] while acquiring a distinctive graphic character thanks to the incorporation of *Jugendstil* imagery in the visual arts and in literature.

What set Cultural Zionism apart from other Jewish-national expressions was its rejection of liberal views,[117] in addition to its particularly racialist foundation. Racial thought was not exclusive to anti-Semitism alone. It was an element of a more general neo-Romantic mood in Germany, which in rejecting positivism, rationalism, and capitalist impersonality emphasized the importance of community and a regeneration of *Volksgeist*.[118] Yet the more prevalent *racialism* that inspired for instance Cultural Zionism should be distinguished from the *racism* that was characteristic of the German *völkisch* ideology. Whereas the first aimed at invigorating national consciousness within a frame of racial difference and equality, a claim of racial superiority was intrinsic to the latter.[119] Cultural Zionism was permeated with racialist perspectives, although there was little consensus on the concept of a Jewish race.[120] Even if it served to arouse a national consciousness, Jewish racialist rhetoric functioned equally as a defense mechanism against the prevalence of anti-Semitic racism.

The First World War: the illusion of a 'community of the trenches'

The Dreyfus Affair in France (1894–1906) is often mentioned as an eye-opening moment for Herzl. The political scandal surrounding the Jewish artillery officer Alfred Dreyfus, who was falsely indicted for treason, convinced Herzl that Zionist political action was necessary. The scandal made it clear to him that assimilation would not secure the acceptance of Jews in society.[121] For the majority of German Jews, however, a more decisive period of disillusionment would arrive with the First World War and its aftermath. The war exposed the incongruence between patriotic and ethnic-national identification by Jews and gentile Germans. According to a "well-trodden historiographical narrative,"[122] the war led to the complete separation of Jews from other Germans. Even so, some nuance to the idea that the Jews had only been guests in a very separate "German war experience"[123] is in order. The isolation of Jewish soldiers was indeed rooted in increasing wartime anti-Semitism. Still, judging from the prominent Jewish involvement in commemoration and veterans' organizations that were not specifically Jewish, it could be argued that "German Jews [...] emerged from the First World War still firmly rooted in wider German society."[124]

Nevertheless, as "the testing ground for the validity of the various prewar German images of the Ostjude," the First World War became a "strange encounter"[125] in several respects: of politics meeting compassion, of myth meeting reality, of comrades-in-arms becoming Jews and Germans again. When war was declared in 1914, most German Jews entered into a nation-wide enthusiasm, "with high hopes of gaining recognition as integral parts of the German *Volksgemeinschaft*."[126] Because the war was directed against anti-Semitic Russian absolutism, it was moreover considered as "an identity of interests."[127] On the battlefield, the notion of shared sacrifice and military experience affected all German soldiers alike, which would also become a key element in the Weimar Republic's memory culture and public remembrance.[128] However, the encounter with Jews on the Eastern Front confronted German-Jewish soldiers with their own precarious position. As German patriots, they approached *Ostjuden* from a political perspective, but they had to act as cultural mediators between the Jews and the German authorities at the same time. While they had to emphasize their distance from Eastern Jewry, they also had to soften the negative impression on German soldiers, by reminding them that the poor conditions in the ghetto were historical and not the result of Jewish character.[129]

Adding to their self-awareness, the Jewish contribution to the war became the new target of intensifying anti-Semitism. Already in 1914, newspapers accused the Jews of spying and unpatriotic behavior. As the war progressed, accusations of lacking national responsibility, shirking (*Drückebergerei*), and even profiteering from the wartime struggle led to the infamous *Judenzählung* in October 1916.[130] The official census subjected German-Jewish soldiers to an official count, so as to determine the level of wartime participation.[131] Rather than confirming the Jews' loyalty, however, the census especially demonstrated how their 'Germanness' was being questioned, and—perhaps because the results were kept a secret— simply intensified the existing allegations. To German Jews, it must have become increasingly clear that "[e]ven the toll of twelve thousand Jewish lives in the battlefield [...] was not sufficient to create the 'community of the trenches.'"[132]

In the aftermath of war and defeat, anti-Semitism surfaced even more vehemently as a response to the economic crisis. Once more, Jews were forced to reassess and redefine their commitment to Jewishness, even for those Jews who did not participate in Jewish community and religious life.[133] Strategies to do so still varied along existing ideological strains, but under the pressure of an increasingly polarizing environment they acquired a more urgent and anxious character.[134] The

Centralverein deutscher Staatsbürger jüdischen Glaubens continued to consider German Jews as a *Stamm* of the German people and to harmonize both identities. Many Jews defined their Jewishness in terms of its similarity with Germanness but visibly struggled with their (perceived) incompatibility. Others still propagated complete assimilation, which sometimes resulted in radical manifestations of Jewish self-hatred and self-denial. Ironically, Zionists 'agreed' with anti-Semites on the necessity of Jewish difference and self-assertion. They would become the only ones "equipped with an ideological and explanatory framework that took seriously the radical nature of anti-Semitism."[135]

The ambivalence of assimilation

The First World War exposed the confrontation between Jewish confidence in inclusion and a society that increasingly rejected their efforts. It remains a question whether or not "das jüdische Projekt der Moderne"[136] ever had a fair chance at success. No matter how divergent assimilationist and Zionist objectives were, they were different answers to the same unease with the Jewish position, and sprouted from common ground: a longing to overcome the ghetto past, and to carve out a space in modern society. Their assimilatory drive seems logically paired with the drive for emancipation. But, as Zygmunt Bauman argues, German-Jewish relations are in fact exemplary of how the concept of assimilation itself produces its own failure.[137] It proposes the vision of a culturally unified body, and implies a social hierarchy in which the majority's 'invitation' to become part of it lends them the power to both "set the exams and mark the performance:"[138]

> The standing invitation was represented as a sign of tolerance. In fact, however, the assimilatory offer derived its sense from the stiffness of discriminatory norms, from the finality of the verdict of inferiority passed or [sic] nonconformist values. The tolerance, understood as the encouragement of 'progressive attitudes' expressed in the search of individual 'self-improvement', was meaningful only as long as the measures of progress were not negotiable. Within the policy of assimilation, tolerance aimed at individuals was inextricably linked with intolerance aimed at collectivities, their values and above all their value-legitimating powers.[139]

In other words, assimilation is a responsibility of the self-improving, Enlightened individual. But that individual and his 'progress' are not the yardstick in assessments of successful integration. It is the quality of the weakest section that determines political evaluations of emancipation, which always apply to the acculturating community as a *whole*. Indeed, Volkov observes a discrepancy between the successful integration of individual Jews, while Jewry as a collective was still regarded as socially distinctive.[140] Assimilants thus can only be perceived as inauthentic: as "suspect[s] of duplicity"[141] they are never fully accepted by a dominant majority. To call this a "birth defect [Geburtsfehler]"[142] of the process sheds an unjustified light of doom on early acculturative efforts. Still, the Jewish endeavor had from the outset suffered from a fundamental asynchronicity:[143] the Jews were pursuing the ideals of the Enlightenment as it was already losing its authority to a German majority. The Jewish attraction to *Bildung*, to the humanistic promise of self-improvement and inclusion into a 'neutral' society of equals became "drawn into the complex [...] process of constructing a compelling collective identity,"[144] cultivated in terms of a German *Volksnation* and an innate sense of *Kultur* and ethnic genealogy.[145] German Jews thus painfully encountered the fundamental tension that shapes European modernity to this day, between Romantic *Kultur* and Enlightened optimism.

In this light, Şenocak's plea for a careful consideration of *Aufklärung*, and especially his reference to German Jews in that context, is interesting. For Jewish 'assimilation' has proven more problematic and complex than a cultural 'symbiosis'; in fact, their history reveals the utterly vulnerable position of minorities in the context of Enlightened acculturation. As I will illustrate in the following chapter section, a similar conflation of *Aufklärung* and *Kultur* marks the contemporary debate as well. Though not immediately visible as a historical process where *Bildung* is instrumentalized in the development of a *Kulturnation*, the tension becomes evident in the debate itself. Throughout the 1980s and 1990s, and after the turn of the century still, Germany struggled with the effects of labor migration and its status as *Einwanderungsland*. Evidence of that struggle are vehement public debates that—just like a century before—paradoxically combine a demand for assimilatory integration of minorities with the clear demarcation of cultures, again enabling liberals to voice anti-liberal concerns about the perceived menace to 'German' culture.

1.3 A reluctant country of immigration

German history is marked deeply by the consequences of people moving across borders but also of borders moving across people.[146] A history of migration from, into, and within Germany is a story of the dislocation of *die Fremde*, of how migration blurs and challenges seemingly clear-cut distinctions between German and non-German, between native and foreign, self and other. Today, about twenty-one percent of the overall German population has a migration background, a number that increases every year.[147] These numbers—as well as the evolution from a country of emigration, of labor import, of immigration, into a country of transit characterized by high transnational mobility[148]—would suggest that Germany has long asserted itself as a country of immigration. Indeed in 2015, with the historical words 'We can do this [Wir schaffen das]', Chancellor Merkel showed remarkable confidence when faced with the humanitarian refugee crisis. Yet the self-perception of the country regarding its status as *Einwanderungsland* has traveled historically and legally complex paths and remains troublesome still.

From emigration to immigration

Since its foundation in 1871, the German state has evolved in phases from a country of primarily emigration into one of immigration.[149] Until the 1890s, employment was the primary reason for German emigration to the United States. As industrial growth stimulated the economy, emigration decreased, and was complemented by an inflow of foreign workers from Russia, Italy, and Galicia. By the beginning of the First World War, over a million foreigners were employed in Germany.[150] Some of them became German citizens, others forced laborers under the Nazi regime. The construction and maintenance of the Third Reich depended on a workforce of 7.5 million laborers of non-German origin—about a quarter of the total.[151] After the Second World War, about 12 million people from Eastern Germany and from German settlement zones in Eastern Europe were expected to 'integrate' into the new *Bundesrepublik*—with mixed results. But the reconstruction of Germany suffered from a shortage of labor force, which could only partially be covered by *Übersiedler* and *Aussiedler*. The German *Wirtschaftswunder* challenged a labor market that was already strained by limited birth surplus, expedited retirement age, prolonged education, and the introduction of military service. In 1955, Germany entered into the first of several recruitment agreements abroad; first with Italy, later with Spain and Greece

(1960), Turkey (1961), Tunisia (1963), Portugal (1964), Morocco (1965), and Yugoslavia (1968).[152]

From the beginning, the agreements were considered to be a European project—the agreement text between Germany and Italy invokes the "spirit of European solidarity [Geist europäischer Solidarität]."[153] Indeed, they did not only serve German economic interests but also allowed for a controlled 'export of unemployment' from the sending countries that benefited from the transfers.[154] Between 1955 and 1973, about 14 million foreigners were employed in Germany, about 11 million of whom returned to their native countries.[155] When in 1973, against the backdrop of the oil crisis, the number of foreign workers peaked at 2.5 million, the German government announced a recruitment ban, which had unexpected long-term effects on society. The recruitment agreements had been aimed specifically at short-term relief of market needs, as implied by the unofficial but widespread term *Gast*arbeiter. But the *Anwerbestopp* overreached itself and accelerated that which it intended to prevent. Laborers who had worked in Germany and returned home—most of them Turkish—were not allowed to return to Germany afterwards. For many, this was a reason not to leave Germany at all, despite increasing unemployment.[156] By the end of the 1970s, most of the mass accommodations for guest workers had turned into more or less separated 'settler colonies', which served both as a refuge from and a stepping stone into a new environment. Rather than the result of (intentional) isolation, such communities were the indicators of a new societal transition. Bade concludes: "Guests had become permanent, resulting in a solid minority of foreigners in a genuine immigration situation. [Aus Gästen waren Dauergäste geworden und daraus eine feste Ausländerminorität in einer echten Einwanderungssituation.]"[157]

A belated country of immigration

For a long time, German legislation lagged behind the reality of that situation. The realization that a short-term economic approach to labor migration could not sufficiently deal with the long-term effects on society took more than ten years to find articulation in legal terms.[158] In 1979, the contested "Kühn-Memorandum"[159] warned against the harm that a continued neglect of the sociocultural and political urgency of the *Einwanderungssituation* would cause. The memorandum demanded immediate political acknowledgement of the reality of immigration, calling on the social responsibilities of the employing country. Its recommendations on education policy, suffrage, and a general revision of the naturalization law were however met with what Bade vehemently criticizes as a "defensive refusal of recognition [defensive Erkenntisverweigerung]"[160] on federal level. For over ten years—he speaks of the 1980s as a "lost decade"[161]—foreigner policy only revolved around the restriction of new non-EEC immigration and the futile promotion of guest workers' return, in accordance with the prevalent motto 'Deutschland ist kein Einwanderungsland'. This resulted in a twofold failure, one that recognized neither the reality of a *de facto* country of immigration without a corresponding policy nor the presence of factual immigrants without a corresponding disposition.[162]

Policy change gained momentum around 2000 with the reformed Citizenship Act and Immigration Act. The 1999 reform of the *Staatsangehörigkeitsgesetz*[163] entailed a liberalization of the *ius sanguinis* by introducing *ius soli* elements into naturalization law. Previously, German citizenship was granted on ancestral grounds only. The new law included birth place as a constitutive factor, granting the offspring of immigrants, in addition to their parents' nationality, immediate German citizenship as well.[164] In 2001, an independent commission on immigration, under the guidance of CDU-politician Rita Süssmuth, published its advice[165] on integration as a demographic, economic, and labor market issue, acknowledging that "Germany is *de facto* an immigration country. [Deutschland ist faktisch ein Einwanderungsland.]"[166] Its recommendations served as the foundation for the 2005 *Zuwanderungsgesetz*,[167] which for the first time addressed issues of immigration and integration from a legal perspective.[168] Additionally, since 2006, a number of sociopolitically oriented initiatives like the annual *Integrationsgipfel* and *Islamkonferenz* have gathered representatives from the political sphere and from religious or immigrants' associations for extensive dialogue on the long-term approach to integration. These initiatives, as well as the gradual legal adaptation to social reality, indicate that migration and integration have entered political consciousness as primary sociopolitical issues—albeit with a delay of more than 25 years.[169]

Kultur in the aftermath of non-policy: *MultiKulti—Leitkultur—*'Deutschland schafft sich ab'

In 2010, on the twentieth anniversary of German reunification, Federal President Christian Wulff caused a stir with his celebratory speech. He elaborated on the contemporary meaning of "Deutschland, einig Vaterland"—a line from the GDR's national hymn, which at the time of the *Wende* also expressed the East-German desire for *Wiedervereinigung*. In his speech, Wulff calls for the same solidarity and courage that once united two separate countries into one. Translating the memory of a shared past to a contemporary social context, Wulff presents a remarkably liberal and inclusive reinterpretation of the German *Vaterland*:

> [We need] an understanding of Germany that does not limit belonging to a passport, a family history, or a faith but is broader in scope. Christianity undoubtedly belongs to Germany. Judaism undoubtedly belongs to Germany. That is our Christian-Jewish heritage. But Islam now also belongs to Germany. Nearly 200 years ago Johann Wolfgang von Goethe expressed it in his *West-östlichen Divan*: 'Whoever knows himself and others will also recognize that Orient and Occident can no longer be separated.'
>
> [[Wir brauchen] ein Verständnis von Deutschland, das Zugehörigkeit nicht auf einen Pass, eine Familiengeschichte oder einen Glauben verengt, sondern breiter angelegt ist. Das Christentum gehört zweifelsfrei zu Deutschland. Das Judentum gehört zweifelsfrei zu Deutschland. Das ist unsere christlich-jüdische Geschichte. Aber der Islam gehört inzwischen auch zu Deutschland. Vor fast 200 Jahren hat es Johann Wolfgang von Goethe in seinem *West-östlichen Divan* zum Ausdruck gebracht: "Wer sich selbst und andere kennt, wird auch hier erkennen: Orient und Okzident sind nicht mehr zu trennen.]"[170]

Wulff's speech represents only one voice in a proliferation of statements and opinions that have constituted a decades-long debate, which around 2000 revolved primarily around the notion of *Leitkultur*. His careful rhetoric indeed conveys his awareness of the German audience's sensitivity to the subject. While a repeated "We are the people [Wir sind das Volk]" appeals to a sense of national unity, his speech also introduces a notion of unity in diversity: Judeo-Christian history should be a self-evident aspect of German identity, and, gradually, Islam has become one as well. It is no coincidence that Wulff inserts a Goethe quote here to highlight the heterogeneity of German culture. The indispensable image of German *Kultur* apparently undermines any notion of a single *Leitkultur*, thus salvaging the notion of unity from culturalistic claims that often dominate the public debate. Much like the *Berliner Antisemitismusstreit* more than a century before, the *Leitkultur* debate became a platform for the definition of national identity—"What the nation is at any given moment for any given individual depends on the narrative accounts and arguments they bring to bear on the subject."[171] The Berlin Antisemitism Dispute illustrates the contradictory conflation of liberal and nationalist considerations in the formation of the German state. The *Leitkultur* debate, too, reveals a remarkable adultery of culturalist and

Enlightened-liberal views, in which the latter become instrumentalized in the defense of *Leitkultur*.

The apparent interchangeability of both perspectives is due to their embeddedness within the same post-racial paradigm—a logic that allows and justifies the culturalization of difference and its translation into political terms.[172] Post-racialism, as Lentin argues, has become the dominant framework in which suspicion of diversity is articulated "in cultural-civilizational terms that attempt to avoid the charge of racism."[173] In the post-racial mode, she argues, "the language of race and racism has been abandoned for that of 'different but equal culture.'"[174] This semantic shift, which denies the significance of racism through a mobilization of the language of culture, has been recognized as the 'culturalization of politics'. It occurs when "differences conditioned by political inequality or economic exploitation are naturalized and neutralized into 'cultural' differences, that is into different 'ways of life' which are something given, something that cannot be overcome."[175] Culture as an explanatory framework for difference thus becomes an equally essentializing mechanism that reduces individuals to their belonging to purportedly homogeneous cultural groups, and in doing so, excludes all other modes of explanation. As such, Lentin concludes, "the post-racial is [...] the dominant mode in which racism finds expression today across a variety of contexts."[176] In what follows, I will illustrate how the notion of *Kultur*, both in terms of culturalism and of culturalization, has dominated several contemporary debates. The disputes on multiculturalism, its proclaimed failure, on integration, on parallel societies, on the headscarf issue, and on German *Leitkultur* all convey the primacy of the notion of culture as static and innate.

The introduction of 'multiculturalism' into public awareness, and with it a reintroduction of *Kultur*, kindled a first debate in the 1980s.[177] The realization that guest workers' residence in Germany had lost its temporary character shifted the focus from their economic to their cultural context. Previously, the perception of labor migrants had been informed primarily in terms of their economic plight.[178] A counterpoint to that one-sided focus would be a more comprehensive view on the 'cultural enrichment' they had brought. An ecumenical announcement on the occasion of the "Tag des ausländischen Mitbürgers" (1980)[179] for instance stated that multicultural reality requires acquaintance with 'foreign' cultures. Greater valorization of cultural specificities would lead to understanding and tolerance. The success of multicultural society, according to the announcement, depended on mutual efforts at integration, defined not in terms of assimilation but of respect for the minority's aspirations and traditions. However, in the elevation of multicultural coexistence as "a new opportunity for the future of the

Federal Republic [eine neue Chance für die Zukunft der Bundesrepublik]," the benevolence of the announcement is overshadowed by a Eurocentric approach of difference: "Achieving creative communication with other cultures is an important contribution to the realization of the common culture of a European Community. [Wenn es gelingt, zu einer schöpferischen Kommunikation mit anderen Kulturen zu kommen, ist dies ein wichtiger Beitrag für die Verwirklichung der gemeinsamen Kultur einer Europäischen Gemeinschaft.]"[180] The phrasing of the statement suggests that multiculturalism requires considerable effort to overcome the distance between cultures as sphere-like, incompatible entities. Despite its good intentions, the attempt at redirecting the perception of immigrants' misery amounted to a problematic shift from a socioeconomic to a culturalized approach of inequality and difference.

Opponents of multiculturalism brought forward a number of anti-pluralist and ethnocultural arguments that insisted on 'insurmountable' differences. Exemplary is the "Heidelberger Manifest,"[181] signed and published by fifteen university professors in 1982, who criticize "euphoric-optimistic economic policy [euphorisch-optimistische Wirtschaftspolitik]" as a menace to German *Kultur*: The rhetoric of the manifesto is reminiscent of Treitschke's contradictory *Einimpfung* imagery. Its core argument is that peoples are mutually exclusive— they are "(biological and cybernetic) organisms [...] with different system properties, passed on genetically and by tradition [(biologisch und kybernetisch) lebende Systeme [...] mit voneinander verschiedenen Systemeigenschaften, die genetisch und durch Traditionen weitergegeben werden]."[182] As such, they naturally resist cultural pluralism on the same territory. However, this does not mean that acculturation is impossible—in fact, the real menace to the *Volk* is a potential *Einschmelzung*. The contradiction in the notion of (in)compatible cultures is shrouded in a constitutional argument: "The constitution of the Federal Republic does not proceed from the concept of the 'nation' as the sum of all peoples within a state. Rather, it is based on the concept of 'people', that is, the German people. [Das Grundgesetz der Bundesrepublik geht nicht aus vom Begriff der 'Nation' als der Summe aller Völker innerhalb eines Staates. Es geht vielmehr aus vom Begriff 'Volk', und zwar vom deutschen Volk.]"[183] Thus adapting a biological-nationalist stance usually associated with racist propaganda, the Heidelberger manifesto functioned as a "discursive bridge"[184] between overt racism and the ethnopluralism of New Right that was gaining ground in the 1980s. It acknowledged the heterogeneous makeup of society yet insisted on the necessary preservation of ethnic and cultural difference. This stance, as Dirke observes, "managed to make larger and larger inroads into public opinion" because it "replaces the concept of race with the seemingly less controversial concept of the *Kulturkreis*."[185] Indeed, opponents of multiculturalism used the notion of *Kultur* to invert an initial ideal of dialogue and mutual tolerance into its exclusionary opposite. Even so, the fact that 'multiculturalism' is susceptible to such an easy inversion illustrates that the argument between defenders and opponents in fact agrees on the very same idea: that of internal cultural homogeneity and mutual incompatibility, which both positions remarkably articulate in terms of 'respect'—"respect for other peoples [die Achtung vor anderen Völkern]" in the *Heidelberger Manifest*; in the ecumenical announcement the claim that "in the coexistence of cultures [...] the majority [should] respect the claims of minorities [im Miteinander der Kulturen [...] die Mehrheit die Ansprüche der Minderheiten respektieren [soll]]."[186]

Since its introduction into public debates, the notion of multiculturalism has suffered from a lack of agreement on its definition. "[O]ver the years the term 'multiculturalism' has come to reference a diffuse, indeed maddeningly spongy and imprecise, discursive field: a train of false trails and misleading universals. Its references are a wild variety of political strategies."[187] The arguments brought forward often entangle prescriptive and descriptive multiculturalism, i.e. multicultural policies and the lived multicultural situation of people from diverse origins coexisting in one society.[188] That vagueness partially explains how "Multikulti" could experience "a symptomatic conversion from a term of endearment to a swear word [eine symptomatische Konversion [...] vom Schmusewort zum Schimpfwort],"[189] eventually culminating in the proclaimed crisis of multiculturalism.[190] Purported evidence of its 'failure' are the so-called *Parallelgesellschaften*. The image of parallel societies as sociotopes, of ethnically homogeneous population segments, separated socially and culturally from society, has more discursive than referential relevance. The arguments in the dispute all agree on the idea that *Parallelgesellschaften* are symbols of incomplete integration: either as its failure or as a transitory stop in the process.[191] As such, the debate on these urban areas conveys a societal unease with the supposed "excessive tolerance and benevolence towards disloyal, unassimilable, culturally different others" supported by multiculturalism.[192] However, the perceived excess of cultural diversity is really the result of long-term non-policy.

The erosion of the term 'multiculturalism' accelerated with the emergence of the notion *Leitkultur*, which in 2000 and 2001 dominated a controversy about the future of German society. Following a proposal by the center-left government to remove the notion of descent from new laws on immigration and citizenship, conservative opponents accused the government of jeopardizing German cultural identity. They set up an immigration commission in order to influence discourse in favor of a definition and protection of that identity.[193] German *Leitkultur*, introduced in the public debate in 2000 by CDU chairman in the Federal Parliament Friedrich Merz, would become the key concept in that attempt. Its resonance relies on its dual connotative power: "Whilst its first lexeme *Leit-* hints at a hierarchical relationship between cultures with the German one taking a lead, the second lexeme *-kultur* denotes the social glue that is traditionally meant to bind Germans together."[194] The term thus reintroduced an assimilatory understanding of integration. But more significantly, it illustrates the pattern of how a universalist notion is mobilized in a discourse of *Kultur*.

Originally, the term *Leitkultur*, formulated by political scientist Bassam Tibi,[195] was indebted to a universalist *Verfassungspatriotismus*. Resisting the idea of a *Kulturnation*, Tibi proposes that Germany should reposition itself by acknowledging a democratic, Enlightened 'European *Leitkultur*' as a set of guiding values: secular democracy, civil rights, the primacy of reason over religion, and civil society. Although Tibi points out that such values are fundamentally incompatible with an ethnocultural understanding of the nation,[196] Friedrich Merz reappropriated the term in a national and cultural context. What he calls the "liberal German guiding culture [freiheitliche deutsche Leitkultur]" carries the constitution and European Enlightenment at its core:

> The constitution is [...] the most important expression of our value system and thus part of the German cultural identity that enables the inner cohesion of our society in the first place. [...] Immigration and integration of foreigners [...] needs orientation to generally applicable value standards.
>
> [Das Grundgesetz ist [...] wichtigster Ausdruck unserer Werteordnung und so Teil der deutschen kulturellen Identität, die den inneren Zusammenhalt unserer Gesellschaft erst möglich macht. [...] Einwanderung und Integration von Ausländern [...] braucht Orientierung an allgemein gültigen Wertmaßstäben.][197]

Paradoxically, by referring to the constitution as an expression of culture, rather than a means of guaranteeing equality, 'generally applicable values' are employed here as a standard for cultural assimilation. The quote is exemplary of a pattern that characterized the course of the debate—as Stefan Manz concludes: "What was conceived as a purely political concept [...] was easily appropriated by the right through an ethnocultural interpretation."[198] Merz's assimilatory notion of *Leitkultur* met with opposition from the political left and representatives of minority groups, who denounced it as "a meaningless slogan [eine inhaltsleere Parole]"[199] prone to misinterpretation by xenophobic groups. Indeed, right-wing press and political parties continued to functionalize it in a strong assertion of Germanness. Evolving from a potentially universalist concept into its (ethno) cultural, exclusionary opposite, "[t]he term *Leitkultur* [...] offered the opportunity to express instinctive fears of the Other in a politically acceptable way." Much like the notion of *Kultur* as a discursive bridge in the *Heidelberger Manifest*, the term *Leitkultur* allowed "[a] taboo in German public discourse [to be] circumvented by reverting to an apparently unsuspicious word."[200]

The antithesis of *Leitkultur* was constructed in the course of several so-called 'headscarf debates'. In 1998, Fereshta Ludin, an Afghani-born German citizen, was prohibited from teaching in Baden-Württemberg's public schools because she chose to wear a headscarf. Her choice was considered as a statement of "resistance against integration or assimilation goals."[201] Yet the central issue in the Ludin case, as opposed to earlier cases, was her emergence as a 'Muslim woman' in the German public domain, and everything it was meant to symbolize: the state, the constitution, and Western democracy. At stake was the symbolic power of the headscarf, which in the course of the trial was transformed from a religious into a cultural symbol. First, Ludin was refused a teaching position on grounds of her inability to represent the state's Christian values.[202] Remarkably, later court decisions against Ludin invoked principles of state neutrality—a justification now based on Ludin's non-secular rather than non-Christian appearance. In the court's inconsistent decisions, the headscarf was set up as 'religious' and therefore in contradiction with state neutrality, whereas Christian values were considered 'cultural' and 'neutral'.[203] As a result, the headscarf became a battleground for a conflict of cultures. Ironically, however, the obsession with 'culture' overshadowed the fact that Ludin herself embodied the opposite of what the scarf was believed to represent: gendered oppression within Islam, and the inability of Muslims to act according to democratic principles. Weber illustrates how Ludin's subjectivity was denied, as she was construed as a non-agent: the acting subject was replaced by the cultural object of the 'Muslim woman'. The actual but implicit symbolic power of the headscarf, then, was its disturbance of the public field: its undeniable visibility "force[d] an acknowledgement of the deceptions necessary to maintain the unity of the German subject and [...] by which the false assumption of unity is created—the German subject, it seems, is not only Christian; its Muslim Other not only silent, backwards, invisible."[204]

The course of the *Kopftuchstreit* is symptomatic of the increasing polarization in Western discourses after the attacks of September 11, 2001. Since then, a number of key incidents and public statements have reignited controversy about multiculturalism, immigrants, and Muslims in particular.[205] The tension between 'civilized West' and an external threat soon equated with 'Islam' in general has been fought out over symbolic content—the construction of a mosque in Köln-Ehrenfeld, or the Swiss ban on minarets. While '*MultiKulti*' and '*Leitkultur*' have gradually lost their discursive power, a rediscovered *Fremd- und Feindbild* of Islam now dominates debates on integration.[206] German Jews a century before were considered suspicious due to their increasing embodiment of modernity and secularism, which irked both conservatives and 'liberals' like Treitschke. Around 2000, it is a 'secularized' *Abendland* that distinguishes itself from the 'religious' other, i.e. Orient. The "Islamisierung" or "Muslimisierung"[207] of difference, sustained by media coverage and reports on immigration,[208] now accompanies—at times replaces—the culturalization of difference. The "diffuse blending of the term 'terrorism' with a religion, as generated in politics and in the media [politisch und medial geschaffene diffuse Verschmelzung des Begriffs Terrorismus mit einer Religion]" has resulted in a tendency whereby Muslims are codified as a collective threat within society.[209]

A century before, Treitschke's anti-liberal liberalism was a symptom of the conflation of national culture and liberal considerations in the early nation-state. Similarly, around 2000 values of *Aufklärung* appear to be instrumentalized in narratives of *Kultur*, allowing yet another anti-liberal liberal to express his concern about an impending loss of *Kultur*. In 2010, Thilo Sarrazin published the highly contentious book *Deutschland schafft sich ab*,[210] which reached bestseller status and acquired a taboo-breaking aura, as if Sarrazin were speaking for a silent majority. In advance of publication, Sarrazin had already courted controversy with statements about the purported cultural and intellectual disintegration of the country.[211] His claims about *Überfremdung* and the foreign menace to German *Kultur* are reminiscent of anti-Semitic rhetoric a century before. Sarrazin's primary concern pertains to a decreasing number of ethnic Germans combined with an increase of lower-class citizens from a migration background,[212] culminating in a doomsday scenario in which "Germany [...] is becoming more ignorant on average as a result of the skewed birth distribution [...]. Intelligence and social class correlate very strongly [Deutschland [...] durchschnittlich dümmer [wird], weil die Geburtenverteilung [...] schief ist. Intelligenz und Schichtzugehörigkeit korrelieren stark positiv]."[213] While repeatedly covering himself against indictments of racism, Sarrazin added fuel to the fire with statements about the existence of a specific Jewish gene[214] and about the "cultural peculiarity of peoples," which he considers the defining constituent of European reality.[215]

Especially controversial about the publication was Sarrazin's political affiliation as a social democrat. His social-Darwinist reasoning[216]—a potent mix of culturalism, economism, and genetics[217]—strongly contradicts any notion of social advancement through education and support. His rhetoric treads on dangerous ground by proposing to inhibit "a dysgenic birth pattern [eine dysgenisch wirkende Geburtenstruktur]" with drastic measures that should be effective first of all and constitutional only secondarily.[218] An extreme example of the culturalist reduction of what is in fact a socio-economic inequality, Sarrazin represents a return of explicit racialism within a post-racial environment. The familiar paradox of demanding assimilation while claiming the unassimilability of the Other shapes his entire argument. As Hofmann concludes, he expresses a "chauvinism that amounts to a separation of population groups and does not strive for integration, yet laments ghettoization while perpetuating it through culturalism at the same time [ein Chauvinismus [...], der auf eine Trennung der Bevölkerungsgruppen hinausläuft und nicht Integration anstrebt, sondern Ghettoisierung beklagt, aber gleichzeitig durch Kulturalismus fortschreibt]."[219]

Assessing the impact of the "Sarrazin phenomenon [Phänomen Sarrazin],"[220] Bade criticizes the *Desintegrationspublizistik* for reinforcing and legitimating ethno- and sociobiological thought patterns, for harming integration optimism among Muslim *Einwanderer*, and most importantly for its failure to establish a transparent discussion on integration.[221] Bade interprets the Sarrazin controversy, and by extension the entire integration debate, as a "surrogate debate [Ersatzdebatte]"[222] for a highly urgent—yet ignored through decades of political amnesia[223]—discussion of Germany's status as an immigration country. The real challenge, he argues, lies in tailoring a comprehensible self-image for *all* Germans—a "tangible new encompassing identity [...] that is already being lived in day-to-day life, but has no name as yet [einer beschreibbaren neuen gruppenübergreifenden Identität [...], die im Alltag schon gelebt wird, aber noch keinen Namen hat]."[224]

1.4 Literature, identity, and singularity

To imagine and to describe such an unnamed inclusive identity is hardly the territory of political debate alone; it is in fact a very productive *literary* matter. Over the years, countless authors have intervened in public debates, considering it their duty to counter the discursive primacy of *Kultur*. Şenocak's *Deutschsein* and Kermani's *Wer ist wir. Deutschland und seine Muslime* (2009),[225] for instance, are Enlightened critiques of the German self-definition as a *Kulturnation*. *Das Manifest der Vielen* (2011), edited by Hilal Sezgin,[226] constructs a counter-identity that defies the notion of *Leitkultur*, weaving together the voices of about thirty authors of diverse origins and confessions who defend their "right to live one's life [Eigenrecht gelebten Lebens]"[227]—their desire to seek refuge from the imperative of identity, and to live their *singular* lives instead. The essays articulate an already existing 'new Germanness', articulating hope for an inclusive, pluralistic, and future-oriented *Wir*: "Even if their past and individual narratives distinguish people from one another, the idea of a sustainable, common German identity could unite them. [Auch wenn die Vergangenheit und die einzelnen Narrative die Menschen voneinander unterscheiden—die Vorstellung von einer tragbaren, gemeinsamen deutschen Identität könnte sie einigen.]"[228]

The optimism and Enlightened overtones of such essays and identity constructions are obvious. However, as the history of German Jews around 1900 illustrates, the optimism in embracing Enlightenment principles may expire in the confrontation with the *Kulturnation*. In this light, Feridun Zaimoglu's contribution to the *Manifest* is worth mentioning explicitly.[229] Hesitant to refer to the public debate as a 'clash of cultures'—it is rather a "battle which we have good reasons to avoid calling *Kulturkampf* [Kampf, den wir aus guten Gründen Kulturkampf zu nennen vermeiden]"[230]—Zaimoglu accurately observes that it is deeply affected by the conflation of *Kultur* and *Aufklärung*. Unduly claimed by "would-be Voltaires [Westentaschen-Voltaires],"[231] Enlightenment principles have been perverted in the declaration of "hostility as the primary duty of occidentally inspired humanism [Feindschaft zur ersten Pflicht des abendländisch inspirierten Humanismus [...]]."[232] Zaimoglu calls instead for a return to a humanism inspired by vulnerability, and by an awareness of the singularity of lived experience:

> It is indecent to see only heaps and hordes, when it is people who perceive this land as their own. They and I feel connected to a humanism to which it is more urgent to relate today than yesterday. This humanism implies standing on the side of the vulnerable.
>
> [Unanständig ist es, nur Haufen und Horden zu sehen, wo es doch Menschen sind, die dieses Land als ihr eigenes Land betrachten. Sie und ich fühlen sich einem Humanismus verbunden, auf den sich zu beziehen heute dringlicher ist als gestern. Dieser Humanismus bedeutet, dass man auf der Seite der Schwachen steht.]233

An author's deliberate embrace of the 'weaker' position implicitly draws the attention to the position of literature within the polarized debate. While that debate at both ends of the twentieth century revolves around the conflation of *Kultur* and *Aufklärung*, many literary texts dealing with the vexed issue of identity move away from clear-cut argumentative and ideological stances, outlining the significance of a humanism of vulnerability, especially in a context of Enlightened optimism.

Of course, literary texts have shown themselves susceptible to ideological instrumentalization or deployment in constructions of national identities—if they are not themselves already explicit in their programmatic nature. In fact, at both ends of the century, a majority of definitions of literature are closely entwined with ideological programs. Exemplary in the case of German-Jewish literary history is the *Kunstwart* debate. In 1912, Moritz Goldstein sparked a controversy among Jewish intellectuals with an article that was "[a]rguably the sharpest invective ever launched against German-Jewish assimilation."234 The essay "Deutsch-jüdischer Parnaß,"235 published in the conservative magazine *Der Kunstwart*, was remarkable for its "head-on [attack of] what Jews of previous generations had so passionately been aspiring to achieve."236 Goldstein posits that a genuine relationship between Jewish and German culture is improbable and interprets the precarious position of German-Jewish authors as exemplary of society at large: "We Jews administer the spiritual heritage of a people that denies us the right and ability to do so. [Wir Juden verwalten den geistigen Besitz eines Volkes, das uns die Berechtigung und die Fähigkeit dazu abspricht]."237 Goldstein's anger with the dilemma faced by German-Jewish authors "is merely a window into the larger Jewish Question."238 His call for Jewish self-assertion and for the establishment of a stronger Jewish cultural sphere in Germany239 is really a demand for a literature in the service of a national program.

Comparable instances of the functionalization of literature can be found along the ideological spectrum. In his interpretation of the *Kunstwart* debate and its aftermath, Kilcher observes that the definition of German-Jewish literature varies according to "the prevalent cultural-political positions of Jewish modernity: assimilation, Zionism, and diaspora theories each implied their own conceptions of literature and culture [den dominanten kulturpolitischen Positionen der jüdischen Moderne: Assimilations-, Zionismus- und Diasporatheorien implizierten alle je eigene Konzeptionen von Literatur und Kultur]."[240] From a liberal perspective, advocated by the historian Ludwig Geiger, German-Jewish literature is both the result and the instrument of acculturation. It should therefore only be considered as 'German' literature, which is intrinsically heterogeneous: "Whoever looks at German literature and art [...] will have to admit that an exclusively German art has hardly ever existed. [Wer die deutsche Literatur und Kunst [...] betrachtet, der wird geradezu sagen müssen, daß es eine ausschließlich deutsche Kunst fast niemals gegeben hat.]"[241] The diasporic model rejects both dissimilatory and acculturative notions of literature and formulates a simultaneously political and aesthetic alternative that elevates (German-) Jewish literature "to a cosmopolitical paradigm of Jewish modernity [zu einem kosmopolitischen Paradigma jüdischer Moderne]."[242] Alfred Wolfenstein's literary program, for instance, rejects any nationalistic and territorial understanding of literature, be it in terms of cultural assimilation, or of dissimilation: "From the weak assimilant to the most courageous Zionist, their one desire is: soil. [Vom schwächlichen Assimilanten bis zum mutigsten Zionisten wünschen sie sich: Boden.]"[243] Instead, modern Jewish literature should celebrate a diasporic existence as a "human, connected dispersion [menschliche, eine verbundene Zerstreuung]."[244]

In the case of contemporary 'literature of migration', the intertwining of ideology and literature is not quite found in cosmopolitan or national claims. Rather, the writers in question appear to move in a field of tension between emancipatory self-assertion and artistic autonomy. In the early years, the works of migrant writers were regarded from a predominantly sociopolitical perspective. With their programmatic article "Literatur der Betroffenheit," for instance, Franco Biondi and Rafik Schami drew attention to a marginalized group of writers and themes. Criticizing the precarious social position of guest workers, the article reserves a particular role for a multinational literature in their emancipation process.[245] Associations such as the politically inspired *PoLiKunst-Verein* (1980–1987) and the publication series *Südwind Gastarbeiterdeutsch* also promoted solidarity among foreign writers. At the same time, several voices rejected such readings, emphasizing the aesthetic qualities of their writings instead.

Turkish-German authors like Yüksel Pazarkaya and Aras Ören represented the perspective of literary autonomy early on.[246] Pazarkaya's programmatic article "Literatur ist Literatur"[247] rejects sociopolitical claims to literature as folkloristic, exoticist reductions. Instead, he draws attention to the often neglected aesthetic dimensions of texts of so-called *Gastarbeiterliteratur*.

Although that aesthetic perspective has become the more dominant one, this literature has far from lost its critical character, even if its 'politics' do not simply reiterate the familiar arguments articulated in the identity debate. As Jacques Rancière puts it:

> Literature does a kind of side-politics or meta-politics. The principle of that 'politics' is to leave the common stage of the conflict of wills in order to investigate in the underground of society and read the symptoms of history. It takes social situations and characters away from their everyday, earth-bound reality and displays what they truly are, a phantasmagoric fabric of poetic signs, which are historical symptoms as well. [...] This 'politics' of literature emerges as the dismissal of the politics of orators and militants, who conceive of politics as a struggle of wills and interests.[248]

Indeed, while the calls for an embrace of *Aufklärung* by Şenocak, Kermani, or Sezgin position the authors on a 'common stage of conflict' that draws them into a narrative of ideological oppositions, a closer look at the 'fabric of signs', at the aesthetic rather than programmatic dimensions of literary texts, we may find many nuanced approaches to the ambivalences of Enlightenment.

CHAPTER 2

AESTHETES BETWEEN IDENTITY AND OPPOSITION

2.1 The authenticity paradox—Writing between identity and opposition

Early 2014, the (Czech-) German writer Maxim Biller caused a stir with a provocative contribution to *Die Zeit*.[1] In his polemical essay 'Letzte Ausfahrt Uckermarck', he comes close to pronouncing the death of contemporary literature. Its deplorable state, Biller contends, is due to the notable absence of *Ruhestörer* who—as once did German-Jewish authors like Peter Weiss or Elias Canetti— disrupt the monotony that seems to pervade the German literary scene:

> The absence of Jewish troublemakers is no good to our literature, which is growing increasingly introspective and therefore feeble and provincial. [...] German literature is like a terminally ill patient who has stopped seeing a doctor yet tells everyone that he is doing well.
>
> [Die Abwesenheit der jüdischen Ruhestörer tut unserer Literatur nicht gut, sie wird immer selbstbezogener, dadurch kraftloser und provinzieller. [...] Die deutsche Literatur ist wie der todkranke Patient, der aufgehört hat, zum Arzt zu gehen, aber allen erzählt, dass es ihm gut geht.][2]

After the failed experiment of the 'German-Jewish symbiosis'[3]—"that century-old attempt to establish a new realistic tradition—literary and political—in romantic cultural backwater Germany [dieser hundert Jahre währende Versuch, im romantischen Krähwinkel Deutschland eine neue Tradition des Realismus— literarisch und politisch—zu etablieren]"—Biller now observes a stark contrast between the bland literary scene and the considerable sociocultural challenges brought on by immigration and integration. Despite that revolutionary potential, he can only witness an obsession with conformity that obstructs any critical intervention by new German citizens, too many of whom enter the public domain as "domesticated SPD politicians [domestizierte SPD-Politiker]"[4] rather than as confident intellectuals and writers. Biller sees that same domestication reflected in the publications of minority writers who "very early on—often already in their debut, which is usually the wide open window into each author's biography— adapt to the prevailing aesthetics [sich sehr früh—oft schon in ihrem Debüt, das normalerweise das weit offene Fenster zur Biografie eines jeden Autors ist—der herrschenden Ästhetik [...] anpassen]."[5] And even when they *do* incorporate their biographies, autobiographical detail hardly ever drives the central conflict and is used only as "folklore or scenic garnish [Folklore oder szenische Beilage]." Resisting the "repressive tolerance [repressive Toleranz]" exercised by the German *Literaturbetrieb*, Biller makes a case for a collective voice of minority writers, pleading for a new realism undaunted by "the shitstorm [den Shitstorm]" of the German *Kulturvolksfront*—a realism authentic to the core that thwarts readers' expectations, and which for this reason, paradoxically, will be appreciated even more.[6]

Truly provocative about Biller's argument—apart from his scathing criticism directed at individual writers—is the equation of the critical value of a text to its visible thematization and incorporation of cultural difference.[7] Biller thus apparently defends the contested "burden of representation"[8] that so many immigrant authors have struggled to shed, and which has gradually entered the awareness of scholarly critics as a particularly sensitive issue. Arguably, as *enfant terrible* of German letters, Biller's primary intention was simply to cause a stir and incite the debate.[9] Possibly, he even satirizes the exoticist desire of the German audience. Yet behind his intervention hides a more fundamental issue, as it revisits the crucial question that has informed the literary debate since the Romantic period, i.e. the question of the critical potential of art and of its social and political relevance. Do the arts constitute an autonomous, "de-humanized" sphere separated from political, economic, and social life[10]—an art for art's sake? Or should the arts on the contrary deliberately and critically engage with the world? Intentionally or not, Biller reveals a field of extremes between which minority writers appear to move: between artistic integrity and conformity to readers' expectations, and between strategic use of cultural difference and the resistance to be received in terms of that difference. Biller suggests that realism and the visibility of difference will revolutionize and vitalize German literature from within. What happens, though, when precisely that difference becomes incorporated into the reader's horizon of expectations? Moreover, is it really only 'ethnic realism' that interrupts, subverts, or questions the assumptions and expectations of an audience? When does cultural difference become a marketing strategy—or worse, a commodity? In other words, Biller's 'authenticity' argument is highly problematic in an aesthetic context. His defense of realism as the only literary mode 'true' to the writer's background—the genre that "speaks in the simplest of terms [...] about people, as they truly are [in den einfachsten Worten [...] über die Menschen [spricht], wie sie wirklich sind]"—is at odds with the aesthetic nature of literature, which always involves mediation, artificiality, and performance to varying extents. Making claims about the 'authenticity' of minority writing thus inevitably invites a paradox. "[T]he dilemma of authenticity," in Jonathan Culler's words,

> is that to be experienced as authentic it must be marked as authentic, but when it is marked as authentic it is mediated, a sign of itself, and hence lacks the authenticity of what is truly unspoiled, untouched by mediating cultural codes. [...] The authentic [...] requires markers, but our notion of the authentic is the unmarked.[11]

The present chapter investigates this field of tension through the lens of the aesthete, focusing on two typical texts from the *Wiener Moderne*—Schnitzler's *Fräulein Else* and Beer-Hofmann's *Der Tod Georgs*—and two contemporary texts—Kermani's *Kurzmitteilung* and Zaimoglu's *Liebesbrand*. In *Fräulein Else* and *Kurzmitteilung*, the aesthete is a performer who attempts to fashion and sell him-/herself as an interesting personality, a beautiful image, a work of art. In both instances, this artistic self-fashioning is inspired by an assimilatory drive. The two aesthetes at first seem to embody a narrative of self-development and conformity to social convention. Having reached the limits of their radical autonomy, however, they see themselves confronted with the dead end of the assimilation process. The texts thus share a critique of radical assimilation, by presenting it as a process of self-aestheticization bordering on self-commodification. The second chapter section picks up where *Fräulein Else* and *Kurzmitteilung* leave off—at the moment of the aesthete's retreat from the world. In *Der Tod Georgs* and *Liebesbrand*, the protagonists' aestheticism reveals itself as a "perceptive disorder."[12] Their distorted perception originates in their submission to idealism, in an everyday as well as a philosophical sense. In very different ways, the novels criticize idealism as an objectifying and essentializing view on reality and identity. The highly pictorial impressions of Beer-Hofmann's aesthete—an outgrowth of his idealism—can be read as an investigation of the assimilated, secularized Jewish mind.[13] In *Liebesbrand*, the (Western) obsession with the 'original' and the 'authentic' is exposed as an idealizing projection onto a reality that is in fact permanently unstable.

At first sight, the process of self-aestheticization described in the first section has little in common with the perceptive disorder described in the second. Yet either manifestation of aestheticism is based on a distorted reality principle. Aestheticism, in a formal definition, involves

> a specifically heightened form of literary 'perception' constituting a different 'reality' that is not immediately bound to the principles of reality. The world finds expression in images and concepts, in the most general sense through 'attributions of meaning' to the objects of the outer world that in themselves are neutral in meaning. Their 'objective' reproduction or representation is therefore impossible, since 'reality' is constituted in the first place by the perceiving subject. [...] Only the 'reality principle' [...] separates [...] perceiving subject and 'objective' reality. Aestheticism rather regards the world not as a field of activity, planning and action, but as an appearance, as an object of mere observation, as a 'meaningful spectacle' [...].
>
> [eine spezifisch gesteigerte Form literarischer 'Anschauung', durch die eine andere 'Realität', die nicht unmittelbar dem Realitätsprinzip verpflichtet ist, konstituiert wird. Welt gewinnt Ausdruck in Bildern und Begriffen, im allgemeinsten Sinn durch 'Bedeutsamkeitszuschreibungen' gegenüber den an sich bedeutungsneutralen Gegenständen der Erscheinungswelt. Ihre 'objektive' Reproduktion bzw. Abbildung ist daher unmöglich, weil sich 'Realität' überhaupt erst durch das wahrnehmende Subjekt hindurch konstituiert. [...] Erst das 'Realitätsprinzip' statuiert [...] die Trennung von wahrnehmendem Subjekt und 'objektiver' Wirklichkeit. [...] Vielmehr betrachtet der Ästhetizismus die Welt nicht als Wirkungsfeld der Aktivität, des Planens und des Handelns, sondern als Erscheinung, als Gegenstand bloßer Betrachtung, als 'bedeutsames Schauspiel' [...].][14]

The aesthetes in the first section emerge as lead *actors* in that 'spectacle'. Fashioning an image of themselves for others to behold, they actively disengage themselves from a reality principle based on "the requirements of knowledge, tradition, religion, morality, and physical laws [den Vorgaben des Wissens, der Tradition, der Religion, der Moral, und der physikalischen Gesetze]."[15] In that respect, their aesthetic self-performance is informed by a narrative of assimilation, and vice versa. The (semi-) aesthetes in the second section are *spectators*, whose distorted perception leads either to the 'mortification' of reality or to idealizing projections. In both texts, the perceiving subject distorts 'objective' reality by submitting it to the order of his perceptive faculties. Aestheticism is not just a matter of indulgence in beauty, however; the suspension of the reality principle also carries a connotation of aesthetic opposition. The many variations of the aesthete discussed here illustrate that the 'politics' of art and literature do not always involve a truthful, 'authentic' correspondence to the writer's biography, but that they reside precisely in its aesthetic, mediated, and anti-mimetic nature.

The fact that Kermani and Zaimoglu revisit the modernist theme of aestheticism suggests that they see themselves confronted with a dilemma not unlike the one Beer-Hofmann and Schnitzler were facing. The four texts at hand indeed bring into focus a comparable "aesthetic anxiety"[16]—the authors' dilemma between the allure of radical artistic autonomy as a refuge from the imperative of identity and, on the other hand, the concern over losing their social relevance as intellectuals. According to Carl Schorske's influential diagnosis of *fin-de-siècle* Vienna, modernism was the escapist response of a bourgeois elite to the failure of political liberalism.[17] As a "political surrogate for a marginalized liberal bourgeoisie,"[18] Viennese modernism was furthermore expressive of a profound crisis of the (Enlightened) individual. By the end of the nineteenth century, economic, social, and political modernizations had cast doubt on collective cultural identities, as well as on individual subjective identity.[19] The liberal ideal of moral and scientific progress of humanity, embodied by the 'rational man', had started giving way to the more changeable, unstable *homo psychologicus*.[20] The Enlightened individual, as a subject in a clear and stable relationship with the objective world, increasingly lost its significance as a reference point. Modernist art, and particularly aestheticism, reflected that 'inward turn' into radical subjectivity.

The failure of liberalism was significant especially to the assimilated Jews of Vienna. With *Bildung* as its prime vehicle, their assimilation had been inspired by notions of progress and self-improvement. But as anti-Semitism became more virulent and politically dominant with the election of Karl Lueger as mayor in 1895, the liberal promise of integration and emancipation appeared to have reached a dead end. Modernist experiment, inspired by and responding to "the upsets caused in all respects of life by the ever more rapid modernization,"[21] appeared particularly well-suited to address the Jewish predicament. "A refuge for Jews who remained nostalgically faithful to liberalism, even after its fall from power, was in *Bildung* and its privileged auxiliary, art, seen as a secular substitute for religion as a source of human values."[22] Indeed, the undeniably Jewish character of Viennese modernism—in terms of their contribution, not of some Jewish 'essence'[23]—can be considered an expression of their enhanced sensitivity to a climate of crisis, which affected their position as artists *and* as Jews:

> Viennese aestheticism was not, of course, the prerogative of Jewish intellectuals. But it can be seen to assume a unique existential significance for them once it is interpreted as a reaction to the loss of political structures and of possible sociocultural identification, as throwing the individual back on certain refuges: beauty, introspection, dreams. It is then easy to see why these Jewish writers were in such a good position to go further than others in pursuing (and at the same time criticizing) the flight from the world and the denial of reality which is 'art for art's sake'. What we call Viennese modernity meant first living through a crisis of subjectivity, and then reacting against it.[24]

Still, apart from the fact that a retreat into "the aesthetic garden"[25] in itself constituted an oppositional response, the retreat never really offered a permanent or absolute refuge from political reality. Adding nuance to the dichotomy in Schorske's thesis—political engagement versus modern art—Spector argues that aestheticism was untenable and ideological by nature:

> [T]he idealized aesthetic moment of 'Vienna 1900' is best conceived not as a realm unto itself but rather as a thin ridge, like the ridge of a mountain range, which as soon as it is reached reveals a vast and radically different terrain before it. [...] The ridge of aestheticist culture is crossed as soon as it is reached in the sense that the 'retreat into culture' was always already ideological and instantly began to decay.[26]

The modernist texts by Beer-Hofmann and Schnitzler highlight that temporary aspect of the aesthete's retreat. Whereas *Fräulein Else* can be read as the birth of the aesthete—the protagonist moves towards the 'ridge' of aestheticism—*Der Tod Georgs* steers the aesthete back towards real life and his cultural heritage—having reached the ridge, the aesthete is already on his way down. The retreat from reality is indeed already a statement of opposition, but at the peak of aestheticism, the liberal assimilation narrative reaches its absolute limit.

In his discussion of the multiple identity crises of *fin-de-siècle* Vienna, Le Rider points out their 'postmodern' character. "The Viennese modernists may indeed have prefigured some of the great postmodern themes: the triumph and crisis of individualism; the nostalgia for a mythology capable of regenerating society [...]; distrust of scientific and technological rationalism [...];" and—especially relevant to the current chapter—"the questioning of the status of modern art, somewhere between elitism and democratization."[27] Although the label 'postmodern' itself may not fit their novels, Zaimoglu and Kermani revisit similar themes. *Liebesbrand* and *Kurzmitteilung* picture a crisis and a critique of Enlightened individualism and progress, embedded in reflections on the status of art and literature. Kermani does so in allusions to Walter Benjamin's writings on the artwork; Zaimoglu by incorporating typically Romantic motifs. Furthermore, their texts can be read as "literary interventions"[28] into a discursive climate of multiple crises as well. The profound cultural and subjective transformation that the era of "mobilized identities"[29] has brought about, is reminiscent of "the (post)modern indeterminacy of identity"[30] that characterized Viennese modernism. The almost frantic clinging to national and cultural identities today can be considered a response to the problematic construction of the self in relation to an increasingly decontextualized and deterritorialized social space. When "globalizing forces and pressures prise open local certainties, local forms of association, affiliation and feeling, local ways of dwelling [...],"[31] their impact is deeply personal, to the extent that individuals seem to lose control over life.[32] In terms of selfhood and community, then, the identity crises today appear not that different from those faced by the modernists. By revisiting the aesthete, Zaimoglu and Kermani articulate their skepticism of radical assimilation from a contemporary perspective. The contrastive comparison of aestheticist themes across two time frames sheds light on how the Enlightened confidence that underpins assimilation narratives gives ground to a vulnerable individual in need of self-transcendence and community.

2.2 The aesthete's retreat: Arthur Schnitzler's *Fräulein Else* (1924) versus Navid Kermani's *Kurzmitteilung* (2007)

The 'value' of cultural difference: Arthur Schnitzler and Navid Kermani

Fräulein Else, published in 1924, was conceived in a period marked by strong anti-Semitic responses to Schnitzler's work. The origins of the novella can be traced back to the 1921 Viennese premiere of his erotically tinted play *Reigen*.[33] The play elicited a scandal and was received by the anti-Semitic press as evidence of the author's supposed "predilection for bordello themes, which, in turn, were interpreted as evidence of an uncanny business sense."[34] As the press continued its attack, the play even became the topic of a heated parliamentary debate. After a mob caused a riot in a theatre, Schnitzler eventually forbade all further performances after 1922. Schnitzler, "[t]rue to his lifelong apolitical habits, [...] did not react to external crisis by publicly confronting it."[35] Instead, he responded to the anti-Semitic reception of his work by reworking material and turning inward.[36] Indeed, in *Fräulein Else*, Schnitzler appears to comment subtly on the impossible position of the Jewish author, whose work for some was 'too Jewish' but for others 'not Jewish enough'.

Kurzmitteilung was published at a comparably tense moment. In the aftermath of the publication of the Mohammed cartoons in the Danish *Jyllands-Posten* in 2005, the "emotive dyad"[37] of 'Islam' versus 'the West' had resurfaced with renewed intensity in the German public debate. The image of Islam as a threat to Western values dominated the debate on the construction of mosques in Cologne (Kermani's residence) and Berlin in 2006. For some, these were a sign of religious tolerance, for others evidence of the development of *Parallelgesellschaften*, and Germany's "silent islamification [stille Islamisierung]."[38] Kermani's interventions in the debate are reminiscent of Edward Said's diagnosis that Western media use the term 'Islam' as "part fiction, part ideological label, part minimal designation of a religion called Islam," which barely corresponds to "the enormously varied life that goes on within the world of Islam, with [...] its dozens of societies, states, histories, geographies, cultures."[39] Like Said, Kermani calls for more nuance in the often polarizing debates:

Authors, speakers, and studio guests are ahead of me in that they seem to know exactly what Islam is. To me it is not so clear. When asked, for example, whether Islam is compatible with modernity, I cannot come up with a straight answer. Which modernity? is to be asked first of all. [...] The second question seems to be even more difficult to answer: Which Islam?

[Die Autoren, Redner und Studiogäste haben mir voraus, daß sie genau zu wissen scheinen, was der Islam ist. Mir ist das nicht so klar. Auf die Frage etwa, ob der Islam mit der Moderne kompatibel sei, will mir keine bündige Antwort einfallen. Welche Moderne? ist zunächst einmal zu fragen. [...] Schwieriger noch zu beantworten scheint die zweite Frage: Welcher Islam?][40]

Without delivering pat answers, *Kurzmitteilung* comments on the position of religion in a (self-perceived) secularized society. In a reversed 'orientalizing' gesture, Kermani paints a highly ironic picture of Western secularism, unmasking it as a capitalist 'religion'.

The pressure to stake a stand on political matters in an increasingly anti-Semitic environment had a particular effect on (the reception of) Schnitzler's work (1862–1931). The idea that, as a writer, he had no adequate answer to the Jewish question shaped his approach to the few Jewish-themed texts he did write.[41] Schnitzler appeared to represent the typical assimilated Jewish intellectual, unfettered by religious tradition or nostalgic sentiments about his family history, while showing little interest in the many paths of Jewish revival. Although his medical education paved the way for a bourgeois life among the acculturated Jews of Vienna, he chose not to become a doctor and to pursue a literary career instead. Still, Schnitzler never rejected his Jewishness, as his diary entries on anti-Semitism and on the many shades and variants of Jewish responses to it reflect.[42] He saw little contradiction in the multiple facets of his identity: "I am a Jew, an Austrian, a German. It has to be that way, for I feel insulted in the name of the Jews, the Austrians, and the Germans when they say something horrible about any of the three. [Ich bin Jude, Österreicher, Deutscher. Es muss wohl so sein—denn beleidigt fühl ich mich im Namen des Judentums, des Österreichertums und des Deutschlands, wenn man einem von den Dreien was Schlimmes nachsagt.]"[43] Despite his obvious affiliation to the fatherland, Schnitzler was skeptical of determinate notions of (collective) identity.[44] Unlike his friend Beer-Hofmann, he opposed both cultural and political Zionism, rejecting it as a questionable notion, "according to which someone who was born in a certain country, grew up there, is always employed there, should regard another country [...] also *emotionally* as his actual homeland [nach der jemand, der in einem bestimmten Land geboren, dort aufgewachsen, dort dauernd tätig ist, ein anderes Land [...] auch *gefühlsmäßig* als seine eigentliche Heimat zu betrachten habe."[45] He felt that a deliberate personal commitment to the Jewish cause would be hard to reconcile with his Enlightened view on autonomy. With his "skeptical individualism" he sought to "reaffirm the autonomy of the inner self in an age of collectivist ideologies [...] which might threaten its integrity."[46]

Not surprisingly, Schnitzler was not known for taking an explicit stand on the position of Austrian Jews. His public silence does not imply, however, that the author was not interested in pressing political matters—as Gillman notes, "history had rendered that position obsolete."[47] Although a direct engagement with Jewish themes is largely absent from his extensive oeuvre,[48] two of his works are directly concerned with Jewish themes: his debut novel *Der Weg ins Freie* (1908) and the play *Professor Bernhardi* (1912). Both texts offer a panoramic view of Viennese Jewish intellectual circles and its range of ideologies—from Jewish socialists, to Zionists, to "assimilatory geckos [assimilatorischen Gecken]."[49] Yet even though these works portray the Jews in an increasingly hostile environment, Schnitzler's apparent engagement with Jewish issues did not really convince his readers. According to Gillman, this was due to the fact that Schnitzler's 'Jewish' texts "respond[ed] to the situation by offering anatomies of failure: works that on formal and thematic levels are all about a hopeless hybridity failing to cohere in the well-made story or political program."[50] Gillman further argues that Schnitzler went to great lengths "to frustrate the expectations of readers and viewers who expected a Jewish writer of Schnitzler's prominence to take a stand [...]."[51] In other words, the author was well aware of how critical pressure to engage with Jewish themes would affect the reception of his work. The choice to write about Jewish themes presented him with a dilemma. On the one hand, if he chose to withhold a clear political argument from his texts, they would be "vulnerable to cooptation by almost every ideological camp."[52] On the other hand, he was convinced that "the aesthetic criteria of successful dramatic art made it impossible for an overtly Jewish dramatist to succeed. Any and every representation of the Jewish question would be seen as polemical from the onset [...]."[53]

So, while critics deemed him a public intellectual obligated to express an opinion on Jewish matters, Schnitzler himself found that political engagement and addressing cultural difference would compromise the integrity of his writing and his status as a skilled novelist. He felt that, either way, he would fail—as being too polemical, or not polemical enough. As I will illustrate, *Fräulein Else*—even if it is not an explicitly 'Jewish' text—evokes a similar artistic predicament, as well as the artist's desire to escape its pressure. I will do so in comparison to Kermani's *Kurzmitteilung,* which explores the artistic 'value' of cultural difference against a contemporary background of consumer culture, culture industry, and Islam in a secularized society.

Navid Kermani (1967) was born of Iranian parents in Siegen, Germany. His interventions in the debate on 'Islam versus *Aufklärung*' have garnered him the status of well-respected public figure. In his fictional, academic, and journalistic writing, he consistently focuses on religion, which he approaches from a variety of perspectives. He has written on political issues in the Muslim world, Iran in particular,[54] but also on the aesthetic perception of the Qur'an[55] and, more recently, on Christian art.[56] In his public role, he does not shy away from criticism, but when compared to, for instance, Zaimoglu's characteristic anti-establishment strategy, Kermani adopts a more reconciliatory tone. The author, who had a seat on the *Deutsche Islamkonferenz* from 2006 until 2009, has revealed himself a staunch defender of interreligious tolerance[57] and strongly encourages intercultural dialogue. In his essay collection *Wer ist Wir?* (2009),[58] for instance, Kermani deplores "that the debate about multiculturalism is in fact a debate about Muslims—not *with* Muslims, by the way, but mainly *about* them [daß die Debatte um den Multikulturalismus faktisch eine Debatte über Muslime ist— übrigens nicht *mit* den Muslimen, sondern hauptsächlich *über* sie]."[59] In his essays, Kermani's personal experiences as a German Muslim convey an Enlightened perspective on religion in a (seemingly) secular society.[60] In doing so, he confronts those voices that surfaced more strongly since September 11, 2001, which claim that Islamic and Western values are fundamentally incompatible. Kermani is, in other words, not reluctant to assume a representational role or to take a nuanced stand in a polarized debate. Still, it is important to note that he does so primarily as an academic: he does not speak only from personal experience but from a more distanced and critical perspective on Islam and religion as well.

As a writer of *literary* texts, on the other hand, he refuses to be pigeonholed as a 'minority writer'. "My literature is German, period—as German as Kafka [...]. [Meine Literatur ist deutsch, Punkt, aus, basta—so deutsch wie Kafka [...]."[61] Tracing his affinity to Kafka—"a German writer who is not German [einem deutschen Schriftsteller, der nicht deutsch [ist]],"[62] yet whose "intellectual *Heimat* [...] is German literature [geistige Heimat [...] die deutsche Literatur [ist]]"[63]—Kermani highlights the fact that 'German' literary history has always been characterized by cultural, linguistic, and geographical heterogeneity and, moreover, has shown itself "remarkably often recalcitrant to concepts such as nation, empire, fatherland [auffallend oft widerspenstig gegenüber Begriffen wie Nation, Reich, Vaterland]."[64] Similarly, as far as his fiction is concerned, he refuses to carry the burden of representation. In an interview for *Die Zeit*, a literary critic confronted Kermani with a question reminiscent of Biller's provocation.[65] She wonders why Kermani's novel *Sozusagen Paris* (2016)—a story about "the very normal life in a goddamn German countryside village [das ganz normale Leben in einer scheißdeutschen Provinz]," to use Kermani's own words—is so tedious. Furthermore, she denounces the metafictional aspect of the text, which is traversed by references to Marcel Proust and directs the reader's attention to the construction of the literary manuscript: "Why this flirtation with the seal of authenticity? [Was soll die Koketterie mit dem Echtheitssiegel?]"[66] Apparently, like Biller, the critic had different expectations about fiction by an author otherwise very much engaged with the relations between Islam and the West. The implied assumption that these issues should at least be reflected in his literary work once more illustrates the pressure to account for one's cultural difference through fiction.

Schnitzler and Kermani address the 'burden of representation' and the 'market value' of cultural difference from a similar perspective. The aesthetes in *Fräulein Else* and *Kurzmitteilung*, who both fashion themselves as performers, represent a conflict between artistic 'codes': between an "aesthetics of opposition" that creates dissonance, and an "aesthetics of identity," in which the artist's code is the same as the audience's.[67] This artistic tension is traversed by narratives of assimilation and cultural difference. To Schnitzler's aesthete, the burden of covert Jewishness aggravates the artistic conflict; Kermani's aesthete fashions a palatable cultural difference, exploiting his Islamic background as a self-marketing strategy. By comparing these protagonists, I will illustrate how cultural difference—like the art object—is vulnerable to commodification and further complicates the already existing tension between artistic autonomy and resonance with the audience, which literature has to negotiate. Furthermore, I will argue that the aesthete, as the embodiment of *Bildung*, conveys a critique of radical assimilation: it merely leads to a dead end of "uselessly advanced self-development."[68] On a metanarrative level, the aesthete—especially Kermani's—subverts exoticist projections on minority writing as being 'original' and 'authentic' and is, rather, a reminder of the essentially mediated and artificial nature of literature.

A conflict of codes:
'aesthetics of opposition' versus 'aesthetics of identity'

Fräulein Else consists of the interior monologue of the young, acculturated Jewish woman Else, whose integrity is compromised by her father's financial difficulties. During a summer retreat with relatives at an Italian spa, Else receives a telegram from her mother, requesting her to approach one of the guests, the vicomte Dorsday, for a loan. Dorsday only accepts the financial transaction on the condition of Else's service in return—to show herself naked in front of him. A considerable part of the novella pictures Else's fretting about the social dilemma she faces: should she protect her father from disgrace by disgracing herself? Or should she resist social and familial pressure and instead give in to her surfacing longing to break through the façade of Viennese bourgeoisie? In a culmination of her mental distress and her desire to reveal herself as a performer, Else enters the hotel's music room dressed in only a coat, undresses in front of the collected guests, and collapses, which the audience perceives as a bout of illness or hysteria. Once she returns to her room, she poisons herself, seemingly fatally, with a dose of barbiturate she has kept at her disposal, and which she has referred to before as an ideal means of escape. Else's Jewish background is not evident at first sight, but can be inferred from the tension between her and Dorsday, a Jewish art dealer, and—in Else's eyes—a parvenu. It is in their conflict that assimilatory and artistic/aestheticist narratives confront each other.

Kurzmitteilung situates the I-narrator Dariusch against a backdrop of culture industry and increased anti-Islamic sentiment. Dariusch is a second-generation German-Iranian event manager—not quite an art dealer but a dealer in *Kultur*—who suffers from a deeply conflicted identity. He struggles to reconcile his position as a successful businessman with his Middle Eastern background, which he considers both an asset and an impediment to his well-manicured image: he claims residual identity as an Iranian Muslim, even though he is not an observant one; he seems very critical of misconstrued versions of Islam in the West but is, due to his profession, complicit in its commercialization. Dariusch has been commissioned to organize a farewell celebration for the Ford AG chairman Patrick Boger. His preparations are interrupted by a text message from his former colleague Korinna. She informs him about the sudden death of his contact at Ford, Maike Anfang, whom he has met only a couple of weeks before. This news coincides with the 7/7 bombings in London,[69] which upsets Dariusch in an unexpected way, causing him to question his lifestyle and eliciting a desire for connection and spirituality. Remarkably, it does not lead him to rediscover his Islamic background. Instead, under the guidance of Boger, he turns to a cultic movement that very much resembles the corporate and capitalist 'religion' Scientology.

Driving the conflict in both stories is a similar short message—a text message in *Kurzmitteilung* and a telegram in *Fräulein Else*. This apparently direct, quick, and effective means of communication in fact exposes a social context from which genuine connection is missing. *Fräulein Else* is well-known for its exposure of bourgeois false fronts and for painting a picture of "a society that has lost its immediacy and grown used to a degree of alienation."[70] Similarly, Dariusch represents the typical "network nomad," "who swing[s] from contact to contact and project to project [...] without insisting on a consistent self-image"[71]—and who does not manage to establish any meaningful connection. In this light, the I-narration in both stories reflects the protagonists' painful isolation, indicating that their individualistic, assimilatory narrative has reached its limits. Furthermore, as I will illustrate, the respective social contexts endorse performance and self-aestheticization. This manifests itself in Else's acute awareness of how others perceive her and in her "self-dramatizing tendency:"[72] to her, social interaction amounts to a theatrical performance. In Dariusch, that tendency is evident in slightly irritating self-justifications feeding the impression that the I-narrator consistently addresses an audience—which in fact he does: it turns out that the story is a book chapter addressed to Boger.

The short message, then, is a crucial narrative element, as it connects the stories to the larger question of artistic communication—of how the writer mediates a message to an audience. As I will illustrate, *Kurzmitteilung* and *Fräulein Else* revolve around a conflict between two literary codes as defined by literary theorist Jurij Lotman.[73] "The perception of an artistic text," he writes,

> is always a struggle between audience and author [...]. The audience takes in part of the text and then 'finishes' or 'constructs' the rest. [...] [The author] outplays the artistic experience, aesthetic norms and prejudices of the reader, and thrusts his model of the world and concept of the structure of reality upon him. [...] The reader, of course, is not passive; he *has an interest* in mastering the model that the artist presents to him.[74]

Based on this relation between potentially conflicting interests, Lotman distinguishes two artistic codes: the "aesthetics of identity" and the "aesthetics of opposition."[75] The first presupposes the identity or near-identity of sender's and receiver's codes. "[T]he rules of the author and of the audience are not one, but two phenomena in a state of mutual identity."[76] This implies, first of all, that a work of art is judged "according to its observation of certain rules,"[77] and, secondly, that the work sets out to meet the audience's expectations. The aesthetics of identity are characteristic of folkloristic, medieval, and classicist art. By contrast, the aesthetics of opposition, typical of Romanticism or the avant-gardes, involve those artistic systems that associate aesthetic worth with originality:

> [Their] code is unknown to the audience before the act of artistic perception begins. [...] The author sets his own, original resolution, which he believes to be the truer one, in opposition to methods of modeling reality that are familiar to the reader. In the first instance the act of artistic perception involves simplification and generalization; here we are dealing with complication.[78]

This does not imply that all rules are abandoned in the aesthetics of opposition. Rather, as Lotman puts it, the rules "must be established in the process of play."[79] This dynamic between artist's and audience's codes, as well as the mutual dependence of artist and onlooker, will prove useful in the interpretation of Else's and Dariusch's artistic self-fashioning and its traversal by assimilatory narratives.

Birth of the aesthete—"Bin nicht geschaffen für eine bürgerliche Existenz [...]"

Fräulein Else has often been read as a case study in hysteria and narcissism and the 'pathology' of Else's mindset as the symptom of pervasive social determination.[80] Others have focused on themes of voyeurism and surveillance as aspects of Viennese bourgeois culture.[81] More recently, the Jewish context of the novella, as well as the Jewish setting of the story have come into the picture,[82] while others have pointed out the significance of Else's theatricality and self-dramatization.[83] As I will argue, Else's covert Jewishness is crucial in her "failed attempt at aesthetic self-fashioning."[84] By asserting herself as an aesthete—a combination of actor and artist—Else seeks to regain control over a situation in which she is at the mercy of social, erotic, and economic pressure—"I'm paralysed [Ich bin gelähmt]." (FE 59) The challenge to resist conformity and social convention is augmented by the fact that she must engage in a "double monitoring [...] as woman and as assimilated Jew."[85] Yet her self-aestheticization makes her complicit in her own commodification: she becomes an art object for male consumption and thus loses the agency that her performance initially affords her. Her dilemma—the choice between her father's integrity or her own—thus entails a more fundamental conflict: between the emancipatory desire to assert herself and her own involvement in the erotic, economic, and Jewish-assimilatory narratives that determine her experience.

Else's theatrical inclination is evident already in the opening scene. Her "autonomous monologue"[86] offers insight into the privacy of her thoughts during social interaction. While it lends an air of veracity and transparency to her account, this "mimesis of consciousness"[87] also reveals a discordance between what she is thinking and what she is saying. When she decides to leave a game of tennis with Paul and Cissy, their interaction is an example of conversational etiquette:

> "Won't you really play any more, Else ?" "No, Paul, I can't play any more—goodbye. Good-bye, gnädige Frau."—"But, Else, call me Frau Cissy—or better still, just Cissy."—"Good-bye, Frau Cissy."—"But why are you going already, Else ? There are two whole hours before dinner."—"Please play your single with Paul, Frau Cissy. It's really no fun playing with me to-day."—"Leave her alone, gnädige Frau, she's in one of her moods to-day—As a matter of fact, Else, being in a bad mood is very becoming to you.—And your red jersey is still more so."—"I hope you'll find me better-tempered in blue, Paul."
>
> [*"Du willst wirklich nicht mehr weiterspielen, Else?"*—"Nein, Paul, ich kann nicht mehr. Adieu.—Auf Wiedersehen, gnädige Frau."—*"Aber, Else, sagen Sie mir doch: Frau Cissy. Oder lieber noch: Cissy, ganz einfach."*—"Auf Wiedersehen, Frau Cissy."—*"Aber warum gehen Sie denn schon, Else? Es sind noch volle zwei Stunden bis zum Dinner."*—"Spielen Sie nur Ihr Single mit Paul, Frau Cissy, mit mir ist's doch heut' wahrhaftig kein Vergnügen."—*"Lassen Sie sie, gnädige Frau, sie hat heut' ihren ungnädigen Tag.—Steht dir übrigens ausgezeichnet zu Gesicht, das Ungnädigsein, Else.—Und der rote Sweater noch besser."*—"Bei Blau wirst du hoffentlich mehr Gnade finden, Paul. Adieu."] (FE 7)

Their brief conversation triggers Else's thoughts, which reveal her ironic distance from the 'reality' of social conduct. This distance suggests that Else has not fully interiorized social convention, and that it requires her to play a role. Here, the bourgeois setting is exposed as theatrical, artificial, and inauthentic:

That was quite a good exit. I hope those two don't think I'm jealous.—
I'll swear there's something between Cousin Paul and Cissy Mohr.
Nothing in the world troubles me less—Now I'll turn round again and
wave to them. Wave and smile. Do I look gracious now?—Oh Lord,
they're playing again. I really play better than Cissy Mohr, and Paul
isn't exactly a champion, but he looks nice—with his open collar and
that naughty boy face. If only he weren't so affected. You needn't worry,
Aunt Emma.

[Das war ein ganz guter Abgang. Hoffentlich glauben die zwei nicht, daß ich
eifersüchtig bin.—Daß sie was miteinander haben, Cousin Paul und Cissy
Mohr, darauf schwöre ich. Nichts auf der Welt ist mir gleichgültiger.—Nun
wende ich mich noch einmal um und winke ihnen zu. Winke und lächle. Sehe
ich nun gnädig aus?—Ach Gott, sie spielen schon wieder. Eigentlich spiele ich
besser als Cissy Mohr; und Paul ist auch nicht gerade ein Matador. Aber gut
sieht er aus—mit dem offenen Kragen und dem Bösen-Jungen-Gesicht. Wenn
er nur weniger affektiert wäre. Brauchst keine Angst zu haben, Tante Emma.]
(FE 7–8)

The ambivalence of *spielen* in the opening sentence—playing tennis or acting—
may not be evident at first. Else's comments on the opening scene suggest, though,
that she is indeed playing a role, as she directs her own performance. Her retreat
from the game into the privacy of her own thoughts is an appropriate exit from
the stage. Her dramaturgical self-address—'Now I'll turn round again'—betrays
the calculation behind her cordiality. Furthermore, the denial of her attraction
to Paul is addressed to an imaginary audience, 'Aunt Emma'. Else is profoundly
aware of the appearances and emotional self-composure that govern bourgeois
interaction—her bad temper, for instance, is reduced to a feature of her beauty,
like the color of her sweater. Yet playing a role herself, she is suspicious of others'
artificiality as well. She mocks Cissy's use of the word 'Dinner' instead of 'Diner'
as "silly affectation [dumme Affektation]" (FE 14), and conversational etiquette
as perfunctory and superfluous (FE 11), even though she continues to participate
in any conversation. Else's interior monologue thus reveals conflicting impulses.
On the one hand, she is tired of 'playing', of keeping up appearances—'I can't
play any more.' On the other, her self-dramatization suggests that she still enjoys
performing and being watched. Apparently, Else longs for a different kind of
performance than required by her relatives. Her parents have been struggling
with financial difficulties for years and have become skillful actors in a theater of
bourgeois conventions:

It's always been the same story for the last seven years—no, longer than that. Who'd think it to look at me? No one would think it to look at me, or Father either. [...] Mother's really an artist. The dinner for fourteen people last New Year's Day—incomprehensible. But my two pairs of evening gloves—there was a regular fuss about them. And when Rudi wanted three hundred gulden the other day Mother almost cried. And Father is always in good spirits. Always? No. Oh no. At the opera the other day at 'Figaro' his eyes—suddenly lost all expression—I was terrified. He seemed to become quite another person.

[Immer diese Geschichten! Seit sieben Jahren! Nein—länger. Wer möcht' mir das ansehen? Niemand sieht mir was an, auch dem Papa nicht. [...] Mama ist wirklich eine Künstlerin. Das Souper am letzten Neujahrstag für vierzehn Personen—unbegreiflich. Aber dafür meine Ballhandschuhe, die waren eine Affäre. Und wie der Rudi neulich dreihundert Gulden gebraucht hat, da hat die Mama beinah' geweint. Und der Papa ist dabei immer gut aufgelegt. Immer? Nein. O nein. In der Oper neulich bei Figaro sein Blick,—plötzlich ganz leer—ich bin erschrocken. Da war er wie ein ganz anderer Mensch.] (FE 24–5)

Her parents' performance, and especially her mother's 'artistry', involves a strategy of concealment. Tailoring their appearances to the expectations of their social circle, Else's family inhabits a *Scheinwirklichkeit*, where the perception of their impending ruination—"such a scandal as there never was before [ein Skandal, wie er noch nicht da war]" (FE 19)—seems even more important than the ruination itself. Obsessed with the rules of bourgeois convention, Else's parents are thus engaged in an aesthetic of identity from which Else wishes to dissociate herself. Resisting to be forced by her father into the role of beggar-woman, or by Dorsday into the role of erotic object, Else attempts to become an artist of (self-) exposure and self-expression instead.

Else's penchant for role-playing seems at first inscribed into the same aesthetic of identity as her parents'. The roles she imagines herself in are all expressions of social status: "I, the high-spirited one, the aristocrat, the Marchesa, the beggar girl, the swindler's daughter! [[I]ch die Hochgemüte, die Aristokratin, die Marchesa, die Bettlerin, die Tochter des Defraudanten]." (FE 29) Her performance seems closely entwined with a liberal-enlightened narrative of social advancement: "No other woman climbs as well as I do, no other has so much go. I'm a sporting girl. I ought to have been born in England, or a Countess. [...] I ought to have gone on the stage. [Keine klettert so gut wie ich, keine hat so viel Schneid,—sporting girl, in England hätte ich auf die Welt kommen sollen, oder als Gräfin. [...] Zur

Bühne hätte ich gehen sollen.]" (FE 29–30) The association between artist and social climber introduces a narrative of assimilation and covert Jewish identity that is not evident from the text at first. As Kelly Comfort argues, in reference to Nietzsche's *The Gay Science*, Else is obviously not an artist in the traditional sense but can be considered one due to her construction of a stylized self.[88] Nietzsche wonders whether "the delight in simulation," "the inner craving for a role and mask," is "perhaps not only peculiar to the actor."[89] He assigns the actor's attributes to larger groups of people—the lower classes, women, and Jews—for whom acting is enforced by societal standards. It is an acquired instinct of those

> who had to survive under changing pressures and coercions, in deep dependency, who had to cut their coat according to the cloth, always adapting themselves again to new circumstances, who always had to change their mien and posture, until they learned gradually to turn their coat with every wind and thus virtually to become a coat [...].[90]

Based on this argument, he likens the Jewish acculturation process to a theatrical performance. Jews are "the people who possess the art of adaptability par excellence," and "one might see them virtually as a world-historical arrangement for the production of actors, a veritable breeding ground for actors."[91] Even if his reasoning may appear questionable due to its echoes of anti-Semitic suspicions about the invisible 'Jewification' of society, the parallel to Schnitzler's novella is striking. Neither Else's Jewishness nor Dorsday's is mentioned explicitly, which ties in with their apparently complete assimilation. Yet from the dynamic between the two characters, especially from the assumptions on Else's part, it can be inferred that the two are indeed assimilated Jews. As I will illustrate, their conflict of aesthetic codes leads to Else's ultimate artistic failure and aestheticist retreat, picturing how the failure of a bourgeois aesthetic produces an aesthetic of opposition, which however remains vulnerable to stereotype and prejudice.

Else's resistance to her parents' aesthetic code is closely connected to her insufficient identification with the "ideal I of the 'educated' [Ideal-Ich des 'Gebildeten']."[92] While she does seem to have developed a critical awareness regarding the false fronts of bourgeois society, she has become a commodity at the mercy of erotic and capitalist demands. Her education leaves her remarkably helpless, and proves of little help in solving her dilemma:

> Why haven't I learnt anything ? Ok, I have learnt something! Who can say I haven't learnt anything? I can play the piano; I know French, English and a little Italian; I've been to lectures on the history of art.— Ha, ha ! And if I had learnt anything more practical, what good would it be to me now?
>
> [Warum habe ich nichts gelernt? O, ich habe was gelernt! Wer darf sagen, daß ich nichts gelernt habe? Ich spiele Klavier, ich kann französisch, englisch, auch ein bißl italienisch, habe kunstgeschichtliche Vorlesungen besucht—Haha! Und wenn ich schon was Gescheiteres gelernt hätte, was hülfe es mir?] (FE 26)

Apparently, she does not acknowledge her education as a means of self-improvement; it does not enable "a reflected detachment, a practical knowledge of the world and thus sovereign disposition over relevant knowledge, emotional differentiation, moral competence and aesthetic tastes at the same time [eine reflektierte Distanznahme, ein praktisches Weltwissen und damit souveräne Verfügung über relevante Kenntnisse, Differenziertheit des Gefühls, moralische Kompetenz und ästhetischen Geschmack zugleich] [...]."[93] In the conflict of aesthetic codes, Else's indeed simplified notion of *Bildung* shares some characteristics with the aesthetics of identity as represented by her family. *Bildung* can be described as a process of "mimetic association" that enables "the connection of our 'I' with the world in the most general, most lively and most free mutual interaction."[94]

> An individual uses his mimetic abilities to extend towards the unfamiliar and incorporate it into his world of images, sounds and imagination. Outer world thus becomes inner world. This transformation, which constitutes the education process, is accomplished through transmitting the outer world in pictures, and through adopting it into the inner image world of the individual. The power of imagination then connects these images with the person's inner image world of memories, desires and other ideas.[95]

The condition for *Bildsamkeit* is the subject's mimetic capacity to creatively incorporate the image of the world and, in doing so, to experience "the difference of the outer world, its non-identity with his own world."[96] Else however mistakes that mimetic negotiation for meaningless imitation. *Bildung* then becomes nothing more than the equivalent of simple *imitatio*, a mimetic process that "degenerate[s] into mimicry [...] with disregard for the creative strengths and energies of the individual."⁹⁷ In other words, to Else, *Bildung* is inscribed into the aesthetic of identity represented by her parents: it is about the rules of convention and about avoiding dissonance.

Indicative of Else's faulty appropriation of *Bildung* is her attitude towards bourgeois practices of literacy. Reading and writing are generally considered to foster emotional and cognitive sensibility and self-awareness.⁹⁸

> The bourgeois self-practices of literacy enable a specifically internally oriented subject to come into existence. Focused in physical motor activity and the intellectual attention, elements of a cognitive and emotional, partly also imaginative 'inner world' emerge: through reflection—e.g. on biographical possibilities and moral dilemmas—self-observation and emotionally sensible inner experience.
>
> [Die bürgerlichen Selbstpraktiken der Schriftlichkeit verhelfen einer spezifisch innenorientierten Subjektform zur Existenz. In der körperlichen Motorik und der Aufmerksamkeit des Geistes fokussiert, bilden sich Elemente einer kognitiven und emotionalen, zum Teil auch imaginativen 'Innenwelt' heraus: über den Weg der Reflexion—etwa über biographische Möglichkeiten und moralische Dilemmata—, der Selbstbeobachtung und des emotional sensibilisierten inneren Erlebens.]⁹⁹

That degree of self-reflection remains largely absent in Else. There is no mention of Else either writing¹⁰⁰ or reading—except for her mother's *Expreßbrief*. Although the inward orientation of her monologue may resemble the self-hermeneutic practice of diary-keeping, she in fact rejects that kind of self-observation: "Why am I reminiscing like this? I'm not writing my memoirs. I don't even keep a diary like Bertha. [Wozu nachdenken, ich schreibe ja keine Memoiren. Nicht einmal ein Tagebuch wie die Bertha.]" (FE 10) Nor does she acknowledge the didactic and moral value in reading novels. In an attempt to evade a confrontation with Dorsday, Else thinks of approaching a friend for help, but she quickly rejects the option:

> Couldn't I go down now, at once, and speak to Dorsday before dinner? O, how horrible!—Paul, if you get me thirty thousand you can have anything you ask of me. *That's out of a novel*. The noble daughter sells herself for her beloved father's sake, and really rather enjoys it. B-r-r ! No, Paul, you can't get me even for thirty thousand. Nobody can.

> [Wenn ich jetzt gleich hinunterginge, Dorsday noch vor dem Diner spräche? Ah wie entsetzlich!—Paul, wenn du mir die dreißigtausend verschaffst, kannst du von mir haben, was du willst. *Das ist ja schon wieder aus einem Roman.* Die edle Tochter verkauft sich für den geliebten Vater, und hat am End' noch ein Vergnügen davon. Pfui Teufel! Nein, Paul, auch für dreißigtausend kannst du von mir nichts haben. Niemand.] (FE 28; emphasis added)

At first sight, the comment 'That's out of a novel' suggests that Else struggles with the "realism effect [Realismus-Effekt]"[101] of bourgeois novels, which "[present] themselves as quasi-didactic examples of reflexive-moral actions and at the same time as mediators of a cognitive 'knowledge of the world' that tries to convey verbal intelligence and subjective sovereignty [[die]sich als quasi-didaktische Exempel reflexiv-moralischen Handelns [präsentieren] und zugleich als Vermittler eines kognitiven 'Weltwissens', das mundane Intelligibilität und subjektive Souveränität zu vermitteln versucht]."[102] The source of Else's irritation is that her life and inspiration seem to imitate art, and that she cannot come up with original solutions. She discards her 'own' idea not due to her desire to comply with a bourgeois moral code, but because the idea might have been affected *a priori* by that code. The authority of novels and *Bildung* alike, in Else's eyes, interferes excessively with 'real' life and original thought. At the same time, Else imagines herself as a character in a fictional plot. In doing so, she embodies the aestheticist motto that "everything in the world exists to end up in a book,"[103] and that art is "the supreme reality" and "life [...] a mere mode of fiction."[104] Her self-dramatization reverses the supposed exemplarity of fiction: her own life provides the example; it *is* the work of art. In other words, her aestheticist inversion of the *Realismuseffekt* robs it of its didactic value. Else's insufficient identification with the ideal of *Bildung* thus enables her to fashion a subversive aesthetic of her own. As I will discuss in more detail, it affords her the sense of agency that had been robbed from her by erotic and economic pressures.

The aesthete as 'ästhetisch-ökonomische Doublette'

Whereas Else's performance resists impending commodification, Dariusch's self-fashioning is motivated by market logic entirely. His aestheticism is informed by an assimilatory drive as well, but unlike Else, whose Jewish identity remains covert, Dariusch fashions a palatable, salable version of cultural difference. A century apart, it seems that the value of cultural difference takes on different but equally critical hues: Schnitzler criticizes the persistence of cultural prejudice in the reception of art, while Kermani mocks the audience's exoticist desire for 'authentic' difference.

Dariusch's performance is not evident from some dramaturgical self-address but, rather, from the tone of self-justification that pervades his account. His personality elicits irritation, as reviewers have noticed as well: "Navid Kermani tells the story of a fundamentally disagreeable man [Navid Kermani erzählt die Geschichte eines gründlich unsympathischen Mannes]," of a "confirmed asshole [ausgemachtes Arschloch]" even, and the novel itself is the "annoying story of a successful loser [irritierend[e] Geschichte einer erfolgreichen Niete]."[105] Of course, the (lacking) appeal of a character is hardly a critical criterion otherwise, but it is relevant in this case, as it is an immediate effect of his all too evident calculation and inauthenticity. In his address to the reader, he presents himself as a German with an Iranian background, and makes quite an effort of demonstrating his estrangement from his cultural and religious heritage. As a child, his Iranian identity felt natural to him, unlike today. Most likely, if he is a businessman in his thirties or early forties, the Iran of his childhood was that of the 1960s or 1970s, before the 1979 Islamic Revolution. In other words, he was able to identify with the country when it still had a pro-Western government. He then curiously leaves out that his parents probably escaped the country, and that he was not allowed to return when in the 1980s Iranian universities were closed and 'cleansed' from un-Islamic influences. Instead, he emphasizes his status as a German citizen by mentioning that he was a conscript and, more importantly, depicts his ties to Iran as an affinity by choice. Jim Jordan describes Dariusch's estrangement from his heritage as an "ironic denial"[106] of his cultural identity, but it is not a denial per se. Rather, he seems to tailor his Iranian image to his German audience. His interest in Persian culture is limited to harmless elements that are interesting in an exoticist way—literature, music, mysticism. Additionally, if he wants to fashion his Iranian identity as an accessory to an otherwise bland German image, of course he must reject Islam as a restrictive or oppressive religion: "Islam has always annoyed me. For me it was all bigoted. Had it been freer, I could have imagined living in Iran. [Der Islam hat mich immer genervt. Für mich war das alles bigott. Wäre es freier gewesen, hätte ich mir vorstellen können, in Iran zu leben]." (KM 32) Whereas Else's self-fashioning is an ambiguous and self-destructive act of resistance, in *Kurzmitteilung* it becomes an act of self-marketing adding greatly to the narrator's excellence, though it eventually proves to be nothing but a sign of his conformation to capitalist demands.

The theme of commodified cultural identity is highlighted by Kermani's allusions to Walter Benjamin's reflections on the 'Aura' of the artwork.[107] In the opening scene, Dariusch recalls his whereabouts at the moment he received Korinna's text message about Maike Anfang's death: the Catalan town Cadaqués.

His favorite retreat from German corporate life—located near Portbou, where Benjamin took his own life—serves as a spatial metaphor for his self-fashioning and image-building:

> Picasso once had a house here, Dalí nearby, too, and something of their *aura* still floods the stone-paved streets [...]. The inhabitants, most of whom have moved here, carefully preserve the image of an artist's village on the Mediterranean: with whitewashed, yet befittingly flaked off walls [...], with bulging flower boxes and picturesque handicraft, delicatessen and wine shops, with restaurants that reinvent their cuisine on chalkboards every day, and studios in which bareheaded painters draw equally broad strokes on the canvas with their windows wide open. I myself have succumbed to the *aura* such that it always draws me back to Cadaqués, even though it may hardly be more than a Disneyland for individualists.
>
> [Picasso hatte hier einmal ein Haus, in der Nähe auch Dalí, und etwas von ihrer *Aura* durchflutet noch immer die steinbepflasterten Gassen [...]. Sorgsam konservieren die Einwohner, die meisten zugezogen, das Bild eines Künstlerdorfes am Mittelmeer: mit weißgetünchten, aber geziemend abgeblätterten Mauern [...], mit prall bestückten Blumenkästen und malerischen Läden für Kunsthandwerk, Delikatessen und Wein, mit Restaurants, die ihre Küche täglich neu auf Kreidetafeln erfinden, und Ateliers, in denen barhäuptige Maler bei weit geöffneten Fenstern ebenso weit geschwungene Striche auf der Leinwand ziehen. Ich selbst bin der *Aura* erlegen, daß es mich immer wieder nach Cadaqués zurückzieht, mag es auch kaum mehr sein als ein Disneyland für Individualisten.] (KM 7; emphasis added)

The references to the aura recall Benjamin's argument about art in the modern age. Benjamin argues that, as an effect of technological innovation, the aura of the artwork—its authority or originality—evaporates in the process of mass reproduction. The artwork loses the authenticity associated to "the here and now of the artwork—its unique existence at the place where it is. [...] The here and now of the original constitutes the notion of its authenticity [das Hier und Jetzt des Kunstwerks—sein einmaliges Dasein an dem Orte, an dem es sich befindet. [...] Das Hier und Jetzt des Originals macht den Begriff seiner Echtheit aus][...]."[108] In Dariusch's description of Cadaqués, however, 'aura' hardly involves originality; he rather describes a *simulation* of authenticity. The town owes its artistic image not to originality but precisely to a reproduction and exploitation of the 'aura' once attributed to Dalí's or Picasso's presence. Benjamin describes such cultivation

Aesthetes between identity and opposition   91

of semblance in terms of a shifting emphasis from *Kultwert* to *Ausstellungswert*. With its 'befittingly flaked off walls', the town indeed cultivates an authenticity that is paradoxically artificial. Originality is reduced to a matter of blackboard advertising by restaurants that 'reinvent' their cuisine everyday. Conserving a template-like 'image of an artist's town', the town has become an amusement park for the consumption of authenticity.

Dariusch personifies that same mechanism, as he incorporates the 'aura' of cultural difference into his self-marketing. Promoting his various qualifications in the field of mass-produced *Kultur*, he represents the contemporary aesthete as an "aesthetic-economic double [ästhetisch-ökonomische Doublette]": an amalgamation of self-stylization, self-entrepreneurship, and explicit market orientation.[109] As in *Fräulein Else*, the narrator's self-fashioning is connected to the trope of the artist. Yet like Cadaqués, the town exploiting the aura of its former inhabitants, Dariusch merely rides the wave of other people's artistry. As an event manager, his professionalism relies on borrowed creativity rather than personal genius. His second-hand creativity is to be distinguished from the types of artistry he recognizes in Korinna, though it is unclear to him whether she represents a Romantic aesthetic of creative genius, or one of imitation:

> With my livelihood as an artist and the character of my life as a dandy, I accommodated her longing for the unconventional and the intellectually superior, of which it was unclear to me whether it arose from an inner impulse or was inspired by the role model of her chairman.
>
> [Ihrer Sehnsucht nach Unkonventionellem und geistig Höherstehendem, von der mir nicht klar war, ob sie einem inneren Antrieb entsprang oder sich dem Vorbild ihres Vorstandsvorsitzendem verdankte, kam ich mit meiner Künstlerexistenz und dem Dandyhaften meines Lebens entgegen.] (KM 14)

Dariusch is, by his own admission, a radical aesthete. Whereas the other aesthetic codes contain a mimetic relation to either an example or to an inner urge, his artistry is entirely anti-mimetic—"Paying attention to style is part of my job [Auf den Stil zu achten, gehört zu meinem Beruf] [...]." (KM 40) He nurtures no other philosophy of life but the conviction that life is art, even though he can convince his colleagues otherwise:

> Maike Anfang emphasized that my ideas and my way of thinking had impressed her, the *philosophy of art being entangled with life* and expressing itself without being articulated. [...] The emotion she put

into her words and eyes *felt so genuine* that for a few seconds I was about to believe in a philosophy of my own self-presentation. Then it occurred to me that in no other business could emotions be applied so effectively as in the communication and public relations department of an international enterprise.

[Maike Anfang sagte mit Nachdruck, daß meine Ideen und die Art meines Denkens sie beeindruckt hätten, die *Philosophie einer Kunst, die mit dem Leben verschränkt sei* und sich ausdrücke, ohne ausgesprochen zu werden. [...] Die Emotion, die sie in ihre wenigen Worte und in ihren Blick legte, *wirkten so echt*, daß ich für ein Paar Sekunden drauf und dran war, selbst an eine Philosophie meiner Präsentation zu glauben. Dann fiel mir ein, daß man Emotionen nirgendwo so perfekt anwenden dürfte wie im Geschäftsbereich Kommunikation und Öffentlichkeit eines internationalen Konzerns.] (KM 12–13; emphasis added)

The flicker of genuineness in Maike's compliment is relegated immediately to the domain of networking strategy, which reveals more about himself than about Maike's (in)sincerity: to Dariusch, authenticity is just a means of self-promotion. He likes to invite business partners to a bar that is pleasantly shocking in its authenticity—"shabby and honest, pure exoticism [schäbig und ehrlich, die reine Exotik] [...]." (KM 17) The ironic use of the authentic in a professional context is a crucial aspect of intertwining economic and creative requirements in so-called "cultural capitalism"—the "new syncretism of economy and forms of life," in which "building and improving their relation is [...] at the heart of the capitalistic enterprise itself."[110] Schnitzler's and Kermani's aesthetes, then, are products of two quite different capitalist regimes—the first a family-based, bourgeois capitalism depending on strong family networks and commitments, the latter a cultural capitalism "characterized by the fact that it has incorporated the *artistic critique* [...] into its justifications."[111] Indeed, Else's performance is an act of resistance, no matter how futile. Dariusch on the other hand has internalized "the new capitalist spirit," in which "authenticity and self-realization are promoted as motives for participation in economic life by the new capitalist justification regime itself."[112] In these capitalist narratives, cultural difference thus acquires a different 'value'. Dariusch exploits his Iranian identity in a capitalist aesthetic of identity, whereas Else's hidden Jewishness thwarts her initially subversive aesthetic. In her confrontation with Dorsday, the convergence of artistic, erotic, and economic narratives is complicated by her assimilatory performance—a code of imitation at odds with her aesthetic of exposure.

"...und Talent habe ich auch keines"—The aesthete's retreat

Due to her failure to internalize the bourgeois code, Else adopts a romantic aesthetic that relies on the "metaphor of an intransparent, irregular 'depth' in the 'interior' of the subject and of a *Hinterwelt* behind phenomena that remains concealed to rationality and perception and is ultimately uncontrollable [Metaphorik einer intransparenten, irregulären 'Tiefe' im 'Innern' des Subjekts und einer für Rationalität und Wahrnehmung nicht sichtbaren, letztlich unkontrollierbaren 'Hinterwelt' hinter den Erscheinungen]."[113] Indeed, Else's new aesthetic is centered around self-exposure: "[N]obody'll suspect that there's nothing under the coat but me, just me. [[K]ein Mensch wird ahnen, daß unter dem Mantel nichts ist, als ich, ich selber.]" (FE 105). Her desire to unveil affords her a means of self-expression, in which her appearance becomes an act of defiance against the erotic and economic narratives that threaten her autonomy: "Hereafter I stand on my own feet. I have pretty legs [...]. [Ich stelle mich jetzt auf meine eigenen Beine. Ich habe schöne Beine [...]]." (FE 83) Her act of exposure creates meaning—it is an exhibitionist performance through which she acquires a sense of self. Standing in front of a window, she imagines herself on a curtained stage:

> I must turn on the light. It's getting chilly. Shut the window. Blind down?—No need. There's no one standing on the mountain over there with a telescope. Worse luck...
>
> [Ich muß Licht Machen. Kühl wird es. Fenster zu. Vorhang herunter?—Überflüssig. Steht keiner auf dem Berg drüben mit einem Fernrohr. Schade.] (FE 30)

Her refusal to close the curtains signals her continued performance in front of an imagined audience, but her awareness of the fact that someone *might* be looking puts her in a slightly dominant position: to some extent, she reverses the power relation implicit in the voyeuristic act of seeing without being seen. Likewise, she transforms Dorsday's indecent proposal into an opportunity to perform. After she requests the loan, he tells her "everything in the world has its price, and that anyone who gives away his money when he might get something in return for it is a consummate fool [dass alles auf der Welt seinen Preis hat und das einer, der sein Geld verschenkt, wenn er in der Lage ist, einen Gegenwert dafür zu bekommen, ein ausgemachter Narr ist]." (FE 58) When he tells her what he expects in return, Else hides her indignation: "Why don't I smack his face? [...] He speaks as he would speak to a female slave. [Warum schlage ich ihm nicht ins Gesicht? [...] Wie zu einer Sklavin spricht er.]" (FE 58) Even so, in her impending 'enslavement'

Else recognizes an artistic opportunity. Her unveiling will be a performance that reasserts her autonomy as a woman and as an artist.[114] Her nakedness then will be a miscalculation, not a transaction, on the part of the men that objectify her: "I'll never sell myself. I'll give myself. [...] I'll be a hussy, but not a prostitute. You have miscalculated, Herr von Dorsday. And so has Father. [Nie werde ich mich verkaufen. Ich schenke mich her. [...] Ein Luder will ich sein, aber nicht eine Dirne. Sie haben sich verrechnet, Herr von Dorsday. Und der Papa auch.]" (FE 65)

Else's aesthetic revolt nevertheless treads a delicate line between self-assertion and self-commodification. Her aesthetic of opposition is not acknowledged by her main onlooker Dorsday, due to which Else is faced with "a threat to self-definition posed by the social definition by others [einer Bedrohung der Selbstdefinition durch die soziale Fremddefinition]."[115] Else thus becomes "complicit in her own 'feminization'"[116] and her ensuing objectification. Dorsday's own assimilatory performance draws Else's act into an aesthetic of imitation that she intended to escape. His Jewish identity is never established as a fact but is insinuated by Else's assessment of his appearance. She considers him her contender in "a struggle over visual effect"[117] but is not convinced by his acting—"He talks like a bad actor. [Spricht wie ein schlechter Schauspieler.]" (FE 60) She identifies him as a Jewish parvenu right away: "He's a social climber. [...] Dorsday! I'm sure your name used to be something else. [Schraubt sich künstlich hinauf. [...] Dorsday! Sie haben sicher einmal anders geheißen.]" (FE 13) Dorsday, in Else's eyes, bears the marks of Jewish assimilation too conspicuously, making him a bad actor inscribed in the aesthetic of imitation she resents. Dorsday's visible performance, however, unsettles her own act, reminding her that she, by contrast, keeps her Jewish background painstakingly hidden, even if she denies doing so:

> [A]nd the way he looks at me. No, Herr Dorsday, I'm not taken in by your smartness and your monocle and your title. You might just as well deal in old clothes as in old pictures.—But, Else, Else, what are you thinking of?—Oh, I can permit myself a remark like that. Nobody notices it in me. I'm positively blonde, a reddish blonde, and Rudi looks a regular aristocrat. Certainly one can notice it at once in Mother, at any rate in her speech, but not at all in Father. For that matter, let people notice it. I don't deny it, and I'm sure Rudi doesn't. Quite the contrary.
>
> [Auch die Art, wie er mich ansieht. Nein, Herr Dorsday, ich glaube Ihnen Ihre Eleganz nicht und nicht Ihr Monokel und nicht Ihre Noblesse. Sie könnten ebensogut mit alten Kleidern handeln wie mit alten Bildern.—Aber Else! Else,

was fällt dir denn ein.—O, ich kann mir das erlauben. Mir sieht's niemand an. Ich bin sogar blond, rötlichblond, und Rudi sieht absolut aus wie ein Aristokrat. Bei der Mama merkt man es freilich gleich, wenigstens im Reden. Beim Papa wieder gar nicht. Übrigens sollen sie es merken. Ich verleugne es durchaus nicht und Rudi erst recht nicht. Im Gegenteil.] (FE 27)

Dorsday is presented here as the embodiment of anti-Semitic stereotype, "the epitome of the lascivious Jewish businessman, obsessed with material possessions and money, devoid of ethical values and with a perverse, voyeuristic sexuality to boot."[118] In his attempt to justify his indecent proposal, he presents himself as a victim of his own desire (FE 56), which confirms the effect of Else's self-feminizing act, while also hinting at his supposed insecure Jewish masculinity. As Susan C. Anderson argues, Dorsday's voyeurism signals his attempt at reasserting the virility that, according to anti-Semitic stereotype, is lacking in Jewish men.[119] Furthermore, compounding the stereotype, his sly business instinct as an art dealer contributes to Else's objectification. Her nakedness becomes part of a financial transaction, and its value is assessed as if she were an image for sale.

Because of her own act, Else is painfully aware of both Dorsday's assimilatory act as well as his "sharp eye [Scharfblick]" (FE 11). She is uncomfortable at its (erotic) intent, because it threatens to see through the effect of her performance and to confront her with her own hidden Jewishness. Dorsday is indeed not just her passive observer; he is Else's threatening complement. His voyeurism matches Else's desire for self-exposure; his economic notion of the aesthetic corresponds to Else's unintentional self-commodification; his capitalist instinct is the socially acceptable version of her father's *Spielleidenschaft*; moreover, his deceptive assimilation is an unwelcome reminder of what Else keeps hidden, despite her drive for exposure. Else's disdain of Dorsday is not based on their difference but, rather, on their complementarity. He reminds her of what she may become when she complies with the same mimetic code: a bad actress in a theater of conformation and mimicry. In other words, the effect of Else's self-fashioned subversive aesthetic is eliminated by an onlooker who reminds her of the assimilatory aspect of her performance. Her covert Jewishness thus inhibits her full identification with an aesthetic of self-exposure.

Else's final act—her public undressing, collapse, and self-poisoning—is her ultimate attempt at rescuing her artistic autonomy. Her unveiling in front of a wider audience, rather than just Dorsday, relieves her from the unbearable notion of being someone's slave. As Comfort explains:

> Whereas a sole spectator such as Dorsday likens the performance to prostitution, a public spectacle allows Else to justify her actions not only in moral but also in artistic terms. [...] [I]n response to the predicament set in motion by her father and Dorsday's various requests, Else stages the performance before a larger public [...] and thereby manages, at least in her own mind, to transform an economic exchange into an aesthetic act.[120]

She carries out her part of the deal with Dorsday but sets the stage on her own terms. By revealing herself in public, she heeds her desire for artistic self-expression. Her aesthetic revolt does not achieve a lasting effect, however, for it is reduced to illness, hysteria, and weakness. Once more, Else's dependence on an audience that does not share her code makes her vulnerable to misinterpretation. She worries that even her ultimate act will be 'confiscated' by Dorsday: "But don't imagine, for Heaven's sake, that you, a miserable creature like you, have driven me to my death. [Aber bilden Sie sich dann um Gottes willen nicht ein, daß sie, elender Kerl, mich in den Tod getrieben haben.]" (FE 84)

In her final performance, both the code of imitation and the code of self-expression reach a dead end—as Else concludes: "I wasn't made for a bourgeois existence, and I've no talent. [Bin nicht geschaffen für eine bürgerliche Existenz, und Talent habe ich auch keines.]" (FE 84). Yet by poisoning herself, she is able to switch artistic codes once more. Her (near-) death represents an aestheticist withdrawal from all linguistic, communicative codes. Finding no adequate, undistorted form of self-expression—"There's not a word of truth in that. [Nicht ein Wort ist wahr.]" (FE 113)—Else's monologue eventually dissolves into stream of consciousness, which reflects more than just her drug-induced confusion. Reaching a state of full self-immersion, her silent, passive body now fails to reach out to its audience (FE 128). In the end, Else loses all linguistic form, her final utterances no more than a string of half-formed words: "I'm flying... I'm dreaming... I'm asleep... I'm drea... drea—I'm fly...... [Ich fliege... ich träume... ich schlafe... ich träu... träu—ich flie......" (FE 136). In death, Else transitions to a purely pictorial code: she becomes an "inanimate object on display."[121] In an imaginary testament prefiguring her self-chosen death, Else dedicates her dead body as the ultimate artwork to the art dealer:

> Herr von Dorsday shall have the right to see my body, my beautiful, naked maiden body. [...] You're getting something for your money. There's nothing in our contract about my still being alive. Oh no. It's

not in writing anywhere. Well then—I bequeath a view of my body to
the art dealer Dorsday.

[Herr von Dorsday hat das Recht, meinen Leichnam zu sehen. Meinen schönen nackten Mädchenleichnam. [...] Sie haben doch was für Ihr Geld. Daß ich noch lebendig sein muß, das steht nicht in unserem Kontrakt. O nein. Das steht nirgends geschrieben. Also den Anblick meines Leichnams vermache ich dem Kunsthändler Dorsday.] (FE 86)

By choosing her own death, she is able "to become both the aesthetic object that the art dealer demands and the commodity that her father needs."[122] Although she becomes an object for male consumption, her retreat into a fully pictorial code[123] still contains an element of resistance: she detects a flaw in Dorsday's stipulations—'Das steht nirgends geschrieben.'—and adapts an economic and erotic exchange to her own artistic needs.

Although the Jewish theme is not central to the novella at first sight, it is crucial in the confrontation of artistic codes that shapes Else' tragedy. Her covert Jewish identity and her instrumentalization by the audience correspond to Schnitzler's consideration that the absence of a Jewish theme leads to unwanted cooptation by ideological camps. Still, that does not imply that exposing her Jewishness would have rescued her artistic autonomy—on the contrary, it would have made her performance polemical from the start. The novella thus reflects the dilemma of the Jewish author who, like Else, seems to find no adequate communicative code to become a successful artist. Caught between an aesthetic of identity and an aesthetic of opposition, Else's aestheticist retreat evokes the writer's desire to escape the burden of representation.

Between *Publikumstauglichkeit* and *Avantgarde*

In Dariusch's case, the aestheticist retreat represents the ultimate—and entirely intentional—conformation to the market. To Else, cultural difference, whether covert or not, has a devaluing effect on her performance. Dariusch, on the other hand, professionally active on a market that craves the 'authenticity' of the cultural Other, fashions his difference as an asset. Within the story, Dariusch may have lost the capacity for critique, but the protagonist nevertheless presents a highly ironic picture of Western secularism. By reversing the Orientalist gaze, Kermani exposes capitalism as the actual religion of the West.

As a representative of the culture industry, Dariusch, like Else, is positioned between two aesthetic codes—or so he likes to believe. In a double entendre in the opening pages, it becomes clear that, to the entrepreneur, '*Kultur*' refers to both the entertainment industry *and* his cultural difference. What appears to be one of the event manager's self-promotional rants can also be read as a highly ironic comment on the 'genuineness' of the native informant and on the truism of intercultural 'enrichment':

> I am famous for my intuition to win people over to culture, also and especially by broadening their horizons. In my experience, the audience does not just want to see the familiar, the well-tried—but you have to take them with you, spur them on, challenge them if you want to lead them to something new, something uncomfortable or even painful. They should not be left alone. I firmly believe that the balancing act between suitability for the public and the avant-garde is possible [...].
>
> [Ich bin bekannt für mein Gespür, Menschen für die Kultur zu gewinnen, auch und gerade indem ich ihren Horizont erweitere. Meiner Erfahrung nach wollen die Zuschauer keineswegs nur das Gewohnte, Bewährte sehen—aber man muß sie mitnehmen, anstiften, herausfordern, will man sie zu etwas Neuem führen, etwas Unbequemem oder gar Schmerzhaftem. Man darf sie nicht allein lassen. Ich glaube fest daran, daß der Spagat zwischen Publikumstauglichkeit und Avantgarde möglich ist [...].] (KM 9)

Unlike Else, who fails to manage a such a balancing act, Dariusch is convinced that he can reconcile a 'vanguard' perspective with accessibility for a wide audience. He believes that his 'authentic' Oriental identity may answer to the audience's desire to have its horizon of expectations challenged and expanded by 'the Other', thus equating cultural difference to artistic novelty. Yet in order to appeal to the Western market, Dariusch must tailor, aestheticize, and commercialize that difference. He thereby loses the presumed authenticity of the native informant. Indeed, as Frauke Matthes remarks, "a transnational heritage does not guarantee intercultural competence and awareness of cultural sensitivities."[124] Kermani's unlikeable, calculating, and inauthentic protagonist thus ridicules exoticist projections onto the work of minority writers, who are expected to advocate their difference, though only in a recognizable and non-threatening way.

This mechanism becomes especially evident in Dariusch's confounded relation to Islam. As it befits the aesthete, he fails to establish a clear cultural or religious identity. Moreover, his calculated self-presentation grows increasingly obvious, leaving the reader in doubt as to the veracity of his assertions about religion. He appears totally immersed in German culture and admits to lack the ambition to actively engage with his heritage.

> I lacked the ambition of my Iranian or Turkish peers to study Islamic Studies in order to get to know my own culture, my identity! Admittedly, after graduating from high school I had been toying with the idea, but when I learned that I would have to learn Arabic for this, the matter was settled for me. The Persian course at the adult education center was sufficient as an excuse to continue to identify myself with something other than Germany.
>
> [Mir fehlte der Ehrgeiz meiner iranischen oder türkischen Altersgenossen, Islamwissenschaft zu studieren, um die eigene Kultur, meine Identität! kennenzulernen. Zugegeben, nach dem Abitur hatte ich mit dem Gedanken gespielt, aber als ich erfuhr, daß ich dafür Arabisch lernen müßte, war die Angelegenheit für mich erledigt. Der Persischkurs an der Volkshochschule genügte als Ausrede, um mich weiterhin mit etwas anderem als Deutschland zu identifizieren.] (KM 47)

Referring to the Persian courses as 'a sufficient excuse', he suggests that he does not really feel the need to explore his identity; his Middle Eastern 'expertise' remains "a commitment thrust upon him."[125] Then, though, he suddenly turns to a coarse register that highlights his rejection of terrorism, while revealing a more fundamental aspect of his self-narration. He reproduces the many opinions in the public debate, as well as their simplifications:

> No doubt about it, the boys who blow themselves up in London or wherever are totally nuts. Somewhere I had read an article explaining all this religious bullshit as a result of sexual frustration. That seemed plausible to me. They all have not fucked enough, I thought.
>
> [Keine Frage, die Jungens, die sich in London oder wo immer in die Luft sprengen, sind vollständig durchgeknallt. Irgendwo hatte ich einen Artikel gelesen, in dem der ganze religiöse Scheißdreck als Folge sexueller Frustration erklärt wurde. Das erschien mir plausibel. Die haben alle nicht genug gefickt, dachte ich.] (KM 48)

Dariusch's ambivalence can be read as an attempt to fashion a tolerable, secularized version of 'Islam'—an alternative to the one disseminated by the media. Dariusch denounces their self-proclaimed expertise, fully aware of their pervasive influence on public opinion: "I can't get that filth out of my head. [Ich bekomme den Dreck ja nicht aus meinem Kopf heraus.]" (KM 143) At the same time, however, he repeats their simplifying discourse on various occasions, with the purpose of displacing the focus from 'Muslims' in general onto 'Arab'—as opposed to Persian—fundamentalists. It helps him to separate a demonized version of Islam from the one that he believes is suitable for commercialization.[126]

His own 'religion' provides the example. He explains that, at times, he instinctively resorts to the ritual prayer recited by "we Shiites [wir Schiiten]" (KM 138). Still, to demonstrate his common ground with a secular audience, he claims that his prayer has no actual religious motivation.[127] Religious custom simply serves his credibility as an Iranian German—it "comes comes in handy as proof of cultural identity […] without putting tolerance to the test with headscarves, prayer times, and other relics [kommt als Ausweis kultureller Identität immer gut aus […] ohne die Toleranz mit Kopftüchern, Gebetszeiten und anderen Rückständen auf die Probe zu stellen.]" (KM 138) Yet no matter how superficial his affinity with Islam or the Middle East, he does not shy away from exploiting it. When he is commissioned to organize a "festival of Middle Eastern cultures [Festival orientalischer Kulturen]" (KM 27), he admits he is on unfamiliar territory, and that he was chosen for the job because of his Middle Eastern 'aura', but he agrees to do it anyway, for financial reasons: "[There was] so much Islam since 9/11 that it could only be financially worthwhile to profile myself in the field. [[Es gab] seit 9/11 derart viel Islam, daß es sich finanziell nur lohnen konnte, mich auf dem Feld zu profilieren.]" (KM 33)

Dariusch exposes an ambivalence of Western society. Despite—or due to—its full submission to an apparently post-traditional and post-religious market logic, it remains intrigued by spirituality and 'Otherness', though only on the condition that it remains within secular limits. According to Jim Jordan, Dariusch's conflicted German-Iranian identity is the result of a defective *Herkunftsbewältigung*, recognizing in Kermani's novel "in part an exhortation to the second generation not to try to ignore real issues arising from their position and their family past." Jordan argues "that Dariusch is intended as a cautionary tale […]: his subscription to a vapid, materialist, postmodern, post-ethnic and post-political lifestyle is only a postponement of his personal day of reckoning."[128] But Dariusch's overall aestheticist disposition seems ironic rather than cautionary. He is not a moralistic device, nor a representation of impending identity crisis. Rather, Dariusch is a canvas of assumptions about the supposed incompatibility of 'Islam' and 'modernity'—an argument paradoxically motivated by fear of its opposite, i.e. islamification and gradual submission to religion. On the most individual level, he illustrates what would happen if religion actually *were* fully compatible with capitalist culture—or 'Islam' and 'die Moderne'. More significantly, though, Dariusch inverts an Orientalist gaze that, as Kermani argues in line with Edward

Said, has established a view on Islam as pure religious dogma:[129] "The secular perception of the West excludes the Orient, which thus exemplarily becomes the locus of religion, where all cultural and political developments and events must be explained causally by religion. [Die säkulare Wahrnehmung des Westens nimmt den Orient aus, der so exemplarisch zum Ort der Religion wird, wo sämtliche kulturellen und politischen Entwicklungen und Ereignisse ursächlich mit dem Glauben begründet werden müssen.]"[130] In a similar vein, Kermani denounces the "widespread German conflation of Middle Eastern cultures with Islam,"[131] and especially its mediatized character, which "[...] which for some years now has 'made' people into Muslims [[...] die Menschen seit einigen Jahren zu Muslimen 'macht'.]"[132] Reversing that secular gaze, Kermani's protagonist suggests that, in the age of cultural capitalism, society and the professional market endorse self-stylization and self-promotion to the point of empty aestheticism. In full conformity with market logic, he must cater to that market's exoticist interest in him as a representative of cultural difference and authenticity. A highly ironic product of colonial mimicry, Dariusch responds to "the desire for a reformed, recognizable Other, *as a subject of a difference that is almost the same, but not quite.*"[133] It affords him a "double vision" that subverts the authority of the discourse he internalizes:[134] the West devoutly adheres to secularism, opposing the religious dogma of Islam, but submits itself to an all-encompassing market logic.

Here, *Kurzmitteilung* echoes another essay by Benjamin. In "Kapitalismus als Religion," Benjamin catches sight of a fundamentally religious streak in capitalist culture, calling it "a pure cult religion [eine reine Kultreligion]"[135] that does not revolve around dogma, theology, or absolution, but which consists of the continuous celebration of utilitarianism. Indeed, bewildered by his colleague's unexpected death, Dariusch recognizes that religion may provide support in times of crisis (KM 138) and appears to go through a conversion process. Ironically, he does not convert to Islam but turns his back on the tradition altogether, finding it to be no more than a "piece of wood too little to keep himself above water [Stück Holz, das zu klein ist, um [s]ich über Wasser zu halten]." (KM 24) Instead, he turns to a *Kultreligion* reminiscent of Scientology.[136] In a final epistolary chapter, Dariusch addresses his manager as a mental coach. This letter is the only indication of his conversion and reveals the foregoing account as a cathartic confession, leading up to some inner transformation—"The text belongs to the person I no longer am. [Der Text gehört zu dem Menschen, der ich nicht mehr bin.]" (KM 148–9) However, given the cult's emphasis on public relations and professional success, Dariusch's conversion does not achieve moral or existential reform. Instead, he has submitted to a *Kultreligion* that "crafts the process of spiritual seeking into an act of capitalist consuming."[137] Dariusch proposes to publish and market the account of his existential 'crisis' (KM 148) and, like Else, wants his life to 'end up in a book'. Whereas her retreat retains a moment of critique, though, Dariusch once more exploits his own life to his professional benefit, retreating into a substanceless aestheticism that aligns itself entirely to a capitalist logic.

Almost a century apart, Schnitzler's and Kermani's aesthetes reflect the burden of representation faced by the minority writer. The aesthete as an artist-performer introduces the pressures of the market and outlines the impact of cultural difference on the integrity of the artist. Else's hidden Jewishness inhibits full identification with a code of artistic resistance; to Dariusch, 'Middle-Easternness' is just an interesting accessory to his well-manicured image. Although the two protagonists inhabit an environment of successful assimilation at first, that narrative soon expires into empty bourgeois performance, or in inauthentic, calculated conformity. Their aestheticist retreat, albeit with different implications in terms of artistic critique, represents the dead end of the Enlightened baseline of assimilation. The (semi-) aesthetes in the following chapter section respond to that failure. Heeding a need for self-transcendence, they discover the meaning of a reality that exists outside of the confines of their own mind.

2.3 The aesthete's awakening: Beer-Hofmann's *Der Tod Georgs* (1900) versus Zaimoglu's *Liebesbrand* (2008)

Jewish aesthete and romantic rebel: Richard Beer-Hofmann and Feridun Zaimoglu

Richard Beer-Hofmann (1866–1945) was born in Vienna to an assimilated Jewish bourgeois family of attorneys. They did not participate in Jewish community life, except for his paternal grandmother, who remained connected to the religious community.[138] With a doctoral degree in law, Beer-Hofmann stood at the beginning of a typical bourgeois career, when he became acquainted with the writers of *Jung Wien* around 1890. He developed close friendships with Schnitzler and Hugo von Hofmannsthal, who valued his meticulous criticism of their work. They encouraged him to start writing as well, even if it was never his intention.[139] Writing in an intellectual climate influenced by

Freudian psychoanalysis, Machian empiriocriticism, and the *Sprachkrise* that affected contemporaries such as Fritz Mauthner and his friend Hofmannsthal, Beer-Hofmann developed a poetic language that reached beyond the limitations of realism.

Despite his family's acculturation, and unlike many (Jewish) contemporaries, Beer-Hofmann was openly committed to his Jewish ancestry—the only "homo judaicus"[140] in the *Jung Wien* circle. He is often associated with Buber's Cultural Zionism,[141] due to his explicit commitment to a cultural Jewish identity without distinctly national elements.[142] Yet his precise conception of Judaism has been up for debate.[143] Some critics have pointed out his familiarity with Herzl's *Der Judenstaat*,[144] though they are quick to interpret his lack of outspoken commitment to Zionism as a sign of an anti-Zionist stance. Others have positively associated the author with Herzl, considering the two as "emblematic of a 'conservative revolution', which transformed their erstwhile aestheticist isolationism into a conscious profession of national identity."[145] As far as *Der Tod Georgs* is concerned, however, Beer-Hofmann's exact notion of Judaism—a religion, a culture, a nation, or a sense of ancestral connection—remains undecided and, it seems, deliberately so. The author's eagerness for modernist experiment allows him to articulate a sense of community that is not predicated on 'institutionalized' religion or nationality. His strikingly pictorial, anti-linear prose appears consistent with the reluctance towards fixated identities, which the open ending of the story reinforces.

During the early 1890s, Beer-Hofmann was "living the very Viennese life of the aesthete, styling his life as a work of art [...]."[146] He engaged in a frivolous dandyism that Karl Kraus, in reference to (fellow) *Jung Wien* members and specifically Hermann Bahr, mocked as their habit "to imply genius through a lock of hair dangling over the brow [Genialität durch eine in die Stirne baumelnde Haarlocke anzudeuten],"[147] and to remain "thoughtful" at all times about "beauty and the utmost precision of any pose [auf Schönheit und möglichste Exactheit einer jeden Pose bedacht].[148] Beer-Hofmann's early novellas *Camelias* and *Das Kind,* both published in 1893, explore the aestheticism that the author epitomized at the time. Yet in these early texts, he already appears to introduce his doubts about the value of that lifestyle—a "narcissistic inward turn"[149] of which he would grow increasingly critical. Around the middle of the 1890s, Beer-Hofmann experienced a profound personal crisis, now perceiving the persona of the aesthete as a shallow caricature and longing for a more genuine relation to the world,[150] even if his work reflects a deliberate engagement with Jewish identity only after 1895.[151] His own Jewish awakening—inspired by marriage and fatherhood, as well as by the publication of Herzl's *Der Judenstaat* (1896)—is reflected in *Der Tod Georgs* (1893–99).[152]

Heeding a modernist impulse to break free from formal tradition, while thematically reverting to the author's heritage, *Der Tod Georgs* is exemplary of a "backward-looking yet highly experimental" Viennese Jewish modernism, which "sought to invent a Jewish countertradition through aesthetic means."[153] Combining a death theme—fashionable around the turn of the century[154]—with literary *Jugendstil*,[155] *Der Tod Georgs* is a typically modern text. In fact, it is one of the very first German-language texts to experiment with techniques that would become central to the modern novel—interior monologue, stream of consciousness, and *erlebte Rede*.[156] Beer-Hofmann's originality extends to the unique interplay of two central themes—"that of the transcending of the deadly selfishness of aestheticism and the return to true life, and that of the return of the 'Jewish mind' to 'the spirit of Jewishness.'"[157] In strikingly ornamental associations, the novella relates the Jewish awakening of an aesthete with narcissistic tendencies—a 'conversion' reminiscent of the author's own. *Der Tod Georgs* is at once representative and critical of aestheticism, exploring it to the point where it exhausts itself. The protagonist Paul suffers from a "perceptive disorder,"[158] due to which "the perceiving subject constitutes his or her own reality and is not directly bound to the reality principle."[159] This worldview is thoroughly challenged by the death of his longtime friend Georg, the shock of which leads Paul to repudiate his dandyism. The aesthete's crisis of meaning is described by Georg Lukács as the moment

> when the soul, utterly exhausted in ever new but eternally repeated games, yearns for truth, for tangible, incontrovertible truth and begins to comprehend as a prison the nature of its ego to fuse everything within itself, to conform everything to itself.
>
> [wenn die Seele, gänzlich erschöpft in immer neuem, doch ewig wiederholten Spiele, sich nach Wahrheit sehnt, nach greifbarer, unumknetbarer Wahrheit und die alles in sich einschmelzende, an alles sich anpassende Art ihres Ichs als Kerker zu begreifen beginnt.][160]

Such longed-for 'truth' arrives in Paul's seemingly sudden awareness of his Jewish ancestry. In the concluding chapter, conspicuous references to a *Gesetz*, a *Volk*, and to the voice of blood convey Paul's new intuition of his genealogy. The novella's critique of aestheticism as narrow individualism is thus traversed by the "hidden dimension of a pathological study of the assimilated, secularized Jewish mind."[161]

Considering aestheticism as a 'perceptive disorder' that first leads to a withdrawal from the world, then to the birth of meaningful connection, *Der Tod Georgs* allows a comparison with Zaimoglu's *Liebesbrand*.[162] A century apart from Beer-Hofmann's aesthete *par excellence*, Zaimoglu portrays a (semi-) aesthete who has rejected the capitalist world, only to be deceived by his recently discovered idealism and Romantic *Sehnsucht*. As does Beer-Hofmann, Zaimoglu depicts a perceptive and spiritual awakening, developing an imagery of 'becoming' and changeable identities that questions any claim to subjective autonomy or radical idealism. *Der Tod Georgs* and *Liebesbrand* thus pick up where the self-aestheticization of Schnitzler's and Kermani's protagonists left off: at the dead end of Enlightened assimilation.

Zaimoglu (1964) has become one of the most 'canonical' voices of Turkish-German writing and one of the most celebrated contemporary German authors *tout court*. Born in Turkey, but raised and educated in Germany, he abandoned his studies in medicine and art in order to start writing and painting. A public figure as well, Zaimoglu balances his position as a literary author and as a (perceived) 'native informant' of the Turkish-German population. Zaimoglu first garnered critical attention—and the reputation of *enfant terrible*—with *Kanak Sprak. 24 Mißtöne vom Rande der Gesellschaft* (1995).[163] With this collection of at times offensive voices of second- and third-generation Turkish-German youth, Zaimoglu propagates a *Kanak* counter-identity in opposition to bourgeois German self-definitions.[164] Yet despite its staged character and its highly stylized use of Turkish-German slang, critics have unduly taken Zaimoglu for the *Kanak* spokesman of "a disaffected and discriminated constituency to which he belonged by virtue of his birth, and whose anger he was challenging."[165] Rather than a realistic testimonial, Zaimoglu's "parodic ethnicisation"[166] is about the creation of "a new language, a new way of experiencing and disrupting differences, rather than communicating and fixing them."[167] Zaimoglu has by now somewhat distanced himself from his beginnings as an agitator[168] and from the text that won him the status of *Sprachrohr*.[169] Still, its reception remains a prime example of the critical misconception that Zaimoglu continues to denounce, namely, how Turkish-German authors are forced into the role of *Alibitürke,* or are expected to exhibit a degree of "Salonradikalität"[170]—a palatable, crowd-pleasing rebelliousness. He strongly resists being confined to a position of 'authenticity' that is, in fact, projected onto him. When for instance *Kindlers Literatur Lexikon* printed his entry as 'Zaimoğlu', including the diacritical mark he has abandoned, he mocks the undue emphasis on his 'difference' as a Turkish-German writer, as if his work solely reflected an 'original' Turkish (-German) experience:[171] "I have eliminated the breve [...]. In the entry to my person one attaches value, however, to faithfulness to the original. [Den Querbalken [...] habe ich abgeschafft. Im Eintrag zu meiner Person legt man jedoch Wert auf Originaltreue.]"¹⁷²

Even more demonstrative of the critical obsession with 'authenticity' and 'originality' is the controversy that ensued after Zaimoglu's (alleged) plagiarism in his 2006 novel *Leyla*. An anonymous critic accused the author of having plagiarized a number of motifs and anecdotes from Özdamar's novel *Das Leben ist eine Karawanserei* (1991)—like *Leyla*, the semi-fictional story of a girl's youth in Turkey and subsequent emigration to Germany. In his defense, Zaimoglu presented the recordings of his mother's memories, which were the inspiration for his novel. The fact that Zaimoglu "mounted this self-defence in terms of documentary evidence and in terms of stories' oral, vernacular origins in real life—that is, in terms of 'authenticity', rather than in terms of the liberty of the imagination,"¹⁷³ is telling. While it may have been wise to provide documentary evidence instead of invoking artistic liberty, it remains striking how critics—some academic, most journalistic—have treated the issue as a question of authenticity, as if a migrant writer's *fictional* text "obeyed specific generic laws, which tied it to the witness of real bodies and citable voices, relating ascertainable facts about documented places and times."¹⁷⁴ Once again, it suggests that, for a writer perceived as a 'native informant', the value of his work is not accepted when not explicitly marked as authentic.¹⁷⁵

Since the 2000s, Zaimoglu has explored themes that tie in with the German Romantic tradition. Most of his protagonists have come in variations of the Romantic hero—

> highly educated and intelligent [...], out of key with his time, belated, discontented with modernity, with the 'rationality' and 'Enlightenment' underpinning consumer capitalism—a rebel against conformism—but a poet-dreamer rather than a social political activist, one who seeks to find an ineffable authenticity or truth in heterosexual love, sex, and travel or flight from the familiar.¹⁷⁶

Although his "Romantic turn"¹⁷⁷ has shifted focus away from the "discords from the social margins,"¹⁷⁸ Zaimoglu continues to undermine the critical obsession with 'authentic' migrant writing. His engagement with the Romantic tradition might be read in terms of a chastened temper, or of artistic 'maturation', but to a limited extent only: an anti-establishment attitude and a "war on the German real"¹⁷⁹ have remained the hallmarks of his writing. This Romantic register has allowed him to voice more generalized criticism of German bourgeois society and European modernity. Zaimoglu indeed characterizes himself as the antithesis of Enlightenment, as someone who "could befriend certain moments of Counter-Enlightenment [[sich] mit gewissen Momenten der Gegenaufklärung anfreunden kann]."[180] Dismissing the 'ludicrous' notions of freedom and autonomy,[181] he senses hubris hiding in intellectuality and *Fortschrittsglaube*:

> [Modern man] believes he is at the zenith of human potential in terms of intelligence. He thinks that everything that existed before has progressed to this climax and is, so to speak, the grand apex of human potential. But these modern people only leave graves, for they believe that what has deceased and is abandoned, what is derelict, has only deserved to have been defeated.
>
> [[Der moderne Mensch] glaubt, er sei von der Intelligenz her am Zenith der menschlichen Möglichkeit. Er denkt alles, was vorher war, sei auf diesen Höhepunkt hin zugelaufen, und sei gewissermaßen die großartige Zuspitzung der menschlichen Möglichkeiten. Doch hinterlassen diese modernen Menschen nur Gräber, denn sie denken, was gestorben und verlassen, was Ruine ist, hat es nicht anders als verdient, als besiegt zu sein.][182]

Conversely, his skepticism extends to ideology and institutionalized religion. Just as he distrusts atheism—"essentially a stomach of modernity [im Grunde genommen ein Magen der Moderne]"[183]—so too does he think of "the clerics, the zealots of faith [die Klerikalen, die Glaubenseiferer]" as the idiots of the modern world.[184] The public debate on religion, he contends, is marked by unnecessary polarization and erroneous reifications on either side:

> The reification of popular faith into publicly debated kitsch, namely complete secularization, and the reification of popular faith of the Church with a high priest as administrator of a legend at the head—both are lies. For there exists a fervent core.
>
> [Die Verdinglichung des Volksglaubens zum öffentlich debattierten Tand, nämlich die totale Säkularisierung, und die Verdinglichung des Volksglaubens der Kirche mit einem Hohepriester als Verwalter einer Legende an der Spitze, beide sind Lügen. Denn es gibt einen Glutkern.][185]

Protecting this highly individualized 'fervent core' from being drowned out by a false modern binary is the driving force behind Zaimoglu's romanticism.

When asked about his artistic motto, he offers two insights: "I do not want to betray that which is real. And I do not want to improve that which is good. [Das Echte will ich nicht verraten. Und das Gute will ich nicht verbessern.]"[186] Valuing authentic self-expression over continuous self-improvement, Zaimoglu indeed advocates a distinctly romantic concept of art: "I do not think highly of size, of expansion, of self-realization. I think highly of self-effacement, in art, in literature. [Ich halte nichts von Größe, von Expansion, von Selbstverwirklichung. Ich halte viel von der Selbstauslöschung, in der Kunst, in der Literatur.]"[187] He even declares himself a "staunch advocate of the rejection of reality [unbedingter Befürworter der Realitätsablehnung],"[188] which bears resemblance to Beer-Hofmann's more radical aestheticist retreat. Like Beer-Hofmann, Zaimoglu is skeptical of a reality governed by instrumental reason, leading him to seek out the intensity of experience that "a 'culture' perceived to be deformed by competitive consumer capitalism and the dictates of cold-hearted reason"[189] fails to provide.

Especially *Liebesbrand* can be considered a "full-blown" experiment "in inventing a contemporary Romanticism for a future Europe."[190] The novel relates the love quest of David, who survives a bus accident in Turkey,[191] and he follows Tyra, a German tourist who offered him first aid, on her travels through Germany, to Prague, and to Vienna. Even if Tyra rejects David, and he eventually resigns himself to it, the novel provides no resolution. As Littler remarks, the story is about "longing itself, and love's transformative power,"[192] about "its unsettling of the integrity of identities."[193] Zaimoglu considers it his as yet most authentic publication—not in terms of biographical veracity but in terms "romantic expressive feeling [romantische[s] Ausdrucksgefühl]."[194] His self-insertion into the Romantic tradition might be read in terms of an assimilatory desire to be included into the German canon. But looking closer, it really resembles a romantic rebellion against determinate identities—national, cultural, or religious, as well as against a deeply ingrained (German) idealism that lies at the core of the Western obsession with the 'authentic' and the 'original'.

In *Liebesbrand*, Zaimoglu takes a more reflective approach to the game of (staged) authenticity he initiated in *Kanak Sprak*.[195] Confronting claims of biographical authenticity with his own romantically inclined notion of authenticity, his focus on intense yet elusive *Sehnsucht* opposes the dual objectification he observes in European modernity: the reduction of reality by instrumental reason and capitalism, and the institutionalization of spiritual experience. The incorporation of romantic motifs in *Liebesbrand*—especially that of 'burning passion'—shapes a worldview that is distinctly anti-idealistic. By the example of the protagonist who is blindly led by the idea of love, the novel questions the essentializing nature of idealism, and its reductive effect on reality. As I will illustrate, the protagonist strives for the 'ideal' love, which renders him blind to everyday manifestations of love as a corporeal-affective, rather than a strictly (im)material, experience.

Liebesbrand and *Der Tod Georgs* are structured by a close entanglement of love and death themes representing the onset of an awakening. Confronted with two radical opposites—the vital intensity of love and the inevitability of death—the two protagonists are challenged to reassess their views and to discover new meanings and connections beyond the confinement of the aesthete's mind. For Zaimoglu's David, this implies a departure first from his capitalist worldview, then from his radical idealism; for Beer-Hofmann's Paul, it means recalibrating his solipsistic surrender to association and superficial perception. Both novels thus picture how Enlightened autonomy yields to spirituality and longing for connection.

Realitätsablehnung & experiences of finitude

"Die Immanenz des Selbstbewußtseins"[196]

"Can a modern consciousness governed by chance associations find its way back from aesthetic detachment to ancestral Judaism?"[197] Abigail Gillman aptly captures the premise of Beer-Hofmann's novella, in which the author sets out to "divert the modernist impulse back towards the ethical."[198] This seems like an irresolvable question, since the aesthete's mind, surrendered to sensations, seems divorced from objective reality:

> How then should [the writer] consolidate chance occurrences into a teleological narrative? And in the case where the conclusion to this narrative (like that of any spiritual journey) is both unforeseen and somehow inevitable, how should he convey that the transformation is at once an outgrowth of the aethete's natural tendencies, as well as a wholly unexpected turning point, an *Erlebnis* or epiphany?[199]

Beer-Hofmann treats Paul's spiritual awakening as a question of form, whereby seemingly disconnected images are layered onto each other and, in the process, acquire symbolic meaning. The rejection of linear narration and the use of interior monologue and *erlebte Rede* convey a psychological change within the aesthete's mind, rather than following a coherent logic. Indeed, with *Der Tod Georgs*,

Beer-Hofmann sought to finish off aestheticism from within, and "to bring the aesthete to an end by means of aestheticism itself [dem Ästheten mit den Mitteln des Ästhetentums ein Ende [zu bereiten]]."[200]

The novella opens with a fairly uneventful frame narrative that starkly contrasts with the intricate, ornamental rendering of Paul's dreams in the encapsulated stories. In four unequally proportioned chapters, *Der Tod Georgs* describes how the aesthete first withdraws from reality, surrenders to a dream reality, and then re-emerges in the frame narrative, which concludes several months after the initial scene. The story opens on the night when Georg has visited Paul in his summer home. From the only instance of dialogue in the novella, the reader indirectly learns of Georg's visit—the event itself remains unnarrated. A seemingly insignificant interaction with some passerby already implies Paul's desire to withdraw; he indicates that he is very tired and will not come outside for a walk. The window motif highlights his disconnection further. Whereas the dialogue above takes place through an open window, subsequent occurrences of the motif[201] involve windows being closed or hidden behind curtains, signifying his disconnection. The motif interconnects several other meanings. The glass matches the transparency of his mind within the text[202] but more significantly represents the aesthete's "sterile interaction with reality," which is "conceived of as a surface,"[203] which I will address later. At this early point in the novella, the window alludes to Paul's confinement within his own mind. Returning home after a walk, Paul is too tired to think, and at the mercy of association and sensory perception:

> Then he lay there and still felt how well the cool pillows nestled into his heated neck. How moonlit the room was! And there on the wall was the black shadow of the window cross. Georg slept in there. The foliage of the lime tree in front of the window looked like a grid of black hearts.—What was that scent the wind carried through the open window? Did it come out of the garden? Or was it freshly mown meadows in the mountains?—He slept.
>
> [Dann lag er da und fühlte noch, wie gut die kühlen Kissen sich in seinen heissen Nacken schmiegten. Wie mondhell das Zimmer war! Und das da an der Wand war der schwarze Schatten des Fensterkreuzes. Georg schlief da drinnen. Wie ein Gitter von schwarzen Herzen sah das Laub der Linde vor dem Fenster aus.—Was das für ein Duft war, den der Wind da durchs offene Fenster trug? Kam er aus dem Garten? Oder waren das frischgemähte Wiesen auf den Bergen?—Er schlief.] (TG 15)

In an evocation of random impressions as he falls asleep, focalized narration gives way to free indirect speech. In this conclusion to the first chapter—the frame narrative—the window is still opened. Yet the window cross casts a dark shadow—a suggestion of confinement reinforced by the black grid of foliage: Paul's reality is now limited to merely his impressions. Correspondingly, his mind is rendered in a Machian fashion, in which "any and all inherent principles of distinction and causality vanish."[204] Beer-Hofmann's extensive use of formal innovation corresponds to the impressionistic atmosphere that Hermann Bahr diagnosed as characteristic of the modern *Zeitgeist*,[205] and which Mach captured in his *Analyse der Empfindungen* (1900)[206] as an all-encompassing suspension of distinctions, as "the physical and the psychological converge, elements and perceptions are one, the ego dissolves and everything is only an eternal flood, which seems to falter here, flows more hastily there [das Physikalische und das Psychologische rinnt zusammen, Element und Empfindung sind eins, das Ich löst sich auf und alles ist nur eine ewige Flut, die hier zu stocken scheint, dort eiliger fließt] [...]."[207]

There is, however, a paradoxical aspect to the impressionistic dissolution of the self. When the distinction between physical and psychological realms ceases to exist, consciousness becomes the sole reference point: "This immanence of self-consciousness is coupled with a high degree of individualization, which hardly leaves any room for overall coherence. [Diese Immanenz des Selbstbewußtseins verbindet sich mit einem Höchstmaß an Individualisierung, die kaum mehr einen Weg zu übergreifenden Zusammenhängen offenläßt.]"[208] Indeed, on several occasions, Paul's worldview is exposed as egocentric to the point of narcissism.[209] After his spiritual awakening, he ponders his previous life as an aesthete and becomes aware of the radical isolation and self-referentiality of the lifestyle: "All around him he had laid loneliness, and inside it he had strayed like one who, lost in deserts, endlessly follows his own traces in circles. [Rings um sich hatte er Einsamkeiten gelegt, und in ihnen war er umhergeirrt wie einer, der, in Wüsten verloren, endlos im Kreise den eigenen Spuren folgt.]" (TG 203) To the radical aesthete, the aspects that define a conventional existence have lost their distinctive power: personal, causal, temporal, or spiritual relations have been sacrificed to the aesthete's associative surface perception. Because he discerns no difference between present and past experience—indeed, he suffers from a kind of memory loss[210]—the aesthete's reality resembles a shadow theatre where vague memories emerge on the same surface as the lives surrounding him:

> Deeds that had long since turned cold, from which only a dull glow, fading, dawned on the living throughout the centuries, he had approached with feverish hands, and still trembling destinies of living people, who surrounded him, walking the earth at the same time with him, he had kept away from him with defensively spreading fingers, until both—dead and living—equally far away from him, seemed to perform like shadows on the same stage.
>
> [Längst kalt gewordene Thaten, von denen nur ein matter Schein, verblassend, durch Jahrhunderte zu den Lebenden herüberdämmerte, hatte er mit fiebernden Händen an sich herangerückt, und noch zuckende Schicksale lebendiger Menschen, die um ihn gedrängt, mit ihm zugleich die Erde traten, solange mit abwehrend sich spreizenden Fingern von sich ferne gehalten, bis Beides—Totes und Lebendiges—gleich weit von ihm, wie auf derselben Bühne, schattenhaft sich selbst zu spielen schien.] (TG 191)

The seeming contradiction, whereby the dissolving self ultimately becomes the center of its own universe, is characteristic of the *Wiener Moderne*. This conspicuous thematization of death in this period reflects the experience of increasing individualization and isolation[211] at the time and articulates the ultimate failure of the ego in the simultaneous "absolute positioning of the ego and its farewell [Absolutsetzung des Ich und seine Verabschiedung]."[212] The accompanying loss of metaphysical reference

> has as its consequence that, in a paradoxical way, the emphatically absolute subject sees itself exposed to transience and destruction. The Archimedean center of thought, the final bastion of transcendental idealism, suddenly proves to be phantasmagoric.
>
> [[hat] zur Folge, daß in widersprüchlicher Weise das emphatisch absolut gesetzte Subjekt sich der Flüchtigkeit und Vernichtung preisgegeben sieht. Der archimedische Punkt des Denkens, die letzte Bastion des transzendentalen Idealismus, erweist sich plötzlich als Phantasmagorie.][213]

Similarly, in *Der Tod Georgs*, the lack of perceptive depth symbolizes the absolute reality of the aesthete's mind, which exists disconnected from external sources of meaning. Paul's confrontation with mortality—even if it takes place within a dream—elicits his transformation, marking the moment when the absolute self-foundation of consciousness reaches its limits. This failure is outlined in the second chapter, the opening scene of which features the same elements that closed the preceding one where Paul fell asleep—the window, the trees, the foliage—the second chapter appears to be the simple continuation of the frame narrative (TG 16). While reiterating the state of Paul's confinement, the window motif now also marks the transition between layers of consciousness,[214] introducing the reader to the all-encompassing reality of Paul's dream on the night of Georg's death. The dream consists of Paul's lengthy reflections about a woman on her deathbed, whose presence is suggested first by "a soft protracted whimpering sound [ein leiser langgezogenen wimmernder Ton]," and then confirmed by the focalizer's associations about the unnamed woman, "who had been laying dying downstairs for weeks [die unten seit Wochen sterbend lag]." (TG 16–7) Georg's death remains unnarrated and is evoked metonymically by the dying woman instead. This obscures a causal relationship between Georg's death and Paul's (spiritual) awakening and ties in with Beer-Hofmann's intention to depict a transformation *within* the aesthete's mind—the emergence of (spiritual) meaning out of chance associations, rather than a causal or teleological process.

More importantly, Georg's unnarrated death indicates the limitations of Paul's self-absorbed state. It suggests that the solipsistic aesthete is unable to witness, let alone access, another person's death without transcending himself, without becoming aware of his own mortality, and thereby undermining the absolute self-foundation of his mind. In this respect, Paul's dream constitutes an experience of finitude in the Nancian sense. His associations about the dying woman culminate in the rupture of the 'immanence' of his self-consciousness. In a concise summary of Nancy's argument, Christopher Fynsk elucidates the estrangement of the modern individual from his own mortality:

> [P]art of the devastation wrought by the technical organization of advanced capitalist societies [...] lies in the isolation of the individual in its very death and thus the impoverishment of that which resists any appropriation or objectification. Death is an experience that a collectivity cannot make its *work* or its property, in the sense of something that would find its meaning in a value or cause transcending the individual. [...] There is a point at which death exposes a radical meaninglessness that cannot be subsumed. And when death presents itself as *not ours*, the very impossibility of representing its meaning suspends or breaches the possibility of self-presentation and exposes us to our finitude. [...] [T]his exposure is also an opening to community: outside ourselves, we first encounter the other.[215]

The three fundamental characteristics of a Nancian experience of finitude—its resistance to appropriation and objectification; its exposure of radical meaninglessness; the impossibility of autonomous self-presentation—are indeed crucial elements in the aesthete's awakening. Paul's realization that mortality is both highly individualized and beyond objectification ruptures the confines of his mind. In his dream, the aesthete ponders his relationship to the woman on her deathbed. It appears to not have been a relationship between equals, but rather one of appropriation, as Paul has subjected her to his own worldview:

> He took away her faith in a benevolent God who steered her destiny, and left her nothing but a consuming yearning for faith [...]. The more he took from her, the more she became his. Empty and unsteady she sank to him, for she believed in him [...].
>
> [Er nahm ihr den Glauben an einen gütigen Gott der ihr Schicksal lenkte, und ließ ihr nichts als verzehrende Sehnsucht nach Glauben [...]. [J]e mehr er ihr nam, desto mehr ward sie sein. Leer und haltlos sank sie ihm zu, denn an ihn glaubte sie [...].] (TG 27–8)

Having robbed her of her beliefs, he feels "that he owes her [dass er ihr etwas zu geben schulde]." Yet what he offers her in return is merely his own aestheticist reverence of "the beauty of everyday things [die Schönheit alltäglicher Dinge]." (TG 28) At the moment of her death, however, Paul witnesses how, despite her submission to him before, she now rejects him, focusing on her very private, "important business: she was about to die [wichtiges Geschäft: Sie hatte zu sterben]." (TG 91) Paul is not allowed to partake in her dying, let alone to appropriate the moment:

> Gradually she seemed to elude his authority. [...] She looked at him, then she seemed to turn her gaze from him contemptuously. He felt like a deceiver; the deal was about immeasurable things, and his beggar's wares should have value to her? She was dying; she had to leave everything alive behind—and he wanted to comfort her with childish caresses? He felt ashamed.
>
> [Langsam schien sie seiner Herrschaft zu entgleiten. [...] Sie sah ihn an, dann schien sie verächtlich ihren Blick von ihm zu wenden. Wie ein Betrüger kam er sich vor; um Unermessliches ging der Handel, und seine Bettelwaare sollte Werth für sie haben? Sie starb; von allem Lebendigen musste sie weg—und mit kindischem Liebkosen wollte er sie trösten? Er empfand Scham.] (TG 90–2)

Aesthetes between identity and opposition   115

The economic terminology here—'Geschäft', 'Handel', 'Bettelwaare', 'Werth'—emphasizes the fact that the woman's death resists commodification or appropriation. Indeed, Paul feels ashamed—an affect stemming from an *ethical* rather than an *aesthetic* realm of experience, which marks the onset of his awakening and return to Judaism. The deathbed scene is thus an illustration of how "the individual Dasein first knows community when it experiences the impossibility of communion or immanence [...] before the dead other."[216] The rupture of immanence is once more highlighted by the window motif. Sitting near the deathbed, Paul notices children outside who are looking in. Angrily he waves his fist at them, forgetting about the window between them, and shatters the glass at the same moment of the woman's death: "The shattering of the broken glass and the children's crying made the voice of the old attendant yell: 'Jesus—the woman is dying'. He stood there breathing heavily; his clenched fist full of piercing glass shards [...]. [Durch das Klirren der Scherben und das Schreien der Kinder gellte die Stimme der alten Wärterin: "Jesus—die Frau stirbt!" Er stand schweratmend da; seine geballte Faust fühlte er voll schneidender Glassplitter [...]]." (TG 95) The now shattered window, symbol of Paul's indirect engagement with the world, now signifies his the opening up of his self-consciousness towards the discovery of external meaning: "He was wide awake now, so well-rested! [[E]r war jetzt so wach, so ausgeschlafen!]" (TG 97) The narrative experiment of *erlebte Rede* and interior monologue that conjures the totality of consciousness now comes to a halt, "where consciousness encounters the inaccessible [wo das Bewußtsein an das Nicht-Verfügbare stößt]."[217] This experience of finitude announces a rejection of the idealism on which Paul's absolute consciousness was founded. As Pfeiffer concludes:

> The absolute self-foundation of consciousness [...] has failed. Thus [Beer-Hofmann] repeats in explicit form the attempt that the early Romantics had already embarked upon, and which led them to renounce the philosophy of German idealism. That is, the attempt to found subjectivity in the gesture of pure self-reflexivity proved unfeasible to the early Romantics [...]. They arrived at the realization that selfhood could not be founded upon immanent consciousness [...].
>
> [Die absolute Selbstbegründung des Bewußtseins [...] mißlingt. Damit wiederholt [Beer-Hofmann] in expliziter Form jenen Versuch, den die Frühromantiker bereits in Ansätzen durchexerzierten und der sie dazu führte, sich von der Philosophie des deutschen Idealismus abzuwenden. Das Bestreben, nämlich, Subjektivität im Gestus reiner Selbstreflexivität zu begründen, erweist sich den

Frühromantikern [...] als undurchführbar. Sie gelangen zu der Überzeugung, daß sich Selbstsein nicht bewußtseinsimmanent begründen lasse [...].]²¹⁸

The subsequent chapters picture how Paul gradually overcomes the enclosure of his thoughts and impressions and eventually finds the source of his existence outside of his mind: in his Jewish ancestry. In the third chapter, Paul travels by train to Georg's funeral; his coffin accompanies him in a freight car. The motif of train travel highlights that the aesthete's associative mind is returning to the 'right track'—devoid of "anything coincidental and capricious [alles Zufällige und Launenhafte]," it reassures him "to be sliding towards his destination on anchored iron rails [auf eisernen festgebetteten Schienen seinem Ziele zuzugleiten.]" (TG 111) In other words, the train ride "encompass[es] his entire being in its motion, it signifies an existential change of state."²¹⁹ During his journey, Paul looks out the window, watching the landscape passing by. Yet his perception is rendered less impressionistically than before—he now seems more reflective, as if coming down from the ridge of aestheticism. In his reflections on Georg's death, Paul becomes increasingly aware of the temporal depth of existence, becoming aware that the meaning of life is found not at resting places, nor in the collection of fulfilled wishes and achievements (TG 113–4), but in the "acceptance of life as duration."²²⁰ Inside that acceptance, there is no room for narcissistic self-examination:

> Or did he belong to those who knew that their lives flowed and that water did not stand still to see itself? And who knew that it could not be contained in pitchers to stare into the captured flood and tell it, 'You are my life.'
>
> [Oder war er von denen, die wussten, dass ihr Leben floss, und das Wasser nicht stillstand, um sich selber zu besehen? Und die wussten, dass man es nicht in Krüge fassen konnte, um in die gefangene Fluth zu starren und ihr zu sagen: "Du bist mein Leben."] (TG 114)

With that acceptance comes his awareness of an age-old "hidden thought [verborgenes Denken]" (TG114) that informs the present and "infiltrates (and unites) phyical and mental life."²²¹ This awareness will enable Paul to acknowledge a transcendent God, as well as the structuring principle he refers to as *Gesetz* and *Gerechtigkeit*. Now, he sees things clearly, no longer in a flurry of impressions:

> The distance did not swim in a haze; in sure lines it distinguished itself from the clouds [...] The way it separated and staggered, he recognized

the coherence. He understood what surrounded him as if he overlooked it from a distance. [...] [He was able] to grasp the silent will of the landscape through which he walked, and its law in the quiet clearing light of autumn.

[Die Fernen schwammen nicht im Dunst; in sicheren Linien schieden sie sich von Wolken. [...] Wie es sich sonderte und stufte, erkannte er die Zusammenhänge. Was ihn umgab, begriff er so, als übersähe er es aus der Ferne. [...] [Er vermochte] im stillen klärenden Licht des Herbstes den stummen Willen der Landschaft zu erfassen, durch die er schritt, und ihr Gesetz.] (TG 170)

Sehnsucht and the inverted *Philister*

Beer-Hofmann's aesthete transitions from radical impressionistic subjectivity—an outgrowth of idealism—to the acknowledgement of a reality beyond the visible. A similar (Romantic) resistance to idealism can be found in Zaimoglu's *Liebesbrand*, a novel featuring "flagrant breaches of modern rationalist propriety."[222] The two novels criticize idealism from different perspectives. *Der Tod Georgs* outlines the limits of philosophical idealism—in short, the theory that 'reality' is founded on human consciousness or reason. *Liebesbrand* adopts the more everyday notion of idealism, as the practice of adopting and living by ideals. In both novels, either form of idealism is criticized as a problematic reduction of reality. In Beer-Hofmann's text, it leads to the solipsistic rejection of any external source of meaning. Likewise, Zaimoglu's "rage against the real"[223] supports a critique of both materialistic and idealistic world views. The protagonist David undergoes a transformation not unlike the aesthete Paul's: in the wake of a near-death experience, he becomes receptive to a reality beyond the objectifiable. Still, the perceptive transformations described in each novel do not parallel each other entirely. Whereas *Der Tod Georgs* describes the protagonist's gradual rediscovery of his forgotten (Jewish) ancestry, and thus his 'cure' from a perceptive disorder, the near-death experience in Zaimoglu first *introduces* that disorder. The protagonist's Romantic focus on intensity of experience—emotional, erotic, religious, or sublime—indeed rejects a rationalist appropriation of reality. But at the same time, that new focus leads to an equally problematic submission, that is, to idealizing projections onto material, corporeal reality.

Like *Der Tod Georgs*, *Liebesbrand* involves a perceptive transformation elicited by a confrontation with mortality. The narrator is a 38-year-old German of Turkish origin who—like Kermani's Dariusch—appears to have adopted a 'westernized', capitalist, and secularized lifestyle. His success on the stock exchange has allowed him to retire early and seems to have grown estranged from his Turkish relations in Germany. His success allows him to settle a family dispute in Turkey by financial intervention, which he mocks as "a very civilized solution [eine sehr zivilisierte [Lösung]]." (LB 22) David considers himself an example of successful assimilation into German society. When confronted with the remark "but you are not a German [doch kein Deutscher]," he responds: "Sure, I just came in a little later… [Doch, ich bin eben etwas später dazugekommen…]" (LB 94) He prides himself for his distinct lack of *Lebensanschauung*. Like Beer-Hofmann's aesthete, he is suspicious of any kind of unifying narrative and incapable of detecting underlying patterns of meaning: "I was skeptical of all the wisdoms of life, not because they were lacking in truth, but because I got out of step immediately when I tried to remember them as great truths. [[I]ch war skeptisch gegenüber allen Lebensweisheiten, nicht etwa, weil sie der Wahrheit entbehrten, sondern weil ich sofort aus dem Tritt kam, wenn ich versuchte, sie mir als große Wahrheiten zu merken.]" (LB 47) Unlike the aesthete, however, David describes himself as someone who has no affinity with the arts whatsoever: "I wanted nothing to do with the arts and much less with artists […]. [Ich wollte von Kunst nichts wissen und viel weniger von Künstlern […]]." (LB 116); "I myself was well versed in the art of bursting beauty in a single stroke. [[I]ch selbst kannte mich in der Kunst aus, die Schönheit mit einem Handstreich zum Platzen zu bringen.]" (LB 98) David's 'anti-aestheticism', reminiscent of the Romantics' *Philister*,[224] is thoroughly challenged when he barely escapes from a bus crash in Turkey—an experience of finitude he describes in both religious and medical terms:

> When one dies—just before the thread is cut—the nerves transmit millions of impulses, and perhaps that impulse explosion is purgatory, the little hell before entering the great paradise. I was not prepared, I was afraid.
>
> [Wenn man stirbt—kurz bevor der Faden reißt—, leiten die Nerven Millionen von Impulsen weiter, und vielleicht ist diese Impulsexplosion das Fegefeuer, die kleine Hölle vor dem Eintritt in das große Paradies. Ich war nicht darauf vorbereitet, ich hatte Angst.] (LB 5)

The combination of two seemingly incompatible registers—death as a neurological versus a purgatorial event—introduces the ambivalent focus of the novel. It resists a completely secular worldview, while pointing to the ambiguous nature of spiritual experiences, which are presented as the "intimation of another world," but are also "mistrusted as fraudulent superstition."[225]

David's near-death experience arouses his acute sensitivity to the sublime. The hospital where he is treated for his injuries functions as a liminal space where the narrator is stripped of his previous lifestyle; his possessions, except for his indispensable mobile phone, have been lost in the crash (LB 14).[226] The hospital is described as "a realm of dividing curtains and small chambers [ein Reich der Trennvorhänge und kleinen Kammern]" (LB 33) where reality may hide from the eye, which alludes to David's impending perceptive transformation. At this stage of his narrative it is not yet clear what his awakening entails exactly, but it is evident that he has grown suspicious of his former lifestyle. Previously, he was preoccupied with the question of earning more money (LB 23); now, he finds himself humbled by questions of fate and truth, and catches himself looking for wisdom in his fellow patients' words—"Perhaps I ought to show my good intentions and listen to the men, perhaps there was a truth hidden in their words [...]. [Vielleicht sollte ich meinen guten Willen zeigen und den Männern lauschen, vielleicht verbarg sich in ihren Worten eine Wahrheit [...].]" (LB 27) David's hospital stay thus recalibrates the "laws of reality [Gesetze der Realität]" (LB 34) as he knows them: his materialism encounters idealism, and his Enlightened sense encounters Romantic sensibility. David befriends a group of patients who refer to each other by the name of their ailments or the cause of their wounds—"Liver [Leber]," "Bruise [Bluterguß]," "Knife [Messer]," "Rib [Rippe]." Their remarkable name-giving alludes to the essentializing mechanisms criticized throughout the novel and first and foremost indicates the "all too embodied,"[227] corporeal business in the hospital: their convalescence. Yet their medical conditions are not their actual concern, as all are preoccupied with love and with adoration of one of the doctors. Quick to observe the absence of a wedding ring on David's finger, they assume that he is a contender in their contest for the doctor's affection. In a hypothetical counterargument that should convince them of his lack of interest, David exaggerates his modern, anti-romantic world view:

> I knew the sparks of lighters, but no burning of love in my heart, I was corrupted in the West, I was a thoroughly degenerate man of the Occident, and I had no idea of the tradition of the Middle Eastern worship of women [...].
>
> [[I]ch kannte Feuerzeugfunken, aber keinen Liebesbrand im Herzen, ich war im Westen verdorben, ich war ein durch und durch degenerierter Mann des Abendlandes, und von der Tradition der orientalischen Frauenanbetung hatte ich keine Ahnung [...]]. (LB 31)

Likewise, the concept of the soul is to him unfamiliar; his view is limited to the material world: "Soul? The soul is my nails, my teeth, my hair. I am matter, and matter perishes. [Seele? Seele sind meine Nägel, sind meine Zähne, sind meine Haare. Ich bin Stoff, und der Stoff verdirbt.]" (LB 43)

But this Enlightened confidence in the material world[228] soon starts showing cracks. The peculiar name-giving at the hospital also alludes to the fragility of bodily boundaries that accompanies David's budding *Sehnsucht*. Feeling "unprotected [ungeschützt]" (LB 14) after the accident, he wonders whether his new propensity to get hurt or ill is perhaps related to Turkey itself, as if in this the country he "attracted evil glances [böse Blicke auf [s]ich zog]" and "curses seemed to unfold their full effect [Flüche ihre volle Wirkkraft zu entfalten [schienen]]." (LB 32–33) Yet he soon realizes that indeed "his era of mercy is over [die Zeit der Verschonung vorbei war]." (LB 191) David's physical vulnerability symbolizes his new worldview, characterized by his receptiveness to an immaterial world that defies "the sovereignty of money and law [Herrschaft des Geldes und des Gesetzes]," and by his alertness to "signs from people who witnessed a different power at work, whose confidence had a different source [Zeichen von Menschen, die eine andere Kraft wirken sahen, deren Vertrauen eine andere Quelle kannte]." (LB 90) At times, that sensitivity ties in with the Platonic notion that the tangible world is merely a shadowy manifestation of the essences and ideals it represents. In the hospital, the distant sounds of a lament cause him to wonder: "Did I see what I wanted to see, or did I see the shadow of that which always withdraws and hides itself? [[S]ah ich, was ich sehen wollte, oder sah ich den Schatten dessen, das sich stets entzieht und verbirgt?]" (LB 44) This perceptual doubt—this "beautiful blurring [schöne Trübung]" (LB 44)—manifests itself more acutely in a strong melancholy desire to uncover a more meaningful connection to the world. It is an exemplary Romantic experience, described in terms of mystery, darkness, and indefinite longing:[229]

> We walked past a place of worship that was lit up unearthly beautifully, and I heard a curious sound, it sounded like rainwater collecting in the roof gutter and flowing down the drainpipe, how much I would have liked to uncover the mystery, but in this darkness I could not strike out on my own, after the accident it was impossible for me. Suddenly I felt a great yearning, I longed for something that would make me greater and happier.

[Wir gingen an einem Gotteshaus vorbei, das überirdisch schön erleuchtet war, und ich lauschte einem seltsamen Geräusch, es hörte sich an wie Regenwasser, das sich in der Dachrinne sammelt und das Fallrohr herunterströmt, wie gerne wäre ich dem Geheimnis auf die Spur gekommen, doch ich konnte in dieser Dunkelheit nicht eigene Wege gehen, nach dem Unfall war es mir unmöglich. Plötzlich verspürte ich eine große Sehnsucht, ich sehnte mich nach etwas, das mich größer und glücklicher machen sollte [...].] (LB 43)

Whereas before he defined his own body in materialistic terms, his Romantic inclination now makes him acutely aware of the soullessness of pure matter. The eery image of dismembered mannequins in a shop window—"naked and dressed dolls [nackte und angezogene Puppen]", "their dismantled limbs on the floor [die abmontierten Glieder auf dem Boden]", "their hard plastic torsos on wooden stools [die Hartplastikrümpfe [...] auf Holzkrücken] (LB 44)—contrasts strongly with David's description of yearning for meaning and unity beyond the material world.[230]

At this point, David's awareness of the sublime corresponds to a Platonic or Kantian idealism.[231] However, the narrator also associates the notion of ideals and essences to deception and fraudulence. Roaming the streets with his hospital friends, David indeed surmises that nothing is exactly as it seems, and that the derelict streets and run-down façades might in fact be false fronts for the dwellings of "renegade gypsy princes, robber lords expelled from the family, who send their children to beg and steal but feign modest living conditions [abtrünnige Zigeunerfürsten, von der Großfamilie verstoßene Räuberherren, die ihre Kinder zum Betteln und Klauen losschicken, aber bescheidene Verhältnisse vortäuschen]." (LB 44) In a similar vein, the narrator is suspicious of his new sensitivity, mistrusting it as merely an "illusion of perspective [Illusion von Perspektive]" (LB 71), which, he assumes, distorts his view of reality—"over and over again a fairytale dream image lay itself onto everyday scenes [immer wieder legte sich ein Märchentraumbild auf die Alltagsszenen] [...]." (LB 70)

Thus playing with the unclear boundary between *Schein* und *Sein*, Zaimoglu sets the scene for a critique of idealism and its essentializing tendency. While David's new, distinctly Romantic vulnerability implies a rejection of reality as pure matter, the idealistic alternative, as I will argue, expires in his futile quest for the ideal of love as well. If David resembled the *Philister* before—"a person without intellectual needs [ein Mensch ohne geistige Bedürfnisse]," whose most defining trait is "that *ideals* do not grant him any diversion [daß *Idealitäten* ih[m] keine Unterhaltung gewähren]," and who therefore, "in order to evade tedium, needs *realities* [um der Langeweile zu entgehen, stets der *Realitäten* bedürf[t]]"²³²—he has now become its inversion: an idealist who has lost sight of the reality in front of him. Renouncing strict idealism and strict materialism alike, Zaimoglu focuses instead on the transformative potential of love as a *corporeal-affective* experience. This particular focus, as I will illustrate, allows the author to imagine identity in terms of a "capacity to become"²³³ rather than a fixed set of characteristics. In this light, his Romantic references are not likely an indication of Zaimoglu's desired absorption into a 'German' canon. Rather, the novel is a subtle critique of a (Western) obsession with defining the 'original', the 'authentic', the 'essence' of people, nationalities, or cultures.

Aesthetics of becoming—The ambivalent rhetoric of blood

Beer-Hofmann's and Zaimoglu's protagonists do not suffer from the same aesthetic 'disorder'. Whereas depth of vision is absent in the former, it is excessively present in the latter. Both views are, however, presented as outgrowths of idealism—either in terms of fully congruent being and consciousness (Beer-Hofmann) or in terms of a radical counterreaction to soulless materialism (Zaimoglu). As I will illustrate, both novels criticize idealism as an objectifying worldview, producing static and 'mortified' images of reality. In both cases, this view is surmounted by a dynamic of 'becoming': a labyrinthine movement that subverts the aesthete's 'mortifying' gaze in *Der Tod Georgs* and an 'ordinary' love experience that consists of fleeting moments of self-transcendence. Correspondingly, both texts propose a notion of identity not in terms of a permanent 'being' but of a continuous 'becoming' that resists static representation. As Nancy writes, "identity never comes to be; it never identifies itself, even as an infinite projection, *because it is already there* [...]."²³⁴

Ornamentation—*Mortifikation*—the labyrinth

To contemporary critics of *Der Tod Georgs*, the transition from a modernist poetics of association to a determinate anchoring in Judaism was remarkable, if not implausible.²³⁵ The novella was regarded as flawed due to its ambiguous conclusion and due to a "disagreeable effect [arising] from prose drawn too taut between its prodigious lyricality and the demands of a sequential narrative."²³⁶ In a letter to Beer-Hofmann, Schnitzler too expresses his reservations. Comparing the text to a precious jewel, he finds fault not with its pictorial character and not even with the apparent lack of purpose of the images. What strikes him is "a cheeky scam [ein frecher Schwindel]" in the final chapter that involves a sudden change of register—"You sit down at another organ, as it were, which also sounds wonderful—but that does not prove anything. [Sie setzen sich sozusagen an eine andre Orgel, die auch herrlich klingt—aber das beweist nichts.]"[237] Schnitzler's remarks—and those of later critics—refer to the improbable shift from an aesthetic to an ethical dimension and are based on the consideration that "a genuine conversion would mandate a shift from the controls of impressionistic feeling (*Stimmung*) to those of cognitive understanding (*Erkenntnis*)."[238] Because the text fails to make an explicit reference to Judaism[239] and does not seem to leave the focalizer's perspective, Paul's conversion could be interpreted as yet another *Stimmung*, as aestheticism in the guise of spirituality. His seemingly abrupt awakening, however, is carefully prepared throughout the text. What may seem like profuse imagery, useless to the sequence of the story, is in fact crucial to Paul's non-linear and non-teleological transformation.

The pictoriality of *Der Tod Georgs* is significant for two reasons. Firstly, it illustrates the effects of the aesthete's perceptive disorder. It is an outgrowth of his idealism: the rich imagery "is symptomatic of the solipsism of the aesthete who turns all beings and all things into ornaments subject to the decrees of his sovereign preferences […]."[240] On a second reading, though, the seemingly inconsequential images acquire symbolic character. When the single images are layered over each other, they create a depth of meaning that was not there at first.

Under the aesthete's gaze, reality is robbed from its conventional dimensions resulting in one-dimensional and timeless images reminiscent of *Jugendstil* art.[241] The object of aesthetic observation here is subordinate entirely to the observer's subjectivity and senses—a reification process diagnosed by Rainer Hank as "Mortifikation."[242] In the first chapter, for instance, as Paul goes out for a short walk, he encounters a woman who strikes him as vaguely familiar.[243] Under his gaze, her presence loses all semblance of life; she morphs into an icon to behold, reminding him of "pictures […] in which archangels in steel gold-inlaid armor push their sword before them into the ground [Bilder […], auf denen Erzengel in stählernem goldtauschiertem Panzer ihr Schwert vor sich hin in den Boden stemmten]." And indeed, the woman is described in painting terminology:

> The deep shadow of the forest and then strayed sunbeams tinged her cheeks and her slightly wavy hair. In the dusty corners of an antique shop stood statuettes of saints who resembled her; her cheeks seemed to have the matte luster of light wood—only on her lips was a pale red, like light cursory overpainting. The hair seemed dark; incense smoke, laying itself heavily in the braids, and the flame of sacred colorful candles, burning fragrantly in wall sconces, had blackened it.

> [Der tiefe Schatten des Waldes und dann wieder verirrte Sonnenstrahlen färbten ihre Wangen und ihr leicht gewelltes Haar. In verstaubten Winkeln eines Antiquitäten-Ladens standen Statuetten von Heiligen, die ihr glichen; ihre Wangen schien den matten Glanz von lichtem Holz zu haben—nur auf den Lippen hing blasses Rot, wie leichte flüchtige Übermalung. Das Haar schien dunkel; Weihrauchqualm, der sich schwer in die Flechten legte, und die Flamme geweihter bunter Kerzen, die in Wandleuchtern duftend brannten, hatten es geschwärzt.] (TG 6–7)

In the aesthete's impressions, the woman is situated not in the foreground of, but on the same surface as the trees and the rays of light. The painting references furthermore suggest that her hair and her facial features derive color from their surroundings, and that the woman lacks substance of her own. Her appearance is measured against icons and statues, rather than the other way around: not the icons are evaluated for their lifelikeness; it is the woman who is scrutinized for her pictorial, iconic likeness. The 'mortifying' gaze of the aesthete renders reality and life as timeless ornaments, an *Erstarrung* articulating the aesthete's desire to stall aging, a yearning for an eternal present: "The death of life marks the beginning of art—the prerequisite for the artistic surmounting of mortality. [Der Tod des Lebens wird zum Anfang der Kunst—zur Voraussetzung einer künstlerischen Überwindung der Vergänglichkeit.]"[244]

However, the string of such still, meaningless images is wound in such a way that their stillness yields to a return of meaning. By elevating imagery and leitmotifs to key elements of narration, Beer-Hofmann refuses a sequential representation of Paul's psychological growth. His "narrative counterstrategy [erzählerische Gegenstrategie]"[245] consists of a central leitmotif: the labyrinth. The spatial metaphor condenses into a single image the thematic and narrative layers of the novella. It represents a non-linear movement with a teleology of its own, symbolizing the intricate pattern of the aesthete's consciousness, as well as the trajectory of the recovery of meaning:

> Their lives ran in winding labyrinthine paths, curiously chained to the lives of others. What seemed like a wrong track led to the destination; what seemed to meander aimlessly and capriciously was integrated into intricate forms, like the artistically conceived, gold-knitted arabesques on the white silk of prayer curtains.
>
> [In gewundenen labyrinthischen Wegen lief ihr Leben, mit dem Anderer seltsam verkettet. Was einem Irrweg glich, führte ans Ziel; was sich planlos launenhaft zu winden schien, fügte sich in vielverschlungene Formen, wie die

künstlich erdachten, goldgewirkten Arabesken auf der weissen Seide der Gebetvorhänge.] (TG 21)

The labyrinth simulates the static dynamism of the aesthete's consciousness, in which the stillness of *Jugendstil* imagery competes with impressionistic association. At first, it seems to invite the wandering mind to meander between images, evoking a continuous movement lacking linear progress. At the same time, the structure compels the mind in a certain direction and, upon its return, forces the mind to revisit familiar images and associative paths.[246] Every time a motif is encountered again, it accumulates meaning. While the horizontal linearity of narrated time remains minimal, the vertical dimension of leitmotivic layering acquires symbolic intensity.[247]

For instance, the lake motif featured in the dream sequence of the second chapter illustrates how initially static ornamentation produces depth of meaning. At first, the lake is simply a part of Paul's view from the window—a man looks outside, perhaps in contemplation, or in search of comfort by beauty, and by chance catches sight of a still life in nature:

> Through a large side window hot light came in. He leaned on the glowing railing and looked out forlornly. Where the glaring green of the treetops ended, the reflecting lake lay still. The mountains at its edges grew black into its depths and reached new heights there, the rich blue sky lay deep below and, flashing, at the bottom the white-blinding sun.
>
> [Durch ein grosses Seitenfenster fiel heisses Licht. Er stützte sich auf das glühende Geländer und sah verloren hinaus. Wo das grellflimmernde Grün der Baumwipfel endete, lag regungslos der spiegelnde See. Die Berge an seinem Saum wuchsen schwarz in seine Tiefe und gipfelten von Neuem darin, der sattblaue Himmel lag tief unten und, blitzend, auf dem Grund die weissblendende Sonne.] (TG 23)

It is only in retrospect, as the motif keeps evolving, that the symbolism of the lake becomes evident as a prefiguration of Paul's awakening. At this point, the lake illustrates the aesthete's 'mortifying' gaze. The perfect stillness of the water betrays the absence of life below the flawless mirror-like surface, obliterating the distinction between reality and illusory reflection. The blinding reflection of the sun as well as the saturated, impenetrable blue of the water prevent from assessing the depth of the lake; in fact, bottom and surface of the lake seem to coincide. The lake image thus symbolizes the aesthete's refusal to distinguish illusion from reality, as well as his spiritual *Bodenlosigkeit*. The position of the lake furthermore emphasizes the aesthete's isolation from reality. The lake escapes the confines of his focalization, as the narrative lens extends beyond the visual scope of a person who is merely looking out the window. It reaches beyond treetops and foliage, even though Paul is located at such a distance that he cannot distinguish individual trees anymore, only their dissolving into 'shimmering green'. The shift outside of his scope of vision suggests that the lake refers to a truth that, for the moment, is out of reach.

In the course of the dream sequence, the image undergoes slight yet significant alterations. Following an almost verbatim repetition of the image above, the lake is suddenly located "[o]nly a few steps away from [Paul] [[n]ur wenige Schritte weit von [Paul]]." The water starts rippling with "air bubbles gleaming [s]ilver [[s]ilbern glänzende Luftblasen]" and bursting the surface; then it settles again—"then the surface became smooth again, settled and revealing nothing of the depth underneath [dann glättete sich wieder der Spiegel und nichts verrieth unter der beruhigten Fläche die Tiefe." (TG 66) Near the end of the dream, the image is revisited, extended and adjusted, so as to illustrate Paul's completed, though still subconscious, transformation. At this point, the lake is at a walking distance from his window. He can now measure its proximity by a strip of grass sloping into the water's edge, suggesting that it has become an accessible reality. The rippling water now suspends Paul's illusion, revealing the depth of the lake:

> A silver flash tore the picture apart; a fish had surged up, [...]. [...] He saw how the clear sea bottom was flat for another stretch, and then slowly sank to the depth between slightly swaying dark water plants. [...] The earlier image was lost; his eyes no longer understood how to see only the dark water surface mirroring the mountains and the sky and the sun.
>
> [Ein silbernes Blitzen zerriss das Bild; ein Fisch war emporgeschnellt, [...]. [...] Er sah, wie der lichte Seeboden noch eine Strecke flach verlief, und dan zwischen leicht schwankenden dunklen Wasserpflanzen sich langsam zur Tiefe senkte. [...] Das frühere Bild war verloren; seine Augen verstanden es nicht mehr, nur die dunkle Fläche des Wassers zu sehen, die spiegelnd die Berge und Himmel und Sonne in sich fing.] (TG 86–8)

The aesthete has recovered from his perceptive disorder as the result of an associative process taking place within his mind. The labyrinthine structure of the narrative thus counteracts the aesthete's 'mortifying' gaze. It accommodates the wandering mind but eventually compels it into one of only two directions—either towards its core, to a culmination of aestheticism, or to its exit, to the real world. The improbable shift from modernist association towards an ethical awakening thus takes place by virtue of association itself—indeed, what may seem to lead to a dead end in fact leads towards a goal. Still, as I will illustrate later on, Paul's awakening remains highly ambiguous, as the labyrinthine imagery of 'becoming' is markedly at odds with a deterministic rhetoric of blood introduced in the final chapter.

Against monuments—"the crossing of love"[248]

Concerned with ideas and ideals rather than tangible realities, the inverted *Philister* may not have a 'mortifying' gaze like the aesthete's. Yet on several occasions, David's new idealism reveals itself as equally distorting. His gaze resembles an idealizing projection, which his friend Messer prefiguratively warns about in the hospital: "We must not shape reality after our wishful dreams. [[W]ir dürfen die Wirklichkeit nicht nach unserem Wunschtraum formen.]" (LB 42) In his quest for love David remains (partially) blind to the relevance of that motto: while striving for the idealized Tyra, he fails to acknowledge his everyday intimacy with Jarmila. His 'idealizing' disorder is exposed in the contrast between these two types of love. Furthermore, the intricate game of *Sein* and *Schein* extends his distorting view to questions of cultural and national identity. Driven by romantic *Sehnsucht*, David's quest for love takes him on travels through Central Europe. His movement is interspersed with images of statues and monuments capturing his attention. As instances of the infinite projection of meaning, they are similar to the ornaments in *Der Tod Georgs*—not in terms of a *lack* of meaning, but in that they conjure a deceptive sense of permanence that does not correspond to a changeable reality. Just as the 'mortified' ornaments in *Der Tod Georgs* evoke the illusion of an eternal present, so too do the stony representations of (Czech) history simulate an eternal past with an unchanging meaning. However, David's quest brings to light the continual 'becoming' of meaning and reality. David's 'disorder' can thus be read as a subtle critique of idealism as an unduly essentializing gesture, which translates to a (Western) obsession with determining and representing the pure idea(l), the essence, the original.

David's idealizing perception is relevant first in the context of national allegiances and cultural memory. On his Central European quest, he finds himself confronted with the anti-idealistic worldview of his tour guide Jarmila. Their conversations are interspersed with Jarmila's (rehearsed) tirades about recent Czech history and with allusions to the 'German' cooptation of 'Czech' culture—to "our Kafka, who has become their Kafka [unser Kafka, der ihr Kafka geworden ist]." (LB 214) Reluctant to ascribe a static, permanent significance to external phenomena, she strongly resists essentializing notions of culture and nationality. This becomes evident at first when David—still taken with his intimation of a hidden reality—asks about the meaning of her name. She responds: "Please break that habit. Jarmila means Jarmila. This name has no inner power... [[G]ewöhn' es dir bitte ab. Jarmila heißt Jarmila. In diesem Namen steckt keine innere Macht...]" (LB 204) In the same vein, she angrily corrects David when he enquires about 'the Czech soul':

> I had asked her about the Czech soul and had encountered bewilderment, what was that supposed to be? she had exclaimed, you Germans are so obsessed with the assumption of a core, a being, an inner force, you become suspicious when another people has simply had enough of the history invoked by all the occupying forces, we Czechs have often fought, mostly unsuccessfully, and we have given up revolting immediately and fiercely, we wait, and perhaps that is why we are considered reserved people. It was curious to hear these words from the mouth of a Czech woman, if I had been asked about the nature of the Germans, I would have shown myself similarly rude.

> [Ich hatte sie nach der tschechischen Seele gefragt und war auf Unverständnis gestoßen, was sollte das sein? hatte sie ausgerufen, ihr Deutschen seid derart versessen darauf, einen Kern, ein Wesen, eine innere Macht zu vermuten, ihr werdet mißtrauisch, wenn ein anderes Volk einfach genug hat von der Geschichte, auf die sich alle Besatzer berufen, wir Tschechen haben uns oft geschlagen, meist erfolglos, und wir haben es aufgegeben, sofort und heftig aufzubegehren, wir warten ab, und vielleicht deshalb gelten wir als reservierte Menschen. Es war seltsam, diese Worte aus dem Munde einer Tschechin zu hören, hätte man mich nach dem Wesen der Deutschen gefragt, hätte ich mich ähnlich unwirsch gezeigt.] (LB 203–4)

Resisting the reduction of reality and history to a nation's 'soul', Jarmila points out to David (albeit in rather generalizing terms about Germans and Czechs) that current appearances are the result of an evolving historical process, rather than the expression of an eternal inner force. Opposing the idea of an inner truth that remains unaffected by expressive forms, she simply rejects the notions of authenticity and originality—echoing Zaimoglu's criticism of the orientalizing/exoticizing reception of migrant writing. During a monologue by Jarmila, David notices "that she had deleted the original and had presented her own version [[dass] sie [...] das Original gestrichen und ihre eigene Fassung dargeboten [hatte]]." (LB 215) Her conviction that expressive form *shapes* meaning, rather than simply articulating it, becomes evident when she shows David a slightly obscene sculpture situated above one of the doors of St. Jacob's Church in Brno. It features "a man showing his exposed bottom, at last no saint and no hero, I liked it, and so did many other tourists [einen Mann, der seinen entblößten Hintern zeigte, endlich kein Heiliger und kein Held, es gefiel mir, und es gefiel auch vielen anderen Touristen [...]]." (LB 222) As the story goes, it is the result of a vengeful sculptor, but in a sarcastic tone Jarmila mocks the onlooking tourists and David as people who willingly let themselves be tricked into 'buying' the story behind the sculpture: "[B]ut here as well, there is a secret and true story that you would like to hear about immediately, no? [[A]ber auch hier gibt es eine geheime und wahre Geschichte, die du jetzt und sofort hören möchtest, oder nicht?]" (LB 223) Unaware of her mocking emphasis on the 'secret truth', David is indeed eager to hear it. He does not understand her, though, and remains blind to the ambiguity of the sculpture:

> When you take a second and third look at the little man, [...] you discover that his body hides the female, so up there you see... Is that what you call... a love act?
> You could, but it sounds a bit technical.
> Skillful love is also perfect technique, she said.
> What was I supposed to say to her, I looked at her, I looked up again, and although I tried hard, I was not able to recognize the concealed woman [...].
>
> [Wenn man auf das Männchen einen zweiten und dritten Blick wirft, fuhr sie fort, entdeckt man, daß es mit seinem Körper das Weibchen verdeckt, dort oben sieht man also... Sagt man das... Liebesakt?
> Kann man, aber es klingt etwas technisch.
> Gekonnte Liebe ist auch perfekte Technik, sagte sie.
> Was sollte ich ihr darauf erwidern, ich schaute sie an, ich schaute wieder hoch, und obwohl ich mir Mühe gab, gelang es mir nicht, die verdeckte Frau zu erkennen [...].] (LB 223)

It is telling that Jarmila shows him a sculpture evoking a love *act*—as opposed to an *idea*—and, moreover, a sculpture that conveys a different meaning once the onlooker's perspective changes. In other words, its 'truth' does not exist independently from its formal expression; it is in fact technical and, most of all, corporeal. As I will illustrate, Jarmila's suspicion of the *idea* shapes her 'common' love affair with David. Furthermore, it informs the tour guide's mockery of tourism as an obsession with the original story—even if it clearly involves commodified or framed authenticity and is as such entangled in the authenticity paradox mentioned earlier.

Jarmila's concentration on the tangible and changeable nature of reality corresponds to a suspicion of static representation that permeates the novel, especially with regard to the monuments adorning the Czech squares and cities. "Frozen in directional gestures [[I]n Gesten der Richtungsweisung eingefroren]," (LB 231) they are deceptive 'signposts' in a permanently evolving reality.[249] For instance, a highly contested monument commemorating the victims of the communist regime is criticized "because of the sense of false reverence it elicits, artificially arresting the flow of life":[250]

> It was said that the people of Prague had stormed it, [...] they wanted to forget about perpetrators and victims. Just forget—what was wrong with no longer dealing with the wrong, leaden times? The old men in short trousers made serious faces, some held their arms close to their sides and looked like a saluting soldier, the monuments only made us citizens freeze in our movements, break off our conversations and experience a sanctity of the moment that was lying and fraudulent.
>
> [Es hieß, die Prager wären dagegen Sturm gelaufen, [...] sie wollten Täter und Opfer vergessen. Einfach vergessen—was war falsch daran, sich nicht länger mit der falschen bleiernen Zeit zu beschäftigen? Die alten Männer in kurzen Hosen machten ernste Gesichter, manch einer hielt die Arme eng an den Seiten und sah aus wie ein salutierender Soldat, die Denkmäler brachten uns Bürger nur dazu, in unseren Bewegungen zu erstarren, unsere Gespräche abzubrechen und ein Gefühl von Heiligkeit des Augenblicks zu bekommen, die erlogen und erschwindelt war.] (LB 271)

The enforced 'sanctity of the moment'—once again mocked by way of tourists in short trousers—conjures an illusion of unchanging national and cultural identification. The monument supports "pedagogical narratives of nation"[251] and a ritual interpretation of the Czech past. By overlaying that narrative with

Aesthetes between identity and opposition   131

a mockery of tourism, Zaimoglu criticizes the nation as an idealistic projection that pays little attention to the intricacies and nuances of present reality. National identification, as the excerpt above implies, is the result of a projection of meaning, of a misguided desire for authenticity that affects the tourist's and the idealist's gaze alike. Whereas static imagery conjures the illusion of an eternal present in *Der Tod Georgs*, it simulates the illusory permanence of the past in *Liebesbrand*.

Yet David's new idealism especially affects his notion of love. His new intimation of a reality beyond the visible is closely tied to his near-death experience and to the *Sehnsucht* it has aroused. Shortly after the accident, he is offered water by Tyra, a German woman who appears as a guardian angel to the injured David. During their brief exchange, David notices a silver ring on her right hand but not much else. The memory of her ring, as well as a hair clip she loses at the crash site, are all David is left with as the woman leaves in her car with German license plate. Upon his return to Germany, David traces the woman to Nienburg. He finds out that she is enrolled for a PhD in history at the University of Göttingen and then follows her on a research trip to Prague. While he chases an idealized woman through Central Europe, though, it is the other woman who keeps him company—the Czech tour guide Jarmila. The contrast between the two women illuminates David's distorted view of love and reality.

Zaimoglu's engagement with romantic motifs of love can be illustrated in reference to Nancy, whose notion of love ties in with his non-identitarian concept of community. In the essay "Shattered Love,"[252] he argues against the notion of love as a 'communion of souls', or even as a mutual complementation and enrichment. Rather, love reveals the fundamental interrelatedness of human beings, even when (or especially when) they conceive themselves as absolute individuals. Love marks the moment when the singular plural being recognizes itself as being 'outside of itself': "Love [...] is once again an experience of finite transcendence: the subject *finds itself* in love, *beyond itself*."[253] As an "act of transcendence,"[254] love does not rely on the presumed pre-existence of autonomous individuals:

> [T]he transcendence of love does not go from the singular being toward the other, toward the outside. It is not the singular being that puts itself outside itself: it is the other, and in the other it is not the subject's identity that operates this movement or this touch.[255]

Nancy's non-identitarian notion of love implies that it never complements one being with another; it does not respond to a lack, nor to an abundance. In fact, it "frustrates the simple opposition between economy and noneconomy:" "Love is precisely […] that which brings an end to the dichotomy between the love in which I lose myself without reserve and the love in which I recuperate myself, to the opposition between gift and property."[256] A similar non-identitarian view informs Zaimoglu's approach in *Liebesbrand*. By opposing an everyday, fleeting experience of love to a proprietary, idealizing notion, Zaimoglu formulates an alternative to the enforced 'sanctity of the moment' associated with national identification.

The highly educated Tyra represents an unattainable ideal, leaving David in the position of "emasculated romantic [entmannter Romantiker]" (LB 54)—submissive and pleading for her attention. In this respect, David emerges as the reversal of Beer-Hofmann's aesthete, whose 'love' for the unnamed woman in his dream consists of his 'mortifying' appropriation of her life and views. David, by contrast, is willing to sacrifice any of his customs and 'beliefs' to attain his ideal—"For your sake, I would even go to a natural history museum on a Sunday, a nightmare […]. [Ich würde dir zuliebe an einem Sonntag sogar in ein Naturkundemuseum gehen, ein Alptraum […].]" (LB 79) Remarkably, in the hospital, David is about to warn his friend Messer about the improbability of a loving relationship between two such extremes—if one person represents the absolute ideal, the other is reduced to a complement on the opposite end of the scale: "[S]he was a woman of learning, of culture, a lily of purity, but he was a large unshaven zero, a quite simple-minded creature on the periphery of life and love. [[S]ie war eine Studierte, eine Kultivierte, eine Lilie der Reinheit, er aber war eine große unrasierte Null, eine recht einfältige Kreatur in der Peripherie des Lebens und der Liebe.]" (LB 31) Oblivious to his own advice, David ends up chasing his own ideal, but he can only ever seem to experience his love through partial images and objects imbued with desire: "I have begun yearning for you, I know it is stupid, but your hands. But your special ring. But your voice. Your business woman's suit [[I]ch habe angefangen, mich nach dir zu sehnen, ich weiß, es ist dumm, aber deine Hände. Aber dein besonderer Ring. Aber deine Stimme. Dein Geschäftsfrauenkostüm.]" (LB 79) His fetishistic reverence suggests that the totality of his ideal remains out of reach. Mistaking the absolute idea(l) of love for reality,[257] David cannot help feeling like an impostor unworthy of Tyra's attention:

> How do you recognize an idiot? He would not listen, he was hooked on an idea, and in his dreams he saw the image of the woman who ridiculed him in reality. […] I was a man who disguised himself as a tourist to cover up his delusions of love, and the idiocy of my deception could not remain hidden from her.

> [Woran erkannte man einen Idioten? Er wollte nicht hören, er hing einer Idee an, und in seinen Träumen sah er das Abbild der Frau, die ihn in der Wirklichkeit verlachte. [...] Ich war ein Mann, der sich als Tourist verkleidete, um seinen Liebeswahn zu verhüllen, und das Idiotische an meinem Betrug konnte ihr nicht verborgen bleiben.] (LB 238)

The actual deceit taking place here is not his attempt to hide his obsession, but rather the *Liebeswahn* itself: it is merely his wishful idea projected onto reality. Nancy's distinction between desire and love fittingly describes David's illusion. Considering himself to be the lesser part of an incomplete relationship, David espouses a proprietary notion of love. Yet as Nancy argues, "love is at once the promise of completion—but a promise always disappearing—and the threat of decomposition, always imminent."[258]

> This is why desire is not love. Desire lacks its object—which is the subject—and lacks it while appropriating it to itself (or rather, it appropriates it to itself while lacking it. Desire [...] is foreign to love because it sublates, be it negatively, the logic of fulfillment. Desire is self extending towards its end—but love does not extend, nor does it extend itself toward an end.[259]

If Tyra represents the ultimate end of David's desire—and, in Nancian terms, the extension to his own self—Jarmila stands for the resistance to such appropriation and for a moment of self-transcendence for David. As his tour guide, she accompanies David on his journey, rather than directing him towards his goal—Tyra. Her guidance offers an alternative kind of love and, subsequently, an alternative approach to reality. David's initial request about her role as a guide—"Just be my seeing-eye dog, please. [[S]eien Sie einfach nur mein Blindenhund, bitte.]" (LB 178)—thus becomes relevant to more than just his visit to Prague.

Indeed, Jarmila reveals herself as far more in touch with reality, representing an anti-idealistic notion of reality, both in the philosophical and in the everyday sense. An actress as well, Jarmila proves highly sensitive to the tension between *Sein* and *Schein*. Wenn she suddenly changes her mind after having invited David to her bed, her justification reveals how she measures wishful dream against reality, carefully assessing their compatibility:

> [S]he was certainly not erratic, she just wanted to separate true from false, and sometimes it happened that her wish came true, but she looked at it, then she looked as one looks at fingerprints on the glass plate, and then undid her wish.
>
> [[S]ie war ganz sicher nicht sprunghaft, sie wollte nur wahr von falsch trennen, und manchmal kam es vor, daß sich ihr Wunsch erfüllte, doch sie sah es sich an, sie schaute dann, wie man Fingerabdrücke auf der Glasplatte ansieht, und machte ihren Wunsch rückgängig.] (LB 230)

Her reaction suggests that the fulfillment of desire may not lead to a desirable reality. Instead, she defends an anti-idealistic view of life and love, in which hopes and desires are not allied with projections: "You hope without seeing. You expect without trusting your eyes. You confess, full of fear and without understanding. [Man hofft, ohne zu sehen. Man erwartet, ohne seinen Augen zu trauen. Man bekennt, voller Angst und ohne zu erkennen.]" (LB 227) This notion of love is reminiscent of what Nancy refers to as "the crossing of love." It strikes beyond one's volition, and exposes the limits of one's ostensible autonomy: "Love arrives, it comes, or else it is not love. But it is thus that it endlessly goes elsewhere than to 'me' who would receive it: its coming is only a departure for the other, its departure only the coming of the other."[260] Precisely this "incessant coming-and-going"[261] of love describes David and Jarmila's budding affair. It seems to happen by accident, without them even realizing it, as an everyday kiss on the cheek grows inadvertently intimate—"I missed her cheek and kissed her on the neck, it was an oversight, but at that moment it was beyond my powers to enlighten her about the misunderstanding. [[Ich verfehlte] ihre Wange und küßte sie auf den Hals, es war ein Versehen, es ging aber in diesem Moment über meine Kräfte, sie über das Mißverständnis aufzuklären.]" (LB 209) Indeed, love happens to them without presenting itself as such. Even before they become actual lovers, they sleep together in an innocent yet intimate way, to which there is a sense of ordinariness—it happens without being questioned:

> I was not surprised […] that she slipped under my cover and lay half on top of me, and because we were ashamed, we were content with just smelling each other's skin, she fell asleep in my embrace and with my hand on her breast.
>
> [[E]s wunderte mich […] nicht, daß sie unter meine Decke schlüpfte und halb auf mir lag, und weil wir schamvoll waren, begnügten wir uns damit, an der

Haut des anderen zu riechen, sie schlief ein in meiner Umarmung und mit meiner Hand auf ihrer Brust.] (LB 232)

The apparent simplicity of their bond stands in stark contrast to David's and Tyra's relationship. Their lovemaking resembles warfare—a battle of appropriation, where her "attack of deliberate ferocity [Anfall von überlegter Wildheit]" (LB 103) is met with his desire to possess: "Fight and war in bed, she loved to be possessed, and I wanted to be possessed by her. [Kampf und Krieg im Bett, sie liebte es, besessen zu sein, und ich wollte von ihr besessen sein.]"[262] (LB 105–6) This battle, from a Nancian perspective, is evidence of two people longing to be appropriated as objects of desire, seeking to restore and complete themselves. Ordinary love on the other hand—the one that does not heed an external, absolute idea of love—comes gradually, by unpredictable strokes. "What characterizes [the] endless forms [of love] is nothing more than its *éclats*; it has no other essence."[263] Its sense of fulfillment does not come with conquering an ideal, but it arrives in fleeting moments.[264] As opposed to the contrived 'sanctity of the moment' enforced by monuments, common love makes David aware of a flow of life. When he makes love to Jarmila for the first time, it happens unexpectedly—not as the result of desire, nor even as the result of subjective agency. Having been rejected by Tyra briefly before, he suddenly finds himself in bed with Jarmila, unaware of how he got there:

> It's over, she said, it's over, I said, and why was I in her arms, one woman had left me, one woman touched me, touched my eyelids, licked my lip groove, and why were we both naked, one woman had not let herself be tamed by all those words, [...] one woman left me, one woman found me [...].
>
> [Es ist vorbei, sagte sie, es ist vorbei, sagte ich, und wieso lag ich in ihren Armen, eine Frau hatte mich verlassen, eine Frau faßte mich an, berührte meine Lider, leckte meine Lippenmulde, und wieso waren wir beide nackt, eine Frau hatte sich durch all die vielen Worte nicht zähmen lassen, [...] eine Frau verließ mich, eine Frau fand mich [...]]. (LB 282)

Indeed, in Nancy's words, David is first presented with 'the unfulfillment of love'—his ideal proves unattainable—yet at the same time he is 'offered its actual advent' in the arms of another woman. In a five-page long sentence of paratactic association (LB 282–6), their lovemaking is described as a jumble of fleeting thoughts and impressions, over which David has no control. This passage marks a moment of self-transcendence for David, who is, for now, not concerned with his ideal but with reality as it takes shape in front of him, with him. Whereas his affair with Tyra is marked by self-involved desire and 'the extension of the self', the ordinary one with Jarmila allows him to witness a corporeal reality that takes him over, rather than the other way around.

Der Tod Georgs and *Liebesbrand* bring into focus the moment when idealism, as an outgrowth of radical autonomy and 'the assimilated mind', starts to lose its hold on reality. Both novels implicitly criticize idealism as leading to a reification of reality. At the same time, they explore how to overcome that 'mortified' stasis and to respond to a need for self-transcendence. They imagine identity in terms of a capacity to *become*, rather than a *state* of being. Still, the 'awakening' of both the aesthete and the inverted *Philister* leads to an open ending, which casts doubt on the probability of their transformation. In *Der Tod Georgs*, the unexpected introduction of a (racial) rhetoric of blood appears at odds with the imagery of 'becoming' developed throughout the text. Likewise, *Liebesbrand* leaves the reader in uncertainty as to whether the protagonist has effectively overcome his perceptive disorder and acknowledges the reality of 'ordinary' love. However, from a comparison of the blood motifs in each novel, that lack of closure reveals itself to be consistent with the protagonists' emerging sense of community, as well as with a resistance against determinate identities conveyed by each novel.

The ambivalent rhetoric of blood

Zaimoglu's engagement with the Romantic tradition puts him in an interesting position as a German author. As Hofmann remarks on Zaimoglu's "Romantic rebellion," there is an ironic aspect to the cliché that Zaimoglu's writings strike readers as 'Middle Eastern', for he draws on a tradition which has apparently become unfamiliar to many Germans. "What German critics and readers think they recognize as a strangeness, an alien, exotic and extravagant quality, is a neglected facet of their own culture which Zaimoglu invites them to rediscover."[265] Hofmann draws on Şenocak's argument that postwar German culture has favored objectivity and realism over romanticism, as the latter is almost invariably associated with nationalism—and thus the catastrophe of Nazism.[266] Immigrant writers, Hofmann argues, have been able to approach and appropriate Romantic traditions far more freely, disassociating them from dangerous ideology. In *Liebesbrand*, the Romantic echoes have indeed been disengaged from the dangers of collectivism. The intimacy between Jarmila and David, marked by 'the crossing of love', acquires a more universal character when she persuades him to accompany her to the hospital to donate blood plasma. After the procedure, David feels as if he has been robbed of an essence—"They have just taken something from us. [Sie haben uns gerade etwas abgenommen.]" (LB 262) Jarmila, on the other hand, feels enriched. Although a regular plasma donor, she is not motivated by the money but by the sense of connection it affords her: "My plasma is needed. It flows in the veins of other people. In this way I acquire kinship. [...] Blood makes relatives. [Mein Plasma wird gebraucht. Es fließt in den Adern anderer Menschen. Auf diese Weise bekomme ich Verwandtschaft. [...] Blut macht Verwandte.]" (LB 263) Jarmila establishes an artificial, "nonfilial yet organic connectedness"[267] that does not involve the kind of family trouble that David had to settle. She single-handedly creates a sense of kinship that ignores, even subverts, the racial overtones usually associated with the rhetoric of blood. Redefining the traditional connection between blood and kinship, Zaimoglu transposes the non-identitarian aspect of their 'ordinary' love to a notion of community that resembles Nancy's 'inoperative community'. The same "*Verwandtschaft* without obligation"[268] informs the lack of closure of the novel. Although ultimately rejected by Tyra, David's quest does not seem to have reached a conclusion. In the final phone conversation with Jarmila—a very banal one, which fits their ordinary love—David appears intent on continuing his journey: "I have finished with everything, I said. [...] See you very soon, Jarmila said and hung up. Then, in the cutting cold wind—I should go. [Ich habe mit allem abgeschlossen, sagte ich. [...] Bis ganz bald, sagte Jarmila und legte auf. Dann, im schneidend kalten Wind— ich sollte gehen.]" (LB 375) The reader is left to wonder whether David flees the banality of love he shares with Jarmila in order to continue his quest for the ideal love. Still, these final lines contain a note of optimism. Closure would imply the standstill that was revealed as suspicious before. Instead, David continues to be driven by *Sehnsucht*, which means that he remains receptive to the 'crossing of love'. The fact that he is not inclined to stay for Jarmila's sake, with whom he remains connected over the phone, ties in with their kinship without obligation.

Der Tod Georgs concludes in similar ambiguity, due to the remarkable insertion of a blood narrative in the final chapter in which the aesthete recovers his Jewish ancestry. Apparently awakened from the aestheticist illusion, Paul is now aware of a signifying dimension behind the ornament that reality had become. Whereas he lived in the illusion of an eternal present before, he now acknowledges his genealogical connectedness, extending his existence into the past and the future:

> Unveiled [...] a realization stared at him. His thoughts had grasped whatever he disregarded otherwise and, *growing* up from them, they had *taken root* backwards into the past, and *ranked* far into the future for what was to come.
>
> [Unverhüllt [...] sah eine Erkenntnis ihn an. Gleichgiltiges das er sonst übersah, hatten seine Gedanken umklammert, und daran *emporwuchernd*, schlugen sie nach rückwärts *Wurzeln* in Vergangenes, und *rankten* zu Kommendem weit in die Zukunft.] (TG 201–2; emphasis added)

This distinctly organic image of rootedness contrasts with the static ornamentation that suffused the aesthete's world before. Yet in the light of Paul's gradual rediscovery of meaning, which occurred as a cognitive, psychological, or in any case *associative* process, it is remarkable—if not problematic—that his turn to Judaism is presented in the language of *Blutverwandtschaft*:[269]

> And behind them all a people, not begging for mercy, struggling to obtain the blessing of their God; wandering through the seas, not held back by deserts, and always so filled with the feeling of the righteous God as the *blood flowing in their veins* [...]. [...] *And of their blood he was as well.*
>
> [Und hinter ihnen allen ein Volk, um Gnaden nicht bettelnd, im Kampf den Segen seines Gottes sich erringend; durch Meere wandernd, von Wüsten nicht aufgehalten, und immer vom Fühlen des gerechten Gottes so durchströmt, wie vom *Blut in ihren Adern* [...]. [...] *Und von ihrem Blute war auch er.*]
> (TG 215–7; emphasis added)

Whereas the process of Paul's awakening pictures identity as changeable, the rhetoric of blood "amounts to the statement that, even for Jews who know it not, Jewishness is an inalienable part of the self."[270] In fact, Paul himself ponders the question if this blood kinship is indeed an essential part of himself or just a fleeting thought: "What sign had been given to him that this was not transient in him [...], that he could feel confident that—like the blood in his veins—it always belonged to him, and only to him? [Welches Zeichen war ihm denn gegeben, dass dies nicht vergänglich in ihm war [...], dass er sich dessen sicher fühlen durfte, dass es—wie das Blut in seinen Adern—immer ihm, und nur ihm gehörte?]" (TG 214–5) What Paul seems to have recovered, indefinitely, is a sense of ancestry and "a 'national energy' hidden deep within the modern individual."[271] Yet the abrupt transition from a cognitive process to the essentializing determinacy of blood raises the question which aspects are more significant in the formation of identity: are they cultural, intellectual, social, or—as the unexpected blood motif suggests—exclusively racial? Moreover, as Gillman notes, from a narrative perspective, would not the elaborate dream sequence and the very act of regaining self-knowledge be rendered useless, if the novella concluded with the assertion that "identity is finally a matter of one's blood heritage?"[272] Beer-Hofmann withholds a clear answer to that question. In doing so, he casts doubt not just over the protagonist's awakening but over the plausibility of an essentialist identity as well. The real focus of the novella thus remains on the subjective, idiosyncratic nature of spiritual awakening itself, not on the specific (cultural, religious, ideological) nature of its outcome. In fact, Paul appears indecisive about the affirmation of his Jewishness (and not simply because the word 'Jewish' is never mentioned). Reluctant to "finish the thought [den Gedanken [...] zu Ende denken]" (TG 219) about what his transformation means exactly, Paul leaves the Schönbrunn park and joins a group of workmen, whose fatigue reminds the reader of the wandering people mentioned above. Paul seems to question his belonging but joins them anyway:

> They spoke to each other in a foreign language that Paul did not understand. He was too tired to go any faster and pass them. Slowly he walked behind them, unconsciously falling into the heavy rhythm of their steps. How dense the fog was and how far the city was! But through all the tiredness Paul felt peace and security. As if a strong hand lay soothing and guiding him on his right; as if he felt its strong pulse. But what he felt was only the beating of his own blood.
>
> [Sie sprachen miteinander in einer fremden Sprache, die Paul nicht verstand. Er war zu müde, um rascher zu gehen und sie zu überholen. Langsam ging er hinter ihnen, unbewusst in den schweren Takt ihrer Schritte verfallend. Wie dicht der Nebel war und wie weit die Stadt lag! Aber durch alle Müdigkeit hindurch empfand Paul, Ruhe und Sicherheit. Als läge eine starke Hand beruhigend und ihn leitend auf seiner Rechten; als fühle er ihren starken Pulsschlag. Aber was er fühlte, war nur das Schlagen seines eigenen Bluts.] (TG 221)

The concluding lines once more emphasize the ambivalence of the rhetoric of blood. While Paul seems to have found a sense of calm and assurance, he is still unable to see clearly through the fog. Even though he joins the group of workers, he does not speak their language. Yet most significantly, the 'aber' in the final sentence seems to convey an objection to the preceding images of

Blutverwandtschaft, which is reinforced by the irrealis mood in the preceding sentence: Paul's sense of community might be "a self-made fiction;"[273] he might not have overcome the immanence of his own mind. What he feels, might be nothing more than the beating of his own heart, not that of a community. As Le Rider concludes: "Tomorrow, perhaps, Paul will no longer hear that 'voice of blood' so clearly. His sense of a Jewish identity remains, irremediably, fragile."[274]

The ambivalent rhetoric of blood in *Liebesbrand* and *Der Tod Georgs* thus demonstrates a reluctance to subscribe to collectivist or individualist notions of identity. Both novels articulate a wavering confidence in absolute autonomy and idealism, but despite the arising need for self-transcendence, the authors remain skeptical of collectivism and essentialism. Instead, the anti-mimetic pictoriality of Beer-Hofmann's text and Zaimoglu's Romantic anti-idealism carve out a space for indeterminate and constantly evolving identities.

Conclusion

> Art's asociality is the determinate negation of a determinate society. [...] Art keeps itself alive through its social force of resistance; unless it reifies itself, it becomes a commodity. Its contribution to society is not communication with it but rather something extremely mediated: It is resistance in which, by virtue of inner-aesthetic development, social development is reproduced without being imitated.[275]

Theodor Adorno's view on the critical potential of art reads like the opposite of Biller's defense of realism as the truly oppositional mode for migrant writing. Yet Adorno's statement might very well serve as the motto of the four aesthetes described here. *Fräulein Else* demonstrates exactly how art must reify itself in resistance to commodification. Indeed, Schnitzler's novella owes its oppositional aspect not to its reference to social reality, but rather to a conflict of aesthetic codes explored *within* the text. Kermani's aesthete is a negative confirmation of Adorno's view, representing the commodified art object tailored to social expectations. The critical aspect of these texts becomes especially evident on a metafictional level, as they share a critique of assimilation as a process of self-aestheticization leading to self-commodification. Beer-Hofmann's and Zaimoglu's (semi-) aesthetes are illustrations of the extremely mediated resistance of literary texts. Tracing the aesthete's 'conversion' from idealistic individualism to tentative forms of community, both novels oppose determinate notions of identity, indeed 'by virtue of an inner-aesthetic development', by fashioning an imagery of becoming that resists fixation. These variations of the aesthete show that the oppositional character of minority writing does not necessarily reside in the explicit thematization of identity issues but precisely in its aesthetic and anti-mimetic nature. Through the lens of the aesthete, the comparison of these four texts has firstly brought into focus the dead end of assimilation narratives and, secondly, an underlying pattern whereby this dead end may give way to the imagination of fleeting forms of community that resist the embrace of collective identities.

CHAPTER 3

CITY DWELLERS BETWEEN DIFFERENCE AND INDIFFERENCE

3.1 Images of the city: emancipatory visions and spatialized difference

In an interview for the journal *Transit*, the Hungarian-born writer Terézia Mora discusses the artistic impetus that comes with her residence in Berlin. Inspiration and creation are, to her, inextricably bound up with living space, and only in Berlin does she experience a sense of artistic liberation:

> It has become clear to me that I need this and no other place to write what I want to write. I have a feeling of insanely irritating alienation everywhere, really everywhere in the world, in every place, even in the place where I was born.

> [[Es] ist mir klar geworden, dass ich diesen und keinen anderen Ort brauche, um das zu schreiben, was ich schreiben will. Ich habe überall, wirklich überall auf der Welt, an jedem Ort, auch an dem Ort, an dem ich geboren wurde, das Gefühl von irrsinnig irritierender Fremdheit.][1]

While *Fremdheit* may be a recurring theme throughout her writings, it is, as she indicates herself, not a matter of 'foreignness'—of autobiography, a lost *Heimat*, or the experience of being displaced. Nor does she consider the city's inspirational quality in terms of its lived character, the visual abundance of architecture, bustling streets, or cultural diversity. Rather, the city releases her from an existential alienation that she associates with being unable to articulate herself:

> I am very susceptible to disturbances, and I work slowly, and I have to get rid of this alienation before I can say a word. And Berlin is the only place that disturbs me so little in my existence that it becomes possible, that there is enough air and space.
>
> [Ich bin sehr störungsanfällig, und ich arbeite langsam, und ich muss mich dieser Fremdheit erst entledigt haben, bevor ich ein Wort sagen kann. Und Berlin ist der einzige Ort, der mich so wenig stört in meiner Existenz, dass das möglich ist, dass da genügend Luft ist und Raum.][2]

A condition of, rather than a challenge to her artistic self-understanding, Berlin offers Mora the exact opposite of the *Reiz* that inspired so many modernists of the early twentieth century; to her, Berlin is a silent backdrop that accommodates her literary voice.

Berlin: image of an unsettled national identity

Mora's statement bespeaks the versatility of the metropolis as a literary concept. Attempts to decode the artistic appeal of the city, beyond that which Klaus Scherpe defined as the "unreality of cities [Unwirklichkeit der Städte],"[3] easily lapse into commonplace. While it may not always have been considered beneficial to one's sense of self—as it does to Mora—Berlin has most certainly and most profoundly inspired several generations of artists in various ways. German literature has featured the metropolis throughout the entire twentieth century, from avant-garde experiment to the *(Post-) Wendeliteratur* of the 1990s, in addition to a revival of *Pop-Literatur* in the early 2000s. Berlin modeled in the development of artistic concepts that explore subjectivity in relation to either real or fictional, textual spaces against the backdrop of German (national) history.[4] Alfred Döblin's *Berlin Alexanderplatz* (1929) and Rainer Maria Rilke's *Die Aufzeichnungen des Malte Laurids Brigge* (1910) are paradigmatic of the modernist urban experience, depicting city dwellers whose visual and corporeal experience in a "shocking perceptual space [schockierender Wahrnehmungsraum]" leads to fragmentation and alienation.[5] While by the end of the twentieth century, focus had shifted from the sensory impact onto imaginary and semiotic significance, the metropolis has remained a typical locus of *Verfremdung*. As Erk Grimm observes, the individual in contemporary texts "cannot simply be resynthesized [kann [...] nicht einfach resynthetisiert werden]" and is best understood as a "polycentric subject [polyzentrisches Subjekt]", "already disintegrated in modernity and trapped in its alienation [schon in der Moderne zerfallen und in seiner Alienation gefangen]."[6]

Berlin furthermore symbolizes a historical and political dimension of alienation and fragmentation. Once the symbol of an ideologically divided world, Berlin remains, even as the capital of a unified Germany, the image of an unsettled national identity. In his acclaimed study *Ghosts of Berlin*,[7] Brian Ladd calls Berlin "a haunted city," where the present always bears the traces of Germany's past, and where remembrance and a desire to forget are in permanent dialogue: "The calls for remembrance—and the calls for silence and forgetting make all silence and all forgetting impossible, and they also make remembrance difficult."[8] Adding to this ambiguity of memory, Berlin symbolizes Germany's contested status as *Einwanderungsland*. Migration and plurality determine its everyday reality—"Large cities are immigration magnets [Großstädte sind Zuwanderungsmagneten]" is the hardly surprising conclusion of a 2013 microcensus.[9] The study observes that a current "renaissance of cities [Renaissance der Städte]" is mostly due to a considerable increase of inhabitants with a migration background, which compensates for tendencies of *Stadtflucht*.[10] Historically as well, urban development has thrived on the dynamism of newcomers and minority cultures[11]—from French Huguenots and Bohemian religious refugees in the seventeenth and eighteenth centuries, to Polish immigrants throughout the twentieth century, and, of course, the Jewish community, which contributed considerably to Berlin's economic and cultural life.[12] The historical normality of transit and intercultural exchange is, of course, not exclusive to Berlin. Large cities are, in Erol Yildiz's words, "sites of uncertainty and unfamiliarity [Orte der Ungewissheit und des Fremden]":

> They hold niches ready for idiosyncratic self-designs, provide a daily experience of transitions, interstices, and new beginnings. [...] This urban diversity is not a static juxtaposition of disparate elements that like mosaic tiles result in a uniform overall picture but, rather, is to be found in movement and counter-movement, alternating mixing and discontinuities that repeatedly force reorientation and a change of perspective.
>
> [[S]ie halten Nischen bereit für eigenwillige Selbstentwürfe, bieten die tägliche Erfahrung von Übergängen, Zwischenräumen und Neuanfängen. [...] Diese urbane Diversität ist kein statisches Nebeneinander unterschiedlicher

Elemente, die wie Mosaiksteine ein einheitliches Gesamtbild ergeben, sondern vor allem in Bewegung und Gegenbewegung, wechselnder Vermischung und Brüchen zu finden, die immer wieder zu Umorientierung und Perspektivenwechsel zwingen.]¹³

As such, the metropolis and Berlin, in particular, challenge notions of national identity defined as a static German *Leitkultur*. Berlin indeed owes its endless artistic appeal to an entanglement of its particular memory with the urban dynamism that resists translation into myths of nation, language, ethnicity, or religion. Its "complex intertwining of history, memory, architecture, and apparitions of national identity," as Azade Seyhan notes, "implicitly and explicitly perform[s] an ongoing discourse of the city [...]."[14] A witness to European history and at the same time a tangible illustration of Germany as a country of immigration, Berlin has become for many artists "a desired object of affiliation, for it represents a territory to which no essentialist national interest can lay claim."[15] Indeed, the metropolis can be regarded as in and of itself cosmopolitan, a place where artists can find refuge from enforced cultural identities and national affiliations: "The writer does not have to swear allegiance to the nation in the cosmopolitan city; she or he is only the citizen of the city."[16] According to James Donald, city life constitutes "a normative ideal" beyond cultural and national belonging. It acknowledges the "desire for the security of home, but also the inevitability of migration, change, and conflict, and so too the ethical need for an openness to unassimilated otherness."[17] The upside of the paradigmatic experience of alienation, in a city where everyone is a stranger, is the opportunity to live according to one's own principles, undisturbed by tradition, culture, or nationality. *Fremdheit*, then, is not merely an isolating but also an emancipatory aspect of city life.

Indifference to difference

As early as 1903, Georg Simmel reflected on the nature of modern metropolitan subjectivity. In his well-known essay "The Metropolis and Mental Life [Die Großstädte und das Geistesleben],"[18] he discusses the significance of urban anonymity in emancipation and liberation. Simmel ascribes the modern city resident a general indifference to difference. Confronted with its elementary form of experience, the shock, the city dweller is forced to develop an "intellectuality [Verstandesmäßigkeit]" that is seen to preserve subjective life against "the overwhelming power of metropolitan life [gegen die Vergewaltigungen der Großstadt]."[19] The metropolitan's "blasé attitude [Blasiertheit]" is at once "stimulus shield and distancing device [Reizschutz und Distanzorgan],"[20] without which he would be at the mercy of an overwhelming abundance of stimuli.

Simmel bridges two seemingly contradictory notions of modern(ist) subjectivity and authorship.[21] On the one hand, the modernist "crisis of the senses" implies a "world-sensitive" subject,[22] characterized by experiences of distraction, disintegration, and a loss of self. On the other hand, modernist fiction is commonly associated with formal mastery and the invention of a unique personal style, implying a strongly individualistic notion of subjectivity and authorship, marked by observational, intellectual, or skeptical distance. This "defensive"[23] approach is, from Simmel's perspective, simply an alternative manifestation of the same loss of self: both the authorial voice embodied in formal mastery and its fragmentation are literary expressions of the same experience. Simmel suggests that, paradoxically, detachment derives from susceptibility to experiences and does not amount to a simple retreat into isolation. The city dweller's blasé character even constitutes a moment of individual liberation, emancipation, and socialization. The internal unity of a group, Simmel writes, loses coherence to the extent that it increases numerically, spatially, or in terms of life purposes, allowing the individual a freedom of movement beyond previous limitations.[24] Due to the abundance of differences and external stimuli in modern city life, the city dweller loses the desire or the capacity to give meaning to it and is encouraged to assert himself beyond familiar differences and relations, thus escaping the exigencies of traditional community life. In this respect, Simmel acknowledges the modern metropolis as a fundamentally social space—not as a collection of isolated individuals, but as a "functional extension beyond its physical boundaries [funktionell[e] Größe jenseits ihrer physischen Grenzen]:"

> Man does not end with the limits of his body or the area comprising his immediate activity. Rather is the range of the person constituted by the sum of effects emanating from him temporally and spatially. In the same way, a city consists of its total effects which extend beyond its immediate confines. Only this range is the city's actual extent in which its existence is expressed.
>
> [Wie ein Mensch nicht zu Ende ist mit den Grenzen seines Körpers oder des Bezirkes [...] sondern erst mit der Summe der Wirkungen, die sich von ihm aus zeitlich oder räumlich erstrecken: so besteht auch eine Stadt erst aus der Gesamtheit der über ihre Unmittelbarkeit hinausreichenden Wirkungen. Dies erst ist ihr wirklicher Umfang, in dem sich ihr Sein ausspricht.][25]

The city as a site of Jewish self-definition

In the context of identity debates, both at the beginning and at the end of the twentieth century, the city has acquired highly ambivalent connotations. It is often associated with cosmopolitan and emancipatory tendencies—Berlin in particular is considered to challenge notions of static cultural identity. Yet the city provides a popular image in support of exclusionary discourse as well. The city then becomes a projection screen for destructive stereotype and irreconcilable difference, a site where liberating encounters are kept at bay.

Many European Jews were drawn to the cosmopolitan aspect of the metropolis,[26] as it provided an alternative to the dilemma between commitment to the Jewish community and pressure to 'dissolve' into their host societies. "The idea of cosmopolitanism in its modern incarnation," as Miller and Ury observe, "presents itself as the standard bearer of the struggle of the universal against the particular, or the interests of humanity against this or that local community."[27] That ideal was to a large extent rooted in urban culture. Urbanization played a significant role in the Jewish process of self-definition and in coming to terms with the challenges of modernity.[28] Processes of acculturation, secularization, and social mobility coincided with (though were not strictly dependent on) that of urbanization,[29] a process that took place two to three times faster in the Jewish community than in society as a whole.[30] In contrast to the old rural *shtetl* and urban immigrant neighborhoods, which were usually strongly influenced by traditional Jewish culture and tradition,[31] the cosmopolitan appeal of the metropolis fit well the adoption of the ethic of *Bildung* as an emancipatory strategy. Berlin stood out as a city inhabited by a wealthy, educated Jewish middle class, and although the Jewish community never constituted more than four percent of Berlin's overall population, their contribution to its intellectual and economic life exceeded their demographic representation.[32] Berlin provided ample opportunity for experiment in the many semi-public places of artistic and cultural creation, which became popular sites for artists of disparate backgrounds and inclinations to meet and exchange ideas.[33]

Noah Isenberg concludes that the city thus became "a place where Jews tend[ed] to define themselves in terms of their Germanness more than their Jewishness."[34] Even so, any acculturative optimism was also met with distinct German-Jewish anti-urban sentiments mourning the loss of authentic Jewish culture in city life. In an article for *Die Freistatt*,[35] Arnold Zweig, who had Zionist and socialist sympathies, counters anti-Semitic attempts "to deny Jews their creativity [den Juden das Schöpferische abzusprechen]."[36] Zweig attributes the perceived inability of German Jews "to produce an ingenious poet [einen genialen Dichter zu erzeugen]"[37] to their enforced urban existence and alienation from their *Volksgemeinschaft*: "The metropolis has become his surrogate for the lost community of the people in his own state. [Die Großstadt wird ihm zum Surrogat für die verlorene Gemeinschaft des Volkes im eigenen Staat.]"[38] What Simmel considered a liberation also signaled to some Jews a loss of authentic identity and rekindled their desire for a unified *Gemeinschaft*. The tension between emancipatory and anti-urban positions grew especially urgent with the mass immigration of *Ostjuden* into larger cities, further fueling the debate on German-Jewish identity. The overwhelming presence of *Ostjuden* in Berlin, in the *Scheunenviertel* ghetto, polarized opinions of German Jewry regarding the potential impact on their self-perception.[39] To convinced Zionists and opponents of assimilation, the *Ostjude* represented an untainted pre-urban authenticity to be protected from "the backlash of emancipation: the massive trend in baptisms, the destruction of Jewish family life, and, most significantly, the disruptive forces of the cities."[40] At the same time, to a majority of Germans Jews, Berlin remained a space of accelerated secularization and acculturation. Early twentieth-century Berlin was, in conclusion, a "laboratory and prism of modernity,"[41] a site of alienation, but at the same time a site of cultural pluralism and emancipation.

Urban stereotype and spatialized difference

The metropolis may thrive on the dynamism of migration and diversity, but discourses of the city are often intent on keeping otherness at bay. Its emancipatory promise then turns into the opposite: the city becomes a projection screen for exclusionary discourse, destructive stereotype, and irreconcilable difference.

Today, the term *Parallelgesellschaft*, having gained currency in German public debates since the 2000s, is part of an urban integration discourse that casts cultural difference into stone. Introduced in urban sociology in the 1990s in the context of ethnic segregation in German cities,[42] there remains a lack of consistent evidence that such areas are indeed monocultural "ethnic colonies."[43] Nevertheless, the notion has been readily deployed in German public debates to denounce the perceived unwillingness to integrate that these areas are thought to represent. Criticizing this *Paniksemantik*, Bade points out that the term creates a false impression of political and scientific consensus, and that spatial separation is unjustly perceived as a withdrawal into anti-Western tendencies.[44] The current usage of the term illustrates how urban imagery serves the discursive consolidation of cultural difference—or "[h]ow strangers are made [[w]ie Fremde gemacht werden]."[45]

The historical example of Berlin Jews reveals a similar discursive ambivalence. In their case, too, the city was not merely a site of self-expression and emancipation but also the source of anti-Semitic stereotype. According to Joachim Schlör, the construction of a Jewish "urban type [Urbantyp]" or "urban race [Stadtrasse]" had been a crucial element in modern Jewish self-definition.[46] At the same time, such types became a device of anti-Semitic, anti-urbanist, anti-modern discourses. As Isenberg summarizes, "[w]hile German Zionists focused on the rapid decline of Judaism due to modernization and urban growth, German nationalists exploited such data to support their claims of the impending [...] Jewish contamination of the German city."[47] The assimilated German Jew thus came to represent cosmopolitan mass society and modernity in general. Exemplary of that reactionary discursive link are the writings of social and economic historian Werner Sombart. In a monograph on Jews and modern economic life,[48] Sombart argues that the Jews are pre-eminently urban people. Despite their assimilation and 'invisibility', their diasporic history and nomadic origins had prepared them exceptionally well for the economic and cultural restlessness of modern city life. Their "intellectual rootlessness, combined with a nomadic adaptability enables [them] to place themselves 'in another's position', a capacity for empathy that allows them to excel in journalism, jurisprudence, and theater—the three most distinctive and, to his mind, most troubling expressions of urban culture."[49] Yet even the *Ostjude*, who lived separated from modernity and was hailed by Zionists as the epitome of authenticity, was perceived to confirm the affinity between Jews and city life. The ghetto Jew represented "the quintessential urban *Volk*"[50] and became "a master icon of identification for Jews at large."[51] The image of the *Ostjude*—his conspicuous difference and stereotypical physiognomy—shaped the suspected invisible cultural difference of assimilated German Jews.

A foil of metropolitan indifference and anonymity, twentieth-century Berlin has provided the scene for intensive identity negotiation and artistic self-expression. Against the backdrop of opposing liberal and reactionary tendencies, the city dweller navigates between emancipatory vision and reductive stereotype, between enforced identity and self-liberation. The current chapter examines four texts with regard to their literary approaches to the intangible experience of *Fremdheit* or *Verfremdung*, an apparent constant in urban narratives of the modern individual. Crucial to these stories is the ambiguity of alienation—the distancing that Simmel interprets as at once defensive and liberating, and which manifests itself as either *differential*, in Ludwig Jacobowski's *Werther, der Jude* (1892) and Terézia Mora's *Alle Tage* (2004); or as *relational*, in Franz Hessel's *Spazieren in Berlin* (1929) and Emine Sevgi Özdamar's story "Der Hof im

Spiegel" (2001). In all four examples, the metropolitan experience supports the recalibration of the autonomous, Enlightened individual. The city emerges as an ambivalent space that exposes the futility of emancipatory effort and erodes individualistic self-assertion but at the same time engenders experiences of vulnerability and the potential for reconnection. The four city dwellers discussed here illustrate how neither radical individualism nor collectivism can lay claim to the city. Rather, the city space enables a resistance to *immanence*.

3.2 The failure of exemplarity—'Figures of immanence': Ludwig Jacobowski's *Werther, der Jude* (1892) versus Terézia Mora's *Alle Tage* (2004)

Exemplarity, identification, alienation

Born in a Jewish merchant's family, Ludwig Jacobowski (1868–1900) moved with his family from Strelno, Posen to Berlin in 1874, where he studied history, literature, and philosophy.[52] After obtaining his doctoral degree in literature, Jacobowski became a prominent figure in the publishing field, as co-editor of several literary anthologies, as founder of the magazine *Der Zeitgenosse*, and as editor-in-chief of *Die Gesellschaft. Halbmonatsschrift für Litteratur, Kunst und Sozialpolitik*, a leading magazine of the naturalist movement. Shortly before he died, Jacobowski founded *Die Kommenden*, a reader's circle attended by Stefan Zweig, Else Lasker-Schüler, and Rudolf Steiner. A prolific writer, Jacobowski published his work in over thirty magazines and newspapers. Both his fictional and essayistic writings are concerned with matters of Jewish life and culture, on the whole reflecting the liberal-humanist views of the *Verein zur Abwehr des Antisemitismus*, of which Jacobowski was a member as well. He was convinced that the solution to increasing anti-Semitic sentiment was to be found in a common ideological platform for Germans and Jews, where a tolerant and progressive German *Geist* would accommodate the aspirations of a new Jewish generation "to participate honestly, genuinely, and warmly in the further development of the German people [um ehrlich, echt und warm theilzunemen an der [...] Fortentwicklung des deutschen Volkes]."[53] When he became acquainted with the idea of Zionism shortly before his death, he remained convinced that German culture and literature would remain not only his personal *Heimat* but also that of Berlin Jews in general.[54]

Werther, der Jude reflects Jacobowski's commitment to the Jewish cause. It appears to be what he considered an instance of successful German-Jewish cultural symbiosis, "the epitome of what German-Jewish literature should be about."[55] The novel transposes the main theme of Johann Wolfgang von Goethe's *Die Leiden des jungen Werthers* (1774) onto the quandary of German Jews. Against a Berlin backdrop, Jacobowski relates the story of Jewish philosophy student Leo Wolff, whose determined effort at ethical improvement through *Bildung* is thwarted by anti-Semitic sentiment encountered in every aspect of his social life: in the streets of Berlin, in the lower middle class family of his (Christian) girlfriend Helene, and most significantly among his fellow fraternity members. Leo's unrequited love of German culture eventually leads to his downfall; he shoots himself and dies in the arms of his (gentile) friend.

Jacobowski's adaptation of Goethe's epistolary novel received wide popular acclaim, particularly from mainstream liberal German Jewry. It remained in print for almost forty years.[56] Its resonance with an assimilated audience was in part due to its claim to exemplarity. Paul Rieger, a prominent figure of the liberal *Centralverein deutscher Staatsbürger jüdischen Glaubens*, praised *Werther, der Jude* for its depiction of the protagonist's individual struggles in such a way that it offered a "symbolic transfiguration of the modern sufferings" of all German Jews.[57] Leo's exemplarity, however tragic, was read as an encouragement to counter anti-Semitism with a Jewish effort at ethical improvement, by "envisioning a scenario in which Jews [would] embody the grandeur of German classical humanism."[58] Indeed, in the preface, Jacobowski presents his novel as a promotion of assimilation, in spite of emerging Jewish nationalist tendencies—he defends "always only the one direction: integral absorption into the German spirit and German morality [immer nur die eine Wegrichtung: Restloses Aufgehen in deutschen Geist und deutsche Gesittung]."[59] However, while *Werther, der Jude* seems to set out as a German-Jewish *Bildungsroman*, the protagonist's aspiration to become a 'better' Jew eventually ends in tragedy. His exemplarity as an assimilated Jew draws on an Enlightened notion of self-improvement. Yet several aspects of the story indicate that that notion is losing ground, setting the novel apart from a tradition of German-Jewish *Bildungsromane*.[60] As an instance of psychological naturalism, *Werther, der Jude* prefigures the dissolution of an autonomous subject seemingly impervious to social influence. Not only does Leo appear to have internalized anti-Semitic prejudice, he is moreover confronted with it in the one paradigmatic locus of *Bildung*—at university. The novel evokes a pervasive anti-Semitism that affects both the vehicle and the optimism of assimilation, thus containing a hint of fatalism regarding its own exemplary purpose, despite Jacobowski's explicit intent.

Alle Tage, too, addresses the destructiveness of stereotype and imposed identification but does so in a very different way than Jacobowski's novel, especially with regard to the role of exemplarity. Exemplarity establishes a relationship between particular characteristics and an abstract, conceptual whole. It aims at reader identification: "The 'whole' [...] is not just the whole of the work but that of a world of which the work is a part, and to which the work and the exemplary instance within it are tied by the work's claim to relevance, to legibility."[61] The exemplarity of *Werther, der Jude* indeed follows an "always-unstated logic according to which readers identify with the characters of a work, or by which they may search in it for indications of how to live."[62] In *Alle Tage*, however, the exemplary protagonist is designed to impede that logic. The narrative structure of the novel fosters alienation, subverting the very principle of identification. The novel portrays the futile efforts of war refugee and language prodigy Abel Nema at finding solid ground in an unspecified German metropolis. As the 'symbolic transfiguration' of 'the stranger', of the rootless immigrant roaming the margins of society, Abel embodies the inversion of Leo Wolff's rational self-sufficiency. Unlike Leo, who believes himself on a linear path of self-improvement, Abel is a decentered, radically 'postmodern' figure, a faltering subject who fails to steer his life into a particular direction. He exists merely through external determination. Whereas Leo embodies the author's programmatic intent and confidence in the Enlightened individual, Abel's non-identity is a device in a narrative, linguistic, and philosophical puzzle that questions the legitimacy of a subject with an appointed subject position. In terms of successful *Subjektwerdung*, each novel suggests that, in the end, neither the 'autonomous' nor the 'deconstructed' extreme is viable.

Jacobowski's and Mora's opposite uses of exemplarity—identification versus alienation—traces back to their poetological views. Jacobowski's novelistic work pursued the same purpose as his contributions for the *Verein zur Abwehr des Antisemitismus*, which "directed its energies both at unmasking the irrational nature of antisemitism and at encouraging internal Jewish efforts at ethical improvement."[63] Mora, on the other hand, claims to have no such educational intentions. When asked about the "vanishing point [Flüchtpunkt]" of her writing—whether it is part of an "Enlightenment project [aufklärerisches Projekt]" or responds to a need for genial self-expression, she states that, to her, "to be a writer and to be present in one's life [Schriftstellerin zu sein und in seinem Leben anwesend zu sein]" are one and the same thing.[64] The significance of her work should be found in existential rather than quantifiable elements: "Art has no purpose, it has a reason. [...] To a successful work of art, there is always this inexplicable and incomprehensible dimension that has come into being, even though I did not make it. [Kunst hat kein Ziel, sondern einen Grund. [...] Es gibt immer diesen unerklärbaren und unfassbaren Bereich, der in einem gelungenen Kunstwerk da ist, der entstanden ist, obwohl ich ihn nicht gemacht habe.]"[65] Her statement indirectly responds to the critical tendency to interpret a text in terms of its author's biography, and, in a similar vein, to attribute a sense of *Fremdheit* to novels by writers of 'non-German' origin, which forces them into an artificial framework of, indeed, exemplarity of cultural difference:

> You are estranged from yourself or have a sense of foreignness because you do not live in the same place you were born, or because you have another or two more mother tongues. But of course otherness does not work at this level at all. I'm sorry, but it's not that way.
>
> [[M]an ist sich selbst entfremdet oder hat ein Fremdheitsgefühl, weil man nicht an dem Ort lebt, an dem man geboren wurde, oder weil man noch eine weitere oder noch zwei weitere Muttersprachen hat. Aber natürlich funktioniert Fremdsein überhaupt nicht auf dieser Ebene. Tut mir leid, aber es ist nicht so!][66]

Mora emphasizes that the significance of any work of art, and its inherent *Fremdheit*, goes beyond intention, purpose, or biography—as her own perspective on her life and works illustrates. Mora was born in 1971 in a Hungarian town, Sopron, near the Austrian border. She belonged to the German-speaking minority that had lived there since the collapse of the Austro-Hungarian dual monarchy. She left for Berlin in 1990, where she completed her education in Hungarian, theatre studies, and screenwriting. When Mora was awarded the Adelbert von Chamisso Prize in 2010, she was lauded for her contribution to intercultural exchange that altered the German "view of one's own culture as well as of the foreign culture [Blick auf die eigene, wie auch auf die fremde Kultur]."[67] However, such references to being a "border crosser [Grenzüberschreiterin]" are, for Mora, relevant only in aesthetic terms, never in terms of her personal history. Crossing boundaries is an indispensable quality for any artist.[68] Likewise, she considers her linguistic sensibility not really as a side-effect of her bilingualism but of her fundamental distrust towards language and narration in general.[69] Additionally, the fact that her work reflects her affinity with the German literary *Moderne*— *Alle Tage* contains allusions and references to the writings of Franz Kafka, Alfred Döblin, and Ingeborg Bachmann—is far from an indication that she strives for an assimilatory, 'integral absorption' into 'German' culture.

'Figures of immanence': the atomic individual versus the *Leerstelle*

In both novels, the city motif highlights the 'failures' of the protagonists—two opposite but equally problematic types of individual. A German Jew and an immigrant attempt to carve out a space for themselves in society, in defiance of stereotype and cultural difference. In the city, the emancipatory promise of *Bildung* or multilingual competence proves inadequate to counter the language of prejudice. At the same time, the city offers them temporary refuge from these exclusionary mechanisms, as urban life initiates fleeting and fragile moments of connection. The tragedies of these city dwellers question radical forms of individualism, on the one hand, and of dissolution into homogeneous collectivities on the other. However, the potential for such 'inoperative' moments of connection is nipped in the bud by repeated acts of linguistic violence.

The protagonists are two opposite types of individuals: in *Werther, der Jude* a centered, atomic individual recognizable as a (mockery of the) Romantic genius; in *Alle Tage* an entirely decentered subject devoid of meaning and identity, a negative space created by expressions of meaning surrounding it. As entirely self-sustaining sources of meaning and absence of meaning, respectively, both individuals represent two extremes of what Nancy considers highly problematic "figures of immanence:"

> [T]he individual is merely the residue of the experience of the dissolution of community. By its nature—as its name indicates, it is the atom, the indivisible—the individual reveals that it is the abstract result of a decomposition. It is [...] [a] figure of immanence: the absolutely detached for-itself, taken as origin and as certainty.[70]

These types of individuals are characterized by a state of undivided (lack of) selfhood: either completely independent from external influence or entirely determined by their environment. While the city motif accentuates the problem of their individualism, the urban experience also disrupts their state of 'immanence'. As such, the city motif is a crucial element of the critique of cultures as monadically, self-enclosed entities which are fully present with themselves—immanent, or identical to itself. In what may appear to be entirely different novels, both Mora and Jacobowski articulate their criticism of cultural self-presence by exposing the unsustainability of the individual as 'absolutely detached for-itself'.

The atomic individual

Werther, der Jude proposes a notion of the subject—and of art itself—that is very different from the one presented by Goethe's epistolary novel. The latter relies on the unique self as a major source of literary material and is an instance of the radical inward turn that marked the transition from the Enlightenment to Romanticism.[71] *Werther, der Jude* on the other hand makes a moral example out of a romantic's troublesome conversion to the principles of Enlightenment. Leo Wolff embodies a conflict between Romantic and Enlightened perspectives on the individual, and symbolically, on German-Jewish culture. Several allusions to (Jewish) Enlightenment thinkers inscribe him into an assimilation paradigm that relies on rationalism, progress optimism, and emancipation. Not only is Leo working on a dissertation on the Dutch-Jewish philosopher Baruch Spinoza (1632–1677), Leo's own name alludes to Christian Wolff (1679–1754), another rationalist at the peak of German Enlightenment. Wolff had been of great influence on Moses Mendelssohn, who became the most prominent advocate of the *Haskalah*.[72] Wolff is especially known for his systemization and adaptation of Gottfried Wilhelm Leibniz' theory of monads—the elementary, individual, independent, and irreducible particles of the universe.[73] Aspects of Wolff's views resonate in Jacobowski's deployment of urban space and his proposal for a comparably monadic understanding of the individual.

Werther, der Jude takes place in Berlin. Although the city does not really acquire a narrative character of its own, as it does in for instance Döblin's *Berlin Alexanderplatz*, the bustling streets do have a very tangible presence in the story. Like Leo himself, the city is 'set up for identification'. His walks on the streets, for instance, when he is looking for his girlfriend Helene, can be traced on a map (WJ 143). The city motif serves a stark demarcation between the cold, grey, wintry streets outside and the warm inside of Leo's home. His mood improves in contrast with the street: "Leo was happy about the winter mood in the street. Snow flurries were part of his genuine, pure winter pleasure and added an even more cosy and intimate atmosphere to his warm, comfortable home. [Leo freute sich über die Winterstimmung der Straße. Schneegestöber gehörte bei ihm zum echten, rechten Wintervergnügen, und machte ihm die Stimmung in seinem warmen, gemütlichen Heim noch heimlicher und traulicher.]"[74] (WJ 116) The city highlights the distinction between the self-contained individual and his environment—even if Leo remains aware of his surroundings and acquires a sense of self by distinguishing himself from the bustling streets—the distance he creates is a difference. Leo thus embodies the notion of atomic self-identity described by Christian Wolff. The atomic elements that constitute the universe are each "defined, or individuated, by its own distinctive internal state."[75] The atomic self, considered as a coherent unity "indivisible in-itself,"[76] acquires self-consciousness in the gesture of placing things outside of the self: "Looking at ourselves, we will find that we are aware of many things as being outside ourselves. But we put them outside ourselves by recognizing that they are different from us. [Wenn wir auf uns acht haben; so werden wir finden, daß wir uns vieler Dinge als außer uns bewußt sind. Wir setzen sie aber außer uns, in dem wir erkennen, daß sie von uns unterschieden sind.]"[77] Leo's experience of the city is portrayed accordingly in terms of individuation and externalization. As long as Leo remains inside, street noises enter the house, conveying an urban reality that, for now, remains in the background: "As if subdued, the noise of the city roared into his room, and occasionally it shuddered when heavy carriages rumbled past him below. [...] Otherwise soft, comforting silence. [Wie gedämpft brauste der Lärm der Großstadt zu ihm ins Zimmer, und manchmal nur zitterte es, wenn schwere Wagen unten kollernd vorbeipolterten. [...] Sonst weiche, wohlige Ruhe.]" (WJ 6–7)

Leo furthermore embodies Wolff's principle of individuation by externalization as determining the position of the atomic self in the order of things: "When we consider things—existing at the same time that they are not another thing—as external to each other, a certain order emerges among them. And as soon as we imagine this order, we imagine space. [Indem nun viele Dinge, die zugleich sind und deren eines das andere nicht ist, als außer einander vorgestellet werden; so entstehet dadurch unter ihnen eine gewisse Ordnung. Und so bald wir uns diese Ordnung vorstellen; stellen wir uns den Raum vor.]"[78] Once Leo goes out into the streets, that order is upset. First, Leo is depicted, in a slightly mocking tone, as a typical romantic—inspired by the beauty of nature, thriving on introspection, and divorced from the real world—"What a dreamer he was! [Was er doch für ein Träumer war!]." (WJ 17) As such, he is out of place in the modern metropolis, which physically startles him out of his reveries:

> Cheerfully he swung his walking stick in his right hand and gazed ahead as if lost in thought. He loved that. He had been a bad observer of life since early on [...]. He much preferred to reflect silently on various chains of thoughts and did not pay attention to what was happening around him. It often happened that he unwittingly collided with a lamppost or a person, jerking him back into reality.

> [Fröhlich schwang er seinen Spazierstock in der rechten Hand und starrte wie gedankenverloren vor sich hin. Er liebte das. Er war von früh auf ein schlechter Beobachter des Lebens [...]. Viel lieber sann er über allerhand Gedankenketten still nach und achtete nicht darauf, was um ihn vorging. Oft kam es vor, daß er unbewußt gegen einen Laternenpfahl oder einen Menschen stieß, welcher Ruck ihn wieder in die Wirklichkeit zurückrief.] (WJ 19–20)[79]

Leo's penchant for daydreaming and a life immersed in thoughts evoke the Romantic idea of an essence that defines the subject, which asserts itself through the exploration of individuality and imagination.[80] Yet as Leo searches for meaning in an inner depth that is "socially indifferent [sozial indifferent],"[81] he has become a bad observer, oblivious to his surroundings. Outside, however, the city acquires a "Physiognomie" (WJ 55) of its own, forcing itself upon Leo more insistently, at times even overpowering him. In the city, the rules of individuation and externalization no longer seem to apply: "He, the provincial man, thirstily absorbed all the impressions that were assailing him. He walked the busiest streets with listening eyes [...]. [Durstig sog er, der Provinziale, all die Eindrücke ein, die auf ihn einstürmten. Er ging die belebtesten Straßen mit horchenden Augen ab [...].]" (WJ 55) The crowd on the street becomes a single, uncanny entity—"an eternally flowing black river [ein ewig flutender, schwarzer Strom]" that sucks him in, while "an unspeakable sense of fear [ein unnennbares Angstgefühl]" creeps up on him. (WJ 55–6) Only by escaping the city center—or rather, by being expelled from it as an incompatible element—does Leo manage to restore his centered self, as well as his capacity to distinguish individualized images and people:

> The pressure of the metropolis would be heavy on his chest, forcing him out of the noise and screeching and hustle and bustle. Then he would flee to the suburbs, where life did not cast such hasty circles on the surface, where the mighty roar of the inner city itself sounded only timid and subdued. Here his eye caught a richly varied abundance of single images; here he observed the common man of the people, the craftsman, the worker, the starving proletarian.
>
> [[S]chwer lag ihm dann der Druck der Großstadt auf der Brust, daß es ihn hinausdrängte aus dem Lärm und Gekreisch und Gewühl. Dann flüchtete er sich in die Vorstädte, wo das Leben nicht so hastige Kreise an der Oberfläche warf, wo das mächtige Brausen der eigentlichen Innenstadt nur zaghaft und gedämpft herausklang. Hier faßte dann sein Auge eine abwechslungsreiche Fülle von Einzelbildern, hier beobachtete er den kleinen Mann des Volkes, den Handwerker, den Arbeiter, den hungernden Proletarier.] (WJ 55–6)

The city motif thus accentuates Leo's initially atomic individuality but exposes the fragility of that self-enclosure at the same time. Gradually, the urban experience—threatening as it is to the unassimilable atomic subject—will force Leo out of his self-involvement and initiate an experience of connection and potential ethical improvement.

The individual as *Leerstelle*

Alle Tage, in contrast, does not focus on a centered and self-determined individual but on the obtrusive force of external identification instead. Abel's incapacity for self-assertion—which makes him the opposite of the enlightened individual—is particularly linguistic in nature, as reflected by Mora's narrative experiment. His *Subjektwerdung* is conceived as the quest for an individual language that sets him free from his quite literal *Unmündigsein*.

Abel Nema is a war refugee in denial of his traumatic past, who attempts to find solid ground in a German metropolis. The absence of a personal history is mirrored by Mora's remarkable polyphonic narrative strategy. Numerous plot threads, as well as a highly inconsistent narrative perspective, complicate a sequential reconstruction of the protagonist's past. Abel appears to have started traveling after the love of his youth Ilia rejected him. On the road he becomes involved in a peculiar accident with gas, which inexplicably takes his memory yet replaces it with the gift of multilingualism. His new talent, however, proves of little help, as he fails to communicate and to establish simple human connection. The moment of the accident coincides with the outbreak of a civil war in his home country, preventing him from returning. He eventually arrives in the unspecified metropolis B., where he is taken care of by several individuals from various social strata. Nevertheless, he fails to settle, remaining rootless and roaming the margins.

Alle Tage is, unlike *Werther, der Jude*, characterized by an emphatic refusal of temporal, spatial, and narrative specificity. The opening sentence—a subtle reference to the opening line of Goethe's *Wahlverwandtschaften*—establishes an undetermined narrative present, in which various focalizing and authorial voices attempt to reconstruct Abel's past: "Let us call the time *now*; let us call the place *here*. Let us describe both as follows. [Nennen wir die Zeit jetzt, nennen wir den Ort hier. Beschreiben wir beides wie folgt.]" (AT 6) That vagueness lends Abel's story a degree of universality and exemplarity. It is clearly situated within a fictional framework generalized enough to allow identification. Yet the lack of specificity is so overstated that identification eventually remains impossible. While the city B. may be reminiscent of Berlin—one narrator describes it as the "*most pulsating metropolis of the hemisphere [pulsierendste […] Metropole [der]*

Hemisphäre]" (AT 96; emphasis in original)—it is never mentioned explicitly. This is not simply a matter of omitted topographical detail; it is a *meaningful* lack of clarity that has been referred to as "circumlocation."[82] The "practice of bordering-on-names"[83] presents the reader with a blurred outline of narrated space yet refuses to focus, fixate, or identify, forever avoiding a center of meaning. As a result, any representation of the city B. negates itself immediately. The city is indeed a negative space marked only by absence and emptiness:

> Brown streets, warehouses empty or full of no one quite knows what, and jampacked human residences zigzagging along the railway line, running into brick walls in sudden cul-de-sacs. [...] No park, just a tiny, desolate triangle of so-called green space left over when two streets came together in a point. An empty corner of land. Sudden gusts of early-morning wind [...] rattle a playground carousel, an old or merely old-looking wooden toy at the edge of the green space. There is a ring nearby, the kind used to pull litter-bins, but free-floating, with no bin attached.
>
> [Braune Straßen, leere oder man weiß nicht genau womit gefüllte Lagerräume und vollgestopfte Menschenheime, im Zickzack an der Bahnlinie entlang laufend, in plötzlichen Sackgassen an eine Ziegelsteinmauer stoßend. [...] Kein Park, nur ein winziges, wüstes Dreieck sogenannte Grünfläche, weil etwas übrig geblieben war am spitzen Zusammenlaufen zweier Gassen, so ein leerer Winkel. Plötzliche Böen frühmorgendlichen Windes [...] rütteln an einer hölzernen Scheibe, einem alten oder nur so aussehenden Kinderspielzeug [...]. Daneben der frei schwebende Tragering eines Mülleimers, der Eimer selber fehlt.] (AT 9)

The avoidance to arrive at a 'center' of meaning is mirrored by the enunciative instability of the novel. Countless voices, some of them familiar, others impersonal, alternate quickly and often even mid-sentence in recovering Abel's story. The continuous change of personal pronouns, otherwise the markers of a stable point of view, blurs the distinction between direct and indirect speech and, furthermore, undermines a hierarchy of supposedly objective, authorial and, on the other hand, subjective, focalizing perspectives. Italics and parenthesized stage directions occasionally attempt to restore a sense of location, restraining the changeable and placeless narration to some extent.

Abel's character is introduced in the same polyphonic fashion as the nondescript setting. Compared to Leo Wolff, whose self-containment makes him a 'figure of immanence' in the Nancian sense, Abel Nema represents its inversion. His name alone is indicative of the absence, negation and absolute *Fremdheit* he evokes: "Nema as in 'nothing'? [Nema. So wie das Nichts?]" (AT 27) The name seals his indefinite, only vaguely perceptible appearance. His pretended wife Mercedes loses grip on his shapeless features:

> From the outside he looks like a perfectly normal man— correction, a perfectly normal person. Correction: delete the entire sentence, because Mercedes realized immediately that even the first part, from the outside, made no sense when applied to a person (man), so there was nothing left, nothing that would hold water. Sometimes I doubt whether a single thought … She felt herself swaying as she stood there. She wanted to look him in the face, but kept having to focus, as in a moving train. My eyes had begun to hurt, and suddenly he seemed no longer to have a specific sex, he was a hermaphrodite.
>
> [Von außen betrachtet, sah er wie ein ganz normaler Mann aus, Korrektur: ein ganz normaler *Mensch*, Korrektur: verwerfe den ganzen Satz, weil Mercedes noch rechtzeitig einfiel, dass auch der erste Teil, dieses von 'außen betrachtet' bei einem *Menschen* (Mann) überhaupt keinen Sinn machte und somit am Ganzen nichts mehr war, das, ausgesprochen, einigermaßen sicher dagestanden hätte. Nichts stand einigermaßen sicher da. Manchmal zweifle ich, ob überhaupt ein einziger Gedanke… Sie hatte das Gefühl, im Stehen zu schwanken, wollte sie ihm ins Gesicht schauen, musste sie immer wieder scharf stellen, wie in einem fahrenden Zug, mir taten schon die Augen weh, und plötzlich schien er überhaupt kein bestimmtes Geschlecht mehr zu haben, ein Ichweißnichtwas, ein seltsamer Zwitter […].] (AT 327–8)

As an inverted figure of immanence, Abel Nema elicits a desire for identification but undermines it at the same time. Lacking all typical identity markers—gender, memory, an accent, and even a voice of his own—he exemplifies 'the stranger' in absolute terms; he is a cipher of non-identity.

Mora's 'circumlocation' technique, which draws a parallel between the urban setting and Abel's *Leerstelle*, temporarily suspends the mechanism of identification. On the technique, which she explored already in her story collection *Seltsame Materie*, she comments that it serves to safeguard the text from interpretive bias: "Some words take over a text completely and immediately. One cannot mention Gestapo, the Yugoslav Wars, or 9/11 just in passing. Such words dominate a text, the text is about them, no matter what it is otherwise supposedly about. [Es gibt Wörter, die reißen einen Text mit Mann und Maus an sich. Man kann Gestapo,

Balkankriege oder 9/11 nicht *nebenbei* erwähnen. Solche Wörter dominieren einen Text, er *handelt* von ihnen, egal, worüber es sonst zu handeln meint.]"[84] In this respect, Mora's strategy of avoidance sets up a space specific enough to interpret Abel's story as that of the immigrant's troublesome settlement in a metropolis. At the same time, it steers away from that exemplary status and, in doing so, exposes that status, or any other specific interpretation, as a potential act of reductive identification.

The narrative instability and polyphony in Mora's text are reminiscent of Alfred Döblin's characteristic montage in *Berlin Alexanderplatz*.[85] In the case of Döblin, montage highlights the local specificity of Berlin, which becomes a "city that narrates itself [Stadt, die sich selbst erzählt]."[86] By lending the city a voice of its own, Döblin firmly anchors the text in reality, which—even as it remains an instrument of his authority—conceals the author's voice.[87] Mora's novel can be regarded as a radicalization of that technique. The loss of authorial stability in *Alle Tage* then parallels the 'deterritorialized' state of the globalized city. The disembedding of social relations from their local contexts results in a loss of familiarity of the local, which thus acquires a phantasmagoric quality.[88] Indeed, whereas Jacobowski's preface unambiguously establishes his intent, Mora's authorial voice remains absent from any diegetic or extradiegetic level. The preface to *Alle Tage* is instead provided by what appears to be an editor, who, however, has no narrative authority whatsoever over any of the countless voices relating Abel's story. It simply summarizes his exoticist expectations about the novel—it should be "extreme and quirky [Extremes und Skurriles]," rather than authentic or true-to-life, as should any foreign or multilingual story: "The Latin countries are particularly fertile. Good old Babylon. And of course Transylvania. The Balkans etcetera. [...] For all I care, you can lie and/or invent. [Die lateinischen Länder sind besonders ergiebig. Gutes altes Babylon. Und natürlich Transsylvanien. Der Balkan etcetera. [...] Meinetwegen lügen undoder erfinden Sie auch." (AT 5). Mocking both exoticist expectations and narrative authority, the seemingly insignificant preface "only examines the *gestures* that might point to the origins of Abel's stories—and not to these origins themselves."[89] It thus sets the stage for the plurality of voices that will interpret Abel's *Leerstelle*: they will attempt to fixate and identify him in a language of assumptions, prejudice, and clichés.

Metropolitan milieus: 'the law of the proper' versus *Verletzbarkeit*

Although they are situated at opposite ends of a spectrum, both Leo and Abel are, as Nancy would refer to it, "set up for identification."[90] Leo exemplifies an Enlightened emancipation ideal; Abel's *Leerstelle* forces him to blend in completely with several social identities enforced upon him. Both protagonists are thus characterized by a state of undivided (lack of) selfhood—either atomically independent from external influence or entirely determined by their environment. They move in social circles that abide by what Nancy calls "[t]he absolute and vertiginous law of the *proper*,"[91] and which sustain themselves through linguistic violence: the language of exclusionary stereotype, nicknaming, insult, or even the mere absence of proper names. In doing so, these communities aim to secure the 'proper'—the identical, the authentic that defines their 'pure' community. In both instances, *Bildung* and multilingual competence prove powerless against such communal desire for unity.

There is an important difference between the lack of proper names as it occurs in *Alle Tage* and *Werther, der Jude*. In Mora's case, it is part of a narrative attempt to suspend the mechanism of identification. In *Werther, der Jude*, nicknaming is all about identity fixation.[92] Yet in the end the effect is the same: nicknaming and lack of proper names are symptoms of a generalized intolerance of difference or singularity. In *Werther, der Jude*, Leo encounters anti-Semitic prejudice in just about every domain of his social life: among his aristocratic friends, from the daughter of his school principal, from the middle class family of his girlfriend Helene, and from strangers in the streets of Berlin. That prejudice affects deeply the primary vehicles of Jewish assimilation: *Bildung* and university life. His father finances Leo's university courses, but Leo is himself highly suspicious of the man's financial dealings, since he works with an Eastern Jew, who represents the anti-Semitic swindler stereotype in the story. And Leo's student league exhibits anti-Semitic traits of an unbearable "cleverness [Patentheit]" (WJ 77), which, as it turns out, forces Leo's story into tragedy. His *Couleurbrüder* address each other by nickname—an innocent marker of camaraderie (WJ 8) that however prefigures the linguistic power that governs the fraternity. Nicknaming and stereotype here become instances of "determinant violence [festschreibende Gewalt]."[93] As Steffen Herrmann argues in reference to Emmanuel Lévinas' thoughts on linguistic violence, stereotypes are aimed at reifying difference and reducing a person's singularity to a single feature. Insults and stereotypes are an "inversion of 'greeting' [Invertierung des 'Grüßens']:"[94] whereas a salutation is a positive gesture establishing proximity, the insult produces distance. The introduction of a new fraternity member Max von Horst illustrates the flipside of this at first companionable manner of speech. Scrutinizing the face of the anti-Semite Max Horst, nicknamed 'Fuchs', Leo concludes "that his face was unappealing to him. He was not quite sure why, was it his nasal speech, his arrogant, all too polished looks, as if 'licked clean'? [daß ihm dessen Gesicht unsympathisch war. Er wußte nicht recht weshalb, ob die näselnde Sprache, ob das hochmütige, das allzu gewichste wie 'abgeleckte' Äußere.]" (WJ 9) Conversely, Horst considers Leo "just a bit 'very' Jewish. [...] The hair and well, you know, his whole manner… A little bit very Jewish. [ein bißchen 'sehr' Jude. [...] Die Haare und na, wißt ihr, so die ganze Manier von ihm… Ein bißchen sehr Jude.]" (WJ 10) Lévinas' phenomenology of the *Antlitz* posits that the Other's countenance, its absolute singularity and otherness, elicits a fundamental *Anspruch* and thus a sense of connection in the beholder. "On the image of a face [Auf der Abbildung eines Gesichts]," to summarize Lévinas,

> our gaze can rest unimpaired. It can absorb the eyes, their color, grain, tint and shade [...] and glide along the contours of the eyes, nose, and cheek. [...] In face-to-face situations, on the other hand, our gaze is unsettled—the other's eyes refuse the observing gaze. [...] It is difficult to stand up to the gaze of the other, for the other calls for and demands a gesture from me.
>
> [kann unser Blick ungestört ruhen. Er vermag die Augen, ihre Farbe, Maserung, Tönung und Schattierung aufzunehmen [...] und die Konturen von Augen, Nase und Wange entlang zu gleiten. [...] In der Situation von Angesicht zu Angesicht dagegen wird unser Blick beunruhigt—die Augen des Anderen verweigern sich dem betrachtenden Blick. [...] Nur schwer lässt sich dem Blick des Anderen standhalten, denn dieser fordert und verlangt von mir eine Geste [...].]⁹⁵

Leo and Horst however scrutinize each other as still images. In other words, their animosity manifests itself in the mutual *Festschreibung* of facial features, which are read in terms of their perceived character or racial identities. Horst's conspicuous Berlin dialect reinforces their antagonism. He masters the 'proper' linguistic marker of Berlin life, whereas Leo speaks the impeccable German of an educated Jew and is thus marked as an outsider. In Leo's defense, other fraternity members attempt to point out his virtue but inadvertently perpetuate yet another anti-Semitic stereotype. While they consider him "quite a good fellow [ein ganz guter Kerl]," they admit he is not a proficient duelist, reminding Horst of the anti-Semitic caricature of the weak, effeminate Jew who gives up immediately in the duel with a Christian. (WJ 10)

The persistence of such stereotype and prejudice inhibits Leo from realizing his journey of ethical improvement. As a single Jew in a fraternity exhibiting increasing German nationalist tendencies, he seems to have little interest in his Jewish heritage—the club is his community of choice. In fact, he actively resists any sense of collective Jewish identity, denouncing it as an "atavistic instinct [atavistische[r] Instinkt]," "a Romantic sentiment, a sentiment of the old Jewish generation [...] that had to be overcome [ein romantisches Gefühl, als ein Gefühl der alten, jüdischen Generation [...] das überwunden werden mußte]." (WJ 35) While Leo acknowledges an instinctive sense of Jewish identity, he refuses to heed the urge to turn inward. Instead, he seeks virtue in an Enlightened Jewish ethical reformation, which will present itself as a typically metropolitan experience of human connection and *Verletzbarkeit*.

In *Alle Tage*, it is not so much stereotype as imposed identity in which the 'law of the proper' manifests itself. Unlike Leo Wolff, whose name is a direct reference to the philosophical and ideological foundation of the novel, Abel Nema's name literally signifies 'nothing' and is as such the opposite of a 'proper' name. His ethnic identity remains undecided—his father is said to be "one half Hungarian, other half unclear [[e]in halber Ungar, die andere Hälfte ungewiss]," since he claimed to carry in him "the blood of all the minorities in the region [das Blut sämtlicher Minderheiten in der Region]." (AT 61) Abel's name is furthermore "related etymologically to the modern Slav word for German [verwandt mit dem slawischen Nemec],"[96] which stands for "any non-Slav language or people, for the mute neighbours or, to put it differently, the barbarians [jede nichtslawische Zunge, für den Stummen also, oder anders ausgedrückt, den Barbaren]." (AT 14) Significantly, it is not Abel himself who provides this etymology. An unspecified commenter, who seems to speak for the 'common people' and for 'common sense', demonstrates this logic of linguistic identification. He presumes an irrefutable connection between not speaking the local, 'proper' language and a 'barbaric', 'improper' nature.

Indeed, carrying Lacanian overtones, Abel's faltering subjectivity—both its constitution and its destruction—are linguistic in nature. His multilingualism is of major symbolic significance. At first, his giftedness is associated with identity loss. Having been rejected by his childhood love, Abel roams the city streets and notices his reflection in a window. In a mushroom-induced psychosis—significantly the sole instance of Abel as a focalizer and as an I-narrator—he explains how, at that moment, he disowned his history and origins. He remembers shattering his mirror image and, along with it, his self-awareness. When the gas accident robs him of "the swarm of memory and projection, of past and future [das Gewusel von Erinnerung und Projektion, Vergangenheit und Zukunft]," (AT 75) he is in exchange endowed with the gift of multilingualism. Abel's untainted linguistic proficiency is what Nancy refers to as an "absolute idiolect," which is "utterly deprived of relations and, therefore, of identity."[97] Because it remains purely conceptual, it fails to establish simple human connection: "[I]n fact he hardly says a word [[I]n der Praxis hört man kaum einen Satz von ihm]," and "everything he says is so [...] *place*less, so uniquely clear—no accent, no dialect, nothing: he speaks like a person who comes from nowhere [ist alles, was er sagt, so [...] ohne *Ort*, so klar, wie man es noch nie gehört hat, kein Akzent, kein Dialekt, nichts—er spricht wie einer, der nirgends herkommt]." (AT 13–4) Abel's linguistic genius, untainted and complete, thus correlates with what Jacques Derrida considers a linguistic "identity disorder."[98] His lack of "autobiographical anamnesis" has led to a failure of his "identificatory modality,"[99] and has robbed him from his capacity to speak as a singular subject.

Hypothetically, the absence of a personal history and his linguistic proficiency make Abel a perfectly assimilable, transcultural subject. However, his gift is really a curse. Indeed, the ambivalence of the gift is a central concept in discussions about linguistic violence and "symbolic vulnerability [symbolische Verletzbarkeit]."[100] "The gift," as Hannes Kuch summarizes,

> can contain a—at times manifest, but often also latent—violent dimension: because it can impose a burden of debt on the recipient; because the giver can usurp a position of moral superiority through it; or, after all, because the recipient of the gift can be humiliated by it—if he or she is unable to return it.
>
> [Der Gabe kann eine—manchmal manifeste, oft aber auch latente—gewaltsame Dimension zu Eigen sein: Weil sie dem oder der Beschenkten eine Schuld aufzubürden vermag; weil der oder die Gebende durch sie die Position moralischer Überlegenheit usurpieren kann; oder schließlich auch deshalb, weil die Empfängerin oder der Empfänger der Gabe durch sie gedemütigt werden kann—wenn sie oder er nicht in der Lage ist, die Gabe zu erwidern.][101]

A lack of anamnesis and the gift of perfect idiom have indeed rendered Abel extremely vulnerable to imposed identification and linguistic violence. Once he arrives in the city B., he finds temporary refuge in several social circles. Abel's

Leerstelle there becomes a blank projection screen for their social identities. Yet he continually fails to conform to their expectations, thus becoming a *Störfaktor* to their communal sense of unity. Although he acquires an identity only as several subject positions are projected onto him, Abel is not considered a 'proper' refugee (because he has obtained a scholarship), nor a 'proper' husband (because he has divorced his pretend wife), and even his language professor questions his actual competence. Indeed, Abel remains at the mercy of communities that sustain themselves by defining their 'proper' identity. When a street gang struggles to identify Abel as nothing more than a "guy [Typ]," they beat him up so badly that it leaves him aphasic. 'Typ' here loses its benign, colloquial meaning, and becomes an instrument of "epistemic violence"[102] that literally mutes the represented subject: Abel is forcefully reduced to the societal stereotype of the immigrant who barely knows the language and utters no more than an insufficient "It's good [Es ist gut]." (AT 432)

Experiences of *Verletzbarkeit*

Yet despite the linguistic violence sustaining these metropolitan communities, the city also produces ephemeral moments of human connection, fragile states of 'being singular plural' which, however briefly, counteract the persistence of stereotype. In *Werther, der Jude*, Berlin emerges simultaneously as an antagonistic force and as a site of dissolving antagonisms, enabling an "armistice on foreign Berlin soil [Waffenstillstand auf fremdem Berliner Boden]." (WJ 36) After Leo's and Horst's confrontation, the bustling city streets seem to overpower and resolve their conflict: "The others steadied the two, they were unsure of whose side they should take, and were glad when they had reached the road, where the hustle and bustle of the metropolis roared towards them like a wild hunt. [Die übrigen beruhigten die beiden, sie wußten nicht recht, wessen Partei sie nehmen sollten, und waren froh, als sie die Straße erreicht hatten, wo das Getöse der Weltstadt wie ein wilde Jagd ihnen entgegenbrauste.]" (WJ 12) More significantly, the city induces moments of vulnerability that support Leo's moral reformation. Witnessing a scene of charity and "human interaction [menschliche Teilnahme]" (WJ 65), Leo refers to it as an adventure, a "city experience, coffee house poetry full of tears [Großstadterlebnis, Caféhauspoesie voll Tränen]." (WJ 69) The event enhances his determination to become a better Jew. Resisting the 'atavistic instinct' of a collective identity, he adopts an Enlightened approach, striving for "an ethical improvement of the single Jew [einer ethischen Besserung der einzelnen Juden]." (WJ 159–60) Yet his moral reformation is less a matter of

Bildung than a typically urban experience. The adoption of a Goethe quote as his life motto—"A Jew, noble, helpful, and good... Yes, that is what he wanted to be! [Ein Jude, edel, hilfreich und gut... Ja, das wollte er sein!]"[103] (WJ 172)—may indicate the author's support of a German-Jewish cultural 'symbiosis', but Leo's character tells a different story. His experience of community does not involve at all the 'restloses Aufgehen' into German culture as advocated by the author—the ultimate dissolution into 'German' culture—his Wertherian suicide—is in fact quite ironic.

Instead, his turbulent love affair with Helene highlights an alternative experience of connection. A symbol of the modern city experience, their relationship deeply challenges Leo's self-involvement. Their love exemplifies a connection that "is not [...] conceived on the basis of the [...] model of communion in one," but rather "exposes [...] the incessant *incompletion* of community."[104] Helene's character embodies the city's ambivalence. She is inscribed into a discourse of stereotype and prejudice but undermines it at the same time. When Leo describes their relationship as a "Berlin-style affair [Verhältnis nach Berliner Art]" (WJ 88), and Helene as a "fair Berlin girl [helle Berlinerin]" (WJ 121), Leo at first hints at her presumed sexual promiscuity. Likewise, Leo is first associated with the stereotype of the effeminate Jew. His tendency to dream is designated by his father and even by himself as "a decidedly unmanly quality, a female weakness in him [eine entschieden unmännliche Eigenschaft, eine weibliche Schwäche an ihm]." (WJ 77–8). Encouraged by his fraternity members to disprove the anti-Semitic prejudice about Jewish effeminacy, Leo first approaches Helene from a comparably bigoted perspective: she must fulfill the stereotype of the loose *Berlinerin*. In line with his conviction that "love without full submission of the woman [Liebe ohne völlige Unterwerfung des Weibes]" is impossible (WJ 167), Leo is driven by the "thought to possess Helene completely [Gedanke, Helene ganz zu besitzen]" (WJ 96), that is, sexually and psychologically. Such appropriation denies her complexity and eventually leads to both her and Leo's destruction. In the meantime, though, Leo grows annoyed at her ambivalence; that on the one hand "she had given up her whole ego, her whole spirit of contradiction to him [sie ihr ganzes Ich, ihren ganzen Widerspruchsgeist aufgegeben [...] habe an ihm]" (WJ 99), while, on the other, she does not quite fit the stereotype—"This eternal prudery, with a Berlin woman to boot, was unbearable! [Diese ewige Prüderei, und noch dazu bei einer Berlinerin, war ja unausstehlich!]" (WJ 120) Apparently, Helene defies the principles of stereotype and appropriation. Her 'urban' promiscuity is indeed a matter of being indiscriminate but not primarily in a sexual way. In defense of their 'mixed' relationship—"first one is human and only then Christian or Jew [erst sei man Mensch und dann Christ oder Jude]" (WJ 289)—she emphasizes human relations over religious identity. Their 'Berlin affair' then does not symbolize a dreamed German-Jewish unison or a successful appropriation of German culture. It is simply a reminder of how simple human connection should not become the instrument of stereotype or of a communal desire for unity. Eventually, however, when Helene becomes pregnant, she sees herself compelled to commit suicide, thereby fueling anti-Semitic sentiment only further, due to her involvement with a Jewish swindler's son. As the press relates the facts: "Another example of the corruption of our affairs by the Jews! The elders deceive the upright, decent, plain German, and the younger ones seduce his daughters! [Wieder ein neues Beispiel von der Korruption unserer Zustände durch die Juden! Die Alten betrügen den biederen, braven Michel, und die Jungen verführen seine Töchter!]" (WJ 355–6) Upon reading about Helene's death, Leo loses all hope for a future, and, like Goethe's Werther, commits suicide.

In *Alle Tage*, a comparable one-on-one relationship briefly redeems the protagonist from linguistic violence. Abel's stepson Omar, who is partially blind, provides a crucial counterpoint to the attempts at fixation that Abel endures. Whereas Abel's gift is in fact a curse, Omar's stigma—a token of *Verletzbarkeit*—reveals itself as a gift of connection. His (im)perfection evens out Abel's transparency and perfect idiom: "[E]verything about him—except for a minor deviation in the amber of the artificial iris in the right eye—was in perfect equilibrium. [A]lles an ihm—bis auf eine winzige Abweichung in der Bernsteinfarbe der künstlichen Iris rechts—war in perfekter Balance." (AT 165) Omar literally sees things differently; his incomplete gaze refuses to focus, fixate, and thus to identify—"I have only one eye. [Ich habe nur ein Auge]," he explains, "I traded the other in for wisdom [[d]as andere habe ich hingegeben für Weisheit]." (AT 165) As a result, Omar's and Abel's relationship can unfold on the basis of communication and shared experience. Yet even when Abel finds a voice of his own—an accent, rather than flawless mastery—he remains at the mercy of collectivities that sustain themselves through identity fixation.

The city motif first articulates and underscores the protagonists' 'undivided selfhood': the atomic individual in *Werther, der Jude*, and its inversion in *Alle Tage*. At the same time, the city also allows short-lived refuge from identity fixation. Real and fragile experiences of community, as these novels suggest, do not take place as the result of autonomous self-improvement or communal desire, of 'integral absorption' into a desired group, or of chameleon-like adaptation to existing collectives. Rather, community takes place as an act of "resistance to immanence," "resistance to the communion of everyone or to the exclusive passion of one or several: to all the forms and all the violences of subjectivity."[105] Such moments being short-lived, both novels also illustrate the fragility of 'being singular plural' when faced with destructive 'law of the proper'. The eventual destruction of the subject in these novels demonstrates the violence of pure and 'proper' identity—"pure identity cancels itself out; it can no longer identify itself. Only what is identical to itself is identical to itself. As such, it turns in a circle and never makes it into existence."[106] The irony that fully realized assimilation—Leo's Wertherian death as a symbol of a full incorporation into 'German' culture—requires the death of the subject criticizes anti-Semitic prejudice *and* the ideal of assimilation as quite similar strategies of 'proper' identity. *Alle Tage* suggests that communication and community cannot be established in disregard of memory and origin, but it also implies that those elements are at permanent risk of becoming sources of violent identity reduction.

The protagonists thus fail to become exemplary figures. In Jacobowski's novel, that failure has its roots in the incongruence between the author's intent, the protagonist's embodiment of an Enlightened ideal, and the tragic conclusion of the story: Leo's optimistic self-cultivation cannot withstand the force of stereotype. In Mora's text, the attempt at exemplarity is subverted from the onset. The protagonist may at first invite identification, albeit then revealed to be a principle of alienation. The exemplary stranger without a past, perfectly transcultural in theory, fails to establish human connection and is headed for destruction as well. Yet precisely by way of that interrupted exemplarity, these novels, as do many other literary texts, remind us "that singular beings are never founding, originary figures for one another, never places or powers of remainderless identification."[107]

3.3 Disoriented city dwellers—Figures of 'distanced proximity': Franz Hessel's *Spazieren in Berlin* (1929) versus Emine Sevgi Özdamar's "Der Hof im Spiegel" (2001)

The protagonists in *Werther, der Jude* and *Alle Tage* are both condemned to an unviable state of 'immanence'. They fall victim to a reification of difference through stereotype and linguistic violence, which undermines the liberating and connective potential of the urban experience. By way of contrast, I will discuss two alternative approaches to the metropolitan experience of *Fremdheit*. In line with Simmel's diagnosis that the 'blasé' city dweller navigates between defensive and socializing strategies, the narrative perspective in both Özdamar's "Der Hof im Spiegel" and Hessel's *Spazieren in Berlin* relies on a *relational*—rather than differential—distance between subject and objective world. Their first-person narrators assume a marginal, detached, or seemingly isolated position yet manage to observe and fashion a sense of connection that is not framed by a collective identity. Their *Fremdheit* enables a perceptional attitude, and reveals itself as neither absolute nor dissociative but as relative and affiliating. These city dwellers act on what Arjun Appadurai describes as a basic "human need for locality,"[108] which he considers a *social* rather than a geographical principle.[109] In a very subtle way, these metropolitans defend a notion of *Heimat* as a highly subjective sense of belonging that emerges on the "intersection of memory and space,"[110] of perception and affect, and which thwarts instrumentalization by territorial narratives of collective identity. Instead, these texts reveal the socializing potential of the city from the perspective of individuals at the moment when they become 'singular-plural'—or, in Simmel's words, how "[m]an does not end with the limits of his body [[w]ie ein Mensch nicht zu Ende ist mit den Grenzen seines Körpers]."[111]

Reading the city

In Emine Sevgi Özdamar's short story collection *Der Hof im Spiegel*, the I-narrator makes an obvious yet essential observation: "Everyone in a city has their own personal city. [Jeder hat in einer Stadt seine persönliche Stadt.]"[112] The statement aptly summarizes Özdamar's narrative strategy in several stories featuring an I-narrator who relates her experiences in familiar and unfamiliar cities. With titles such as "Mein Berlin" and "Mein Istanbul," Özdamar reveals a highly personalized perspective on the city, which also characterizes stories like "Der Hof im Spiegel" or "Fahrrad auf dem Eis" (which, as Liesbet Minnaard notes, might just as well have been titled "Mein Amsterdam").[113] Özdamar's statement is reminiscent of the "mental map," introduced by Kevin Lynch in his seminal *The Image of the City* (1960). Enabling individuals to orient themselves in the city, it is a mental image of the exterior world, composed of immediate sensations and past experiences, of both *Erlebnis* and *Erfahrung*:[114]

> Looking at cities can give a special pleasure, however commonplace the sight may be. [...] At every instant, there is more than the eye

can see, more than the ear can hear, a setting or a view waiting to be explored. Nothing is experienced by itself, but always in relation to its surroundings, the sequences of events leading up to it, the memory of past experiences. [...] Every citizen has had long associations with some part of his city, and his image is soaked in memories and meanings.[115]

Lynch's diagnosis that the physical city can only ever be perceived partially, and is always a matter of subjectivity and experience, is reinforced by a large number of literary texts. The constellation of the individual in the city has been a rewarding motif in literary portrayals of human existence: as a struggle of life, as a way of life, but also as a way of living together. Whether as a 'social imaginary,'[116] or as a "spatialized symbol of a culture [verräumlichtes Sinnbild einer Kultur],"[117] the literary metropolis is a mental-subjective and a sociocultural space at once, where issues of identity and community are very likely to be at stake. Lynch himself highlights why the city lends itself particularly well to narrative experiment. The mental map enables the "legibility"[118] of an environment that otherwise remains hard to grasp. It coherently patterns the city dweller's typically fragmented and ambivalent perspective, which alternates between participation and observation, between mobility and standstill:

> Moving elements in a city, and in particular the people and their activities, are as important as the stationary physical parts. We are not simply observers of this spectacle, but are ourselves a part of it, on the stage with the other participants. Most often, our perception of the city is not sustained, but rather partial, fragmentary, mixed with other concerns. Nearly every sense is in operation, and the image is the composite of them all.[119]

A device of legibility and coherence, the mental map has, aside from practical relevance, emotional importance as well: it prevents the "mishap of disorientation."[120] As Lynch indicates, "[t]he very word 'lost' [...] means much more than simple geographical uncertainty; it carries overtones of utter disaster."[121] The mental picture of the city thus provides a frame of reference enabling orientation in the broadest sense of the term—"a possibility of choice and a starting-point for the acquisition of further information. A clear image of the surroundings is thus a useful basis for individual growth."[122]

While Lynch emphasizes the principle of legibility, the mental map as a wayfinding *and* hermeneutic device has particular literary potential as well—it easily translates into aspects of style, narration, and story. Fragmented and partial impressions of the city find a suitable form in short prose, or the "kleine Form,"[123] which favors the incompleteness of the particular over the clarity of the whole. Also, the city dweller's ambivalence as both a spectator and a participant lends itself to experiment with first-person narration or unstable narrative authority, as the individual becomes the final reference point in a city that can only be grasped purely subjectively. And finally, the personal map tells the story of an individual who attempts to carve out a space, to establish a sense of belonging in an otherwise disorienting modern city.

Özdamar's story "Der Hof im Spiegel" is, indeed, the literary counterpart of the mental map. The story, which contains fictionalized autobiographical elements typical of Özdamar's writing,[124] relates the experience of a seemingly isolated immigrant woman in a German city. The exploration of the I-narrator's personal city takes place primarily inside her apartment building. Her fellow inhabitants make up a metropolitan microcosm that represents a culturally and socially heterogeneous composite of craftsmen, salesmen, nuns, and African immigrants—which, as they only have their residence in common, can hardly be defined as a community in a traditional sense. The typically partial and personalized aspect of the narrator's mental map extends to the perception of her neighbors, whom she observes as individuals with a unique history. As Dirk Göttsche notes, the apartment building reflects the narrator's "partly already lived, partly only aspired sociality [teils bereits gelebten, teils erst erhofften Sozialität],"[125] which is charted in a "personal city map [persönliche[r] Stadtplan]" (HS 21) that affords her a sense of emotional security, connection, and orientation.

The city as a textual metaphor—as a book to be opened, read, and interpreted by any one of its countless inhabitants who turn it into their own 'persönliche Stadt'—has been a literary concept since the early twentieth century. Lynch's approach is in fact remarkably reminiscent of Franz Hessel's famous quote from *Spazieren in Berlin*, a collection of impressions and *Städtebilder* from an ever-transforming and vibrant Weimar Berlin:

> The flaneur reads the street, and human faces, displays, window dressings, cafe terraces, trains, cars, and trees become letters that yield the words, sentences, and pages of a book that is always new.
>
> [Flanieren ist eine Art Lektüre der Straße, wobei Menschengesichter, Auslagen, Schaufenster, Café-Terrassen, Bahnen, Autos, Bäume zu lauter gleichberechtigten Buchstaben werden, die zusammen Worte, Sätze und Seiten eines immer neuen Buches ergeben.] (SB 156)

His close friend and collaborator Walter Benjamin[126] hailed Hessel's observations as "the return of the flâneur [die Wiederkehr des Flaneurs],"[127] and ever since, Hessel has been considered the German counterpart of the idle city stroller and detached observer who first emerged in nineteenth-century French culture.[128] In Benjamin's study of Baudelaire's writings (1939),[129] the flâneur emerges as the emblem of urbanism and modernity. Yet whereas Benjamin "merely reconstructs the flaneur retrospectively as an anachronistic type of nineteenth-century Paris streetlife,"[130] Hessel introduces the type in 1920s Berlin, where he embodies the typical *Blasiertheit* that Simmel diagnosed as a defense mechanism for the overstimulated city dweller. Hessel's "picture book in words [Bilderbuch in Worten]" is the author's account of "a few shy attempts to go walking in Berlin, round about and through the middle [ein paar schüchterne Versuche, in Berlin spazieren zu gehen, rund herum und mitten durch]." (SB 283) In the afterword addressed to his Berlin readers, Hessel considers himself to be a cartographer of the opposites that distinguish his beloved object of observation—"the thing that is Berlin, in its combination and chaos of luxury and meanness, solidity and spuriousness, peculiarity and respectability [das Ding Berlin in seinem Neben- und Durcheinander von Kostbarem und Garstigem, Solidem und Unechtem, Komischem und Respektablem] [...]." (SB 285) His strolling narration will reveal itself as a mental map much like Özdamar's—highly individualized, but always with an eye to the aesthetics of sociality. At first, Hessel's flânerie—his mobile, noncommittal observation of the urban spectacle—seems to have little in common with the imagery, immobility, and staging of perspective in "Der Hof im Spiegel." Nevertheless, both narrators emerge as similarly active readers of their cities. Their observational detachment illustrates at once their sense of autonomy and their complex entanglement with their surroundings. A comparison of these texts will reveal a hermeneutic distance and *Fremdheit* that enable the legibility of the urban space and, moreover, an existential relationality and fragile sense of community.

From Istanbul to Berlin

Özdamar belongs to a generation of German-Turkish authors who announced a second phase of 'migrant writing',[131] those who shifted focus away from the everyday struggle to find solid ground in a foreign, often hostile environment—a common trope in '*Gastarbeiterliteratur*' of the preceding 1960s and 1970s. Özdamar has become one of the most 'canonical' voices in German 'literature of migration'. She was the first non-German-born writer to have been awarded the prestigious Ingeborg Bachmann Prize, and has been widely acclaimed for her innovative use of language, combined with an engaged perspective on historical developments in postwar German and Turkish history.¹³² Berlin, and cities in general, have played a key role in both Özdamar's life and writings. Born in 1946 in the eastern Turkish region Malatya, she came to Berlin in the 1960s as a factory worker, in pursuit of her dream of becoming an actress. She went to Istanbul to study theater but returned to East Berlin in the 1970s to work at the *Volksbühne*, with Bertolt Brecht's disciple Benno Besson. Her affinity with the stage, and with Brechtian epic theatre specifically, is a distinctive characteristic of her writings. In Özdamar's acclaimed semi-autobiographical novel *Die Brücke vom goldenen Horn* (1998), Berlin is shown to realize its emancipatory potential. Conceived as a kind of *Entwicklungsroman*, the novel describes the sexual, professional, and political coming-of-age of a young Turkish woman, the author's *alter ego* Sevgi. As she moves between Istanbul, Paris, and Berlin, the city emerges as a site of experiment, providing a stage for her performance of various roles and identities. Indeed, the novel is "an ode to Berlin as a city that fulfills its promise to liberate and educate,"¹³³ while securing a sense of home at the same time:

> Berlin had been like a street to me. As a child, I had stayed in the street until midnight, in Berlin I had found my street again. From Berlin I had returned to my parents' house, but now it was like a hotel, I wanted to go back on to the street again.
>
> [Berlin war für mich wie eine Straße gewesen. Als Kind war ich bis Mitternacht auf der Straße geblieben, in Berlin hatte ich meine Straße wiedergefunden. Von Berlin war ich in mein Elternhaus zurückgekehrt, aber jetzt war es für mich wie ein Hotel, ich wollte wieder auf die Straße.]¹³⁴

In the condensed space of a short story, "Der Hof im Spiegel" elaborates aspects already present in *Die Brücke vom Goldenen Horn*. As Monika Shafi observes about the latter, the protagonist "develops a kind of personal topography that helps not only navigate parts of her new environment but through which she crafts a kind of intimate, private space."¹³⁵ Similarly, the novel is constructed around the image of building and crossing bridges—a metaphor of connection present in "Der Hof im Spiegel" as well. In both texts, the subjectivized topography allows the crossing of boundaries and the bridging of differences. This is the reason why neither Berlin nor Istanbul emerge as the 'divided cities' they are usually perceived in geographical, political, or historical terms. As Shafi argues:

> [N]either Istanbul with its rich history as a meeting point between Europe and Asia, a location alternately "invoked in Western discourse either as a bridge between East and West or as a quintessentially Oriental city,"[136] nor the divided city of Berlin are relegated to an exclusively Western or Eastern sphere. [137]

In "Der Hof im Spiegel," too, the strict focus on the narrator's 'personal city' charts the narrator's multiple attachments, which allow her to overcome the presumed divide between between *Diesseits* and *Jenseits*, between familiar and foreign, between East and West. Özdamar presents a picture of the city dweller as cosmopolitan, not in terms of an ideological conviction but in terms of the ability to produce a sense of belonging through various relations. The narrator's personalized city map thus brings into view how "the original cultural imprint of a particular home, family and nation can be modified and remolded and superseded with new [...] affinities and communities."[138]

In *Die Brücke vom Goldenen Horn* this renegotiation of *Heimat* takes place against the backdrop of both the German and the Turkish historical struggle to come to terms with the challenges of modernity. By juxtaposing the 'divided' cities of Berlin and Istanbul, Özdamar comments on "the ways Enlightenment concepts of normative humanism, equality, and progress have failed both in [her] homeland that embraced a belated modernity and in [her] adopted land where it turned [...] into an epochal betrayal of the masses."[139] In view of that failure, Berlin and Istanbul are more alike than an Orientalizing division between East and West would suggest. Both cities have witnessed the "different but equally problematic legacies of modernity that present generations of Germans, Turks, and Turkish Germans have inherited."[140] In Özdamar's portrayal, the city is not merely the backdrop to the immigrant's experience in terms of a predictable tension. Rather, the (modern) city posits a critical counterpoint to the modern nation-state, which "relies for its legitimacy on [...] its meaningful presence in a continuous body of bounded territory."[141] Although this political dimension remains implicit in "Der Hof im Spiegel," the story is a kind of blueprint for the condensed, metaphorical way one's individual map challenges the stereotypical concept of *Heimat*, the connotation of a determinate 'cultural imprint', and the illusion of a homogeneous, originary identity that underlies it it.

From Paris to Berlin

Just as Özdamar, whose writings reflect her divided attention to Berlin and Istanbul, so too Hessel can be considered a mediator between two metropolitan cultures—

Paris and Berlin.¹⁴² For that reason, Hessel remained an "eternal outsider," "regarded in Germany as a Jew and in France as a German."¹⁴³ Hessel was born in 1888 in Stettin, the son of an assimilated and prosperous Jewish banker, but was baptized as a Lutheran. Hessel spent his childhood in Berlin and moved to München to study literature and philosophy. Drawn to the arts scene there, he became acquainted with the aestheticist circle around Stefan George. He moved to Paris in 1906, where he perfected the art of strolling that would become his literary trademark. His relationship with Helen Grund served as a model for his friend Henri-Pierre Roché's novel *Jules et Jim* (1953), which in turn inspired François Truffaut's famous film adaptation (1961). During the 1920s, Hessel contributed substantially to the literary culture of Weimar Berlin, working as a writer and an editor for the Rowohlt publishing house, and he even continued to edit and translate for the house after his own works had fallen under Nazi publication ban. Only briefly before the 1938 pogroms could he be convinced to go into Parisian exile.

Hessel's Jewish descent was not a primary thematic concern of his writings, nor did it invite him onto a quest for identity. But in a social climate marked by intensifying anti-Semitism, it is not an insignificant aspect of his identity. For no matter how secondary it may have been to his self-understanding as a writer, the course of Hessel's life was inavoidably influenced by his 'ancestry': neither his family's conversion nor his marriage to a Christian woman would eventually shield him from anti-Semitic sentiment. His biographically inspired novel *Der Kramladen des Glücks* (1913) touches briefly on the Jewishness to which he felt uncommitted. From the perspective of the protagonist Gustav, the novel evokes the identity crisis of a Jewish generation born in the 1880s, which felt increasingly alienated from their parents' liberal worldview. As Gustav notes: "My father loves Nathan the Wise, Uriel Acosta, the universally human. For all my love for him, that is just as repugnant to me as is Prussia's compulsory education. [Mein Vater liebt Nathan den Weisen, Uriel Acosta, das allgemein Menschliche. Das ist mir—bei all meiner Liebe zu ihm—ebenso zuwider wie die Preußenpflicht der Schule.]"¹⁴⁴ When a schoolmate taunts him as a Jew, he does not seem to understand why, yet he is acutely aware of being excluded. At the sixth Zionist Congress in Basel of 1903—which Hessel himself attended with Karl Wolfskehl—he feels like an outside observer. Gustav's impressions may reflect Hessel's own, as Robert Stam concludes:

> Hessel was equally alienated from a wide variety of contemporaneous lifestyles and ideological currents, equally distant "from the progressive enlightened ideas of his Jewish father; from the Christianity that, for

sentimental reasons, he tried to adopt; from the Zionism in which he could not see himself; and from the bohemian life which seduced but did not convince him."[145]

His ideological, religious, and even artistic *Heimatlosigkeit* became the foundation of Hessel's *Lebensphilosophie* and aesthetic program. His aimless flânerie involves "the greatest possible openness to the world and the utmost enjoyment [eine grösstmögliche Weltoffenheit und ein Höchstmaß an Genuß],"[146] a hedonistic detachment that can be read as a critique of the materialistic fixation of his time. In *Spazieren in Berlin*, the most visible 'shocks' of the modern city— consumerism and exploitation of human labor—are countered by his particularly aesthetic subjectivity.[147] His observations remain detached but never unaffected, which brings into focus again the connection, the humanity, and the memory of the modern city. At once a product and a critic of modernity, city-reader Hessel is a "liminal writer [Schwellenliterat]," a "border crosser between the spheres of traditional, humanistic, intellectually oriented culture, bound to language and writing, and the transitory 'surface culture' of the social sphere [Grenzgänger zwischen den Sphären der traditionellen, humanistischen, geistig orientierten, an Sprache und Schrift gebundenen Kultur und der transitorischen 'Oberflächenkultur' der sozialen Sphäre]."[148] Yet perhaps more so than on the border, Hessel's position was on the outside—raised according to the principles of an inclusive ideal of Enlightened humanism, but betrayed all the same, being forced into exile. His initial refusal to leave Berlin, despite the ever more violent persecution of Jews, was based on a new sense of shared fate and solidarity with the Jews; Hessel remarked "that he had not considered himself entitled to escape the fate of the Jews as a privileged one [daß er sich nicht dazu berechtigt gesehen habe, als ein Bevorzugter dem Schicksal der Juden zu entgehen]."[149].

Hessel's pre-exile residence in Paris was decisive for his artistic self-understanding. During his years in the city, Hessel combined his familiarity with German aestheticism—which largely ignored urban themes—with the particularly metropolitan character of the French avant-garde, which had enthusiastically rediscovered Charles Baudelaire as the literary pioneer of urbanism and flânerie.[150] Hessel's novel *Pariser Romanze* (1920), which he completed after returning to Berlin, already contains narrative features he would refine in his reading of Berlin. *Pariser Romanze* depicts the affair between a soldier and a young German woman, but focuses especially on the protagonist's affection for the physical city.[151] Hessel's beloved Paris is not found in historic sites and landmarks but in the richness of the everyday, which reveals itself as in a "picture book [Bilderbuch]."[152]

When Hessel returned to Berlin in the 1920s, he realized that his *Heimatstadt* could become an object of artistic observation as well. The first edition of *Spazieren in Berlin* was aptly subtitled "A textbook of the art of strolling in Berlin very close to the magic of the city she hardly knows about herself—A picture book in words [Ein Lehrbuch der Kunst in Berlin spazieren zu gehn ganz nah dem Zauber der Stadt von dem sie selbst kaum weiß—Ein Bilderbuch in Worten]." As the title suggests, the text heeds the same principle as *Pariser Romanze*: to observe the city as an aesthetic object. To do so, Hessel approached the two cities from different perspectives. In Paris, Hessel was the stranger, who wanted to become more familiar; in Berlin, as a former inhabitant, he wanted to become a stranger again. By juxtaposing childhood memory and his immediate perception, his *Erfahrung* and *Erlebnis*, Hessel's focus is not exclusively on archiving his past.[153] Instead, Hessel directs his attention to the metropolitan capacity for renewal—in terms of architecture, as well as people breaking free from their past.

In his 1929 review of *Spazieren in Berlin*, Walter Benjamin hails the improbable 'return of the flâneur', whom he believed to be a forgotten figure and, moreover, unknown to Berliners: "And now, here in Berlin, where it never flourished, it was to renew itself? [Und nun sollte es hier, in Berlin, wo es niemals in hoher Blüte stand, sich erneuern?]" But then he sums up a number of conditions favorable to the emergence of the flâneur in Berlin:

> We must add that the Berliners have become other people. Gradually their problematic foundation pride in the capital begins to make way for Berlin as their hometown. At the same time, a sense of reality, a sense of chronicle, document, and detail has sharpened in Europe.
>
> [Dazu muß man wissen, daß die Berliner andre geworden sind. Langsam beginnt ihr problematischer Gründerstolz auf die Hauptstadt der Neigung zu Berlin als Heimat Platz zu machen. Und zugleich hat in Europa der Wirklichkeitssinn, der Sinn für Chronik, Dokument, Detail sich geschärft.][154]

The city stroller's anecdotal style indeed corresponded to an increasing interest in documentary representation. The *Neue Sachlichkeit* and the objective portrayal of metropolitan and economic life distinguished the arts of 1920s Berlin. Yet a change of mentality, especially, and an overall sense of regeneration enabled the flâneur to become a detached observer of his hometown. Interestingly, Benjamin differentiates between the pride in establishing a new, democratic republic after the First World War and, on the other hand, an increasing sense of belonging and attachment that the Berliners' *Gründerstolz* did not necessarily reflect. Hessel's focus is on those attempts at creating a *Heimat*. By the time he strolls through Berlin, he has cultivated his own *Heimatlosigkeit* into a deliberate balancing act between future and past and between observer and participant. In his personal topography, he traces and narrates Berlin as a *Heimat* revealing itself in scattered memories and subtle everyday impressions, emerging in-between modern architecture and reminders of the Wilhelmine past. As someone who is equally detached and affected, the flâneur embodies the city dweller as Simmel defined him—drawn to the *Reiz* but keeping a distance at the same time.

Disoriented/dis-Oriented city dwellers

"Verschränkung von Heimwelt und Fremdwelt"

Over half a century, the catastrophe of the *Shoah* and the strained aftermath of the Second World War set Özdamar's Berlin apart from Hessel's. In Özdamar's globalized Berlin, the immigrant city dweller is challenged to secure a sense of locality in a transnational context and to familiarize the unfamiliar. Hessel's Berlin, by contrast, is the capital of a newly founded republic, which translates its new sense of nationhood into architectural renewal.[155] For him, the challenge is not so much in finding a home in an unfamiliar city but in harmonizing the two stories the city represents—his personal memories of Wilhelmine Berlin, and the story of a modern city that asserts itself in grand architectural gestures.

In both texts, the image of the city emerges according to the principle of Lynch's mental map. The mental image assuages the fear that comes with disorientation; it is a reminder "that the sweet sense of home is strongest when home is not only familiar but distinctive as well."[156] For Hessel, a distinctive and legible Berlin requires his defamiliarization and his deliberate effort "to regain the distance to the world of which he himself is very much a part [die Distanz zu der Welt zu gewinnen, der er selbst ganz angehört]."[157] Özdamar's narrator keeps her neighborhood at a reading distance, too, with the (implicit) purpose of charting and familiarizing her local connectedness. Their reading strategy engages them in what Appadurai describes as the "production of locality."[158] Writing about cultural global flows, Appadurai wonders "what locality might mean in a situation where the nation-state faces particular sorts of transnational destabilization"[159] or, in Hessel's context, where the nation-state has taken a new and still unstable form. Both *Spazieren in Berlin* and "Der Hof im Spiegel" illustrate several aspects of Appadurai's view. He considers locality as primarily relational and contextual rather than as scalar or spatial. [He sees] it as a complex phenomenological quality, constituted by a series of links between the sense of social immediacy, the technologies of interactivity, and the relativity of contexts. This phenomenological quality, which expresses itself in certain kinds of agency, sociality, and reproducibility, is the main predicate of locality as a category.[160]

That phenomenological quality becomes evident in the hermeneutic distance and *Teilbetrachtung* adopted by both Özdamar and Hessel. The individualized perspective of the I-narrators corresponds with the key principle of phenomenology, i.e. that the meaning of phenomena—the city, here—is only ever known through subjective experience, and cannot be known objectively or outside of that perception. Rather than a given and knowable reality to which the subject reacts in a causal manner, the urban space is a *phenomenon*: its meaning is shaped and conditioned only by and through a perceiving subject. Hessel's and Özdamar's anecdotal storytelling resists the illusion of a unified perspective; or of a reality that can be fully captured by linear, realistic, and progressive plot. Instead, they develop an aesthetics of disorientation, which, as I will illustrate, allows sociality to become aesthetic and meaningful—"a pattern of relations [...] out of which an unexpected sense of belonging may be discerned."[161]

In a comparison of *Spazieren in Berlin* and "Der Hof im Spiegel," I will discuss how each 'reading' of the city revolves around *Fremdheit* as at once a narrative, a subjective, and a socializing principle. As opposed to the figures of immanence which, in *Alle Tage* and *Werther der Jude*, inhabit cities determined almost entirely by stereotype and linguistic violence, the I-narrators here are witnesses of, and actors in, an urban network thriving on potential human encounter. As such, they actively produce a sense of locality and social immediacy that is not tied to known identities and communities.

Werther, der Jude and *Alle Tage* question the atomic notion of (cultural) selfhood that Nancy describes as a state of *immanence*—the concept of an undivided self or community that requires protection from external influences, from which it differentiates and distances itself. The 'self' introduced in "Der Hof im Spiegel" and *Spazieren in Berlin* is relational, depending on an external, unfamiliar, and unappropriated outside—not in terms of a 'constitutive outside,' which implies a self that emerges *ex negativo*, but in terms of a self that only comes into being by virtue of a pattern of relations. This self originates on the spot "where the transition from one's self to the world and to the other occurs, where these paths intersect [wo der Übergang vom eigenen Selbst in die Welt und zum

Anderen geschieht, dort, wo die Wege sich kreuzen]," as Bernhard Waldenfels writes.[162] The urban space substantiates such an "entanglement of home world and foreign world [Verschränkung von Heimwelt und Fremdwelt],"[163] from which the self emerges.

> The concept [of entanglement] resists the extreme opposition between complete coverage or complete fusion on the one hand and complete disparity on the other. If we apply it to the opposition of the self and the foreign, entanglement means, on the one hand, that the self and the foreign are *more or less* intertwined [...], and, on the other hand, that there exist only *blurred boundaries* between the self and the foreign [...]. The entanglement opposes every form of purity, be it the purity of a race, a culture, an idea [...].
>
> [Diese Denkfigur [der Verschränkung] widersetzt sich dem extremen Gegensatz von vollständiger Deckung oder völliger Fusion einerseits und vollständiger Disparatheit andererseits. Wenn wir sie auf den Gegensatz von Eigenem und Fremdem anwenden, so besagt Verschränkung zum einen, daß Eigenes und Fremdes *mehr oder wenig* ineinander verwickelt sind [...], und es besagt zum anderen, daß zwischen Eigenem und Fremdem immer nur *unscharfe Grenzen* bestehen [...]. Die Verschränkung widersetzt sich jeder Form von Reinheit, sei es die Reinheit einer Rasse, einer Kultur, einer Idee [...].]"[164]

As such, the entanglement, rather than disparity, of the familiar and the unfamiliar relies on a positive, relational understanding of difference and therefore counteracts any state of immanent selfhood. Özdamar's and Hessel's city dwellers embody this notion of *Verschränkung* in different yet comparable ways.

Permeability & *Spiegelraum*

"Der Hof im Spiegel" is, on the surface, a story of loss, displacement, and disorientation. The narrator, an actress, lives in an apartment in a German city that remains unspecified.[165] She frequently makes emotional phone calls to her mother in Turkey—"My mother in Istanbul and I in front of the mirror were crying on the phone. [Meine Mutter in Istanbul und ich vor dem Spiegel weinten am Telefon.]" (HS 25)—and in the course of the story her parents die. She appears to live in isolation, as suggested by a conversation with a homeless man on the street. He remarks:

"The city itself is very nice, but the people are stupid.' I said: 'You know, maybe the city is not to blame. I used to work at the theater in other cities. In this city I have no theater, I have no friends, I only work at home."

["Die Stadt ist an sich sehr nett, aber die Menschen sind dumm." Ich sagte: "Wissen Sie, vielleicht hat die Stadt keine Schuld. Ich habe früher in anderen Städten immer am Theater gearbeitet. In dieser Stadt habe ich kein Theater, ich habe keine Freunde, ich arbeite nur zu Hause."] (HS 18)

It is significant that, unlike the man, she does not differentiate between the city and its inhabitants—to her, they are almost one and the same. Her "personal city map [persönliche[r] Stadtplan]" (HS 17), which takes up over seven pages, lists anecdotes of her encounters on the street and in shops—a pet shop with German-speaking parrots; a buxom baker who keeps her informed about her love affairs; the homeless man who has forgotten that she once gave him 300 marks; a bereaved butcher's wife; a Moroccan shoemaker; and the like. (HS 17–24) The few physical landmarks she does include in her map are the train station and the bridges (HS 21). Although these are symbolic locations, their symbolism remains ambivalent. The train station may refer to the narrator's unique memory of displacement and arrival as a newcomer in Germany; to the ubiquity of people in transit (in an existential or a migrational sense); or simply to a place of encounters and farewells. Likewise, her love of bridges may evoke nostalgia for Istanbul, or on the contrary signal her capacity for recognizing and constructing a home wherever there are bridges. These ambivalent landmarks represent neither *Fremdheit* nor complete familiarity with the city; they symbolize the way she bridges and connects those aspects. Instead of a displaced and alienated individual, her personal city map gradually brings into focus a person whose apparent isolation dissolves as she explores her city map.

An important motif illustrating this entanglement of *Heimwelt* and *Fremdwelt* is the architecture of her apartment overlooking a courtyard. Although the yard separates her from her neighbors, she has a rather intimate view into their lives. She observes them closely through a construction of mirrors positioned in such a way that they reflect outside images into each other, bringing her neighbors' lives into her own home. Although the narrative transpires primarily inside her apartment, it becomes clear early on that the distinctions between inside and outside, between here and there, between *Eigenes* and *Fremdes*, have become meaningless:

> In the stairwell, the lights went on, someone went down the stairs. Through the frosted window of my apartment door the light spread to the kitchen, and I saw my waiting face in the mirror. That must have been Mr. Volker going down the stairs. His steps used to be much louder than they are now. [...] The young man upstairs was sewing beautiful costumes for himself and for Mr. Volker on a sewing machine. The rattling of the machine made Mr. Volker's wooden floor shudder, and my ceiling shuddered too. And because of the shuddering ceiling, the plates stacked in the kitchen cupboard also began to shudder.
>
> [Im Treppenhaus ging das Licht an, jemand ging die Treppe hinunter. Durch das Milchglasfenster meiner Wohnungstür wuchs das Licht bis zur Küche, und ich sah mein wartendes Gesicht im Spiegel. Das mußte Herr Volker sein, der die Treppen heruntergeht. Seine Schritte waren früher viel lauter als jetzt. [...] Der junge Mann nähte oben an einer Nähmaschine schöne Kostüme für sich und für Herrn Volker. Durch das Rattern der Nähmaschine zitterte der Holzboden von Herrn Volker, und meine Decke zitterte mit. Und durch die zitternde Decke fingen auch die Teller, die übereinander im Küchenschrank standen, an zu zittern.] (HS 11)

The physical boundaries that apparently separate the narrator from her neighbors are actually permeable: a frosted glass door that carries light into her kitchen, which vibrates along with the rattling sewing machine of the upstairs neighbor. The wooden floor is a ceiling at the same time and transmits the sounds between seemingly separate spaces. These images highlight how the familiar and the unfamiliar meet. The central motif of the story—the mirror—illustrates that this permeability does not involve a *crossing* or *overcoming* of boundaries but is indeed an entanglement of seemingly separate spheres:

> All the people who died dwelled in that mirror. [...] And now, I think, the old nun in the yard has died too. The dead in the mirror make room when a new dead person arrives. Sometimes a bee flies through the window and flies in the mirror among the dead. [...] Or a bird flies through the open window and flies around in the mirror. I take a shower in the bathtub, see myself naked among the dead people in the mirror.
>
> [Alle Toten wohnten in diesem Spiegel. [...] Und jetzt, jetzt denke ich, die alte Nonne im Hof ist auch gestorben. Die Toten im Spiegel machen Platz, wenn ein neuer Tote kommt. Manchmal fliegt eine Biene durch das Fenster und

fliegt im Spiegel zwischen den Toten. [...] Oder ein Vogel fliegt durchs offene Fenster und fliegt im Spiegel umher. Ich dusche in der Badewanne, sehe mich nackt zwischen den Toten im Spiegel.] (HS 24)

The mirror produces a virtual space, a *Spiegelraum*[166] that not only unites distinct, physical details into a single image,[167] but which also condenses physical and spiritual realms. As residence of the deceased, the mirror suspends the ultimate boundary between *Diesseits* and *Jenseits*. The mirror motif thus reveals the story's overarching theme: death signifies loss and grief, but it is also the one thing, despite all differences, that all humans have in common. The mirror imbues the narrator's observations with, in Nancian terms, a sense of *finitude* and as such establishes her self-image, enabling her to speak *as* a subject—"I loved the mirror hanging over the kitchen table. You could make the room speak. Only there did I hear my voice. [Ich liebte den Spiegel, der über dem Küchentisch hing. Man konnte den Raum zum Sprechen bringen. Ich hörte nur dort meine Stimme.]" (HS 27)

An outsider on the inside

In the case of the flâneur, the entanglement of familiar and unfamiliar spheres becomes evident in his aesthetic detachment. Hessel opens his reading of Berlin with what could be interpreted as the flâneur's poetological statement. Under the first heading "The Suspect [Der Verdächtige]," Hessel introduces his ambivalent position in-between participation and observation, as well as his assumptions about his perception by the crowd:

> Walking slowly down bustling streets is a particular pleasure. Awash in the haste of others, it's a dip in the surf. [...] I attract wary glances whenever I try to play the flaneur among the industrious; I believe they take me for a pickpocket.
>
> [Langsam durch belebte Straßen zu gehen, is ein besonderes Vergnügen. Man wird überspült von der Eile der andern, es ist ein Bad in der Brandung. [...] Ich bekomme immer mißtrauische Blicke ab, wenn ich versuche, zwischen den Geschäftigen zu flanieren. Ich glaube, man hält mich für einen Taschendieb.] (SB 23)

The flâneur enjoys being overwhelmed by the bustling streets, indicating that he is very much involved in the present moment; his *Erlebnis* is a sign of the narrator's proximity to his surroundings. At the same time, he deliberately remains an onlooker and outsider to the spectacle, in which he participates at the same time by being observed. The flâneur's aesthetic detachment distinguishes him from the other emblematic street type that co-emerged with mass culture: the *badaud*. Unlike the flâneur, who is the urban equivalent of the artist-poet, the 'gawker' or 'rubberneck' loses his individuality in the street crowd, "that faceless mass that the *flâneur*" define[s] himself against."[168] The *badaud* carries connotations ranging from "idle curiosity" to more negative ones, such as "gullibility, simpleminded foolishness, and gaping ignorance."[169] In other words, the flâneur "is a man *in* the crowd, but not *of* the crowd [...]."[170] That preservation of his autonomy and his refusal to merge completely with the crowd elicit suspicion:

> The swift, firm big-city girls with their insatiably open mouths become indignant when my gaze settles on their sailing shoulders and floating cheeks. That's not to say they have anything against being looked at. But the slow-motion stare of the impassive observer unnerves them.
>
> [Die hurtigen, straffen Großstadtmädchen mit den unersättlich offnen Mündern werden ungehalten, wenn meine Blicke sich des längeren auf ihren segelnden Schultern und schwebenden Wangen niederlassen. Nicht als ob sie überhaupt etwas dagegen hätten, angesehn zu werden. Aber dieser Zeitlupenblick des harmlosen Zuschauers enerviert sie.] (SB 23)

As in Jacobowski's *Werther, der Jude*, the metropolitan experience is articulated by an image of femininity. In the former, Helene's character represents and subverts the problematic stereotype of the promiscuous *Berlinerin*. Hessel portrays Berlin women as at once consumers and objects of consumption in the predominantly visual culture of 1920s Berlin. They share some aspects with the *badaud*, their gaping mouths a sign of curiosity and astonishment.[171] Still, the flâneur recognizes them as individuals in a crowd, as they show their irritation and suspicion towards the *Fremdkörper* of the flâneur. The flâneur, here, is reminiscent of Simmel's definition of 'the stranger'. In his "Exkurs über den Fremden,"[172] Simmel considers European Jews as exemplary of "the stranger [der Fremde]" as "an element of the group itself—an element that includes at once an outside and an opposite [ein Element der Gruppe selbst [...]—ein Element, [das] zugleich ein Außerhalb und Gegenüber einschließt."[173] Although Hessel does not explain his ambivalent position in terms of his Jewish 'ancestry' or his ideological *Heimatlosigkeit*, it resembles the position of Weimar Jews, who have been described as "outsiders on the inside."[174] Hessel recognizes that his *Fremdheit*—Jewish or not—allows him to recover "the first sight of the city [den Ersten Blick auf die Stadt]"

(SB 23)—an unbiased view of Berlin that partially resembles the tourist's gaze. In the chapter "A Tour [Rundfahrt]," Hessel illustrates how his perspective can be at once that of an inhabitant and that of a stranger. Embarking on a sightseeing bus tour, the flâneur comments:

> So now I'm seated on a leather seat, surrounded by real foreigners. They all seem sure that they'll finish the tour between eleven and one [...]. Red writing in English on the white flag in front of me: 'Sightseeing'. What insistent redundancy!—All at once, the entire right half of our travel group rises, while I and the others on the left are commanded to remain seated and present our faces to the photographer, who is lifting the cap from his lens on the sidewalk, turning me into a permanent piece of tourism in his group photo. From out of the depths, a native hand reaches up with picture postcards. We lord over it all, we tourists, we foreigners!
>
> [Da sitze ich nun auf Lederpolster, umgeben von echten Fremden. Die andern sehen alle so sicher aus, sie werden die Sache von 11 bis 1 erledigen [...]. Auf weißer Fahne vor mir steht in roter Schrift: *Sight seeing*. Welch eindringlicher Pleonasmus!—Mit einmal erhebt sich die ganze rechte Hälfte meiner Fahrtgenossen, und ich nebst allen andern Linken werde aufgefordert, sitzen zu bleiben und mein Gesicht dem Photographen preiszugeben, der dort auf dem Fahrdamm die Kappe vor der Linse lüftet und mich auf seinem Sammelbild nun endgültig zu einem Stückchen Fremdenverkehr macht. Fern aus der Tiefe streckt mir eine eingeborene Hand farbige Ansichtskarten herauf. Wie hoch wir thronen, wir Rundfahrer, wir Fremden!] (SB 67)

By joining a group of 'real foreigners' on the bus, the stroller seeks to reintroduce some distance into his perspective, as if he could then see the city through their unfamiliar eyes. The interesting word 'native' furthermore indicates that he now presents himself as a visitor looking at 'the Other'. He willingly lets himself be identified with the sightseeing crowd, as a photographer permanently documents his participation. Merging with the anonymous *Fremdenverkehr*, the flâneur extends and alienates his familiar perspective, so that his proximity as a former Berlin inhabitant becomes entangled with the tourist's distant perspective. At the same time, he feels that revealing his face for a picture feels like a disclosure ('preisgeben') of something he would rather keep to himself—his identity, his anonymity, his ambivalence as both outsider and insider. With his "mimicry with the stranger [Mimikry mit den Fremden]"[175] the flâneur embodies the stranger as Simmel describes him—not as the sightseer or "the wanderer who arrives today and leaves tomorrow [der Wandernde, der heute kommt und morgen geht]," but as someone "who arrives today and stays tomorrow—that is, the potential wanderer who, despite not having moved on, has not entirely overcome the detachment of coming and going [der heute kommt und morgen bleibt— sozusagen der potentiell Wandernde, der, obgleich er nicht weitergezogen ist, die Gelöstheit des Kommens und Gehens nicht ganz überwunden hat]."[176] Indeed, the tourist's perspective only suits him temporarily. Again, he refuses to merge with a crowd of sightseers, dismounts, and sees them off—"Drive on without me, you *real* foreigners! [Fahrt ohne mich weiter, ihr richtigen Fremden!]" (SB 149) Instead of going to see more of monumental Berlin, the flâneur continues on his very personal and social sightseeing tour; he now turns to the familiar again, meeting his friends in a café. His earlier remark about the pleonasm of 'sightseeing' indeed reveals a slightly defiant attitude: not only does he refuse to become a part of any crowd, he refuses to be told by a tourist guide which official 'sights' are worth being seen. Guided by his own map, the flâneur instead continues to read and narrate the fragmented story of the city. As Benjamin concludes: "The great remnants, the historical sights—to the true flâneur, they are rubbish, which he gladly leaves to the traveller. [Die großen Remineszenzen, die historischen Schauer—sie sind dem wahren Flaneur ja ein Bettel, den er gerne dem Reisenden überläßt]."[177]

Labyrinthine (dis)orientation & 'distanced proximity'

As a symbolic articulation of the entanglement of *Heimwelt* and *Fremdwelt*, Özdamar's and Hessel's texts both deploy a dynamics of orientation and disorientation—the image of the mental map is complemented, implicitly or explicitly, by the image of a labyrinth or a maze—which obviously has a lot with a city map in common. As in Beer-Hofmann's *Der Tod Georgs*, the labyrinth is an ambivalent symbol. As an image of non-linear movement, it evokes a loss of direction and a sense of confusion. In *Der Tod Georgs* there is a coercive aspect to the labyrinth, as it steers the aesthete towards the exit. In Hessel's and Özdamar's texts, emphasis is not on the resolution provided by center or exit of the labyrinthine structure. Rather, the labyrinth or the maze symbolizes the phenomenological entanglement of *Heimwelt* and *Fremdwelt*; it represents a condensed space, where distance and nearness overlap.[178] As opposed to the atomic city dwellers earlier, who are surrounded by isolating distance, these narrators embody a paradoxical experience that Nancy calls the "almost-there [...] of distanced proximity."[179] Their distance and detachment not only enable the legibility of the city, they also allow the narrators to witness or produce a sense of intimacy and relationality. In Özdamar's text, the *mise-en-scène* of mirrors inside the narrator's apartment produces a similar 'distanced proximity', while Hessel's purposeless and associative movement reflects his antinormative and antirepresentational reading of the city.

In "Der Hof im Spiegel," the labyrinthine experience first presents itself as a moment of apparent loss and disorientation. The narrator is waiting in fear that the nun who lives across the courtyard, and whom she has been observing attentively for years, has passed away:

> I was standing in the kitchen, leaning my back against the radiator, waiting for the sad light in her room, in the building where she lived, across the courtyard, to appear in the large mirror attached to the wall above my kitchen table. Her light from the house on the other side of the courtyard had been my setting sun for years. When I saw her illuminated window in the kitchen mirror, only then did I turn on the light in the apartment.
>
> [Ich stand in der Küche, meinen Rücken an den Heizkörper gelehnt, und wartete, daß im großen Spiegel, der über meinem Küchentisch an der Wand festgemacht war, das traurige Licht in ihrem Zimmer, im Haus gegenüber, wo sie lebte, anging. Ihr Licht aus dem Haus auf der anderen Seite des Hofes war seit Jahren meine untergehende Sonne. Wenn ich ihr beleuchtetes Fenster im Küchenspiegel sah, erst dann machte ich das Licht in der Wohnung an.] (HS 11)

The nun's light has been her primary point of orientation, and apparently—perhaps surprisingly—it is not the East. As her 'setting sun', the signal of nightfall, the nun's light conveys that this 'Orient' is not or no longer her frame of reference. Özdamar thus establishes from the beginning that the narrator inhabits a space that has overcome the presumed divide between West and East. It is furthermore an unconventional space, where distance is variable and adaptable, and, as Littler argues, that is deeply invested with affect.[180] While the nun's light is a point of 'dis-Orientation', her possible death is announced as the moment of actual disorientation. The duration of the narrator's waiting—in a strung-out sentence—accentuates the distance between her and the nun's residence; as she waits, she traces the path that the nun's light would travel from across the courtyard to her mirror. As such, that distance becomes meaningful, since it represents not a disparity, nor an "interstice between two members of a relationship [Zwischenraum zwischen zwei Relationsgliedern],"[181] but a significant affective relation.[182]

The setup of mirrors reinforces the labyrinthine 'distanced proximity' established by the narrator. Their reflections of the courtyard and her neighbours' lives into her apartment remind the narrator of "residential aesthetics of the East [die Wohnästhetik des Orients]":

> The people there extended their houses as far as creating alleys. Suddenly a window would be in front of the neighbors' windows. The houses mingled with each other, almost building labyrinths. The neighbors woke up nose to nose. I, too, had extended this apartment with three mirrors to the courtyard building. In the kitchen one mirror, from the kitchen one could go left and right into two rooms. In the room on the right there was a large mirror in the corner, and in the room on the left there was also a very large mirror that hung above a painter's cupboard, and which was suspended from the high ceiling. The three mirrors assembled all the windows and floors and the nunnery garden from three different perspectives. [...] We all lived together in three mirrors, nose to nose.
>
> [Die Menschen dort verlängerten ihre Häuser bis zu Gassen. Plötzlich befand sich so ein Fenster vor dem Fenster der Nachbarn. Die Häuser mischten sich ineinander, und so entstanden fast Labyrinthe. Die Nachbarn wachten Nase an Nase auf. Auch ich hatte diese Wohnung mit drei Spiegeln bis zum Hofhaus verlängert. In der Küche ein Spiegel, von der Küche aus konnte man links und rechts in zwei Zimmer gehen. Im Zimmer rechts stand ein großer Spiegel in der Ecke, und im linken Zimmer hing über einem Malerschrank ebenso ein sehr großer Spiegel, der an der hohen Decke aufgehängt war. Die drei Spiegel sammelten alle Fenster und Etagen und den Garten des Nonnenhauses aus drei verschiedenen Perspektiven. [...] Wir lebten alle in drei Spiegeln Nase an Nase zusammen.] (HS 25–6)

The narrator's indirect and mediated observation, as well as her memory of a Middle Eastern aesthetics of dwelling, could be read in terms of alienation and displacement. However, it soon becomes evident that the *Fremdheit* of her distanced perspective is not framed in cultural terms but, rather, reveals her "idiosyncratic staging of her view [eigenwillige Inszenierung des Blicks]"[183]— different from Hessel's 'first sight of the city', yet comparable in their artificiality. Extending her view from the inside, while closing the distance between herself and the mirrors' object of reflection, these mirrors produce a condensed and adaptable space where distance and nearness are closely entwined. The labyrinthine structure of the house of mirrors is not simply disorienting but a deliberate redirection of her view, opening it towards potential community. According to Littler, this virtual mirror space suspends a Kantian dualistic notion of self that is "established in oppositional relationship to permanent, inert matter," and which "fixes selfhood and otherness at a distance, precluding the notion of identities which gradually evolve, hybridise or transform."[184] Instead of a displaced and alienated individual, the mirrors bring into focus "a person whose passionate curiosity conveys a sense of community which is not actually there"[185]—at least not yet. For the mirrors conjure an unexpected experience of connection: "I was happy in the mirror because like that I was in several places at the same time. My mother and six nuns and a priest, we all lived together. [Ich war glücklich im Spiegel, weil ich so an mehreren Orten zur gleichen Zeit war. Meine Mutter und sechs Nonnen und ein Pfarrer, alle wohnten wir zusammen.]" (HS 31)

In *Spazieren in Berlin*, the flâneur's deliberate disorientation allows an antinormative reading of the city. His perspective resists the authority of 'official' history, enabling him to uncover an urban sociality that goes beyond familiar class distinctions. Particularly aware of the ambiguities of city life, he reveals unexpected associations between human and industrial spheres.

To recover an unbiased view, the flâneur requires a complete lack of direction and purpose—"To stroll properly, one must not have anything too specific in mind. [Um richtig zu flanieren, darf man nichts allzu Bestimmtes vorhaben.]" (SB 156; own translation)—as opposed to the street crowd—"Here, you don't walk, you walk *somewhere*. [Hier geht man nicht wo, sondern wohin.]" (SB 26) Purposelessness and idleness indeed allow him to explore the distanced proximity of the city, which enforces a continuous change of perspective. In "Berlin's Boulevard [Berlins Boulevard]" he writes:

> Glass and artificial light are two great helps, the latter especially when it's combined with a bit of remaining daylight and twilight. Then everything becomes multiple, *new nearnesses and distances* come into being, the happiest mixture "où l'indécis au précis se joint". Incandescent advertisements light up and disappear, scroll away and return, altering the height, depth, or shape of their buildings.
>
> [Zwei große Helfer sind Glas und künstliches Licht und dies letztere besonders im Wettstreit mit einem Rest Tageslicht und Dämmerung. Da wird alles vielfacher, es entstehen *neue Nähen und Fernen*, und die glückhafte Mischung, "où l'indécis au précis se joint." Die aufleuchtenden und verschwindenden, wandernden und wiederkehrenden Lichtreklamen ändern noch einmal Tiefe, Höhe und Umriß der Gebäude.] (SB 156; emphasis added)

As his quote from Paul Verlaine's poem 'Art Poétique' accentuates,[186] the actual "unforeseen adventures of the eyes [ungeahnten Abenteuer des Auges]" are those highly ambiguous places where one sphere becomes entangled in another. Glass, artificial lights, neon signs—all markers of the modern metropolis—generate an indeterminate yet 'fortunate' space where the night is never quite dark, and where the physical city takes on new dimensions, changing depth, height, and contours. This space where distance and proximity are interchangeable—as in a labyrinth—is the flâneur's habitat; wandering and being lost are his primary mode of perception. On his sightseeing trip, he advises tourists emphatically to become lost in maze-like "Alt-Berlin," a neighborhood that usually falls off the map:

> But I advise you [...]: when you're in the area again and have the time, get a little lost here. There are still real alleys here, still tiny houses huddled together with their gables thrust forward, completely unknown except to a few connoisseurs [...]. [...] There, into the inconspicuous you should go. That is an important Berlin landmark.
>
> [Ich aber rate dir, [...] wenn du noch einmal in diese Gegend kommst und Zeit hast, dich hier ein wenig zu verirren. Hier gibt es noch richtige Gassen, noch Häuserchen, die sich aneinanderdrängen und mit ihren Giebeln vorlugen, gar nicht weiter berühmt außer bei ein paar Kennern [...]. [...] Dort in das unscheinbare mußt du gehn. Das ist eine wichtige Berliner Stätte.] (SB 79–80; author's translation)

Seeking out the inconspicuous parts of Berlin, the places that have no historical landmark value, the flâneur once again evokes an aspect of the stranger described by Simmel—who is "by nature no landowner, whereby land is conceived not only in the physical sense, but also in the figurative sense of a substance of life, which is attached, if not to a spatial, then to an ideal place in the social sphere [seiner Natur nach kein Bodenbesitzer, wobei Boden nicht nur in dem physischen Sinne verstanden wird, sondern auch in dem übertragenen einer Lebenssubstanz, die, wenn nicht an einer räumlichen, so an einer ideellen Stelle des gesellschaftlichen Umkreises fixiert ist]."[187] Indeed, Hessel translates his *Boden-* and *Heimatlosigkeit* into an aesthetic(ist) critical counterpoint to the territorial and official story of the city. Seeking out the private stories of the public, his strolls will teach him "new pasts of the city [immer neue Vergangenheiten der Stadt]" and to appreciate the past in the present, to enjoy "in what is still visible that which has disappeared [im noch Sichtbaren Verschwundenes] [...]." (SB 285) Flânerie thus reveals the true meaning of a city *Heimat*, which many Berliners have yet to discover—"We

Berliners must dwell in our city to a much greater degree. [Wir Berliner müssen unsere Stadt noch viel mehr—bewohnen.]" (SB 285) Benjamin praises Hessel for his exceptional understanding of *Wohnen*, which takes place not in houses, but on the streets, for the streets are "the home of the eternally restless, eternally moving being [die Wohnung des ewig unruhigen, ewig bewegten Wesens]."[188] Whereas Özdamar's notion of dwelling entails an extension of the interior, the flâneur seeks out the 'private' or unconventional side of the streetscape. His refusal to be guided or to take a deliberate direction renders his perspective typically antinormative:

> [We] wanted to stay out in the city and on the street. For a short visit to the museums, Baedeker is excellent; its single and double stars inform us as to what the *consensus gentium* deems exceptionally beautiful and valuable, although this doesn't prevent anyone from making their own discoveries.
>
> [[W]ir wollen in der Stadt und auf der Straße bleiben. Für einen kurzen Besuch der Museen unterrichtet der Baedeker ausgezeichnet, seine einfachen und Doppelsternchen orientieren über das, was eine Art *consensus gentium* letzthin für besonders schön und wertvoll hält, und das hindert niemanden, seine eignen Entdeckungen zu machen.] (SB 108)

As opposed to the flâneur's antinormative perspective, the *Baedeker* travel guide promotes a formalized and institutionalized experience of culture and is furthermore adapted to the generic expectations of mass tourism.[189] The *Baedeker* and the sightseeing tour are typical nineteenth-century "media of urban appropriation [Medien der Stadtaneignung],"[190] which not only 'read' the city in terms of highlights and landmarks, but also function as "signposts that standardize the movement of travellers in urban space [Wegweiser, die die Bewegung der Reisenden im Stadtraum [...] normieren]."[191] The flâneur opposes that educational and normative intention, although in "I Learn a Thing or Two [Ich lerne]," he mentions, with irony, that he does care about his education:

> I really must 'culture' myself. Just walking around won't do it. I'll have to educate myself in local history, take an interest in both the past and future of this city, a city that's always on the go, always in the middle of becoming something else.
>
> [[I]ch muß etwas für meine Bildung tun. Mit dem Herumlaufen allein ist es nicht getan. Ich muss eine Art Heimatkunde treiben, mich um die Vergangenheit

und Zukunft dieser Stadt kümmern, dieser Stadt, die immer unterwegs, immer im Begriff, anders zu werden, ist.] (SB 28)

Visiting an architect, however, who instructs him on the future development of the expanding city, the flâneur soon becomes aware that the man's ideas will not convey its true character. Instead, looking out over a field, he realizes—in a vision of distanced proximity—that the architectural future and the implied notion of progress are meaningless when separated from the city past. The effect of grandiose modern architecture is only visible in relation to its complement:

> I am shown *at close range* the giant's tiny neighbor, a little house 'so wind-worried', standing *far afield*. [...] The *juxtaposition* of the towering halls and this hut is like an emblem of Berlin's silhouette.
>
> [[G]anz *nah* bekomme ich des Riesen winzigen Nachbar gezeigt, ein Häuschen, "so windebang,"[192] das da *tief im Felde* steht. [...] Das *Nebeneinander* der ragenden Hallen und dieser Hütte ist wie ein Wahrzeichen des Weichbildes von Berlin.] (SB 32; emphasis added; author's translation)

From the flâneur's individualized *Städtebilder*, the modern metropolis first emerges as a non-unitary and fragmented space. Yet there is a cinematic aspect to his detachment that registers unexpected connections and relations. As in the fragment above, Hessel finds beauty in complementarity, rather than contrast. This allows him to perceive humanity in images that might otherwise be read as illustrations of modern exploitation. In the chapter "A Bit of Work [Etwas von der Arbeit]," the flâneur observes Berlin's "particular and visible beauty, whenever and wherever it is at work [besondere und sichtbare Schönheit, wenn und wo es arbeitet]." (SB 35) In the Siemens factory, he notices alongside the mechanical a distinctly human aspect of factory work: "Just like the machine parts, so too do mugs and cups for the girls' tea, coffee, and cocoa wander on the conveyor belt, returning from their circuit through the kitchen heated and ready. [[W]ie die Maschinenteile, so wandern auf laufendem Bande auch Tassen und Becher, in welche die Mädchen ihren Tee, Kaffee und Kakao getan haben, und der kommt dann von seinem Rundgang durch die Küche gekocht und fertig zu ihnen zurück.]" (SB 37; author's translation) Then, with a sensitive but camera-like eye, the flâneur switches effortlessly between descriptions of mechanical and architectural structures inside the factory, close-ups of human detail, and establishing shots of what their working hands accomplish (SB 38):

[I]t's so fantastic to look down into the hall, from the stairs or the gallery, at the whirring, gyrating machines; so gripping is the view of the necks and hands of those pottering about there, and when their upward-glancing eyes meet your own. The things these people make fill your little room with light—a light that wanders from house to house, illuminates, extols, advertises, and outlines.

[[S]o großartig es ist, im Saal, von der Treppe, von der Galerie auf die kreisenden und surrenden Maschinen zu sehn, so ergreifend ist der Anblick der Nacken und Hände derer, die da werkeln, und die Begegnung des Auges mit ihren aufschauenden Augen. Aus dem, was diese Menschen schaffen, kommt Licht in dein kleines Zimmer und wandert Häuserfronten entlang, bestrahlt, preist an, wirbt, und baut um.] (SB 38)

Truly soulless and dehumanizing to the flâneur is not factory work but, rather, the new consumerism. Standing in front of a shop window, he notices a number of mannequins whose "cool mixture of insolence and distinction [kühle Mischung von Frechheit und Distinktion]" and "determined expression [dezidierte[r] Ausdruck]" (SB 44) at first remind him of the new type of woman he identifies with the metropolis.[193] Yet when he notices single, decontextualized mannequin parts in the window—"individual legs [Beine einzeln]," "puzzling frameworks [rätselhafte Gestelle]," "a female torso ends in one stylized arm and one cut-off stump [eine Art Frauentorso, der in einen stilisierten Arm und einen abgeschnittenen Armstumpf endet]," they leave the observer in bewilderment. (SB 44–5) Reduced to their purpose in a new consumerist society, the mannequin parts lose any semblance of humanity, whereas the view of necks, hands, and eyes in the fragment above bespeaks a still distinctly human aspect of factory work: those body parts are connected to and contribute to a larger urban existence.

The flâneur's ability to contextualize and connect seemingly separated spheres is particularly significant in his observations of urban social life. With a similar sensitivity to the complementarity rather than opposition of polarities, the flâneur—in line with Simmel's diagnosis of modern city life—charts the emergence and disappearance of different forms of sociality. From his conversation with the urban planner, he has learned that the *Scheunenviertel*, which houses a large Jewish community, has to make way for the "big orderly settlements [planmäßige Großsiedlung]" that will thoroughly change "the old city body [den alten Stadtkörper]." (SB 28) In his detachment, there is no trace of affiliation with the old Jewish ghetto of the *Jüdenstraße*, which he describes as an anachronistic "idyll in the middle of the chaotic city [Idyll mitten in der lärmenden Stadt]."

(SB 93) Similarly, he detects "something similar to a ghetto [etwas Ghettoähnliches]" in the disintegrating *Scheunenviertel* of the Eastern Jewish community. While there is a hint of sympathy and appreciation in his description, the flâneur takes on an ethnographer's perspective, which indicates that their community is to him as *fremd* as to any other Berliner:

> These streets are still a world of their own, home to the eternal wanderers, who long ago were propelled out of the east in one great wave. Eventually, they will have so acclimated themselves to Berlin that they can be tempted to push farther into the west of the city and to discard the most evident signs of their peculiarity. And it's too bad; the way they live in the Scheunenviertel is nicer than the way they may live later in the clothing factories or the stock exchange.
>
> [Noch sind diese Straßen eine Welt für sich und den ewigen Fremden eine Art Heimat, bis sie, die vor noch nicht langer Zeit von einem Schub aus dem Osten hergetragen worden sind, sich soweit in Berlin akklimatisiert haben, daß es sie verlockt, tiefer in den Westen vorzudringen und die allzu deutlichen Zeichen ihrer Eigenart abzutun. Es ist oft schade darum, sie sind eigentlich so, wie sie im Scheunenviertel herumgehen, schöner als nachher in der Konfektion und an der Börse.] (SB 94)

The *Scheunenviertel* exemplifies a different kind of *Heimat* than the one the flâneur seeks to uncover. In "Der Hof im Spiegel," the narrator's sense of locality lies in tentative relations, whereas Hessel's *Städtebilder* reveal locality in terms of complementarity and context. The *Scheunenviertel*, as an isolated— not contextualized, and therefore anachronistic—neighborhood, gradually surrenders to the expanding metropolis, encouraging its inhabitants to explore new identities—no matter how little the flâneur may think of professions in factories or the stock exchange. It is interesting that Hessel describes this community as 'eternal strangers', given that his flânerie is constructed around his own (partially chosen) outsider position. While the flâneur is not inclined to frame his *Heimatlosigkeit* in terms of ancestry, he is himself an illustration of how modern city life encourages him to define himself independently from tradition and background. In the imminent dissolution of the ghetto, Hessel witnesses the early stages of an acculturation process that he himself has already completed.

Yet the disintegration of old neighborhoods and traditional community life is only one aspect of Berlin's ever-changing image. Hessel describes Berlin society as "a concept that's both hard to grasp and to define [[e]in schwer zu erfassender und zu begrenzender Begriff]." (SB 56) The flâneur witnesses the emergence of a new kind of sociality that gradually transcends the familiar class distinctions and is instead characterized by complementary oppositions:

> Hospitable houses unify art and the haute bourgeoisie, and at the tables of great bank barons, socialist delegates meet with princes of former ruling houses. [...] With youthful enthusiasm, the ambitious Berliner plunges into this new conviviality [...].
>
> [Gästliche Häuser vereinen Kunst und hohe Bourgeoisie, und am Tische großer Bankherren begegnen sich sozialistische Abgeordnete mit Prinzen aus dem früheren Herrscherhaus. [...] Mit jugendlichem Eifer stürzt sich der ehrgeizige Berliner in die neue Geselligkeit [...].] (SB 56–7)

Berlin's 'neue Geselligkeit' is, in the flâneur's eyes, not representational or hierarchical, but relational. In this respect, the flâneur's antinormative 'erster Blick' has more in common with Özdamar's 'inszenierter Blick' than one might expect. By keeping the city at a reading distance, the narrators allow the city to reveal itself as a site of interconnection, context, and of myriad individualized stories at the same time. They register a sense of proximity that is not tied to known identities and communities, and which refuses to be incorporated into national and territorial narratives of *Heimat*. As opposed to the city dwellers discussed earlier, who due to dogmatic identity discourses of difference and stereotype fail to realize themselves as singular human beings, Özdamar's and Hessel's narrators read the city in relational rather than differential terms. By adopting a hermeneutic perspective, they can assert themselves in terms of social and contextual proximity.

Conclusion

Simmel captured the ambivalence of the modern metropolitan experience as early as 1903, but his views are still relevant in a transnational context. At both ends of the twentieth century, the city is not a silent backdrop but a catalyst. It encourages city dwellers to assert themselves beyond familiar differences and relations, thereby escaping the exigencies of traditional community life. At the same time, despite this detachment, the city dweller remains receptive to new connections and does not retreat into isolation. The city becomes the locus of reshaping the modern individual beyond "[t]he most radical forms of solitude and of community, autonomous separateness and homogeneous unison."[194] The four city dwellers—even when they are a century apart—suggest that neither enlightened confidence in the individual nor dissolution into a collective will guarantee a sense of connection. And neither radical individualism nor absolute collectivism can lay claim to the city. Although images of the city can be used to emphasize difference—from *Westjuden* living in the cities as "paradigmatic agents of modernity,"[195] to ghetto Jews as a distrusted urban *Volk*, to '*integrationsunwillige*' residents of Germany's 'parallel societies'—the urban experience does not lend itself to such instrumentalization. Rather, the city is a site of recalibration. It enables tentative, fragile experiences of community, which are not the result of Enlightened, autonomous individuals seeking connection through self-development, nor of deconstructed individuals who are denied an origin, a history, or an identity. Instead, in the city, differences may become relations and proximities. As such, the urban experience constitutes an anti-essentializing moment—a fundamental 'resistance to immanence'.

CHAPTER 4

FAMILY HEROES BETWEEN MYTH AND STORYTELLING

4.1 Writing in the shadow of an empire

A cursory glance at the list of Chamisso Prize winners of the last few years reveals a considerable number of writers from Eastern Europe and former Yugoslavia.[1] Having settled in German-speaking countries since the fall of communism and the disintegration of Yugoslavia, these writers make a substantial contribution to German-language literature in varied and original ways. Among them are established names—Herta Müller and Richard Wagner, for instance, both ethnic Germans from Romania. More recently, younger voices have entered the stage. Mainstream prizes such as the Leipzig Book Fair Prize and the German Book Prize indicate that this new generation has come to achieve more general recognition beyond their status as 'migrant writers'. Some of the texts by, for example, Bulgarian-born Ilja Trojanow (*Der Weltensammler*, 2006), the Bosnian-German Saša Stanišić (*Wie der Soldat das Grammaphon repariert*, 2006), or the Russian-born Wladimir Kaminer (*Russendisko*, 2000) have indeed achieved bestseller status.

"The Eastern turn," as Brigid Haines coined this wave of writing,[2] complements what Leslie Adelson famously identified as the "Turkish turn" in German literature.[3] Like many (first-generation) Turkish-German authors, they are often inspired by migration experiences, although their stylistic and thematic preferences can hardly be contained by that single denominator. Rather, as Haines observes, the body of texts derives provisional unity from an "underlying Cold War metanarrative."[4] They share a thematic concern with the communist period in the Eastern Bloc, as well as with the aftermath of its demise.[5] The individual stories reveal a plurality of historical situations across former communist states, providing an often autobiographically inspired "micronarrative of a particular trajectory."[6] At the same time, they collectively reflect the enormous impact of the Soviet regime, its supporting regimes, as well as the violent consequence of its collapse—the outburst of nationalist sentiment and the Yugoslav wars of the 1990s. Their postcommunist narrative takes a relatively new angle on questions of national and cultural identity. Broadly speaking, the 'Turkish turn' in literature has charted the effects of globalization on individual lives and, more importantly, has thoroughly questioned the notion of a static German identity in a globalized world. Eastern European 'migrant writing' works beyond individual narratives, too, and furthermore puts current European identity debates in an interesting historical perspective. As Haines concludes:

> [B]y writing in German of eastern Cold War experiences from distinct national or regional perspectives, this new wave of migrant writing frames German, Austrian and Swiss debates in a longer historical, and a wider geographical context and contributes to the work of overcoming the divided memory cultures that characterised the Cold War period, challenging conceptions of Europe grounded in the Franco-German heart of the EU. This remapping of Europe looks to move beyond the Cold War division in the awareness of globalisation, but also of Europe's roots in empires.[7]

The Soviet regime is just the latest instance of imperialisms that shaped—and divided—twentieth-century Europe; the Yugoslav Wars of the 1990s only the latest violent conflict to arise on the shards of a disintegrated empire.[8] Yet it is Sarajevo that, in an almost symbolic manner, relates the events of Europe's imperial history. Twice in the course of the twentieth century, the city suffered the consequences of modern war, ethnic and nationalist conflict; twice, it witnessed the crumbling of hegemonies. History does not repeat itself, exactly, but as the saying goes, it does rhyme. The recent wave of eastern 'migrant writing' reintroduces into German literatures a theme of imperial (dis)continuity in European history, which due to the perceived historical rupture of 1989 has remained understated.

To some extent, the emphatic symbolism of '1989' in literary history "stands for Cold-War Germany's privileged position in a chronology that determines post-communist history."⁹ In all their diversity and plurality, the eastern voices in German literature tend to subvert a biased, Germany-centered perspective, reminding audiences that the communist past has determined the lives of millions of Germans and Europeans and is, more than two decades after the *Wende*, still not over and done with. By re-establishing a sense of continuity with the socialist past—and even before that—they tone down the significance of national paradigms. With their "long historical consciousness and a heightened awareness of empires,"¹⁰ they contribute to a reframing and remapping of Europe from an angle beyond the familiar East-West distinction—a remnant from the Cold War. In doing so, they are inviting their audiences to reassess the long-term imperial political projects that have shaped European history.

In her 1991 introduction to the English translation of Joseph Roth's *Radetzkymarsch*, Nadine Gordimer articulates her awareness of such historical analogies. She points out the striking similarity between her time of writing and the Austro-Hungarian Empire on the eve of the Great War:

> [T]he wheel of karma—or historical consequence?—has brought Roth's territory back to a reenactment of the situation central to his work. [...] [W]e see the deterioration of a society, an empire, in which disparate nationalities have been forced into political unity by an overriding authority and its symbol: the Austro-Hungarian Empire and the personality of Emperor Franz Joseph. There the rise of socialism and fascism against royalism led to Sarajevo and the First World War. After World War II the groups that had won autonomy were forced together again, if in a slightly different conglomerate, by another all-powerful authority and its symbol: the Communist bloc and the personality of Joseph Stalin. Now restlessness and rebellion, this time against the socialism that has not proved to be liberation, brings once again the breakup of a hegemony. Passages in Roth's work, about the Slovenes, Croats, and Serbs, could with scarcely a change describe what has happened in Yugoslavia in 1991.¹¹

The current postcommunist narrative in German literature traces tendencies and events similar to those in pre-war Austria-Hungary—like the Soviet Union a multiethnic conglomerate directed towards a common future but unable to defuse emerging internal division and opposition. The decline of both communism and the Austro-Hungarian Empire can be read as instances of the "metanarrative of empire to nation," according to which "the rise of national consciousness is [...] an inescapable facet of modernity and the driving force in imperial dissolution."[12] It is a common understanding that the transition to modernity coincided with the decline of empires and the rise of nations. The emergence of nations is, moreover, seen as "the natural manifestation of a will to self-determination of subject peoples." However, even as a "teleology of the nation"[13] continues to shape the historiography of declining empires, emphasis on the novelty of the national form has yielded to an awareness of nations as discursive constructs—"imagined communities"[14] relying on "invented traditions."[15]

Indeed, Sarajevo and its history of declining hegemonies is exemplary of multiple tendencies towards foundational and post-imperial mythologization. The collapse of communism effected, especially in eastern Europe, a "return of memory" and with it, as Tony Judt argues, "a revival of the national units that framed and shaped that memory and give meaning to the collective past."[16] Whereas the West seems to have developed an increasingly desacralized and democratized national collective memory, the Yugoslav Wars resulted from an apparent "desperate need for founding myths" in postsocialist states, "despite—or perhaps because of—the fact that communism had a 'desacralising' effect in many countries."[17] They were an immediate result of the demise of socialist rule, but they were also the long-term effect of "geopolitical 'business' left over from the Second World War," which had been 'suspended' for decades under communist rule. In the 1990s, the "*nachholende* nation-building" of ethnic and religious groups was "being finished off [...] in an extremely bloody manner."[18] Indirectly, the conflicts were also related to tensions that laid the foundations of the First World War—its immediate cause the assassination of Austria-Hungary's successor to the throne by a Serbian radical nationalist. The reasons for the empire's decline are much debated and generally attributed to a potent mixture of "[i]mperial overreach, the corruption of autocratic rule, international competition, defeat in war, and changes in economic and political life [...]."[19] In the end, though, its demise was a matter of one imperial myth losing its foundational appeal and being succeeded by several national or ethnic ones. During the reign of Emperor Franz Joseph—the period evoked in Roth's novel—the empire legitimized itself as an "absolute necessity," as a counterbalance to powerful Russia, but also "in the interest of humanity."[20] From a post-imperial perspective, this legitimation appears less obvious. The multitude of political and historical interpretations of its demise suggests that, of course, a single diachronic narrative does not exist. Its multiethnic composition of eleven main nationalities was interpreted as an

"Austrian prison of the nations" briefly after the First World War but, more recently, also as a "peaceful family of nations."[21] Now, the empire is remembered as either "an obsolete system of authoritarian, suppressive and disintegrating imperial power" or, on the contrary, as an exemplary "framework for the relatively peaceful coexistence as well as the economic and political integration of various nationalities, language and confessional groups on their way to nation building."[22]

The gap between these extremes leaves a lot of room for interpretation. For some, the collapse of an empire is evidence of the eventual triumph of peoples' right to self-determination; for others, the ensuing conflicts and social and political insecurities often feed into imperial nostalgia. A phenomenon like postcommunist nostalgia—'Yugo-nostalgia' or its eastern German counterpart *Ostalgie*—is not an uncommon cultural response to the disintegration of authoritarian systems[23]—if they were not too violent, that is. It expresses a longing not for the socialist regime itself but for the security, stability, and prosperity it guaranteed.[24] 'Nostalgia' may carry connotations of sentimentality and can be considered as "the programmatic equivalent of bad memory," or even "the abdication of memory."[25] Even so, it does not necessarily articulate a people's yearning for the return to a past that in the process of remembrance grows mythical or utopian. Instead, nostalgic expressions "may be a style or design or narrative that serves to comment on how memory works. Rather than an end reaction to yearning, it is understood as a technique for provoking a secondary reaction."[26] As a form of selective remembrance, nostalgia is a strategy of "dealing with the past by creating continuity where discontinuity should be."[27] As such, it is a means of discussing the present and imagining a future, rather than a simple idealization of the past.

The postcommunist response is reminiscent of what Claudio Magris has famously coined "the Habsburg myth [der habsburgische Mythos]."[28] Magris argues that with the collapse of the Austro-Hungarian Empire, many intellectuals saw their cultural foundations in ruins. In the same fashion as postcommunist authors who express a longing for stability and security, these Austrian writers attempted to cope with an insecure political climate, by looking back upon the empire as "a fortunate and harmonious era, an orderly and enchanting Middle Europe [...]. [...] In their memory, that Austria became 'a golden age of security' [eine glückliche und harmonische Zeit, als geordnetes und märchenhaftes Mitteleuropa [...]. [...] In ihrer Erinnerung wurde dieses Österreich zu einem 'goldenen Zeitalter der Sicherheit']."[29] Writers like Joseph Roth and Stefan Zweig were undoubtedly aware of the flaws of this past 'golden age'. Still, their written memories set in motion a "fantastic and poetic transformation of the vanished Danube Monarchy [phantastisch[e] und poetisch[e] Verwandlung der untergegangenen Donaumonarchie]"[30] which, according to Magris, characterizes a substantial part of post-1918 Austrian literature. Even the most sensible, ironic, or critical authors, who did not revert to an idealization of the past, found themselves "prisoners of the fairytale-like and wistful glorification of the Danube Monarchy [Gefangene [der] märchenhaften und sehnsüchtigen Verklärung der Donaumonarchie]."[31] This fictional transfiguration is not a matter of shared themes or motifs, but rather of a specific undertone and "cultural humus [kulturelle[r] Humus]."[32] As Magris argues, this—partly conscious, partly unintended—distortion of the past signals their shared desire to make sense of an emotional landscape that had been irrevocably destroyed. By altering a sociohistorical reality, and replacing it with an illusory one, their writings attribute metahistorical meaning to a past reality they cannot fully recover.

Like postcommunist nostalgia, the 'Habsburg myth' created a narrative of continuity after an experience of historical disruption. According to Magris, this narrative was the literary extension of a historical deformation process that shaped the reality of the empire itself. Especially towards its end, the myth was a useful instrument in the continued effort "to justify the existence of an increasingly anachronistic state structure [für ein immer anachronistischer werdendes Staatsgefüge eine Daseinsberechtigung zu finden]."[33] Moreover, it had influenced everyday life and personal ideals to such an extent that it created a deceptive sense of peace in a reality that was full of contradictions. The Habsburg myth provided, in other words, not just a "backward-looking utopia [rückwärts gewandte Utopie];"[34] it also served as an instrument of political estrangement, on which the Empire could further build its enlightened claim to "perpetual peace."[35] Under the banner of 'absolute necessity' and 'peaceful coexistence', the Austro-Hungarian mosaic of "heterogeneous components and irreconcilable contradictions"[36] found a common goal in the imperial claim to eternal peace:

> [The Austrian did not] identify with the individual nationalities grouped together under the Dual Monarchy: rather, he was the ribbon that tied the bundle together, the invisible element that was common to them all and identical with none. The Austrian existed in the abstract idea of unity, in a non-material or *hinternational* dimension.[37]

A similar abstract idea of unity also sustained the communist regime, which, as Nancy argues in *The Inoperative Community*, is another textbook example of "mythic thought"—"the thought of a founding fiction, or a foundation by fiction."[38] He distinguishes two types of immanentism based on mythologization. As discussed earlier, the first involves the tendency of nations and communities to define themselves based on their undivided yet common selfhood, which needs to be shielded from external influence. The other is evident in the former socialist regimes, which defined the communist ideology as the ultimate destination of humanity.[39] Communism understands community in terms of the "desire to discover or rediscover a place of community at once beyond social divisions and beyond subordination to technopolitical dominion."[40] The communist framework of nations aimed to overcome differences by striving for the final goal—to reach a transparent way of life, where "all alienation of the capitalist way of life would disappear and society would finally be harmoniously present with itself."[41] Whether myth presents itself as a final destiny or as a foundational narrative, its claim to absolute or eternal truth strives for integral fusion or identification: "[M]yth represents multiple existences as immanent to its own unique fiction, which gathers them together and gives them their common figure in its speech and as this speech."[42] Put another way, "[m]yth signifies itself, and thereby converts its own fiction into foundation or into the inauguration of meaning itself."[43]

The current chapter focuses on authors who, at both ends of the twentieth century, have chronicled imperial myths at work and in demise. From a variety of perspectives, Joseph Roth, Zsusza Bank, and Dimitré Dinev trace narrative and unifying aspects of (post-) imperial mythology—and its eventual failure to assert a claim to eternity. Firstly, a contrastive comparison of Roth's famous generation novel *Radetzkymarsch* and Dinev's (post-) communist family saga *Engelszungen* addresses the intertwined narratives of family and imperial history. The family motif in these novels reveals the fissures in the smooth surface of imperial myth, which robs people of any sense of individuality. Contrastively, Zsuzsa Bank's *Der Schwimmer* and Joseph Roth's *Hiob* feature disintegrated families against a backdrop of stifling authoritarianism and insistent modernity. Despite the overall sense of vanishing (comm)unity, these families manage to carve out a space for the modern individual.

Previous chapters focused on the vulnerability of the radical individual, whose Enlightened confidence starts wavering in the confrontaion with pervasive stereotype, isolation, or mortality. In the present chapter section, focus is on individuals who attempt to resist their dissolution into radical collectivism and identification. Obstructed to assume an identity of their own, they seek to recover a sense of autonomy. *Engelszungen* and *Radetzkymarsch* bring into focus the highly ambivalent, Enlightened foundations of the Habsburg Empire and the communist regime—both of which advocated supranationality, tolerance, equality, and progress, though in their practice—as Roth and Dinev suggest—they could only sustain themselves by way of exclusion and suppression of cultural and religious difference.

The shadow of declining empires has offered fertile ground for many authors. Writers of the recent 'Eastern turn' in German literature and, more generally, those who are "writing postcommunism"[44] navigate between their desire to forget and their inescapable memory. As Judt argues, the period under communism seems to have been "consigned to a limbo between history and memory." "[I]n a region whose recent past offers no clear social or political descriptors, it is tempting to erase from the public record any reference to the communist era [...]."[45] At the same time, having witnessed the downfall of an authoritarian system that shaped the course of (European) history, these authors have of course been deeply influenced by their lived memory. In the last two decades, several German writers from the former Eastern Bloc have explored their memory of communist rule and their migration experiences. A convenient form, in many cases, has been the generation or family novel. The family—whether in its nuclear form or as consecutive generations—can be regarded as a "mnemonic community" in its most condensed form.[46] The family novel thus instantiates a fundamental question of cultural memory studies—"how 'the past' is created and recreated within sociocultural contexts."[47] In the case of postcommunist writing, family histories usually function as a counternarrative to official history, or they address the tension between personal memory and communicative memory—the narrative process of remembrance taking place within families.[48]

Furthermore, the process of imperial decline, as Eric Hobsbawm notes, lends itself gratefully to narration and fictionalization, especially in the Austrian context:

> Austrian minds had time to reflect on the death and disintegration of their empire, while it struck all the other empires suddenly, at least by the measure of the historical clock, even those in visibly declining health, like the Soviet Union. But perhaps the perceived and accepted multi-linguality, multi-confessionality and multi-culturality of the monarchy helped them to a more complex sense of historical perspective. Its subjects lived simultaneously in different social universes and different historical epochs.[49]

It can indeed be argued that authors like Roth—a westernized Jew born in Brody, Galicia—developed a 'complex sense of historical perspective' due to their keen awareness of imperial decline, but also their social position in a multicultural, yet increasingly hostile, environment. 'Austro-Modernism,'[50] as Perloff calls it, developed a remarkable impact especially right after the First World War, "when artists and writers from the far-flung frontiers of the dismembered empire—writers, mostly Jewish, who had received a classical German education, as authorized by the centralized *k. & k. (kaiserlich und königlich)* government—came on the scene."[51] Despite the constitutional changes of 1867, which established the dual monarchy and a parliamentary system, and which granted a plurality of nationalities a chance at political representation, German-Austrians retained their political and cultural predominance.[52] Austro-Modernism is indeed closely entwined with the paradoxical situation of Jewish authors. Their intellectual horizon was shaped by the imperial Habsburg high culture scene,[53] yet they were not considered a part of it. The First World War contributed to an increasingly anti-Jewish climate, as the arrival of a large group of Eastern Jewish immigrants, often working as peddlers, irked the anti-Semitic mayor of Vienna Karl Lueger. The overrepresentation of Jews in finance, culture, and the political left added to his suspicions about the Jews as capitalist exploiters and a threat to the fatherland.[54] The Jewish situation is a salient example of the contradictions and tensions within the abstract unity of the empire. Perloff associates the paradoxical situation of Jewish authors—enjoying equal rights, while perceived as a threat—with their particular sensitivity to nuance and complexity. Distinguishing Austrian modernism from the formal experiment of its English or German counterparts, she detects among Jewish post-empire writers a keen "fondness of paradox and contradiction as modes of understanding."[55] As chroniclers of a collapsed empire, Jewish Austrians wrote from a perspective that forced them away from quick and careless judgment.

The authors discussed in the present chapter share a complicated vantage point between official history and personal memory and experience. As children of collapsed empires and, moreover, as voices from the East, Joseph Roth, Zsuzsa Bánk, and Dimitré Dinev explore imperial myths, their disintegration, and attempts at restoring a sense of continuity. The comparison of two distinct time frames suggests that the recent 'Eastern turn' does not quite describe a *Wende* but, rather, really harks back to Europe's history of imperial decline. Firstly, I focus on (de)generational narratives in Roth's *Radetzkymarsch* and Dinev's *Engelszungen*, where the entanglement of family history and imperial downfall brings out the narrative and mythical character of the empire. Furthermore, the novels bring into focus the destructive effect of imperial myths on individual self-determination—no matter how 'enlightened' and 'universalistic' they may present themselves. Finally, they suggest that when a state considers the principles of Enlightenment as already realized in its own structure and program, rather than an ongoing commitment of single individuals, its Enlightened foundation becomes a myth itself.

4.2 Family heroes redefined: Joseph Roth's *Radetzkymarsch* (1932) versus Dimitré Dinev's *Engelszungen* (2003)

Storytellers between empires and nations: Joseph Roth and Dimitré Dinev

In his essay "Kaddisch für Österreich," W.G. Sebald praises Roth as not quite a chronicler of historical time, but as a writer who is finely attuned to the world outside of historical categories, for "the other world time, which is the concern of a chronicler who sees the round years rolling by one after the other, that is the time of naive poetry [[d]ie andere Weltzeit, um die es einem Chronisten geht, der die runden Jahre nacheinander abrollen sieht, diese Zeit ist die der naiven Dichtung][...]."[56] The year 1930, in which Roth published *Hiob* and started working on *Radetzkymarsch*, is often held to mark his transition from critical engagement with issues of the present towards nostalgic and melancholy recreations of vanished worlds. Yet Sebald is not referring to that apparent change of focus; Roth's strength is not in his escape from *Weltzeit*. Roth indeed remained concerned with the issues that had shaped both his time of writing and his own life—the disintegration of the Austro-Hungarian Empire, the westward migration of Eastern Jews, and the crisis of the modern individual.[57] Characteristic of Roth's remarkable ease of storytelling, as Sebald emphasizes, is his skill to line these topics with "fringes of eternity [die Ränder der Ewigkeit]."[58] He masters an "artistic exercise that, despite its apparent modesty, is by no means satisfied with superficiality [Kunstübung, die, ihrer scheinbaren Anspruchslosigkeit zum Trotz, nirgends mit dem Vordergründigen sich zufriedengibt]."[59] Roth confronts a fragmented experience of modernity with the longing for an unlimited experience that transcends nations and territories. His idea of a timeless Judaism, for instance, ties in with the supranational Jewish tradition that sought to transcend national oppositions in favor of common European roots.[60] At the same time, he considered the ideal of tolerance and unity as already realized in the Empire. Especially as anti-Semitic sentiment became more prominent, Roth seemed to value the

Empire as a multicultural, multiethnic political formation allowing its citizens to be both Jewish and Austrian.[61] As his biographer David Bronsen observes, Roth's novels, stories, and journalistic writing reveal his "double consciousness,"[62] his craving for "a possibility of belonging."[63] He figures both as "an eminently Austrian writer"—as illustrated by his novels set in the Austro-Hungarian Empire (e.g. *Radetzkymarsch, Die Kapuzinergruft*) and, conversely, as "a storyteller of the *shtetl* culture of Eastern European Jewry"[64] (e.g. *Hiob, Juden auf Wanderschaft*).

According to Bronsen, Roth's 'split' personality is firmly rooted in his biography. In a letter to a fellow journalist for the *Frankfurter Zeitung*, Benno Reifenberg, Roth emphasized his contradictory personality as "a Frenchman from the East, a humanist, a rationalist with religion, a Catholic with a Jewish mind."[65] Born in 1894 in Brody, Galicia, a mostly Jewish town in the easternmost province of the Empire, he later moved to Lemberg/Lviv and Vienna to study German literature. At an early age, he refused to take part in the Zionist movement, calling himself an Austrian assimilationist, loyal to the Emperor. However, as an adult, even as he supported the universalistic claims of the Empire, he continued to celebrate the particularism of the *shtetl*.[66] In the course of his life, Roth adopted still other seemingly contradictory views. In his early journalistic work for a number of leftist papers, he assumed a rather distanced perspective on the monarchy and its defenders. Like many others, Roth set his hopes on the promised solidarity of socialism as a remedy for postwar Europe and the ills of capitalism.[67] In his later years, however, on the eve of the Second World War, his anti-Habsburg stance made way again for sympathy for the humanitarian qualities of the monarchy.[68]

These swift changes in attitude have been ascribed to the political rise of Hitler and to Roth's association of the figure of the emperor with his personal past. Briefly before he went into exile, he wrote how deeply the Empire's downfall had upset him: "My most powerful experience was the war and the downfall of my fatherland, the only one I have ever possessed [...]. Even today I am still a patriotic Austrian and love the rest of my homeland like a sacred relic. [Mein stärkstes Erlebnis war der Krieg und der Untergang meines Vaterlandes, des einzigen das ich je besessen habe [...]. Auch heute noch bin ich durchaus patriotischer Österreicher und liebe den Rest meiner Heimat wie eine Reliquie]."[69] The absence of a meaningful father figure, in addition to his mother's silence about his father's mental illness, added to his confounded sense of self. As Bronsen remarks, it left Roth to "grope his entire life with the question of his origins and identity," and to invent "genealogies for himself to fill the void that represented his paternal line."[70] He makes a connection between Roth's absent father and the author's search for a fatherland and, likewise, between the crumbling empire and a lost childhood. While one could object to such a biographical reading, a recurring motif throughout his work is indeed the replacement of territorial notions of *Heimat* with mythical ones.[71] Two of the current corpus texts, *Hiob* and *Radetzkymarsch*, translate Roth's ambivalence to two family histories—the first a traditional Jewish family, the latter three Trotta generations that mirror the Empire's demise. In both, Roth's presumably sentimental nostalgia for a lost *Heimat* reveals itself instead as a subtle critique on the illusory, mythical nature of the fatherland.

Dimitré Dinev's *Engelszungen* harks back to Roth's imperial memories in *Radetzkymarsch*. The similarities between the two novels, as well as Dinev's variation on a theme introduced by Roth, suggest that the former follows in Roth's footsteps, more or less establishing an Austrian-German 'tradition' of post-imperial writing. With more picaresque overtones, though in an equally subversive way as *Radetzkymarsch,* Dinev evokes a "utopia contrary to political reality [gegenläufige Utopie zur politischen Realität],"[72] a reality that determined his childhood and his experiences as an immigrant in Austria.

Born in 1968 in Plovdiv, Bulgaria, Dinev witnessed the political and everyday reality of a life under communist rule. He attended the German-language Bertolt-Brecht-Gymnasium in Pasardschik, where he started writing in Bulgarian and Russian. In the late 1980s, Dinev participated in the oppositional movement against the regime of Todor Shivkov, who was convicted for abuse of power in the early 1990s. The collapse of the socialist regime led to a brief moment of euphoria, as the system was exposed as empty and corrupt. However, in June 1990, former communists, who had refashioned themselves as the 'Bulgarian Socialist Party', won the first free elections with an outright majority. In a matter of days, a disillusioned Dinev decided to leave the country to start a new life in Austria. Conquering the barbed wire fences at the Czech-Austrian border, he came 'crawling' into the country, lived at the Traiskirchen refugee camp, and, for several years, continued to live "crouched down [in geduckter Haltung]," in fear of deportation.[73] Working in temporary employment, Dinev studied Russian philology and philosophy in Vienna. Since 1992, he has been publishing his work in German; it includes prose, drama, screenplays, and radio features. He has received several awards for his debut novel *Engelszungen*, as well as for his short story collection *Ein Licht über dem Kopf* (2005).

About his German proficiency, Dinev explains that it was initially of vital importance when he first came to Austria: "My survival in Austria was dependent on the German language, so I am more dependent on this language than a native author. [Mein Überleben in Österreich war von der deutschen Sprache abhängig, also bin ich von dieser Sprache mehr abhängig als ein einheimischer Autor.]"[74] Nevertheless, Dinev is highly critical of the way language has become a yardstick for the degree of one's integration, while at the same time critics refuse to apply the same principle for literary authors—"One is isolated again, regarded as an exception in literary studies, and categorized into the field of migration literature, instead of being regarded as a natural part of literature. So one is betrayed. [Man wird wieder isoliert, als Sonderfall in der Literaturwissenschaft betrachtet und in den Bereich der Migrationsliteratur eingeordnet, anstatt als natürlicher Teil der Literatur angesehen zu werden. Man wird also verraten."[75] Denouncing the word "author of migration [Migrationsautor]" as really "the ultimate anti-advertising [die ultimative Antiwerbung],"[76] Dinev strongly emphasizes that an author should carefully guard his creative autonomy, unless he is willing to risk being instrumentalized as "showcase migrant [Vorzeigemigrant]."[77] Resisting any notion of *Migrantenliteratur* as itself the symptom of a society that does build on acceptance, exchange, or inclusion, Dinev advocates a notion of integration that combines individual *Verantwortung* and compassion. Rather than an assimilatory trajectory, in which the individual must shed all markers of difference, integration is to be understood as the "lifelong duty of each individual, insofar as one wishes to be part of a society [[l]ebenslange Aufgabe eines jeden Individuums, insofern es Teil einer Gesellschaft sein will]."[78] Yet this responsibility can only be realized in relation to the other. In *Barmherzigkeit* (2010), Dinev further explores the idea in a philosophical reflection on compassion as the one true common language, and the one true "power of the individual [Macht des Einzelnen]."[79] With clear echoes of Lévinas' philosophy of the Other,[80] and also reminiscent of Nancy's 'being singular plural', Dinev recovers the notion from the theological sphere. Compassion, Dinev argues, is a particularly individual privilege, which cannot be instrumentalized for the purpose of ideology or state. Involving a resistance to violence, it cannot serve the founding of a state, which always already implies the *Gewaltakt* of demarcation and exclusion. Compassion, therefore, can grow political—it becomes "the oppositional force *par excellence* [die oppositionelle Kraft schlechthin]"[81]—an idea that seems to permeate *Engelszungen* as well.

In the preface to the serialized newspaper publication of *Radetzkymarsch*, Roth writes that the empire allowed him to be "a patriot and a cosmopolitan at the same time, [...] an Austrian and a German among all Austrian peoples [ein Patriot und Weltbürger zugleich, [...] ein Österreicher und ein Deutscher unter allen österreichischen Völkern]."[82] A primary theme of his novel, however, is that the self-mythologizing tendency of the empire, as well as an implicit German bias, did not really allow the free formation of an identity.[83] Rather, it suggests that the individual is tragically determined by the past and by preceding generations. On the surface, the novel follows, as J.M. Coetzee summarizes, "the fortunes of three generations of the Trotta family, servants of the crown; the first Trotta a simple soldier elevated to the minor nobility for an act of heroism; the second a high provincial administrator; the third an army officer whose life dissolves into futility as the Habsburg mystique loses its hold on him, and who perishes without issue in the war."[84] As this genealogy progresses, it exposes the self-referential nature of an empire desperately seeking to uphold its unity and order. Carl Joseph, who has grown up with the image of an embellished heroic past, fails to take responsibility for a life that appears to have been predefined by his family history. His life serves as evidence of how the imperial myth robs people of their individuality: seeing himself at the mercy of a deterministic course of history, he denies himself both individual agency and responsibility.

In *Engelszungen*, Dinev takes Roth's thematic constellation—imperial allegiance, family heroes, and the power of fiction—beyond the fall of the Iron Curtain into twenty-first-century Vienna.[85] The novel relates the eventful histories of two Bulgarian families, which, as in *Radetzkymarsch*, mirror the history of a country overshadowed by a powerful regime. Eventually focusing on the experiences of the younger sons, Iskren Mladenov and Svetljo Apostolov, the novel traces their attempts at designing their own lives in the two symbolic realms they inhabit—Bulgarian *Realsozialismus* and, later on, Austrian/Western capitalism. The power of speech and fiction reveals itself not just in the orations of party leaders, but also, unlike in *Radetzkymarsch*, as a means of individual agency. The art of storytelling will support the roguish protagonists in their adolescent search for lovers and, especially, after the collapse of the communist regime, when they emigrate to Austria and struggle to survive as undocumented immigrants.

"Listening to the same story"—
Heroic grandfathers and the power of fiction

In the opening lines of the essay "Myth Interrupted," Nancy inserts a family image to highlight the unifying effect of storytelling. Alluding to the comparable narrative origins of religion, ideology, or nationalism, Nancy describes "the scene of myth, the scene of its invention, of its recital and its transmission."[86] The sense of community arising from a shared narrative, he suggests, is thought to resemble an organic family bond:

> We know the scene: there is a gathering, and someone is telling a story. We do not yet know whether these people gathered together form an assembly, if they are a horde or a tribe. But we call them *brothers and sisters* because they are gathered together and because they are listening to the same story. [...] They were not assembled like this before the story; the recitation has gathered them together. Before, they were dispersed [...], shoulder to shoulder, working with and confronting one another without recognizing another.[87]

The power of the word gathers isolated individuals into an assembly, which from that moment on shares a story of their origin. While their family-like community is based on a principle of sameness, the person reciting the story takes up an ambivalent position, right at the border between inclusion and exclusion:

> We do not yet know whether the one speaking is from among them or if he is an outsider. We say that he is one of them, but different from them because he has a gift, or simply the right—or else it is his duty—to tell the story.[88]

Because the authority of storytelling comes at the risk of revealing an 'outside' where alternative sources of meaning exist, the storyteller makes himself redundant. By means of continued recitation, the community incorporates the story as its own:

> He is his own hero, and they, by turns, are the heroes of the tale and the ones who have the right to hear it and the duty to learn it. In the speech of the narrator, their language for the first time serves no other purpose than that of presenting the narrative and of keeping it going.[89]

Heroism and storytelling as the foundation of family-like bonds is an important shared theme of *Radetzkymarsch* and *Engelszungen*. The motif of the family hero brings into focus the narrative aspect of collective identities, as well as the authority involved in storytelling, particularly that of history textbooks. On the other hand, the generational setup of the two novels disturbs images of organic unity conjured by such narratives of origin or common destiny. The novels ask the question if and how individuals can resist the myth of state authority, no matter how 'enlightened' it may present itself. In each text, a family hero and a (grand)son living in his shadow furnish the account of declining imperial and ideological allure. As such, the motif presents an anti-teleological counternarrative to imperial claims at progress, universality, and eternity. Significantly, the crucial figures, i.e. the ones who see through the illusory image of unity and authority, are situated on the margins of social, imperial, and military order: the Jew Max Demant in *Radetzkymarsch* and the undocumented immigrants Svetljo and Iskren in *Engelszungen*. Whereas Roth presents the family hero in a context of eroded formalistic codes that serve to perpetuate the imperial myth, Dinev emphasizes the heroics of storytelling as a subversive and connecting, rather than a mythologizing, strategy.

Roth and Dinev furthermore deploy similar images to underline the unifying effect of 'listening to the same story': the portrait and the military uniform. In *Radetzkymarsch*, a picture of the 'Hero of Solferino'—a last remainder of Joseph von Trotta's life—symbolizes how the myth of his heroism is carried forward into the next generations: "The portrait was and remained the only one ever done of old Trotta. Later it hung in his son's study and even haunted his grandson's imagination. [Das Porträt war und blieb das einzige, was man jemals vom alten Trotta angefertigt hatte. Es hing später im Wohnzimmer seines Sohnes und beschäftigte noch die Phantasie des Enkels...]." (RM 23) Indeed, the example of his legendary grandfather, rather than the person, intrigues Carl Joseph to the extent that his life becomes centered around an idealized image: "The grandson's curiosity constantly focused on his grandfather's blurring figure and vanished fame. [Die Neugier des Enkels kreiste beständig um die erloschene Gestalt und den verschollenen Ruhm des Großvaters.]"[90] (RM 42)

In *Engelszungen*, too, pictures of communist party leaders accompany Svetljo and Iskren in their classrooms. As in *Radetzkymarsch*, the portrait has an educational and exemplary function, symbolizing the authority over the story being told and instilling into the pupils a sense of compliance—"So Svetljo grew and learned, with comrade Shivkov's familiar gaze directed at his dirty fingernails [...]. [So wuchs Svetljo und lernte, mit dem vertrauten Blick des Genossen Shivkov auf seine schmutzigen Fingernägel gerichtet [...]]." (EZ 283–4) Likewise, the portrait of comrade Dimitrov printed on Bulgarian banknotes "smiled at Iskren [...] in various colors [lächelte Iskren [...] in unterschiedlichen Farben an [...]]," which, as the narrator mocks, is not actually an indication of Dimitrov's historical merit, but rather of the party's interference with lives—"[T]he party wanted to be certain, to avoid any kind of misunderstanding, and to state clearly and plainly who was responsible for well-being and smiling in society. [[D]ie Partei wollte sichergehen, jede Art von Mißverständnissen vermeiden und klar und deutlich darauf hinweisen, wer für das Wohl und das Lächeln in der Gesellschaft zuständig war."] (EZ 431)

The pervasive pictorial presence of state authority in both texts is supported by military images such as the uniform—a crucial performative element of allegiance.[91] The Trottas, employed as either military or state officials, are staged as "Kakanian representatives [kakanische Repräsentanten]," and "relics of an era fading away [Relikte einer verwehenden Zeit]."[92] Their adherence to military codes and myths, as Torsten Voß demonstrates, indicates their resistance toward the change of paradigms on the eve of the First World War.[93] The uniform, in this context, further emphasizes their imperial identity, however anachronistic it has become. Similar to the Trottas, Jordan Apostolov and Mladen Mladenov are employed as officials of the Bulgarian *Volkmiliz* and the communist party, respectively. As representatives of both the repressive and the ideological state apparatus, they actively contribute to an image of uniformity that the party upholds and enforces. Furthermore, as I will illustrate, they derive a strong sense of identity from their endorsement of the regime, to the extent that they lose their individuality. In both novels, then, the portrait and the military theme highlight a desire for 'immanence', shaping both imperial myth and communist ideology and driving individuals to dissolve into the homogeneity of collective identity.[94]

In what follows, I will focus, for the two novels separately, on manifestations of this desire: firstly, the motif of the family hero as an element of imperial myth-making in *Radetzkymarsch*, and secondly, the 'language of the people' as an expression of 'absolute community' in *Engelszungen*. Despite different historical contexts and novelistic approaches, Dinev and Roth bring into view the destructive effects of the strong communal desire for a closed identity.

Heroism in demise: *Radetzkymarsch*

Ever since it was published, *Radetzkymarsch* has occupied critics with the question of its historical accuracy.[95] The novel steers an ironic course between idealization and reality, between fiction and fact, between "a sense of possibility and a sense of reality [*Möglichkeitssinn* and *Wirklichkeitssinn*]."[96] In one of the earliest reactions to the novel, Georg Lukács brings up this historicity paradox—which Magris would later summarize as the 'Habsburg myth'—in a remarkable way:

> The great artistic value of this work, even though it does not emerge from the ideological weakness of the author, is still strongly connected to it. If Roth had not had his illusions, he could hardly have succeeded in looking so profoundly into the world of his officials and officers, and in depicting so completely and truthfully the process of their moral and social decay.

> [[D]er große künstlerische Wert dieses Werkes ist, wenn er auch nicht aus der ideologischen Schwäche des Autors hervorgeht, so doch damit stark verbunden. Hätte Roth nicht seine Illusionen, so hätte es ihm kaum gelingen können, so tief in die Welt seiner Beamten und Offiziere hineinzublicken und so voll und ganz und wahrhaftig den Prozeß ihres sittlichen und sozialen Verfall darzustellen.][97]

Lukács makes two rather bold assumptions: first, that because Roth depicts the empire in a convincing way, he must have shared in its illusory tendency; second, that the novel claims to be a realistic historical depiction of imperial downfall. It is doubtful that Roth really was led by 'illusions' or 'ideological weakness'. Conceived between 1930 and 1932, at a time when Nazis were gaining political ground, Roth may have been inclined to mourn the vanished Habsburg world of his childhood, a world in which modern nationalism and the atrocities of modern warfare had not yet presented themselves. As Kati Tonkin writes, "[f]or Roth, the privilege of one element of identity—the national—over all others lay at the root of all postwar problems."[98] Still, it has been demonstrated time and again that even despite hints of nostalgia, Roth does not shy away from satire and subtle criticism.[99] As for the historical and realist claim, *Radetzkymarsch* actually reveals itself as a transitional novel: it introduces a modernist aesthetics, and it questions the plausibility of realist convention.[100] The real artistic value of the novel, then, is rather the opposite of Lukács's description: Roth skillfully creates an illusion of historical realism and, in doing so, subverts the categories of historicity and realism themselves. Paradoxically, the novel thus aligns with Lukács's own definition of the historical novel, which he does not consider to be "the retelling of great historical events" but a mediated form that allows readers to

> re-experience the social and human motives which led men to think, feel and act just as they did in historical reality. And it is a law of literary portrayal which first appears paradoxical, but then quite obvious, that in order to bring out these social and human motives of behaviour, the outwardly insignificant events, "the smaller [...] relationships are better suited than the great monumental dramas of world history."[101]

In other words, Roth's novel does not claim to demonstrate a historical truth but, rather, explores history to discover insight via fiction.

The opening chapter is remarkably brief, yet of critical importance to the reader's understanding of the rest of the novel. Like an exemplum,[102] it introduces the major themes, as well as the origins of the foundational myth that determines the rise and fall of the Trottas. Almost like an encyclopedia entry, concise and factual, the introductory sentences create the impression of a historical narrative told by an omniscient narrator:

> The Trottas were a young dynasty. Their progenitor had been knighted after the Battle of Solferino. He was a Slovene. Sipolje—the German name for his native village—became his title of nobility. Fate had elected him for a special deed. But he then made sure that later times lost all memory of him.
>
> [Die Trottas waren ein junges Geschlecht. Ihr Ahnherr hatte nach der Schlacht bei Solferino den Adel bekommen. Er war Slowene. Sipolje—der Name des Dorfes, aus dem er stammte—wurde sein Adelsprädikat. Zu einer besondern Tat hatte ihn das Schicksal ausersehn. Er aber sorgte dafür, daß ihn die späteren Zeiten aus dem Gedächtnis verloren.] (RM 5)

The introduction already confronts the conflicting world views that traverse the novel. On the one hand, there is a premodern narrative of heroism, aristocratic honor, and belief in an inherent order depicted as fate, which collides, on the other hand, with a notion of individual agency. The final sentence, although not obvious at first, also hints at the potential unreliability of historical narrative. As the chapter progresses, it becomes clear that, despite his efforts to intervene in historiography, Trotta in fact has no influence whatsoever over the way he will be remembered.

The initial chapter introduces two additional themes: the question of identity in the multiethnic Empire and the generational patterns that connect the past and the present.[103] These elements shape the central theme of heroism in demise, which constitutes an anti-teleological counternarrative to imperial myth. Firstly, it illustrates a process of degeneration subverting the imperial claim to eternity. The continued reference to the grandfather's act of heroism is a circular gesture that does not take into account chance occurrences or simply the changes inherent in generational evolution. For degeneration is an integral part of evolution: it is "a progressive movement that increases over generations, thus connecting the futurizing character of the generation with the idea of waste and destruction [eine durch die Generationen hindurch zunehmende, fortschreitende Bewegung und verknüpft so den futurisierenden Charakter der Generation mit der Idee von Abfall und Ende]."[104] Secondly, the narrative of the empire's demise as an inevitable historical destiny is unmasked as an imposed narrative order. The eroded family hero thus exposes—'interrupts', as Nancy calls it—the mythical foundations of the empire.

An accidental hero

Roth's narrator goes on to describe the Battle of Solferino, in which Lieutenant Joseph von Trotta rescues Emperor Franz Joseph from being shot. When the emperor comes onto the battlefield, asking for field glasses, Trotta senses imminent danger: someone raising binoculars draws attention to the Emperor's higher rank, thus making him a target. Trotta's heroic act consists of his receiving a bullet intended for the *Kaiser*. Adding to the impression that Trotta and the Emperor are interchangeable—they also share a part of their names—is Trotta's instinct, which betrays his complete, corporeal identification with the empire. He fears the Emperor's death as his own, and by extension the collapse of the Empire as the end of the world as he knows it—"Terror at the inconceivable, immeasurable catastrophe that would destroy Trotta, the regiment, the army, the state, the entire world drove burning chills through his body. His knees quaked. [Die Angst vor der unausdenkbaren, der grenzenlosen Katastrophe, die ihn selbst, das Regiment, die Armee, den Staat, die ganze Welt vernichten würde, jagte glühende Fröste durch seinen Körper. Seine Knie zitterten.]" (RM 6) In contrast to the narrator's earlier factual description, which offered no insight into Trotta's consciousness, the significance of his emotions is now brought to the fore. The heroic rescue reflects his instinctive and physical conformity with the imperial order—precisely the kind of unconditional identification of which Roth was suspicious.[105] Yet while his reflexes suggest that Trotta's belief system is entirely congruent with the imperial order, he soon grows uncomfortable with his loyalty, because it alienates him from his modest Slovenian background and, most of all, because his absolute 'truth' reveals itself to have no basis in reality. The rescue may represent a culmination of identification, it signals the beginning of Trotta's estrangement at the same time.

The ironic distance in the narrator's account is a first indication that Trotta's allegiance is more problematic than it seems. Despite his omniscience, he fails to provide the year in which the battle took place (1859), nor does he point out its symbolic importance to the unity of the Habsburg Empire: it was the first battle lost to the principle of national self-determination.[106] Furthermore, his ironic description of the actual rescue does not quite distort historical 'truth', but it is nonetheless indicative of his wavering impartiality. As the only historical character in the novel, the emperor serves as "the interface of fiction and history,"[107] yet his portrayal suggests that history and fiction do not align. When the emperor arrives at the battlefield, he is presented, in a slightly mocking tone, as a god-like apparition. While the introductory paragraph led one to believe that his rescue was determined by fate, the narrator presents it instead as a succession of chance occurrences and even clumsy actions:

> And the eternal grudge of the subaltern frontline officer against the high-ranking staff officers [...] dictated the action that indelibly stamped the lieutenant's name on the history of his regiment. Both his hands reached toward the monarch's shoulders in order to push him down. The lieutenant probably grabbed too hard; the Kaiser promptly fell. His escorts hurled themselves upon the falling man. That same instant, a shot bored through the lieutenant's left shoulder, the very shot meant for the Kaiser's heart. As the emperor rose, the lieutenant sank.
>
> [[D]er ewige Groll des subalternen Frontoffiziers gegen die hohen Herren des Generalstabs [...] diktierte dem Leutnant jene Handlung, die seinen Namen unauslöslich in die Geschichte seines Regiments einprägte. Er griff mit beiden Händen nach den Schultern des Monarchen, um ihn niederzudrücken. Der Leutnant hatte wohl zu stark angefaßt. Der Kaiser fiel sofort um. Die Begleiter stürzten auf den Fallenden. In diesem Augenblick durchbohrte ein Schuß die linke Schulter des Leutnants, jener Schuß eben, der dem Herzen des Kaisers gegolten hatte. Während er sich erhob, sank der Leutnant nieder. (RM 6)

Should the sequence of events have taken a different course, Trotta's action might have been considered as insubordinate, since he acts on a grudge towards his careless superiors. Furthermore, the explicit mention of the random moment at which the bullet is fired—"that same instant [[i]n diesem Augenblick]"— suggests that Trotta's heroism is entirely coincidental. The narrator's "implied privileging of contingency over causality," as Landwehr notes, "undermines the concept of fate as a cosmic or historical force [...]."[108] It exposes *Schicksal* as a projected historical and narrative order, rather than intrinsic to reality.

"In fremden Stiefeln": a reluctant hero

The discrepancy between contingent reality and its recuperation in terms of causality, fate, and honor is the source of Trotta's estrangement. Ennobled for his rescue, Trotta is absorbed into an imperial narrative that adheres to an anachronistic and formalistic code of honor. Now a member of the German-speaking minor nobility, Hauptmann Joseph Trotta von Sipolje feels uncomfortable in his new role, "as if his own life had been traded for a new and alien life manufactured in a workshop [[a]ls hätte man ihm sein eigenes Leben gegen ein fremdes, neues, in einer Werkstatt angefertigtes vertauscht], and as if "he had been sentenced to wear another man's boots for life [er von nun ab sein Leben lang verurteilt [wäre], in fremden Stiefeln auf einem glatten Boden zu wandeln [...]]." (RM 7–8) Sentenced by "an incomprehensible destiny [das unbegreifliche Schicksal]," Trotta experiences his new identity—the official confirmation of his imperial loyalty—as fabricated and inauthentic. Previously, he considered the rank of lieutenant to be "natural and suitable [natürlich und angemessen]" for the son of an *Unteroffizier* and *Wachtmeister*, and the grandson of a peasant (RM 8). Now, he now stumbles around in unfamiliar boots—his ennoblement having uprooted the modesty of his descent, as well as his sense of intergenerational continuity: "But to the decorated, aristocratic captain, who went about in the alien and almost unearthly radiance of imperial favor as in a golden cloud, his own father had suddenly moved far away. [Dem adeligen und ausgezeichneten Hauptmann aber, der im fremden und fast unheimlichen Glanz der kaiserlichen Gnade umherging wie in einer goldenen Wolke, war der leibliche Vater plotz ferngerückt [...]." (RM 8) At first sight, the Trottas' family history simply mirrors the empire's gradual disintegration. More significantly, though, it is a reflection on the effects of myth-making and allegiance, be it national or supranational. The increasing estrangement of the Trottas exposes the effects of loyalty to an empire that seeks to sustain itself through an anachronistic code of honor, and it illustrates that unconditional dedication to the fatherland, no matter how diverse and tolerant to a range of identities it may be, divides rather than unites people.

In the introductory lines, Trotta's pre-Solferino identity is stated straightforwardly as "He was a Slovene. [Er war Slowene.]" But the simplicity of the statement belies a complex problem of national sentiment in an ostensibly supranational organization. When the recently ennobled Trotta visits his father in the country, who lives in most humble circumstances, he is portrayed in hyperbolic terms as an out-of-place "military god, wearing a gleaming officer's scarf [militärischer Gott, mit glitzernder Feldbinde]" (RM 10). Furthermore, a conspicuous contrast between registers highlights the rigidity of military code, on the one hand, and the elusive character of memory, sentiment, and familiarity on the other. Trotta's obligatory audience with the emperor is summarized succinctly, in accordance with the formal character of military ceremony. Its hurried and factual rendition—reminiscent of the *Neue Sachlichkeit* which Roth denounced, but with which he has often been associated[109]—stands out from a more poetic register. His father's house is described in slower, novelistic language brimming with color and detail. The stark contrast between Trotta's shining armor and his father's mundane life furthermore corresponds to their linguistic estrangement. His father does not address him in his Slovenian mother tongue but in the German *Amtssprache* that he only speaks with a heavy accent:

> Just five years ago he had still been speaking Slovenian to his son, although the boy understood only a few words and never produced a single one himself. But today it might strike the old man as an audacious intimacy to hear his mother tongue used by his son, who had been removed so far by the grace of Fate and Emperor, while the captain focused on the father's lips in order to greet the first Slovenian sound as a familiar remoteness and lost homeyness.
>
> [Vor fünf Jahren noch hatte er zu seinem Sohn slowenisch gesprochen, obwohl der Junge nur ein paar Worte verstand und nicht ein einziges selbst hervorbrachte. Heute aber mochte dem Alten der Gebrauch seiner Muttersprache von dem so weit durch die Gnade des Schicksals und des Kaisers entrückten Sohn als eine gewagte Zutraulichkeit erscheinen, während der Hauptmann auf die Lippen des Vaters achtete, um den ersten slowenischen Laut zu begrüßen, wie etwas vertraut Fernes und verloren Heimisches.] (RM 10–11)

Trotta looks for a sense of familiarity in his father's mother tongue, but their difference in rank does not allow it, establishing their estrangement. But what is more, by refusing to speak Slovenian, "the father is symbolically excluding him from Slovenian identity, or preventing him from having recourse to this identity."[110] Again, the younger Trotta understands their estrangement as an inevitable intervention of fate. But since he himself barely speaks Slovenian, it becomes clear that a generation gap was already developing before Trotta's ennoblement.[111] The formal confirmation of his imperial allegiance thus crowns a gradual alienation from his Slovenian forebears. His close ties to a political body, even to one as diverse as Austria-Hungary, comes with partial identity loss: "Captain Trotta was severed from the long procession of his Slavic peasant forebears. [Losgelöst war der Hauptmann Trotta von dem langen Zug seiner bäuerlichen slawischen Vorfahren.]" (RM 11) The only remainder from his family history is the formalistic marker of his Slovene origin in his new title: Sipolje.

Trotta's estrangement reveals a powerful undercurrent at work within the empire. Despite its banner of supranationality, being a loyal Austrian implied being free from national sentiment only to a limited extent. Trotta's linguistic alienation suggests that his dedication to the fatherland requires relinquishing parts of one's identity in favor of a profile oriented on a German intellectual horizon. As Tonkin points out, the monarchy "recognized German as the language of culture, and its bureaucrats, while they were not German nationalists, 'never supposed that the empire could be anything other than a German state.'"[112] While Trotta increasingly embodies imperial allegiance, as confirmed by its code of honor, he has also grown estranged from his Slovenian background. He may consider the distance from his forebears as just one of the machinations of an incomprehensible fate, but what is really at work is an imperial tendency towards 'immanence'—a desirable idea of unity believed to be more powerful than the nationalist stirrings emerging across the empire.

"Ritter der Wahrheit": an anachronistic hero

Radetzkymarsch engages the reader in a game of truth and fiction that renders unconditional loyalty to a political formation as a matter of belief in a narrative construct—a construct that, in accordance with the narrator's ironic puncturing of the illusion of historical realism, is exposed as imperial myth. Just like readers let themselves be persuaded by a narrative order of causality or *Schicksal*, so too does the empire achieve unity by imposing a narrative of natural order.

The different registers, of military order on the one hand and of contingent events and sentiment on the other, convey a modernist consciousness struggling with the notion of representation. As Trotta corresponds with his father after his rescue act, he is struck by his inability to render his extraordinary experience and personal reflections in a soldier's mundane language and letter format:

> But now, especially since his new rank exempted him from the old rotation, how should he refashion the official epistolary form, which was designed for a whole military lifetime, and how should he intersperse the standardized sentences with unusual statements about conditions that had become unusual and that he himself had barely grasped?
>
> [Wie aber sollte man jetzt, zumal da man dank dem neuen Rang nicht mehr den alten Turnus mitmachte, die gesetzmäßige, für ein ganzes Soldatenleben berechnete Form der Briefe ändern und zwischen die normierten Sätze ungewöhnliche Mitteilungen von ungewöhnlich gewordenen Verhältnissen rücken, die man selbst noch kaum begriffen hatte?] (RM 9)

Trotta's inability to communicate effectively with his father foreshadows a process of intergenerational estrangement, culminating in Carl Joseph's uneventful, unheroic death. The passage can also be read as a metafictional comment, drawing attention to the rendering of imperial disintegration in a coherent narrative construct. Most significantly, though, it refers to a fissure at the foundations of the empire. As a self-proclaimed Enlightened organization, it relies on a belief in the coherence and orderliness of reality, in "berechnete Form" and "normiert[e] Sätze." It is however an outdated aristocratic code that fails to account for the unexpected, the unreliable, the unquantifiable, and thus fails to contain emerging desire for national self-determination. This tension between an increasingly fragmented modern reality and a belief in natural order—be it Enlightened or premodern—lies at the root of the crumbling myth.

The self-mythologizing mechanism becomes painfully evident to Trotta, when he discovers that his son's history book relates the events of the Battle of Solferino in a distorted way—"[B]ut how utterly transformed! [Aber in welcher Verwandlung!]" (RM 13). As opposed to the earlier depiction of successive clumsy actions and mistakes on the part of the emperor's men, the book presents an embellished and historicized version of events.[113] Guns have been replaced with swinging sabers, so as to create the illusion of a grand historical battle. The emperor is not a passive observer but a dauntless fighter, who assesses the danger of the situation himself. "At that moment of supreme need [In diesem Augenblick der höchsten Not [...]]," as the textbook says, Trotta's intervention is not depicted as a fortuitous action but as born out of necessity or fate (RM 13). Enraged by the falsehood of textbook history, Trotta sets out to correct the lie—"And now began the martyrdom of Captain Joseph Trotta von Sipolje, the Knight of Truth. [Und nun begann das Martyrium des Hauptmanns Joseph Trotta, Ritter von Sipolje, des Ritters der Wahrheit.]" (RM 15) Yet when he attempts to explain the abuse to a notary, he is at a loss of words, thus giving, implicitly and inadvertently, credit to the fictionalized rendition: "He should have brought the primer along. With that odious object in hand, he would have had a far easier time explaining things. [Er hätte das Lesebuch mitnehmen müssen. Mit diesem odiosen Gegenstand in Händen wäre ihm die Erklärung bedeutend leichter gefallen.]" (RM 14) Indeed, even as a knight of truth, he submits to the authority of fabrication. His insistence on the absolute truth thus becomes a futile, if not ridiculous quest—much like Don Quixote's, another knight who is all alone is his chase after anachronistic standards.[114]

Trotta's futile mission to restore the truth conveys his lack of individual agency within the imperial order. The ministry of education, as well as the emperor himself, advise Trotta to just let things be. Lies, they suggest in resignation, are an inherent part of the imperial structure:

"Listen, my dear Trotta!" said the Kaiser. "The whole business is rather awkward. But neither of us comes off all that badly. Let it be!" "Your Majesty," replied the captain, "it's a lie!" "People tell a lot of lies," the Kaiser confirmed.

["Sehn Sie zu, lieber Trotta!" sagte der Kaiser. "Die Sache ist recht unangenehm. Aber schlecht kommen wir beide dabei nicht weg! Lassen S' die Geschicht'!" "Majestät," erwiderte der Hauptmann, "es ist eine Lüge!" "Es wird viel gelogen," bestätigte der Kaiser.] (RM 16–7)

The words "Let it be! [Lassen S' die Geschicht'!]"—repeated twice, and furthermore marked as "fatherly [väterlich]" (RM 16)—really seem to imply that one cannot and should not intervene in the course of history—although, ironically, Trotta has been decorated with the Maria-Theresien-Orden, rewarding a soldier's self-initiative in the battlefield.[115] The 'Ritter der Wahrheit', now incorporated into the myth indefinitely, cannot escape the imperial grasp, even when he requests to be discharged from army duty to retire in the country— "Imperial favor did not abandon him. [Die kaiserliche Gnade verließ ihn nicht.]" (RM 17) Much to his discontent, the emperor assigns a large sum of money for the education of Trotta's son and elevates Trotta himself to the rank of Baron— gifts he accepts "sullenly, as insults [mißmutig [...], wie Beleidigungen]." (RM 17) At the emperor's request, the fictionalized passage eventually disappears from the history books. Nevertheless, the ghost of Trotta, "the unknown bearer of ephemeral fame [der unbekannte Träger früh verschollenen Ruhms]," (RM 18) will haunt future generations, his grandson Carl Joseph in particular. Whereas the 'Ritter der Wahrheit' still attempted to resist the empire's self-referential myth, his grandson fails to discern it altogether.

In *Radetzkymarsch*, the demise of the family hero exposes the mythical foundations of the empire. It subverts the myth of supranationality by revealing an implicit German bias at the heart of imperial bureaucracy and military. Secondly, the imperial claim to historical necessity and its pretension of representing a natural order are revealed as fictions. Its ostensibly enlightened and supranational structure leaves no room for self-determination and requires the dissolution of autonomy in favor of imperial order. Paradoxically, the novel suggests, the empire's disintegration was caused precisely by its stifling insistence on unity and self-preservation: it drove constituent peoples to act on their right to self-determination, which culminated in the violent triumph of nationalist differences.

The language of the people: *Engelszungen*

"[S]tumm, doch verläßlicher als jedes Lehrbuch [...]"
Engelszungen opens quite literally on the shards of the Austro-Hungarian Empire. At the *Wiener Zentralfriedhof*, we are introduced to the grave of Miro, a framework figure to which the opening and closing chapters are dedicated.[116] His remarkable grave is located in a prominent alley of the cemetery, and is "surrounded by the best, most honorable company [[v]on bester, ehrenwertester Gesellschaft [...] umgeben]." (EZ 7) The description of the grave's surroundings explicitly connects the novel to the vanished world of the Austro-Hungarian Empire, and furthermore the mention of the questionable reliability of history textbooks is a clear reference to Roth's novel:

> A Danube-Swabian poetess, whose voice, silent for many years now, flowed only like an underground river, lay beside him. A few widowed countesses also lay beside Miro, who now could finally discard their widowhood in the earth, like the *k.u.k.* officers their medals. For there were also *k.u.k.* officers there, scattered around Miro like heavy shrapnel. A *k.u.k.* lieutenant-colonel of the artillery, who couldn't hear any cannons any more, a *k.u.k.* staff physician, who no longer needed to treat his deafness. [...] Surrounded by artists, officers, and high officials who reflected Austrian history silently and yet more reliably than any textbook, Miro rested.
>
> [Eine donauschwäbische Dichterin, deren Stimme, seit vielen Jahren still geworden, nur noch wie ein unterirdischer Fluß dahinfloß, lag neben ihm. Auch einige verwitwete Gräfinnen lagen neben Miro, die sich ihrer Witwenschaft nun endlich in der Erde entledigen konnten, so wie die k.u.k. Offiziere ihrer Orden. Denn es lagen dort auch k.u.k. Offiziere, zerstreut um Miro wie große Granatsplitter. Ein k.u.k. Oberstleutnant der Artillerie, der keine Kanonen mehr hören konnte, ein k.u.k. Generalstabsarzt, der seine Taubheit nicht mehr zu behandeln brauchte. [...] Umgeben von Künstlern, Offizieren und hohen Beamten, die die österreichische Geschichte stumm, doch verläßlicher als jedes Lehrbuch widerspiegelten, ruhte Miro.] (EZ 7–8)[117]

During his lifetime, Miro was a cunning businessman and criminal, but now he is the guardian angel of Vienna's immigrants, who will provide them with residence and work permits. His transfiguration into an angel introduces a picaresque reversal of truths characteristic of the rest of the novel. His birthplace and his parents unknown, Miro has led a nomadic existence, unfettered by family or descent. With a biblical reference to immaculate conception—"'A virgin has given birth to me.' ['Eine Jungfrau hat mich geboren.']"—he elevates his marginalized existence to a universal theme: "No matter where I go, I'm at home. No matter where I arrive, I am a guest. [Egal, wo ich hingehe, bin ich zuhaus. Egal, wo ich ankomme, bin ich ein Gast.]"; "We're all just guests on this earth. [Wir sind alle nur Gäste auf dieser Erde.]" (EZ 10) Just like the surrounding widows and officers who, in death, have rid themselves of all markers of status and rank, so too does Miro represent a notion of impermanence, a reminder that in birth and death all are alike. His grave provides a safe, unbiased haven for the stories that have shaped the postcommunist Austrian past—the most singular stories of immigrants and war refugees. It is at Miro's grave that Bulgarian immigrants Svetljo and Iskren encounter each other for the first time, both in desperate need of help and money. Yet Miro's grave is not just a place of naive worship for those who have "nothing left to smile about, nothing to hope for [nichts mehr zu lachen und zu hoffen [...]]." (EZ 11) It has become an almost sacred space of encounter and storytelling. Countless fresh flowers on his grave are evidence of how many people from different nations come to his grave and leave again with their "shadows [...] much firmer and denser, their faces much brighter [Schatten [...] viel fester und dichter [...], ihre Gesichter viel heller]." (EZ 11) Miro listens to the unique histories of the utterly hopeless which—like the *k.u.k.* artists, widows, and officials—narrate Austrian history in a more reliable or at least more authentic way than history textbooks.

Whereas *Radetzkymarsch* is constructed around the divergence of a linear-genealogical narrative from a circular, self-referential myth, *Engelszungen* alternates between two family histories that repeatedly touch and briefly intertwine. The dialectical framework puts the individual stories in a wider historical and philosophical perspective, as it brings to mind the notion of historical determinism present in the communist ideology. As in *Radetzkymarsch*, the generational motif in *Engelzungen* challenges a belief that the course of history depends on predetermined patterns. Against the backdrop of Bulgaria's communist history, the novel arrives dialectically at a truth of human interconnection and *Barmherzigkeit* that transcends all antitheses—between ideologies, between state-imposed determinism and individual responsibility.

Another parallel to *Radetzkymarsch* involves the relationship between truth and fiction. In *Radetzkymarsch*, Roth's modernist narrative game punctures an illusion at the heart of the Austro-Hungarian Empire. Dinev's text focuses instead on the redeeming and subversive potential of narration and fiction. Woven into the two family histories are—beside the history of the Bulgarian *Volksrepublik*—various aspects of storytelling, belief in fiction, and intergenerational communication—a thematic focus Dinev associates with his indebtedness to Bulgarian oral culture: "Everything is done much more immediately, [...] in Bulgaria you do not get analytical answers, you tell a story as an answer instead. Or you simply do not give an answer at all and just tell a story. [Alles geschieht viel unmittelbarer, [...] man bekommt in Bulgarien keine analytischen Antworten, sondern man erzählt als Antwort eine Geschichte. Oder man gibt gleich gar keine Antwort und erzählt nur eine Geschichte.]"[118] Highlighting the importance of language and speech, both the motif of the tongue[119] and the multilayered title *Engelszungen*[120] reveal the novel's focus on narrative connection as a subversive power. Throughout the novel, the many variations of narrative—or mute—bonds between family members defy the unifying narrative of communist ideology as embodied by the father figures. The expression *mit Engelszungen reden*[121] refers to an act of persuasion through eloquence, reminiscent of the propagandistic orations by party leaders.[122] Furthermore, the title contains a religious dimension involving the opposite of eloquence: it might be associated with glossolalia, or its biblical equivalent 'speaking in tongues', or to 'angelic tongues'. Adding to these Christian, Jewish, and occult references, the tongue motif also comes to symbolize a language of silent communication and love.[123] The title thus imagines a multitude of voices that confront the propagandastic narrative, resisting its desire for uniformity. Not even members of the one truly 'organic' community, as the family motif underscores, keep listening to the same story; it is a multitude of stories and beliefs that shape families, generations, and history.

 The Mladenovs and Apostolovs each represent one of the two pillars of the communist regime, the same ones as featured in *Radetzkymarsch*: bureaucracy and the military. The Mladenovs' story primarily focuses on Iskren and his parents Mladen and Dorothea. Mladen is a high-ranking party official, focused solely on climbing the communist career ladder. He is a gifted orator, whose speeches impress even comrade Shivkov. Mladen is in love with the high-class prostitute Isabella but is married to Dorothea, a Chekov-quoting actress struggling with career and mental health. Their son Iskren is held to be an intelligent young boy—"he started to speak very early on [er habe sehr früh zu reden angefangen]." (EZ 197) Iskren's childhood revolves around the magic of storytelling and imagination, which contrasts with his father's insistence on a good, traditional education—a German education in Plovdiv, in particular.[124] His grandmother Sdravka, who takes over the maternal role from the often absent Dorothea, shares with Iskren her love for cinema. She takes him on her visits to the grave of her husband, to whom she continues to tell stories. Cinema and conversations beyond the grave afford her a sense—albeit an imaginary one—of the connection and agency missing from her life. (EZ 97) During his frequent visits to his grandfather's grave, Iskren learns how to read and to write. His inherited love for the imagination will prove essential later in life.

If the Mladenovs represent a 'bourgeois' class, the Apostolovs represent their counterpart in *Kleinbürgertum*. Svetljo's father Jordan works as a loyal interrogator for the secret service of the *Volksmiliz*. He is famous for his uncanny ability to get suspects to talk: "He could make anyone talk. Since he lacked the words himself, he easily pulled them out of other people. [...] 'He can even make iron talk', his colleagues said admiringly and yet not without disgust. [Er konnte jeden zum Reden bringen. Da ihm selber die Worte fehlten, holte er sie leicht aus den anderen heraus. [...] 'Er kann sogar das Eisen zum Reden bringen', sagten die Kollegen voller Bewunderung und doch nicht ohne Abscheu von ihm.]" (EZ 52–3) His son Svetljo, as opposed to Iskren, refuses to speak for a very long time, until the age of five. His first words are a subversive truth disguised as a joke: "'Comrade Shivkov poops from below and from above', Svetljo said and laughed. [Der Genosse Shivkov kackt von unten und von oben', sagte Svetljo und lachte.]" (EZ 160) Svetljo is named after his famous grandfather Svetlin, "like the partisan, like the hero [so wie der Partisan, so wie der Held]." (EZ 61) But Svetlin's fame as a hero, it turns out, has no basis in reality. Reminiscent of Trotta's accidental heroism, which at least still consisted of a real rescue, Svetlin's is a fortunate coincidence of circumstances, which he transforms into a heroic story. When the anti-fascist, mostly pro-Communist Partisan movement arrived in his village,[125] Svetlin rides the wave of its increasing popularity, by 'joining' them in a most opportunistic way:

> He had sensed in time which way the wind was blowing, had hidden in the corn field with a rusty pistol and a Stalin photo [...]. When the partisans passed by, he had joined them [...]. From now on he could no longer be separated from the partisans. One night a vineyard guard had shot him in the thigh. Svetlin said that he had suffered the bullet wound while pursuing a fascist and thus became a hero.
>
> [Er hatte rechtzeitig gerochen, woher der Wind wehte, hatte sich mit einer rostigen Pistole und einem Stalin-Foto im Maisfeld versteckt [...]. Als dann die Partisanen vorbeigekommen waren, hatte er sich zu ihnen gesellt [...]. Von nun an war er nicht mehr von den Partisanen zu trennen. Eines nachts hatte ein Weinbergwächter auf ihn geschossen und seinen Oberschenkel getroffen.

Svetlin sagte, er habe die Schußwunde bei der Verfolgung eines Faschisten ab-
bekommen und wurde zum Helden.] (EZ 44)

Svetlin's opportunistic allegiance lays the foundations for the picaresque overtones of the novel.[126] Both Svetljo and Iskren grow up to become impostors and masters of deception. Inventiveness, storytelling, and impersonation will guide them as anti-heroes through the hardship of an immigrant's existence.

'Absolute community'—*Bildsamkeit* as compliance

As agents of the "ideological state apparatus" and the "repressive state apparatus,"[127] party official Mladen Mladenov and member of the *Volksmiliz* Jordan Apostolov embody the mythical foundations of the regime, illustrating the de-individualizing effects of propaganda. The speech motif renders them as products of a totalitarian desire to establish a homogenous people. Depicted as, respectively, producer and recipient of the 'myth' of the people's voice, Mladen and Jordan's allegiance comes with a symptomatic absence of individuality, revealing the "will of community"[128] that governs communist authority. As personifications of the connection between speech, myth, and community, both father figures can be interpreted as exponents of what Nancy calls the "absolute community":

> Absolute community—myth—is not so much the total fusion of individuals, but the *will* of community: the desire to operate, through the power of myth, the communion that myth represents and that it represents as a communion or communication of wills. Fusion ensues: myth represents multiple existences as immanent to its own unique fiction, which gathers them together and gives them their common figure in its speech and as this speech. This does not mean only that community is a myth, that communitarian communion is a myth. It means that myth and myth's force and foundation are essential to community and that there can be, therefore, no community outside of myth.[129]

In a personal meeting, Shivkov compliments Mladen's ability to persuade: "'This person has an angel's tongue, says everyone who has heard it. [Dieser Mensch hat eine Engelszunge, erzählt mir jeder, der sie gehört hat.]'" Mladen's remarkable response reveals not just his unfamiliarity with figurative language, but also his de-individualized position in the system: "'I have tasted beef and veal and lamb tongue. But I do not know what an angel's tongue is and what it can be used

for, Comrade Shivkov. I simply speak the language of the people, that's all' [...].
[Ich habe schon Rinds- und Kalbs- und Lammszunge gekostet. Aber was eine Engelszunge ist und wofür man sie verwenden kann, weiß ich nicht, Genosse Shivkov. Ich rede einfach mit der Sprache des Volkes, das ist alles' [...].]" (EZ 333–4) Mladen embodies an illusory correspondence between people and state. Obviously, as a party official, Mladen does not really address the people as if he were one of them—he speaks "mit," rather than "in" the language of the people. Still, by reducing the multitude of individualized voices to the idea of a single 'language', the state creates the impression of full, integral communion of people and state. As Nancy writes, "myth is essential to community—but only in the sense that it completes it and gives it the closure and the destiny of an individual, of a completed totality."[130] Mladen's speeches thus perform the power of the myth, fusing singular people into apparent unity, at the expense of even his own individuality: his humble self-assessment, as well as his lack of imagination, are signs of his compliance with party expectations.

Reminiscent of Roth's imperial myth—the 'imperial favor' that leaves the knight of truth powerless—the communist system is governed by an irrational force that Mladen is aware of, though he cannot escape or oppose it. He can merely seek out the margins where these uncanny forces at least still have the shape of law and order:

> He knew the laws of authority, and he preferred to wander far from their center. Not too far, but also not too close, for he did not know the center, nobody knew the center. There were no laws there, there were only forces.
>
> [[E]r kannte die Gesetze der Macht, und er bewegte sich lieber weit weg von ihrem Zentrum. Nicht zu weit, aber auch nicht zu nahe, denn das Zentrum kannte er nicht, das Zentrum kannte keiner. Dort gab es keine Gesetze, dort gab es nur Kräfte.] (EZ 104–5)

While these forces—the 'will of community'—may drive the individual to the margins, it will remain in its sphere of influence and thus powerless to assert itself. Even when Mladen's ambitions—a sign of his individual desire—are thwarted by the system, he cannot step outside of the myth, as it is the only source of meaning that exists in the absolute community.[131] He assuages his disappointment by repeating the communist motto, thus reinforcing the perceived necessity of collectivism: "After all, it was better to work collectively. And what exactly is an individual compared to that? A collective is always more powerful, and the mass of the proletariat is the most powerful. [Man arbeitete ja besser im Kollektiv. Was ist dagegen ein Individuum? Ein Kollektiv ist immer stärker und die Masse des Proletariats am stärksten.]" (EZ 99)

Jordan Apostolov is positioned at the receiving end of the regime's propaganda. As his name suggests, he is, like an apostle, "captivated by the power of words [von der Macht der Worte gefangen]." (EZ 152) Because his father Svetlin did not see much potential in his son, he sent him to join the *Volksmiliz*, acknowledging that Jordan, with his "strong muscles, cheeky tongue, and meager intellect [starke Muskeln, eine freche Zunge und wenig Verstand]" (EZ 45), would become the ideal, compliant state official. Jordan's education is a training in complete identification, as illustrated by his perfectly tailored uniform: "[H]e had received a new, blue, magical uniform that not only shrouded him, but also filled his life with content. [[E]r hatte eine neue, blaue, magische Uniform bekommen, die ihn nicht nur umhüllte, sondern sein Leben mit Inhalt füllte.]" (EZ 45–6) As in *Radetzkymarsch*, the uniform symbolizes utter conformity to state authority. Listening to one of Shivkov's speeches, in which secret service officials are praised as "the most faithful sons [[die] treuesten Söhn[e]]", Jordan experiences the distinctly corporeal effects of his dissolution into the body of authority:

> Shivkov's words penetrated Jordan's flesh and penetrated deep into his bones. Jordan's body shivered. 'Their most faithful sons,' repeated his lips and remained open. Every word should go into him. [...] 'Great mission,' repeated Jordan's flesh [...].
>
> [Shivkovs Worte drangen in Jordans Fleisch und bohrten sich tief in seine Knochen. Jordans Körper erzitterte. 'Ihre treuesten Söhne,' wiederholten seine Lippen und blieben offen. Jedes Wort sollte in ihn hineingehen. [...] 'Große Mission,' wiederholte Jordans Fleisch [...].] (EZ 149–50)

Succumbing to the myth of absolute community, Jordan can only repeat the words spoken to him. Indeed, his ability to get suspects to talk without speaking himself, is connected to his endorsement of the regime. An incident with baby Svetljo, who accompanies his father to an oration, demonstrates that loss of voice. Startled from his nap by the cheering crowd, Svetljo is frightened by the "many faces [...], all of them screaming, all of them uncanny [viele Gesichter [...], alle schreiend, alle unheimlich]". (EZ 151) Almost choking on his own tongue, he refuses to speak for several more years. Shivkov's orations render not just baby Svetljo mute but really the entire Bulgarian people, of which the common voice is less valuable than a single orator's, who, ironically, claims to speak the language of the people.[132]

Just as state propaganda deploys the family image of loyal sons to conjure a sense of absolute community, indeed a sense of 'organic' unity, so too do the father figures attempt to transfer that illusion onto their sons, by designing their educational programs after the image of the state—"After all, the party does the same with the proletariat. What the party could do, Jordan could do as well. [Das gleiche macht nämlich auch die Partei mit dem Proletariat. Was die Partei konnte, konnte auch Jordan.]" (EZ 277) Yet such education hardly fosters versatility or development—or individual aspirations, for that matter, as the narrator concludes cynically:

> Shadowing intellectuals had by no means turned [Jordan] into an intellectual, as he believed. True, a few small shifts had taken place in his soul, but no lasting changes. While he had picked up some quotes he had struggled to learn and often used incorrectly, he was still the old Jordan. A dream of an official of order and a nightmare for anyone who threatened that order. But who had dreams like that.
>
> [Das Beschatten von Intellektuellen hatte aus [Jordan] noch lange keinen Intellektuellen gemacht, wie er sich einbildete. In seiner Seele hatten zwar ein paar kleine Verschiebungen stattgefunden, aber keine Veränderungen. Zwar hatte er sich einige Zitate zugelegt, die er mit Mühe gelernt hatte und die er oft falsch verwendete, aber er war immer noch der alte Jordan. Ein Traum von einem Beamten der Ordnung und ein Alptraum für jeden der diese Ordnung bedrohte. Aber wer hatte schon solche Träume.] (EZ 280–1)

The absolute community, as represented by the father figures, sustains itself through the dissemination of an illusion of collective progress. *Bildsamkeit*, then, does not enable emancipation; to the contrary, it reinforces conformity. At the expense of all expressions of individual difference or aspiration, absolute community amounts to a standstill.

Dinev brings up a particularly telling illustration of that mechanism. Enacted by Todor Shivkov between 1984 and 1989, the so-called Revival Process sought to forcibly assimilate the sizable Turkish and Muslim minority in Bulgaria. In what was initially a secret operation, police and army units were dispatched to southern Bulgaria, in order to provide the Turkish minority with new documents. They were forced to adopt 'Bulgarian' names and were no longer allowed to speak Turkish in public.[133] Growing resistance led the Sofia government to open the border to Turkey in early 1989, encouraging the minority to leave the country.[134] Dinev mentions this episode as the reason for Mladen's increasing estrangement from the communist party. He denounces the forced assimilation as "a betrayal of communist ideals [ein Verrat an den kommunistischen Idealen]" (EZ 380), recalling the ideals for which he entered the party: internationalism and equality of all people. Yet Dinev's inclusion of this episode surpasses a simple indictment of the communist regime. He describes a demand for assimilation that, of course, ties in with the contemporary Western debate on immigration. More significantly, what Mladen experiences as a betrayal of the communist ideal, is really an instrumentalization of Enlightenment values by a nationalist project. Another ironic comment by the narrator renders the forcible assimilation as the government's encouragement of Turkish emancipation and equality:

> [The Turkish minority] was still too attached to its customs and name, tied to the heavy burden of a reactionary tradition. They wanted to help that minority free itself from such tradition. It was to look to the future again, and the future belonged to only a progressive unified socialist nation only.
>
> [[Die türkische Minderheit] hing noch zu sehr an ihren Gebräuchen und ihren Namen, gefesselt von der schweren Last einer reaktionären Tradition. Man wollte ihr helfen, sich davon zu befreien. Sie sollte wieder in die Zukunft blicken, und die Zukunft gehörte nur einer progressiven einheitlichen sozialistischen Nation.] (EZ 398)

The ostensibly Enlightened, educational project of the communist regime reveals itself as an instrument to achieve homogeneity, rather than a society based on equality. In an interrogation about Mladen's refusal to endorse the forced assimilation, a party official admits as much: "We hoped that industrialization and education would equalize all ethnic differences. Unfortunately, it did not come to that, humankind loves the past far too much. [Wir haben gehofft, die Industrialisierung und die Bildung würden alle ethnischen Unterschiede ausgleichen. Leider ist es nicht dazu gekommen, der Mensch liebt viel zusehr die Vergangenheit] [...]." (EZ 380) Even though the party official justifies Turkish assimilation as a necessary measure due to the failure of the state's 'Enlightened' project, he implicitly admits the defeat of communism itself. For what really motivates the assimilation is increasingly nationalist and xenophobic sentiment, which communism, despite its ideals, has not managed to keep at bay:

> The majority of this country consists of Bulgarians, and which one of them really likes the Turks. Which of them can forget that they slaughtered, massacred, and violated our ancestors 500 years ago? People still sing about it in folk songs to this day. People hear these songs with tears in their eyes.
>
> [Die Mehrheit dieses Landes besteht aus Bulgaren, und welcher von ihnen mag schon die Türken wirklich. Welcher von ihnen kann es vergessen, daß sie unsere Vorfahren vor 500 Jahren gemetzelt, geschlachtet und geschändet haben. Heute noch wird in den Volksliedern davon gesungen. Mit Tränen in den Augen hören Menschen diese Lieder.] (EZ 379)

Engelszungen thus brings into focus the ambivalent indebtedness of the communist regime to the Enlightenment. While apparently devoted to the principles of reason, progress, and education of the masses, it also practiced ideals deeply at odds with those principles: "monolithic authority, class-relative truth, central economic planning, [...] the religion of the party-state," and obviously, the utter disregard of individual rights.[135]

"Against the confines of the image"— Un-/antiheroic grandsons and the power of storytelling

Carefully exposing the illusion at the heart of both the Austro-Hungarian Empire and the Bulgarian communist regime, Roth's and Dinev's family sagas come to a similar conclusion. In *Die Kapuzinergruft* (1938), a continuation of *Radetzkymarsch* narrated by the grandson of Joseph von Trotta's brother, Roth confirms explicitly what his saga only suggests: "Austria is not a state, not a homeland, not a nation. It is a religion. [Österreich ist kein Staat, keine Heimat, keine Nation. Es ist eine Religion.]"[136] Likewise, Dinev portrays the communist regime as a question of belief, a utilitarian substitute for religion: "The synagogue had become a bakery. [...] The manna that had once fallen from the heavens was now planned and produced in a socialist manner. [Aus der Synagoge war eine Bäckerei geworden. [...] Das Manna, das einmal vom Himmel gefallen war, wurde jetzt sozialistisch geplant und produziert.]" (EZ 264–5) Icons of these secular religions are the portraits mentioned briefly above of the 'hero of Solferino' and the communist party leaders. As *Abbild* and *Vorbild* at once, such portraits depict their subject as actually present in the onlooker's reality.[137] They demonstrate authority and perform it at the same time; they are an image of unity and bring about unity through identification. However, in the stories of the (grand)sons, these static representations gradually lose their identity-establishing allure. Instead, their stillness becomes associated with alienation, disintegration, and the inflation of value. For the still, unifying image masks a heterogeneous reality of multiple stories and experiences. As Nancy writes about the confines of the picture:

> Why is it that an 'identification photo' is most often poorer, duller, and less 'lifelike' than any other photo? And even more, why are ten identity photos of the same person so different from one another? When does someone resemble *himself* [in a photo]? Only when the photo shows something of him, or her, something more than what is identical, more than the 'face', the 'image', the 'traits' or the 'portrait', something more than a copy of the diacritical signs of an 'identity' [...]. It is only when it evokes an unending *mêlée* of peoples, parents, works, pains, pleasures, refusals, forgettings, transgressions, expectations, dreams, stories, and all that trembles within and struggles against the confines of the image. This is not something imaginary; it is nothing but what is real: what is real has to do with the *mêlée*. A *true* identification photo would be an indeterminant *mêlée* of photos and scribbles [...] that resemble nothing, under which one would inscribe a proper name.[138]

In *Engelszungen*, it is the power of storytelling that challenges the confines of the absolute community, in that it restores a sense of individual agency in the protagonists, and enables fleeting moments of connection. In *Radetzkymarsch*, the struggle is less evident within the diegetic realm, as the Trottas seem to remain trapped within the mythical confines. It is the myopic Jewish figure Max Demant who, moving in the margins of imperial order, sees through the myth yet falls victim to it all the same.

Travesty of heroism

In the story of Carl Joseph von Trotta, grandson of the hero of Solferino, the portrait symbolizes the influence of the family hero on later generations, while conveying their increasing alienation at the same time. Although Carl Joseph's father Franz von Trotta is *Bezirkshauptmann*, a district administrator[139] outside the officers' corps, he has internalized the military attitude and lives according to the myth of the officer.[140] Carl Joseph's upbringing is strict and military-like, according to the principle of "subordination, [...] the duty of unconditional obedience [Subordination, [...] "die Pflicht des unbedingten Gehorsams]"

(RM 31), which has nurtured a strong sense of obedience in Carl Joseph. In contrast to his grandfather, the tenacious 'knight of truth', Carl Joseph is ascribed a childlike naivety, who "with a childishly devoted heart [mit einem kindlich ergebenen Herzen]" (RM 31–32) identifies with the myth of his grandfather's heroism, and who draws on his father's status as a state official. His military training as a cadet as well as his father's demanding upbringing have stifled his development as an autonomous individual,[141] producing "an impotent young man easily influenced by others"[142] and led from one crisis to the next. The anti-hero accumulates gambling debts, develops a drinking problem, gets involved in an affair with his friend's wife, and, worst of all, regards his crises as the workings of fate, rather than the result of his own poor judgment:

> He believed he could detect the insidious machinations of some dark power; [...] and gradually the lieutenant saw all the somber events of his life fitting together in a somber mosaic as if manipulated by some powerful, hateful, invisible wire puller who was intent on destroying him.
>
> [Er glaubte, die tückischen Schliche einer finsteren Macht zu erkennen, [...] und allmählich sah er auch alle düsteren Ereignisse seines Lebens in einen düsteren Zusammenhang gefügt und abhängig von irgendeinem gewaltigen, gehässigen, unsichtbaren Drahtzieher, dessen Ziel es war, den Leutnant zu vernichten.] (RM 313)

In this son, his father Franz recognizes "a *Zeitgeist* phenomenon against the soldierly tradition [ein Zeitgeistphänomen wider die soldatische Tradition],"[143] but also a victim of circumstance. He sees, as Voß summarizes, "his son Carl Joseph at the mercy of the deterministic powers of time and history [seinen Sohn Carl Joseph als den deterministischen Mächten von Zeit und Geschichte ausgeliefert]" and as such robs him of "individual failure, but in fact also of individual development [individuelles Versagen, aber eigentlich auch individuelle Entwicklung]."[144] Due to intergenerational determinism, furthermore, Carl Joseph has become the exact opposite of the 'Ritter der Wahrheit', who acted on personal initiative bordering on insubordination yet refused to become a legend. Carl Joseph, by contrast, focused on his legendary grandfather, has been molded according to formalistic military life but has lost all sense of individual agency. His education, in this respect, is merely formalistic and not at all focused on his personal development—despite his lack of talent in horsemanship or trigonometry, he passes with a good score simply because he is the grandson of the hero of Solferino (RM 44). His family history has, as Reidel-Schrewe argues, obstructed the "autonomy of his ego [Autonomie seines Ichs]:"[145] "This character is not distinguished by a loss of identity or self-alienation, but rather by the inability to assume an identity. [Nicht Identitätsverlust oder Selbstentfremdung kennzeichnen diesen Charakter, vielmehr das Unvermögen, eine Identität anzunehmen.]"[146] Indeed, as the case of the embellished history textbook already showed, the purpose of education is not to raise autonomous individuals, or to teach a truthful history, but to serve a self-referential narrative instead.

The portrait of his grandfather shows the first cracks in that self-referentiality. At the time of its making, the portrait did resonate with the depicted elder Trotta. Skeptical at first about how a single surface image could possibly represent his entire being, he eventually reconciles himself to it. To Trotta, it becomes a meaningful image heightening his self-awareness:

> Only now did he grow acquainted with his features; he sometimes had a mute dialogue with his own face. It aroused unfamiliar thoughts and memories, baffling, quickly blurring shadows of wistfulness. He had needed the portrait to experience his early old age and his great loneliness; from the painted canvas loneliness and old age came flooding toward him.
>
> [Er lernte erst jetzt sein Angesicht kennen, er hielt manchmal stumme Zwiesprache mit seinem Angesicht. Es weckte in ihm nie gekannte Gedanken, Erinnerungen, unfaßbare, rasch verschwimmende Schatten von Wehmut. Er hatte erst des Bildes bedurft, um sein frühes Alter und seine große Einsamkeit zu erfahren, aus der bemalten Leinwand strömten sie ihm entgegen, die Einsamkeit und das Alter.] (RM 23)

Trotta's eventual acceptance of the portrait—even though, like his heroic act, it may not be an entirely accurate rendering—is a sign of his coming to terms with his previous disillusionment, a sign that he has come to a true understanding of himself and society.[147] To Carl Joseph, however, the portrait fails to communicate its meaning. Although at first the portrait feeds into Carl Joseph's fascination with his grandfather, it soon becomes a symbol of their alienation and their adherence to entirely different paradigms. From up close, the painting disintegrates into fragmented colors, brush strokes, and contrasting tones:

> It splintered into countless deep shadows and bright highlights, into brush strokes and dabs, into a myriad weave of the painted canvas, into a

hard colored interplay of dried oil. [...] The dead man revealed nothing; the boy learned nothing. From year to year, the portrait seemed to be growing paler and more otherworldly, as if the Hero of Solferino were dying once again and a time would come when an empty canvas would stare down upon the descendant even more mutely than the portrait.

[Es zerfiel in zahlreiche tiefe Schatten und helle Lichtflecke, in Pinselstriche und Tupfen, in ein tausendfältiges Gewebe der bemalten Leinwand, in ein hartes Farbenspiel getrockneten Öls. [...] Nichts verriet der Tote. Nichts erfuhr der Junge. Von Jahr zu Jahr schien das Bildnis blasser und jenseitiger zu werden, [...] als müßte eine Zeit kommen, in der eine leere Leinwand aus dem schwarzen Rahmen noch stummer als das Porträt auf den Nachkommen niederstarren würden.] (EZ 42–3)

From these painted fragments, Carl Joseph fails to discover meaning; the painting remains mute, and the disconnection between the past and the present, he feels, will only increase. The painting thus reinforces the theme of imperial disintegration into separate nations, underscored by the estrangement of grandfather and grandson. To Carl Joseph, the painting is a collection of material characteristics, rather than an artwork speaking to its onlooker: there is no person or subject for him to identify. Only at a distance do the fragments yield a semblance of unity again—"the dabs and brush strokes merged back into the familiar but unfathomable physiognomy [die Pinselstriche und Tupfen fügten sich wieder zu der vertrauten, aber unergründlichen Physiognomie][...]." (RM 42) Although Carl Joseph surmises a different truth behind the legend of his grandfather, he remains in the dark about what really happened at Solferino— even the old servant Jaccques cannot restore the connection between past and present. Having nothing but the legend at his disposal, he only repeats, "like a good twenty times in the past [wie immer und wie schon gute zwanzig Mal]" the same common knowledge: "Everyone knew he had saved the Kaiser's life at the Battle of Solferino, but he kept mum about it, never a peep out of him. [Alle haben gewußt: Er hat dem Kaiser das Leben gerettet, in der Schlacht bei Solferino, aber er hat nichts davon gesagt, keinen Mucks hat er gegeben.]" (RM 43)

Summoned by a "looming super-ego [dräuendes Über-Ich]"[148] to an imitation of his grandfather's glory, Carl Joseph's attempts amount to a travesty of heroism. As it is no longer possible to repeat the aged Emperor's rescue on the battlefield, he can only resort to inferior imitations, such has the 'rescue' of a miniature portrait of the Emperor from the officers' brothel, as if to protect a holy relic from desecration. (RM 93–4) More significantly, Carl Joseph's unheroic death reinforces the idea that his attempt to emulate can only result in failure. Taking place on the margins of the battlefield,[149] his death is, as the narrator comments, unfit for textbook history:

> The end of the grandson of the Hero of Solferino was a commonplace end, not suitable for textbooks in the elementary schools and high schools of Imperial and Royal Austria. Lieutenant Trotta died holding not a weapon but two pails.
>
> [So einfach und zur Behandlung in Lesebüchern für die kaiser- und königlichen österreichischen Volks- und Bürgerschulen ungeeignet war das Ende des Enkels des Helden von Solferino. Der Leutnant Trotta starb nicht mit der Waffe, sondern mit zwei Wassereimern in der Hand.] (RM 391)

Ironically, Carl Joseph's unheroic death is in itself the product of mythologization through history textbooks. His lack of autonomy, agency, and responsibility represent not only a failure of *imitatio*, they are also evidence of a process of *Bildung* gone awry. With his death, not only a story of premodern heroism comes to an end. It also casts doubt on the merits of *Bildung* as an emancipatory strategy.

In this respect, a crucial role is reserved for the Jewish regimental doctor Max Demant. The Trottas, each one in his own way, move within the confines of the myth. Even if they might be aware of its existence, they cannot expose it from within or discover a source of meaning external to it. Demant's character serves both as a mirror image and a counter-image to Carl Joseph, who feels a brotherly connection to his friend:

> "There are so many graves," said the regimental surgeon. "Don't you feel as I do the way we live off the dead?" "I live off my grandfather," said Trotta. He saw the portrait of the Hero of Solferino blurring under the ceiling of his father's house. Yes, something brotherly came from the regimental surgeon, brotherliness rushed like a small flame from Dr. Demant's heart. "My grandfather," the regimental surgeon said, "was an old, tall Jew with a silver beard." Carl Joseph saw the old, tall Jew with the silver beard. They were grandsons, they were both grandsons.
>
> ["Es gibt so viele Tote," sagte der Regimentsarzt. "Fühlst du nicht auch, wie man von den Toten lebt?" "Ich lebe vom Großvater," sagte Trotta. Er sah das Bildnis des Helden von Solferino, verdämmernd unter dem Suffit des väterlichen Hauses. Ja, etwas Brüderliches klang aus dem Regimentsarzt, aus dem

> Herzen Doktor Demants schlug das Brüderliche wie ein Feuerchen. "Mein Großvater," hat der Regimentsarzt gesagt, "war ein alter großer Jude mit silbernem Bart!" Carl Joseph sah den alten, großen Juden mit dem silbernen Bart. Sie waren Enkel, sie waren beide Enkel.] (RM 108)

Carl Joseph situates the roots of their friendship in their shared fate as grandsons, in their determination by an image of the past looming over them. However, Demant's relationship with his grandfather is quite the opposite of Carl Joseph's.[150] His recollection of the old Jew is much clearer and realistic than the disintegrating portrait in the Trottas' house, which suggests that Demant has a more tangible connection to his past. Even so, Demant's assimilation history also mirrors Carl Joseph's predicament. What they have in common, or what gives Carl Joseph a sense of familiarity with Demant, is not just their status as grandsons, it is their lack of autonomy.

Once a Galician Jew and now an army doctor, Demant at first seems to exemplify a story of Jewish assimilation. Unlike Carl Joseph, who is paralyzed by imposed expectations, Demant has broken free from his grandfather's views: "Had he known that his grandson would some day stroll through the world murderously armed and in an officer's uniform, the old man would have cursed his old age and the fruit of his loins. [Wenn er gewußt hätte, daß sein Enkel einmal in der Uniform eines Offiziers und mörderisch bewaffnet durch die Welt spazieren würde, hätte er sein Alter verflucht und die Frucht seiner Lenden.]" (RM 95–6) Yet although his army career breaks any sense of intergenerational determinism, Demant himself regards his assimilation in fatalistic terms, rather than as an outcome of self-improvement and agency. Referring to himself with the indefinite pronoun *man*, he excludes his own volition from the course of events:[151]

> He literally sank into the arms of the military. Seven years of food, seven years of drink, seven years of clothing, seven years of shelter: seven, seven long years! He became an army doctor. And he remained one. [...] And before he even made a decision he was an old man.
>
> [Man sank der Armee geradezu in die Arme. Sieben Jahre Essen, sieben Jahre Trinken, sieben Jahre Kleidung, sieben Jahre Obdach, sieben, sieben lange Jahre! Man wurde Militärarzt. Und man blieb es. [...] Und ehe man einen Entschluß gefaßt hatte, war man ein alter Mann.] (RM 97–8)

Demant's assimilation, in other words, does not resemble a process of emancipation, but rather his resignation to an inescapable imperial order. While his story at first seems to tie in with an Enlightened emancipation ideal that shaped Roth's own life, Demant's true 'enlightenment' is of a different nature. Ranked as major, and as such familiar with the military code, he has a position in the margins of social and military order. As Torsten Voß argues, his liminal position as a Jew is reinforced by the fact that, as a doctor, Demant does not share the martial duty and thus the self-conception of people in uniforms.[152] Moreover, being very shortsighted, he is exempted from battle and, as such, becomes a "a border crosser who, on the one hand, is excluded from the corps spirit but, on the other, cannot completely withdraw from the regulations of the corps due to his uniform. [Grenzgänger, welcher auf der einen Seite vom Korpsgeist ausgeschlossen ist, auf der anderen Seite aber aufgrund der Uniform sich nicht den Reglements des Korps vollständig entziehen kann]."[153] Furthermore, Demant's shortsightedness actually symbolizes his *clear*sightedness—much like Omar's impaired sight in *Alle Tage*—and reinforces his already liminal perspective. In one of the very few but significant instances of anti-Semitism in the novel, Demant's apparent lack of vision enables him to unmask the military codes as redundant social constructs. When he is taunted as a Jew by *Rittmeister* Tattenbach, Demant challenges the man to a duel. Shortly before the fight, Demant expresses his frustration at the outdated code of honor, which—if he wants to perform it correctly—requires that he remain blind to its pointlessness. His "little revenge [kleine Rache]" consists of taking off his glasses, thus refusing to recognize the code:

> "This death is senseless," the doctor went on. "As senseless as my life was." [...] Tomorrow I'm going to the like a hero, a so-called hero, completely against my grain, and against the grain of my forebears and my tribe and against my grandfather's will. [...] But I'm nearsighted. I'm not going to take aim. [...] Without my glasses, I can see nothing at all, nothing at all, and I will shoot without seeing. That will be more natural, more honest, and altogether fitting."
>
> [Dieser Tod ist unsinnig! [...] So unsinnig, wie mein Leben gewesen ist! [...] Ich werde morgen wie ein Held sterben, wie ein sogenannter Held, ganz gegen meine Art und ganz gegen die Art meiner Väter und meines Geschlechts und gegen den Willen meines Großvaters. [...] Aber ich bin kurzsichtig, ich werde nicht zielen. [...] Wenn ich die Brille abnehme, sehe ich gar nichts, gar nichts. Und ich werde schießen, ohne zu sehn! Das wird natürlicher sein, ehrlicher und ganz passend!] (RM 125)

As the duel leaves both participants dead, producing no winner, Demant's death underscores the utter meaninglessness of the code. By dying a hero "according to the code of honor and military regulations [nach Ehrenkodex und Dienstreglement]" (RM 134), Demant may have broken free from previous generations and seemingly have completed an acculturation process. Still, what brought the duel about is an anti-Semitic undercurrent that the imperial order has failed to eliminate, despite its claims of supranationality and tolerance. At first glance, Demant thus embodies the paradoxical position of German and Austrian Jews, who strongly identified with the Enlightened concept of inclusion in exchange for acculturation yet continued to be singled out as outsiders. His individual story initially reveals the implicit exclusionary nature of the Austrian identity. Yet through the family motif—his brotherly connection to Carl Joseph—Demant's figure acquires a more universal meaning. Demant's and Carl Joseph's "shared burden and sense of commonality"[154] is not really a matter of their status as *Enkel*, but rather of their equally powerless position within the imperial order. Their family histories are alike in the sense that they are each marked by a process of estrangement from their Galician and Slovenian origins—in the Trottas' case due to social progress and ennoblement, in the Demants' case due to acculturation and *Bildung*. Yet the juxtaposition of the two characters reveals that even an Enlightened, educational process still leaves the individual defenseless:

> [Demant's] wise mind, inherited from a long long line of wise forebears, was as helpless as the simple mind of the lieutenant, whose ancestors had been the simple peasants of Sipolje. An obtuse iron-clad law had no loophole.
>
> [[Demants] kluger Kopf, ererbt von einer langen, langen Reihe kluger Väter, wußte ebensowenig Rat wie der einfache Kopf des Leutnants, dessen Ahnen die einfachen Bauern von Sipolje gewesen waren. Ein stupides, eisernes Gesetz ließ keinen Ausweg frei.] (RM 131)

Educated or not, Enlightened or not, both families fall victim to the mechanism of myth all the same—be it the myth of supranationality, or that of the nationalisms emerging across the empire. Demant may see through it, but his 'enlightened' position is eventually of little help in his predicament. The character thus reinforces the notion that the imperial order, no matter how Enlightened its foundations, leaves room for neither religious tolerance nor individual agency.

Storytelling heroics—"Die Liebe hinkt"[155]

Engelszungen, as opposed to *Radetzkymarsch*, does seem to allow its characters to develop agency, by reserving space for the redeeming potential of storytelling. Its narrative structure suggests that fiction does not merely serve the enforcement of conformity, but also the resistance to power of myth. While in Roth's novel the grandfathers embody a notion of determinism, Dinev's ironic narrator mocks such an association. Svetljo's grandfather is, so he believes, in charge of his grandson's destiny, but his indecisiveness gets in the way of that determinism:

> His grandfather Svetlin, the partisan, had spent two weeks with Svetljo's umbilical cord in his trousers because he still hadn't decided what his grandson should become. He may not believe in God, but he was strongly convinced that the place where an umbilical cord was laid or thrown would continue to determine the fate of its owner. [...] "Just make sure you don't lose it in a tavern," the peasants mocked. He had actually forgotten it in the tavern. [...] The next day Svetlin drove into town, bought a medical book, and hid the umbilical cord between the pages. [...] His grandson was to become a doctor.
>
> [Sein Großvater Svetlin, der Partisan, hatte zwei Wochen mit Svetljos Nabelschnur in der Hose verbracht, weil er immer noch nicht entschieden hatte, was aus seinem Enkel werden sollte. Er mochte nicht an Gott glauben, aber er war fest davon überzeugt, daß der Ort, wohin eine Nabelschnur gelegt oder geworfen wird, das Schicksal seines Besitzers weiter bestimmen wird. [...] "Schau nur, daß du sie nicht in einer Schenke verlierst," spotteten die Bauern. Er hatte sie dann tatsächlich in der Schenke vergessen. [...] Am nächsten Tag fuhr Svetlin in die Stadt, kaufte ein medizinisches Buch und versteckte die Nabelschnur zwischen den Seiten. [...] Aus seinem Enkel sollte ein Arzt werden.]
> (EZ 141–142)

The grandfather is quite careless with his 'authority', and his choice over his grandson's 'fate' is moreover open to the influence of random tavern visitors. As it turns out, Svetljo does not become a doctor. While his destiny may not be predetermined, however, he did inherit the storytelling heroics from his grandfather, a partisan by happenstance. On the school playground, Svetljo soon discovers the power of fiction and practices in stretching the boundaries of truth:

> Svetljo had long since discovered that one could win friends with beautiful toys or objects or with beautiful stories. [...] Svetljo decided to tell stories. The stories should not exceed a certain degree of credibility, but other than that anything could be told [...].
>
> [Svetljo hatte längst entdeckt, daß man Freunde mit schönen Spielzeugen oder Gegenständen oder mit schönen Geschichten gewinnen konnte. [...] Svetljo entschied sich für das Erzählen. Die Geschichten sollten nur nicht ein gewisses Maß an Glaubwürdigkeit übersteigen, aber sonst konnte man alles erzählen [...]]. (EZ 282)

Although he is aware of their persuasive power, Svetljo's 'schöne Geschichten' are of an entirely different nature than the mythic speech of communist orators that rendered him mute as a baby. Whereas the latter seeks to shape a 'collective individual', Dinev presents the reader with a multitude of stories that underscore the *singularity* of the individual: storytelling, as opposed to mythic speech, connects individuals without erasing differences. The fabricated nature of Svetlin's partisan heroism, then, does not serve a myth and, as such, is different from the embellishment of Trotta's heroism. When Svetljo's teacher invites Svetlin to speak in class about his partisan past, the teacher justifies it as "incredibly important for the education of pupils and indispensable for the development of their value systems [unglaublich wichtig für die Erziehung der Schüler und unersetzbar für die Bildung ihrer Wertsysteme]." (EZ 313) Yet Svetlin has no intention of teaching children the value of the communist or any other ideology:

> He may never have been a hero, but he had always been a good narrator. What difference did that make, anyway? People often preferred stories to heroes, for with a story they knew what to do more than with a hero.
>
> Mag sein, daß er nie ein Held gewesen war, aber ein guter Erzähler war er immer schon gewesen. Was machte das schon für einen Unterschied? Den Leuten waren die Geschichten oft lieber als die Helden, denn mit einer Geschichte wußten sie viel mehr anzufangen als mit einem Helden. (EZ 312)

The real nature of heroism, according to him, is fundamentally narrative and even fictional, as it affects people more than a static heroic past. As in *Radetzkymarsch*, there is a clear narrative connection between generations, but in *Engelszungen* its deterministic and mythic elements aspects are markedly absent. The grandfather's story does not incite the grandson to imitation but evidences a loving, playful connection instead. When the teacher then invites him for future talks, Svetlin refuses to become part of an ideological narrative that must repeat itself: "'I only did it this once, because of my grandson.' ['Ich hab's nur dieses eine Mal gemacht, wegen meines Enkels.']" (EZ 313)

In Dinev's text, the anti-mythic nature of the narrative connection between generations is underscored by the female characters. Iskren's grandmother Sdravka and his mother Dorothea are engaged in a narrative dynamic that brings the two women closer. Living with her daughter-in-law, Sdravka is determined to teach her how to cook, which turns out to be more difficult than expected, as Dorothea is engrossed in theater rehearsals. Still, Sdravka helps her out with both—"Sometimes it was a word, sometimes a spice that Sdravka added. [Einmal war es ein Wort, einmal ein Gewürz, das Sdravka ergänzte.]" (EZ 237) Although they do no spontaneously become friendly with one another, the two women find a way to add to each other's 'stories': "Dorothea also liked to listen to Sdravka when she talked about the old days. [...] Dorothea was attentive, she was touched, she was actually the ideal listener. [Dorothea hörte Sdravka auch gerne zu, wenn sie von den alten Zeiten erzählte. [...] Dorothea war aufmerksam, sie war berührt, war eigentlich die ideale Zuhörerin.]" (EZ 237–8) They thus establish a narrative connection that, at the same time, refuses to become a perfect union or absolute community:[156] "Sdravka was unsure what to think of her daughter-in-law. For hating her, she lacked a reason; for loving her, she lacked sometimes a word, sometimes a spice. [Sdravka wußte nicht, was sie von ihrer Schwiegertochter halten sollte. Um sie zu hassen, fehlte ihr der Grund, um sie zu lieben, fehlte ihr einmal ein Wort, einmal ein Gewürz.]" (EZ 237)

Their imperfect relationship, based on the exchange of scraps of meaning, provides an important counter-image to the mythic speech of orators, who address a collective individual with an ultimate truth. Whereas father figures Mladen and Jordan, as willing recipients of the myth, appear to dissolve into the collective, the exchange of meaning between Sdravka and Dorothea reflects what Nancy calls 'being singular plural'. Storytelling, as opposed to originary mythic speech, is the material of sharing and 'being-with':

> There is no meaning if meaning is not shared, and not because there would be an ultimate or first signification that all beings have in common, but because *meaning is itself the sharing of Being*. Meaning begins where presence is not pure presence but where presence comes apart [...].
> [...] Pure, unshared presence—presence to nothing, of nothing, for nothing—is neither present nor absent. It is the simple implosion of a being that could never have *been*—an implosion without any trace.[157]

Storytelling implies a shared moment in which meaning is created and exchanged, whereas mythic speech robs the individual of a voice, imposing on it its 'ultimate signification'.

Symbol of Sdravka's and, by extension, Iskren's, resistance to the 'pure, unshared presence' of the absolute community is her physical limp. Reminiscent of Demant's myopia in *Radetzkymarsch*, or Omar's incomplete vision in *Alle Tage*, Sdravka carries a 'stigma' that enables an alternative kind of 'enlightenment' and community to Mladen's educational program. Indeed, the close relationship between Sdravka and his son irritates Mladen, due the fact that his "half-educated mother [halbgebildete Mutter]" has taught his son how to read and to write. (EZ 238) Furthermore, due to an association Iskren made as a child between limping and affection—"Did it always take a limp to love him? [Mußte man denn immer hinken, um ihn lieben zu können?]" (EZ 223)—he develops a fondness for people with physical deficiencies, for "the flawed ones found the easiest way to his heart [diejenigen, die einen Makel hatten, fanden am leichtesten den Weg zu seinem Herzen]." (EZ 329) A sign of vulnerability, the limp here represents a fault that confounds the purity of absolute community; a weak spot in a perfectly smooth surface. Iskren first deploys it as a subversive strategy to undermine his father's authority, feigning a limp in order to skip school (EZ 234), thus interfering with his father's perfectly planned education: "The thought that his own child—the child of comrade Mladenov, who had so perfectly planned his advancement, his marriage, and his house—might become a cripple didn't appeal to him at all. [Der Gedanke, daß sein eigenes Kind, das Kind des Genossen Mladenov, der seinen Aufstieg, seine Ehe und sein Haus so perfekt geplant hatte, womöglich ein Krüppel würde, gefiel ihm gar nicht.]" (EZ 247–8) Iskren thus introduces a *Störfaktor*, an aspect of degeneration, that opposes his father's ostensibly Enlightened "view of a dialectical materialist [Blick eines dialektischen Materialisten]" (EZ 248)—a cripple cannot march to the rhythm of ideology, so to speak. Iskren's emancipation is, in other words, based on his subversion of education: it is not his intellectual improvement that will rescue his sense of autonomy, but rather his talent for impersonation and storytelling.

His feigned limp is his first experience as an impostor, "the best game he had every played [das beste Spiel, das er je gespielt hatte]." (EZ 234) Like Svetljo's knack for 'schöne Geschichten', it lays the foundation for a picaresque lifestyle that inverts common values and truths, and which rescues the protagonists' sense of autonomy. As roguish antiheroes, both Iskren and Svetljo "assert themselves in a loosely composed series of episodes with shrewdness and morally not harmless means against a hostile and corrupt world [...], creating a satirically drawn panorama of this world [[behaupten] sich in einer locker gefügten Folge von Episoden mit Gewitztheit und moralisch nicht unbedenklichen Mitteln gegen eine feindliche und korrupte Welt [...], wobei von dieser Welt ein satirisch gezeichnetes Panorama entworfen wird]."[158] Their impersonation and storytelling heroics underscore the changeable, relative nature of the values supported by a society or a political system. In terms of *Wertverlust*, the image of comrade Dimitrov on the lev banknotes is telling:

> With Bulgarian levs you did not get very far in the world. Comrade Dimitrov was still depicted on them, and there, where the border of the People's Republic ended, they also lost their significance, because who in the world wanted to know about the comrade. Even in Bulgaria itself he gradually lost value. His embalmed corpse, which had been in the mausoleum for decades, was now buried in the earth and left to the worms. The same was about to happen with the Bulgarian currency.
>
> [Mit bulgarischen Lewa kam man in der Welt nicht sehr weit. Auf ihnen war immer noch der Genosse Dimitrov abgebildet, und dort, wo die Grenze der Volksrepublik endete, verloren sie auch ihre Bedeutung, denn wer in der Welt wollte schon von dem Genossen wissen. Sogar in Bulgarien selbst verlor er von Tag zu Tag an Wert. Seine einbalsamierte Leiche, die seit Jahrzehnten im Mausoleum gelegen war, wurde nun in der Erde beigesetzt und den Würmern überlassen. Das gleiche drohte auch mit der bulgarischen Währung zu geschehen.] (EZ 526)

Putting ideology on a par with currency, Dinev points out the irony of the comrade's depiction on a symbol of capitalism, suggesting that the ideology he represents is simply interchangeable. Moreover, his still, 'embalmed' image, once symbol of an equally still collective individual, is now at the mercy of the forces of disintegration. The now devalued currency/personification of communism thus mirrors Svetljo's and Iskren's struggle 'against the confines of the image'.

However, as they move to the capitalist realm, they encounter yet another mythic narrative. As undocumented and unemployed immigrants in Vienna, they soon learn the most important German phrase for any refugee: "I am looking for a job. [Ich suche eine Arbeit.]" (EZ 538) And indeed, for several years, their lives are determined by fear of losing the humble jobs that reflect their low social capital: "The fear of being left unemployed again was much greater and stronger than anything else. It determined their thought, it determined their being. [[D]ie Angst, wieder ohne Arbeit zu bleiben, war viel größer und stärker als alles andere.

Sie bestimmte ihr Denken, sie bestimmte ihr Wesen.]" (EZ 552) Having escaped the determinism of the communist regime, Svetljo and Iskren are now confronted with the capitalist mantra of money and employment, a myth that robs them from their aspirations just as well—"So it happened that employment had turned into meaning and the search for it into a way of being. [So war die Arbeit zu Sinn und aus der Suche nach ihr eine Seinsweise geworden.]" (EZ 574)

Whereas their subversive tactics safeguarded their autonomy from a collectivist grasp, their insistence on individualism now proves insufficient. This is where the paradoxical character of the *Pikaro* as a marginal figure reveals itself. As someone who "is never able to establish lasting affective relationships [niemals beständige affektive Beziehungen einzugehen vermag]," the picaro may end up in painful isolation:

> He betrays and deceives in order to be recognized by his fellow men and to obtain a place in their world, but precisely this prevents intimacy and lasting proximity from being able to develop at all. Because continuous masquerades conceal the essence of the picaro, he becomes a mystery to himself and his surroundings.
>
> [Er betrügt und täuscht, um von seinen Mitmenschen anerkannt zu werden und einen Platz in ihrer Welt zu gewinnen, doch eben dies verhindert, dass Intimität und dauerhafte Nähe überhaupt entstehen können. Weil kontinuierliche Maskeraden das Wesen des Pikaros verhüllen, wird er sich selbst und seiner Umgebung zum Rätsel.][159]

Indeed, if they want to recover their humanity, their singular stories, Iskren and Svetljo have to adapt their insistent individualism by becoming trusting of others' compassion. Svetljo, for instance, is at first uncomfortable with the hospitality of Egyptian immigrant Altaf—Arabic for 'kindness'—who offers offers him shelter expecting nothing in return. Svetljo considers it "a painful situation [eine peinliche Situation]," (EZ 542–3) because Altaf's compassion exposes a vulnerability that he is unwilling to admit. Yet Altaf's *Barmherzigkeit* is not an expression of pity, or even altruism. As Nancy writes, compassion is not

> a pity that feels sorry for itself and feeds on itself. Com-passion is the contagion, the contact of being with one another in this turmoil. Compassion is not altruism, nor is it identification; it is the disturbance of violent relatedness.[160]

As a slightly contemptuous sympathy with the sorrows of others, pity distances the self from the pitied one. Altruism, on the other hand, implies selflessness and thus identification with the other. Compassion, however, implies an act of *sharing*, a moment that neither confirms nor denies a selfhood; it represents a brief moment of humanity in a context of violence and exclusion. This restored sense of humanity is what Dinev refers to when he argues that *Barmherzigkeit* is the ultimate oppositional power. It is truly subversive, disruptive, and inclusive, because it stands outside of societal definitions.[161] Compassion is moreover fundamentally linguistic and dialogic in nature:

> Compassion cannot be promised, perhaps because it enables language itself, because in its original intention it is itself language, perhaps because it is itself the origin of language, that first gesture of attention that redeems the other from his solitude [...]. [...] The act of compassion is always a dialogue, a duality, a multiplicity.
>
> [Die Barmherzigkeit lässt sich nicht versprechen, vielleicht weil sie selber die Sprache ermöglicht, weil sie selber in ihrer ursprünglichen Intention Sprache ist, vielleicht weil sie selbst der Ursprung der Sprache ist, jene erste Geste der Zuwendung, die den anderen von seiner Einsamkeit erlöst [...]. [...] Der Akt der Barmherzigkeit ist immer ein Dialog, ein Zu-zweit-, Zu-mehrt-sein.][162]

Indeed, in *Engelszungen*, the power of language allows the protagonists to reconnect. If at first their storytelling heroics symbolized the individual's resistance to collectivist dissolution, it now rescues them from isolated individualism. The novel concludes with the recovery of Svetljo's story, which indeed constitutes an awareness of 'duplicity', of 'being singular plural'. As Svetljo retraces his personal (hi)story, he initially only gets as far as a list of decisive moments in his migratory existence, written down on playing cards.[163] Yet inspired by his visit to the guardian angel Miro, Svetljo realizes that his identity extends far beyond the factual and geographical markers of his past. His personal history is traversed by experiences of friendship and affection that render these markers of migration meaningless: "If I did not tell about my friends or simply about the others, the last eleven years of my life would be limited to these words. I would have had nothing to report... I have experienced nothing else... [Würde ich nicht von meinen Freunden oder einfach von den anderen erzählen, würden sich die letzten elf Jahre meines Lebens nur auf diese Worte beschränken. Ich hätte nichts zu berichten gehabt... Ich hab sonst nichts erlebt...]" (EZ 598)

By juxtaposing two symbolic realms, *Engelszungen* refrains from a simple indictment of either communism or the tough circumstances of undocumented immigrants in Austria. Instead, it brings into focus the struggle against the deterministic confines of ideology or economy. Svetljo's and Iskren's subversion starts well before their emigration, so their antiheroics are not a strategy acquired along with their immigrant status. In the communist realm, their roguish antiheroism symbolizes a triumph of the individual over stifling collectivism. Yet when they are at the mercy of the opposite—a capitalist system that paradoxically promotes individualism and *Selbstverantwortung* but reduces people to their economic contribution—their subversive individualism yields to an awareness of their 'being singular plural'.

Through the lens of the family hero, *Engelszungen* and *Radetzkymarsch* reflect on the meaning of myth and self-determination—a notion particularly significant in the historical contexts of Roth's and Dinev's writing, for it heralded the First World War and was radically absent from the 'collective individual' produced by the communist regime. The family hero stands for a collection of interrelated themes: identification with state authority, the narrative nature of heroism, and the sense of generational determinism. Although *Radetzkymarsch* is often held to be a 'nostalgic' evocation of a glorious, multicultural Austrian past, the novel subtly criticizes exactly an idealizing obsession with that past. Roth has been reported to have declared his similarity to Carl Joseph: "Lieutenant Trotta, that is me. [Der Leutnant Trotta, der bin ich.]"[164] Although Carl Joseph's story is not one of *Jewish* assimilation, it is indeed, like Roth's biography, a story of 'assimilation', of identification with the Emperor, and of estrangement from one's forebears. Most of all, though, Carl Joseph's unheroic life evokes a deep sense of disillusionment with the Enlightened ideal—an ideal that did not manage to fend off the triumph of nationalist differences. Following in Roth's footsteps, Dinev reverts to the same thematic constellation. His postcommunist perspective reinforces a key issue in Roth's novel: that a collective identity—be it an abstract supranational unity or a 'collective individual'—may only realize itself by suppressing cultural and religious difference. Moreover, if Enlightened ideals of tolerance and equality are no longer seen as individualized but as institutionalized responsibilities, they become the material of myth themselves. Dinev's emphasis on storytelling brings into view an individual that does not emerge on the premise of Enlightened individualism. Rather, storytelling as an at once subversive, emancipatory, and connective strategy enables *Barmherzigkeit* and the awareness of 'being singular plural'. Furthermore, while storytelling may share the medium of mythic speech, it does not reiterate it: the ironic tone of Dinev's and Roth's narrators prevents the stories from blending in entirely with the mythic narrative they seem to reproduce. As Nancy concludes, in the literary interruption of myth "there is nothing new to be heard, there is no new myth breaking through; it is the old story one seems to hear;"[165] but it is an interruption nonetheless.

4.3 "Diaspora's children"[166]—Heroics of endurance and hope: Joseph Roth's *Hiob* (1930) versus Zsusza Bánk's *Der Schwimmer* (2002)

In *Radetzkymarsch* and *Engelszungen*, the family motif highlights the disintegration of an imperial unity that was illusory to begin with. Furthermore, as a perspective on the notion of determinism, the family motif also features in the context of future-oriented perspectives. Roth's *Hiob* (1930) and Bánk's *Der Schwimmer* (2002), for instance, feature nomadic and diasporic families, which at first appear to mirror a sense of vanishing (comm)unity. Against the background of failed revolutions and insistent modernity, however, their experiences of *Heimatlosigkeit* also provide the conditions for transformation—in terms of either a new, postcommunist temporality (in *Der Schwimmer*) or a renewed religious experience (in *Hiob*). Art and storytelling, in these novels, are crucial elements of endurance, whenever confidence in modern progress, or in God's benevolence, has reached a dead end.

Between East and West—Between pathos and hope: Joseph Roth and Zsuzsa Bánk

Although situated in entirely different historical, social, and political contexts, these two stories share an existential(ist) theme, highlighted by motifs of diaspora and nomadism. The authors portray their characters as painfully torn between their worldly existence and their desire to transcend it; between their need to escape their misfortune and their longing to leave a trace. What does it mean to endure, the novels seem to ask, and how does it affect one's presence in the world? Does endurance imply abandoning all responsibility to a righteous God, to state authority, or does it instead encourage the individual to take charge and to discover meaning by himself?

In *Hiob*, that question takes on a religious hue. It translates the biblical story of Job to the predicament of Eastern Jewish communities facing the pressure of modernity. Set in the fictional *shtetl* Zuchnow, the novel relates the story of Mendel Singer, family father and devout Talmud teacher. Like the biblical Job, Mendel's faith in the word of God is put to the test when he fathers a disabled child Menuchim and witnesses how his other children give in to the allure of secular life. Mendel's emigration to America barely improves his outlook, unable to stop thinking about the sick child he had to leave behind. Misfortune strikes again when his Americanized son Schemarjah/Sam perishes in the war, their younger son Jonas goes missing, his daughter Mirjam is admitted to a psychiatric hospital, and his wife Deborah dies. While *Hiob*, in this respect, shares with *Radetzkymarsch* a deep sense of disillusionment with the promise of modernity, Roth reserves a conspicuously optimistic—perhaps even contrived[167]—conclusion to his novel. Mendel renounces his religion, but eventually, and surprisingly, his faith in God is restored when Menuchim returns to him, fully healed, and when Mendel envisions the promise of returning home.

In *Der Schwimmer* the question of endurance is related to life under a repressive regime. The protagonists experience a deep sense of alienation after their mother escapes Hungary in the wake of the failed 1956 revolt.[168] Moving aimlessly through 1950s and 1960s Hungary, they struggle not to succumb to a sense of angst-burdened paralysis. After the Soviet regime violently suppressed the twelve-day uprising, harsh reprisals by the Kádár government—mass internment, interrogations, police surveillance—continued into the 1960s.[169] This had a lasting effect on the families of those who were imprisoned or executed. Such intimidation, augmented by social and economic devastation, especially affected the psyche and life stories of children who grew up in those families.[170] While *Der Schwimmer* leaves that political background largely unspoken, it vividly evokes its psychological impact. Narrated in retrospect by daughter Kata, the story depicts the family's travels from relative to relative. For what appears to be quite some time, they recover stability near Lake Balaton, but their peace is disturbed when their hosts' house is set on fire. After moving again, her brother Isti nearly drowns and dies of pneumonia shortly afterwards. As does *Hiob*, *Der Schwimmer* ends on a remarkably optimistic note, however, which contrasts with the subdued despair permeating the story. As Kata's recollections reach the diegetic present, she decides that one day she will escape. Telling the story of her family, it seems, is a necessary step in leaving that history, and the country, behind.

If *Radetzkymarsch* can be read as a declaration of Roth's (problematic) Austrian identity, *Hiob* can be regarded as the affirmation of his Jewish heritage.

The novel is often considered a turning point in Roth's fiction, marking a transition from committed leftist journalism to an increasing disillusionment with Western civilization; from the poignancy of his earlier writings to more lyrical, melancholy prose.[171] Stefan Zweig, in his review, is surprised by its simultaneous simplicity and sentimentality. Roth narrates "in a very simple (but deliberately artistic) way the simplest of all stories [in einer denkbar einfachen (aber wissend kunstvollen) Weise die schlichteste aller Geschichten] [...]."[172] Such simplicity, Zweig adds, lends the story a universal character. It is about "none of the beloved themes of the era [...] but about a present day, relevant to yesterday and tomorrow and relatable to anyone who understands with the heart [[k]eines der beliebten Probleme der Zeit [...], sondern ein Heute, das für gestern und morgen und jederzeit gilt und jedem verständlich ist, der mit dem Herzen versteht]."[173] However, this stylistic change does not involve a loss of commitment or Roth's escape from *Weltzeit*. Just as ostensible nostalgia conveys Roth's more fundamental criticism of the imperial past, so too his portrayal of Eastern Jewry is not simply born of fond memories of a vanished Galician childhood. As Ritchie Robertson remarks, Roth's "complex irony conveys that the Imperial dynasty and the Galician shtetl are [...] [each] in terminal decline."[174] For all its simplicity and apparent sentimentality, the novel shares with *Radetzkymarsch* a profound disillusionment with modernity, characteristic of most of Roth's work. Before he published *Hiob*, he had already written his impressions about Eastern Jews in European cities. *Juden auf Wanderschaft* (1927)[175] is not primarily an indictment of their circumstances, or the anti-Semitic sentiment they encountered, even if the essay does address those issues. Nor is it a romanticizing depiction of devotion, of 'premodern' religiousness, as can be found in Arnold Zweig's *Das ostjüdische Antlitz*.[176] Rather, the essay holds a mirror up to its Western audience. It is concerned with the bias against Eastern Jews that existed among gentile Germans and assimilated Jews alike. He explicitly addresses the audience with the "foolish hope that there are still readers before whom one need not defend the Eastern Jews [törichte Hoffnung, daß es noch Leser gibt, vor denen man die Ostjuden nicht zu verteidigen braucht] [...]."[177] Roth is thus obviously well aware of how the *Ostjuden* are perceived by western(ized) readers, who "with a cheap and sour benevolence look down upon the nearby East from the swaying towers of western civilization [mit einem billigen und sauren Wohlwollen von den schwanken Türmen westlicher Zivilisation auf den nahen Osten hinabschielen] [...]."[178] A similar weariness with the Western world permeates *Hiob*, as some of its protagonists trace various dead-ended paths of assimilation. Roth reverses the traditional valences of East and West, rediscovering Eastern culture as an alternative to modern rationalism and materialism. The *Ostjude*, in Roth's portrayal, is "no longer perceived as an embarrassing reminder of Judaism's difference from modern Western culture, but as the embodiment of an authenticity purportedly lost in the process of emancipation and acculturation."[179] Still, *Hiob* is not simply a story of antimodern or dissimilatory desire. Its optimistic and somewhat cinematic conclusion imagines an embrace of modernity without losing sight of the divine or the sublime; conversely, it pictures a revived religious experience that refuses to detach itself from the world. In other words, Roth's optimism involves a restored sense of humanity in a disenchanted world; neither the word of God nor the path of secular modernity holds the key.

Like Roth, Bánk is a storyteller situated between East and West. *Der Schwimmer* spans the years between the failed Hungarian Revolution of 1956 and Jan Palach's self-immolation in Prague in 1969—still two decades removed from an at the time improbable future symbolized by the year 1989. Looking back upon a period that some may have assigned "to an inert past,"[180] Bánk "confronts readers with a still open but [...]"—in the light of the suppressed revolution by the Soviet regime—"still bleak future."[181] Yet by focusing on a period of paralysis, when 'resolution' in terms of revolution had proven ineffective, Bánk is careful not to pit East against West. Her story does not align with a teleological narrative positing that 1989 represents the inevitable triumph of liberalism over communism. If her novel ends on a hopeful note, it is not because a downfall of the regime is in the making, but because the narrator secures her personal (hi)story from the misfortune and paralysis surrounding her. Kata's history, the novel suggests, may bear the traces of a suppressive political regime, but it is decidedly independent from 'official' history as well.

As opposed to Dimitré Dinev, who spent his childhood under communist rule, Bánk (1965) has witnessed the collapse of communism only indirectly, through her family history. She was born in Frankfurt to Hungarian immigrants who fled to the West after the Hungarian Revolution of 1956. She was trained as a bookseller and studied politics and literature afterwards. In a review of her acclaimed debut *Der Schwimmer*, Péter Nádas describes her story as a "a profoundly Hungarian novel written in German, yet about a time she did not experience [zutiefst ungarische[r] Roman auf Deutsch geschrieben, jedoch über eine Zeit, die sie nicht erlebt hat]."[182] Although Bánk strongly resists autobiographical readings,[183] her novels do reflect her affinity with Hungarian history, subtly weaving elements of its political past or linguistic quirks[184] into the stories. By her own admission, *Der Schwimmer* was inspired by her upbringing in a family that kept half an eye on its Hungarian origins. "It definitely played a role

[…]. All my relatives still live in Hungary, and we've always visited them eagerly. [Das spielte bestimmt immer eine Rolle […]. Meine ganzen Verwandten leben noch in Ungarn, die haben wir auch immer eifrig besucht]," she remembers. It led to a double awareness about her life: "I was always happy not having to live in that everyday life, which was always very simple, very raw, and just not as complicated and remarkable as life here can be. It was an absolutely opposite world. It has inspired me and has left a lasting impression on me. [Ich war immer ganz glücklich, nicht in diesem Alltag leben zu müssen, der immer sehr einfach war, sehr rau und eben nicht […] so kompliziert und merkwürdig wie manchmal hier. Es war die absolute Gegenwelt. Das hat mich inspiriert und nachhaltig beeindruckt.]"[185] Still, even though she is often addressed as a 'witness', her Hungarian background merely reverberates in her work.[186] *Der Schwimmer* is about rumors, about "what you overhear [das, was man überhört]."[187] Although her publisher requested her to do otherwise, the implicit political background with vague references to, for instance, the public mourning of Stalin's death in 1953,[188] was Bánk's deliberate choice: "I will not undertake any educational effort for those who have already forgotten everything. [Ich unternehme keine Bildungsanstrengung für jene, die alles schon vergessen haben.]"[189] *Der Schwimmer* is indeed not an account of Hungarian history, intended to educate a possibly amnesic Western audience; it traces the effects of political history in a much more subtle and complex manner. Nádas praises Bánk for her remarkable "capability of twofold vision [Fähigkeit zum doppelten Blick]," which is evident at first in her 'translation' of Hungarian history into German. Perhaps more riveting than this intercultural exchange is Bánk's narrative perspective, which walks a fine line between the child narrator's uninformed, unbiased representation of events and an undercurrent of tacit yet palpable emotion. Besides a German and a Hungarian Bánk, as Nádas writes,

> [there is] a third one that positions itself in the incredibly tense and utterly mysterious relationship that soon emerges between object and language, between language and emotion. This third is the spirit of the narrative itself […].[…] With ascetic objectivity she banishes pathos from tragedy.
>
> [[gibt es] noch eine Dritte, die sich selbst in dem unglaublich gespannten und äußerst geheimnisvollen Verhältnis positioniert, das sich bald zwischen Gegenstand und Sprache, bald zwischen Sprache und Gefühl herausbildet. Diese Dritte ist der Geist der Erzählung selbst […]. […] Mit asketischer Sachlichkeit verbannt sie das Pathos aus der Tragödie.][190]

Bánk's subdued pathos and Roth's near-sentimentality may seem to have little in common. As Zweig remarks, *Hiob* is a novel which "one experiences, rather than reads. And one is not ashamed to finally be shaken quite sentimentally by a true work of art. [[m]an erlebt, statt zu lesen. Und man schämt sich nicht, endlich auch einmal von einem wirklichen Kunstwerk ganz sentimentalisch erschüttert zu sein.]"[191] Still, the novels share a narrative perspective that refuses to blend in entirely with the tragedies they portray. To Bánk's narrator, this is crucial, since her storytelling aims to distance herself from the past, as well as from the paralysis that threatens to overpower her. In *Hiob*, it is a "gifted super-ego [begnadetes Über-Ich]"[192] that accompanies the narrator: it lends Mendel Singer's story an exemplary status, and his misfortune a universal meaning. As Zweig adds, its potential for sentimentality is evened out by Roth's simplicity of style—"No arabesque disturbs his determined and yet never jagged lines [...], no pathos violates the folk-song naturalness of his brilliantly clear [...] language. [Keine Arabeske stört seine entschlossenen und dennoch niemals schroffen Linien [...], kein Pathos verletzt die volksliedhafte Natürlichkeit dieser durchleuchtend klaren [...] Sprache.]"[193] Striking a careful balance between emotion and restraint, both writers lay the foundations for the crucial theme of their stories: hope, a powerful sentiment that, once it crosses the border to pathos, turns into its opposite: despair.

Their 'heroes', then, are quite different from the ones discussed earlier. Whereas the hero motif in *Radetzkymarsch* and *Engelszungen* serves to expose the narrative, even deceitful, nature of imperial unity, the present heroes outline the emergence of courage out of misfortune. Nancy writes: "If [...] the hero traces the interruption of the heroic myth, this does not mean that his acts are deprived of something that we can perhaps no longer correctly call heroism, but that is no doubt at least courage."[194] The current texts focus on that latter aspect, emphasizing an alternative side to the 'interruption' discussed before. "This courage," Nancy continues,

> is not—as one might at first think—the courage to say something that it would be dangerous to dare to proclaim. Of course, such courage exists—but the courage of interruption consists rather in daring to be silent, or rather, [...] it consists in *allowing to be said* something that no one—no individual, no representative—could ever say [...].[195]

Der Schwimmer and *Hiob* indeed display a meaningful tension between silence on the one hand and, on the other, speech, words, or storytelling. Here, the tension is not engaged in a subversive game of truth and fiction. It is related instead to the heroism of recovering a degree of humanity from an authoritarian God, from the oppressive stasis of communist society, and from a disenchanted modern world.

Communities of violence—Communities of silence

In each novel, a process of historical change taking place in the background—a suppressed revolution, or insistent modernity—is mirrored by a traditional family unit falling apart. Bánk and Roth depict these processes by focusing on the authority of the fathers, who are portrayed in their desperate effort to keep the family unit intact, and to resist the changes they are facing. But it is precisely the violence of their attempt that lays bare the disintegration of their families.

"[D]ie grauenhafte Stille einer ganzen gestorbenen Welt"

Roth's novelistic Job is Mendel Singer, who is introduced to the reader as "a pious, God-fearing and ordinary, an entirely everyday Jew [fromm, gottesfürchtig und gewöhnlich, ein ganz alltäglicher Jude]", who practices "the modest profession of a teacher [den schlichten Beruf eines Lehrers]" "without spectacular success [ohne aufsehenerregenden Erfolg]." (H 7) Already from the introductory lines, the reader is to gather that Mendel excels in mediocrity. In no way does he stand out from the religious tradition he carries forward. Because of the emphasis on his plainness, the blows of misfortune that strike him will appear unjust and disproportionate. In Mendel's life, it seems, there is not a single cause for offense to a righteous God, because he lives by piety and ritualized prayer. As a *melamed*,[196] someone who teaches children the Talmud and the Torah, Mendel furthermore derives a sense of authority from his closeness to the divine and his responsibility to disseminate the word of God. Instructing a class of six-year-olds in reading and memorizing the Bible, he recites while his pupils repeat after him: "The bright choir of children's voices repeated word after word, sentence after sentence, it was as if the Bible were being tolled by many bells. Like bells the students' upper bodies swung forward and back [...]. [Der helle Chor der Kinderstimmen wiederholte Wort für Wort, Satz auf Satz, es war als würde die Bibel von vielen Glocken geläutet. Wie Glocken schwangen auch die Oberkörper der Lernenden vorwärts und zurück [...].]" (H 19) The synchronicity of body movement and recitation articulates a profound sense of unity with the *word* of God, which is reinforced by Mendel's disregard of *visual* representation. Loyally respecting the biblical prohibition of mediation of the divine, Mendel evokes the aniconic aspect of Jewish religion:[197] "His upright mind was directed toward the simple earthly things and tolerated no miracle within range of his eyes. [...] His simple piety required no mediating power between God and man. [Sein gerader Sinn vertrug kein Wunder im Bereich der Augen. [...] Seine schlichte Frömmigkeit bedurfte keiner vermittelnden Gewalt zwischen Gott und den Menschen.]" (H 18) It is remarkable, indeed, that there is no mention of Mendel teaching the Talmud (which, as opposed to the Torah, is not considered the law of God but consists of rabbinic teachings and opinions). Mendel's devotion to God's word leaves no room for interpretation or discussion; his immediacy to the divine is absolute. Yet as Nancy observes:

> To strive against idolatry presupposes that one has the highest and most demanding idea of God, or of the absence of all gods. That is precisely what shows up the limits of criticism of idols. For in opposition to the idol there is no *idea* we can form of God, nor of his absence [...].[198]

An important aspect of Mendel's religious renewal, as I will illustrate, involves distancing himself from his immediacy to the idea of God and redirecting his gaze to the world.

It soon becomes evident that tradition and religion yield to an increasingly disenchanted world. Early in the novel, a Sabbath scene—reminiscent of typically idealizing descriptions in Jewish ghetto fiction[199]—appears to start out as a peaceful, uncomplicated family moment:

> [Mendel] sat down, sang a little song, then the parents and children slurped the hot soup, smiled at the plates and spoke not a word. Warmth rose in the room. It swarmed from the pots, the bowls, the bodies. The cheap candles in the nickel silver candlesticks couldn't stand it, they began to bend. Stearin dripped on the brick-red and blue checkered tablecloth and encrusted in no time. The window was flung open, the candles braced up and burned peacefully to their end. [...] [T]he parents remained sitting and gazed with troubled solemnity into the last little blue flames, which shot up jaggedly [...]. The stearin smoldered, thin blue threads of smoke drifted upward to the ceiling from the charred remains of the wick.
>
> [[Mendel] setzte sich, sang ein Liedchen, dann schlürften die Eltern und die Kinder die heiße Suppe, lächelten den Tellern zu und sprachen kein Wort.

Wärme erhob sich im Zimmer. Sie schwärmte aus den Töpfen, den Schüssel, den Leibern. Die billigen Kerzen in den Leuchtern aus Alpaka hielten es nicht aus, sie begannen sich zu biegen. Auf das ziegelrote, blaukarierte Tischtuch tropfte Stearin und verkrustete im Nu. Man stieß das Fenster auf, die Kerzen ermannten sich und brannten friedlich ihrem Ende zu. [...] [D]ie Eltern [...] sahen mit bekümmerten Festlichkeit in die letzten blauen Flämmchen, die gezackt aus den Höhlungen der Leuchter emporschossen [...]. Das Stearin schwellte, blaue dünne Fäden aus Rauch zogen von den verkohlten Dochtresten aufwärts zur Decke.] (H 9–10)

There is more to this scene of 'troubled solemnity' than a simple demonstration of the poverty of the Singer family. What should be a picture of worship and unity actually conveys how the sacred gives way to the material, and beauty to simplicity. Disenchantment seeps into the intimacy of a family gathering. Not once using religious terminology, Roth's narrator robs the scene of any spirituality or devotion. The traditional song at the start of the Sabbath meal is reduced to 'ein Liedchen', and the blessing (*kiddush*) is skipped altogether. Instead, the narrator points out slurping noises, emphasizing the worldly and material aspects of the scene. The candelabrum, for instance, is merely made of poor man's silver. Likewise, the cheap candles—an important attribute of worship otherwise—lose their symbolism as the narrator refers to them as a chemical substance—'stearin', rather than 'candle wax'. More significantly, the holy candles struggle to stay alight in the room without oxygen. The tradition that once held the family together is on the verge of being extinguished. Indeed, as the family does not speak a single word, the warmth in the room should not be mistaken for connection and love, it is just the heat spread by the food on the table.

The word of God, then, does not unite the Singer family at all. On the contrary, whenever God's will seems to manifest itself in blows of misfortune, ripping the family apart, they remain shrouded in deafening silence. When the two eldest sons return with the news that they have been "genommen," i.e. enlisted to join the army, "a terrible silence [ein furchtbares Schweigen]" overtakes the room, "a silence without bounds, much vaster than the space it had captured [ein Schweigen ohne Grenzen, um vieles gewaltiger als der Raum, der seine Beute geworden war]." (H 35) Their loss of words evidences God's retreat and "the harsh reality of modern experience: namely, that divinity [is] withdrawing infinitely from immanence."[200] Indeed, when Deborah implores a *Wunderrabbi* to help her son, her loud, desperate cries convey "the terrible silence of a whole dead world [die grauenhafte Stille einer ganzen gestorbenen Welt]." (H 17)

Menuchim's birth accelerates the family's disintegration. Thirteen months after he is born, it becomes evident that he is severely disabled:

> His broad brow folded and furrowed all over like a crumpled parchment. His legs were curved and lifeless like two wooden bows. His scrawny little arms wriggled and twitched. His mouth stammered ridiculous sounds.
>
> [Seine breite Stirn fächelte und furchte sich kreuz und quer, wie ein zerknittertes Pergament. Seine Beine waren gekrümmt und ohne Leben wie zwei hölzerne Bögen. Seine dürren Ärmchen zappelten und zuckten. Lächerliche Laute stammelte sein Mund.] (H 11)

Roth's conspicuous use of alliteration here draws attention to the storytelling process itself and, as such, to Menuchim's symbolic position within that story. Although eventually he emerges as a redemptory figure who enables Mendel to restore his faith, his disability is of a different symbolic value. The 'crumpled parchment' of his skin likely refers to the scriptures, exemplifying the fragile condition of his father's religion, which has started to lose its unifying power over the family. Moreover, Menuchim grows up without ever uttering more than the word 'Mama'. His speech impairment is like an antidote to Mendel's rigid religiosity. Menuchim may not speak, but his voice is, from birth on, louder than the word of God: "Seine Stimme krächzte über den heiligen Sätzen der Bibel. [His voice croaked over the holy sentences of the Bible.]" (H 10) Menuchim's disability and speech impairment, as the story suggests, are loud reminders of Mendel's responsibility to the world, to his family, rather than to the God he fears. Reminiscent of the redeeming flaws and imperfections in previously discussed texts (in *Alle Tage*, Abel's exchange of perfect proficiency for an accent; Omar's imperfect eyesight; or Dinev's references to 'limping love'), the crippled, babbling child undermines the 'perfect idiom' of the father, his embodiment of the divine word. Menuchim, as I will illustrate, initiates a transformation of Mendel's religious experience, in which the immediacy to the divine word, or immanence, opens up towards an experience of the world, without however giving in to disenchanted secularism. This process requires the recovery of Mendel's human nature and the insertion of distance into his proximity to God. Mendel's transformation thus resembles, to summarize Nancy, "a non-secular experience that would be without a Book, without a Temple, and without God, and for which even the epithet 'divine' would no longer be suitable."[201]

At the heart of Roth's story lies a conflict between conceptions of mankind's relation to the divine, and between the different notions of endurance they imply. Deborah and Mendel argue over the typical distinction between a benevolent God and the wrathful one from the Old Testament. To Mendel, enduring misfortune means submission and resignation to God's authority—"Against the will of heaven there is no power. [Gegen den Willen des Himmels gibt es keine Gewalt.]" (H 38) Deborah, on the other hand, questions Mendel's strict interpretation of the scriptures, and counters that man remains in charge of his own life: "Man must seek to help himself, and God will help him. So it is written, Mendel! You always know the wrong sentences by heart. [Der Mensch muß sich zu helfen suchen, und Gott wird ihm helfen. So steht es geschrieben, Mendel! Immer weißt du die falschen Sätze auswendig.]" (H 39) To the pious Mendel, the signs of imminent modernity are God's punishment, which he undergoes without protest. When, due to an outbreak of smallpox, the authorities subject the Jewish community to forced vaccination, the narrator elevates Mendel's piety above the others: "Some hid. But Mendel Singer, the righteous, fled no divine punishment. Even the vaccination he awaited calmly. [Manche verbargen sich. Mendel Singer aber, der Gerechte, floh vor keiner Strafe Gottes. Auch der Impfung sah er getrost entgegen.]" (H 11) Likewise, Mendel considers Menuchim's illness as a sign of God's will, which he should accept silently. Therefore he rejects a doctor's offer to cure him:

> "No doctor can cure him if God doesn't will it. [...] One is not healed in strange hospitals." Like a hero Mendel held out his scrawny white arm for the vaccination. But he did not give Menuchim away.
>
> ["Gesund machen kann ihn kein Doktor, wenn Gott nicht will. [...] Man wird nicht geheilt in fremden Spitälern." Wie ein Held hielt Mendel seinen dürren weißen Arm zum Impfen hin. Menuchim aber gab er nicht fort.] (H 12–3)

The absurdity of Mendel's 'heroism' is revealed here: both his son's illness *and* modern medical science are God's punishment, but despite that contradiction Mendel persists in his obstinate acquiescence. Deborah, on the other hand, is open to the doctor's suggestion, because it would cost her nothing. Her religious experience is represented in terms of favors, her God is a benefactor. In contrast to Mendel's proximity to God's word, though, Deborah feels distanced from the divine: "She no longer dared appeal to God, He seemed to her too high, too great, too remote, infinitely far beyond infinite heavens, she would have needed a ladder of a million prayers to reach even a hem of God's garment. [Sie wagte nicht mehr Gott anzurufen, er schien ihr zu hoch, zu groß, zu weit, unendlich hinter unendlichen Himmeln, eine Leiter aus Millionen Gebeten hätte sie haben müssen, um einen Zipfel von Gott zu erreichen.]" (H 15) Instead, she looks for help from 'advocates' of God—the deceased, the patriarchs, the bones of Moses—in other words, for a mediated spiritual experience that, just like her obsession with wealth, borders on idolatry. Disheartened when her appeals are not answered, she decides to visit a *tsaddik*. The *Wunderrabbi* prophesies that Menuchim will heal and grow up to be a good man, but only after a very long time. While this knowledge gives her hope, her real predicament will be to endure the long wait and to not let hope turn into despair. The intensity of Deborah's hope is reflected in her neglect of her daily "duty at the stove [Dienst am Herd]," resulting in a house falling into ruin. (H 13) Likewise, Mendel cannot prevent the family from falling apart. When he hears that Menuchim's healing will take a long time, Mendel's despair is portrayed after the image of his own vengeful God:

> He unbuckled his belt and swung it through the air. As if the leather were part of his body, as if it were the natural continuation of his hand, Mendel Singer felt each slapping lash that struck his sons' backs. An uncanny roar broke out in his head. His wife's warning cries fell into his own noise and died away meaninglessly in it.
>
> [Er schnallte den Hosengurt ab und schwang ihn durch die Luft. Als gehörte das Leder noch zu seinem Körper, als wäre es die natürliche Fortsetzung seiner Hand, fühlte Mendel Singer jeden klatschenden Schlag, der die Rücken seiner Söhne traf. Ein unheimliches Getöse brach los in seinem Kopf.] (H 19)

Mendel's outburst, it seems, is a violent attempt at restoring the authority of God's word. The rabbi's prophecy will turn out to be correct, but in the meantime neither Mendel's nor Deborah's prayers will succeed in warding off misfortune, the disintegration of their family, or the arrival of modernity. Mendel's rage drowns out the disenchanted silence that his God has left behind.

A history submerged in silence

Silence, in *Der Schwimmer*, is not the symbol of divine retreat, but it reveals an absence as well: the absent mother represents the prohibition of free speech under communist rule. Katalin's departure to Germany leaves her family in a state of bewilderment and paralysis. The implosion of the family,[202] as in *Hiob*, finds expression in closely intertwining motifs of silence and violence. Opening with a chapter entitled "*Wir*" and closing with her own name "*Kata*," the narrator aligns the account of her family history to the gradual emergence of her singular voice. Her focus on the everyday lives of relatives and friends, who thus appear to be the protagonists, deflects from the 'heroism' of telling her own story. In the opening chapter, Kata paints the picture of a family that has lost its center; a family shrouded in silence, holding on to a past represented by photographs of the mother:

> I had few memories of my mother. Actually, I only knew her from photographs my father kept in a little box. [...] I looked at the pictures often. There were times when I did nothing else. It was that way for my father too. He spent whole days spreading the pictures out on the tablecloth and reshuffling them over and over again [...]. I knew this could go on for days, knew it even though at that age I surely had no real grasp of time. For me there were only the times that were bearable and those that were almost unbearable.
>
> [Ich hatte wenige Erinnerungen an meine Mutter. Im Grunde kannte ich sie nur von Fotos, die mein Vater in einem kleinen Kasten aufbewahrte. [...] Ich schaute mir die Bilder häufig an. Es gab Zeiten, in denen ich nichts anderes tat. Mit meinem Vater war es ähnlich. Er verbrachte ganze Tage damit, die Bilder auf dem Tischtuch auszubreiten und die immer wieder neu zu mischen [...]. Daß es Tage waren, wußte ich, obwohl ich damals sicher keinen Begriff von Zeit hatte. Für mich gab es nur Zeiten, die ich ertragen, und Zeiten, die ich kaum ertragen konnte.] (DS 7)

The narrator's sense of time, as these opening lines indicate, is based entirely on memory and impressions, and her highly personal evaluation of 'the times'. To the children, time tables were "nothing but numbers, numbers next to each other [nichts mehr als Zahlen, nebeneinanderstehende Zahlen]." (DS 24) Indeed, in *Der Schwimmer*, external historical time plays a minor narrative role, even if the chronology of communist history is crucial in understanding some of the protagonists' motivations. The tacit historical background inhibits a reading of Kata's account as a teleological narrative. "[E]nding as it does in 1969," Katarina Nousek observes, "the novel conspicuously ignores the events of 1989, a year that has become a crucial point of orientation for historical accounts of twentieth-century European communism. Whereas historical accounts of communism tend to be anchored in a happy ending coincident with the dissolution of dictatorships, the figures in Bánk's novel [...] have yet to question the permanence of the communist government in Hungary."[203] Yet even while Kata does not relate official Hungarian history, she tells a story of enduring and escaping the fear that stifled individual lives. When, at first, Kata's father evades the questions about the mother's departure, and then answers that she left for work, Kata intuits that something outside of her experience, in historical reality, has changed: "[I] knew that something had changed, that something had shifted that morning and the night before. [[I]ch wußte, etwas war anders, etwas hatte sich verschoben, an diesem Morgen und in der Nacht davor.]" (DS 13) The connection between her mother's departure and the events of 1956 are never made explicit, but Kata's description of the immobility and the lack of future prospects that overpowers her family undeniably reflects the sense of disillusionment and paralysis afterwards: "A gluey strip, black with flies, hung from the lamp overhead. I wondered how they died, those flies, from what. Could you die because you were stuck to something? [Von der Lampe über mir hing ein Klebestreifen, der schwarz von Fliegen war. Ich fragte mich, wie sie starben, diese Fliegen, an was. Konnte man sterben, weil man festklebte?]" (DS 10–11)

Against that seemingly silent historical background, Kata's storytelling counters the void of her mother's unexpected departure. Father Kálmán withdraws into silence time and again, keeping a picture of his wife close to him, oblivious to his children—"We called it diving. Father has gone diving. We'd ask each other, Has Father come back from diving? [Wir nannten es tauchen. Vater taucht. Vater ist zum Tauchen gegangen. Ist Vater zurück vom Tauchen?, fragten wir einander.]" (DS 7–8) Her brother Isti, especially, seems to suffer. Along with his mother, the world has been robbed from a sense of wonder. Instead of the fairytales their mother told them, which Isti would take for truth, the children are now repeatedly told the painful truth of their current situation—"[t]he story about my mother, who left the country without saying a word [[d]ie Geschichte meiner Mutter, die das Land ohne ein Wort verlassen hatte]." (DS 8) In an interview, Bánk clarifies that the absent mother indeed represents "the dark center of the book [das dunkle Zentrum des Buches],"[204] but that she is decidedly not condemned for leaving. She is not the object of a "glorification of the mother image [Verklärung des Mutterbildes]," nor does she represent an "ideal vision of security, of care [Wunschbild der Geborgenheit, der Fürsorge]," nor a utopian "projection screen for the power that binds the 'holy' family together [Projektionsfläche für die Kraft, die die 'heilige' Familie zusammenhält] [...]."[205] Rather, her departure represents an act of empowerment by a woman who refuses to acquiesce in an all-encompassing stasis under communist rule.[206] As I will illustrate, Katalin's *Leerstelle* acquires meaning through contextual associations that anchor the story more firmly in Hungarian history. She symbolizes a liberating aspect of language and communication, which only comes to the surface *ex negativo*, in the silence of her absence.

Her husband Kálmán, on the other hand, evokes the latent yet palpable aggression that marks the village community and the family. Even before Katalin's departure, Kálmán prohibited his children from naming their dog, and any potential for caring is nipped in the bud afterwards. Isti is elated when he spends all his money on seven fish, but Kálmán, in a terrible rage, deliberately and offensively destroys his son's delight—"The fish were on the table, laid neatly in a row. My father had cut off their heads. [Die Fische lagen auf dem Tisch, fein säuberlich nebeneinander. Mein Vater hatte ihnen die Köpfe abgeschnitten.]" Isti then sinks into a "dazed state that was worse than Father's diving [Dämmerzustand, der schlimmer war als Vaters Tauchen]." (DS 22) The violent atmosphere that causes Isti to withdraw is also implied as the reason for Katalin's wordless departure. As in *Engelszungen*, where the fathers as officials embody state authority, Kálmán seems to function as "code name for the institution of the state [Deckname für die Institution des Staates],"[207] though in a far more evocative way. His unpredictable attitude towards the children, alternating between intimidation, occasional commitment, and complete indifference, is indeed reminiscent of the unreliable, repressive regime. The Kádár government, for instance, took measures to silence revolutionaries and their families and to act as if the 1956 events had never happened. Events and periods that were considered "politically undesirable were simply treated [...] in such a way that people were afraid to mention them."[208] School textbooks rendered falsified facts, and people

> were made to forget [...] their experiences, feelings and opinions. They kept silent, and accepted—at least seemingly—the official ideology [...]. Not only on an official level, but on a personal level too: in most families [...] [1956] and the recriminations which followed were taboo subjects.[209]

Katalin's *Leerstelle*, her departure, as well as the silence overpowering her family evoke precisely that 'forbidden' part of Hungarian history. Although she wanted no part in the "hierarchy of violence [Hierarchie der Gewalt]" that defined her family and village life,[210] she did not succeed in staying out of its reach: "Once when she slapped my brother and he started to cry, she cried, too. [Meinen Bruder hat sie einmal geohrfeigt. Als er anfing zu weinen, weinte sie auch.]" (DS 11) Leaving Kálmán, in other words, meant escaping an authoritarian regime: "[M]y father's wishes were law. My mother never contradicted my father. She deserted him. [[D]ie Wünsche meines Vaters waren Gesetz. Meine Mutter hat meinem Vater nie widersprochen. Sie hat ihn verlassen.]" (DS 12)

The motif of silence further connects Katalin's departure to Hungarian history in different indirect ways. Several passages strongly suggest that Katalin was an outsider: a Roma woman and thus presumably a victim of exclusion. In pictures, she is wearing sandals, even when "nobody wore sandals in those days, certainly not in the fields [[n]iemand [...] damals Sandalen [trug], schon gar nicht auf dem Feld]." (DS 7) Her eyes are black, which as a child she had tried to make lighter with soap, because she had been called a gypsy girl in the village (DS 10). She furthermore has a particularly figurative way of speaking (DS 45), and especially her accent or dialect stands out from the others'. Introducing her future husband Kálmán to her parents, she carefully tries on her new name:

> Mrs. Katalin Várhegyi Kálmán Velencei, and she repeated the name again and again, this long name with two V's and two K's, as if to practice it, as if to hear what it sounded like [...]. [...] Kálmán liked the way she pronounced it, her new name, as only she could pronounce words, and now [...] I remembered how our mother had pronounced words: not the way our father did; different from the way we did and from all the other people in our village and all the other villages that we knew.
>
> [Frau Velencei Kálmán Várhegyi Katalin, und dann wiederholte sie diesen Namen, immer wieder, diesen langen Namen, mit zweimal V und zweimal K, als wolle sie ihn einüben, als wolle sie hören, wie er klinge [...]. [...] Kálmán mochte es, wie sie ihn betonte, ihren neuen Namen, so wie nur sie die Worte betonte, und jetzt [...] erinnerte ich mich, wie sie die Worte betont hatte, anders als unser Vater, als wir, als alle anderen im Dorf und in den nächsten Dörfern.] (DS 262)

The way she slowly practices her new name conveys her pride in marrying Kálmán, as if it promises long-awaited social advancement,[211] and announces her way out of an unwelcome (Roma) minority. Yet that emancipatory outlook, Kata's account suggests, must have hit a wall of local prejudice. When Kata and Isti arrive in Szerencs, their host Éva chases away a couple of barefoot boys following them, "as if she were shooing away a cat [als würde sie eine Katze vertreiben]." She even warns the children: "Don't look at them. They're Gypsies. [[S]chaut nicht hin, es sind Zigeuner [...]]." (DS 27) The incident not only illustrates the existing prejudice against the Gypsy population, but the fact that Éva forbids the children to so much as look also implies an assimilatory drive on her part, as she does not seem to want the children to rediscover their original ethnic belonging.[212]

Moreover, Katalin's desire to break free from traditional community life was likely crushed by the forceful emancipation by the state. The history of Hungarian Roma is marked by exclusion and non-policy on the part of various governments,[213] but after the communist seizure of power in 1948, the government started a process of large-scale industrialization. This affected the Roma population in particular, as they were largely active in agricultural professions. "The leaders of the party-state, besides seeking quick and violent solutions to social problems, viewed the Gypsy population as a backup labor force for extensive industrialization [...]." They also emphasized that "social 'integration' [...] of Gypsies could not proceed, because they migrated within the country's borders and traditionally made a living from 'begging.'"[214] Although industrialization and collectivization involved radical changes for all parts of the population equally, the government "surely did seek to induce the Gypsy populations to fit into the new forms of society—i.e. to send their children to schools, to abandon their separate living arrangements, to hold down regular jobs, and to stop migrating."[215] In other words, the socialist regime enforced a process of assimilation under the banner of modernization. When nationalization reached its peak in the early 1950s, the party tried to 'solve' the Roma problem by criminalizing traditional occupations—all in order to "speed up the forceful assimilation of Gypsies."[216] In that way, Katalin's absence and silence, to return to *Der Schwimmer*, are not only reminiscent of the voicelessness of a repressed people, as in *Engelszungen*. From indications in Kata's ingenuous narration, her mother's 'silence' reveals itself as an effect of intensified work in the weaving industry:

> Working in the factory had destroyed my mother's larynx, or so she said. She held the cotton threads taut in her teeth while the machine cleaned them. [...] Little bits of cotton kept getting into my mother's throat, and over the years she swallowed many small scraps.
>
> [Die Arbeit in der Fabrik hatte ihren Kehlkopf zerstört, wie meine Mutter sagte. Zwischen ihren Zähnen hatte sie Fäden aus Baumwolle festgehalten, während eine Maschine die Fäden säuberte. [...] Stückchen aus Baumwolle hatte meine Mutter in den Hals bekommen, über Jahre hatte sie kleine Abfälle geschluckt.] (DS 9)

The effect of the authoritarian regime and her forced employment in socialist labor are presented here as the cause of her voicelessness. Katalin's *Leerstelle* thus invites the reader to trace an ambivalent story of emancipation, in which the escape from traditional community life only encounters continued prejudice and a compelled conformity masquerading as the socialist emancipation of the people.

Even if Kata's account is not an active reconstruction of her mother's history, the narrator does assume a vital position, namely, that of the tradition of oral (family) history that suffered severely in the long wake of 1956. Bánk's deliberate choice for an absent mother instead of a father at first sight reverses historical family roles. In general, the persecuted, imprisoned, or executed revolutionaries of 1956 were men, whose families then had to deal with their absence.[217] Families, and mothers in particular, played a crucial role in their children's knowledge about the the revolt, as well as the perception of their fathers. Bánk underscores that communicative role, by demonstrating the effects of its absence, and then reintroducing it from Kata's perspective. Years after her mother's departure, Kata overhears a conversation between her father and Zsófi, with whom they are currently staying. Her son Jenő is a student whose awareness of the political situation is mirrored in a collection of newspaper photographs "of large stone heads lying amid heaps of rubble on a street [von diesen großen Köpfen aus Stein, die zwischen Trümmern auf einer Straße lagen]." (DS 250) In the wake of the Prague Spring, he leaves unexpectedly, without a word, too. But Zsófi, unlike Kálmán years before, does not withdraw into silence, as the abundant speech verbs in Kata's rendering suggest:

> She had been summoned to the police station, Zsófi *said*, but she wasn't able to *tell* them anything. What could she have *told* them, except that Jenő was gone? "Even if you can't *tell* them a thing, they still summon you, [...] just like they did with you, Kálmán." Isti and I hadn't known our father had been sent for back then, to *tell* the police what had happened to our mother and why, and Zsófi *talked* about it now as if it were alright to *talk* about it [...].
>
> [Zur Polizei habe man sie bestellt, *erklärte* Zsófi, und nichts habe sie *sagen* können. Was hätte sie *sagen* sollen, außer daß Jenő weg war? Man kann ihnen nichts *sagen* und trotzdem bestellen sie einen, [...] wie dich, Kálmán. Isti und ich, wir wußten nichts davon, daß unser Vater bestellt worden war, um zu *reden*, um zu *erzählen*, wie alles gekommen war und warum, und Zsófi *sprach* jetzt so darüber, als dürfe man darüber *sprechen* [...].] (DS 251; emphasis added)

In Kata's eyes, Zsófi—like her mother—evokes a freedom of speech that is crucial in political as well as historical terms. Whereas Kálmán adopts a policy of (coerced) silence, Zsófi recovers a sense of liberation and understanding by discussing history, talking about 'what had happened and why'. Breaking a silence entwined with repression, authoritarianism, and failed emancipation, Zsófi embodies the necessity of communicative memory as an act of resistance: it undermines the official yet falsified narrative of the regime, and it allows a story to be told that might otherwise vanish into oblivion. Kata's account, as I will illustrate, is indeed about leaving a trace in history, about the courage to resist a silence that seems to consume everyone around her.

Allowing something to be said— Hope emerging from silence

Despite different historical and ideological contexts, the families in *Der Schwimmer* and *Hiob* are both confronted with the effects of enforced modernization—by an authoritarian socialist government, by Russian authorities, by the rhythm of American life, or by the gradual disenchantment of religious practice. In terms of modernization, socialist and capitalist worldviews have an important characteristic in common. Sharing an emancipatory future vision, states adhering to either worldview consider "themselves and their time as the beginning of the future and as its depositories [...]. The basic phenomena associated with modernization—industrialization and urbanization—are viewed as the only possible logic for social progress."[218] However, Bánk and Roth outline a hopeful future vision that is not founded on the promise—or 'orthodoxy'—of modern progress, nor does it place the accompanying emphasis on the individual. Their stories do trace the emergence of individuals, acting independent from religion or from a silencing authority, but that emancipaton originates in experiences of community and being in the world. Their hopeful conclusions convey an almost utopian belief in future possibilities—not in the sense that they advocate a clear, unified vision of the future, but simply in the sense that "utopia becomes the capacity to imagine alternative subjectivities and social temporalities."[219]

More specifically, Bánk imagines a new kind of collective experience and temporality; Roth an alternative kind of religious experience allowing the sublime to re-enter modernity. Storytelling and art, as these novels suggest, do not imagine a future that hinges on external attribution (to a divine or state authority; to a future telos; to a miracle). Instead, they picture the future as a matter of people seeking connection to the world at present.

The impact of modernization, in each text, is highlighted by various motifs of nature: landscapes, the sky, the ocean, a lake, or the wind all bring into focus the position of the modern individual in the world. In addition to these, the diasporic and nomadic themes conjure a modern sense of *Heimatlosigkeit* and alienation from nature: in *Der Schwimmer*, an agricultural lifestyle gives way to collectivized factory labor; in *Hiob*, traditional religious practice in the Galician countryside becomes increasingly exposed to modernity. Looking closer, these motifs also convey a drive to withstand those influences—not in terms of desperately and obstinately holding on to tradition or the past, but rather in terms of readjustment to the present world.

"[K]ein Wunder im Bereich der Augen"

In the first chapter of *Juden auf Wanderschaft*, Roth traces the defining aspects that shape the existence of Eastern Jewry. Their history of exclusion and forced displacements, combined with unconditional devotion to the word of God, has culminated in their estrangement from nature and in a preference for abstract concepts over visual perception:

> The Eastern Jew does not perceive the beauty of the East. He was forbidden to live in villages and in large cities as well. The Jews live in filthy streets and dilapidated houses. [...] They become acquainted with the painful hopelessness of Jewish prayer in their earliest childhood; the fierce struggle with a God who punishes more than he loves, and who chalks up a pleasure like a sin; the strict duty of learning and searching for the abstract with young eyes that are still hungry for perception. [...] The great majority do not recognize the soil that nourishes them.
>
> [Der Ostjude sieht die Schönheit des Ostens nicht. Man verbot ihm, in Dörfern zu leben, aber auch in großen Städten. In schmutzigen Straßen, in verfallenen Häusern leben die Juden. [...] Die schmerzliche Aussichtslosigkeit des jüdischen Gebets lernen sie im frühesten Kindesalter kennen; den leidenschaftlichen Kampf mit einem Gott, der mehr straft, als er liebt, und der einen Genuß, wie eine Sünde ankreidet; die strenge Pflicht, zu lernen und mit jungen Augen, die noch hungrig nach der Anschauung sind, das Abstrakte zu suchen. [...] Die große Mehrzahl kennt den Boden nicht, der sie ernährt.][220]

By the same token, the *Ostjude*, who does not acknowledge "the boundless width of the horizon [die grenzenlose Weite des Horizonts]" or "the advantages of his homeland [die Vorzüge seiner Heimat]," unjustly considers the West as a paradise where Jews can live protected from pogroms and exclusion.[221] In *Hiob*, Roth pictures Mendel Singer's predicament against the same background, situated between religious *Weltabgewandtheit* and utopian vision. His complete identification with the word of God reveals itself in (learned) disregard for his natural surroundings, a distrust of visual representation that ties in with an aniconic religious practice. Only in retrospect do these images acquire value: after emigration, and after God's abandonment, they emerge as memories of a lost *Heimat* (see below). Yet *Hiob* is not a story of dissimilatory desire; it describes a careful mutual embrace of traditional religion and secular modernity.

The many references to nature in *Hiob*—landscapes and skies in particular—are reminders of the natural roots of Jewish religion,[222] with holidays inspired by the cycle from sowing to first and final harvest, monthly greetings of the new moon, and blessings spoken at the sight of natural phenomena like the sea, the mountains, rainbows, or blossoming trees.[223] Looking closer, though, the motif really brings out the opposite, namely, "the very substance of the existence of the Eastern Jews who live alienated from nature [das Wesen der naturentfremdeten Existenz der Ostjuden]."[224] A gathering of Jews in an open field illustrates how, despite their celebration of the new moon, elements of nature have little bearing on their religious experience:

> And they hastened, silent and black, in disorderly little groups, behind the houses, saw in the distance the forest, which was black and silent like them, but eternal in its rooted persistence, saw the veils of night over the wide fields and finally stopped. They looked to the sky and sought the curved silver of the new heavenly body that today was born once again as on the day of its creation. They formed a tight group, opened their prayer books, white shimmered the pages, black stared the angular letters before their eyes in the night's bluish clearness, and they began to murmur the greeting to the moon and to rock their upper bodies back and forth so that they looked as if shaken by an invisible storm.
>
> [[S]ie hasteten, stumm und schwarz, in regellosen Grüppchen, hinter die Häuser, sahen in der Ferne den Wald, der schwarz und schweigsam war wie sie, aber ewig in seinem verwurzelten Bestand, sahen die Schleier der Nacht über den weiten Feldern und blieben schließlich stehn. Sie blickten zum Himmel

und suchten das gekrümmte Silber des neuen Gestirns, das heute noch einmal geboren wurde, wie am Tage seiner Erschaffung. Sie schlossen sich zu einer dichten Gruppe, schlugen ihre Gebetbücher auf, weiß schimmerten die Seiten, schwarz starrten die eckigen Buchstaben vor ihren Augen in der nächtlichbläulichen Klarheit, und sie begannen, den Gruß an den Mond zu murmeln und die Oberkörper hin und her zu wiegen, daß sie aussahen wie von einem unsichtbaren Sturm gerüttelt.] (H 61–2)

From a distanced perspective, the narrator points out a visual likeness between the gathering Jews and the dark and silent woods, but he quickly acknowledges their fundamental difference. Unlike the trees, the Jewish community is *entwurzelt*, disconnected from nature altogether. Even though gathered to celebrate the new moon, their sense of unity does not derive from their natural surroundings. The collection of individuals only becomes a closed unit once their upward gaze turns downward, towards the written word, on which the narrator suddenly focuses, as if he were standing among them. When they start moving to the rhythm of their prayer, the narrator again likens them to shaking trees, but the 'invisible wind' that moves them is born of their recitation, rather than their connection to surrounding nature. In fact, the images of nature emphasize their existential *Heimatlosigkeit* and disconnection from the earth—"Alien to them was the earth on which they stood, hostile the forest, which stared back at them, spiteful the yapping of the dogs, whose mistrustful ears they had awakened, and familiar only the moon [...]. [Fremd war ihnen die Erde, auf der sie standen, feindlich der Wald, der ihnen entgegenstarrte, gehässig das Kläffen der Hunde, deren mißtrauisches Gehör sie geweckt hatten, und vertraut nur der Mond [...].] (H 62)

Underscoring the estrangement of the Jewish 'people of the Book' from its natural origins, Roth's narrator emphasizes that their sense of home exists only in relation to (the word of) God.[225] Indeed, Mendel's devotion is accompanied by an inability, fear even, to establish a relation with his surroundings, "afraid of the unknown earth and the dangerous worms it most likely harbored [hatte Angst vor der unbekannten Erde und dem gefahrvollen Gewürm, das sie höchstwahrscheinlich beherbergte]." (H 62) To Mendel, the divine does not manifest itself in nature, as Roth's concise, factual renditions of nature underscore. Focalizing through Mendel's promiscuous daughter Mirjam, by contrast, who has abandoned Jewish tradition, the narrator presents a far more poetic and encompassing picture of nature (H 73–4). When she sleeps with cossacks in a cornfield, "in the middle of the field, embedded among the fruits of the earth, surrounded and overarched by the heavy grain [mitten im Feld, eingebettet zwischen den Früchten der Erde, umgeben und überwölbt vom schweren

Korn]," the grain ears seem to willingly give in to her presence (H 88). In other words, Mendel's daughter has been incorporated by physical nature, whereas the orthodox Jews remain foreign bodies.[226]

Mendel's *Weltabgewandtheit* and inability to connect with the world are rooted in his religious mistrust of the visual. As mentioned earlier, his identification with the biblical word prohibits representation and mediation of the divine. In Mendel's experience, therefore, the physical and aesthetic appearance of nature does not convey a divine presence; it only impedes an immediate relation to God.[227] Nature has an intellectual rather than a spiritual effect on him—it conceals rather than reveals the divine:

> He saw above him the sky and the stars and thought, they conceal God. All this the Lord created in seven days. And when a Jew wants to go to America, it takes years! "Do you see how beautiful the country is?" asked Sameshkin.
>
> [Er sah über sich den Himmel und die Sterne und dachte, sie verdecken Gott. All das hat der Herr in sieben Tagen geschaffen. Und wenn ein Jude nach Amerika fahren will, braucht es Jahre! "Siehst du, wie schön das Land ist?" fragte Sameschkin.] (H 81)

Here, Roth reiterates his observation of *Juden auf Wanderschaft*—that the Eastern, orthodox Jew, who has trained himself to look for abstract concepts, is no longer able to perceive beauty or transcendence in nature. Mendel's devotion to God's word does not allow him to establish a relation with the world as it presents itself to him, let alone to *act* in it. His concept of endurance—resignation and immobility—is thus tied to the ambivalence of his crisis: on the one hand, his devotion does not allow him to partake in the world but, on the other, his religious practice is not immune to the disenchantment of modernity, either. Mendel's emigration to America, despite its largely negative connotations, is a necessary stage in breaking free from that immobility, enabling a double recalibration: it encourages a religious embrace of the modern world and, conversely, allows the spiritual and the sublime to find their way to modernity and to nature again.

Although the Singers continue to suffer the blows of misfortune in America, and Mendel even rejects his faith in anger, the second part of the novel subtly paves the way towards the uncharacteristically happy ending.[228] On his way to America, his perception of the ocean carries a promise of hope and future change. "[C]alm and without fear [[R]uhig und ohne Furcht]," Mendel is comforted by the "the endlessness of the choppy water [Unendlichkeit des bewegten Wassers.]"

Here, he is humbled by the infinity of God's presence—"[H]e turned [...] in a semicircle and murmured the blessing that is to be spoken at the sight of the sea. [[E]r drehte sich [...] im Halbkreis und murmelte den Segen, der zu sprechen ist beim Anblick des Meeres.]" (H 98) Even so, this tentative acknowledgement of the divine does not affect his notion of endurance just yet. His inability to be present in the world is compounded by his position in-between utopian ideals. In Galicia, Mendel and Deborah felt that their endurance has reached its limits. There, America held the promise for a better future. Yet American life, to Mendel and Deborah, is a far cry from the emancipatory promise symbolized by their son, and self-made man, Sam/Schemarjah. In a typically modernist evocation of metropolitan pace, confusion, stench, and ugliness (H 102–3), the city image comprises truly dystopian traits. Their arrival in New York leads to Mendel's breakdown, now portrayed as a victim of modern life—"America besieged him, America broke him, America shattered him. [Amerika drang auf ihn ein, Amerika zerbrach ihn, Amerika zerschmetterte ihn.]" (H 103) Mendel's almost perfunctory identity crisis in the city as well as Roth's ostensibly simplified portrayal of America have been criticized as a narrative failure, for "America is for Joseph Roth a failed literary location: the settings are caricatured and false, the characters underdeveloped and flat, and the pervasive negative tone takes its toll on the novel."[229] However, just as Roth's portrayal of the Empire in *Radetzkymarsch* does not claim to be historically accurate, so too is his dystopian characterization of the modern city—which he knew from a distance only[230]— significant primarily in a narrative and symbolic respect. Taking into account Mendel's exemplarity, his diasporic movement between different locations symbolizes a transformation that is both 'territorial' and spiritual. America provides the locus for Mendel's "Job-like trial—seemingly senseless suffering at the hands of a higher power,"[231] but it lays the foundations for his triumph and miraculous happiness as well.

As a literary device, the American metropolis at first conveys a profound disillusionment with the project of modernity. Roth's narrator barely contains his cynicism as he paints the picture of the American dream—a paramount picture of modern Enlightenment optimism—and reduces it to absurdity: "Soon people will fly like birds, swim like fish, see the future like prophets, live in eternal peace and in perfect harmony build skyscrapers to the stars. [Bald werden die Menschen fliegen wie Vögel, schwimmen wie Fische, die Zukunft sehn wie Propheten, im ewigen Frieden leben und in vollkommener Eintracht bis zu den Sternen Wolkenkratzer bauen.]" (H 120) Its Enlightened "belief in oneself [Glaube an sich selbst]" (H 120) mocks Mendel's earlier subjective disintegration. What is more, to Mendel and Deborah, the American promise entails a complete denial of their individual agency: "It was as if they, Deborah and Mendel, had not voluntarily made the decision to go to America, but rather as if America had come over them, set upon them. [Es war, als hätten sie [...] nicht freiwillig den Entschluß gefaßt, nach Amerika zu gehn, sondern als wäre Amerika über sie gekommen, über sie hergefallen [...]]." (H 92) Witnessing such hyperbolic, indeed utopian, optimism, Mendel withdraws into reminiscence, which however suffers from a lack of nuance and backward oriented idealization itself—"Those meadows had been there, and those flowers! [...] If we had stayed there—thought Mendel—nothing at all would have happened! [Diese Wiesen hatte es dort gegeben und diese Blumen! [...] Wären wir dort geblieben—dachte Mendel,— gar nichts wäre geschehen!" (H 137) Mendel's lament is ambiguous. Obviously, in his idealized hypothetical past, misfortune would not have struck again. His exclamation also suggests, though, that had they not moved to America, they would have remained stuck in immobility—literally 'nothing would have happened', neither misfortune nor a chance for hope.

Indeed, beneath the crushing disillusionment with modern life, Mendel's American experience maps out "a positive, or at least *possible*, model of Jewish existence in modernity,"[232] an existence averse to utopian/dystopian visions. Mendel's attitude towards his God and towards the world transforms in such a way that he recaptures a sense of agency and acknowledges the sublime within the modern. In the angry rejection of his faith, Mendel discovers an authority of his own: "Why did he appear taller and statelier to them all? [Warum erschien er allen größer und stattlicher?]" (H 139) Refusing to partake in the "deception [Trug]" that his daily rituals had offered him (H 150), he redirects his gaze to the world surrounding him, helping his neighbors out with the daily chores and preparations for religious holidays (H 150–1). On the broken shards of his faith, Mendel experiences a renewal that is religious and aesthetic in nature but, first and foremost, distinctly modern. Eventually, Mendel's endurance is rewarded by his reunion with Menuchim, who is fully healed and travelling the world as a famous orchestra conductor. Although his re-emergence in Mendel's life most definitely carries messianic overtones,[233] the decisive moment of their reunion involves an *aesthetic* experience. Listening to a new record on his neighbor's gramophone, Mendel is deeply moved by one of the "new songs from Europe [neue Lieder aus Europa]"—"How is it possible that the whole world is engraved on such a small disk? [Wie ist es möglich, daß die ganze Welt auf so einer kleinen Platte eingraviert ist?]" (H 156) As it turns out, the song is called "Menuchim's Lied" and has been recorded by his abandoned son. Yet the actual miracle of their reunion, it seems, is that of modern technology—"no miracle within range of his eyes [kein Wunder im Bereich der Augen]," but rather an unexpected musical encounter. Although a secular experience, it strongly reminds him of ritual chanting and singing to his infant son. A symbolic association between Menuchim, once a crippled child, and the gramophone presages Mendel's musical awakening:[234]

> [Sam] already owns a gramophone, Miriam borrows it sometimes from her sister-in-law and carries it in faithful arms through the streets, *as if it were a sick child.* The gramophone can play many waltzes, but also Kol Nidre.
>
> [Ein Gramophon besitzt [Sam] schon, Mirjam leiht es manchmal bei der Schwägerin aus und trägt es in getreuen Armen durch die Straßen, *wie ein krankes Kind.* Das Gramophon kann viele Walzer spielen, aber auch Kol-Nidre.] (H 108; emphasis added)

The latter statement underscores the versatility of modern technology—useful for worldly entertainment, as well as for the declaration of vows on Yom Kippur. From a Nancian perspective, the gramophone furthermore yields an experience of 'distanced proximity' in several ways. Technologically, it brings together spatially and/or temporally separated senders and receivers; psychologically, it allows the listener to relive past emotions; and spiritually, it allows an encounter with the sublime, which comprises the divine and the aesthetic at once. As Nancy describes the proximity, yet fundamental difference, between the sacred and the aesthetic:

> Though all art is sacred, and though there is doubtless nothing sacred except where there is art, art and the divine are nevertheless two totally distinct things. Which is to say that when the divine manifests itself, art itself is reduced to nothing. Selfsame with whatever thing the divine is made manifest (for example, a thing of nature, an animal, a stone, or else man himself), this manifestation places the thing within the sphere of art. But at the same time it reduces art as such to nothing.[235]

Mendel's acoustic reawakening, in this respect, does not breach the prohibition of iconic mediation. Unlike previously, when he considered his immediacy to the word of God and to the idea of the divine as absolute and therefore not suitable for mediation, his aesthetic reconnection with the sublime stakes no claim in absolute knowledge. Rather, art allows him brief glimpses into the sacred, while never allowing him full access, due to its secular nature. It provides a "face-to-face encounter that remains blind and unavowable inasmuch as gods and humans are present to one another in utter strangeness."[236] Indeed, in the final scene, Mendel seems to have recovered his sense of humanity, feeling "a strange and also forbidden longing to take off the cap of old silk rep and let the sun shine on his old pate. And for the first time in his life Mendel Singer voluntarily uncovered his head [ein merkwürdiges und auch verbotenes Verlangen, die Mütze aus altem Seidenrips abzulegen und die Sonne auf seinen alten Schädel scheinen zu lassen. Und zum erstenmal in seinem Leben entblößte Mendel Singer aus freiem Willen sein Haupt] [...]." (H 186–7) Although prohibited by religious law, taking off his hat resembles a touching gesture that underscores Mendel's recaptured humanity and his humility toward the world he now embraces. *Hiob* thus traces a tentative mutual recalibration of traditional religion and secular modernity, a slight touch that Robertson sees reflected in Roth's conspicuous style as well:

> [T]he very thinness of Roth's realism leaves space for the mysterious and the miraculous. [...] [M]odernism, which might seem to be the literary mode appropriate for a disenchanted world, in fact allows the spiritual to re-enter, not as a matter of dogmatic certainty, but as a vivid and tantalizing possibility.[237]

Leaving with(out) a trace

In Bánk's novel, the nature motif and the multilayered images of both water and swimming highlight the protagonists' conflicting desires to escape stasis, yet to leave a trace of their personal history at the same time. When Kata's family first moves to Budapest, she describes their life in the city as an experience of immobility, both physically and temporally:

> Wherever I looked, I saw nothing but brick walls, house walls, doors. [...] I longed to get away. [...] It was as if someone had stopped all the clocks, as if time were not passing for us. As if someone had dropped Isti and me in syrup and then forgotten about us.
>
> [Wo ich hinsah, sah ich nichts als Mauern, Türen, Wände. [...] Ich wollte weg. [...] Es war, als habe jemand alle Uhren zum Stehen gebracht, als liefe die Zeit für uns nicht weiter. So, als habe man Isti und mich in Sirup fallen lassen und dort vergessen.] (DS 17)

To Kata, the fear of being forgotten and of disappearing without a trace just like her mother is closely entwined with feelings of physical entrapment and of time standing still. The family's nomadic mobility, then, is more than a simple allusion to the Roma background of the mother. It articulates the protagonists' desire to escape and, at the same time, to regain control over their lives—"As long as we kept moving, our world also continued to move, to turn, and we thought we could make it stop turning whenever we wished. [Bewegten wir uns, dann bewegte sich, drehte sich auch unsere Welt weiter, und wir glaubten, sie könne in einem Augenblick zum Stehen kommen, in dem wir es wünschten.]" (DS 102) Interestingly, as Lengl observes, the family's nomadic existence echoes an implied Hungarian idiom that further emphasizes their hopelessness and political impotence. Lengl is reminded of the phrase "megszoksz, vagy megszöksz," which she translates as "you either get used to it, or you run [du gewöhnst dich dran, oder fliehst]."[238] Indeed, Kata is used to being constantly on the move, because it creates an illusion of mobility and change that is not actually there—"the way you become used to something you know will always stay, whether you like it or not [wie man sich gewöhnt an etwas, von dem man weiß, es wird bleiben, ob man möchte oder nicht]." (DS 230) But whereas most characters seem to have adopted a mindset of 'abwarten', of biding their time—an attitude reflecting the political stagnation of their country,[239] Katalin apparently could not get used to waiting and enduring and had to escape: "At some point, all you can do with this life is endure it [...], but Kálmán's wife wasn't suited for enduring. [Irgendwann gehe es allein ums Ertragen, [...] um nichts anderes mehr, aber fürs Ertragen sei Kálmáns Frau nicht gemacht] [...]." (DS 264)

For a long time—"but what did long really mean in the way we measured time [aber was soll das schon heißen, was soll das schon sein in unserer Zeitrechnung [...]: lange]" (DS 101)—Kata and Isti seem to find stability near Lake Balaton, where they learn how to swim. In *Der Schwimmer*, the image of water is not solely associated with more obvious meanings such as freedom, nor does it substitute a missing female element.[240] Rather, water, and the lake in particular, symbolizes existence itself, as well as its inherent contradictions. Associated with questions of integration and synthesis, memory and narration, the swimming motif serves as "paradigmatic sign for a tentative search for new orientations and locations [paradigmatische[r] Zeichen für eine behutsame Suche nach neuen Orientierungen und Verortungen]."[241] In *Der Schwimmer*, the oppositional themes that structure the story are merged into a single experience. Mobility versus stasis, community versus isolation, life versus death—the swimming motif "connects the oppositions into a utopia of universal fusion [[verbindet] die Gegensätze zu einer Utopie der All-Verschmelzung]."²⁴² Yet Kata's rendering leaves a dark lining around their days near the lake, a sense of foreboding that conveys the lake's ambivalent symbolism and the fragility of its utopian effect.

When they first arrive near Lake Balaton, Kata's impressions are quite different from hers of Budapest. Instead of physical obstructions and a syrup-like slowing down of time, she observes the absence of boundaries and even of time itself: "It was as if there were no demarcation between day and night here, no definite time when one ended and the other began. [Es war, als gebe es hier keine Grenze zwischen Tag und Nacht, als sei keine Zeit bestimmt, in der das eine für das andere aussetzten mußte, um Stunden später wieder anzufangen.]" (DS 59) The lake indeed appears to be a catalyst for the dissolution of differences and violence, as the children suddenly stop fighting with each other (DS 78), and its proximity renders family arguments harmless—a source of amicable connection, even: "For weeks afterward we argued, my father, Isti, and I about whether the water that day was green or blue. [Ob das Wasser an diesem Tag eher grün oder eher blau gewesen war—darüber stritten wir noch Wochen später, mein Vater, Isti und ich.]" (DS 63) Although her memories are "covered in a leaden melancholy [von einer bleiernen Melancholie überzogen]"²⁴³ otherwise, Kata vividly remembers scarce, ephemeral moments of belonging while swimming with her father and brother:

> Isti and I, we ran into the water so quickly that it splashed up to our shoulders, and then we swam out, side by side this time, at the same level, our father not even a bit faster than Isti and I, and I was not sure whether it was because we were swimming better, because he had slowed down, or because he was really waiting for us.
>
> [[I]sti und ich, wir liefen ins Wasser, so schnell, daß es hochspritzte, bis zu unseren Schultern, und dann schwammen wir hinaus, diesmal nebeneinander, auf gleicher Höhe, unser Vater kein bißchen schneller als Isti und ich, und ich wußte nicht, war es, weil wir schon besser schwammen, war es, weil er langsamer geworden war oder weil er wirklich auf uns wartete.] (DS 224; author's translation)

Although indeed a short reprieve from their reality as well as their 'territorial' existence,²⁴⁴ their swimming escapism does little to allay the fear of disappearing into oblivion. When Kata's father returns ashore, he does not notice her presence (DS 77–8), which an image of erased footprints underscores: "My father's footprints were the only ones here. I always wiped mine away before leaving.

[Die Fußspuren meines Vaters waren die einzigen, die ich hier entdecken konnte. Meine verwischte ich jedesmal, bevor ich ging.]" (DS 77) At first, this may seem to indicate her desire to shed her *Landexistenz* as well, just like her father and her brother. On other occasions, though, she deliberately leaves traces of her nomadic existence, as if to ward off the force of oblivion:

> They would forget us as soon as we boarded a train or climbed into some stranger's car. [...] No traces of us. We left nothing behind. [...] Later I would hide stones, feathers, and coins in the houses we lived in and left. I hid them in closets, above door frames, behind windows, and in stoves. I never forgot a single one of my hiding places.
>
> [Sobald wir uns wieder in den Zug setzten oder in einen fremden Wagen stiegen [...] hatte man uns hier vergessen. [...] Von uns gab es keine Spuren. Wir hinterließen nichts. [...] Später fing ich an, Steine, Federn oder Geldstücke in den Häusern zu verstecken, in denen wir eine Zeitlang gelebt hatten [...]. Ich versteckte sie in Schränken, über Türrahmen, hinter Fenstern und in Öfen. Ich vergaß nicht eines meiner Verstecke.] (DS 39)

So, if Kata deliberately erases her footsteps in the sand, it either means that she does not want to leave the place, since she only hides traces in places she has to leave. Or, from a more distant perspective, the erased marks in the sand rather convey her fear of disappearing without a trace; as if she senses that the lake, offering an all too easy escape, will dissolve her as it seems to dissolve anything. For a lake is not the same as a river, as their host Virág implies at their arrival—"'We've lived by the water, too,' Isti said. 'After all, a river is water, isn't it?' Virág said yes, but it sounded like a no. [Isti erwiderte, auch wir haben am Wasser gelebt, schließlich sei auch ein Fluß Wasser, oder nicht? Ja, sagte Virág, aber es klang wie ein Nein.]" (DS 64) Indeed, for all the relief it offers, the lake's standing water, unlike a river's flow, implies stagnation, holding no promise for progress or change. Whereas Kálmán and Isti submerge themselves in the silence of their 'diving'—be it in the lake or in their heads—Kata resists losing herself in memory or in a substitute for reality. For a while, Kata and Isti make up their own stories to explain their mother's absence but, unlike her brother, she remains aware of the fact that they are merely fictions (DS 98).[245] Isti, on the other hand, withdraws into a world of his own making, where he hears "things that made no sound [Dinge [...] die keinen Laut von sich gaben]" (DS 72–3) and speaks "in a language of his own [in seiner eigenen Sprache]." (DS 61) For Isti, that re-enchantment of the world has a fatal outcome. He nearly drowns when he follows a vision of his mother into a freezing river: "He had seen his mother walking across the water and just wanted to follow her. [[E]r habe sie übers Wasser laufen sehen, seine Mutter, und er habe ihr bloß folgen wollen.]" (DS 277) He dies of a lung infection shortly afterwards.

Searching for a balance between remembrance and forgetting, Kata gradually reveals several stages in the "mythical timelessness of swimming [mythische Überzeitlichkeit des Schwimmens]"[246] and the image of water as a symbol of memory and oblivion. In a first stage, swimming allows the children to forget about the reality of their mother's abandonment, but it also threatens to draw them into oblivion themselves. Taking into account the Hungarian context, it furthermore hints at a truth withheld or erased from history. Additionally, from an even broader perspective, with an eye to the tacit political background, the lake also represents the course of history itself, which may submerge individual stories and tragedies in silence. Kata, though not overtly, takes a decidedly different approach. Whereas the image of water, like memory, lacks coherence and intention, and furthermore "eludes verbalization [sich der Versprachlichung entzieht],"[247] Kata assumes the role required of oral history and communicative memory. Kata remembers their stay at the lake with the sense that they remained stuck in a stagnant present—"the feeling that they were living on a spinning top, on a point, where you turn it and let it go, and we, we spinned along with it, always on the same spot, always under the same sky [das Gefühl, wir lebten auf einem Kreisel, auf einer Spitze, dort, wo man ihn dreht und losläßt, und wir, wir drehten uns mit ihm, immer auf der einen Stelle, immer unter demselben Himmel]." (DS 270; own translation) Tearing herself away from that all-encompassing state of paralysis, her account suggests that submerging stories in silence is not a viable strategy for a future, even if she wonders about the accuracy of her perspective (DS 207). By recording her family history, however subjective it may be, Kata has 'immortalized' their traces and is able to look forward: "The narrator Kata collects the (memory) images of her life in order to protect them from oblivion. [Die Erzählerin Kata sammelt die (Erinnerungs)Bilder ihres Lebens zusammen, um diese vor dem Vergessen in Sicherheit zu bringen.]"[248]

Kata's restored sense of agency emerges against the background of the Prague Spring. Only months after the fact does she learn that someone set himself on fire in Prague.[249] In the final chapter bearing her own name—only at this point does the historical context become more explicit—Kata narrates from a diegetic present in which she is still on the fence about looking into the past or towards the future,[250] as do her friends, who are still divided over the meaning and implications of Palach's act in Czechoslovakia. Narrating as an indefinite 'we', here, Kata believes that a future outlook requires a collective. Yet an incident a few months earlier demonstrates that collective action also depends on individual effort. A few months ago, their lake house was destroyed by a fire—an allusion to the events in Prague, connecting the passage to the political context more explicitly. While everyone rushes to extinguish the flames, their host Ági would rather remain in a familiar state of immobile endurance:

> [Ági] kept holding on to the back of a chair and said she'd rather stay, rather stay and wait, sit by the water until it was over [...]. But Isti took both her hands and pulled her across the wooden boards, out of the restaurant, up the path, and I pressed against Ági's back with the palms of my hands [...]. Isti let go of Ági's hands, and Ági put them to her mouth, and we stood there until Ági dropped her hands and said, hurry, let's go.
>
> [[Ági] hielt sich weiter fest an einer Stuhllehne und sagte, daß sie lieber bleiben wolle, lieber bleiben und warten, am Wasser sitzen, bis es vorbei, bis es ausgestanden war [...] aber Isti zog sie an beiden Händen über den Kies, über die Holzplatten, hinaus aus dem Lokal, den Weg hoch, und ich drückte meine flachen Hände auf Ágis Rücken [...]. Isti ließ Ágis Hände los, und Ági legte sie auf ihre Lippen, und so standen wir, bis Ági ihre Hände fallen ließ und sagte, schnell, gehen wir.] (DS 214)

It is only due to Kata's and Isti's individual yet joined efforts that Ági breaks away from her paralysis, taking control over the situation, and ordering the townspeople around, "as if there was nothing she could do better than shout orders, as if she had always done that and nothing else [als könne sie nichts besser als Befehle schreien, als habe sie immer schon das getan und nichts anders]." (DS 214–5) Relating how people become engaged "to collectively move their storyworld toward crucial action,"[251] Kata's oral history reveals its political and historical significance. In line with Palach's ethical appeal,[252] it demonstrates that withdrawal into passive silence holds no future; only present action and engagement with the world. Through her narration, Kata recasts an otherwise static, silent past into a source of meaning for the future.[253] While her imagination of that future remains unspecified, it involves a collective future that does not exclude the value of the individual. In the final lines, Kata intends to leave the country, with her father's approval:

> I have been told that it will take time, I will have to wait, perhaps longer than I think, certainly longer, and I have said that it doesn't matter, it doesn't matter at all, I can wait, and then I said again: I can wait, yes.
>
> Man hat mir erklärt, es wird dauern, ich werde warten müssen, vielleicht länger, als ich denke, bestimmt länger, und ich habe gesagt, es macht nichts, es macht gar nichts, ich kann warten, und dann hab ich noch einmal gesagt: Ich kann warten, ja. (DS 284; author's translation)

Even though she is still waiting—be it for an official permit or just for the right opportunity[254]—the tone of this final passage is subtly different from the paralysis and despair that permeate the story elsewhere. For the first time, she speaks from her own wishes, confirming the triumph of her voice over oppressive silence. Her 'waiting' thus implies a different temporality than before: stagnation has yielded to a future perspective. Just as in *Radetzkymarsch*—another storyworld marked deeply by stagnation—so too should the melancholy tone of *Der Schwimmer* not be mistaken for nostalgia. Bánk does not present a picture of childhood innocence, of a time when political history had not yet arrived in her everyday experience. Nor does she "direct attention to a communist past in order to mourn the post-communist absence of collective labour."[255] Instead, reminiscent of Roth's novel, Bánk describes the disruption of a static past and reflects on how it may inform the present and the future, without lapsing into utopian images.

If Bánk's and Roth's masterful balance between pathos and restraint allows for any message, for 'something to be said', it must be that art and storytelling are crucial in a re-enchantment of the world. Against different ideological backgrounds, both authors picture the emergence of hope in a world that has fallen silent—under the authority of a repressive regime and while facing the challenge of modernity. In *Hiob*, that silence is interrupted by modern art, allowing miracles to enter the world again; in *Der Schwimmer*, storytelling and oral history allow individuals to leave traces in a postcommunist world. Enlightened modernity, as these novels suggest, becomes oppressive and hard to endure when it is robbed of the sublime, but withdrawal into religion, or into a stagnant past, holds no promise for a future, either. While family connections force the protagonists to stay present in the world, art and storytelling make the endurance of misfortune bearable.

Conclusion

Every myth produces its own heroes. Roth and Dinev explore notions of heroism that expose the myth itself. The storytelling heroics of a partisan grandfather or the futile quest of the 'Ritter der Wahrheit' both engage the reader in a game of truth and fiction, of history and textbooks, laying bare the narrative origins of the 'imagined community'. As Nancy summarizes:

> [T]he mythic hero—and the heroic myth—interrupts his pose and his epic. He tells the truth: that he is not a hero, not even, or especially not, the hero of writing or literature, and that there is no hero, there is no figure who alone assumes and presents the heroism of the life and death of commonly singular beings. He tells the truth of the interruption of his myth, the truth of the interruption of all founding speeches, [...] of speech that schematizes a world and that fictions an origin and an end.[256]

Der Schwimmer and *Hiob* picture the heroics of hope and endurance and the emergence of courage out of misfortune. By recovering their sense of humanity and their individual voices from the 'orthodoxy' of modernity and from an oppressive regime, these unusual heroes resist the schematization of the world in terms of originary fictions and utopian outcomes. All four novels, then, represent the triumph of art and storytelling over the authority of myth—even if their heroes remain the victims of these myths.

CONCLUSION

THE FALLIBILITY OF *BILDUNG*

Any conclusion to be drawn from the comparative close readings gathered in this study extends well beyond the status of the authors' position on the constitutive outside, beyond the preliminary denominators 'literature of migration' and 'German-Jewish literature', and even beyond the German (-language) context. In a variety of themes and motifs—ranging from the position of the artist, to the metropolitan experience, to the disintegration of imperial myth—the examined texts can be read as attempts to subvert, renegotiate, or adapt the narrative of *Aufklärung* as the sole bearer of modernity. Indeed, they reverberate with the ambivalence of Enlightenment that, to this day, shapes European modernity. Especially within a polarized social context, when Enlightenment values become drawn into a rhetoric of *Kultur* and national identity, many literary texts—more implicitly than explicitly—revisit the principles of the Enlightenment, revealing how its promise—emancipation, the embrace of secularism, and self-development as tickets to a society of equals—fails to be redeemed, proving insufficient in breaking down walls of cultural prejudice and exclusion.

Particularly the Enlightenment ideal of *Bildung*, the 'vessel' of German-Jewish assimilation, is shown to lose its appeal, in a contemporary, 'transnational' context as well. In a traditional definition, *Bildung* is seen as a teleological identification process towards the harmonious and unified recognition of selfhood, a process "that requires a complex, well-calibrated dialectical integration of the individual and the community."[1] In several selected works, that identification process is presented as deficient. Kermani and Schnitzler, for instance, thoroughly question the outcomes of self-cultivation as an effective strategy of emancipation and developing selfhood. Else, who has clearly been raised according to the bourgeois principles of *Bildung*, is unable to free herself from the same 'aesthetic' code that supports her assimilation, and forces her into the role of an aesthetic commodity. Kermani, with his aesthete Dariusch, makes a subtle mockery of self-cultivation, as it leads to irritating compliance with market demands. The narrator's education merely consists of Persian language courses that furnish his well-manicured exotic appeal. The city dwellers in Mora's and Jacobowski's stories expose the limitations of *Bildung* in confronting stereotypes and prejudice. Leo Wolff—Enlightenment optimism personified—cannot prevent prejudice from affecting his fraternity and university life. He becomes the tragic hero of the failure of a German-Jewish 'symbiosis'. Although gifted with an eminently transnational competence, the multilingual Abel Nema has been robbed of his singular history. Despite his efforts to find solid ground in a university milieu, he is violently muted by prejudice and stereotype. Finally, the history textbooks in Roth's and Dinev's novels are not designed to educate or emancipate; they are instruments of imperial myth-making, and of the communist production of a collective individual, which robs people of their singular voices and histories.

Yet the apparent dead end of *Bildung* as an emancipatory strategy does not herald the ultimate failure of Enlightenment ideals themselves. *Bildung*, although it is a "holistic and unifying" process, contains a fundamental "antinomy between the absolute harmony of achieved selfhood and the open-ended risk of 'spontaneous cooperation' with others, an antinomy that prevents *Bildung* from ever attaining its ideal form."[2] That instability allows the subject to transform the failure of *Bildung* "into the knowledge of failure."[3] Indeed, at the moment when Enlightened autonomy reaches its limits, a new vulnerability emerges, a sensitivity to transient forms of intimacy and community. Exemplary of this becoming 'singular plural' are the awakened aesthetes, the city readers, and the once silenced family heroes. Beer-Hofmann and Zaimoglu picture a transformation from radical idealism to an awareness of genealogical connection and universal kinship without obligation. Özdamar's and Hessel's urban dwellers adopt a hermeneutic distance that allows them to discern and experience the city as a site of contextuality and relationality. And through art and storytelling, the unusual family heroes in Roth's and Bánk's stories recover their singularity from the oppressive silence imposed by a communist regime or by insistent modernity.

At both ends of the twentieth century, these literary texts—and with them many others—articulate nuances that would be drowned out on the 'common stage of the conflict of wills'. By looking at the history of Jews in Germany around 1900, and at their once hopeful embrace of Enlightenment values, the references to *Aufklärung* today are put in a revealing perspective. Both around

1900 and around 2000, many writers stay away from the stage of conflict, and in their work they subtly trace the wavering belief in promises of equality and inclusion. At the same time, their writings imagine unforeseen experiences of *Verletzbarkeit* and *Barmherzigkeit* which, due to their ephemeral nature, resist the allure of collective identity. By uncovering that undercurrent in the writings of constitutive outsiders, the historical comparison in this study not only points out similar literary approaches to exclusion, stereotype, and (forcible) assimilation across the twentieth century, it also brings into clear focus a deeply vulnerable Enlightened individual, and reveals European modernity as not simply the territory of autonomy, rationality, and intellect. These constitutive outsiders instead picture fleeting moments of intimacy, a re-enchantment of modernity, and the recovery of singularity through art and storytelling. That is the resistance to immanence that shapes the politics of literature.

NOTES

Introduction

1. Preliminary remark: all English translations from the original German are the author's own, unless indicated otherwise.
2. Ulrich Beck, "Das kosmopolitische Empire. Ein Plädoyer für ein Europa jenseits des Nationaalstaats," in: *Internationale Politik*. July 2006, pp. 6–12. Reprinted by Deniz Göktürk, David Gramling, Anton Kaes, Andreas Langenohl (eds.), *Transit Deutschland: Debatten zu Nation und Migration*. Munich: Wilhelm Fink Verlag, 2011, pp. 718–25 (p. 719).
3. Beck, "Das kosmopolitische Empire," p. 719.
4. Ibid.
5. Stuart Hall, "The Question of Cultural Identity," in: Stuart Hall, David Held and Anthony McGrew (eds.), *Modernity and Its Futures*. Cambridge: Polity Press, 1992, p. 314.
6. Ibid.
7. Anthony Giddens, *The Consequences of Modernity*. Cambridge: Polity Press, 1990, p. 65.
8. That is about 21 percent of the entire population, according to statistics by the Statistisches Bundesamt. Statistisches Bundesamt (Destatis), *Bevölkerung und Erwerbstätigkeit. Bevölkerung mit Migrationshintergrund. Ergebnisse des Mikrozensus 2015*. Statistisches Bundesamt (Destatis), 2017.
9. Charles Taylor, *Modern Social Imaginaries*. Durham and London: Duke University Press, 2004, p. 23.
10. *Literaturen*, "Ich bin ein Teil der deutschen Literatur, so deutsch wie Kafka," in: *Literaturen*. 4, 2005, pp. 26–31 (p. 26).
11. *Literaturen*, "Ich bin ein Teil der deutschen Literatur," p. 28.
12. Arno Herzig, *Jüdische Geschichte in Deutschland. Von den Anfängen bis zur Gegenwart*. Munich: C.H. Beck, 2002.
13. Shmuel Feiner, David Sorkin (eds.), *New Perspectives on the Haskalah*. London, Portland: The Littman Library of Jewish Civilization, 2001.
14. Shulamit Volkov, *Das jüdische Projekt der Moderne. Zehn Essays*. Munich: C.H. Beck, 2001.
15. Marcel Stoetzler, *The State, the Nation, and the Jews. Liberalism and the Anti-Semitism Dispute in Bismarck's Germany*. Lincoln: University of Nebraska Press, 2008.

16 Sander L. Gilman, Jack Zipes (eds.), *The Yale Companion to Jewish Writing and Thought in German Culture, 1096–1996.* New Haven: Yale University Press, 1997; Andreas B. Kilcher, *Metzler Lexikon der deutsch-jüdischen Literatur. Jüdische Autorinnen und Autoren deutscher Sprache von der Aufklärung bis zur Gegenwart.* Stuttgart/Weimar: J.B. Metzler, 2000.

17 Mark H. Gelber, *Melancholy Pride: Nation, Race, and Gender in the German Literature of Cultural Zionism.* Tübingen: De Gruyter, 2000.

18 Barbara Hahn, *Die Jüdin Pallas Athene. Auch eine Theorie der Moderne.* Berlin: Berlin Verlag, 2002.

19 Arlene A. Teraoka and Heidrun Suhr were among the first to publish overview articles on early migrant writing in Germany, locating its emergence in the early 1980s. Their articles can be considered as the onset of research on 'literature of migration' in Germany. See: Arlene A. Teraoka, "Gastarbeiterliteratur: The Other speaks back", in: *Cultural Critique.* 7, 1987, pp. 77–101. Heidrun Suhr, "Ausländerliteratur: Minority Literature in the Federal Republic of Germany," in: *New German Critique,* 46 (Winter), 1989, pp. 71–103.

20 Carmine Chiellino (ed.), *Interkulturelle Literatur in Deutschland. Ein Handbuch.* Stuttgart: Metzler, 2000.

21 Tom Cheesman, *Novels of Turkish German Settlement: Cosmopolite Fictions.* Rochester, New York: Camden House, 2007; Leslie A. Adelson, *The Turkish Turn in Contemporary German Literature. Toward a New Critical Grammar of Migration.* New York: Palgrave, 2005.

22 Lyn Marven, Stuart Taberner (eds.), *Emerging German-Language Novelists of the Twenty-First Century.* Rochester, New York: Camden House, 2011.

23 Lyn Marven, Brigid Haines (eds.), *Contemporary Women's Writing in German: Changing the Subject.* Oxford: Oxford University Press, 2004.

24 Yasemin Yildiz, *Beyond the Mother Tongue: The Postmonolingual Paradigm.* New York: Fordham University Press, 2012, pp. 2–4.

25 Liesbeth Minnaard, *New Germans, New Dutch. Literary Interventions.* Amsterdam: University Press, 2008, p. 48.

26 Ibid.

27 Armin Pfahl-Traughber argues that the term 'islamophobia' does not satisfyingly distinguish between criticism of Islam and animosity directed at Muslims, and proposes the alternative terms "Muslimenfeindlichkeit" or "Antimuslimismus." Armin Pfahl-Traughber, "Die fehlende Trennschärfe des 'Islamophobie'-Konzepts für die Vorurteilsforschung," in: Gideon Botsch, Olaf Glöckner, Christoph Kopke, Michael Spieker (eds.), *Islamophobie und Antisemitismus: Ein umstrittener Vergleich.* Berlin/Boston: Walter de Gruyter, 2012, pp. 11–28.

28 Monika Schwarz-Friesel, Evyatar Friesel, "'Gestern die Juden, heute die Muslime...?' Von den Gefahren falscher Analogien," in: Botsch et al., *Islamophobie und Antisemitismus,* pp. 29–50.

29 Natalie Melas, "Versions of incommensurability," in: *World Literature Today.* 69(2), 1995, pp. 275–88 (p. 275).

30 Andreas B. Kilcher, "Was ist 'deutsch-jüdische Literatur'? Eine historische Diskursanalyse," in: *Weimarer Beiträge.* 45 (4), 1999, pp. 485–517 (p. 485). Alternative discussions of the concept 'German-Jewish literature' are provided by, among others: Hans-Otto Horch, Itta Schedletzky, *Die deutsch-jüdische Literatur und ihre Geschichte,* in: Julius H. Schoeps (ed.): *Neues Lexikon des Judentums.* Gütersloh: Bertelsmann, 1998; Hans-Otto Horch, "Was heißt und zu welchem Ende studiert man deutsch-jüdische Literaturgeschichte? Prolegomena zu einem Forschungsprojekt," in: *German Life and Letters.* 49, 1996, pp. 124–35; Hana Wirth-Nesher (ed.), *What is Jewish Literature?.* Philadelphia: Jewish Publication Society, 1994.

31 Kilcher, "Was ist 'deutsch-jüdische Literatur'?," p. 485.
32 "The determination of a Jewish identity in the sense of an objectifiable, measurable quality, recognizable in the biography of an author and also in the semantic layers and aesthetic features of his literary texts, is [...] a highly problematic venture for literary studies. [...] [It must] seem questionable to reduce literature to a representation of ethnic, religious, or cultural values, as is at least implicitly done in the debate on German-Jewish literature. Here literature becomes the function of a cultural identity, its aesthetic qualities are instrumentalized—and thus ignored. [Die Bestimmung einer jüdischen Identität im Sinne einer objektivierbaren, meßbaren Qualität, die sich in der Biographie eines Autors und ebenso in den semantischen Schichten und ästhetischen Aspekten seiner literarischen Texte ablesen lassen müßte, ist [...] für die Literaturwissenschaft ein höchst problematisches Unterfangen. [...] [Es muß] als fragwürdig erscheinen, Literatur auf die Representation ethnischer, religiöser oder kultureller Werte zu reduzieren, wie es in der Rede von der deutsch-jüdischen Literatur zumindest implizit getan wird. Literatur wird hier zur Funktion einer kulturellen Identität, ihre ästhetischen Qualitäten werden instrumentalisiert—und damit ignoriert.]" Kilcher, "Was ist 'deutsch-jüdische Literatur'?," p. 486.
Ernst Gombrich vehemently rejects this line of reasoning as well, arguing that the thought of a 'German-Jewish culture' is dangerously reminiscent of the National-Socialists' argumentation, and "that the concept of Jewish culture was invented by Hitler and his predecessors and successors [daß der Begriff der jüdischen Kultur von Hitler und seinen Vor- und Nachläufern erfunden wurde]." Ernst Gombrich, *Jüdische Identität und jüdisches Schicksal. Eine Diskussionsbemerkung*. Vienna: Passagen, 1997, p. 33.
33 In his discourse analysis, Kilcher lists three interpretations of German-Jewish literature between 1871 and 1933: as a polemical category defined by the *völkische Germanistik*, in order to fixate and exclude 'Jewish elements' from German literature; as a Jewish-assimilatory counterreaction to that anti-Semitic concept, in an attempt to demonstrate the "Wahlverwandtschaft oder Symbiose der beiden Kulturen und Literaturen"; and, finally, as a Jewish nationalist definition of literature and culture that resists the assimilatory concept.
34 On the terminological issue, see for instance: Helmut Schmitz, "Einleitung: Von der nationalen zur internationalen Literatur," in Helmut Schmitz (ed.) *Von der nationalen zur internationalen Literatur. Transkulturelle deutschsprachige Literatur und Kultur im Zeitalter globaler Migration*. Amsterdam/New York: Rodopi, 2009, pp. 7–15; Yildiz, *Beyond the Mother Tongue*, pp. 19–20; Chiara Cerri, "Interkulturelle Literatur. Ein erneutes Plädoyer für eine dringende begriffliche Entscheidung," in: *Weimarer Beiträge*. 54(3), 2008, pp. 424–36.
35 The publication of the programmatic article "Literatur der Betroffenheit. Bemerkungen zur Gastarbeiterliteratur" by Franco Biondi and Rafik Schami marked a first moment of visibility for these writers. Franco Biondi, Rafik Schami, "Literatur der Betroffenheit. Bemerkungen zur Gastarbeiterliteratur," in: Christian Schaffernicht (ed.), *Zu Hause in der Fremde*. Fischerhude: Atelier im Bauernhaus, 1981, pp. 136–150.
36 Irmgard Ackermann, Harald Weinrich (eds.), *Eine nicht nur deutsche Literatur. Zur Standortbestimmung der 'Ausländerliteratur'*. Munich: Piper, 1986.
37 Heidi Rösch, *Migrationsliteratur im interkulturellen Kontext*. Frankfurt am Main: Verlag für interkulturelle Kommunikation, 1992.
38 Leslie A. Adelson, *The Turkish Turn in Contemporary German Literature. Toward a New Critical Grammar of Migration*. New York: Palgrave, 2005.
39 Cheesman, *Novels of Turkish German Settlement*, p. 12.

40   See, for instance: Michael Hofmann, *Interkulturelle Literaturwissenschaft. Eine Einführung*. Paderborn: Fink/UTB, 2006.
41   Schmitz, *Von der nationalen zur internationalen Literatur*, p. 8.
42   See: Margaret Littler, "Intimacy and Affect in Turkish-German Writing: Emine Sevgi Özdamar's 'The Courtyard in the Mirror'," in: *Journal of Intercultural Studies*. 29(3), 2008, pp. 331–345 (p. 343); Volker C. Dörr, "'Third Space' vs. Diaspora. Topologien transkultureller Literatur," in Helmut Schmitz (ed.), *Von der nationalen zur internationalen Literatur*, pp. 59–75.
43   Dörr, "'Third Space' vs. Diaspora," p. 60.
44   Littler, "Intimacy and Affect," p. 343.
45   Hofmann's *Interkulturelle Literaturwissenschaft*, for instance, adopts a clearly postcolonial perspective, as he refers to Homi K. Bhabha's concepts of 'hybridity' and 'third space'.
46   Dörr, "'Third Space' vs. Diaspora," p. 60.
47   Homi K. Bhabha, *The Location of Culture*. New York: Routledge, 1994/2005.
48   Of course, as Dörr adds, 'intercultural literature' is the result of a social situation similar to those "constellations that have emerged from the political and conceptual dissolution of colonial contexts and that exist, at least from a metaphorical point of view, even if—as in the case of so-called 'German-Turkish literature', for example—there has never been a colonial context [Konstellationen, die aus der politischen wie begrifflichen Auflösung kolonialer Zusammenhänge entstanden sind und die, mindestens in metaphorischer Sicht, auch dann vorliegen, wenn es—wie im Falle etwa der sogenannten 'deutsch-türkischen Literatur'—nie koloniale Zusammenhänge gegeben hat]." Dörr, "'Third Space' vs. Diaspora," p. 60.
49   Jonathan Rutherford, "The Third Space. Interview with Homi K. Bhabha," in Jonathan Rutherford (ed.), *Identity: Community, Culture, Difference*. London: Lawrence & Wishart, 1990, pp. 207–21.
50   Dörr, "'Third Space' vs. Diaspora," p. 64.
51   Jim Jordan, "More Than a Metaphor: The Passing of the Two Worlds Paradigm in German-Language Diasporic Literature," *German Life and Letters*. 59(4), 2006, pp. 488–499.
52   Leslie A. Adelson, *The Turkish Turn in Contemporary in Contemporary German Literature: Toward a New Critical Grammar of Migration*. New York: Palgrave MacMillan, 2005.
53   Leslie A. Adelson, "Against Between: A Manifesto," in: Iftikhar Dadi, Salah Hassan (eds.), *Unpacking Europe; Towards a Critical Reading*. Rotterdam: Museum Boijmans van Beuningen and NAi Publishers, 2001, pp. 244–56 (p. 245).
54   See: Moray McGowan, "Brücken und Brücken-Köpfe: Wandlungen einer Metapher in der türkisch-deutschen Literatur," in: Manfred Durzak, Nilüfer Kuruyazıcı (eds.), *Die andere deutsche Literatur. Istanbuler Vorträge*. Würzburg: Königshausen & Neumann, 2004, pp. 31–40.
55   Jordan, "More Than a Metaphor," p. 488.
56   Adelson, *The Turkish Turn*, pp. 3–4.
57   See, for instance: David Sorkin, "Emancipation and Assimilation. Two Concepts and their Application to German-Jewish History," in: *Leo Baeck Institute Yearbook*. 35, 1990, pp. 17–33; Shulamit Volkov, "The Dynamics of Dissimilation: *Ostjuden* and German Jews," in: Jehuda Reinharz, Walter Schatzberg (eds.), *The Jewish Response to German Culture: From the Enlightenment to the Second World War*. Hanover: University Press of New England, 1985, pp. 195–211.

58   Jonathan Skolnik, *Jewish Pasts, German Fictions*. Stanford: Stanford University Press, 2014, p. 2.
59   Scott Spector, "Forget assimilation: Introducing Subjectivity to German-Jewish History," in: *Jewish History*. 20 (3/4), 2006, pp. 349–61.
60   Spector, "Forget assimilation," p. 351.
61   Vivian Liska, *When Kafka Says We. Uncommon Communities in German-Jewish Literature*. Bloomington/Indianapolis: Indiana University Press, 2009, p. 7.
62   Liska, *When Kafka Says We*, p. 2.
63   Liska, *When Kafka Says We*, p. 3.
64   Ignaas Devisch, "Jean-Luc Nancy," in: *The Internet Encyclopedia of Philosophy* (s.d.) [June 2016]; http://www.iep.utm.edu/nancy/.
65   Jean-Luc Nancy, *The Inoperative Community*. Edited by Connor, Peter. Minneapolis/London: University of Minnesota Press, 1991; Jean-Luc Nancy, *Being Singular Plural*. Translated by Richardson, R.D. & O'Byrne, A.E. Stanford: Stanford University Press, 2000.
66   Devisch, "Jean-Luc Nancy," s.p.
67   Liska lists Nancy among thinkers who theorize "uncommon forms of community," such as Maurice Blanchot and Giorgio Agamben. Liska, *When Kafka Says We*, p. 4.
68   Devisch, "Jean-Luc Nancy," s.p.
69   Jed Deppman, "Jean-Luc Nancy, Myth, and Literature," *Qui Parle*. 10 (2), 1997, pp. 11–32 (p. 20).
70   Devisch, "Jean-Luc Nancy," s.p.
71   Devisch, "Jean-Luc Nancy," s.p.
72   Bart Philipsen, "Literature and the Profane Community in Jean-Luc Nancy's *Being Singular Plural*," in: Birgit M. Kaiser (ed.), *Singularity and Transnational Poetics*. New York: Routledge, 2015, pp. 27–46 (p. 27).
73   Deppman, "Jean-Luc Nancy, Myth, and Literature," p. 14.
74   Nancy, *The Inoperative Community*, p. 78.
75   Nancy, *The Inoperative Community*, p. 78–9.
76   Richard Beer-Hofmann, *Der Tod Georgs*. Berlin: S. Fischer Verlag, 1900. Referenced in the text as 'TG', English translations from this text are the author's own; Arthur Schnitzler, *Fräulein Else: Novelle*. Berlin: Zsolnay, 1924. Referenced in the text as 'FE', English translations by F.H. Lyon; Navid Kermani, *Kurzmitteilung*. Zürich: Ammann Verlag, 2007. Referenced in the text as 'KM', English translations from this text are the author's own; Feridun Zaimoglu, *Liebesbrand*. Cologne: Kiepenheuer & Witsch, 2008/2010. Referenced in the text as 'LB', English translations from this text are the author's own, unless indicated otherwise.
77   Ludwig Jacobowski, *Werther, der Jude*. Dresden: Pierson, 5th edition, 1905. Referenced in the text as 'WJ', English translations from this text are the author's own; Franz Hessel, *Spazieren in Berlin*. Berlin: Bloomsbury, 2012. Referenced in the text as 'SB', English translations by Amanda de Marco, unless indicated otherwise; Emine Sevgi Özdamar, *Der Hof im Spiegel. Erzählungen*. Cologne: Kiepenheuer & Witsch, 2001/2005. Referenced in the text as 'HS', English translations from this text are the author's own; Terézia Mora, *Alle Tage*. Munich: Random House, 2006. Referenced in the text as 'AT'. English translations by Michael Henry Heim.
78   Joseph Roth, *Radetzkymarsch*. Munich: Deutscher Taschenbuch Verlag, 2009. Referenced in the text as 'RM', English translations by Joachim Neugroschel; Dimitré Dinev, *Engelszungen*. Munich: btb Verlag, 2003/2006. Referenced in the text as 'EZ', English translations from this text are the author's own.

79   Joseph Roth, *Hiob*. Munich: Deutscher Taschenbuch Verlag, 2002. Referenced in the text as 'H'. English translations by Ross Benjamin; Zsuzsa Bánk, *Der Schwimmer*. Frankfurt am Main: S. Fischer Verlag, 2002/2004. Referenced in the text as 'DS'. English translations by Margot Bettauer Dembo, unless indicated otherwise.

Chapter 1: Constitutive outsiders

1   Paul Mendes-Flohr, *German Jews. A Dual Identity*. New Haven/London: Yale University Press, 1999, p. 5.
2   Steven E. Aschheim, *Brothers and Strangers. The East European Jew in German and German Jewish Consciousness 1800–1923*. London/Madison: Wisconsin University Press, 1982, p. 52.
3   Stuart Hall, "Who needs identity?," in: Paul du Gay et al. (eds.), *Identity: a reader*. London: Sage Publications, 2000, pp. 15–30 (p. 17–18).
4   Konrad H. Jarausch, "Reshaping German Identities: Reflections on the Post-Unification Debate," in: Konrad H. Jarausch (ed.), *After Unity: Reconfiguring German Identities*. Providence: Berghahn, 1997, pp. 1–24.
5   As Todd Kontje remarks, the pattern even dates back to before the German *Reichsgründung*. Strictly speaking, since it did not have a colonial policy before 1884, Germany had no immediate national interest in the construction of an Oriental Other. "If, however, we define *national interest* more broadly as an intellectual effort to locate and preserve a sense of communal identity, then we can indeed speak of a German national interest in the East. In fact, the very lack of a unified nation-state and the absence of empire contributed to the development of a peculiarly German Orientalism." Todd Kontje, *German Orientalisms*. Ann Arbor: University of Michigan Press, 2004, pp. 2–3.
6   Minnaard, *New Germans, New Dutch*, p. 38.
7   Jeffrey Peck et al., "Natives, Strangers, and Foreigners. Constituting Germans by Constructing Others," in: Konrad Jarausch (ed.), *After Unity: Reconfiguring German Identities*. Providence: Berghahn, 1997, pp. 61–102 (p. 63ff.).
8   Birgit Rommelspacher, *Anerkennung und Ausgrenzung. Deutschland als multikulturelle Gesellschaft*. Frankfurt/New York: Campus Verlag, 2002, pp. 48–49. Minnaard remarks in this context that "the defeated German nation state was made up of a fairly homogeneous mono-ethnic population," and that "this exceptional, atypical situation of the 1950s often still functions as an agreed-upon point of reference in debates on German identity and on the postwar ethnic transformation of German society." Minnaard, *New Germans, New Dutch*, p. 37.
9   Minnaard, *New Germans, New Dutch*, pp. 37–8.
10   Minnaard, *New Germans, New Dutch*, p. 40.
11   Ibid.
12   Andreas Huyssen, "The Inevitability of Nation: German Intellectuals after Unification," in: *October*. 61, 1992, pp. 65–73 (p. 72).
13   Alana Lentin, "Post-race, post politics: the paradoxical rise of culture after multiculturalism," in: *Ethnic and Racial Studies*. 37(8), 2014, pp. 1268–85 (p. 1270).
14   Steven Vertovec and Susanne Wessendorf, *The Multiculturalism Backlash. European discourses, policies and practices*. New York: Routledge, 2010, pp. 1–28.
15   Marcel Stoetzler, *The State, the Nation, and the Jews. Liberalism and the Anti-Semitism Dispute in Bismarck's Germany*. Lincoln: University of Nebraska Press, 2008, p. 204ff.

16 The essentialist notions of 'race' and 'culture' emerge in these contexts as *myths*: they are discursive categories, in the sense that they generate meaning, thus shaping a value system and providing the terminology to make sense of everyday social reality. In this respect, they resemble the foundational myth that Nancy describes as the spoken expression that "takes on a whole series of values that amplify, fill, and ennoble this speech, giving it the dimensions of a narrative of origins and an explanation of destinies." Nancy, *The Inoperative Community*, p. 48.

17 Christopher Douglas, *A Genealogy of Literary Multiculturalism*. New York: Cornell University Press, 2009, p. 320.

18 Also see: Rita Chin et al., *After the Nazi Racial State. Difference and Democracy in Germany and Europe*. Ann Arbor: University of Michigan Press, 2009.

19 Lentin, "Post-race, post politics," p. 1271.

20 A *Staatsnation*, as Sigrid Weigel clarifies, represents a unity of territory and state and consists of an ethnically, linguistically, or culturally diverse population. In a *Kulturnation*, the ethnic-cultural homogeneity of a population is not represented by territorial unity of the state; it is potentially stateless. Sigrid Weigel, "Die Phantome der Kulturnation," in: Christoph Bartmann, Carola Dürr, Hans-Georg Knopp (eds.), *Wiedervorlage: Nationalkultur. Variationen über ein neuralgisches Thema*. Göttingen: Steidl Verlag, 2010, pp. 79–88 (p. 83). Also see: Sigrid Weigel, "Flucht ins Erbe. Alle wollen die 'Kulturnation'—warum?," in: *Süddeutsche Zeitung*. 1 February 2008, s.p.

21 For instance, in Friedrich Meinecke's classic definition, the nation is grounded in a natural core of blood kinship, a precondition for the development of a community consciousness into a national one. Friedrich Meinecke, *Cosmopolitanism and the Nation State*, Princeton University Press, 1970 [1928], p. 9. Also see: Sabine von Dirke, "Multikulti: The German Debate on Multiculturalism," in: *German Studies Review*. 17(3), 1994, pp. 513–36 (p. 513).

22 Weigel, "Die Phantome der Kulturnation," p. 83.

23 Weigel, "Flucht ins Erbe," s.p.

24 Ibid.

25 Norbert Elias, *The Civilizing Process. The History of Manners*. New York: Urizen Books, 1978.

26 Elias, *The Civilizing Process*, p. 4.

27 Ibid. Similarly, Wolfgang Welsch describes the exclusionary notion of *Kultur* as homogenizing and separatist: "Erstens soll eine Kultur das Leben des betreffenden Volkes im ganzen wie im einzelnen prägen und jede Handlung und jedes Objekt zu einem unverwechselbaren Bestandteil gerade *dieser* Kultur machen: das Konzept ist stark vereinheitlichend. Zweitens soll Kultur immer die Kultur eines *Volkes* sein; sie stellt—so drückt Herder das aus—*'die Blüte'* des Daseins eines Volkes dar: das Konzept ist volksgebunden. Drittens ergibt sich daraus eine entschiedene *Absetzung* nach außen, jede Kultur soll, als Kultur *eines* Volkes, von den Kulturen *anderer* Völker spezifisch unterschieden und abgegrenzt sein: das Konzept ist separatistisch." Wolfgang Welsch, "Auf dem Weg zu transkulturellen Gesellschaften," in: Lars Allolio-Näcke, Britta Kalscheuer, Arne Manzeschke (eds.), *Differenzen anders denken. Bausteine zu einer Kulturtheorie der Transdifferenz*. Frankfurt am Main/New York: Campus Verlag, 2005, pp. 314–41 (p. 316–7; emphasis in original).

28 Weigel, "Die Phantome der Kulturnation," p. 84.

29 Elias, *The Civilizing Process*, p. 4–5.

30 Elias, *The Civilizing Process*, p. 50.

31 Exemplary is the term *Leitkultur*, which was originally conceived as an enlightened, universalist principle, but became instrumentalized in the rhetoric of a normative, exclusionary *Kultur*. Stefan Manz, "Constructing a Normative National Identity. The *Leitkultur* Debate in Germany, 2000/2001," in: *Journal of Multilingual and Multicultural Development*. 25 (5–6), 2004, pp. 481–496.
32 Zafer Şenocak, *Deutschsein. Eine Aufklärungsschrift*. Hamburg-Bergedorf: Edition Körber Stiftung, 2011.
33 Şenocak, *Deutschsein*, p. 166.
34 Şenocak, *Deutschsein*, p. 167.
35 Şenocak, *Deutschsein*, p. 114.
36 Şenocak, *Deutschsein*, p. 114–5.
37 Şenocak, *Deutschsein*, p. 115.
38 George Mosse, "Jewish Emancipation. Between *Bildung* and Respectability," in: Jehuda Reinharz, Walter Schatzberg (eds.), *The Jewish Response to German Culture. From the Enlightenment to the Second World War*. Hanover: University Press of New England, 1985, pp. 1–16 (p. 10).
39 Mendes-Flohr, *German Jews*, p. 9.
40 Stoetzler, *The State, the Nation, and the Jews*, p. 7.
41 Aschheim, *Brothers and Strangers*, p. 52.
42 See: Shmuel Feiner, "Towards a Historical Definition of the Haskalah," in: Shmuel Feiner, David Sorkin (eds.), *New Perspectives on the Haskalah*. London, Portland: The Littman Library of Jewish Civilization, 2001, pp. 184–217.
43 For a more extensive account of the sociopolitical background of the *Haskalah* and Jewish emancipation, see for instance: Arno Herzig, *Jüdische Geschichte in Deutschland. Von den Anfängen bis zur Gegenwart*. Munich: C.H. Beck, 2002, pp. 150–185; Julius Schoeps documents the debates on Jewish emancipation in: Julius H. Schoeps, *Deutsch-jüdische Symbiose oder die mißglückte Emanzipation*. Darmstadt: Wissenschaftliche Buchgesellschaft, 1996, pp. 13–146.
44 Herzig, *Jüdische Geschichte*, p. 162.
45 George L. Mosse analyzes how German Jews turned to *Bildung* and Enlightenment ideals to craft an identity as Germans and Jews. George L. Mosse, *German Jews Beyond Judaism*. Bloomington: Indiana University Press, 1985.
46 George L. Mosse, "Jewish Emancipation. Between *Bildung* and Respectability," in: Jehuda Reinharz, Walter Schatzberg, *The Jewish Response to German Culture: From the Enlightenment to the Second World War*. Hanover, N.H.: University Press of New England, 1985, pp. 1–16 (p. 14).
47 Mosse, "Jewish Emancipation," p. 14.
48 Mendes-Flohr, *German Jews*, p. 10.
49 Mosse, "Jewish Emancipation," p. 14. Also see: Mosse, *German Jews Beyond Judaism*, p. 22. He points out that "Weimar culture was largely the creation of left-wing intellectuals, among whom there was such a disproportionate number of Jews that Weimar culture has been been called, somewhat snidely, an internal Jewish dialogue."
50 Herzig, *Jüdische Geschichte*, p. 163.
51 George Mosse points out that *Bildung* entailed more than intellectual cultivation. *Sittlichkeit*, or respectable comportment, was considered equally important in the modernization process. While adopting the ethic of *Bildung* would bring about cultural and intellectual integration, *Sittlichkeit* aimed at a greater conformity in manners. The emphasis on self-control and

moderation as outward signs of respectability implied discarding the discernibility of 'Jewishness', such as the traditional caftan and sidelocks, as well as any linguistic distinctiveness. Mosse, "Jewish Emancipation," p. 15. Considered an inferior derivative, a "profanation" of the German language, Yiddish acquired a negative connotation. It defined the counter-image of what the modern Jew had to become. Aschheim, *Brothers and Strangers*, pp. 8–11.

52 Amos Elon, *Zu einer anderen Zeit. Porträt der jüdisch-deutschen Epoche (1743–1933)*. Munich: Carl Hanser Verlag, 2003, p. 206; based on statistics in: *Leo Baeck Institute Yearbook*. 28, 1983, p. 79ff. Also see: Herzig, *Jüdische Geschichte*, pp. 191–193.

53 Shulamit Volkov, "Die Erfindung einer Tradition. Zur Entstehung des modernen Judentums in Deutschland," in: Shulamit Volkov, *Das jüdische Projekt der Moderne. Zehn Essays*. Munich: C.H. Beck, 2001, pp. 118–37 (p. 123).

54 Volkov, "Die Erfindung einer Tradition," pp. 118–37; Volkov, "The Dynamics of Dissimilation," pp. 197–198.

55 David Sorkin, *The Transformation of German Jewry, 1780–1840*. New York: Oxford University Press, 1987, pp. 113–23 (p. 113). This separation appeared especially true during the earlier decades of the nineteenth century, but probably less so after the 1860s, when bourgeois Jews no longer had to rely on 'simulated' participation, because they had become affiliated with both Jewish and general associations. Till van Rahden, "Jews and the Ambivalences of Civil Society in Germany, 1800–1933: Assessment and Reassessment," in: *The Journal of Modern History*. 77(4), 2005, pp. 1024–47 (p. 1037).

56 For a more detailed analysis of 'emancipation' and 'assimilation' as indifferentiated and thus increasingly inadequate terms, see: Sorkin, "Emancipation and Assimilation"; pp. 17–33. Also see: Spector, "Forget assimilation," in: *Jewish History*. 20, 2006, pp. 349–61.

57 Sorkin lists the terms used before 'assimilation' gained currency: "*Annäherung, Anpassung, Amalgamierung, Eingliederung, Verschmelzung.*" Sorkin, "Emancipation and Assimilation," p. 19.

58 The liberal rabbi Benno Jacob made a similar distinction between "Assimilation im Akkusativ und im Dativ, ob ich mich oder mir assimiliere." Benno Jacob, "Prinzipielle Bemerkungen zu einer zionistischen Schrift," in: *Der Morgen*. 5, 1927, p. 529.

59 Volkov, "The Dynamics of Dissimilation," p. 195.

60 Ibid.

61 Sorkin, "Emancipation and Assimilation," p. 24.

62 Mendes-Flohr, *German Jews*, pp. 92–93.

63 Gerschom Scholem, "Jews and Germans," in: *On Jews and Judaism in Crisis: Selected Essays*. Philadelphia: Paul Dry Books, 2012 [1976], pp. 71–92 (p. 77).

64 Mendes-Flohr, *German Jews*, p. 92.

65 Ibid.

66 Mendes-Flohr, *German Jews*, p. 93.

67 Sorkin, "Emancipation and Assimilation," p. 32–33.

68 Volkov, "The Dynamics of Dissimilation," p. 196.

69 In 1878, Adolf Stöcker founded the anti-Semitic *Christlichsoziale Arbeiterpartei*. The year 1879 witnessed outbursts of anti-Semitic street violence and the formation of radically anti-Semitic groupings, such as Wilhelm Marr's *Antisemiten-Liga*, who also coined the term 'antisemitic'. Peter G.J. Pulzer, *The Rise of Political Anti-Semitism in Germany and Austria*. Cambridge, MA: Harvard University Press, 1988 [1964]. Helmut Berding: *Moderner Anti-Semitismus in Deutschland*, Frankfurt am Main, 1988.

70 Alana Lentin, *Racism & Anti-Racism in Europe*. London: Pluto Press, 2004, p. 38.

71 Lentin, *Racism & Anti-Racism*, p. 65.
72 Lentin, *Racism & Anti-Racism*, p. 37–8.
73 Étienne Balibar, "Racism and Nationalism," in: Étienne Balibar, Immanuel Wallerstein (eds.), *Race, Nation, Class: Ambiguous Identities*. London: Verso, 1991, pp. 37–68.
74 Lentin, *Racism & Anti-Racism*, p. 39.
75 On the history of the term, see: Shulamit Volkov, *Die Juden in Deutschland 1780–1918*. Munich: Oldenbourg, 2000, pp. 21–23.
76 Eugen Dühring, *Die Judenfrage als Racen-, Sitten- und Culturfrage. Mit einer weltgeschichtlichen Antwort*. Karlsruhe/Leipzig: Reuther, 1881.
77 Steven Aschheim, "'The Jew within': The Myth of 'Judaization' in Germany," in: Reinharz, Schatzberg, *The Jewish Response to German Culture*. Hanover: University Press of New England, 1985, pp. 212–241.
78 Dühring, *Die Judenfrage*, p. 3–4 (emphasis added).
79 Julius Schoeps, *Deutsch-jüdische Symbiose oder die mißglückte Emanzipation*. Darmstadt: Wissenschaftliche Buchgesellschaft, 1996, pp. 155–6; Reinhard Rürup, *Emanzipation und Anti-Semitismus: Studien zur 'Judenfrage' der bürgerlichen Gesellschaft*. Göttingen: Vandenhoeck & Ruprecht, 1975, p. 102ff.
80 Rürup specifies the *Modernisierungsverlierer* as follows: "Social bearers of the movement united under the name of anti-Semitism were groups that felt disadvantaged by the liberal capitalist system: Craftsmen, small traders, and an initially still small proportion of farmers, as well as members of former classes of government and education, whose prospects in society as a whole seemed threatened by the dynamics of capitalist development; in addition there were the ideologically motivated forces of integral nationalism, romantic-pessimistic cultural criticism, anxiety about the Christian way of life, or anti-liberalism and anti-capitalism. [Sozialer Träger der unter dem Begriff des Anti-Semitismus vereinten Bewegung waren Gruppen, die sich durch das liberalkapitalistische System benachteiligt fühlten: Handwerker, Kleinhändler und ein zunächst noch geringer Teil der Landwirte, sowie Angehörige der alten Führungs- und Bildungsschichten, deren Aussichten im Gefüge der Gesamtgesellschaft durch die Dynamik der kapitalistischen Entwicklung bedroht zu sein schienen; dazu kamen die ideologisch—vom integralen Nationalismus, von der romantisch-pessimistischen Kulturkritik, von der Sorge um die christliche Lebensgestaltung des Volkes oder vom Antiliberalismus und Antikapitalismus — motivierten Kräfte.]" Rürup, *Emanzipation und Anti-Semitismus*, p. 106.
81 Slezkine, Yuri, *The Jewish Century*. Princeton/Oxford: Princeton University Press, 2004, pp. 63–73 (p. 63.)
82 Schoeps, *Deutsch-jüdische Symbiose*, p. 157.
83 Shulamit Volkov, "Antisemitismus und Antifeminismus: Soziale Norm oder kultureller Code," in: Volkov, *Das jüdische Projekt der Moderne*, pp. 62–81.
84 Stoetzler, *The State, the Nation, and the Jews*, p. 5.
85 Heinrich von Treitschke, "Unsere Aussichten," in: *Preußische Jahrbücher*. 44, 1879, pp. 559–576.
86 Also see: Stoetzler, *The State, the Nation, and the Jews*, p. 63.
87 Treitschke, "Unsere Aussichten," p. 573.
88 Stoetzler, *The State, the Nation, and the Jews*, p. 6.
89 Marcel Stoetzler, "Cultural difference in the national state: from trouser-selling Jews to unbridled multiculturalism," in: *Patterns of Prejudice*. 42(3), 2008, pp. 245–79 (p. 271).
90 Stoetzler, "Cultural difference," p. 268.

91 Stoetzler, "Cultural difference," p. 272.
92 Stoetzler, *The State, the Nation, and the Jews*, p. 9.
93 Stoetzler, "Cultural difference," p. 274.
94 See: Stoetzler, *The State, the Nation, and the Jews*, p. 7, 291ff. In this context, Stoetzler refers to Adorno and Horkheimer, who distinguish between 'liberal' anti-Semitism and post-bourgeois, fascist anti-Semitism. Stoetzler suggests that since fascism has been historically defeated by liberal society, the recurrence of 'liberal' anti-Semitism requires more urgent analysis than its fascist variety.
95 Volkov, "The Dynamics of Dissimilation," p. 199–200.
96 Volkov, "The Dynamics of Dissimilation," p. 200.
97 Zygmunt Bauman describes a similar "community of assimilants," albeit from a negative perspective (see below). Zygmunt Bauman, "Modernity and Ambivalence," in: *Theory, Culture & Society*. 7, 1990, pp. 143–69 (pp. 162–63).
98 Volkov, "The Dynamics of Dissimilation," pp. 200–206.
99 They had not been integrated by neo-orthodox associations and were different from their German counterparts professionally as well, as they consisted of a substantial group of craftspeople and proletariat. Herzig, *Jüdische Geschichte*, p. 199.
100 Aschheim, *Brothers and Strangers*, p. 34.
101 Aschheim, *Brothers and Strangers*, p. 33ff.
102 Aschheim, *Brothers and Strangers*, pp. 246–252.
103 Aschheim, *Brothers and Strangers*, p. 11.
104 On the relationship between Zionism and (the image of) Eastern Jews, see: Aschheim, *Brothers and Strangers*, pp. 80–99 (p. 84). Exemplary of such glorification is the literary cult of the *Ostjude*, represented most notably by Arnold Zweig's *Das ostjüdische Antlitz* (1920), a collection of observations of Eastern Jewish life, illustrated by Hermann Struck. Arnold Zweig, *Das ostjüdische Antlitz*. Berlin: Welt-Verlag, 1920.
105 Aschheim, *Brothers and Strangers*, p. 252.
106 Max Nordau, for instance, considered the Zionist transformation of Eastern Jewry as a necessity in the self-interest of German bourgeois Jewry, arguing that "the most lowly Jew" had to become a source of pride, which was a responsibility of Western Jews, for "the contempt created by the impudent, crawling beggar in dirty caftan [...] falls back on all of us." Max Nordau, "Der Zionismus und seine Gegner," in: Max Nordau, *Schriften*. 1898, pp. 117ff.; as quoted by Aschheim, *Brothers and Strangers*, p. 88.
107 On Nordau's and Herzl's perpetuation of assimilationist views, see: Aschheim, *Brothers and Strangers*, pp. 84–89.
108 Yitzhak Conforti, "East and West in Jewish Nationalism: conflicting types in the Zionist vision?," in: *Nations and Nationalism*. 16(2), 2010, pp. 201–219 (p. 216). For an extensive overview of the origins and history of Zionism, see: Walter Laqueur, *A History of Zionism*, New York: Schocken Books, 1976.
109 Theodor Herzl, *Der Judenstaat. Versuch einer modernen Lösung der Judenfrage*. Vienna: M. Breitenstein's Verlags-Buchhandlung, 1896.
110 On this East-West antagonism in Zionism, see: Aschheim, *Brothers and Strangers*, pp. 89–99. The distinction between the two Zionist strains is, however, not clear-cut. In an analysis of the 1902/1903 conflict between Herzl and Achad Ha'am on the publication of Herzl's *Altneuland*, Yitzhak Conforti points out that the two strains share ethnic-cultural and civic-political foundations. Conforti, "East and West in Jewish Nationalism," pp. 201–219.
111 Theodor Herzl, *Altneuland*. Leipzig: Seemann, [1902].

[112] Achad Ha'am, "Altneuland," in: *Ost und West*. 3(4), 1903, pp. 227–44 (p. 244).
[113] Achad Ha'am, "Dr. Pinsker und seine Broschüre," in: Achad Ha'am, *Am Scheidewege*. Berlin: Jüdischer Verlag, 1916, pp. 64–82 (p. 73).
[114] Martin Buber, "Jüdische Renaissance," in: *Ost und West*. 1, 1901, pp. 7–10. On Cultural Zionism and the *jungjüdische Bewegung*, see especially: Mark Gelber, *Melancholy Pride. Nation, Race, and Gender in the German Literature of Cultural Zionism*. Tübingen: Max Niemeyer, 2000.
[115] Buber, "Jüdische Renaissance," p. 7.
[116] On Jewish fraternity life and youth gymnastics clubs like *Bar Kochba*, see: Gelber, *Melancholy Pride*, pp. 55–86. The *jungjüdische Bewegung* should be regarded simultaneously within German Cultural Zionism and against the background of Central European *fin-de-siècle* culture. See: Gelber, *Melancholy Pride*, p. 20ff.
[117] Inka Bertz points out that national-Jewish cultural efforts already emerged before the rise of Zionism, but that they took place within Jewish liberalism. Cultural Zionism was characterized by precisely an anti-bourgeois habitus and its rejection of assimilation and liberalism. Inka Bertz, "Jüdische Renaissance," in: Diethart Kerbs, Jürgen Reulecke (eds.), *Handbuch der deutschen Reformbewegungen 1880–1933*. Wuppertal: Peter Hammer, 1998, pp. 551–63 (p. 553).
[118] Aschheim, *Brothers and Strangers*, pp. 101–102.
[119] Gelber, *Melancholy* Pride, p. 125
[120] Nathan Birnbaum, an influential figure in Cultural Zionism, posited that the most secure Jewish nationality would be the one founded on the Jewish race. He rejected Herzl's political Zionism as empty chauvinism, because it contained no 'geistiges Vollblutjudentum'. Instead, he formulated a racialist view that connected biological, intellectual, and psychological characteristics of the Jewish race. Buber, Birnbaum's disciple, succeeded in institutionalizing a racialist foundation of Cultural Zionism and introduced *völkisch* ideas, especially those of the Jewish *Volksseele* and *Blutstamm*, into its aesthetic program. In his attempt to define a Jewish 'Rassenwesen', he deployed a similar flexible definition of 'race' as a combination of genetic, sociological, historical, geographical, and spiritual considerations. Gelber, *Melancholy Pride*, pp. 133–4.
[121] See: Julius Schoeps, "Theodor Herzl und die Affäre Dreyfus," in: Schoeps, *Deutsch-jüdische Symbiose*, pp. 325–342.
[122] Tim Grady, "Creating difference: the racialization of Germany's Jewish soldiers after the First World War," in: *Patterns of Prejudice*. 46 (3/4), 2012, pp. 318–38 (p. 319).
[123] George Mosse, *Jews and the German War Experience, 1914–1918*. New York: Leo Baeck Institute, 1977.
[124] Grady, "Creating difference," p. 324. His main argument is that the National Socialist regime successfully reshaped narratives of the First World War and German memory culture, by excluding Jews from its racialized interpretation of war and memory. In doing so, the regime created the idea of very separate German and Jewish war experiences. Additionally, this resulted in an inward turn of Jewish war commemoration, which reinforced the idea of separation and isolation *during* rather than after the war.
[125] Aschheim, *Brothers and Strangers*, p. 139.

126 Michael Brenner, "1916: The German army orders a census of Jewish soldiers, and Martin Buber launches his cultural magazine *Der Jude*," in: Sander L. Gilman, Jack Zipes (eds.), *The Yale Companion to Jewish Writing and Thought in German Culture, 1096–1996*. New Haven: Yale University Press, 1997, pp. 348–54 (p. 349).
127 Aschheim, *Brothers and Strangers*, p. 142.
128 Grady, "Creating difference," p. 321ff.
129 Aschheim, *Brothers and Strangers*, pp. 153–6.
130 Grady, "Creating difference," p. 321.
131 Michael Brenner, "1916: The German army...," pp. 348–54 (p. 349).
132 Ibid.
133 Herzig, *Jüdische Geschichte*, p. 220ff.
134 Aschheim, *Brothers and Strangers*, pp. 215–52.
135 Aschheim, *Brothers and Strangers*, p. 244.
136 Volkov, *Das jüdische Projekt der Moderne*, pp. 120–23.
137 Bauman, "Modernity and Ambivalence," pp. 143–169.
138 Bauman, "Modernity and Ambivalence," p. 159.
139 Bauman, "Modernity and Ambivalence," pp. 159–60.
140 Herzig, *Jüdische Geschichte*, p. 149, 184.
141 Bauman, "Modernity and Ambivalence," p. 162.
142 Herzig, *Jüdische Geschichte*, p. 149.
143 Volkov, "Die Erfindung einer Tradition," p. 133.
144 Mendes-Flohr, *German Jews*, p. 9. Mendes-Flohr refers to Aleida Assmann's *Arbeit am nationalen Gedächtnis*, in which she explains how *Bildung* transformed from a cosmopolitan into a socially privileged and eventually nationalized and exclusive ethos. Aleida Assmann, *Arbeit am nationalen Gedächtnis. Eine kurze Geschichte der deutschen Bildungsidee*. Frankfurt am Main: Campus Verlag, 1993.
145 Mendes-Flohr, *German Jews*, pp. 8–9, 16.
146 Klaus J. Bade, *Deutsche im Ausland, Fremde in Deutschland*. Munich: C.H. Beck, 1992, p. 17.
147 Statistisches Bundesamt (Destatis), *Bevölkerung und Erwerbstätigkeit. Bevölkerung mit Migrationshintergrund. Ergebnisse des Mikrozensus 2015*. Statistisches Bundesamt (Destatis), 2017.
148 Deniz Göktürk, David Gramling, Anton Kaes, Andreas Langenohl (eds.), *Transit Deutschland: Debatten zu Nation und Migration*. Munich: Wilhelm Fink Verlag, 2011, pp. 23–41.
149 This appears to be a matter of legal and public perception. Legally, Germany has considered itself as a country of immigration since 2002/2005, although statistically, the migration balance since 2006 becomes increasingly negative. This is primarily due to the fact that in statistics, *Spätaussiedler* (*Aussiedler* who migrated to Germany after 1993) also count as German citizens. Stricter linguistic requirements in the 2005 immigration law caused the number of *Spätaussiedler* to plummet. See: Klaus J. Bade, "Von der Arbeitswanderung zur Einwanderungsgesellschaft," in: Susanne Stemmler (ed.), *Multikultur 2.0. Willkommen im Einwanderungsland Deutschland*. Göttingen: Wallstein, 2011, pp. 154–185 (p. 158).

150 Klaus J. Bade, *Ausländer, Aussiedler, Asyl. Eine Bestandsaufnahme*. Munich: Beck, 1994, p. 38.
151 Bade, *Ausländer, Aussiedler, Asyl*, p. 52.
152 Barbara Dietz, Pawel Kaczmarczyk, "On the demand side of international labour mobility: The structure of the German labour market as a causal factor of seasonal Polish migration," in: Corrado Bonifazi, Marek Okólski, Jeanette Schoorl, Patrick Simon (eds.), *International Migration in Europe. New Trends and New Methods of Analysis*. Amsterdam: Amsterdam University Press, 2008, pp. 37–64 (p. 39).
153 "Hunderttausend italienische Arbeiter kommen," in: *Frankfurter Allgemeine Zeitung*. 21 December, 1955. Reprinted in Göktürk, *Transit Deutschland*, pp. 45–6.
154 Bade, "Von der Arbeitswanderung," p. 160.
155 Ibid.
156 Bade, *Ausländer, Aussiedler, Asyl*, p. 52.
157 Klaus J. Bade, *Deutsche im Ausland, Fremde in Deutschland. Migration in Geschichte und Gegenwart*. Munich: Beck, pp. 396–398. The *Einwanderungssituation* was complicated by several more problem areas. During the 1980s, the number of refugees from Eastern Europe and the Third World increased significantly; possibly about a million people resided in Germany without permits. Also, in the late 1980s, the integration of a significant number of *Aussiedler*—ethnic German emigrants, who could still rely on their German nationality or ethnicity (*Staatszugehörigkeit* and *Volkszugehörigkeit*)—was challenged not by legal issues, but often by a language barrier and a difference in values. Furthermore, the German reunification of 1990 initiated inner-German integration problems. *DDR-Flüchtlinge* and *Übersiedler* experienced a German-German culture shock resulting from the difference in both mentality and material standards. Also, the largely unilateral reform after the Western example of the five 'new' *Bundesländer* caused inhabitants to feel like foreigners in their own country. Bade associates their identity problem with a defensive, at times aggressive, attitude towards newcomers, and with the origin of 'ethclass' thinking. Amplified by other radical (nationalist, racist, anti-Semitic) undercurrents, which manifested themselves in the disintegration of the Eastern Bloc, the new immigration situation urgently required a coherent and contemporary redefinition of the concept *Einwanderungsland* as primarily a sociocultural challenge. Bade, *Deutsche im Ausland*, pp. 443–446.
158 In 1965, for instance, the German *Bundesanstalt für Arbeitsvermittlung* called for the organization of care for guest workers, articulating their demand for integratio as a *quid pro quo*. In return for their support of the economic growth of Germany, guest workers "may expect to be supported to the best of our ability in the organization of their personal sphere [erwarten dürfen, bei der Gestaltung ihres persönlichen Bereiches nach besten Kräften unterstützt zu werden]." Bundesanstalt für Arbeitsvermittlung und Arbeitslosenversicherung, "Betreuung der ausländischen Arbeitnehmer," in: *Amtliche Nachrichten der Bundesanstalt für Arbeitsvermittlung und Arbeitslosenversicherung*, 1965. Reprinted partially in Stemmler, *Multikultur 2.0*, pp. 149–53.
159 Heinz Kühn, *Memorandum des Beauftragten der Bundesregierung*. Bonn, 1979. Reprinted as "Stand und Weiterentwicklung der Integration der ausländischen Arbeitnehmer und ihrer Familien in der Bundesrepublik Deutschland," in: Göktürk, *Transit Deutschland*, pp. 358–60. Heinz Kühn was an SPD-politician, governor of Nordrhein-Westfalen from 1966 until 1978, and the first *Ausländerbeauftragter der Bundesregierung* (Commissioner of the Federal Government for Migration and Integration).

160 Klaus J. Bade, "Versäumte Integrationschancen und nachholende Integrationspolitik," in: Klaus J. Bade, Hans-Georg Hiesserich (eds.), *Nachholende Integrationspolitik und Gestaltungsperspektiven der Integrationspraxis*. Göttingen: V&R Unipress, 2007.

161 "Anfang der 1990er Jahre blickt man deshalb zurück auf ein in der Gestaltung der Problembereiche von Migration, Integration und Minderheiten in vieler Hinsicht verlorenes Jahrzehnt." Bade, *Deutsche im Ausland*, p. 449.

162 Bade detects a clear correlation between the two: "In the end, a reluctant country of immigration should not be surprised by occasionally reluctant immigrants. [...] A lifeguard, who for decades has affixed a sign at the gate of his swimming pool with the inscription 'This is not a swimming pool', should not be surprised that the aging visitors on the sunbathing lawn have not turned into passionate swimmers. [Ein Einwanderungsland wider Willen darf sich am Ende über gelegentlich widerwillige Einwanderer nicht wundern. [...] Ein Bademeister, der jahrzehntelang an der Pforte seines Schwimmbads ein Schild mit der Aufschrift angebracht hat ‚Dies ist keine Badeanstalt!', sollte sich später nicht wundern, dass die alt gewordenen Besucher der Liegewiese keine leidenschaftlichen Schwimmer geworden sind.]" Bade, "Von der Arbeitswanderung," pp. 163–4.

163 "Gesetz zur Reform des Staatsangehörigkeitsrechts der Bundesrepublik Deutschland," in: *Bundesgesetzblatt*, 1999, pp. 1618–1623.

164 Fatima El-Tayeb observes that the 1913 German citizenship law, grounded in *ius sanguinis*, reflected the at the time dominant racial definition of nation but continued to influence the further evolution of its definition throughout the twentieth century. Fatima El-Tayeb, "Foreigners, Germans, and German Foreigners: Constructions of National Identity in Early Twentieth Century Germany," in: Iftikhar Dadi, Salah M. Hassan, *Unpacking Europe. Towards a Critical Reading*. Rotterdam: Museum Boijmans van Beuningen and NAi Publishers, 2001, pp. 72–81. The permission of double nationality was implemented for the purpose of European integration but limited by an *Optionspflicht*, the obligation to choose one of the two before the age of 18. Although about a third of the *Optionspflichtigen* would rather retain both nationalities, about 98 percent of them decide on the German nationality. See: http://www.bmi.bund.de/DE/Themen/Migration-Integration/Optionspflicht/optionspflicht_node.html.

165 Bundesministerium des Innern, "Zuwanderung gestalten—Integration fördern." 4 July, 2001; http://www.bmi.bund.de/cae/servlet/contentblob/123148/publicationFile/9076/Zuwanderungsbericht_pdf.

166 Ibid.

167 "Gesetz zur Steuerung und Begrenzung der Zuwanderung und zur Regelung des Aufenthalts und der Integration von Unionsbürgern und Ausländern," in: *Bundesgesetzblatt*, 2004, p. 1950.

168 It distinguishes temporary work permits (*Aufenthaltserlaubnis*) from long-term settlement permits for highly qualified foreigners (*Niederlassungserlaubnis*). It also stipulates the stimulation of economic, cultural, and social integration by means of language and orientation courses.

169 With a recurring self-critical metaphor of sleep, several politicians have acknowledged the historical failure of Germany's non-policy on integration. For instance, *Bundespräsident* Horst Köhler regretted that Germany "[has] slept through integration [die Integration verschlafen [hat]]," and similarly, Armin Laschet, state minister of integration in Nordrhein-Westfalen, confirmed that the country "has slept for decades [jahrzehntelang geschlafen [hat]]" in matters of integration. Bade, "Von der Arbeitswanderung," pp. 164–165.

170 Christian Wulff, "Vielfalt schätzen, Zusammenhalt fördern. Rede zum 20. Jahrestag der Deutschen Einheit." 3 October, 2010; http://www.bundespraesident.de/SharedDocs/Reden/DE/Christian-Wulff/Reden/2010/10/20101003_Rede.html.
171 Michael Lane Bruner, *Strategies of Remembrance. The Rhetorical Dimensions of Identity Construction*. Columbia: University of South Carolina Press, 2002, p. 1.
172 Lentin, "Post-race, post politics," pp. 1–19. Also see: Alana Lentin and Gavin Titley, *The Crises of Multiculturalism. Racism in a Neoliberal Age*. 2011, New York: Palgrave Macmillan. On post-racialism, see especially pp. 49–84.
173 Lentin, "Post-race, post politics," p. 1.
174 Lentin, "Post-race, post politics," p. 9.
175 Slavoj Žižek, *Violence*. London: Profile Books, 2008, p. 119.
176 Lentin, "Post-race, post politics," p. 3.
177 Dirke, "Multikulti," pp. 513–536.
178 Jürgen Micksch (ed.), *Deutschland—Einheit in kultureller Vielfalt*. Frankfurt am Main: Otto Lembeck, 1991, pp. 5–16.
179 Der Ökumenische Vorbereitungsausschuss für den Tag des ausländischen Mitbürgers, "'Wir leben in der Bundesrepublik in einer multikulturellen Gesellschaft.' Thesen vom 24. November 1980, Tag des ausländischen Mitbürgers," in: Jürgen Micksch (ed.), *Deutschland—Einheit in kultureller Vielfalt*. Frankfurt am Main: Otto Lembeck, 1991, pp. 182–185.
180 Ibid.
181 Heidelberger Kreis, "Heidelberger Manifest," in: *Frankfurter Rundschau*. 4 March 1982. Reprinted in Göktürk, *Transit Deutschland*, pp. 155–157. There were two versions of the text, one intended for publication and another for signatories only, which was leaked to the press. The primary difference between both is the more moderate rhetoric in the public version, in which terms like "Unterwanderung" and "Überfremdung" are left out. The signatories' version is available at *Antifaschistisches Pressearchiv und Bildungszentrum Berlin*, at http://www.apabiz.de/archiv/material/Profile/Heidelberger%20Kreis.htm.
182 From the signatories' version.
183 Remarkably, these sentences were left out of the public version of the manifesto, and replaced by an argument anticipating criticism on a racist "Mißbrauch des Wortes Volk": "Wer aus diesem Begriff folgert, daß es auch nichterhaltenswerte Völker gäbe, interpretiert gegen die Regeln wissenschaftlicher Hermeneutik, und mißdeutet gröblich unser Anliegen." Göktürk, *Transit Deutschland*, p. 156.
184 Dirke, "Multikulti," pp. 519–20.
185 Dirke, "Multikulti," p. 522.
186 'Respect' conveys a discursive distance towards the Other that can be considered as a primary marker of the post-racial framework of multiculturalism. In his critique of multiculturalism, Slavoj Žižek detects a superior claim of universality in this respectful distance, and therefore considers it as an indirect form of racism: "[M]ulticulturalism involves patronizing Eurocentrist distance and/or respect for local cultures without roots in one's own particular culture. In other words, multiculturalism is a disavowed, inverted, self-referential form of racism, a 'racism with a distance'—it 'respects' the Other's identity, conceiving the Other as a self-enclosed 'authentic' community towards which he, the multiculturalist, maintains a distance rendered possible by his privileged universal position. Multiculturalism is a racism which empties its own position of all positive content (the multiculturalist is not a direct racist, he doesn't oppose to the Other the *particular* values of his own culture), but nonetheless retains this position as the privileged *empty point of universality* from which one is able to

appreciate (and depreciate) properly other particular cultures—the multiculturalist respect for the Other's specificity is the very form of asserting one's own superiority." Slavoj Žižek, "Multiculturalism, Or, the Cultural Logic of Multinational Capitalism," in: *New Left Review.* 225, 1997, pp. 28–51 (p. 44, emphasis in original).

187 Stuart Hall, *The multicultural question*. Pavis Papers in Social and Cultural Research no. 4. Milton Keynes: Open University, 2001, p. 3.

188 Lentin, "Post-race, post politics," p. 10–11.

189 Claus Leggewie, Susanne Stemmler, "Begriffsgeschichte Multikulturalismus. Claus Leggewie im Gespräch mit Susanne Stemmler," in: Stemmler (ed.), *Multikultur 2.0.*, pp. 37–51 (p. 37).

190 Vertovec, Wessendorf, *The Multiculturalism Backlash*, pp. 1–28. Instances of the discourse on the 'failure' or 'death' of multiculturalism can be found in Heinz Buschkowksy (SPD), district mayor of Berlin-Neukölln, who in 2004 denounced 'multicultural romanticism' as ignorant of ethnic separatism. Heinz Buschkowsky, *Neukölln ist überall*. Berlin: Ullstein, 2012. Similarly, in his publication *Abschied von Multikulti*, political scientist Stefan Luft claimed that multiculturalism as a politics of recognition sustains identities-of-origin and thus promotes segregation and ethnic conflict. Stefan Luft, "Multikulti ist gescheitert," in: *Tagesspiegel.* 17 January, 2008.

191 Werner Schiffauer distinguishes three argumentative positions in the discussion. A first argument considers them to be a symbol of the failure of integration: as Islamic worlds regulated by the value system of honor, which reject Western culture and are a breeding ground of Islamic fundamentalism. A second, optimistic position emphasizes their transitory character as an 'entrance hall' into society, which is usually defined in economic terms. A third one emphasizes the significance of power relations and exclusion mechanisms in the emergence of subsocieties. Werner Schiffauer, *Parallelgesellschaften. Wie viel Wertekonsens braucht unsere Gesellschaft? Für eine kluge Politik der Differenz.* Bielefeld: Transcript, 2008, pp. 7–18.

192 Lentin, "Post-race, post politics," p. 6.

193 See: Hartwig Pautz, "The politics of identity in Germany: the *Leitkultur* debate," in: *Race & Class.* 46(4), 2005, pp. 39–52; Stefan Manz, "Constructing a Normative National Identity: The *Leitkultur* Debate in Germany, 2000/2001," in: *Journal of Multilingual and Multicultural Development.* 25 (5–6), 2004, pp. 481–496.

194 Manz, "Constructing a Normative National Identity," p. 483.

195 Bassam Tibi, *Europa ohne Identität. Die Krise der multikulturellen Gesellschaft.* Munich: Bertelsmann, 1998.

196 Tibi, *Europa ohne Identität*, p. 57.

197 Friedrich Merz, "Einwanderung und Identität," in: *Die Welt,* 25 October, 2000.

198 Manz, "Constructing a Normative National Identity," p. 485.

199 Nadeem Elyas, chairman of the *Zentralrat der Muslime in Deutschland*, in: *Frankfurter Rundschau*, 31 October, 2000. Cited by Manz, "Constructing a Normative National Identity," p. 493.

200 Manz, "Constructing a Normative National Identity," p. 495.

201 Weber cites Baden-Württemberg's Minister of Culture Annette Schavan. Beverly Weber, "Cloth on her Head, Constitution in Hand. Germany's Headscarf Debates and the Cultural Politics of Difference," in: *German Politics and Society.* 22(3), 2004, pp. 33–64 (p. 43).

202 The right-wing *Republikaner* brought the Ludin case before parliament, citing the Baden-Württemberg constitution, which explicitly states that children are to be educated "in the fear of God" and on the basis of Christian and Western cultural values. Weber, "Cloth on her Head," p. 43.

203 Weber, "Cloth on her Head," p. 49.
204 Weber, "Cloth on her Head," p. 46.
205 In the Netherlands, the political rise and death (2001–2002) of politician Pim Fortuyn, as well as the murder of filmmaker Theo van Gogh by a Muslim extremist; in Britain, the 2001 riots between British Bangladeshi and White youths, but especially the 2005 London terrorist bombings; in Spain, the 2004 train bombings; in Denmark, the publication of the Muhammad cartoons. Vertovec, Wessendorf, *The Multiculturalism Backlash*, pp. 4–6.
206 See, for instance: Werner Ruf, *Der Islam. Schrecken des Abendlandes. Wie sich der Westen sein Feindbild konstruiert*. Cologne: PapyRossa, 2012.
207 Göktürk, *Transit Deutschland*, p. 31; Caroline Fetscher, "Die Muslimisierung des Anderen. Eine Diskussion mit Sawsan Chebli, Sema Kaygusuz, Cem Özdemir und Hilal Sezgin, moderiert von Caroline Fetscher," in: Susanne Stemmler (ed.), *Multikultur 2.0, Willkommen im Einwanderungsland Deutschland*, pp. 206–14.
208 See for instance: Christoph Butterwegge, Gudrun Hentges, *Massenmedien, Migration und Integration*. Wiesbaden: Verlag für Sozialwissenschaften, 2006, p. 7.
209 Ruf, *Der Islam*, p. 57.
210 Thilo Sarrazin, *Deutschland schafft sich ab. Wie wir unser Land aufs Spiel setzen*. Munich: Deutscher Verlags-Anstalt, 2010.
211 For instance, in 2009, he claimed: "Ich muß niemanden anerkennen, der vom Staat lebt, diesen Staat ablehnt, für die Ausbildung seiner Kinder nicht vernünftig sorgt und ständig neue kleine Kopftuchmädchen produziert." Sarrazin in an interview with Frank Berberich, "Klasse statt Masse," in: *Lettre International*. 86, 2009, p. 197.
212 Sarrazin, *Deutschland schafft sich ab*, p. 259.
213 Bernd Ulrich, Özlem Topçu, "Sind Muslime dümmer?," in: *Die Zeit*. 26 August, 2010; http://www.zeit.de/2010/35/Sarrazin/komplettansicht.
214 For a discussion of this statement in the context of contemporary discussions of race, see Sander L. Gilman, "Thilo Sarrazin and the Politics of Race in the Twenty-First Century," in: *New German Critique*. 117(39/3), 2012, pp. 47–59.
215 A. Seibel, H. Schuhmacher, J. Fahrun, "Mögen Sie keine Türken, Herr Sarrazin?," in: *Die Welt*. 29 August, 2010; http://www.welt.de/politik/deutschland/article9255898/Moegen-Sie-keine-Tuerken-Herr-Sarrazin.html; "Thilo Sarrazin—,Ich bin kein Rassist'," in: *Berliner Morgenpost*. 28 October, 2010; http://www.morgenpost.de/berlin-aktuell/article1385382/Thilo-Sarrazin-Ich-bin-kein-Rassist.html
216 Sarrazin refers to Darwin to elucidate the correlation between intelligence and heredity, a key argument in his views on demography. Sarrazin, *Deutschland schafft sich ab*, p. 92.
217 Michael Hofmann, "Handicap Islam? Die Sarrazin-Debatte als Herausforderung des deutsch-türkischen Diskurses," in: Şeyda Ozil, Yasemin Dayıoğlu-Yücel, Michael Hofmann (eds.), *Türkisch-deutscher Kulturkontakt und Kulturtransfer. Kontroversen und Lernprozesse*. Göttingen: V&R, 2011, pp. 33–44 (p. 38).
218 "If there is political will to carry out a reasonable measure, there will be a way to make it constitutional—if necessary by amending the Constitution. [Besteht der politische Wille, eine vernünftige Maßnahme durchzuführen, so wird sich ein Weg finden, sie verfassungsrechtlich zu gestalten—notfalls, indem man die Verfassung ändert.]" Sarrazin, *Deutschland schafft sich ab*, p. 378.
219 Hofmann, "Handicap Islam?," p. 39.
220 Hofmann, "Handicap Islam?," p. 34.

221 Klaus J. Bade, *Kritik und Gewalt. Sarrazin-Debatte, 'Islamkritik' und Terror in der Einwanderungsgesellschaft*. Schwalbach: Wochenschau, 2013, pp. 356–57.
222 Bade, *Kritik und Gewalt*, p. 33.
223 Bade, *Kritik und Gewalt*, p. 366.
224 Bade, *Kritik und Gewalt*. p. 366.
225 Navid Kermani, *Wer ist wir. Deutschland und seine Muslime*. Munich: C.H.Beck, 2009.
226 Hilal Sezgin (ed.), *Manifest der Vielen. Deutschland erfindet sich neu*. Berlin: Blumenbar Verlag, 2011.
227 Sezgin, *Manifest der Vielen*, p. 46.
228 Naika Foroutan, "Gemeinsame Identität im pluralen Deutschland," in: Sezgin (ed.), *Manifest der Vielen*, pp. 153–162 (p. 161).
229 Feridun Zaimoglu, "Es tobt in Deutschland ein Kulturkampf," in: Sezgin (ed.), *Manifest der Vielen*, pp. 11–15.
230 Zaimoglu, "Es tobt in Deutschland ein Kulturkampf," p. 11.
231 Ibid.
232 Ibid.
233 Zaimoglu, "*Es tobt in Deutschland ein Kulturkampf*," p. 15.
234 Noah Isenberg, *Between Redemption and Doom. The Strains of German-Jewish Modernism*. Lincoln/London: University of Nebraska Press, 1999, p. 8.
235 Moritz Goldstein, "Deutsch-jüdischer Parnaß," in: *Kunstwart*. 25 March, 1912, pp. 281–294.
236 Isenberg, *Between Redemption and Doom*, pp. 8–9.
237 Goldstein, "Deutsch-jüdischer Parnaß," p. 283 (emphasis in original).
238 Isenberg, *Between Redemption and Doom*, p. 9.
239 Moritz Goldstein, *Begriff und Programm einer jüdischen Nationalliteratur*. Berlin: Jüdischer Verlag, 1912. Another (Cultural) Zionist approach was formulated by Gustav Krojanker, whose essay collection resists an assimilatory universalism that threatens to destroy Jewish particularity. Gustav Krojanker, *Juden in der deutschen Literatur*. Berlin, 1922.
240 Andreas B. Kilcher, "Interpretationen eines kulturellen Zwischenraums. Die Debatte um die deutsch-jüdische Literatur 1900 bis 1933," in: Julius H. Schoeps, Karl E. Grözinger, Willi Jasper, Gert Mattenklott (eds.), *Deutsch-Jüdischer Parnaß. Rekonstruktion einer Debatte*. Menora: Jahrbuch für deutsch-jüdische Geschichte, 13. Berlin/Vienna: Philo, 2002, pp. 289–312.
241 Ludwig Geiger, *Die deutsche Literatur und die Juden*. Berlin: Reimer, 1910, p. 5.
242 Kilcher, "Interpretationen," p. 290.
243 Alfred Wolfenstein, *Jüdisches Wesen und neue Dichtung*. Berlin, 1922.
244 Wolfenstein, *Jüdiches Wesen*, p. 8.
245 Biondi, Schami, "Literatur der Betroffenheit," pp. 136–150.
246 Minnaard, *New Germans, New Dutch*, pp. 59–60.
247 Yüksel Pazarkaya, "Literatur ist Literatur," in: Irmgard Ackermann, Harald Weinrich (eds.), *Eine nicht nur deutsche Literatur. Zur Standortbestimmungen der Ausländerliteratur*. Munich: Piper, 1986, pp. 59–69.
248 Jacques Rancière, "The Politics of Literature," in: *SubStance*. 33(1/103), 2004, pp. 10–24 (pp. 19–20).

Chapter 2: Aesthetes between identity and opposition

1. Maxim Biller, "Letzte Ausfahrt Uckermarck," in: *Die Zeit*. 20 February, 2014, s.p.; http://www.zeit.de/2014/09/deutsche-gegenwartsliteratur-maxim-biller.
2. Ibid.
3. Biller refers to the death of the renowned literary critic Marcel Reich-Ranicki in 2013, who edited the essay collection *Über Ruhestörer*. Marcel Reich-Ranicki, *Über Ruhestörer: Juden in der deutschen Literatur*. Stuttgart: Deutsche Verlags-Anstalt, 1989.
4. Biller, "Letzte Ausfahrt Uckermarck," s.p.
5. For Biller, the Bosnian-German author Saša Stanišić exemplifies such domestication. While praising Stanišić' debut *Wie der Soldat das Grammophon repariert* as a "universell verständlicher Roman über das Lieben, Leben und Töten im Bosnien der neunziger Jahre," he criticizes his second novel *Vor dem Fest*, a *Heimatroman* about life in the Uckermarck region east of Berlin. Biller questions "dieser radikale, antibiografische Themenwechsel": "Ist es ihm wichtiger als Neudeutscher über Urdeutsche zu schreiben als über Leute wie sich selbst?" Ironically, Stanišić himself has expressed his annoyance at precisely this kind of simplifying conflation of biography and "exoticism of style and technique [...], as if this quality is a talent one has brought along from one's homeland." Saša Stanišić, "Three Myths of Immigrant Writing: A View from Germany," 2008, http://wordswithoutborders.org/article/three-myths-of-immigrant-writing-a-view-from-germany#ixzz3YhoPp1VZ.
6. Biller, "Letzte Ausfahrt Uckermarck," s.p.
7. In this respect, Biller's argument appears to rest on a fairly strict interpretation of Gilles Deleuze's and Félix Guattari's concept of "minor literature." Characterized by "the deterritorialization of language, the connection of the individual to a political immediacy, and the collective assemblage of enunciation," they understand minor literature to designate "the revolutionary conditions for every literature within the heart of what is called great (or established) literature." Likewise, Biller suggests that the authenticity of realism delivers on a revolutionary promise of minority writing. It conveys an unreflective, genuine experience of a collective in the middle of a social transformation and is as such capable of subverting existing norms from within. Gilles Deleuze, Félix Guattari, *Kafka: Toward a Minor Literature*. University of Minnesota Press, 1986, p. 18.
8. Tom Cheesman, "Juggling Burdens of Representation: Black, Red, Gold and Turquoise," in: *German Life and Letters*. 59/4, 2006, pp. 471–487.
9. Provocation and (staged) breach of taboo are crucial aspects of Biller's public appearance. He proclaimed the (near-) death of contemporary literature (at least) twice before, on similar grounds: its presumed *Langweiligkeit* and its negligence of harsh social reality. See, for instance: Christof Siemes, "Schwäne in goldenem Nebel," in: *Die Zeit*. 15, 6 April, 2000; Roger Willemsen, "Fahrtwind beim Umblättern," in: *Der Spiegel*. 52, 1992.
10. Kelly Comfort describes the "de-humanization" of art in a variety of terms, as "the process of eliminating the human from art's subject matter; the method of isolating art in its own autonomous sphere; the desire to free art from human utility or usefulness; the act of of rejecting a universal, communal, or collective experience of art [...]." Kelly Comfort, *Art and Life in Aestheticism: De-Humanizing and Re-Humanizing Art, the Artist, and the Artistic Receptor*. New York: Palgrave, 2008, p. 4.
11. Jonathan Culler, "Semiotics of Tourism," in: *American Journal of Semiotics*. 1(1–2), 1981, pp. 127–40 (p. 137).

12   Jacques Le Rider, *Modernity and Crises of Identity. Culture and Society in Fin-de-Siècle Vienna*. Cambridge: Polity Press, 1993, p. 281.
13   Le Rider, *Modernity and Crises of Identity*, p. 279.
14   Stefan Scherer, *Richard Beer-Hofmann und die Wiener Moderne*. Tübingen: Max Niemeyer Verlag, 1993, p. 203.
15   Ibid.
16   Robert Archambeau, "The Aesthetic Anxiety: Avant-Garde Poetics, Autonomous Aesthetics and the Idea of Politics," in: Kelly Comfort (ed.), *Art and Life in Aestheticism*. New York: Palgrave, 2008, pp. 139–58 (p. 139).
17   Carl E. Schorske, *Fin-de-Siècle Vienna: Politics and Culture*. New York: Random House, 1980. Around the 1880s, the fairly recent political authority of Viennese liberals was challenged by the emergence of mass political groupings—the anti-Semitic Christian Social Party, socialists, the Pan-German Movement, and Slavic nationalists. Viennese liberalism would suffer ultimate defeat in 1895, when the anti-Semitic Christian Karl Lueger was elected mayor.
18   Scott Spector, "Beyond the Aesthetic Garden: Politics and Culture on the Margins of *Fin-de Siècle* Vienna," in: *Journal of the History of Ideas*. 59(4), 1998, pp. 691–710.
19   Le Rider, *Modernity and Crises of Identity*, p. 27.
20   Schorske, *Fin-de-Siècle Vienna*, pp. 9–22.
21   Le Rider, *Modernity and Crises of Identity*, p. 28.
22   Le Rider, *Modernity and Crises of Identity*, p. 191.
23   Even if biographical narratives of identity were rejected by many leading cultural figures, Steven Beller argues that the Jewish contribution to Viennese modernism was not entirely incidental. Supported by statistics about education, training, and professional activities of cultural figures of Jewish descent, he argues that while the Jews were certainly only one force among others within the avant-garde, "it was indeed its Jews which made Vienna what it was in the realm of modern culture." Steven Beller, *Vienna and the Jews, 1867–1938*. Cambridge: Cambridge University Press, 1989, p. 244.
24   Le Rider, *Modernity and Crises of Identity*, p. 199.
25   Spector, "Beyond the Aesthetic Garden," p. 691.
26   Spector, "Beyond the Aesthetic Garden," p. 695.
27   Le Rider, *Modernity and Crises of Identity*, pp. 26–7.
28   Minnaard, *New Germans, New Dutch*, p. 54.
29   Cameron McCarthy (ed.), *Mobilized Identities: Mediated Subjectivity and Cultural Crisis in the Neoliberal Era*. Champaign, Illinois: Common Ground Publishing, Kindle Edition, 2013.
30   Le Rider, *Modernity and Crises of Identity*, p. 294.
31   McCarthy, *Mobilized Identities*, Introduction, s.p.
32   Ibid.
33   Andrew Barker, "Race, Sex and Character in Schnitzler's *Fräulein Else*," in: *German Life and Letters*. 54(1), 2001, pp. 1–9 (p. 2).
34   Gerd K. Schneider, "The Social and Political Context of Arthur Schnitzler's *Reigen* in Berlin, Vienna, and New York: 1900–1933," in: Dagmar C. Lorenz (ed.), *A Companion to the Works of Arthur Schnitzler*. Rochester: Camden House, 2003, pp. 27–57 (p. 46).
35   W. Edgar Yates, *Schnitzler, Hofmannsthal and the Austrian Theatre*. London/New Haven: Yale University Press, 1992, p. 170.
36   Ibid.

37 Frauke Matthes, "Islam in the West: Perceptions and Self-Perceptions of Muslims in Navid Kermani's *Kurzmitteilung*," in: *German Life and Letters*. 64(2), 2011, pp. 305–316 (p. 306).
38 Jim Jordan, "Identity, Irony and Denial: Navid Kermani's *Kurzmitteilung*," in: Brigid Haines, Stephen Parker, Colin Riordan (eds.), *Aesthetics and Politics in Modern German Culture: Festschrift in Honour of Rhys W. Williams*. Oxford: Peter Lang, 2010, pp. 165–77 (p. 168).
39 Edward Said, *Covering Islam. How the Media and the Experts Determine How We See The Rest of The World*. London: Random House, 1997/1981, p. l.
40 Kermani, *Wer ist wir?*, pp. 112–13.
41 For an extensive discussion of the cultural dynamics of reception of Schnitzler's 'Jewish' works, see: Abigail Gillman, *Viennese Jewish Modernism. Freud, Hofmannsthal, Beer-Hofmann, and Schnitzler*. University Park: Pennsylvania State University Press, 2009, pp. 101–26.
42 Hans-Peter Bayerdörfer, "Arthur Schnitzler," in: Andreas B. Kilcher (ed.), *Metzler Lexikon der deutsch-jüdischen Literatur: jüdische Autorinnen und Autoren deutscher Sprache von der Aufklärung bis zur Gegenwart*. Stuttgart: Metzler, 2000, pp. 519–23.
43 Arthur Schnitzler, Letter to Elisabeth Steinrück, December 22–26, 1914, in: Arthur Schnitzler, *Briefe 1913–1931*. Edited by Peter Michael Braunwarth et al. Frankfurt am Main: S. Fischer, 1984, p. 69.
44 Bayerdörfer, "Arthur Schnitzler," p. 520.
45 Arthur Schnitzler, *Jugend in Wien: Eine Autobiographie*. Frankfurt am Main: Fischer, 1981, p. 13.
46 Robert S. Wistrich, *The Jews of Vienna in the Age of Franz Joseph*. New York: Littman Library of Jewish Civilization/Oxford University Press, 1989, pp. 610–11. An oft-cited quote of Schnitzler's sums up his position: "I do not feel solidarity with anyone because they happen to belong to the same nation, the same class, the same race, the same family as I do. It is exclusively my own business to whom I wish to feel related. [Ich fühle mich mit niemandem solidarisch, weil er zufällig derselben Nation, demselben Stand, derselben Rasse, derselben Familie angehört wie ich. Es ist ausschließlich meine Sache, mit wem ich mich verwandt zu fühlen wünsche.]" Arthur Schnitzler, "Bekenntnis" (1904), in: Arthur Schnitzler, *Aphorismen und Betrachtungen II: Der Geist im Wort und der Geist in der Tat*. Edited by Robert O. Weiss. Frankfurt am Main: Fischer, 1993, p. 109.
47 Gillman, *Viennese Jewish Modernism*, p. 102.
48 Egon Schwarz, "Arthur Schnitzler und das Judentum," in: Gunter E. Grimm, Hans-Peter Bayersdörfer (eds.), *Im Zeichen Hiobs: Jüdische Schriftsteller und deutsche Literatur im 20. Jahrhundert*. Königstein: Athenäum, 1985, p. 82.
49 Bayersdörfer, "Arthur Schnitzler," p. 521.
50 Gillman, *Viennese Jewish Modernism*, p. 103.
51 Ibid.
52 Gillman, *Viennese Jewish Modernism*, p. 104. This is indeed what happened with the critical reception of *Der Weg ins Freie*. Liberal papers praised its accurate depiction of Viennese society, while Zionist critics read it as a pro-Zionist pamphlet. Left-wing papers strongly identified with the socialist heroine, but were critical of the novel's focus on the upper class. *Professor Bernhardi* was met with similar contradictory reviews. See: Gillman, *Viennese Jewish Modernism*, pp. 104–5.
53 Gillman, *Viennese Jewish Modernism*, p. 107.
54 Navid Kermani, *Iran: Die Revolution der Kinder*. Munich: C.H. Beck, 2000.
55 Navid Kermani, *Gott ist schön: Das ästhetische Erleben des Koran*. Munich: C.H. Beck, 1999.

56   Navid Kermani, *Ungläubiges Staunen*. Munich: C.H. Beck, 2015.
57   In 2009, Kermani was awarded the *Hessischer Kulturpreis*, which was organized that year under the banner of interreligious tolerance.
58   Navid Kermani, *Wer ist Wir? Deutschland und seine Muslime*. Munich: C.H. Beck, 2009.
59   Kermani, *Wer ist wir?*, p. 35.
60   Similarly, in his 2014 address to the *Bundestag* on the celebration of the 65th anniversary of the *Bundesgesetz*, he seized the opportunity to emphasize the constitutional principle of religious freedom. See: https://www.bundestag.de/dokumente/textarchiv/2014/-/280688.
61   Kermani, *Wer ist wir?*, pp. 132–3. Kermani refers to the *Literaturen* interview mentioned in the introduction. *Literaturen*, "Ich bin ein Teil der deutschen Literatur, so deutsch wie Kafka," in: *Literaturen*. 4, 2005, pp. 26–31.
62   Navid Kermani, "Was ist deutsch an der deutschen Literatur?," in: Bernhard Vogel/Konrad-Adenauer-Stiftung e.V. (ed.), *Was eint uns? Verständigung der Gesellschaft über gemeinsame Grundlagen*. Freiburg im Breisgau: Herder Verlag, 2008, pp. 78–98 (p. 79).
63   Kermani, "Was ist deutsch," p. 83.
64   Ibid.
65   Iris Radisch, "Es gibt nun mal Menschen, die Jutta heißen," in: *Die Zeit*. 40, 22 September, 2016, p. 41.
66   Ibid.
67   Jurij Lotman, *The Structure of the Artistic Text*. Translated from the Russian by Gail Lenhoff and Ronald Vroon. Ann Arbor: University of Michigan, 1977.
68   Yves Petry describes the protagonist of his novel *De Maagd Marino* (2010) as the embodiment of radical enlightened autonomy, which becomes a source of vulnerability: "[He experiences] his feeling for life, the fruit of thousands of hours of reading and years of autonomous reflection, more and more as a source of vulnerability. And finally even as a stage of uselessly advanced self-development. [[Hij ervaart] zijn levensgevoel, de vrucht van duizenden leesuren en jaren van autonome reflectie, hoe langer hoe meer als een bron van kwetsbaarheid. En finaal zelfs als een stadium van zinloos geavanceerde zelfontwikkeling.]" Yves Petry, "Besta je wel echt?," in: *De Morgen*. 30 March 2016, s.p.
69   The inspiration for Kermani's novel was in part autobiographical. It is dedicated to actress Claudia Fenner, Kermani's theatre colleague, who died unexpectedly one day after the London bomb attacks of 7 July 2005. Jordan "Identity, Irony and Denial," p. 170.
70   Bettina Matthias, "Arthur Schnitzler's *Fräulein Else* and the end of the bourgeois tragedy," in: *Women in German Yearbook*. 18, 2002, pp. 248–66 (p. 254).
71   Jörn Lamla, "Consuming Authenticity: A Paradoxical Dynamic in Contemporary Capitalism," in: Phillip Vannini, J. Patrick Williams, *Authenticity in Culture, Self, and Society*. London/New York: Routledge, 2009, pp. 171–186 (p. 176).
72   Yeo, Siew Lian, "'Entweder oder': Dualism in Schnitzler's Fraulein Else," in: *Modern Austrian Literature*. 32(2), 1999, pp. 15–26.
73   Lotman, *The Structure of the Artistic Text*, p. 288ff.
74   Lotman, *The Structure of the Artistic Text*, p. 288 (emphasis in original).
75   Lotman, *The Structure of the Artistic Text*, p. 289.
76   Lotman, *The Structure of the Artistic Text*, 290.
77   Ibid.
78   Lotman, *The Structure of the Artistic Text*, 292.
79   Ibid.

80 Frederick J. Beharriell, "Schnitzler's *Fräulein Else*: 'Reality' and Invention," in: *Modern Austrian Literature: Journal of the International Arthur Schnitzler Research Association.* 10(3-4), 1977, pp. 247-64; Dorrit Cohn, *Transparent Minds: Narrative Modes for Presenting Consciousness in Fiction.* Princeton: Princeton UP, 1978.
81 Andreas Huyssen, "The Disturbance of Vision in Vienna Modernism," in: *Modernism/Modernity.* 5(3), 1998, pp. 33-47; Susan C. Anderson, "Seeing Blindly: Voyeurism in Schnitzler's *Fräulein Else* and Andreas Salomé's *Fenitschka*," in: Joseph P. Strelka (ed.), *Die Seele...ist ein weites Land: Kritische Beiträge zum Werk Arthur Schnitzlers.* Bern: Peter Lang, 1996, pp. 13-27; Susan C. Anderson, "The Power of the Gaze: Visual Metaphors in Schnitzler's Prose Works and Dramas," in: Dagmar C. G. Lorenz (ed.), *A Companion to the Works of Arthur Schnitzler.* Rochester: Camden House, 2003, pp. 303-324.
82 Andrew Barker situates the story's genesis within a very specific Viennese sociopolitical context, and establishes a connection between Else's characterization and Otto Weininger's *Geschlecht und Charakter.* Barker, "Race, Sex and Character," pp. 1-9. Achim Aurnhammer comments on the neglect of Else's Jewish identity, due to which "her self-reference acquires a social-historical justification [ihre Selbstbezogenheit eine sozial-historische Begründung erhält]." Achim Aurnhammer, "'Selig, wer in Träumen stirbt.' Das literarisierte Leben und Sterben von *Fräulein Else*," in: *Euphorion: Zeitschrift für Literaturgeschichte.* 77(4), 1983, pp. 500-10 (p. 504).
83 Kelly Comfort, "Artist for art's sake or artist for sale: Lulu's and Else's failed attempts at aesthetic self-fashioning," in: *Women in German Yearbook.* 22, 2006, pp. 189-210; Yeo, "Dualism in Schnitzler's *Fräulein Else*," pp. 15-26; Cathy Raymond, "Masked in Music: Hidden Meaning in Schnitzler's *Fräulein Else*," in: *Monatshefte.* 85(2), 1993, pp. 170-88.
84 Comfort, "Artist for art's sake," p. 189.
85 Anderson, "The Power of the Gaze," p. 19.
86 Cohn, *Transparent Minds*, p. 217ff.
87 Cohn, *Transparent Minds*, p. 8.
88 Comfort, "Artist for art's sake," p. 189.
89 Friedrich Nietzsche, *The Gay Science: With a Prelude in Rhymes and an Appendix of Songs.* Trans. Walter Kaufmann. New York: Random, 1974.
90 Nietzsche, *The Gay Science*, pp. 316-7.
91 Ibid.
92 Andreas Reckwitz, *Das hybride Subjekt. Eine Theorie der Subjektkulturen von der bürgerlichen Moderne zur Postmoderne.* Weilerswist: Velbrück, 2006/2010, p. 171.
93 Ibid.
94 Wilhelm von Humboldt, as quoted in Christoph Wulf, "Perfecting the Individual: Wilhelm von Humboldt's concept of anthropology, Bildung, and mimesis," in: *Educational Philosophy and Theory.* 35(2), 2003, pp. 241-249 (p. 246).
95 Wulf, "Perfecting the Individual," p. 246.
96 Ibid.
97 Ibid.
98 Reckwitz, *Das hybride Subjekt*, pp. 155-78.
99 Reckwitz, *Das hybride Subjekt*, p. 156.
100 Close to the end, when she has taken the dose of Veronal and reaches a state of full self-immersion, she decides that Fred should have her neglected diary, which represents her final distance from her education. It also symbolizes her transition from a linguistic to a purely visual communication code.

101. Reckwitz, *Das hybride Subjekt*, p. 167.
102. Reckwitz, *Das hybride Subjekt*, p. 158.
103. "[Le] monde est fait pour aboutir à un beau livre." Remark from Stéphane Mallarmé to his interviewer Jules Huret. "Symbolistes et Décadents," in: Jules Huret (ed.), *Enquête sur l'évolution littéraire*. Charpentier, 1891, p. 65.
104. Oscar Wilde, *De Profundis*. London: Methuen, 1915, pp. 33–34.
105. Jochen Jung, "Einer dieser Typen von Scientology," in: *Die Zeit*. 21 August, 2007; http://www.zeit.de/2007/34/L-Kermani.
106. Jim Jordan, "Identity, Irony and Denial," p. 170.
107. Walter Benjamin, "Das Kunstwerk im Zeitalter seiner technischen Reproduzierbarkeit" (Dritte Fassung, 1935), in: Walter Benjamin, *Gesammelte Schriften*. Band I, Teil 2. Edited by Rolf Tiedemann and Hermann Schweppenhäuser. Frankfurt am Main: Suhrkamp, 1974, pp. 471–508.
108. Benjamin, "Das Kunstwerk," p. 476.
109. "As a creative subject, it is the bearer of semiotic innovation dispositions and seeks in working the challenge of 'inner growth'; 'creative work' is a central element of its self-stylization. As an 'entrepreneur of the self', he is constantly striving to optimize his profile according to the market's labor force requirements and to model his career biography in calculated acts of choice. [Als Kreativsubjekt ist es Träger von semiotischen Innovationsdispositionen und sucht in der Arbeit nach der Herausforderung seines 'inneren Wachstums'; 'Kreativarbeit' ist ein zentrales Element seiner Selbststilisierung. Als 'Unternehmer seiner selbst' ist es fortlaufend bemüht, sein Profil nach Maßgabe des Marktes an Arbeitskräften zu optimieren und seine Arbeitsbiografie in kalkulatorischen Akten der Wahl zu modellieren.]" Reckwitz, *Das hybride Subjekt*, p. 500.
110. Lamla, "Consuming Authenticity," p. 177 (emphasis in original). Similarly, Reckwitz comments on the postmodern aesthete as a compound of contradictory social and self-oriented inclinations: "The creative-entrepreneurial subject is [...] not only an egoistic self-made man and internally oriented post-romantic 'artist'—both decidedly anti-social figures—but necessarily incorporates that team spirit that not only makes him suitable for collective project work, but also makes the team appear to him as a necessary, affectively engaged community of creativity without which he could not be creative. [Das kreativ-unternehmerische Subjekt ist [...] nicht allein ein egoistischer *self-made man* und innenorientierter post-romantischer 'Künstler'—beide dezidiert anti-soziale Figuren—, sondern inkorporiert notwendig jene Teamfähigkeit, die es nicht nur für kollektive Projektarbeit geeignet macht, sondern ihm selbst auch das Team als notwendige, affektiv besetzte Kreativitätsgemeinschaft erscheinen lässt, ohne die es nicht kreativ sein könnte.]" Reckwitz, *Das hybride Subjekt*, p. 525.
111. Lamla, "Consuming Authenticity," p. 175.
112. Ibid.
113. Reckwitz, *Das hybride Subjekt*, p. 209.
114. Also see: Comfort, "Artist for art's sake," p. 200.
115. Reckwitz, *Das hybride Subjekt*, p. 238.
116. Anderson, "The Power of the Gaze," p. 314.
117. Ibid.
118. Barker, "Race, Sex and Character," p. 5.
119. Anderson, "The Power of the Gaze," p. 314.
120. Comfort, "Artist for art's sake," pp. 203–4.
121. Comfort, "Artist for art's sake," p. 204.

122 Comfort, "Artist for art's sake," p. 205.
123 Comfort points out Else's increasing interest in the plastic arts, and her self-comparison to the portraits of Florentine ladies. Comfort, "Artist for art's sake," pp. 205–6.
124 Matthes, "Islam in the West," p. 309.
125 Jordan, "Identity, Irony, and Denial," p. 176.
126 "Financially, Sufism in Germany would also have potential outside of esoterism, not in the least as onanism for left-wing socialized racists who don't have anything against Muslims but only something against fundamentalism. [Finanziell hätte der Sufismus in Deutschland Potential auch außerhalb der Esoterik, nicht zuletzt als Onanie für linkssozialisierte Rassisten, die nichts gegen Muslime haben wollen, sondern nur etwas gegen den Fundamentalismus.]" (KM 100)
127 "I am not a believer, but when I have something important in mind or someone has died, I speak the Fatiha, the first sura of the Koran, although I don't remember the meaning exactly. [...] The Arabic verses lie well on my lips and help me through the seconds when I don't know what I'm supposed to do or think. [Ich bin nicht gläubig, aber wenn ich etwas Wichtiges vorhabe oder jemand gestorben ist, spreche ich die Fatiha, die erste Sure des Korans, obwohl ich mich gar nicht mehr genau an den Sinn erinnere. [...] Die arabischen Verse liegen gut auf meinen Lippen und helfen mir über die Sekunden hinweg, in denen ich nicht weiß, was ich tun oder denken soll.]" (KM 18–9)
128 Jordan, "Identity, Irony, Denial," p. 177.
129 Similarly, his hypersexuality is a reaction against the perception of 'Muslims' as a homogeneous group of sexual conservatives. By asserting his virility, he positions himself on the market as a legitimate and, especially, stronger counterpart to the Germans' "pale competition [bleiche Konkurrenz]." (KM 126) Dariusch thus inverts the Orientalist dichotomy that distinguishes masculinized Occident from feminized Orient. See: Matthes, "Islam in the West," p. 310.
130 Kermani, *Wer ist wir?*, p. 121.
131 Matthes, "Islam in the West," p. 310.
132 Navid Kermani in an interview with *Reset DOC*, 4 June, 2007; http://www.resetdoc.org/de/Kermani-interview.php.
133 Bhabha, "Of Mimicry and Man," in: *The Location of Culture*, pp. 121–31 (p. 122; emphasis in original).
134 Bhabha, "Of Mimicry and Man," p. 126.
135 Walter Benjamin, "Kapitalismus als Religion," in: Walter Benjamin, *Gesammelte Schriften*. Band VI. Edited by Rolf Tiedemann and Hermann Schweppenhäuser. Frankfurt am Main: Suhrkamp, 1991, pp. 100–102.
136 There is no explicit mention of Scientology, but the final chapter, especially the 'auditing' relation to his counselor, is reminiscent of the cult's practices.
137 Erika Spohrer, "The Seeker-Consumer: Scientology and the Rhetoric of Consumerism," in: *Journal of Religion and Popular Culture*. 26(1), 2014, pp. 107–23.
138 Hillary Hope Herzog, *Vienna is different. Jewish writers in Austria from the fin de siècle to the present*. New York: Berghahn, 2011, p. 78.
139 "I never knew what I wanted to be. [...] Had I not met Hugo Hofmannsthal, Schnitzler, and Bahr by pure chance just one summer, I might never have come to write. But in that circle one was convinced that I would write, and that I would write something good. [Ich wußte nie, was ich werden wollte. [...] Hätte ich nicht durch reinen Zufall in einem einzigen Sommer den Hugo Hofmannsthal, Schnitzler und Bahr kennengelernt, wäre ich vielleicht nie zum Schreiben gekommen. Aber in jenem Kreis war man überzeugt, ich würde schreiben, und

zwar etwas Gutes.]" Beer-Hofmann, quoted in Stefan Scherer, *Richard Beer-Hofmann und die Wiener Moderne*. Tübingen: Niemeyer/De Gruyter, 1993, p. 3.

140 Harry Zohn, "German Jewry as Spirit and Legacy," in Abraham J. Peck (ed.), *The German-Jewish Legacy in America, 1938–1988: From* Bildung *to the Bill of Rights*. Detroit: Wayne State University Press, 1989, pp. 41–46 (p. 41).

141 See especially: Le Rider, *Modernity and Crises of Identity*, p. 285ff.; Ulrike Peters, "Das Problem des Judentums bei Richard Beer-Hofmann," in: *Zeitschrift für Religions- und Geistesgeschichte*. 48(3), 1996, pp. 262–271.

142 Stefan Scherer, "Richard Beer-Hofmann und das Judentum," in: Norbert Otto Eke, Günter Helmes (eds.), *Richard Beer-Hofmann (1866–1945). Studien zu seinem Werk*. Würzburg: Königshausen und Neumann, 1993, pp. 13–33 (p. 14).

143 See: Matti Bunzl, "The Poetics of Politics and the Politics of Poetics: Richard Beer-Hofmann and Theodor Herzl Reconsidered," in: *The German Quarterly*. 69(3), 1996, pp. 277–304.

144 Bunzl, "The Poetics of Politics," pp. 277–278.

145 Bunzl refers to Rainer Hank, in particular. Bunzl, "The Poetics of Politics," p. 278. Rainer Hank, *Mortifikation und Beschwörung: Zur Veränderung ästhetischer Wahrnehmung in der Moderne am Beispiel des Frühwerkes Richard Beer-Hofmanns*. Frankfurt a.M.: Peter Lang, 1984.

146 Herzog, *Vienna is different*, p. 78.

147 Karl Kraus, "Die demolirte Literatur I," in: *Wiener Rundschau*. 1, 15 November 1896, pp. 19–27 (p. 21).

148 Karl Kraus, "Die demolirte Literatur II," in: *Wiener Rundschau*. 2, December 1896, pp. 68–72 (p. 71).

149 Herzog, *Vienna is Different*, p. 78.

150 Bunzl, "The Poetics of Politics," p. 288.

151 Herzog, *Vienna is Different*, p. 78.

152 Gillman, *Viennese Jewish Modernism*, p. 79.

153 Gillman, *Viennese Jewish Modernism*, pp. 8–9.

154 See: Pfeiffer, Joachim. *Tod und Erzählen. Wege der literarischen Moderne um 1900*. Tübingen: Niemeyer, 1997.

155 Konstanze Fliedl, "Richard Beer-Hofmann: Der Tod Georgs," in: Cornelia Niedermeier, Karl Wagner (eds.), *Literatur um 1900. Texte der Jahrhundertwende neu gelesen*. Cologne/Weimar/Vienna: Böhlau, 2001, pp. 155–160 (p. 157).

156 Scherer, *Richard Beer-Hofmann*, p. 184ff.

157 Le Rider, *Modernity and Crises of Identity*, p. 279.

158 Le Rider, *Modernity and Crises of Identity*, p. 281.

159 Herzog, *Vienna is different*, pp. 79–80.

160 Georg Lukács, "Der Augenblick und die Formen" (1908), in: Georg Lukács, *Die Seele und die Formen*. Berlin: Egon Fleischel & Co, 1911, pp. 231–63 (p. 236–7).

161 Le Rider, *Modernity and Crises of Identity*, p. 279.

162 Pfeiffer points out the common ground between Viennese modernism and early Romantic aesthetics, which are both literary counterreactions against the disenchantment of modern rationalism. Pfeiffer, *Tod und Erzählen*, p. 103. On a related note, Bryan Aja argues that Zaimoglu's *Liebesbrand* indeed clearly inserts itself into the Romantic tradition but establishes a connection to Viennese modernism as well. Unlike Aja, who diagnoses the narrator as a "neurotic philanderer" and associates him with for instance Peter Altenberg's writings and Schnitzler's *Anatol*, I prefer to found my comparison on the observation that Zaimoglu's and

Beer-Hofmann's protagonists struggle with very similar crises of meaning and perception. Bryan Aja, "The Shameless Little Man: Narrative Obstruction in Feridun Zaimoğlu's *Liebesbrand*," in: *EDGE—A Graduate Journal for German and Scandinavian Studies*. 3(1), 2013, s.p.

163 Feridun Zaimoglu, *Kanak Sprak. 24 Mißtöne vom Rande der Gesellschaft*. Hamburg: Rotbuch Verlag, 1995/2004.

164 For a discussion of the *Kanak* counter-identity in Zaimoglu's early works, see, for instance: Minnaard, *New Germans, New Dutch*, pp. 143–177.

165 Tom Cheesman, Karin E. Yeşilada (eds.), *Feridun Zaimoglu*. Oxford: Peter Lang, 2012, p. 1.

166 Cheesman, "Juggling Burdens of Representation," p. 477.

167 Cheesman/Yeşilada, *Feridun Zaimoglu*, p. 1.

168 Zaimoglu was co-founder of *Kanak Attak*, a "pan-ethnic social cultural movement" (1998) that, according to its own manifesto, sought to actively attack the "*kanakisation* of certain groups of people through racist attributions [Kanakisierung bestimmter Gruppen von Menschen durch rassistische Zuschreibungen," and to reject any form of nationalist or racist identity politics feeding on ethnological designations. Zaimoglu split from the movement in 2000, paradoxically "to avoid being confined to ethnic positions." Cheesman/Yeşilada, *Feridun Zaimoglu*, p. vii.; The manifesto *Kanak Attak und Basta!* Is accessible at http://www.kanak-attak.de/ka/about.html.

169 Minnaard, *New Germans, New Dutch*, p. 144.

170 Feridun Zaimoglu, Julia Abel, "Migrationsliteratur ist ein toter Kadaver. Ein Gespräch," in: Arnold, Heinz Ludwig (ed.), *Text + Kritik. Zeitschrift für Literatur. Sonderband Literatur und Migration*. 9, 2006, pp. 159–66 (p. 162).

171 Cheesman/Yeşilada, *Feridun Zaimoglu*, p. 3.

172 Zaimoglu, quoted in Cheesman/Yeşilada, *Feridun Zaimoglu*, p. 3.

173 Tom Cheesman, "For Feridun Zaimoglu's Leyla: Crime Facts and Fictions," in: *German as a Foreign Language*. 3, 2008, pp. 4–25 (p. 11). Also see: Yasemin Dayioğlu-Yücel, "Authorship and Authenticity in Migrant Writing: The Plagiarism Debate on *Leyla*," in: in: Tom Cheesman, Karin E. Yeşilada (eds.), *Feridun Zaimoglu*. Oxford: Peter Lang, 2012, pp. 183–99.

174 Cheesman/Yeşilada, *Feridun Zaimoglu*, p. 7.

175 Zaimoglu also intervened in the debate to point out that Özdamar and his aunts had resided in the same migrant workers' hostel in Berlin. He suggested that they might have exchanged stories that were picked up in Özdamar's and Zaimoglu's respective novels. Dayioğlu-Yücel, "Authorship and Authenticity," p. 185.

176 Cheesman/Yeşilada, *Feridun Zaimoglu*, p. 5.

177 On Zaimoglu's engagement with the Romantic tradition, see: Margaret Littler, "Between Romantic Love and War Machine: *Liebesbrand*," in: Tom Cheesman, Karin E. Yeşilada (eds.), *Feridun Zaimoglu*. Oxford: Peter Lang, 2012, pp. 219–38; Michael Hofmann, "Romantic Rebellion: Feridun Zaimoglu and Anti-bourgeois Tradition," in: Tom Cheesman, Karin E. Yeşilada (eds.), *Feridun Zaimoglu*. Oxford: Peter Lang, 2012, pp. 239–58. For a more detailed overview of Romantic approaches throughout his work, see: Cheesman/Yeşilada, *Feridun Zaimoglu*, pp. 4–11.

178 In his subsequent novels *Abschaum* (1997), and to a lesser extent *Koppstoff* (1998), Zaimoglu continues in the same politically engaged tone, using a similar "crafted bricolage of slangs, dialects, jargons and neologisms." Cheesman/Yeşilada, *Feridun Zaimoglu*, p. 4.

179 Cheesman/Yeşilada, *Feridun Zaimoglu*, p. 8.

180 Tom Cheesman, Karin E. Yeşilada, "'Ich bin nicht modern'/ 'I'm not Modern': Interviews with Feridun Zaimoglu," in: Tom Cheesman, Karin E. Yeşilada (eds.), *Feridun Zaimoglu*. Oxford: Peter Lang, 2012, pp. 39–70 (p. 56). In the same interview, he explains in similar terms: "I am not modern, not in my writing, nor in my thoughts and actions. I do not like the modern, this plastic, polyester, this genital shit. [...] I [...] feel very skeptical about the Enlightenment. I am at least as skeptical of the old ideology, and it is just as well that it has disintegrated [...]. [Ich bin nicht modern, nicht in meinem Schreiben, und auch nicht in meinem Denken und Handeln. Ich mag die Moderne nicht, dieses Plastik, Polyester, diesen Genitalscheiß. [...] Ich [...] habe eine große Skepsis gegenüber der Aufklärung. Mindestens genau so eine Skepsis habe ich gegenüber der alten Ideologie, und es ist gut, dass sie zerfallen ist [...].]" Cheesman/Yeşilada, "'Ich bin nicht modern,'" p. 46.
181 Ibid.
182 Ibid.
183 Ibid.
184 Cheesman/Yeşilada, "'Ich bin nicht modern,'" p. 48.
185 Cheesman/Yeşilada, "'Ich bin nicht modern,'" p. 46.
186 Cheesman/Yeşilada, "'Ich bin nicht modern,'" p. 50.
187 Cheesman/Yeşilada, "'Ich bin nicht modern,'" p. 52.
188 Cheesman/Yeşilada, "'Ich bin nicht modern,'" p. 56.
189 Cheesman/Yeşilada, *Feridun Zaimoglu*, p. 2.
190 Cheesman/Yeşilada, *Feridun Zaimoglu*, p. 7.
191 In 2006, Zaimoglu escaped from a bus crash in Turkey. But in the aforementioned interview, he emphasizes that the crash in *Liebesbrand* is not a realistic depiction of his experience. Cheesman/Yeşilada, "'Ich bin nicht modern,'" p. 66.
192 Littler, "Between Romantic Love and War Machine," p. 219.
193 Littler, "Between Romantic Love and War Machine," p. 220.
194 Cheesman/Yeşilada, "'Ich bin nicht modern,'" p. 66.
195 On its claim of authenticity, see: Minnaard, *New Germans, New Dutch*, pp. 143–177.
196 Pfeiffer, *Tod und Erzählen*, p. 137.
197 Gillman, *Viennese Jewish Modernism*, p. 21.
198 Gillman, *Viennese Jewish Modernism*, p. 78.
199 Gillman, *Viennese Jewish Modernism*, pp. 78–9.
200 Beer-Hofmann in an interview with Werner Vordtriede, quoted in Scherer, *Richard Beer-Hofmann*, p. 217.
201 The motif appears at the beginning of the second and third chapters, and at the conclusion of the first two.
202 Gillman, *Viennese Jewish Modernism*, p. 85.
203 Ibid.
204 Gillman, *Viennese Jewish Modernism*, p. 83.
205 Bahr describes Mach's *Analyse der Empfindungen* as "the book that expresses at the greatest our sense of the world, the spirit of the new generation [das Buch, das unser Gefühl der Welt, die Lebensstimmung der neuen Generation auf das größte ausspricht]." Hermann Bahr, *Dialog vom Tragischen*. Berlin: S. Fischer, 1904, p. 113.
206 Ernst Mach, *Die Analyse der Empfindungen und das Verhältnis des Physischen zum Psychischen*. Jena: Gustav Fischer, 1922.
207 Ibid.
208 Pfeiffer, *Tod und Erzählen*, p. 138.

209 Near the end, in a scene alluding to Narcissus, Paul observes his reflection in a pool, and regrets his previous attitude: "He had only searched himself in all those who had encountered him [...] [I]n everything he had searched only himself and had found only himself in everything. [Sich selbst nur hatte er in Allen gesucht die ihm begegnet waren [...] [I]n Allem hatte er nur sich gesucht und sich nur in Allem gefunden." (TG 199–200)

210 Gillman discusses the aesthete's awakening in terms of *mémoire involontaire*. Paul's turn to Judaism is elicited by a recovery of memory by means of association, which is at once the operating principle of the aesthete's mind, and the mechanism of the remembering mind. Gillman, *Viennese Jewish Modernism*, p. 80.

211 Pfeiffer, *Tod und Erzählen*, p. 101.

212 Ibid.

213 Ibid.

214 Gillman, *Viennese Jewish Modernism*, p. 85.

215 Christopher Fynsk, "Foreword: Experiences of finitude," in: Jean-Luc Nancy, *The Inoperative Community*. Ed. Connor, Peter. Minneapolis/London: University of Minnesota Press, 1991, pp. vii-xxxv (p. xvi; emphasis in original).

216 Fynsk, "Experiences of finitude," p. xv.

217 Pfeiffer, *Tod und Erzählen*, p. 139.

218 Pfeiffer, *Tod und Erzählen*, p. 138.

219 Gillman, *Viennese Jewish Modernism*, p. 90.

220 Gillman, *Viennese Jewish Modernism*, p. 92.

221 Ibid.

222 Cheesman/Yeşilada, *Feridun Zaimoglu*, p. 8.

223 Cheesman/Yeşilada, *Feridun Zaimoglu*, p. 5.

224 The Romantics' philistine, as Michael Hofmann points out, emerges in Zaimoglu's writings as the 'Spießer'—a prominent theme in his work. Michael Hofmann, "Romantic Rebellion," p. 240. Also see: Joseph Twist, "'The Crossing of Love': The Inoperative Community and Romantic Love in Feridun Zaimoglu's 'Fünf klopfende Herzen, wenn die Liebe springt' and Hinterland," in: *German Life and Letters*. 67(3), 2014, pp. 399–417.

225 Littler, "Between Romantic Love and War Machine," p. 222.

226 To some extent, Zaimoglu's David resembles himself a liminal person. "The attributes of liminality or of liminal *personae*," according to Victor Turner's definition in the context of rites of passage, "are necessarily ambiguous, since this condition and these persons elude or slip through the network of classifications that normally locate states and positions in cultural space. [...] Liminal entities [...] may be represented as possessing nothing [...]. [A]s liminal beings, they have no status, property, insignia, secular clothing indicating rank or role, position in a kinship system—in short, nothing that may distinguish them from their fellow neophytes or initiands. Their behaviour is normally passive or humble [...]. It is as though they are being reduced or ground down to a uniform condition to be fashioned anew and endowed with additional powers to enable them to cope with their new station in life." Victor Turner, "Liminality and Communitas," in: Victor Turner, *The Ritual Process: Structure and Anti-Structure*. Chicago: Aldine Publishing 1969, pp. 94–130 (p. 95–96).

227 Littler, "Between Romantic Love and War Machine," p. 223.

228 In a slightly mocking tone, the protagonist is shown to soothe himself to sleep with an exemplary story of enlightened self-development, in which a destitute child roaming the streets manages to climb up the social ladder to become a wealthy doctor. (LB 42–43)

229 Likewise, Frauke Matthes connects David's desire to German Romanticism and its focus on "the miraculous, the exotic, the adventurous, the sensual, the sinister, the renunciation of modern civilization and the attention to the inner and outer nature of mankind [das Wunderbare, Exotische, Abenteuerliche, Sinnliche, Schaurige, die Abwendung von der modernen Zivilisation und die Hinwendung zur inneren und äußeren Natur des Menschen] [...]." Frauke Matthes, "Männliche Sehnsucht in (türkisch-) deutscher Gegenwart in Feridun Zaimoğlus *Liebesbrand*," in: *Studien zur deutschen Sprache und Literatur*. 24(2), 2010, pp. 85–102 (p. 89).

230 This passage is remarkably similar to Franz Hessel's description of equally fragmented and meaningless mannequins in *Spazieren in Berlin*. See Chapter 3.

231 Littler, "Between Romantic Love and War Machine," p. 224.

232 Arthur Schopenhauer, Karl-Maria Guth (ed.), *Aphorismen zur Lebensweisheit*. Berlin: Hofenberg, 2016, p. 33 (emphasis in original).

233 Littler, "Between Romantic Love and War Machine," p. 222.

234 Jean-Luc Nancy, "Eulogy for the Mêlée," in: Jean-Luc Nancy, *Being Singular Plural*. Translated by Robert D. Richardson and Anne E. O'Byrne. Stanford: Stanford University Press, 2000, pp. 145–158 (p. 155; emphasis in original).

235 Gillman, *Viennese Jewish Modernism*, p. 80ff.; Scherer, *Richard Beer-Hofmann*, p. 179ff.

236 Gillman, *Viennese Jewish Modernism*, p. 80. In his review for *Die Zeit*, for instance, Alfred Gold compares the novella to a piece of jewelry—"Artificial about the book is the ornamental overload in the detail. Each sentence is built in the most intricate way from small parts, each part is polished, weighed, and colored, as if it were meant to shine for itself. [Gekünstelt ist an dem Buch die Schmucküberladenheit im Detail. Jeder Satz ist auf das Umständlichste aus kleinen Teilen aufgebaut, jeder Teil ist zugeschliffen, abgewogen und getönt, als sollte er leuchtend für sich selber wirken.]" Alfred Gold, "Ästhetik des Sterbens," in: *Die Zeit (Wien)*. 7(22/282), 24 February 1900, p. 121ff. Published in Sören Eberhardt, Charis Goer (eds.), *Über Richard Beer-Hofmann. Rezeptionsdokumente aus 100 Jahren*. Hamburg: Igel Verlag, 1996/2012, pp. 39–42.

237 Konstanze Fliedl (ed.), *Arthur Schnitzler—Richard Beer-Hofmann. Briefwechsel 1891–1931*. Vienna/Zürich: Europa Verlag, 1992, p. 144.

238 Gillman, *Viennese Jewish Modernism*, p. 80.

239 Also see: Gillman, *Viennese Jewish Modernism*, p. 5.

240 Le Rider, *Modernity and Crises of Identity*, p. 282.

241 Pfeiffer notes that *Jugendstil* in the visual arts is characterized by a suspended spatial dimension. In their literary counterpart, especially the temporal dimension is affected: "Der Versuch, das Leben in ein Bild zu fassen und es dadurch seiner historisch-zeitlichen Dimension zu berauben, gehört sicher zu einem vorrangigen Gestaltungsverfahren des literarischen Jugendstils." Pfeiffer, *Tod und Erzählen*, p. 128.

242 See: Rainer Hank, *Mortifikation und Beschwörung. Zur Veränderung ästhetischer Wahrnehmung in der Moderne am Beispiel des Frühwerkes Richard Beer-Hofmanns*. Frankfurt am Main: Peter Lang, 1984.

243 She is very likely the same woman who lies dying in the dream sequence.

244 Pfeiffer, *Tod und Erzählen*, p. 130. In this respect, Beer-Hofmann's and Schnitzler's aesthetes are very much alike, with the only exception that Else subjects herself to the observer's mortifying gaze, in a paradoxical attempt to avoid commodification.

245 Pfeiffer, *Tod und Erzählen*, p. 127.

246 The labyrinth as a metaphor of the path to spiritual enlightenment emerges in several religious traditions, including Judaism. It is also a common motif in Hasidic literature. Geoffrey Dennis, "Finding the Center, Entering the Land: The Labyrinths of Jewish Imagination," in: *Parabola: Tradition, Myth, and the Search for Meaning*. 34, 2009, pp. 31–42. Penelope Reed Doob distinguishes the unicursal labyrinth, where there is only one path winding towards a center, from the multicursal maze, where the wanderer faces a series of choices and may have to retrace his steps. Beer-Hofmann's spatial metaphor appears to be the unicursal labyrinth, since it is suggested that, despite his associations, the aesthete's wandering mind follows a single path, where even a seemingly wrong direction leads towards the goal. Penelope Reed Doob, *The Idea of Labyrinth: From Classical Antiquity Through the Middle Ages*. Ithaca, New York: Cornell University Press, 1990, pp. 17–38.

247 Pfeiffer, *Tod und Erzählen*, p. 130.

248 Nancy, "Shattered Love," in: Jean-Luc Nancy, *The Inoperative Community*. Ed. by Peter Connor, translated by Peter Connor et al. London/Minneapolis: University of Minnesota Press, pp. 82–109 (p. 98).

249 In one particular scene, the tension between static image and dynamic meaning is evoked in a way reminiscent of the *Jugendstil* imagery in *Der Tod Georgs*—the peacock and its feathers (e.g. TG 16): "A female peacock stood not four steps away from me and stared at me, I hadn't noticed it, Jarmila immediately began to address it with nicknames, therefore she detached her hand from my hand and walked carefully towards it, but it retreated and hid behind the pedestal of a bronze statue. [Ein Pfauenweibchen stand keine vier Schritte von mir entfernt und starrte mich an, ich hatte es nicht bemerkt, Jarmila fing sofort an, es mit Kosenamen anzusprechen, dafür löste sie ihre Hand von meiner Hand und ging vorsichtig auf das Weibchen zu, doch es zog sich zurück und versteckte sich hinter dem Sockel einer Bronzestatue.]" (LB 268) The (inconspicuous, female) peacock eludes Jarmila, and hides behind a more impressive statue, which can be interpreted as a metaphor for the game of *Sein* and *Schein* in which both Zaimoglu and Beer-Hofmann are engaged. The peacock (feather) is a recurring feature of *Jugendstil*, of which the Prague-based artist Alphons Mucha is a well-known representative. Indeed, set in Prague, and featuring a typical *Jugendstil* motif, this otherwise insignificant scene connects Zaimoglu's novel more explicitly to the theme addressed by Beer-Hofmann.

250 Littler, "Between Romantic Love and War Machine," p. 236.

251 Littler, "Between Romantic Love and War Machine," p. 237.

252 Nancy, "Shattered Love," pp. 82–109.

253 Fynsk, "Experiences of Finitude," p. xviii (emphasis in original).

254 Nancy, "Shattered Love," p. 97.

255 Ibid.

256 Nancy, "Shattered Love," p. 96.

257 At one moment, David explicitly elevates the idea of love above the reality of Tyra's rejection. He pities her for not experiencing the same desire: "Wie schade, daß du mich nicht liebst, Tyra. Wie schade, daß du nicht von mir träumst, daß du mich nicht vermißt hast." (LB 246)

258 Nancy, "Shattered Love," p. 93.

259 Nancy, "Shattered Love," p. 98.

260 Nancy, "Shattered Love," p. 98.

261 Ibid.

262 In this context, Littler points out the intertextual echoes to Kleist's *Penthesilea*, and its reading by Deleuze and Guattari as an instance of 'literature of war', which is concerned with "the convergence of forces which maintain social formations in a far-from-equilibrium or 'intensive crisis' state, in contrast to the stabilizing forces of state apparatuses." In her Deleuzian reading, Littler considers Tyra's and David's affair in similar terms as an "unrestricted play of violence and eros." Littler, "Between Romantic Love and War Machine," pp. 230–1.

263 Fynsk, "Experiences of Finitude," p. xviii.

264 For instance, David feels pleasantly idle in Jarmila's company: "For an hour we silently pursued our thoughts, and for the first time in a long time I had the feeling that it was neither too early nor too late, I couldn't think of any activity to which I wanted to devote myself, rather than looking at the people strolling about. [Eine Stunde lang hingen wir stumm unseren Gedanken nach, und ich hatte seit langer Zeit das erste Mal das Gefühl, daß es weder zu früh noch zu spät war, mir fiel keine Beschäftigung ein, der ich mich hätte widmen wollen, statt die schlendernden Menschen zu betrachten.]" (LB 225–6) In this scene, there is no indication of David's desire to shape reality according to his own ideas. Instead, he simply experiences reality as it is in the present moment, rather than how it could or should be.

265 Hofmann, "Romantic Rebellion," p. 240.

266 Şenocak, *Deutschsein*, pp. 76–77.

267 Littler, "Between Romantic Love and War Machine," p. 227.

268 Ibid.

269 At the time of Beer-Hofmann's writing, the biological rhetoric of blood was not exclusive to German and Austrian nationalism but adopted by Jewish nationalists as well, for whom "heeding one's blood was a metaphor for unearthing the inalienable Jew within." Gillman, *Viennese Jewish Modernism*, p. 96.

270 Gillman, *Viennese Jewish Modernism*, p. 95.

271 Le Rider, *Modernity and Crises of Identity*, p. 277.

272 Gillman, *Viennese Jewish Modernism*, p. 96.

273 Le Rider, *Modernity and Crises of Identity*, p. 293.

274 Ibid.

275 Theodor W. Adorno, *Aesthetic Theory*. Gretel Adorno and Rolf Tiedemann (eds.), translated by Robert Hullot-Kentor. London: Bloomsbury, 2013 [1970], p. 308.

Chapter 3. City dwellers between difference and indifference

1 Anke Biendarra, "'Schriftstellerin zu sein und in seinem Leben anwesend zu sein, ist für mich eins': ein Gespräch mit Terézia Mora," in: *Transit. A Journal of Travel, Migration, and Multiculturalism in the German-speaking World*. 3(1), 2007, s.p.

2 Ibid.

3 Klaus Scherpe, *Die Unwirklichkeit der Städte. Großstadtdarstellungen zwischen Moderne und Postmoderne*. Reinbek bei Hamburg: Rowohlt, 1988.

4 Erk Grimm, *Semiopolis. Prosa der Moderne und Nachmoderne im Zeichen der Stadt*. Bielefeld: Aisthesis Verlag, 2001, pp. 9–26.

5 Grimm, *Semiopolis*, p. 25.

6 Ibid.

7 Brian Ladd, *Ghosts of Berlin: Confronting German History in the Urban Landscape*. Chicago: Chicago University Press, 1997.

8   Ladd, *Ghosts of Berlin*, p. 1.
9   Stefan Alscher, "Großstädte sind Zuwanderungsmagnete," *Migration und Bevölkerung. Das Online-Portal zur Migrationsgesellschaft*. 11 June 2015; http://www.migration-info.de/artikel/2015-06-11/grossstaedte-sind-zuwanderungsmagneten.
10 Ibid.
11 Frank Gesemann (ed.), *Migration und Integration in Berlin. Wissenschaftliche Analysen und politische Perspektiven*. Opladen: Leske & Budrich, 2001, pp. 11–28.
12 See: Andreas Nachama, Julius Hans Schoeps, Hermann Simon (eds.), *Jews in Berlin*. Oxford: Berghahn, 2002.
13 Erol Yildiz, Birgit Mattausch-Yildiz, "Kultur der Urbanität. Stadt und Migration," in: *kulturrisse. Zeitschrift für radikaldemokratische Kulturpolitik*. 2, 2011, s.p.; http://kulturrisse.at/ausgaben/urbane-raeume-zwischen-verhandlung-und-verwandlung/oppositionen/kultur-der-urbanitaet.-stadt-und-migration.
14 Azade Seyhan, "From Istanbul to Berlin. Stations on the Road to a Transcultural/Translational Literature," in: *German Politics and Society*. 74(23/1), 2005, pp. 152–170 (p. 153).
15 Seyhan, "From Istanbul to Berlin," p. 153.
16 Seyhan, "From Istanbul to Berlin," p. 154.
17 James Donald, "This, Here, Now: Imagining the Modern City," in: Salle Westwood and John Williams (eds.) *Imagining Cities: Script, Sign, Memory*. New York: Routledge, 1997, p. 200.
18 Georg Simmel, "Die Großstädte und das Geistesleben," in: Theodor Petermann (ed.), *Die Grosstadt. Vorträge und Aufsätze zur Städteausstellung*. Dresden: Gehe-Stiftung, 1903, pp. 185–206. English translations by Kurt H. Wolff.
19 Simmel, "Die Großstädte und das Geistesleben," p. 189.
20 Lothar Müller, "Die Großstadt als Ort der Moderne," in: Klaus Scherpe (ed.), *Die Unwirklichkeit der Städte*. Reinbek bei Hamburg: Rowohlt, 1988, pp. 14–36 (p. 16).
21 Ernst van Alphen, "Configurations of Self: Modernism and Distraction," in: Astradur Eysteinsson, Vivian Liska (eds.), *Modernism*. Amsterdam: John Benjamins Publishing Company, 2007, pp. 339–346.
22 van Alphen, "Configurations of Self," p. 344.
23 Ibid.
24 Simmel, "Die Großstädte und das Geistesleben," p. 197.
25 Simmel, "Die Großstädte und das Geistesleben," p. 200.
26 Michael L. Miller, Scott Ury (eds.), *Cosmopolitanism, Nationalism and the Jews of East Central Europe*. London/New York: Routledge, 2014.
27 Michael L. Miller, Scott Ury, "Cosmopolitanism: the end of Jewishness?," in: *European Review of History: Revue européenne d'histoire*. 17(3), pp. 337–359.
28 Joachim Schlör, *Das Ich der Stadt. Debatten über Judentum und Urbanität, 1822–1938*. Berlin: Vandenhoeck & Ruprecht, 2005.
29 Tobias Metzler nuances the direct equation of Jewish secularization and urbanization processes, as well as the implication that city life constituted a threat to religiousness. He argues that the metropolis was at once a site of secularizing tendencies and new forms of religion, and that Berlin in particular became a "space for diverse new expressions of Jewish identity and different conceptualizations of Jewishness and Judaism rather than a hostile environment [...]." Tobias Metzler, "Secularization and Pluralism: Urban Jewish Cultures in Early Twentieth-Century Berlin," in: *Journal of Urban History*. 37 (6), 2011, pp. 871–96 (p. 871).
30 Amos Elon, *Zu einer anderen Zeit*, pp. 206–7; Herzig, *Jüdische Geschichte*, pp. 191–3.

31 Steven M. Lowenstein, "Was Urbanization Harmful to Jewish Tradition and Identity in Germany?," in: Ezra Mendelsohn (ed.), *People of the City. Jews and the Urban Challenge.* New York: Oxford University Press, 1999, pp. 80–106.
32 Paul Mendes-Flohr, "The Berlin Jew as Cosmopolitan," in: Emily D. Bilsky (ed.), *Berlin Metropolis. Jews and the New Culture 1890–1918.* Berkeley/Los Angeles: University of California Press/New York: The Jewish Museum, 1999, pp. 14–30 (p. 17).
33 Emily D. Bilsky (ed.), *Berlin Metropolis. Jews and the New Culture 1890–1918.* Berkeley/Los Angeles: University of California Press/New York: The Jewish Museum, 1999, p. 7.
34 Isenberg, *Between Redemption and Doom*, p. 91.
35 Arnold Zweig, "Zum Problem des jüdischen Dichters in Deutschland," in: *Die Freistatt: Alljüdische Revue. Monatsschrift für jüdische Kultur und Politik.* 1 (5), August 1913, pp. 375–80.
36 Zweig, "Zum Problem des jüdischen Dichters," p. 376.
37 Zweig, "Zum Problem des jüdischen Dichters," p. 377.
38 Zweig, "Zum Problem des jüdischen Dichters," p. 379.
39 Isenberg, *Between Redemption and Doom*, pp. 90–94.
40 Isenberg, *Between Redemption and Doom*, p. 92.
41 Metzler, "Secularization and Pluralism," p. 889.
42 Astrid Ouahyb Sundsbø, *Grenzziehungen in der Stadt. Ethnische Kategorien und die Wahrnehmung und Bewertung von Wohnorten.* Wiesbaden: Springer, 2014; pp. 48–49.
43 Ethnic colonies are characterized by a duplication of independent economic, social, cultural, policital *and* judicial infrastructure, which is not true for ethnic concentrations in Berlin. Hartmut Häußermann, "Ihre Parallelgesellschaften, unser Problem. Sind Migrantenviertel ein Hindernis für Integration?," in: *Leviathan.* 35(4), 2007, pp. 458–69 (pp. 460–61).
44 Häußermann, "Ihre Parallelgesellschaften," p. 459.
45 Wolfgang Kaschuba, "Wie Fremde gemacht werden," in: *Tagesspiegel.* January 14, 2007. Reprinted in: Göktürk, *Transit Deutschland*, pp. 487–491.
46 Schlör, *Das Ich der Stadt*, p. 30.
47 Isenberg, *Between Redemption and Doom*, pp. 92–93.
48 Werner Sombart, *Die Juden und das Wirtschaftleben.* Leipzig: Duncker & Humblot, 1911.
49 Mendes-Flohr, "The Berlin Jew as Cosmopolitan," pp. 17–18.
50 Isenberg, *Between Redemption and Doom*, p. 97.
51 Isenberg, *Between Redemption and Doom*, p. 93.
52 Michael Schardt, "Jacobowski, Ludwig," in: Andreas B. Kilcher, *Metzler Lexikon der deutsch-jüdischen Literatur. Jüdische Autorinnen und Autoren deutscher Sprache von der Aufklärung bis zur Gegenwart.* Stuttgart/Weimar: J.B. Metzler, 2000, pp. 271–2.
53 Schardt, "Jacobowski," p. 272.
54 Ibid.
55 Jonathan M. Hess, "Fictions of a German-Jewish Public: Ludwig Jacobowski's *Werther the Jew* and its Readers," in: *Jewish Social Studies.* 11(2), 2005, pp. 202–30 (p. 202).
56 The novel was reprinted twice during Jacobowski's lifetime and five times posthumously. It was translated into six different languages, among them Yiddish, and was reprinted several times in mass-market editions between 1910 and 1930. Hess, "Fictions of a German-Jewish Public," pp. 202–3.
57 *Im deutschen Reich: Zeitschrift des Centralvereins deutscher Staatsbürger jüdischen Glaubens.* 13, March 1907, pp. 171–3. As quoted by Hess, "Fictions of a German-Jewish Public," p. 203.
58 Hess, "Fictions of a German-Jewish Public," p. 204.

59 Preface to the third edition; Ludwig Jacobowski, *Werther, der Jude*. Third edition. Dresden: Pierson, 1898.
60 See: Florian Krobb, "Scheidewege. Zum Judenbild in deutschen Romanen der 1890er Jahre," in: Pól Ó Dochartaigh (ed.), *Jews in German Literature Since 1945: German-Jewish Literature?* Amsterdam/Atlanta: Rodopi, 2000, pp. 1–20.
61 Timothy Bewes, "Against Exemplarity: W.G. Sebald and the Problem of Connection," in: *Contemporary Literature*. 55(1), 2014, pp. 1–31 (p. 1).
62 Ibid.
63 Hess, "Fictions of a German-Jewish Public," p. 204.
64 Biendarra, "'Schriftstellerin zu sein und in seinem Leben anwesend zu sein, ist für mich eins': ein Gespräch mit Terézia Mora," in: *Transit*. 3(1), 2007.
65 Ibid.
66 Ibid.
67 Robert Bosch Stiftung, "Pressemitteilung: 26. Adelbert-von-Chamisso-Preis in Munich verliehen."; http://www.bosch-stiftung.de/content/language1/html/28641.asp.
68 Thomas Köster, "'Ich bin durchs Schreiben im Leben angekommen.' Terézia Mora im Gespräch." Goethe Institut. June 2010; http://www.goethe.de/kue/lit/aug/de6062887.htm.
69 Ibid.
70 Nancy, *The Inoperative Community*, p. 3.
71 See, for instance: Eugene L. Stelzig, *The Romantic Subject in Autobiography. Rousseau & Goethe*. London/Charlottesville: University Press of Virginia, 2000.
72 David Sorkin, *The Religious Enlightenment: Protestants, Jews, and Catholics from London to Vienna*, Princeton University Press, 2008, p. 174ff.
73 Hettche, Matt, "Christian Wolff," in: Edward N. Zalta (ed.), *The Stanford Encyclopedia of Philosophy*. 2014; http://plato.stanford.edu/archives/win2014/entries/wolff-christian.
74 Similarly, Leo is irritated when the streets at Christmas time are not covered in snow, disappointing the poetic expectations of his Romantic imagination (WJ 68–9).
75 Hettche, "Christian Wolff," s.p.
76 Ibid.
77 Ibid.
78 Ibid.
79 Similarly: "Da stand er nun visavis dem Geschäft, [...], und spann seine krausen Gedanken weiter fort. Das Gebrause der großstädtischen Flut brachte ihn wieder zu sich. Er wollte seine Gedankenkette wieder aufnehmen, trotzdem er mehr als einmal in dem Gedränge gestoßen und weitergetrieben wurde, aber es gelang ihm nicht." (WJ 60).
80 Reckwitz, *Das hybride Subjekt*, p. 204ff.
81 Reckwitz, *Das hybride Subjekt*, p. 211.
82 Paul Buchholz, "Bordering on Names: Strategies of Mapping in the Prose of Terézia Mora and Peter Handke," in: *Transit. A Journal of Travel, Migration, and Multiculturalism in the German-speaking World*. 7(1), 2011.
83 Buchholz, "Bordering on Names," p. 10.
84 Terézia Mora, *Das Kreter-Spiel*, p. 6; accessible via: http://www.tereziamora.de.
85 For a comparison of *Alle Tage* and *Berlin Alexanderplatz*, see: Christian Sieg, "Von Alfred Döblin zu Terézia Mora: Stadt, Roman und Autorschaft im Zeitalter der Globalisierung," in: Wilhelm Amann et al. (eds.), *Globalisierung und Gegenwartsliteratur. Konstellationen—Konzepte—Perspektiven*. Heidelberg: Synchron, 2010, pp. 193–208.

86 Klaus Scherpe, "Nonstop nach Nowhere City? Wandlungen der Symbolisierung, Wahrnehmung und Semiotik der Stadt in der Literatur der Moderne," in: Scherpe, *Die Unwirklichkeit der Städte*, pp. 129–152 (p. 135).
87 Sieg, "Von Alfred Döblin zu Terézia Mora," pp. 197–8.
88 Sieg refers to Anthony Giddens' definition of globalization as an intensification of global social relations, which makes causal relations between remote places possible and ever more likely. Sieg, "Von Alfred Döblin zu Terézia Mora," p. 195.
89 Buchholz, "Bordering on names," p. 12.
90 Nancy, *The Inoperative Community*, p. 78.
91 Nancy, *Being Singular-Plural*, p. 154.
92 Proper names were of great significance in the Jewish acculturation process. They indicated the willingness to adapt one's identity to become part of society. Adapting a name or assuming a new one was considered a telling signal of successful German-Jewish identity. At the same time, name changing fueled anti-Semitic suspicions about the invisible 'Jewification' of German society. See: Elon, *Zu einer anderen Zeit*, p. 207.
93 Steffen K. Herrmann, "Gespräch und Gewalt. Verantwortung und Verletzbarkeit im Denken von Lévinas," in Sybille Krämer, Elke Koch (eds.), *Gewalt in der Sprache. Rhetoriken verletzenden Sprechens*. Munich: Wilhelm Fink, 2010, pp. 157–78 (p. 174).
94 Herrmann, "Gespräch und Gewalt," p. 173.
95 Herrmann, "Gespräch und Gewalt," p. 161.
96 'Nemec' is Slovakian for 'German'.
97 Nancy, *Being Singular Plural*, p. 154.
98 Jacques Derrida, *Monolingualism of the Other; or, The Prosthesis of Origin*. Stanford: Stanford University Press, 1998, p. 14.
99 Derrida, *Monolingualism of the Other*, p. 28.
100 Hannes Kuch, "Sprache, Gabe, Gewalt. Lacan und die symbolische Verletzbarkeit," in: Krämer, Koch (eds.), *Gewalt in der Sprache*, pp. 179–99.
101 Kuch, "Sprache, Gabe, Gewalt," p. 180.
102 Gayatri Chakravorty Spivak conceives of 'epistemic violence' as the discursive crafting of the Other, and creating the terms by which the Other can speak and know itself and its own position. Gayatri Chakravorty Spivak, "Can the Subaltern Speak?," in: C. Nelson, L. Grossberg (eds.), *Marxism and the Interpretation of Culture*. Basingstoke: Macmillan Education, 1988, pp. 271–313 (p. 75).
103 The quote is an adaptation of the first lines of Goethe's poem "Das Göttliche" (1789): "Edel sei der Mensch, hilfreich und gut!"
104 Nancy, *The Inoperative Community*, p. 138 (emphasis in original).
105 Nancy, *The Inoperative Community*, p. 35.
106 Nancy, *Being Singular Plural*, p. 153.
107 Nancy, *The Inoperative Community*, p. 79.
108 Friederike Eigler, Jens Kugele (eds.), *Heimat: At the Intersection of Memory and Space*. Berlin/Boston: de Gruyter, 2012, p. 1.
109 Arjun Appadurai, "The Production of Locality," in: Arjun Appadurai, *Modernity at Large. Cultural Dimensions of Globalization*. Minneapolis: University of Minnesota Press, 1996, pp. 178–200 (p. 178).
110 Eigler, *Heimat*, p. 1.
111 Simmel, "Die Großstadt und das Geistesleben," p. 200.
112 Emine Sevgi Özdamar, *Der Hof im Spiegel*, p. 17.

113 Minnaard, *New Germans, New Dutch*, p. 257 (note 42).
114 Kevin Lynch, *The Image of the City*. Cambridge, Massachusetts/London: The MIT Press, 1960, p. 4.
115 Lynch, *Image of the City*, pp. 1–2.
116 James Donald describes the city as an "*imagined environment*. What is involved in that imagining—the discourses, symbols, metaphors, and fantasies through which we ascribe meaning to the modern experience of urban living—is as important a topic for the social sciences as the material determinants of the physical environment." James Donald, "Metropolis: The City as Text," in: Robert Bocock, Kenneth Thompson (eds.), *Social and Cultural Forms of Modernity*. Cambridge: Polity Press, pp. 417–70 (p. 427).
117 Sigrid Weigel, "Zur Weiblichkeit imaginärer Städte. Eine Forschungsskizze," in: Gotthard Fuchs et al. (eds), *Mythos Metropole*. Frankfurt am Main: Suhrkamp, 1995, pp. 35–45 (p. 36).
118 Lynch, *Image of the City*, pp. 2–3.
119 Lynch, *Image of the City*, p. 2.
120 Lynch, *Image of the City*, p. 4.
121 Ibid.
122 Ibid.
123 See: Eckhardt Köhn, *Straßenrausch. Flanerie und kleine Form. Versuch zur Literaturgeschichte des Flaneurs bis 1933*. Berlin: Das Arsenal, 1989, pp. 7–15.
124 Elizabeth Boa, "Özdamar's Autobiographical Fictions: Trans-national Identity and Literary Form," in: *German Life and Letters*. 59(4), 2006, pp. 526–39.
125 Dirk Göttsche, "Emine Sevgi Özdamar's Erzählung 'Der Hof im Spiegel'. Spielräume einer postkolonialen Lektüre deutsch-türkischer Literatur," in: *German Life and Letters*. 59 (4), 2006, pp. 515–525 (p. 520).
126 Benjamin and Hessel knew each other since the middle of the 1920s, through their cooperation on the magazine *Vers und Prosa* published by Rowohlt.
127 Walter Benjamin, "Die Wiederkehr des Flaneurs," in: Walter Benjamin, *Gesammelte Schriften*. Band III. Edited by Rolf Tiedemann, Hermann Schweppenhäuser. Frankfurt am Main: Suhrkamp, 1980, pp. 194–199.
128 See, for instance: Gregory Shaya, "The Flaneur, the Badaud, and the Making of a Mass Public in France, circa 1860–1910," in: *The American Historical Review*. 109(1), 2004, pp. 41–77; Peter Sprengel (ed.), *Berlin-Flaneure. Stadt-Lektüren in Roman und Feuilleton 1910–1930*. Berlin: Weidler Buchverlag, 1998; Jörg Plath, *Liebhaber der Großstadt. Ästhetische Konzeptionen im Werk Franz Hessels*. Paderborn: Igel Verlag, 1994; Michael Opitz, Jörg Plath (eds.), *Genieße froh, was du nicht hast. Der Flaneur Franz Hessel*. Würzburg: Königshausen & Neumann, 1997; Eckhardt Köhn, *Straßenrausch. Flanerie und kleine Form. Versuch zur Literaturgeschichte des Flaneurs bis 1933*. Berlin: Das Arsenal, 1989.
129 Walter Benjamin, "Über einige Motive bei Baudelaire," in: Walter Benjamin, *Gesammelte Schriften*. Band I. Edited by Rolf Tiedemann, Hermann Schweppenhäuser. Frankfurt am Main: Suhrkamp, 1974, pp. 605–653.
130 Anke Gleber, *The Art of Taking a Walk. Flanerie, Literature, and Film in Weimar Culture*. Princeton: Princeton University Press, 1999, p. 63.
131 Sargut Solçün, "Literatur der türkischen Minderheit," in: Carmine Chiellino (ed.), *Interkulturelle Literatur in Deutschland: Ein Handbuch*. Stuttgart: Metzler, 2000, pp. 138–44.
132 More specifically, the international student movement of the 1960s, and the Turkish military coup of 1971.

133 Seyhan, "From Istanbul to Berlin," p. 161.
134 Emine Sevgi Özdamar, *Die Brücke vom goldenen Horn*. Cologne: Kiepenheuer & Witsch, 1998, p. 193. English translation by Martin Chalmers.
135 Monika Shafi, "Joint Ventures: Identity Politics and Travel in Novels by Emine Sevgi Özdamar and Zafer Şenocak," in: *Comparative Literature Studies*. 40(2), 2003, pp. 193–214 (p. 203).
136 Moray McGowan, "'The Bridge of the Golden Horn': Istanbul, Europe and the 'Fractured Gaze from the West' in Turkish Writing in Germany," in: Andy A. Hollis, *Beyond Boundaries—Textual Representations of Europen Identities*. [Yearbook of European Studies]. 15, 2000, Amsterdam: Rodopi, pp. 53–69 (p. 54).
137 Shafi, "Joint Ventures," p. 199.
138 Shafi, "Joint Ventures," p. 205.
139 Seyhan, "From Istanbul to Berlin," p. 155.
140 Seyhan, "From Istanbul to Berlin," p. 156.
141 Appadurai, "The Production of Locality," p. 189.
142 Köhn, *Straßenrausch*, p. 153; Hartmut Vollmer, "Hessel, Franz," in: Kilcher, *Metzler Lexikon der deutsch-jüdischen Literatur*, pp. 235–7.
143 Robert Stam, *François Truffaut and Friends: Modernism, Sexuality, and Film Adaptation*. New Brunswick, New Jersey/London: Rutgers University Press, 2006, p. 50.
144 Franz Hessel, *Der Kramladen des Glücks*. Berlin: Hofenberg, 2015, p. 48.
145 Stam, *François Truffaut and Friends*, p. 48. Stam cites Manuela Ribeiro Sanches, "Franz Hessel ou a provocação da insolência," in: *Runa. Revista Portuguesa de Estudos Germanísticos*. 13/14, 1990, pp. 405–415.
146 Vollmer, "Franz Hessel," p. 236.
147 Arndt Potdevin, "Franz Hessel und die Neue Sachlichkeit," in: Sprengel, *Berlin-Flaneure*, pp. 101–35 (p. 118).
148 Potdevin, "Franz Hessel und die Neue Sachlichkeit," p. 105.
149 Claudia Becker, "Helen Grund," in: Michael Opitz, Jörg Plath (eds.), *Genieße froh, was du nicht hast. Der Flaneur Franz Hessel*. Würzburg: Königshausen & Neumann, 1997, pp. 191–210 (p. 195).
150 Köhn, *Straßenrausch*, pp. 153–8.
151 Köhn, *Straßenrausch*, p. 164–5.
152 In a conversation between Lotte and the protagonist, Lotte remarks: "You promised to show me everything in Paris, and now that a new page is coming, you are closing the picture book. [Sie haben doch versprochen, mir alles Paris zu zeigen, und nun, wo eine neue Seite kommt, machen Sie das Bilderbuch zu.]" Franz Hessel, *Pariser Romanze. Papiere eines Verschollenen*. Berlin: E. Rowohlt, 1920, p. 110.
153 Hessel's *Heimatkundler* is, in this respect, very different from Baudelaire's flâneur, who easily slides into melancholy lament of the transience of life. Harald Neumeyer, *Der Flaneur: Konzeptionen der Moderne*. Würzburg: Königshausen & Neumann, 1999, p. 297.
154 Walter Benjamin, "Die Wiederkehr des Flaneurs," in: Walter Benjamin, *Gesammelte Schriften* III. Edited by Hella Tiedemann-Bartels. Frankfurt am Main: Suhrkamp, 1972, pp. 194–199 (p. 194).
155 Potdevin, "Franz Hessel und die Neue Sachlichkeit," p. 124ff.
156 Lynch, *The Image of the City*, p. 5.
157 Köhn, *Straßenrausch*, p. 183.
158 Also see: Adelson, *The Turkish Turn*, p. 42; Littler, "Intimacy and Affect," p. 336.
159 Appadurai, "The Production of Locality," p. 178.

160　Ibid.
161　Littler, "Intimacy and Affect," p. 335.
162　Waldenfels refers to the phenomenology of Maurice Merleau-Ponty. Bernhard Waldenfels, *Topographie des Fremden. Studien zur Phänomenologie des Fremden 1*. Frankfurt am Main: Suhrkamp, 1997, p. 66.
163　Waldenfels, *Topographie des Fremden*, p. 66.
164　Waldenfels, *Topographie des Fremden*, p. 67 (emphasis in original).
165　She does mention the "luxury shopping street Königsallee [Luxuseinkaufsstraße Königsallee]" (HS 18), which along with a reference to Heinrich Heine's birthplace and Joseph Beuys' residence (HS 21) suggests that she lives in Düsseldorf. The fact that the city remains anonymous is more relevant, however, as it ties in with the story's concept of the 'personal city'.
166　Angela Weber, *Im Spiegel der Migrationen. Transkulturelles Erzählen und Sprachpolitik bei Emine Sevgi Özdamar*. Bielefeld: Transcript Verlag, 2009, p. 131.
167　Still, the narrator remains aware of the illusory aspect of this condensed image, and the actual distance that separates these spaces: "If this tree had not grown there, I could believe that the nunnery would not be a real house but instead a large photograph hanging there in the sky. [Wenn dieser Baum dort nicht vor sich hin gewachsen wäre, könnte ich glauben, daß das Nonnenhaus nicht ein echtes Haus, sondern ein großes Foto wäre, das dort im Himmel hängt.]" (HS 25)
168　Shaya, "The Flaneur, the Badaud,...," p. 49.
169　Benjamin contrasts the two figures as follows: "In the flâneur, curiosity celebrates its triumph. It may focus on observation—which results in the amateur detective; it may stagnate in the gaper—then the flâneur has become a badaud. [Im Flaneur feiert die Schaulust ihren Triumph. Sie kann sich in der Beobachtung konzentrieren—das ergibt den Amateurdetektiv; sie kann im Gaffer stagnieren—dann ist aus dem Flaneur ein badaud geworden.]" Walter Benjamin, "Das Paris des Second Empire bei Baudelaire," in: Walter Benjamin, *Gesammelte Schriften*. Band I. Edited by Rolf Tiedemann, Hermann Schweppenhäuser. Frankfurt am Main: Suhrkamp, 1974, pp. 511–603 (p. 572).
170　Shaya, "The Flaneur, the Badaud,...," p. 49.
171　Shaya refers to a definition in the *Grand dictionnaire universel* (1867), which describes the *badaud* as "[...] curious; he is astonished by everything he sees; he believes everything he hears, and he shows his contentment or his surprise by his open, gaping mouth." Shaya, 49.
172　Georg Simmel, "Exkurs über den Fremden," in: Georg Simmel, *Soziologie. Untersuchungen über die Formen der Vergesellschaftung*. Berlin: Duncker & Humblot, 1908, pp. 509–12 (p. 509).
173　Simmel, "Exkurs über den Fremden," p. 509.
174　Peter Gay, *Weimar Culture: The Outsider as Insider*. New York/London: W.W. Norton, 1968/2001, p. xiv.
175　Lothar Müller, "Peripatetische Stadtlektüre. Franz Hessels *Spazieren in Berlin*," in: Michael Opitz, Jörg Plath (eds.), *Genieße froh, was du nicht hast. Der Flaneur Franz Hessel*. Würzburg: Königshausen & Neumann, 1997, pp. 75–104 (p. 93).
176　Simmel, "Exkurs über den Fremden," p. 509.
177　Benjamin, "Die Wiederkehr des Flaneurs," p. 195.
178　As such, the labyrinth is reminiscent of Simmel's definition of *Fremdheit*. The distance of the unfamiliar is a defining element in human relations and proximity: "The unity of proximity and remoteness, which every relationship between people contains, has here reached a constellation that can be formulated in the shortest possible way: the distance within the

relationship means that proximity is remote, but foreignness that remoteness is near. [Die Einheit von Nähe und Entferntheit, die jegliches Verhältnis zwischen Menschen enthält, ist hier zu einer, am kürzesten so zu formulierenden Konstellation gelangt: die Distanz innerhalb des Verhältnisses bedeutet, dass der Nahe fern ist, das Fremdsein aber, dass der Ferne nah ist.]" Simmel, "Exkurs über den Fremden," p. 509.

179 Nancy, *Being Singular Plural*, p. 98.
180 Littler, "Intimacy and Affect," p. 337.
181 Waldenfels, *Topographie des Fremden*, p. 67.
182 The *Spiegelraum* may resemble a kind of postcolonial 'third space', in which the narrator negotiates her supposed in-between Turkish-German identity. Given the 'dis-Oriented' frame of the story, however, the mirrors appear to evoke a more generalized entanglement of spheres, "expressing the potential difference within the real." See: Littler, "Intimacy and Affect," p. 340. Angela Weber, by contrast, does consider the mirror as an in-between space in a stricter postcolonial sense: "The mirror initially [functions] as a metaphor for the narrator's specific situation of shifting between different cultures, in that the mirror—as a place without a place—expresses the paradoxical experience of not belonging entirely to a place without being placeless. [[D]er Spiegel [fungiert] zunächst als Metapher für die spezifische Situation der Erzählerin, sich zwischen verschiedenen Kulturen zu bewegen, insofern der Spiegel—als Ort ohne Ort—der paradoxen Erfahrung, keinem Ort ganz anzugehören ohne ortlos zu sein, Ausdruck verleiht.]" Weber, *Im Spiegel der Migrationen*, p. 131.
183 Göttsche, "Emine Sevgi Özdamar's Erzählung 'Der Hof im Spiegel,'" p. 520.
184 Littler, "Intimacy and Affect," p. 334.
185 Littler, "Intimacy and Affect," p. 335.
186 Paul Verlaine, *Jadis et Naguère*. Paris: Léon Vanier, 1891.
187 Simmel, "Exkurs über den Fremden," p. 510.
188 Benjamin, "Wiederkehr des Flaneurs," p. 196.
189 In this respect, one particular scene in 'Rundfahrt' is significant. The flâneur responds sarcastically to the tour guide's enthusiasm about their next stop at *Café Vaterland*, while only briefly mentioning the *Völkerkundemuseum* they drive by. *Café Vaterland* was an amusement palace located near Potsdamer Platz, which housed a number of theme restaurants showcasing the cuisine of various nations. To the flâneur, it is the epitome of consumer culture. He remarks: "What good do our old palaces and museums do them? What they want is colossal Germany. [Was helfen ihnen unsre alten Paläste und Museen? Sie wollen doch das Monsterdeutschland.]" What follows is a description of "this monster establishment [dieses Monsteretablissement]," "this culinary ethnological museum [dies kulinarische Völkermuseum]" that stands in ironic contrast to the neglected museum. *Café Vaterland* emerges as the commercialized and consumerist counterpart of ethnography. (SB 71-2)
190 Müller, "Peripatetische Stadtlektüre," p. 95.
191 Ibid.
192 The quote refers to the poem "Der Knabe und das Immlein" by Eduard Friedrich Mörike.
193 Hessel repeatedly uses the image of the 'neue Berlinerin' to illustrate the complementarity of modern architecture and a new lifestyle. Hessel compares modern architecture to the *Bubikopf*—the characteristic 1920s hairstyle: "As soon as one of the buildings becomes dilapidated or even just needs repair, the new architecture cuts it into the bob of a simple, clear and linear façade. [[S]obald eins der Häuser baufällig oder wenigstens reparaturbedürftig wird, schneidet ihm die junge Architektur den Bubenkopf einer einfachen linienklaren Fassade.]" (SB 157; own translation). Also see: Müller, "Peripatetische Stadtlektüre," p. 88.

[194] Liska, *When Kafka Says We*, p. 15.
[195] Liska, *When Kafka Says We*, p. 9.

Chapter 4. Family heroes between myth and storytelling

[1] They include, among others, Magdalena Sadlon, Zsuzsanna Gahse, Zsuzsa Bank, Ilma Rakusa, and Ilja Trojanow. The Chamisso *Förderpreis*, for unpublished work, has been awarded to Dimitré Dinev, Marica Bodrožić, Vladimir Vertlib, and Terézia Mora.
[2] Brigid Haines, "The Eastern Turn in Contemporary German, Swiss and Austrian Literature," in: *Debatte: Journal of Contemporary and Central and Eastern Europe*. 16(2), 2008, pp. 135–149 (p. 135).
[3] Leslie Adelson, *The Turkish Turn in Contemporary German Literature: Towards a New Critical Grammar of Migration*. New York: Palgrave, 2005.
[4] Haines, "The Eastern Turn," p. 142.
[5] More specifically, Haines discerns "[f]ive recurring scenarios" that reflect the "shifting perspective of the westward-moving migrant": "the lived reality of communist rule during the stagnant period before the fall of communism; the alienating experience of migrations westwards; the disillusionment with life during and after the economic and political liberalisation of the east in the early 1990s; the shocking conflicts in former Yugoslavia in the 1990s; and the disorientation of life in post-Cold War Europe today." Haines, "The Eastern Turn," p. 139.
[6] Haines, "The Eastern Turn," p. 145.
[7] Haines, "The Eastern Turn," p. 148.
[8] On the imperial continuity in European history, see for instance: Karen Barkey, Mark Von Hagen (eds.), *After Empire: Multiethnic Societies and Nation-building: The Soviet Union and the Russian, Ottoman, and Habsburg Empires*. Colorado: Westview Press, 1997.
[9] Katrina Nousek, "A future-oriented *Zeitrechnung*: Narrating post-communist temporality and subjectivity in Zsuzsa Bánk's *Der Schwimmer*," in: *German Life and Letters*. 68(2), 2015, pp. 302–23 (p. 303–4). For similar reasons, Georgina Paul advocates the term 'post-socialist literature' rather than the commonly used '*Wendeliteratur*'. Georgina Paul, "The Privatization of Community: The Legacy of Collectivism in the Post-Socialist Literature of Eastern Germany," in: *Oxford German Studies*. 38(2), 2009, pp. 288–98.
[10] Haines, "The Eastern Turn," p. 145.
[11] Nadine Gordimer, "Introduction. The Empire of Joseph Roth," in: Joseph Roth, *The Radetzky March*. Translation by Joachim Neugroschel. New York: The Overlook Press, 1991/1995, p. vii.
[12] Joseph Esherick et al. (eds.), *Empire to Nation: Historical Perspectives on the Making of the Modern World*. Oxford: Rowman & Littlefield, 2006, p. 2.
[13] Esherick, *Empire to Nation*, pp. 2–3.
[14] Benedict Anderson, *Imagined Communities. Reflections on the Origins and the Spread of Nationalism*. London/New York: Verso, 1983/2006, p. 25ff.
[15] Eric Hobsbawm, Terence Ranger (eds.), *The Invention of Tradition*. Cambridge University Press, 1983, p. 1.
[16] Tony Judt, *A Grand Illusion? An Essay on Europe*. New York/London: New York University Press, 1996/2011, p. 118.

17 Jan-Werner Müller (ed.), *Memory and Power in Post-War Europe. Studies in the Presence of the Past*. Cambridge University Press, 2002, p. 9.
18 Ibid.
19 Esherick, *Empire to Nation*, pp. 1–2.
20 Konstantinos Raptis, "Discord or Achievement? Reflections on the Habsburg Empire, 1848–1918," in: *Historein*. 5, 2005, pp. 118–129 (p. 120).
21 Klaus Koch, "The End of Empire and the Beginning of Nostalgia," in: Emil Brix et al. (eds.), *The Decline of Empires*. Vienna: Verlag für Geschichte und Politik, 2011, pp. 174–83.
22 Raptis, "Discord or Achievement?," p. 118.
23 Breda Luthar and Maruša Pušnik, "The Lure of Utopia: Socialist Everyday Spaces," in: Breda Luthar and Maruša Pušnik (eds.), *Remembering Utopia: The Culture of Everyday Life in Socialist Yugoslavia*. Washington: New Academia Publishing, 2010, pp. 1–36.
24 Maria Nikolaeva Todorova, "Introduction: From Utopia to Propaganda and Back," in: Todorova and Zsusza Gille (eds.), *Post-communist Nostalgia*. New York: Berghahn 2002, pp. 1–16 (p. 7).
25 Todorova, "Introduction: From Utopia to Propaganda and Back," p. 2.
26 Sean Scanlan, "Introduction: Nostalgia," in: *Iowa Journal of Cultural Studies*. 5(1), 2004, pp. 3–9.
27 Luthar /Pušnik, "The Lure of Utopia," p. 18.
28 Claudio Magris, *Der habsburgische Mythos in der modernen osterreichischen Literatur*. Paul Zsolnay Verlag 1963/2000.
29 Magris, *Der habsburgische Mythos*, p. 19. Magris refers to Stefan Zweig's famous characterization of the imperial 'golden age of security': "Everything in our almost thousand-year-old Austrian monarchy seemed based on permanency, and the State itself was the chief guarantor of this stability. [...] In this vast empire, everything stood firmly and immovably in its appointed place, and at its head was the aged emperor; and were he to die, one knew (or believed) another would come to take his place, and nothing would change in the well-regulated order. No one thought of wars, of revolutions, or revolts. All that was radical, all violence, seemed impossible in an age of reason. [Alles in unserer fast tausendjährigen österreichischen Monarchie schien auf Dauer gegründet und der Staat selbst der oberste Garant dieser Beständigkeit. [...] Alles stand in diesem weiten Reiche fest und unverrückbar an seiner Stelle und an der höchsten der greise Kaiser; aber sollte er sterben, so wußte man (oder meinte man), würde ein andere kommen und nichts sich ändern in der wohlberechneten Ordnung. Niemand glaubte an Kriege, an Revolutionen und Umstürze. Alles Radikale, alles Gewaltsame schien bereits unmöglich in einem Zeitalter der Vernunft.]" Stefan Zweig, *Die Welt von Gestern. Erinnerungen eines Europäers*. Frankfurt am Main: S. Fischer Verlag, 1942/2012, pp. 15–6. English translation by Benjamin W. Huebsch and Helmut Ripperger.
30 Magris, *Der habsburgische Mythos*, p. 20.
31 Magris, *Der habsburgische Mythos*, p. 22.
32 Magris, *Der habsburgische Mythos*, p. 20.
33 Magris, *Der habsburgische Mythos*, p. 22–23.
34 Martha Wörsching, "Die rückwärts gewandte Utopie. Sozialpsychologische Anmerkungen zu Joseph Roths Roman 'Radetzkymarsch'," in: Heinz Ludwig Arnold (ed.), *Joseph Roth*. Munich: Edition Text u. Kritik, 1982, pp. 90–100.
35 For a discussion of the enlightened and rationalist foundations of the Austro-Hungarian Empire, see: James R. Sofka, "Metternich's Theory of European Order: A Political Agenda for 'Perpetual Peace'," in: *The Review of Politics*, 60(1), 1998, pp. 115–149.

36 Marjorie Perloff, *Edge of Irony: Modernism in the Shadow of the Habsburg Empire*. Chicago: University of Chicago Press, 2016, p. 102.
37 Claudio Magris, cited by Perloff, *Edge of Irony*, p. 102.
38 Nancy, *The Inoperative Community*, p. 53.
39 Devisch, "Jean-Luc Nancy," s.p.
40 Nancy, *The Inoperative Community*, p. 1.
41 Devisch, "Jean-Luc Nancy," s.p.
42 Nancy, *The Inoperative Community*, p. 57.
43 Nancy, *The Inoperative Community*, p. 53.
44 David Williams, *Writing Postcommunism. Towards a Literature of the East European Ruins*. Basingstoke: Palgrave Macmillan, 2013.
45 Cited by Müller, *Memory and Power*, p. 10.
46 Astrid Erll, "Locating Family in Cultural Memory Studies," in: *Journal of Comparative Family Studies*. 42(3), 2011, pp. 303–318 (p. 308).
47 Erll, "Locating Family," p. 303.
48 See: Andrada Savin, "Auswanderung im Familiengedächtnis' als Themenkomplex und Komposition im deutschsprachigen Gegenwartsroman," in: *Lingua. Language and Culture*. 2, 2012, pp. 167–174.
49 Eric Hobsbawm, *Interesting Times. A Twentieth-Century Life*. New York: Pantheon Books, 2007, pp. 415–6.
50 Perloff, *Edge of Irony*, pp. 3–4.
51 Perloff, *Edge of Irony*, p. 2.
52 Raptis, "Discord or Achievement?," pp. 121–2.
53 Perloff, *Edge of Irony*, p. 3.
54 Perloff, *Edge of Irony*, p. 10.
55 Perloff, *Edge of Irony*, p. 7.
56 W.G. Sebald, "Ein Kaddisch für Österreich—Über Joseph Roth," in: W.G. Sebald, *Unheimliche Heimat. Essays zur österreichischen Literatur*. Frankfurt am Main: Fischer Taschenbuch Verlag, 2012, pp. 104–117 (p. 113).
57 Eva Raffel, *Vertraute Fremde. Das östliche Judentum im Werk von Joseph Roth und Arnold Zweig*. Tübingen: Günter Narr Verlag, 2002, p. 19.
58 Sebald, "Ein Kaddish für Österreich," p. 112. Sebald quotes from Roth's *Radetzkymarsch*, p. 276.
59 Sebald, "Ein Kaddish für Österreich," p. 112.
60 Raffel, *Vertraute Fremde*, pp. 16–17.
61 David Bronsen, "The Jew in Search of a Fatherland: The Relationship of Joseph Roth to the Habsburg Monarchy," in: *Germanic Review*. 54(2), 1979, pp. 54–61 (p. 57).
62 Bronsen, "The Jew in Search of a Fatherland," p. 54.
63 Bronsen, "The Jew in Search of a Fatherland," p. 57.
64 Ibid.
65 Joseph Roth, *Briefe 1911–1939*. Edited by Hermann Kesten. Cologne: Kiepenheuer & Witsch, 1970, p. 98.
66 Bronsen, "The Jew in Search of a Fatherland," pp. 54–55.
67 David Bronsen, *Joseph Roth: Eine Biographie*. Cologne: Kiepenheuer & Witsch, 1974, p. 391.
68 Bronsen, *Joseph Roth*, p. 302.
69 Roth, *Briefe*, pp. 239–40.

70 Bronsen, "The Jew in Search of a Fatherland," p. 55. David Bronsen has illustrated Roth's tendency to tinker with the facts of his own past; see: David Bronsen, *Joseph Roth:* p. 13ff.
71 Eva Raffel, *Vertraute Fremde*, p. 21.
72 Paul Jandl, "Generation Lada: Dimitré Dinev—ein bulgarischer Schriftsteller in Berlin," in: *Neue Zürcher Zeitung*, 18 December 2003; http://www.nzz.ch/article99L38-1.341448.
73 Ibid.
74 Iris Fenkart, "Europäischen Geist gibt es längst: Schrifsteller Dimitré Dinev im Gespräch über Integration, Assimilation und den Begriff Migrantenliteratur," in: *Wiener Zeitung*. 7 July 2010; http://www.wienerzeitung.at/nachrichten/kultur/mehr_kultur/41577_Europaeischen-Geist-gibt-es-laengst.html [March 2017].
75 Ibid.
76 Ibid.
77 Marina Delcheva, "Dimitré Dinev spricht über das Problem der Eliten," in: *Das Biber*, 2015: https://www.dasbiber.at/content/dimitré-dinev-spricht-über-das-problem-der-eliten [March 2017].
78 Ibid.
79 Dimitré Dinev, *Barmherzigkeit—Unruhe bewahren*. Salzburg/Vienna: Residenz Verlag 2010.
80 Also see: Ulrike Freitag, "Es ist fast ärgerlich einfach. Interview mit Dimitré Dinev," in: *Ausreißer. Die Grazer Wandzeitung*. 28 May/June 2009: http://ausreisser.mur.at/ausgaben/ausgaben-1-50/28-l-mai-juni-09/.
81 Dinev, *Barmherzigkeit,* p. 21.
82 Cited by Kati Tonkin, *Joseph Roth's March into History. From the Early Novels to* Radetzkymarsch *and* Die Kapuzinergruft. Rochester, New York: Camden House, 2008, p. 112.
83 Tonkin remarks that Roth's preface itself belongs in the author's "game of truth and fiction." Tonkin, *March into History*, p. 112.
84 J.M. Coetzee, "Emperor of Nostalgia," in: *New York Review of Books*. 28 February, 2002.
85 Dinev indeed mentions Roth as one of his many "teachers and examples [Lehrer und Vorbilder]." See: Ljudmila Dimova, "Die Intimität der Geschichte. Ein Interview aus der bulgarischen Zeitschrift LIK," in: *Der Hammer. Zeitung der Alten Schmiede*. 9, 2005. p. 4.
86 Nancy, *The Inoperative Community*, p. 44.
87 Nancy, *The Inoperative Community*, 43; emphasis added.
88 Ibid.
89 Nancy, *The Inoperative Community*, 44.
90 The painting evokes that other famous image embedded in the collective *k.u.k.* memory, namely, the portrait of Emperor Franz Joseph I in a white, decorated general's uniform.
91 The image of the uniform comprises the denotational and connotational aspects of the soldier's identity. The uniform provides an easy to read indication about rank and decorations but also contains an important emotional and aesthetic dimension related to the soldier's inclusion into a collective. The strongly visual and performative character of the uniform contributes to the visibility of soldiers to others, as well as to fellow soldiers. Most importantly, it signals and performs the soldier's inclusion into the institution of the military. See: Torsten Voß, *Körper, Uniformen und Offiziere. Soldatische Männlichkeiten in der Literatur von Grimmelshausen und J.M.R. Lenz bis Ernst Jünger und Hermann Broch*. Bielefeld: Transcript Verlag, 2016, pp. 28–30.

92 Torsten Voß, "Kakanische Repräsentanten des melancholischen Untergangs. Offiziere, soldatische Zivilisten, Ikonen und maskulin aufgeladene Dingsymbole in Joseph Roths 'Radetzkymarsch' (1932) und Alexander Lernet-Holenias 'Die Standarte' (1934)," in: *Studia Austriaca XXII*. 2014, pp. 139–160 (p. 141).
93 Voß, "Kakanische Repräsentanten," p. 139.
94 Georges Bataille describes the unifying power of military symbols in a similar vein: "Die Armee findet zur Totalität ihrer Existenz erst in dem Moment, in dem sie mit ihrem Schicksal das Leben all derer verbindet, die sie zu einem Angriffskörper und einer einzigen Seele vereint. Damit diese gemeinsame Hingabe ihre korrekte und formelle Verwirklichung findet, gruppiert die Armee die Soldaten um ein sakrales Emblem herum, ganz so, wie eine Kirche die Häuser, die das Dorf ausmachen, um sich versammelt. Dieses Emblem ist häufig ein Gegenstand, ein Abzeichen oder eine Fahne." Georges Bataille, "Struktur und Funktion der Armee," in: Dennis Hollier (ed.), *Das Collège de Sociologie 1937–1939. Aus dem Französischen von Horst Brühlmann*. Berlin: Suhrkamp, 2012, pp. 175–188 (p. 184).
95 For a thorough discussion on the contested status of *Radetzkymarsch* as a historical novel, see: Tonkin, *March into History*, pp. 103–112.
96 David Dollenmayer, "History and Fiction: The Kaiser in Joseph Roth's *Radetzkymarsch*," in: *Modern Language Studies*. 16 (3), 1986, pp. 302–310 (p. 302).
97 Georg Lukács, "Radetzkymarsch," in: *Literaturnaja Gazeta* (Moscow). 8 August 1939. Cited in the German translation by Fritz Hackert, *Kulturpessimismus und Erzählform: Studien zu Joseph Roths Leben und Werk*. Bern: Herbert Lang, 1967, p. 148.
98 Tonkin, *March into History*, p. 19.
99 On the satirical aspects of the novel, see for instance: Bruce Thompson, "'Schlecht kommen wir beide dabei nicht weg!' Joseph Roth's satire on the Emperor Franz Joseph in his novel *Radetzkymarsch*," in: *Neophilologus*. 81, 1997, pp. 253–267; Werner Hoffmeister, "Satirische Elemente in Joseph Roths *Radetzkymarsch*," in: *Modern Language Studies*. 3(2), 1973, pp. 106–113.
100 Margarethe Johanna Landwehr, "Modernist Aesthetics in Joseph Roth's *Radetzkymarsch*: The Crisis of Meaning and the Role of the Reader," in: *German Quarterly*. 76(4), 2003, pp. 398–410.
101 Georg Lukács, *The Historical Novel*. Translated by Hannah and Stanley Mitchell. London: Merlin Press, 1962, p. 42.
102 Dollenmayer, "History and Fiction," p. 303. Similarly, Landwehr interprets the initial chapter and, in particular, the embellished schoolbook version of Franz Joseph's rescue as "paradigmatic for the novel itself." Landwehr, "Modernist Aesthetics," p. 399. Tonkin refers to the first chapter as an "extended prologue." Tonkin, *March into History*, p. 112.
103 Tonkin, *March into History*, pp. 112–117.
104 Ohad Parnes et al. (eds.), *Das Konzept der Generation. Eine Wissenschafts- und Kulturgeschichte*. Frankfurt am Main: Suhrkamp, 2008, p. 187.
105 "Believing that each individual's identity was both intricate and mutable, Roth was highly distrustful of an ideology which demanded absolute allegiance to one language, one culture, one people, and which sought to categorize people according to a biologically defined and one-dimensional nationality." Tonkin, *March into History*, p. 112.
106 Dollenmayer, "History and Fiction," p. 303. The Battle of Solferino was the first in a series of losses that would lead to the final collapse of the monarchy. At Solferino, the monarchy experienced a decisive defeat against a Franco-Piedmontese alliance, leading to the cession of Lombardy to Sardinia-Piedmont. Tonkin, *March into History*, pp. 129–30.

107 Dollenmayer, "History and Fiction," p. 302.
108 Landwehr, "Modernist Aesthetics," p. 401.
109 In his famous 1930 essay "Schluß mit der 'Neuen Sachlichkeit'!," Roth rejects the central tenet of the *Neue Sachlichkeit* that genuine literature is documentary and the writer an objective reporter. Instead, Roth argues that "erst das Kunstwerk [...] echt wie das Leben [ist]." Joseph Roth, *Werke 3. Das journalistische Werk 1929–1939*. Edited by Klaus Westermann. Büchergilde Gutenberg. Cologne: Kiepenheuer & Witsch, 1989, pp. 153–163 (p. 156).
110 Tonkin, *March into History*, p. 114.
111 Ibid.
112 Tonkin, *March into History*, p. 114. Tonkin refers to A.J.P. Taylor, *The Habsburg Monarchy: 1809–1918: A History of the Austrian Empire and Austria-Hungary*. London: Penguin, 1990.
113 As Ziolkowski points out, such historicization is emphasized once more later in the novel, when officials remember the battle as having taken place in the sixteenth century, rather than in the recent past. Saskia Ziolkowski, "The Ends of an Empire: Pier Antonio Quarantotti Gambini's *Il cavallo Tripoli* and Joseph Roth's *Radetzkymarsch*," in: *Comparative Literature Studies*. 25(2), 2015, pp. 349–78 (p. 364).
114 Ziolkowski, "The Ends of an Empire," p. 364.
115 The regulations for decoration articulate the requirement of self-initiative as follows: "Only those valiant deeds which any officer of honour could have omitted without the slightest reproach, but which have nevertheless been undertaken with excellent wisdom, courage, and *self-reliant, free willed motivation*, are entitled to the decoration. [Anspruch auf den Orden gründen nur jene herzhafte Thaten, die jeder Officier von Ehre ohne dem geringsten Vorwurf hätte unterlassen können, die aber dennoch mit ausgezeichneter Klugheit, Tapferkeit und *aus selbsteigenem, freywilligen inneren Antriebe unternommen* worden sind.]" (emphasis added) *Statuten des löblichen militärischen Maria-Theresien-Ordens*, k.k. Hof- und Staatsdruckerey, Vienna, 1811, p. 36.
116 Dinev was inspired by an actual grave on a Viennese cemetery that fits his description in the text: a conspicuous tombstone in black and brown marble, featuring the photograph of a well-dressed man carrying a mobile phone. His picture is framed by two marble wings, creating the image of an angel. See: Barbara Mader, "Dinev: wo die 'Engelszungen' herkommen," in: *kurier.at*, 5 December 2011; https://kurier.at/kultur/dinev-wo-die-engelszungen-herkommen/735.454.
117 Interestingly, Dinev's *k.u.k.* reference also offers a kind of corrective to historical forgetfulness. His focus is first on female 'representatives' of the empire, which contrasts with Roth's evocation of a strikingly male-dominated world. The forgotten Danube-Swabian poetess very likely refers to Marie Eugenie Delle Grazie, who is considered one of the most prominent Austrian (from the Banat region) female writers around 1900.
118 "Dimitré Dinev: Schriftsteller im Gespräch mit Dr. Eberhard Büssem," BR-ONLINE Das Online-Angebot des Bayerischen Rundfunks, 30 May 2005; http://www.br-online.de/alpha/forum/vor0505/20050530.shtml.
119 In Bulgarian, the word 'език' straddles the two denotations of the German words 'Sprache' and 'Zunge'.
120 On the motif of the tongue in *Engelszungen*, see: Sandra Vlasta, *Contemporary Migration Literature in German and English: A Comparative Study*. Leiden/Boston: Brill/Rodopi, 2015, pp. 96ff. With the title *Engelszungen*, Dinev also includes the theme of Bulgarian migration history in German-language literature. The title refers to the memoirs of the Bulgarian-born author Elias Canetti. In *Die gerettete Zunge*, Canetti describes an incident where he was threatened to have his tongue cut off. The incident acquires symbolic value, as it comes to

represent his 'rescued tongue': the beloved German language of an exiled author without a real mother tongue. Furthermore, as Penka Angelova points out, Canetti's memoir also introduced into the German language the topos of Bulgaria as a fatherland. Penka Angelova, "The Other Road: On the Bulgarian Topos in the Work of Three Writers Awarded the Adelbert von Chamisso Prize," in: Elka Agoston-Nikolova (ed.), *Shoreless Bridges: South East European Writing in Diaspora*. Amsterdam/New York: Rodopi, 2010, pp. 83–95 (p. 84).

121 The expression goes back to a verse from the apostle Paul, in the First Epistle to the Corinthians 13.1: "If I speak in the tongues of men or of angels, but do not have love, I am only a resounding gong or a clanging cymbal." The verse aptly summarizes Dinev's exploration of the relationship between speech, storytelling, and interpersonal connection.

122 Dinev repeatedly quotes from Todor Shivkov's orations, collected in *Einheit auf der Grundlage des Marxismus/Leninismus. Reden, Berichte, Artikel*. Sofia-Press, s.d.

123 As Vlasta points out, even the cut-off tongue as a symbol of muteness leads to alternative, pre-verbal, sensual, or sexual forms of communication. Vlasta, *Contemporary Migration Literature*, p. 96.

124 Dinev's mentioning of an education in German not only refers to his own biography. It also positions the story against the backdrop of a particular aspect of German-Bulgarian migration history. In the second half of the nineteenth century, the city Plovdiv housed a colony of German, Austrian, and Swiss railroad workers. In 1901, they founded a school that would provide German-language education. The organization set out to focus only on the German language as "single common denominator [einziges gemeinsames Bindeglied]," and for that purpose "to exclude all national and also religious tendencies of any kind [alle, wie immer gearteten nationalen und auch religiösen Tendenzen auszuschließen] [...]." Anna Slavtcheva-Raiber, *Geschichte, Entwicklung und Sprachwerbetätigkeit der deutschen Schulen in Bulgarien im Zeitraum 1900–1939*. Doctoral dissertation. Universität Mannheim, 2005, p. 37.

125 The Bulgarian Partisans first emerged during the Second World War as a largely pro-communist resistance movement against both the German *Wehrmacht* and the authorities of the Kingdom of Bulgaria. After the German invasion of the Soviet Union in June 1941, the Partisans opposed the Bulgarian government and its German ally. Richard C. Hall, "Partisans, Bulgaria," in: Richard C. Hall (ed.), *War in the Balkans: An Encyclopaedic History from the Fall of the Ottoman to the Breakup of Yugoslavia*. Santa Barbara/Denver/Oxford: ABC-CLIO, 2014, pp. 225–6.

126 On picaresque elements in *Engelszungen*, see: Maria Brunner, "Paradigmen des Pikaresken in Kumpfmüllers *Hampels Fluchten* (2000), Terézia Moras *Alle Tage* (2004), Dimitré Dinevs *Engelszungen* (2003) und Helmut Kraussers *Fette Welt* (1992)," in: *Studien zur deutschen Sprache und Literatur*, 1, 2013, pp. 35–64.

127 Althusser distinguishes the ideological state apparatus, which produces willing compliance, from the repressive state apparatus, which enforces compliance through military and police. Louis Althusser, "Ideology and ideological state apparatuses," in: Louis Althusser, *'Lenin and Philosophy' and other Essays*. London: New Left Books, 1989, pp. 170–86.

128 Nancy, *The Inoperative Community*, p. 57.

129 Nancy, *The Inoperative Community*, p. 57.

130 Nancy, *The Inoperative Community*, p. 62.

131 Nancy describes this as the "tautegorical" construction of absolute community: "Myth signifies itself, and thereby converts its own fiction into foundation or into the inauguration of *meaning* itself." Nancy, *The Inoperative Community*, p. 53 (emphasis in original).

132 Vlasta, *Contemporary Migration Literature*, p. 98.

133 Tatiana Vaksberg, Alexander Andreev, "Recalling the fate of Bulgaria's Turkish minority," in: *Deutsche Welle*. 24 December 2014; http://www.dw.com/en/recalling-the-fate-of-bulgarias-turkish-minority/a-18149416.
134 Clyde Haberman, "Bulgaria Forces Turkish Exodus of Thousands," in: *The New York Times*. 22 June 1989; http://www.nytimes.com/1989/06/22/world/bulgaria-forces-turkish-exodus-of-thousands.html.
135 Nikolas K. Gvosdev (ed.), *The Strange Death of Soviet Communism. A Postscript*. New Brunswick/London: Transaction Publishers, 2008, p. 206. Isaiah Berlin was one of the first scholars to make a connection between communism and Enlightenment. He argues that the 'monist' conception of Enlightenment philosophers, i.e. their conviction that the world is subject to a set of universal, eternal, and knowable laws, inevitably leads to utopian or totalitarian solutions to all problems. Isaiah Berlin, "The Counter-Enlightenment," in: Henry Hardy and Roger Hausheer (eds.), *Isaiah Berlin. The Proper Study of Mankind: An Anthology of Essays*. New York: Farrar, Straus and Giroux, 1998), pp. 243–46.
136 Joseph Roth, *Die Kapuzinergruft*, in: Joseph Roth, *Werke 6. Romane und Erzählungen 1936–1940*. Edited by Fritz Hackert. Büchergilde Gutenberg. Cologne: Kiepenheuer & Witsch, 1989, pp. 225–345 (p. 337).
137 Nicholas John Cull et al. (eds.), *Propaganda and Mass Persuasion. A Historical Encyclopedia, 1500 to the Present*. Santa Barbara: ABC Clio, 2003, p. 206.
138 Nancy, *Being Singular Plural*, p. 157 (emphasis in original).
139 His father Joseph von Trotta has forbidden his son to join the army. (RM 21)
140 Voß, "Kakanische Repräsentanten," p. 153.
141 Tonkin, *March into History*, p. 120.
142 Landwehr, "Modernist Aesthetics," p. 403.
143 Voß, "Kakanische Repräsentanten," p. 154.
144 Ibid.
145 Ursula Reidel-Schrewe, "Im Niemandsland zwischen Indikativ und Konjunktiv," in: *Modern Austrian Literature*, 24, 1991, pp. 59–78 (p. 64).
146 Ibid.
147 Tonkin, *March into History*, p. 121.
148 Voß, "Kakanische Repräsentanten," p. 157.
149 Voß remarks that Carl Joseph has even come to resemble a 'Marketenderin', a sutler, since he dies in an act of "utterly unmartial care [ganz und gar unmartialischer Fürsorge]." Voß, "Kakanische Repräsentanten," p. 160.
150 As Tonkin points out, Demant is mentioned to have known his grandfather in person and to have a clear recollection of him, as opposed to Carl Joseph, who only knows the image in his father's house. Tonkin, *March into History*, pp. 124–125.
151 Also see: Tonkin, *March into History*, p. 126.
152 Voß, "Kakanische Repräsentanten," p. 155.
153 Ibid.
154 Tonkin, *March into History*, p. 125.
155 Dinev, *Engelszungen*, p. 224.
156 Similarly, Dinev's descriptions of family gatherings provide a telling contrast to the absolute community. When Mladen's sister, now an American citizen, visits her Bulgarian family, her reunion with Sdravka on the railway platform is depicted as the *mêlée* that Nancy refers to—not a collection of individuals but an uncontrolled hustle of bodies and movement: "Windows and doors opened. Hands and heads came out, suitcases and people got out,

names were called, hands raised, waved, pressed, shaken, spread out, necks stretched out and embraced, shoulders patted, pushed, shaken, and pressed, bodies on tiptoes, embraced and surrounded, faces sought and kissed, heads stroked. [Fenster und Türen gingen auf. Hände und Köpfe kamen raus, Koffer und Menschen stiegen aus, Namen wurden gerufen, Hände gehoben, gewunken, gedrückt, geschüttelt, ausgebreitet, Hälse hinaufgestreckt und umschlungen, Schultern geklopft, geschubst, gerüttelt und gepreßt, Körper auf Zehenspitzen gestellt, umarmt und umzingelt, Gesichter gesucht und geküßt, Köpfe gestreichelt.]" (EZ 257–8) Likewise, the description of their farewell underscores the family as a composite of simultaneously singular and plural beings, rather than a unified collective: "[They] joked together, shouted together, waved together, and yet each waved for himself, one longer, the other shorter. Together they were cheerful, and yet each was sad on his own. [[Sie] scherzten gemeinsam, riefen gemeinsam, winkten gemeinsam, und doch winkte jeder für sich, der eine länger, der andere kürzer. Gemeinsam waren sie fröhlich, und doch war jeder traurig für sich.]" (EZ 270)

157 Nancy, *Being Singular Plural*, p. 2 (emphasis in original).
158 Jürgen Jacobs, "Bildungsroman und Picaroroman. Versuch einer Abgrenzung," in: Gerhart Hoffmeister (ed.): *Der moderne deutsche Schelmenroman. Interpretationen*. Amsterdam: Rodopi, 1985/1986, pp. 9–19 (p. 18).
159 See: Robert Fajen, "Gefühlsleere und Erotomanie. Zur pikaresken Liebenssemantik in Literatur und Film," in: Christoph Ehland, Robert Fajen (eds.), *Das Paradigma des Pikaresken*. Heidelberg: Universitätsverlag Winter, 2007, pp. 241–59 (p. 241).
160 Nancy, *Being Singular Plural*, p. xiii.
161 "A society can be social, solidary, and many other things, but never compassionate. Solidarity often has to do with ideological views, but compassion is beyond ideology. To be in solidarity with someone means to exclude a third person (for example the aggressor). Compassion is exactly the opposite. [...] It is open to anyone. [Eine Gesellschaft kann sozial, solidarisch und vieles andere sein, aber niemals barmherzig. Solidarität hat oft mit ideologischen Anschauungen zu tun, die Barmherzigkeit dagegen steht jenseits der Ideologie. Solidarisch sein mit jemandem heißt einen Dritten ausschließen (zum Beispiel den Aggressor). Die Barmherzigkeit ist genau das Gegenteil. [...] Sie steht jedem zu.]" Dinev, *Barmherzigkeit*, p. 20.
162 Dinev, *Barmherzigkeit*, p. 21.
163 The card game is another shared motif of *Radetzkymarsch* and *Engelszungen*. In both novels, the game symbolizes the tension between individual agency and being at the mercy of fate or coincidence.
164 Bronsen, *Joseph Roth*, p. 398.
165 Nancy, *The Inoperative Community*, p. 62.
166 Robert Murray Davis, "Diaspora's Children," in: *World Literature Today*. 80(6), 2006, pp. 55–8.
167 The 'flaws' in *Hiob* typically pointed out by critics are, aside from its remarkably happy ending, the tension between biblical parable and novelistic form, as well as its simplified depiction of America. See, for instance: Sidney Rosenfeld, "Joseph Roths *Hiob*: Glaube und Heimat im Bild des Raumes," in: *The Journal of English and Germanic Philology*. 66(4), 1964, pp. 489–500; Kata Gellen, "The Media Myth of America: Joseph Roth's *Hiob* and *Tarabas*," in: *Journal of Austrian Studies*. 45(3–4), 2012, pp. 1–29.

168 In an attempt to ward off an explosive situation after Stalin's death in 1953, Soviet and Hungarian party leaders decided to remove the reform communist Imre Nagy from his position as prime minister in 1955. It led to the outbreak of an armed revolution on October 23, 1956, which demanded independence and the guarantee of basic human and civil rights. Nagy, as well as his multiparty government were reinstated, leading to a brief stabilization. On October 31, Soviet leadership intervened, though, leading to a week-long conflict that defeated the revolutionaries. Zsuzsanna Kőrösi, Adrienne Molnár, "The handing down of experiences in families of the politically condemned in Communist Hungary," in: *9th International Oral History Conference*. Göteborg, 1996, pp. 1160–7 (p. 1160).

169 Nousek, "A future-oriented *Zeitrechnung*," p. 317; Gyorgy Gyarmati, Tibor Valuch, *Hungary under Soviet Domination. 1944–1989*. New York: Columbia University Press, 2009.

170 See: Zuzsanna Kőrösi, Adrienne Molnár, *Carrying a Secret in My Heart...: Children of Political Victims of the Revolution, 1956 Hungary—An Oral History*. Budapest: Central European University Press, 2002.

171 Ritchie Robertson, *The 'Jewish Question' in German Literature, 1749–1939: Emancipation and its Discontents*. New York: Oxford University Press, 1999, p. 421.

172 Stefan Zweig, "Der Roman 'Hiob' von Joseph Roth," in: Stefan Zweig, *Begegnungen mit Büchern: Aufsätze und Einleitungen aus den Jahren 1902–1939*. Edited by Knut Beck. Kapitel 17. Fischer Taschenbuch Verlag, 1983.

173 Ibid.

174 Ibid.

175 Joseph Roth, *Juden auf Wanderschaft*. Berlin: Die Schmiede, 1927. The essay was first published in six installments in a book series for the progressive Berlin publishing house Die Schmiede. Sigurd Paul Scheichl, "*Juden auf Wanderschaft*—2009 neu gelesen," in: Johann Georg Lughofer, Mira Miladinović Zalaznik (eds.), *Joseph Roth: Europäisch-jüdischer Schriftsteller und österreichischer Universalist*. Berlin/Boston: De Gruyter, 2011, pp. 11–22 (p. 11).

176 Arnold Zweig, *Das ostjüdische Antlitz*. Berlin: Welt-Verlag, 1922.

177 Roth, *Juden auf Wanderschaft*, p. 7.

178 Ibid.

179 Katja Garloff, "Femininity and assimilatory desire in Joseph Roth," in: *Modern Fiction Studies*. 51 (2), 2005, pp. 354–373 (p. 354).

180 Katrina Nousek refers to a discourse represented by Samuel Huntington's 'The Clash of Civilizations' and Francis Fukuyama's 'The End of History', in which the events of 1989 are considered as evidence of a teleological historical process that would eventually lead towards th triumph of liberalism and democracy after a Western example. Katrina Nousek, "A future-oriented *Zeitrechnung*," p. 304.

181 Nousek, "A future-oriented *Zeitrechnung*," p. 305.

182 Péter Nádas, "Ein Lob des doppelten Blicks," in: *Die Zeit*. 31 December 2002.

183 When, for instance, she is asked about the origins of the Hungarian character Évi in *Die hellen Tage,* she quickly clarifies that there are no autobiographical similarities. Rather than about herself, she likes to write about "people that do not exist in [her] real life [Menschen, die in [ihrem] wirklichen Leben nicht existieren]," "people she likes to spend time with in her head [Menschen, mit denen sie gerne Zeit in [ihrem] Kopf verbring[t]]." In other words, creative imagination is to her far more important than the characters' migration background. Andrea Pollmeier, "Dynamik des Dreiecks: 'Die hellen Tage' von Zsusza Bánk"; http://faustkultur.de/237-0-Gespraech-mit-Zsuzsa-Bnk.html#.V9coxFv5jIU.

184 For a thorough discussion on the "latent language [latente Sprache]" of the novel, i.e. the echoes of Hungarian idiom, see: Szilvia Lengl, *Interkulturelle Frauenfiguren im deutschsprachigen Roman der Gegenwart*. Dresden: Thelem 2012, pp. 135–98.
185 Fridtjof Küchemann, "Scheiden tut weh—Zsuzsa Bánk und ihr Roman 'Der Schwimmer,'" in: *Frankfurter Allgemeine Zeitung*. 22 August 2002; http://www.faz.net/aktuell/feuilleton/buecher/rezensionen/belletristik/debuet-scheiden-tut-weh-zsuzsa-bank-und-ihr-roman-der-schwimmer-174414.html.
186 Zsuzsa Bánk, "Da bebt etwas nach. Was der ungarische Aufstand von 1956 für die Nachgeborenen bedeutet," in: *Die Welt*. 25 October 2006.
187 Lengl, *Interkulturelle Frauenfiguren*, p. 184.
188 The public mourning is evoked as time standing still: "They walked through the city and suddenly had to stand still. At that moment, everything and everyone came to halt [...] because the order to do so had been given over loudspeakers or with sirens. [Sie waren durch die Stadt gelaufen und irgendwann stehengeblieben, weil man stehenzubleiben hatte in dieser Minute, weil alles und jeder stehenblieb, [...] weil es so bestimmt worden war, über Lautsprecher oder Sirenen.]" (DS 252)
189 Sieglinde Geisel, "Trauerzauber und Abschiedsreigen. Ein Gespräch mit der Schriftstellerin Zsuzsa Bánk," in: *Neue Zürcher Zeitung*. 7 July 2003; http://www.nzz.ch/article8TC4E-1.274677.
190 Nádas, "Ein Lob des doppelten Blicks," s.p.
191 Zweig, "Der Roman 'Hiob,'" s.p.
192 Sebald, "Kaddisch für Österreich," p. 111.
193 Zweig, "Der Roman 'Hiob,'" s.p.
194 Nancy, *The Inoperative Community*, p. 79.
195 Nancy, *The Inoperative Community*, pp. 79–80 (emphasis in original).
196 Robertson, *The 'Jewish Question'*, p. 423.
197 The Second Commandment—"Thou shalt not make unto thee any graven image"—strongly forbids the worship of idols and images. On the significance of aniconism in Jewish art, see: Kalman P. Bland, *The Artless Jew: Mediaeval and Modern Affirmations and Denials of the Visual*. Princeton: Princeton University Press, 2000.
198 Nancy, *The Inoperative Community*, p. 141.
199 Robertson, *The 'Jewish Question'*, p. 423.
200 Nancy, *The Inoperative Community*, p. 10.
201 Fynsk, "Experiences of Finitude," p. xxx.
202 Lengl, *Interkulturelle Frauenfiguren*, p. 172.
203 Nousek, "A future-oriented *Zeitrechnung*," p. 309.
204 Caroline Neubaur, "Mutter ohne Mythos," in: *Literaturen*. 4, 2003, pp. 12–19.
205 Lengl, *Interkulturelle Frauenfiguren*, p. 170.
206 Neubaur, "Mutter ohne Mythos," p. 14. Lengl even inscribes Bánk's mother figure into a tradition of "rebellious, sometimes murderous mothers [aufrührerisch[e], teilweise mörderisch[e] M[ü]tter]," which goes back to the mythical Lilith and to Medea, who as symbols of empowerment have shed the image of the caring, loving mother. Lengl, *Interkulturelle Frauenfiguren*, pp. 168–9.
207 Neubaur, "Mutter ohne Mythos," p. 15.
208 Kőrösi, Molnár, "The handing down of experiences," p. 1160.
209 Ibid.

210 Lengl gives an extensive overview of the latent violence that permeates the lives of the majority of the characters, either in terms of repressed physical aggression, illnesses, or self-aggression. Lengl, *Interkulturelle Frauenfiguren*, pp. 172–183 (p. 183).
211 Between the two World Wars, government censuses counted Magyar speaking Gypsies as Hungarian citizens, which indicates that language was a crucial factor in the perception of their assimilation. William O. McCagg, "Gypsy Policy in Socialist Hungary and Czechoslovakia, 1945–1989," in: *Nationalities Papers: The Journal of Nationalism and Ethnicity*. 19 (3), 1991, pp. 313–336.
212 Lengl, *Interkulturelle Frauenfiguren*, p. 168.
213 See: Balázs Majtényi, György Majtényi, *A Contemporary History of Exclusion: The Roma Issue in Hungary from 1945 to 2015*. Budapest: Central European University Press, 2016, p. 31ff.
214 Majtényi, *A Contemporary History of Exclusion*, p. 37.
215 McCagg, "Gypsy Policy in Socialist Hungary," p. 317.
216 Majtényi, *A Contemporary History of Exclusion*, p. 39.
217 Kőrösi's and Molnár's study of family communication regarding the fathers' involvement in the revolution reveals strategies ranging from complete transparency to total secrecy. Kőrösi, Molnár: "The handing down of experiences," p. 1160ff.
218 Majtényi, *A Contemporary History of Exclusion*, p. 45.
219 Nousek, "A future-oriented *Zeitrechnung*," p. 302.
220 Roth, *Juden auf Wanderschaft*, p. 10.
221 Ibid.
222 Sarah Fraiman-Morris, "Naturgefühl und Religiosität in den Werken österreichisch-jüdischer Schriftsteller: Franz Werfel, Stefan Zweig, Joseph Roth, Richard Beer-Hofmann," in: *Modern Austrian Literature*. 38(1/2), 2005, pp. 29–48.
223 Fraiman-Morris, "Naturgefühl und Religiosität," p. 31.
224 Rosenfeld, "Glaube und Heimat," pp. 490–1.
225 Fraiman-Morris remarks in this context that this disconnection from nature echoes the (internalized) anti-Semitic stereotype of *Naturferne*, which is equivalent to the anti-Semitic prejudice of Jews as agents of modernity and urbanization.
226 Fraiman-Morris, "Naturgefühl und Religiosität," p. 38.
227 Fraiman-Morris, "Naturgefühl und Religiosität," p. 39.
228 As Gellen points out, in the majority of *Hiob* readings, the happy ending is considered unexpected. However, looking more closely at Mendel Singer's relationship with modern technology and connecting it to his former mistrust of visuality and mediation, the foreshadowing of his 'wondrous' transformation—his faith regained, and his family (partially) reunited—becomes more obvious. Gellen, "The Media Myth of America," p. 24.
229 Gellen, "The Media Myth of America," p. 1.
230 Roth's view of America was informed mainly by media—film and radio but also print media and newspapers. In countless articles on film and the film industry, Roth presents a highly critical picture of America, especially when it comes to the exploitation of new technology in the interest of profit. Yet despite his apparent disdain for American culture, Roth had made plans to visit the United States by the time of his death in 1939. Gellen, "The Media Myth of America," pp. 3–4; Jon Hughes. *Facing Modernity: Fragmentation, Culture, and Identity in Joseph Roth's Writing in the 1920s*. London: Maney Publishing, 2006, p. 165.
231 Gellen, "The Media Myth of America," p. 9.

232 Gellen, "The Media-Myth of America," p. 2 (emphasis in original).
233 Like the prophet Elijah, Menuchim arrives at Mendel's house during the Passover seder. Gellen, "The Media Myth of America," p. 10.
234 The way Mirjam carries the gramophone furthermore refers to the way she and her brothers "dragged Menuchim through the town like a misfortune, they left him unattended, they dropped him [Menuchim wie ein Unglück durch die Stadt [schleppten], sie ließen ihn liegen, sie ließen ihn fallen]." (H 20)
235 Nancy, *The Inoperative Community*, p. 129.
236 Fynsk, "Experiences of Finitude," p. xxxii.
237 Robertson, *The 'Jewish Question'*, p. 428.
238 Lengl, *Interkulturelle Frauenfiguren*, pp. 182–3.
239 Lengl, *Interkulturelle Frauenfiguren*, p. 177. Likewise, Christof Hamann observes an underlying "Poetik des Wartens, die die Möglichkeit einer erzählend auf sinnvolle Bewältigung des Vergangenen sich hinbewegenden Subjektivität annuliert." While I agree that Kata's narration does not intend to 'overcome' the past, I want to argue that her account, no matter how subjective it may be, allows her to break through stagnation and paralysis. Christof Hamann, "'Ich kann warten, ja.' Raum und Zeit in Zsuzsa Bánk's Roman *Der Schwimmer*," in: Petra Meurer et al. (eds.): *Interkulturelles Lernen*. Bielefeld: Aisthesis, 2009, pp. 19–34.
240 Lengl, *Interkulturelle Frauenfiguren*, p. 190. About gender specificity and water metaphors, see: Ute Seiderer, *Flusspoeten und Ozeansucher. Konstruktionen von Kultur und Männlichkeit*. Würzburg: Königshausen & Neumann, 2009.
241 Andrea Bartl, "'Der Wechsel von einem vertrauten Element in das Andere, Fremde': Das Schwimm-Motiv in der deutschen Gegenwartsliteratur," in: *German Life and Letters*. 62(4), 2009, pp. 482–495 (p. 482).
242 Bartl, "Das Schwimm-Motiv in der deutschen Gegenwartsliteratur," p. 486.
243 Bartl, "Das Schwimm-Motiv in der deutschen Gegenwartsliteratur," p. 485.
244 Bartl, "Das Schwimm-Motiv in der deutschen Gegenwartsliteratur," p. 487.
245 Their fabricated stories are, again, reminiscent of the lies and secrecy that governed many families of condemned fathers: "Mothers either lied outright to their children or prevaricated, or avoided their questions. [...] They explained away the absence of a father with stories of natural death or defection. The child believed all this for a while — until he suddenly hit upon the fact that his/her mother had been lying. After this he/she would not listen to anything his/her mother had to say on the subject, even if it was the truth. The silence and avoidance of the topic became permanent." Kőrösi, Molnár: "The handing down of experiences," p. 1160.
246 Bartl, "Das Schwimm-Motiv in der deutschen Gegenwartsliteratur," p. 489.
247 Bartl, "Das Schwimm-Motiv in der deutschen Gegenwartsliteratur," p. 491.
248 Lengl, *Interkulturelle Frauenfiguren*, p. 195.
249 Although Bánk does not mention him by name, she obviously refers to Jan Palach, the 21-year-old university student who torched himself to protest against the 1968 Soviet invasion and occupation of Czechoslovakia.
250 In order to illustrate Kata's subtle shift in focalisation, from a past to a present and future orientation, Nousek makes a careful analysis of Bánk's use of tenses and conjunctive mood. Nousek: "A future-oriented *Zeitrechnung*," especially pp. 318–23.
251 Nousek, "A future-oriented *Zeitrechnung*," p. 322.
252 Nousek, "A future-oriented *Zeitrechnung*," p. 318.

253 Nousek refers to Kata's account as the "formal construction of a future-present age," and the diegetic present of her final sentence as a "historical present that connects the communist past—as meaningful past-present age—to the post-communist future." Nousek, "A future-oriented *Zeitrechnung*," p. 321.
254 Lengl interprets the final lines in terms of waiting for official travel documents; Nousek is hesitant to attribute a referent (the authorities) to the indefinite pronoun 'man'. Lengl, *Interkulturelle Frauenfiguren*, 195; Nousek, "A future-oriented *Zeitrechnung*," 319. Reading the passage while leaving the 'man' unresolved may indeed invite the reader to reflect on the question why Kata's 'waiting' has a more hopeful undertone than before.
255 Nousek, "A future-oriented *Zeitrechnung*," p. 323.
256 Nancy, *The Inoperative Community*, p. 79.

Conclusion: The fallibility of *Bildung*

1 Gregory Castle, "Destinies of *Bildung*: Belatedness and the Modernist Novel," in: Gregory Castle (ed.), *A History of the Modernist Novel*. New York: Cambridge University Press, 2015, pp. 483–508 (p. 486).
2 Castle, "Destinies of *Bildung*," p. 486. *Bildung* "runs on the double bind of identification," for "the subject must identify with the model in order to become what the subject already is; however, this also means that the subject must *not* identify with anything—particularly not a master or exemplar—that is not always already the subject itself." Marc Redfield, *Phantom Formations. Aesthetic Ideology and the* Bildungsroman. Ithaca/London: Cornell University Press, 1996, p. 49.
3 Redfield, *Phantom Formations*, p. 64.

BIBLIOGRAPHY

Ackermann, Irmgard, and Harald Weinrich (eds.). *Eine nicht nur deutsche Literatur. Zur Standortbestimmung der Ausländerliteratur*. Munich: Piper, 1986.
Adelson, Leslie A. *The Turkish Turn in Contemporary German Literature. Towards a New Critical Grammar of Migration*. New York: Palgrave, 2005.
——. "Against Between: A Manifesto," in: Hassan, Salah, and Iftikhar Dadi (eds.). *Unpacking Europe; Towards a Critical Reading*. Rotterdam: Museum Boijmans van Beuningen and NAi Publishers, 2001, pp. 244–256.
Adorno, Theodor W. *Aesthetic Theory*. Edited by Adorno, Gretel, and Rolf Tiedemann. Translated by Robert Hullot-Kentor. London: Bloomsbury, 2013 [1970].
Agoston-Nikolova, Elka (ed.). *Shoreless Bridges: South East European Writing in Diaspora*. Amsterdam/New York: Rodopi, 2010.
Aja, Bryan. "The Shameless Little Man: Narrative Obstruction in Feridun Zaimoğlu's Liebesbrand," in: *EDGE—A Graduate Journal for German and Scandinavian Studies*. 3 (1), 2013, s.p.
Allolio-Näcke, Lars, Britta Kalscheuer, and Arne Manzeschke (eds.). *Differenzen anders denken. Bausteine zu einer Kulturtheorie der Transdifferenz*. Frankfurt am Main/New York: Campus Verlag, 2005.
Alscher, Stefan. "Großstädte sind Zuwanderungsmagnete," in: *Migration und Bevölkerung. Das Online-Portal zur Migrationsgesellschaft*, 2015: http://www.migration-info.de/artikel/2015-06-11/grossstaedte-sind-zuwanderungsmagneten [March 2017].
Althusser, Louis. "Ideology and ideological state apparatuses," in: Althusser, Louis. *Lenin and Philosophy and other Essays*. London: New Left Books, 1989, pp. 170–86.
Amann, Wilhelm et al. (eds.). *Globalisierung und Gegenwartsliteratur. Konstellationen—Konzepte—Perspektiven*. Heidelberg: Synchron, 2010.
Anderson, Benedict. *Imagined Communities. Reflections on the Origins and the Spread of Nationalism*. London/New York: Verso, 1983/2006.
Anderson, Susan C. "Seeing Blindly: Voyeurism in Schnitzler's Fräulein Else and Andreas Salomé's Fenitschka," in: Strelka, Joseph P. (ed.). *Die Seele ... ist ein weites Land: Kritische Beiträge zum Werk Arthur Schnitzlers*. Bern: Peter Lang, 1996, pp. 13–27.
——."The Power of the Gaze: Visual Metaphors in Schnitzler's Prose Works and Dramas," in: Lorenz, Dagmar C. G. (ed.). *A Companion to the Works of Arthur Schnitzler*. Rochester: Camden House, 2003, pp. 303–324.

Angelova, Penka. "The Other Road: On the Bulgarian Topos in the Work of Three Writers Awarded the Adelbert von Chamisso Prize," in: Agoston-Nikolova, Elka (ed.). *Shoreless Bridges: South East European Writing in Diaspora.* Amsterdam/New York: Rodopi, 2010, pp. 83–95.
Antifaschistisches Pressearchiv und Bildungszentrum Berlin e.V. Profil: Heidelberger Kreis: http://www.apabiz.de/archiv/material/Profile/Heidelberger%20Kreis.htm [April 2017].
Appadurai, Arjun. "The Production of Locality," in: Appadurai, Arjun. *Modernity at Large. Cultural Dimensions of Globalization.* Minneapolis: University of Minnesota Press, 1996, pp. 178–200.
Archambeau, Robert. "The Aesthetic Anxiety: Avant-Garde Poetics, Autonomous Aesthetics and the Idea of Politics," in: Comfort, Kelly (ed.). *Art and Life in Aestheticism: De-Humanizing and Re-Humanizing Art, the Artist, and the Artistic Receptor.* New York: Palgrave, 2008, pp. 139–58.
Arnold, Heinz Ludwig (ed.). *Joseph Roth.* Munich: Edition Text u. Kritik, 1982, pp. 90–100.
Aschheim, Steven E. *Brothers and Strangers. The East European Jew in German and German Jewish Consciousness 1800–1923.* London/Madison: Wisconsin University Press, 1982.
——— "'The Jew within': The Myth of 'Judaization' in Germany," in: Reinharz, Jehuda, and Walter Schatzberg (eds.). *The Jewish Response to German Culture.* Hanover: University Press of New England, 1985, pp. 212–241.
——— *At the Edges of Liberalism. Junctions of European, German, and Jewish History.* New York: Palgrave Macmillan, 2012.
Assmann, Aleida. *Arbeit am nationalen Gedächtnis. Eine kurze Geschichte der deutschen Bildungsidee.* Frankfurt am Main: Campus Verlag, 1993.
Aurnhammer, Achim. "'Selig, wer in Träumen stirbt.' Das literarisierte Leben und Sterben von Fräulein Else," in: *Euphorion: Zeitschrift für Literaturgeschichte.* 77 (4), 1983, pp. 500–510.
Bade, Klaus J. "Versäumte Integrationschancen und nachholende Integrationspolitik," in: Bade, Klaus J., and Hans-Georg Hiesserich (eds.). *Nachholende Integrationspolitik und Gestaltungsperspektiven der Integrationspraxis.* Göttingen: Vandenhoeck & Ruprecht Unipress, 2007.
———. "Von der Arbeitswanderung zur Einwanderungsgesellschaft," in: Stemmler, Susanne (ed.). *Multikultur 2.0. Willkommen im Einwanderungsland Deutschland.* Göttingen: Wallstein, 2011, pp. 154–185.
———. *Ausländer, Aussiedler, Asyl. Eine Bestandsaufnahme.* Munich: Beck, 1994.
———. *Deutsche im Ausland, Fremde in Deutschland. Migration in Geschichte und Gegenwart.* Munich: C.H. Beck, 1992.
———. *Kritik und Gewalt: Sarrazin-Debatte, 'Islamkritik' und Terror in der Einwanderungsgesellschaft.* Schwalbach: Wochenschau Verlag, 2013.
Bade, Klaus J., and Hans-Georg Hiesserich (eds.). *Nachholende Integrationspolitik und Gestaltungsperspektiven der Integrationspraxis.* Göttingen: Vandenhoeck & Ruprecht Unipress, 2007.
Bahr, Hermann. *Dialog vom Tragischen.* Berlin: S. Fischer Verlag, 1904.

Balibar, Etienne. "Racism and Nationalism," in: Balibar, Etienne, and Immanuel Wallerstein (eds.). *Race, Nation, Class: Ambiguous Identities*. London: Verso, 1991, pp. 37–68.
Bánk, Zsuzsa. *Der Schwimmer*. Frankfurt am Main: S. Fischer Verlag, 2002/2004.
——. *The Swimmer*. Translated by Margot Bettauer Dembo. Orlando: Harcourt, 2004.
——. "Da bebt etwas nach. Was der ungarische Aufstand von 1956 für die Nachgeborenen bedeutet," in: *Die Welt*. 24 October, 2006: https://www.welt.de/kultur/article89605/Da-bebt-etwas-nach.html [March 2017].
Barker, Andrew. "Race, Sex and Character in Schnitzler's Fräulein Else," in: *German Life and Letters* 54 (1), 2001, pp. 1–9.
Barkey, Karen, and Mark Von Hagen (eds.). *After Empire: Multiethnic Societies and Nation-building: The Soviet Union and the Russian, Ottoman, and Habsburg Empires*. Colorado: Westview Press, 1997.
Bartl, Andrea. "'Der Wechsel von einem vertrauten Element in das Andere, Fremde': Das Schwimm-Motiv in der deutschen Gegenwartsliteratur," in: *German Life and Letters*. 62 (4) 2009, pp. 482–495.
Bartmann, Christoph, Carola Dürr, and Hans-Georg Knopp (eds.). *Wiedervorlage: Nationalkultur. Variationen über ein neuralgisches Thema*. Göttingen: Steidl Verlag, 2010.
Bataille, Georges. "Struktur und Funktion der Armee," in: Hollier, Dennis (ed.). *Das Collège de Sociologie 1937–1939*. Berlin: Suhrkamp, 2012, pp. 175–188.
Bauman, Zygmunt. "Modernity and Ambivalence," in: *Theory, Culture & Society*. 7, 1990, pp. 143–169.
Bayersdörfer, Hans-Peter. "Arthur Schnitzler," in: Kilcher, Andreas B. (ed.). *Metzler Lexikon der deutsch-jüdischen Literatur. Jüdische Autorinnen und Autoren deutscher Sprache von der Aufklärung bis zur Gegenwart*. Stuttgart/Weimar: J.B. Metzler, 2000, pp. 519–23.
Beck, Ulrich. "Das kosmopolitische Empire. Ein Plädoyer für ein Europa jenseits des Nationaalstaats," in: *Internationale Politik*. July 2006, pp. 6–12. Reprinted by: Göktürk, Deniz, David Gramling, Anton Kaes, and Andreas Langenohl (eds.). *Transit Deutschland: Debatten zu Nation und Migration*. Munich: Wilhelm Fink Verlag, 2011, pp. 718–725.
Becker, Claudia. "Helen Grund," in: Opitz, Michael, and Jörg Plath (eds.). *Genieße froh, was du nicht hast. Der Flaneur Franz Hessel*. Würzburg: Königshausen & Neumann, 1997, pp. 191–210
Beer-Hofmann, Richard. *Der Tod Georgs*. Berlin: S. Fischer Verlag, 1900.
Beharriell, Frederick J. "Schnitzler's Fräulein Else: 'Reality" and Invention," in: *Modern Austrian Literature: Journal of the International Arthur Schnitzler Research Association*. 10 (3–4), 1977, pp. 247–64.
Beller, Steven. *Vienna and the Jews, 1867–1938*. Cambridge: Cambridge University Press, 1989.
Benjamin, Walter. "Das Kunstwerk im Zeitalter seiner technischen Reproduzierbarkeit" (Dritte Fassung, 1935), in: Benjamin, Walter. *Gesammelte Schriften*. Band I. Edited by Rolf Tiedemann, Hermann Schweppenhäuser. Frankfurt am Main: Suhrkamp, 1974, pp. 471–508.

———. "Das Paris des Second Empire bei Baudelaire," in: Benjamin, Walter. *Gesammelte Schriften*. Band I. Edited by Rolf Tiedemann, Hermann Schweppenhäuser. Frankfurt am Main: Suhrkamp, 1974, pp. 511–603.

———. "Die Wiederkehr des Flaneurs," in: Benjamin, Walter: *Gesammelte Schriften*. Band III. Edited by Rolf Tiedemann, Hermann Schweppenhäuser. Frankfurt am Main: Suhrkamp, 1980, pp. 194–199.

———. "Über einige Motive bei Baudelaire," in: Benjamin, Walter. *Gesammelte Schriften*. Band I. Edited by Rolf Tiedemann, Hermann Schweppenhäuser. Frankfurt am Main: Suhrkamp, 1974, pp. 605–653.

Berberich, Frank. "Klasse statt Masse," in: *Lettre International*. 86, 2009, p. 197.

Berding, Helmut. *Moderner Anti-Semitismus in Deutschland*. Frankfurt am Main: Edition Suhrkamp, 1988.

Berlin, Isaiah. "The Counter-Enlightenment," in: Hardy, Henry, and Roger Hausheer (eds.). *The Proper Study of Mankind: An Anthology of Essays*. New York: Farrar, Straus and Giroux, 1998 [1973], pp. 243–46.

Bertz, Inka. "Jüdische Renaissance," in: Kerbs, Diethart, and Jürgen Reulecke (eds.). *Handbuch der deutschen Reformbewegungen 1880–1933*. Wuppertal: Peter Hammer, 1998, pp. 551–63.

Bewes, Timothy. "Against Exemplarity: W.G. Sebald and the Problem of Connection," in: *Contemporary Literature*. Volume 55, 1, 2014, pp. 1–31.

Bhabha, Homi K. "Of Mimicry and Man: The ambivalence of colonial discourse," in: Bhabha, Homi K. *The Location of Culture*. London/New York: Routledge, 1994/2005, pp. 121–31.

———. *The Location of Culture*. New York: Routledge, 1994/2005.

Biendarra, Anke. "'Schriftstellerin zu sein und in seinem Leben anwesend zu sein, ist für mich eins': ein Gespräch mit Terézia Mora," in: *Transit*. 2007, 3 (1), s.p.

Biller, Maxim. "Letzte Ausfahrt Uckermarck," in: *Die Zeit*. 9, 20 February 2014: http://www.zeit.de/2014/09/deutsche-gegenwartsliteratur-maxim-biller [March 2017].

Bilsky, Emily D. (ed.). *Berlin Metropolis. Jews and the New Culture 1890–1918*. Berkeley/Los Angeles: University of California Press/New York: The Jewish Museum, 1999.

Biondi, Franco, and Rafik Schami. "Literatur der Betroffenheit. Bemerkungen zur Gastarbeiterliteratur," in: Schaffernicht, Christian (ed.). *Zu Hause in der Fremde*. Fischerhude: Atelier im Bauernhaus, 1981, pp. 136–150.

Bland, Kalman P. *The Artless Jew: Mediaeval and Modern Affirmations and Denials of the Visual*. Princeton: Princeton University Press, 2000.

Boa, Elizabeth. "Özdamar's Autobiographical Fictions: Trans-national Identity and Literary Form," in: *German Life and Letters*. 59 (4), 2006, pp. 526–39.

Botsch, Gideon, Olaf Glöckner, Christoph Kopke, and Michael Spieker (eds.). *Islamophobie und Antisemitismus: Ein umstrittener Vergleich*. Berlin/Boston: Walter de Gruyter, 2012.

Brenner, Michael. "1916: The German army orders a census of Jewish soldiers, and Martin Buber launches his cultural magazine Der Jude," in: Gilman, Sander L., and Jack Zipes (eds.). *The Yale Companion to Jewish Writing and Thought in German Culture, 1096–1996*. New Haven: Yale University Press, 1997, pp. 348–54.

Brix, Emil et al. (eds.). *The Decline of Empires*. Vienna: Verlag für Geschichte und Politik, 2011.

Bronsen, David. *Joseph Roth: Eine Biographie*. Köln: Kiepenheuer & Witsch, 1974.

——. "The Jew in Search of a Fatherland: The Relationship of Joseph Roth to the Habsburg Monarchy," in: *Germanic Review*. 54 (2), 1979, pp. 54–61.

Bruner, Michael Lane. *Strategies of Remembrance. The Rhetorical Dimensions of Identity Construction*. Columbia: University of South Carolina Press, 2002.

Brunner, Maria. "Paradigmen des Pikaresken in Kumpfmüllers *Hampels Fluchten* (2000), Terézia Moras *Alle Tage* (2004), Dimitré Dinevs *Engelszungen* (2003) und Helmut Kraussers *Fette Welt* (1992)," in: *Studien zur deutschen Sprache und Literatur*. 1, 2013, pp. 35–64.

Buber, Martin. "Jüdische Renaissance," in: *Ost und West*. 1, 1901, pp. 7–10.

Buchholz, Paul. "Bordering on Names: Strategies of Mapping in the Prose of Terézia Mora and Peter Handke," in: *Transit. A Journal of Travel, Migration, and Multiculturalism in the German-speaking World*. 7(1), 2011.

Bundesanstalt für Arbeitsvermittlung und Arbeitslosenversicherung, "Betreuung der ausländischen Arbeitnehmer," in: *Amtliche Nachrichten der Bundesanstalt für Arbeitsvermittlung und Arbeitslosenversicherung*, 1965. Reprinted partially by Stemmler, Susanne (ed.). *Multikultur 2.0. Willkommen im Einwanderungsland Deutschland*. Göttingen: Wallstein, 2011, pp. 149–153.

Bunzl, Matti. "The Poetics of Politics and the Politics of Poetics. Richard Beer-Hofmann and Theodor Herzl Reconsidered," in: *The German Quarterly*. 69 (3), 1996, pp. 277–304.

Buschkowsky, Heinz. *Neukölln ist überall*. Berlin: Ullstein, 2012.

Büssem, Eberhard. "Dimitré Dinev: Schriftsteller im Gespräch mit Dr. Eberhard Büssem," Bayerischer Rundfunk. 30 May 2005: http://www.br-online.de/alpha/forum/vor0505/20050530.shtml [March 2017].

Butterwegge, Christoph, and Gudrun Hentges. *Massenmedien, Migration und Integration*. Wiesbaden: Verlag für Sozialwissenschaften, 2006.

Castellani Perelli, Daniele. "Endlich befasst sich Deutschland mit dem Problem," in: *Reset DOC*, 4 June 2007: http://www.resetdoc.org/de/Kermani-interview.php [March 2017].

Castle, Gregory. "Destinies of *Bildung*: Belatedness and the Modernist Novel," in: Gregory Castle (ed.), *A History of the Modernist Novel*. New York: Cambridge University Press, 2015, pp. 483–508.

Cerri, Chiara. "Interkulturelle Literatur. Ein erneutes Plädoyer für eine dringende begriffliche Entscheidung," in: *Weimarer Beiträge*. 54 (3), 2008, pp. 424–436.

Cheesman, Tom. *Novels of Turkish German Settlement: Cosmopolite Fictions*. Rochester, New York: Camden House, 2007.

——."Juggling Burdens of Representation: Black, Red, Gold and Turquoise," in: *German Life and Letters*, 59/4, 2006, pp. 471–487.

——. "For Feridun Zaimoglu's *Leyla*: Crime Facts and Fictions," in: *German as a Foreign Language*. 3, 2008, pp. 4–25.

Cheesman, Tom, and Karin E. Yeşilada. "'Ich bin nicht modern'/ 'I'm not modern': Interviews with Feridun Zaimoglu," in: Cheesman, Tom, and Karin E. Yeşilada (eds.). *Feridun Zaimoglu.* Oxford: Peter Lang, 2012, pp. 39–70

Chiellino, Carmine (ed.). *Interkulturelle Literatur in Deutschland: Ein Handbuch.* Stuttgart: Metzler, 2000.

Chin, Rita, Geoff Eley, Heide Fehrenbach, and Atina Grossmann. *After the Nazi Racial State. Difference and Democracy in Germany and Europe.* Ann Arbor: University of Michigan Press, 2009.

Coetzee, John Maxwell. "Emperor of Nostalgia," in: *New York Review of Books.* 28 February 2002, s.p.

Cohn, Dorrit. *Transparent Minds: Narrative Modes for Presenting Consciousness in Fiction.* Princeton: Princeton University Press, 1978.

Comfort, Kelly (ed.). *Art and Life in Aestheticism: De-Humanizing and Re-Humanizing Art, the Artist, and the Artistic Receptor.* New York: Palgrave, 2008.

——. "Artist for art's sake or artist for sale: Lulu's and Else's failed attempts at aesthetic self-fashioning," in: *Women in German Yearbook.* 22, 2006, pp. 189–210.

Conforti, Yitzhak. "East and West in Jewish Nationalism: conflicting types in the Zionist vision?," in: *Nations and Nationalism.* 16 (2), 2010, pp. 201–219.

Cull, Nicholas John et al. (eds.). *Propaganda and Mass Persuasion. A Historical Encyclopedia, 1500 to the Present.* Santa Barbara: ABC Clio, 2003.

Culler, Jonathan. "Semiotics of Tourism," in: *American Journal of Semiotics.* 1 (1–2), 1981, pp.127–140.

Davis, Robert Murray. "Diaspora's Children," in: *World Literature Today.* 80 (6), 2006, pp. 55–8.

Dayioğlu-Yücel, Yasemin. "Authorship and Authenticity in Migrant Writing: The Plagiarism Debate on *Leyla*," in: Cheesman, Tom, and Karin E. Yeşilada (eds.). *Feridun Zaimoglu.* Oxford: Peter Lang, 2012, pp.183–199.

Delcheva, Marina. "Dimitré Dinev spricht über das Problem der Eliten," in: *Das Biber*, 2015: http://www.dasbiber.at/content/dimitr%C3%A9-dinev-spricht-%C3%BCber-das-problem-der-eliten [March 2017].

Deleuze, Gilles, and Félix Guattari. *Kafka: Toward a Minor Literature.* University of Minnesota Press, 1986.

Dennis, Geoff. "Finding the Center, Entering the Land: The Labyrinths of Jewish Imagination," in: *Parabola: Tradition, Myth, and the Search for Meaning.* 34, 2009, pp. 31–42.

Deppman, Jed. "Jean-Luc Nancy, Myth, and Literature," in: *Qui Parle.* 10 (2) 1997, pp. 11–32.

Derrida, Jacques. *Monolingualism of the Other; or, The Prosthesis of Origin.* Stanford: Stanford University Press, 1998.

Devisch, Ignaas. "Jean-Luc Nancy," in: *The Internet Encyclopedia of Philosophy*, s.d.: http://www.iep.utm.edu/nancy/ [June 2016].

Dietz, Barbara, and Pawel Kaczmarczyk, "On the demand side of international labour mobility: The structure of the German labour market as a causal factor of seasonal Polish migration," in: Bonifazi, Corrado, Marek Okólski, Jeanette Schoorl, Patrick Simon (eds.). *International Migration in Europe. New Trends and New Methods of Analysis.* Amsterdam: Amsterdam University Press, 2008, pp. 37–64.

Dimova, Ljudmila. "Die Intimität der Geschichte. Ein Interview aus der bulgarischen Zeitschrift LIK," in: *Der Hammer. Zeitung der Alten Schmiede*. 9, 2005, p. 4.
Dinev, Dimitré. *Barmherzigkeit—Unruhe bewahren*. Salzburg/Vienna: Residenz Verlag, 2010.
——. *Ein Licht über dem Kopf*. Munich: Random House/btb Verlag, 2007.
——. *Engelszungen*. München: btb Verlag, 2003/2006.
Dirke, Sabine von. "Multikulti: The German Debate on Multiculturalism," in: *German Studies Review*. 17 (3), 1994, pp. 513–536.
Dollenmayer, David. "History and Fiction: The Kaiser in Joseph Roth's *Radetzkymarsch*," in: *Modern Language Studies*. 16 (3), 1986, pp. 302–310.
Donald, James. "Metropolis: The City as Text," in: Bocock, Robert, and Kenneth Thompson (eds.). *Social and Cultural Forms of Modernity*. Cambridge: Polity Press, pp. 417–470.
——. "This, Here, Now: Imagining the Modern City," in: Westwood, Salle, and John Williams (eds.). *Imagining Cities: Script, Sign, Memory*. New York: Routledge, 1997, pp. 179–200.
Doob, Penelope Reed. *The Idea of Labyrinth: From Classical Antiquity Through the Middle Ages*. Ithaca, New York: Cornell University Press, 1990.
Dörr, Volker C. "'Third Space' vs. Diaspora. Topologien transkultureller Literatur," in: Schmitz, Helmut (ed.).*Von der nationalen zur internationalen Literatur. Transkulturelle deutschsprachige Literatur und Kultur im Zeitalter globaler Migration*. Amsterdam/New York: Rodopi, 2009, pp. 59–75.
Douglas, Christopher. *A Genealogy of Literary Multiculturalism*. New York: Cornell University Press, 2009.
du Gay, Paul et al. (eds.). *Identity: a reader*. London: Sage Publications, 2000.
Dühring, Eugen. *Die Judenfrage als Racen-, Sitten- und Culturfrage. Mit einer weltgeschichtlichen Antwort*. Karlsruhe/Leipzig: Reuther, 1881.
Durzak, Manfred, and Nilüfer Kuruyazıcı (eds.). *Die andere deutsche Literatur. Istanbuler Vorträge*. Würzburg: Königshausen & Neumann, 2004.
Eberhardt, Sören, and Charis Goer (eds.). *Über Richard Beer-Hofmann. Rezeptionsdokumente aus 100 Jahren*. Hamburg: Igel Verlag, 1996/2012.
Eigler, Friederike, and Jens Kugele (eds.). *Heimat. At the Intersection of Memory and Space*. Berlin/Boston: Walter de Gruyter, 2012.
Eke, Norbert Otto, and Günter Helmes (eds.). *Richard Beer-Hofmann (1866–1945). Studien zu seinem Werk*. Würzburg: Königshausen & Neumann, 1993.
Elias, Norbert. *The Civilizing Process. The History of Manners*. New York: Urizen Books, 1978.
Elon, Amos. *Zu einer anderen Zeit. Porträt der jüdisch-deutschen Epoche (1743–1933)*. München: Carl Hanser Verlag, 2003.
El-Tayeb, Fatima. "Foreigners, Germans, and German Foreigners. Constructions of National Identity in Early Twentieth Century Germany," in: Hasan, Salah, and Iftikhar Dadi (eds.). *Unpacking Europe. Towards a Critical Reading*. Rotterdam: NAi Publishers, 2001, pp. 72–81.
Erll, Astrid. "Locating Family in Cultural Memory Studies," in: *Journal of Comparative Family Studies*. 42 (3), 2011, pp. 303–318.

Esherick, Joseph et al. (eds.). *Empire to Nation: Historical Perspectives on the Making of the Modern World.* Oxford: Rowman & Littlefield, 2006.

Eysteinsson, Astradur, and Vivian Liska (eds.). *Modernism.* Amsterdam: John Benjamins Publishing Company, 2007.

Fajen, Robert. "Gefühlsleere und Erotomanie. Zur pikaresken Liebessemantik in Literatur und Film," in: Ehland, Christoph and Robert Fajen (eds.). *Das Paradigma des Pikaresken.* Heidelberg: Universitätsverlag Winter, 2007, pp. 241–259.

Feiner, Shmuel, and David Sorkin (eds.). *New Perspectives on the Haskalah.* London/Portland: The Littman Library of Jewish Civilization, 2001.

Fenkart, Iris. "Europäischen Geist gibt es längst: Schriftsteller Dimitré Dinev im Gespräch über Integration, Assimilation und den Begriff Migrantenliteratur," in: *Wiener Zeitung.* 7 July 2010: http://www.wienerzeitung.at/nachrichten/kultur/mehr_kultur/41577_Europaeischen-Geist-gibt-es-laengst.html [March 2017].

Fetscher, Caroline. "Die Muslimisierung des Anderen. Eine Diskussion mit Sawsan Chebli, Sema Kaygusuz, Cem Özdemir und Hilal Sezgin," in: Stemmler, Susanne (ed.). *Multikultur 2.0, Willkommen im Einwanderungsland Deutschland.* Göttingen: Wallstein, 2011, pp. 206–14.

Fliedl, Konstanze (ed.). *Arthur Schnitzler—Richard Beer-Hofmann. Briefwechsel 1891–1931.* Vienna/Zürich: Europa Verlag, 1992.

——. "Richard Beer-Hofmann: Der Tod Georgs," in: Niedermeier, Cornelia, and Karl Wagner (eds.). *Literatur um 1900. Texte der Jahrhundertwende neu gelesen.* Cologne/Weimar/Vienna: Böhlau Verlag, 2001, pp. 155–60.

Foroutan, Naika. "Gemeinsame Identität im pluralen Deutschland," in: Sezgin, Hilal (ed.), *Manifest der Vielen. Deutschland erfindet sich neu.* Berlin: Blumenbar Verlag, 2011, pp. 153–162.

Fraiman-Morris, Sarah. "Naturgefühl und Religiosität in den Werken österreichisch-jüdischer Schriftsteller: Franz Werfel, Stefan Zweig, Joseph Roth, Richard Beer-Hofmann," in: *Modern Austrian Literature.* 38 (1/2), 2005, pp. 29–48.

Frankel, Jonathan, and Steven J. Zipperstein (eds.). *Emancipation and Assimilation. The Jews in Nineteenth-Century Europe.* Cambridge University Press, 1992/2004.

Freitag, Ulrike. "Es ist fast ärgerlich einfach. Interview mit Dimitré Dinev," in: *Ausreißer. Die Grazer Wandzeitung.* 28 May/June 2009: http://ausreisser.mur.at/ausgaben/ausgaben-1-50/28-l-mai-juni-09 [March 2017].

Fynsk, Christopher. "Foreword: Experiences of Finitude," in: Nancy, Jean-Luc. *The Inoperative Community,* Edited by Peter Connor. Minneapolis/Oxford: University of Minnesota Press, 1991.

Garloff, Katja. "Femininity and assimilatory desire in Joseph Roth," in: *Modern Fiction Studies.* 51 (2), 2005, pp. 354–373.

Gay, Peter. *Weimar Culture: The Outsider as Insider.* New York/London: W.W. Norton, 1968/2001.

Geiger, Ludwig. *Die deutsche Literatur und die Juden.* Berlin: Reimer, 1910.

Geisel, Sieglinde. "Trauerzauber und Abschiedsreigen. Ein Gespräch mit der Schriftstellerin Zsuzsa Bánk," in: *Neue Zürcher Zeitung.* 7 March 2003: http://www.nzz.ch/article8TC4E-1.274677 [March 2017].

Gelber, Mark H. *Melancholy Pride: Nation, Race, and Gender in the German Literature of Cultural Zionism*. Tübingen: De Gruyter, 2000.
Gellen, Kata. "The Media Myth of America: Joseph Roth's *Hiob* and *Tarabas*," in: *Journal of Austrian Studies*. 45 (3–4), 2012, pp. 1–29.
Gesemann, Frank (ed.). *Migration und Integration in Berlin. Wissenschaftliche Analysen und politische Perspektiven*. Opladen: Leske & Budrich, 2001.
Giddens, Anthony. *The Consequences of Modernity*. Cambridge: Polity Press, 1990.
Gillman, Abigail. *Viennese Jewish Modernism: Freud, Hofmannsthal, Beer-Hofmann, and Schnitzler*. University Park: Penn State University Press, 2009.
Gilman, Sander L., and Jack Zipes (eds.). *The Yale Companion to Jewish Writing and Thought in German Culture, 1096–1996*. New Haven: Yale University Press, 1997.
Gilman, Sander L. "Thilo Sarrazin and the Politics of Race in the Twenty-First Century," in: *New German Critique*. 117 (39/3), 2012, pp. 47–59.
Gleber, Anke. *The Art of Taking a Walk. Flanerie, Literature, and Film in Weimar Culture*. Princeton: Princeton University Press, 1999.
Goethe, Johann W. von. *Goethe's Schriften*. Vol. 8. Leipzig: G. J. Göschen, 1789.
Göktürk, Deniz, David Gramling, Anton Kaes, and Andreas Langenohl (eds.). *Transit Deutschland: Debatten zu Nation und Migration*. München: Wilhelm Fink Verlag, 2011.
Gold, Alfred. "Ästhetik des Sterbens," in: *Die Zeit (Wien)*. 7(22/282), 24 February 1900.
Goldstein, Moritz. *Begriff und Programm einer jüdischen Nationalliteratur*. Berlin: Jüdischer Verlag, 1912.
——. "Deutsch-jüdischer Parnaß," in: *Kunstwart*. 25 March 1912, pp. 281–94.
Gombrich, Ernst. *Jüdische Identität und jüdisches Schicksal. Eine Diskussionsbemerkung*. Vienna: Passagen, 1997.
Gordimer, Nadine. "Introduction. The Empire of Joseph Roth," in: Joseph Roth, *The Radetzky March*. Translation by Joachim Neugroschel. New York: The Overlook Press, 1991/1995.
Göttsche, Dirk. "Emine Sevgi Özdamar's Erzählung 'Der Hof im Spiegel'. Spielräume einer postkolonialen Lektüre deutsch-türkischer Literatur," in: *German Life and Letters*. 59 (4), 2006, pp. 515–25.
Grady, Tim. "Creating difference: the racialization of Germany's Jewish soldiers after the First World War," in: *Patterns of Prejudice*. 46 (3/4), 2012, pp. 318–38.
Grimm, Erk. *Semiopolis. Prosa der Moderne und Nachmoderne im Zeichen der Stadt*. Bielefeld: Aisthesis Verlag, 2001.
Grimm, Gunter E., and Hans-Peter Bayersdörfer (eds.). *Im Zeichen Hiobs: Jüdische Schriftsteller und deutsche Literatur im 20. Jahrhundert*. Königstein: Athenäum, 1985.
Gvosdev, Nikolas K. (ed.). *The Strange Death of Soviet Communism. A Postscript*. New Brunswick/London: Transaction Publishers, 2008.
Gyarmati, Gyorgy, and Tibor Valuch. *Hungary under Soviet Domination. 1944–1989*. New York: Columbia University Press, 2009.
Ha'am, Achad. "Altneuland," in: *Ost und West*. 3 (4), 1903, pp. 227–44.
——. "Dr. Pinsker und seine Broschüre," in: Ha'am, Achad (ed.). *Am Scheidewege*. Berlin: Jüdischer Verlag, 1916, pp. 64–82.

Haberman, Clyde. "Bulgaria Forces Turkish Exodus of Thousands," in: *The New York Times*. 22 June 1989: http://www.nytimes.com/1989/06/22/world/bulgaria-forces-turkish-exodus-of-thousands.html [March 2017].

Hackert, Fritz. *Kulturpessimismus und Erzählform: Studien zu Joseph Roths Leben und Werk*. Bern: Herbert Lang, 1967.

Haines, Brigid. "The Eastern Turn in Contemporary German, Swiss and Austrian Literature," in: *Debatte: Journal of Contemporary and Central and Eastern Europe*. 16 (2), 2008, pp. 135–49.

Haines, Brigid, Stephen Parker and Colin Riordan (eds.). *Aesthetics and Politics in Modern German Culture: Festschrift in Honour of Rhys W. Williams*. Oxford: Peter Lang, 2010.

Hall, Richard C. "Partisans, Bulgaria," in: Hall, Richard C. (ed.). *War in the Balkans: An Encyclopaedic History from the Fall of the Ottoman to the Breakup of Yugoslavia*. Santa Barbara/Denver/Oxford: ABC-CLIO, 2014, pp. 225–6.

Hall, Stuart. *The multicultural question*. Pavis Papers in Social and Cultural Research no. 4. Milton Keynes: Open University, 2001.

——. "The Question of Cultural Identity," in: Hall, Stuart, David Held, and Anthony McGrew (eds.), *Modernity and Its Futures*. Cambridge: Polity Press, 1992, pp. 247–316.

——. "Who needs 'identity'?', in: du Gay, Paul, Jessica Evans, and Peter Redman (eds.). *Identity. A Reader*. London: Sage Publications, 2000, pp. 15–30.

Hall, Stuart, David Held, and Anthony McGrew (eds.). *Modernity and Its Futures*. Cambridge: Polity Press, 1992.

Hamann, Christof. "'Ich kann warten, ja.' Raum und Zeit in Zsuzsa Bánk's Roman *Der Schwimmer*," in: Meurer, Petra, Martina Ölke, and Sabine Wilmes (eds.). *Interkulturelles Lernen*. Bielefeld: Aisthesis, 2009, pp. 19–34.

Hank, Rainer. *Mortifikation und Beschwörung: Zur Veränderung ästhetischer Wahrnehmung in der Moderne am Beispiel des Frühwerkes Richard Beer-Hofmanns*. Frankfurt am Main: Peter Lang, 1984.

Hasan, Salah, and Iftikhar Dadi (eds.). *Unpacking Europe. Towards a Critical Reading*. Rotterdam: NAi Publishers, 2001.

Häußermann, Hartmut. "Ihre Parallelgesellschaften, unser Problem. Sind Migrantenviertel ein Hindernis für Integration?," in: *Leviathan*. 35 (4), 2007, pp. 458–469.

Heidelberger Kreis, "Heidelberger Manifest," in: *Frankfurter Rundschau*. 4 March 1982. Reprinted in: Göktürk, Deniz, David Gramling, Anton Kaes, and Andreas Langenohl (eds.). *Transit Deutschland: Debatten zu Nation und Migration*. Munich: Wilhelm Fink Verlag, 2011, pp. 155–157.

Hentges, Gudrun. "Das Plädoyer für eine ‚deutsche Leitkultur'-Steilvorlage für die extreme Rechte?," in: Butterwegge, Christoph et al. (eds.). *Themen der Rechten-Theme der Mitte*. Opladen: Leske u. Budrich, 2002, pp. 95–121.

Herrmann, Steffen K. "Gespräch und Gewalt. Verantwortung und Verletzbarkeit im Denken von Lévinas," in: Krämer, Sybille and Elke Koch (eds.). *Gewalt in der Sprache. Rhetoriken verletzenden Sprechens*. Munich: Wilhelm Fink, 2010, pp.157–78.

Herzig, Arno. *Jüdische Geschichte in Deutschland. Von den Anfängen bis zur Gegenwart*. Munich: C.H. Beck, 2002.

Herzl, Theodor. *Altneuland*. Leipzig: Seemann, [1902].
——. *Der Judenstaat. Versuch einer modernen Lösung der Judenfrage*. Vienna: M. Breitenstein's Verlags-Buchhandlung, 1896.
Herzog, Hillary Hope. *Vienna is different. Jewish writers in Austria from the fin de siècle to the present*. Oxford: Berghahn, 2011.
Hess, Jonathan M. "Fictions of a German-Jewish Public. Ludwig Jacobowski's *Werther the Jew* and Its Readers," in: *Jewish Social Studies*. 11 (2), 2005, pp. 202–230.
Hessel, Franz. *Der Kramladen des Glücks*. Frankfurt am Main: Literarische Anstalt Rütten & Loening, 1913.
——. *Pariser Romanze: Papiere eines Verschollenen*. Berlin: Ernst Rowohlt Verlag, 1920.
——. *Spazieren in Berlin*. Berlin: Bloomsbury, 2012.
——. *Walking in Berlin: a flaneur in the capital*. Translated by Amanda de Marco. London: Scribe Publications, 2016.
Hettche, Matt. "Christian Wolff," in: Zalta, Edward N. (ed.). *The Stanford Encyclopedia of Philosophy*, 2014: http://plato.stanford.edu/archives/win2014/entries/wolff-christian [June 2016].
Hobsbawm, Eric, and Terence Ranger (eds.). *The Invention of Tradition*. Cambridge University Press, 1983.
Hobsbawm, Eric. *Interesting Times. A Twentieth-Century Life*. New York: Pantheon Books, 2007.
Hoffmeister, Gerhart (ed.). *Der moderne deutsche Schelmenroman. Interpretationen*. Amsterdam: Rodopi, 1985/1986.
Hoffmeister, Werner. "Satirische Elemente in Joseph Roths *Radetzkymarsch*," in: *Modern Language Studies*. 3 (2), 1973, pp.106–113.
Hofmann, Michael. *Interkulturelle Literaturwissenschaft. Eine Einführung*. Paderborn: Fink/UTB 2006.
——. "Handicap Islam? Die Sarrazin-Debatte als Herausforderung des deutsch-türkischen Diskurses," in: Ozil, Şeyda, Yasemin Dayıoğlu-Yücel, and Michael Hofmann (eds.). *Türkisch-deutscher Kulturkontakt und Kulturtransfer. Kontroversen und Lernprozesse*. Göttingen: Vandenhoeck & Ruprecht, 2011, pp. 33–44.
——. "Romantic Rebellion: Feridun Zaimoglu and Anti-bourgeois Tradition," in: Cheesman, Tom, and Karin E. Yeşilada (eds.). *Feridun Zaimoglu*. Oxford: Peter Lang, 2012, pp. 239–258.
Holzinger, Michael (ed.). *Arthur Schnitzler, Jugend in Wien: Eine Autobiographie. Entstanden 1915–1918*. Berliner Ausgabe, 2014.
Horch, Hans-Otto, and Itta Schedletzky. "Die deutsch-jüdische Literatur und ihre Geschichte," in: Schoeps, Julius H. (ed.). *Neues Lexikon des Judentums*. Gütersloh: Bertelsmann-Lexikon-Verlag, 1998.
——. "Was heißt und zu welchem Ende studiert man deutsch-jüdische Literaturgeschichte? Prolegomena zu einem Forschungsprojekt," in: *German Life and Letters*. 49, 1996, pp. 124–135.
"Hunderttausend italienische Arbeiter kommen," in: *Frankfurter Allgemeine Zeitung*. 21 December, 1955. Reprinted in: Göktürk, Deniz, David Gramling, Anton Kaes, and Andreas Langenohl (eds.). *Transit Deutschland. Debatten zu Nation und Migration*. Paderborn: Konstanz University Press, 2011, pp. 45–6.

Hughes, Jon. *Facing Modernity: Fragmentation, Culture, and Identity in Joseph Roth's Writing in the 1920s*. London: Maney Publishing, 2006.
Huret, Jules (ed.). *Enquête sur l'évolution littéraire*. Charpentier, 1891.
Huyssen, Andreas. "The Disturbance of Vision in Vienna Modernism," in: *Modernism/Modernity*. 5(3), 1998, pp. 33–47.
——. "The Inevitability of Nation: German Intellectuals after Unification," in: *October*. 61, 1992, pp. 65–73.
Isenberg, Noah. *Between Redemption and Doom. The Strains of German-Jewish Modernism*. Lincoln/London: University of Nebraska Press, 1999.
Jacob, Benno. "Prinzipielle Bemerkungen zu einer zionistischen Schrift," in: *Der Morgen*. 5, 1927, p. 529.
Jacobowski, Ludwig. *Werther, der Jude*. Dritte Auflage. Dresden: Pierson, 1898.
——. *Werther, der Jude. Roman*. Fünfte Auflage. Dresden: Pierson, 1905.
Jacobs, Jürgen. "Bildungsroman und Picaroroman. Versuch einer Abgrenzung," in: Hoffmeister, Gerhart (ed.). *Der moderne deutsche Schelmenroman. Interpretationen*. Amsterdam: Rodopi, 1985/1986, pp. 9–19.
Jandl, Paul. "Generation Lada: Dimitré Dinev—ein bulgarischer Schriftsteller in Berlin," in: *Neue Zürcher Zeitung*, 18 December 2003: http://www.nzz.ch/article99L38-1.341448 [March 2017].
Jarausch, Konrad H. (ed.). *After Unity: Reconfiguring German Identities*. Providence: Berghahn, 1997.
Jordan, Jim. "Identity, Irony and Denial: Navid Kermani's *Kurzmitteilung*," in: Haines, Brigid, Stephen Parker, and Colin Riordan (eds.). *Aesthetics and Politics in Modern German Culture: Festschrift in Honour of Rhys W. Williams*. Oxford: Peter Lang, 2010, pp. 165–77.
——. "More Than a Metaphor: The Passing of the Two Worlds Paradigm in German-Language Diasporic Literature," in: *German Life and Letters*. 59 (4), 2006, pp. 488–99.
Judt, Tony. *A Grand Illusion? An Essay on Europe*. New York/London: New York University Press, 1996/2011.
Jung, Jochen. "Einer dieser Typen von Scientology," in: *Die Zeit*. 16 August 2007: http://www.zeit.de/2007/34/L-Kermani [March 2017].
Kaiser, Birgit M. (ed.). *Singularity and Transnational Poetics*. New York: Routledge, 2015.
Kanak Attak, "Kanak Attak und Basta!": http://www.kanak-attak.de/ka/about.html [March 2017].
Kaschuba, Wolfgang. "Wie Fremde gemacht werden," in: *Tagesspiegel*. 14 January 2007. Reprinted in: Göktürk, Deniz, David Gramling, Anton Kaes, and Andreas Langenohl (eds.). *Transit Deutschland. Debatten zu Nation und Migration*. Paderborn: Konstanz University Press, 2011, pp. 487–91.
Kerbs, Diethart, and Jürgen Reulecke (eds.). *Handbuch der deutschen Reformbewegungen 1880–1933*. Wuppertal: Peter Hammer, 1998.
Kermani, Navid. *Gott ist schön: Das ästhetische Erleben des Koran*, Munich: C.H. Beck, 1999.
——. *Iran: Die Revolution der Kinder*. Munich: C.H. Beck, 2000.

——. *Kurzmitteilung*. Zürich: Ammann Verlag, 2007.
——. *Ungläubiges Staunen*. München: C.H. Beck, 2015.
——. *Wer ist wir. Deutschland und seine Muslime*. Munich: C.H.Beck, 2009.
——. "Rede zur Feierstunde 65 Jahre Grundgesetz": https://www.bundestag.de/dokumente/textarchiv/2014/-/280688 [March 2017].
——. "Was ist deutsch an der deutschen Literatur?," in: Vogel, Bernhard /Konrad-Adenauer-Stiftung e.V. (ed.). *Was eint uns? Verständigung der Gesellschaft über gemeinsame Grundlagen*. Freiburg: Herder Verlag, 2008, pp. 78–98.
Kilcher, Andreas B. (ed.). *Metzler Lexikon der deutsch-jüdischen Literatur. Jüdische Autorinnen und Autoren deutscher Sprache von der Aufklärung bis zur Gegenwart*. Stuttgart/Weimar: J.B. Metzler, 2000.
——. "Interpretationen eines kulturellen Zwischenraums. Die Debatte um die deutsch-jüdische Literatur 1900 bis 1933," in: Schoeps, Julius H., Karl E. Grözinger, Willi Jasper, and Gert Mattenklott (eds.). *Deutsch-Jüdischer Parnaß. Rekonstruktion einer Debatte*. Menora: Jahrbuch für deutsch-jüdische Geschichte, 13. Berlin/Vienna: Philo, 2002, pp. 289–312.
——. "Was ist 'deutsch-jüdische Literatur'? Eine historische Diskursanalyse," in: *Weimarer Beiträge*. 45 (4), 1999, pp. 485–517.
Koch, Klaus. "The End of Empire and the Beginning of Nostalgia," in: Brix, Emil et al. (eds.). *The Decline of Empires*. Vienna: Verlag für Geschichte und Politik, 2011, pp. 174–83.
Köhn, Eckhardt. *Straßenrausch. Flanerie und kleine Form. Versuch zur Literaturgeschichte des Flaneurs bis 1933*. Berlin: Das Arsenal, 1989.
Kontje, Todd. *German Orientalisms*. Ann Arbor: University of Michigan Press, 2004.
Kőrösi, Zuszanna, and Adrienne Molnár. *Carrying a Secret in My Heart...: Children of Political Victims of the Revolution, 1956 Hungary—An Oral History*. Budapest: Central European University Press, 2002.
—— "The handing down of experiences in families of the politically condemned in Communist Hungary," in: *9th International Oral History Conference*. Gothenburg, 1996, pp. 1160–7.
Köster, Thomas. "'Ich bin durchs Schreiben im Leben angekommen.' Terézia Mora im Gespräch." Goethe Institut. June 2010: http://www.goethe.de/ins/it/lp/prj/lit/bue/gelit/de6062887.htm [March 2017].
Krämer, Sybille, and Elke Koch (eds.). *Gewalt in der Sprache. Rhetoriken verletzenden Sprechens*. Paderborn/Munich: Wilhelm Fink, 2010.
Kraus, Karl. "Die demolirte Literatur I," in: *Wiener Rundschau*. 1, November 1896, pp. 19–27.
——. "Die demolirte Literatur II," in: *Wiener Rundschau*. 2, Dezember 1896, pp. 68–72.
Krobb, Florian. "Scheidewege. Zum Judenbild in deutschen Romanen der 1890er Jahre," in: Ó Dochartaigh, Pól (ed.). *Jews in German Literature Since 1945: German-Jewish Literature?* Amsterdam/Atlanta: Rodopi, 2000, pp. 1–20.
Krojanker, Gustav (ed.). *Juden in der deutschen Literatur. Essays über zeitgenössische Schriftsteller*. Berlin: Welt-Verlag, 1922.

Kuch, Hannes. "Sprache, Gabe, Gewalt. Lacan und die symbolische Verletzbarkeit," in: Krämer, Sybille, and Elke Koch (eds.). *Gewalt in der Sprache. Rhetoriken des verletzenden Sprechens*. Paderborn/Munich: Wilhelm Fink Verlag, 2010, pp. 179–99.

Küchemann, Fridtjof. "Scheiden tut weh—Zsuzsa Bánk und ihr Roman 'Der Schwimmer,'" in: *Frankfurter Allgemeine Zeitung*. 22 August 2002: http://www.faz.net/aktuell/feuilleton/buecher/rezensionen/belletristik/debuet-scheiden-tut-weh-zsuzsa-bank-und-ihr-roman-der-schwimmer-174414.html [March 2017].

Kühn, Heinz. *Memorandum des Beauftragten der Bundesregierung*. Bonn, 1979. Reprinted as "Stand und Weiterentwicklung der Integration der ausländischen Arbeitnehmer und ihrer Familien in der Bundesrepublik Deutschland," in: Göktürk, Deniz, David Gramling, Anton Kaes, and Andreas Langenohl (eds.). *Transit Deutschland: Debatten zu Nation und Migration*. München: Wilhelm Fink Verlag, 2011, pp. 358–60.

Ladd, Brian. *Ghosts of Berlin: Confronting German History in the Urban Landscape*. Chicago: Chicago University Press, 1997.

Lamla, Jörn. "Consuming Authenticity: A Paradoxical Dynamic in Contemporary Capitalism," in: Vannini, Phillip, and J. Patrick Williams (eds.). *Authenticity in Culture, Self, and Society*. London/New York: Routledge, 2009, pp. 171–186.

Landwehr, Margarethe Johanna. "Modernist Aesthetics in Joseph Roth's *Radetzkymarsch*: The Crisis of Meaning and the Role of the Reader," in: *German Quarterly*. 76 (4), 2003, pp. 398–410.

Laqueur, Walter. *A History of Zionism*. New York: Schocken Books, 1976.

Le Rider, Jacques. *Modernity and Crises of Identity: Culture and Society in Fin-De-Siecle Vienna*. New York: Continuum, 1993.

Ledanff, Susanne. *Hauptstadtphantasien. Berliner Stadtlektüren in der Gegenwartsliteratur 1989–2008*. Bielefeld: Aisthesis, 2009.

Leggewie, Claus. "Begriffsgeschichte Multikulturalismus. Claus Leggewie im Gespräch mit Susanne Stemmler," in: Stemmler, Susanne (ed.). *Multikultur 2.0. Willkommen im Einwanderungsland Deutschland*. Göttingen: Wallstein, 2011, pp. 37–51.

Lengl, Szilvia. *Interkulturelle Frauenfiguren im deutschsprachigen Roman der Gegenwart*. Dresden: Thelem, 2012.

Lentin, Alana. *Racism & Anti-Racism in Europe*. London: Pluto Press, 2004.

——. "Post-race, Post Politics. The Paradoxical Rise of Culture after Multiculturalism," in: *Ethnic and Racial Studies*. 37 (8), 2014, pp. 1268–85.

Lentin, Alana, and Gavin Titley. *The Crises of Multiculturalism. Racism in a Neoliberal Age*. New York: Palgrave Macmillan, 2011.

Liska, Vivian. *When Kafka Says We. Uncommon Communities in German-Jewish Literature*. Bloomington/Indianapolis: Indiana University Press, 2009.

Literaturen. "Ich bin ein Teil der deutschen Literatur, so deutsch wie Kafka," in: *Literaturen*. 4, 2005, pp. 26–31.

Littler, Margaret. "Intimacy and Affect in Turkish-German Writing: Emine Sevgi Özdamar's 'The Courtyard in the Mirror,'" in: *Journal of Intercultural Studies*. 29 (3), 2008, pp. 331–45.

———. "Between Romantic Love and War Machine: *Liebesbrand*," in: Cheesman, Tom, and Karin E. Yeşilada (eds.). *Feridun Zaimoglu*. Oxford: Peter Lang, 2012, pp. 219–38.

Lorenz, Dagmar C. (ed.). *A Companion to the Works of Arthur Schnitzler*. Rochester: Camden House, 2003.

Lotman, Jurij. *The Structure of the Artistic Text*. Translated from the Russian by Gail Lenhoff and Ronald Vroon. Ann Arbor: University of Michigan, 1977.

Lowenstein, Steven M. "Was Urbanization Harmful to Jewish Tradition and Identity in Germany?," in: Mendelssohn, Ezra (ed.). *People of the City. Jews and the Urban Challenge*. New York: Oxford University Press, 1999, pp. 80–106.

Luft, Stefan. *Abschied von Multikulti*, in: *Tagesspiegel*. 17 January 2008, s.p.

Lughofer, Johann Georg, and Mira Miladinović Zalaznik (eds.). *Joseph Roth: Europäisch-jüdischer Schriftsteller und österreichischer Universalist*. Berlin/Boston: De Gruyter, 2011.

Lukács, Georg. "Der Augenblick und die Formen" (1908), in: Lukács, Georg. *Die Seele und die Formen*. Berlin: Egon Fleischel & Co, 1911, pp. 231–63.

Lukács, Georg. "Radetzkymarsch," in: *Literaturnaja Gazeta* (Moscow), 8 August 1939. Cited in the German translation by Hackert, Fritz. *Kulturpessimismus und Erzählform: Studien zu Joseph Roths Leben und Werk*, Bern: Herbert Lang, 1967.

Lukács, Georg. *The Historical Novel*, Moscow, 1937. Translated by Hannah and Stanley Mitchell. London: Merlin Press, 1962.

Luthar, Breda and Maruša Pušnik. "The Lure of Utopia: Socialist Everyday Spaces," in: Luthar, Breda and Maruša Pušnik (eds.). *Remembering Utopia: The Culture of Everyday Life in Socialist Yugoslavia*. Washington: New Academia Publishing, 2010, pp. 1–36.

Lynch, Kevin. *The Image of the City*. Cambridge, Massachusetts/London: The MIT Press, 1960.

Mach, Ernst. *Die Analyse der Empfindungen und das Verhältnis des Physischen zum Psychischen*. Jena: Gustav Fischer, 1922.

Mader, Barbara. "Dinev: wo die 'Engelszungen' herkommen," in: *kurier.at*. 05 December 2011: https://kurier.at/kultur/dinev-wo-die-engelszungen-herkommen/735.454 [March 2017].

Magris, Claudio. *Der habsburgische Mythos in der modernen österreichischen Literatur*. Vienna: Paul Zsolnay Verlag, 1963/2000.

Majtényi, Balázs, and György Majtényi. *A Contemporary History of Exclusion: The Roma Issue in Hungary from 1945 to 2015*. Budapest: Central European University Press, 2016.

Marven, Lyn, and Brigid Haines (eds.). *Contemporary Women's Writing in German: Changing the Subject*. Oxford: Oxford University Press, 2004.

Marven, Lyn, and Stuart Taberner (eds.). *Emerging German-Language Novelists of the Twenty-First Century*. Rochester: Camden House, 2011.

Matthes, Frauke. "Islam in the West: Perceptions and Self-Perceptions of Muslims in Navid Kermani's *Kurzmitteilung*," in: *German Life and Letters*. 64 (2), 2011, pp. 305–16.

———. "Männliche Sehnsucht in (türkisch-)deutscher Gegenwart in Feridun Zaimoğlus *Liebesbrand*," in: *Studien zur deutschen Sprache und Literatur*. 24(2), 2010, pp. 85–102.

Matthias, Bettina. "Arthur Schnitzler's *Fräulein Else* and the end of the bourgeois tragedy," in: *Women in German Yearbook*. 18, 2002, pp. 248–66.
McCagg, William O. "Gypsy Policy in Socialist Hungary and Czechoslovakia, 1945–1989," in: *Nationalities Papers: The Journal of Nationalism and Ethnicity*. 19 (3), 1991, pp. 313–336.
McCarthy, Cameron (ed.). *Mobilized Identities: Mediated Subjectivity and Cultural Crisis in the Neoliberal Era*. Champaign, Illinois: Common Ground Publishing, 2013.
McGowan, Moray. "'The Bridge of the Golden Horn': Istanbul, Europe and the 'Fractured Gaze from the West' in Turkish Writing in Germany," in: Andy A. Hollis, *Beyond Boundaries—Textual Representations of Europen Identities*. [Yearbook of European Studies]. 15, 2000, Amsterdam: Rodopi, pp. 53–69.
———. "Brücken und Brücken-Köpfe: Wandlungen einer Metapher in der türkisch-deutschen Literatur," in: Durzak, Manfred, and Nilüfer Kuruyazıcır (eds.). *Die andere deutsche Literatur. Istanbuler Vorträge*. Würzburg: Königshausen & Neumann, 2004, pp. 31–40.
Meinecke, Friedrich. *Cosmopolitanism and the Nation State*. Princeton: Princeton University Press, 1970 [1928].
Melas, Natalie. "Versions of incommensurability," in: *World Literature Today*. 69 (2), 1995, pp. 275–288.
Mendelsohn, Ezra (ed.). *People of the City. Jews and the Urban Challenge*. New York: Oxford University Press, 1999.
Mendes-Flohr, Paul. "The Berlin Jew as Cosmopolitan," in: Bilsky, Emily D. (ed.). *Berlin Metropolis. Jews and the New Culture 1890–1918*. Berkeley/Los Angeles: University of California Press; New York: The Jewish Museum, 1999, pp.14–30.
Mendes-Flohr, Paul. *German Jews. A Dual Identity*. New Haven/London: Yale University Press, 1999.
Merz, Friedrich. "Einwanderung und Identität," in: *Die Welt*. 25 October 2000, s.p.
Metzler, Tobias. "Secularization and Pluralism. Urban Jewish Cultures in Early Twentieth Century Berlin," in: *Journal of Urban History*. 37 (6), 2011, pp. 871–896.
Meurer, Petra, Martina Ölke, and Sabine Wilmes (eds.). *Interkulturelles Lernen*. Bielefeld: Aisthesis, 2009.
Micksch, Jürgen (ed.). *Deutschland—Einheit in kultureller Vielfalt*. Frankfurt am Main: Otto Lembeck, 1991.
Miller, Michael L., and Scott Ury (eds.). *Cosmopolitanism, Nationalism and the Jews of East Central Europe*. London/New York: Routledge, 2014.
———. "The End of Jewishness?," in: *European Review of History: Revue européenne d'histoire*. 17 (3), 2010, pp. 337–359.
Minnaard, Liesbeth. *New Germans, New Dutch. Literary Interventions*. Amsterdam: University Press, 2008.
Mora, Terézia. *Alle Tage*. München: Random House, 2006.
———. *Day in day out*. Translated by Michael Henry Heim. New York: HarperCollins, 2007.
———. "Das Kreter-Spiel": http://www.tereziamora.de [March 2017].
Mosse, George L. *German Jews Beyond Judaism*. Bloomington: Indiana University Press, 1985.

———. *Jews and the German War Experience, 1914–1918*. New York: Leo Baeck Institute, 1977.
———. "Jewish Emancipation. Between *Bildung* and Respectability," in: Reinharz, Jehuda, and Walter Schatzberg (eds.). *The Jewish Response to German Culture. From the Enlightenment to the Second World War*. Hanover: University Press of New England, 1985, pp. 1–16.
Müller, Jan-Werner (ed.). *Memory and Power in Post-War Europe. Studies in the Presence of the Past*. Cambridge University Press, 2002.
Müller, Lothar. "Die Großstadt als Ort der Moderne," in: Scherpe, Klaus (ed.). *Die Unwirklichkeit der Städte*. Reinbek bei Hamburg: Rowohlt, 1988, pp. 14–36.
Müller, Lothar. "Peripatetische Stadtlektüre. Franz Hessels *Spazieren in Berlin*.," in: Opitz, Michael and Jörg Plath (eds.). *Genieße froh, was du nicht hast. Der Flaneur Franz Hessel*. Würzburg: Königshausen & Neumann, 1997, pp. 75–104
Nachama, Andreas, Julius Hans Schoeps and Hermann Simon (eds.). *Jews in Berlin*. Oxford: Berghahn, 2002.
Nádas, Péter. "Ein Lob des doppelten Blicks," in: *Die Zeit*. 31 December 2002.
Nancy, Jean-Luc. *The Inoperative Community*. Minneapolis/Oxford: University of Minnesota Press, 1991.
———. *Being Singular Plural*. Translated by Richardson, R.D. & O'Byrne, A.E. Stanford: Stanford University Press, 2000.
Neubaur, Caroline. "Mutter ohne Mythos," in: *Literaturen*. 4, 2003, pp. 12–19.
Niedermeier, Cornelia, and Karl Wagner (eds.). *Literatur um 1900. Texte der Jahrhundertwende neu gelesen*. Köln/Weimar/Vienna: Böhlau Verlag, 2001.
Nietzsche, Friedrich. *The Gay Science: With a Prelude in Rhymes and an Appendix of Songs*. New York: Random, 1974.
Nousek, Katrina. "A future-oriented *Zeitrechnung*: Narrating post-communist temporality and subjectivity in Zsuzsa Bánk's *Der Schwimmer* (2002)," in: *German Life and Letters*. 68 (2), 2015, pp. 302–323.
Ökumenischer Vorbereitungsausschuss für den Tag des ausländischen Mitbürgers. "'Wir leben in der Bundesrepublik in einer multikulturellen Gesellschaft.' Thesen vom 24. November 1980, Tag des ausländischen Mitbürgers," in: Micksch, Jürgen (ed.). *Deutschland—Einheit in kultureller Vielfalt*. Frankfurt am Main: Otto Lembeck, 1991, pp. 182–185.
Opitz, Michael, and Jörg Plath (eds.). *Genieße froh, was du nicht hast. Der Flaneur Franz Hessel*. Würzburg: Königshausen & Neumann, 1997.
Özdamar, Emine Sevgi. *Der Hof im Spiegel. Erzählungen*. Köln: Kiepenheuer & Witsch, 2001/2005.
———. *Die Brücke vom goldenen Horn*. Cologne: Kiepenheuer & Witsch, 1998.
———. *The Bridge of the Golden Horn*. Translated by Martin Chalmers. London: Profile Books, 2007.
Ozil, Şeyda, Yasemin Dayıoğlu-Yücel, and Michael Hofmann (eds.). *Türkisch-deutscher Kulturkontakt und Kulturtransfer. Kontroversen und Lernprozesse*. Göttingen: Vandenhoeck & Ruprecht, 2011.
Parnes, Ohad et al. (eds.). *Das Konzept der Generation. Eine Wissenschafts- und Kulturgeschichte*. Frankfurt am Main: Suhrkamp Verlag, 2008.

Paul, Georgina. "The Privatization of Community: The Legacy of Collectivism in the Post-Socialist Literature of Eastern Germany," in: *Oxford German Studies*. 38 (2), 2009, pp. 288–98.

Pautz, Hartwig. "The politics of identity in Germany: the *Leitkultur* debate," in: *Race & Class*. 46 (4), 2005, pp. 39–52.

Pazarkaya, Yüksel. "Literatur ist Literatur," in: Ackermann, Irmgard, and Harald Weinrich (eds.). *Eine nicht nur deutsche Literatur. Zur Standortbestimmungen der Ausländerliteratur*. Munich: Piper, 1986, pp. 59–69.

Peck, Abraham J. (ed.). *The German-Jewish Legacy in America, 1938–1988: From 'Bildung' to the Bill of Rights*. Detroit: Wayne State University Press, 1989.

Peck, Jeffrey et al. "Natives, Strangers, and Foreigners. Constituting Germans by Constructing Others," in: Jarausch, Konrad H. (ed.). *After Unity: Reconfiguring German Identities*. Providence: Berghahn, 1997, pp. 61–102.

Perloff, Marjorie. *Edge of Irony: Modernism in the Shadow of the Habsburg Empire*. Chicago: University of Chicago Press, 2016.

Peters, Ulrike. "Das Problem des Judentums bei Richard Beer-Hofmann," in: *Zeitschrift für Religions- und Geistesgeschichte*. 48 (3), 1996, pp. 262–271.

Petry, Yves. "Besta je wel echt?," in: *De Morgen*. 30 March 2016, s.p.

Pfahl-Traughber, Armin. "Die fehlende Trennschärfe des 'Islamophobie'-Konzepts für die Vorurteilsforschung," in: Botsch, Gideon, Olaf Glöckner, Christoph Kopke, and Michael Spieker (eds.). *Islamophobie und Antisemitismus: Ein umstrittener Vergleich*. Berlin/Boston: Walter de Gruyter, 2012, pp. 11–28.

Pfeiffer, Joachim. *Tod und Erzählen. Wege der literarischen Moderne um 1900*. Tübingen: Niemeyer, 1997.

Philipsen, Bart. "Literature and the Profane Community in Jean-Luc Nancy's *Being Singular Plural*," in: Kaiser, Birgit M. (ed.). *Singularity and Transnational Poetics*. New York: Routledge, 2015, pp. 27–46.

Plath, Jörg. *Liebhaber der Großstadt. Ästhetische Konzeptionen im Werk Franz Hessels*. Paderborn: Igel Verlag, 1994.

Pollmeier, Andrea. "Dynamik des Dreiecks: 'Die hellen Tage' von Zsusza Bánk," in: *Edition Faust, Faust Kulturstiftung*. 16 February 2011: http://faustkultur.de/237-0-Gespraech-mit-Zsusza-Bnk.html#.V9eoxFv5jIU [March 2017].

Potdevin, Arndt. "Franz Hessel und die Neue Sachlichkeit," in: Sprengel, Peter (ed.). *Berlin-Flaneure. Stadt-Lektüre in Roman und Feuilleton, 1910–1930*. Berlin: Weidler Verlag, 1998, pp. 101–135.

Pulzer, Peter G.J. *The Rise of Political Anti-Semitism in Germany and Austria*. Cambridge, Massachusetts: Harvard University Press, 1988 [1964].

Radisch, Iris. "Es gibt nun mal Menschen, die Jutta heißen," in: *Die Zeit*. 22 September 2016, p. 41.

Raffel, Eva. *Vertraute Fremde. Das östliche Judentum im Werk von Joseph Roth und Arnold Zweig*. Tübingen: Günter Narr Verlag, 2002.

Rancière, Jacques. "The Politics of Literature," in: *SubStance*. 33 (1/103), 2004, pp. 10–24.

Raptis, Konstantinos. "Discord or Achievement? Reflections on the Habsburg Empire, 1848–1918," in: *Historein*. 5, 2005, pp. 118–129.

Raymond, Cathy. "Masked in Music: Hidden Meaning in Schnitzler's *Fräulein Else*," in: *Monatshefte*. 85.2, 1993, pp. 170–88.
Reckwitz, Andreas. *Das hybride Subjekt. Eine Theorie der Subjektkulturen von der bürgerlichen Moderne zur Postmoderne*. Weilerswist: Velbrück, 2006.
Redfield, Marc. *Phantom Formations. Aesthetic Ideology and the Bildungsroman*. Ithaca/London: Cornell University Press, 1996.
Reich-Ranicki, Marcel. *Über Ruhestörer: Juden in der deutschen Literatur*. Stuttgart: Deutsche Verlags-Anstalt, 1989.
Reidel-Schrewe, Ursula. "Im Niemandsland zwischen Indikativ und Konjunktiv," in: *Modern Austrian Literature*. 24, 1991, pp. 59–78.
Reinharz, Jehuda, and Walter Schatzberg (eds.). *The Jewish Response to German Culture: From the Enlightenment to the Second World War*. Hanover: University Press of New England, 1985.
Robert Bosch Stiftung. "Pressemitteilung: 26. Adelbert-von-Chamisso-Preis in München verliehen," 4 March 2010: http://www.bosch-stiftung.de/content/language1/html/28641.asp [March 2017].
Robertson, Ritchie. *The 'Jewish Question' in German Literature, 1749–1939: Emancipation and its Discontents*. New York: Oxford University Press, 1999.
Rommelspacher, Birgit. *Anerkennung und Ausgrenzung. Deutschland als multikulturelle Gesellschaft*. Frankfurt/New York: Campus Verlag, 2002.
Rösch, Heidi. *Migrationsliteratur im interkulturellen Kontext*. Frankfurt am Main: Verlag für interkulturelle Kommunikation, 1992.
Rosenfeld, Sidney. "Joseph Roths *Hiob*: Glaube und Heimat im Bild des Raumes," in: *The Journal of English and Germanic Philology*. 66 (4), 1964, pp. 489–500.
Roth, Joseph. *Briefe 1911–1939*. Edited by Hermann Kesten. Köln: Kiepenheuer & Witsch, 1970.
———. *Die Kapuzinergruft*, in: Joseph Roth, *Werke 6. Romane und Erzählungen 1936–1940*. Edited by Fritz Hackert. Köln: Kiepenheuer & Witsch, 1989, pp. 225–345.
———. *Hiob*. München: Deutscher Taschenbuch Verlag DTV, 2002.
———. *Job. The Story of a Simple Man*. Translated by Ross Benjamin. Brooklyn: Archipelago Books, 2010.
———. *Juden auf Wanderschaft*, Berlin: Verlag Die Schmiede, 1927.
———. *Radetzkymarsch. Roman*. Munich: Deutscher Taschenbuch Verlag DTV, 2009.
———. *The Radetzky March*. Translated by Joachim Neugroschel. London: Penguin Books, 1995.
———. *Werke 3. Das journalistische Werk 1929–1939*. Edited by Klaus Westermann. Cologne: Kiepenheuer & Witsch, 1989, pp. 153–163.
Ruf, Werner. *Der Islam. Schrecken des Abendlandes. Wie sich der Westen sein Feindbild konstruiert*. Cologne: PapyRossa, 2012.
Rürup, Reinhard. *Emanzipation und Anti-Semitismus: Studien zur 'Judenfrage' der bürgerlichen Gesellschaft*. Göttingen: Vandenhoeck & Ruprecht, 1975.
Rutherford, Jonathan. "The Third Space. Interview with Homi K. Bhabha.", in: Rutherford, Jonathan (ed.). *Identity: Community, Culture, Difference*. London: Lawrence & Wishart, 1990, pp. 207–21.

Said, Edward. *Covering Islam. How the Media and the Experts Determine How We See The Rest of The World*. London: Random House, 1997/1981.
Sarrazin, Thilo. *Deutschland schafft sich ab. Wie wir unser Land aufs Spiel setzen*. Munich: Deutscher Verlags-Anstalt, 2010.
Savin, Andrada. "'Auswanderung im Familiengedächtnis' als Themenkomplex und Komposition im deutschsprachigen Gegenwartsroman," in: *Lingua. Language and Culture*. 2, 2012, pp.167–174.
Scanlan, Sean. "Introduction: Nostalgia," in: *Iowa Journal of Cultural Studies*. 5(1), 2004, pp. 3–9.
Schardt, Michael. "Jacobowski, Ludwig," in: Kilcher, Andreas B. (ed.). *Metzler Lexikon der deutsch-jüdischen Literatur. Jüdische Autorinnen und Autoren deutscher Sprache von der Aufklärung bis zur Gegenwart*. Stuttgart/Weimar: J.B. Metzler, 2000, pp. 271–2.
Scheichl, Sigurd Paul. "*Juden auf Wanderschaft*—*2009 neu gelesen*," in: Lughofer, Johann Georg, and Mira Miladinović Zalaznik (eds.). *Joseph Roth: Europäisch-jüdischer Schriftsteller und österreichischer Universalist*. Berlin/Boston: De Gruyter, 2011, pp. 11–22.
Scherer, Stefan. "Richard Beer-Hofmann und das Judentum," in: Eke, Norbert Otto, and Günter Helmes (eds.). *Richard Beer-Hofmann (1866–1945). Studien zu seinem Werk*. Würzburg: Königshausen & Neumann, 1993, pp. 13–33.
——. *Richard Beer-Hofmann und die Wiener Moderne*, Tübingen: Max Niemeyer/De Gruyter, 1993.
Scherpe, Klaus (ed.). *Die Unwirklichkeit der Städte. Großstadtdarstellungen zwischen Moderne und Postmoderne*. Reinbek bei Hamburg: Rowohlt, 1988.
——. "Nonstop nach Nowhere City? Wandlungen der Symbolisierung, Wahrnehmung und Semiotik der Stadt in der Literatur der Moderne," in: Scherpe, Klaus (ed.). *Die Unwirklichkeit der Städte. Großstadtdarstellungen zwischen Moderne und Postmoderne*. Reinbek bei Hamburg: Rowohlt, 1988, pp. 129–152.
Schiffauer, Werner. *Parallelgesellschaften. Wie viel Wertekonsens braucht unsere Gesellschaft? Für eine kluge Politik der Differenz*. Bielefeld: Transcript, 2008.
Schlör, Joachim. *Das Ich der Stadt. Debatten über Judentum und Urbanität, 1822–1938*. Berlin: Vandenhoeck & Ruprecht, 2005.
Schmitz, Helmut. "Einleitung: Von der nationalen zur internationalen Literatur," in: Schmitz, Helmut (ed.). *Von der nationalen zur internationalen Literatur. Transkulturelle deutschsprachige Literatur und Kultur im Zeitalter globaler Migration*. Amsterdam/New York: Rodopi, 2009, pp. 7–15.
Schneider, Gerd K. "The Social and Political Context of Arthur Schnitzler's *Reigen* in Berlin, Vienna, and New York: 1900–1933," in: Lorenz, Dagmar C. (ed.). *A Companion to the Works of Arthur Schnitzler*, Camden House, 2003, pp. 27–57.
Schnitzler, Arthur. *Fräulein Else: Novelle*. Berlin: Zsolnay, 1924.
——. *Fräulein Else: A Novelette*. Translated by F. H. Lyon. London: A. M. Philpot, 1925.
——. "Bekenntnis" (1904), in: Weiss, Robert O. (ed.). *Aphorismen und Betrachtungen II: Der Geist im Wort und der Geist in der Tat*. Frankfurt am Main: Fischer Taschenbuch, 1993, p. 109.
——. *Briefe 1913–1931*. Edited by Peter Michael Braunwarth et al. Frankfurt am Main: S. Fischer, 1984.

Schoeps, Julius H. (ed.). *Deutsch-jüdische Symbiose oder die mißglückte Emanzipation*. Darmstadt: Wissenschaftliche Buchgesellschaft, 1996.

——. "Theodor Herzl und die Affäre Dreyfus," in: Schoeps, Julius (ed.). *Deutschjüdische Symbiose oder die mißglückte Emanzipation*. Darmstadt: Wissenschaftliche Buchgesellschaft, 1996, pp. 325–342.

Schoeps, Julius H., Karl E. Grözinger, Willi Jasper, and Gert Mattenklott (eds.). *Deutsch-Jüdischer Parnaß. Rekonstruktion einer Debatte*. Menora: Jahrbuch für deutschjüdische Geschichte, 13. Berlin/Vienna: Philo, 2002.

Scholem, Gerschom. "Jews and Germans," in: *On Jews and Judaism in Crisis: Selected Essays*. Philadelphia: Paul Dry Books, 2012 [1976], pp. 71–92.

Schopenhauer, Arthur. "Aphorismen zur Lebensweisheit," in: Guth, Karl-Maria (ed.). Berlin: Hofenberg, 2016.

Schorske, Carl E. *Fin-de-Siècle Vienna: Politics and Culture*. New York: Random House, 1980.

Schwarz, Egon. "Arthur Schnitzler und das Judentum," in: Grimm, Gunter E. and Hans-Peter Bayersdörfer (eds.). *Im Zeichen Hiobs: Jüdische Schriftsteller und deutsche Literatur im 20. Jahrhundert*. Königstein: Athenäum, 1985.

Schwarz-Friesel, Monika, and Evyatar Friesel. "Gestern die Juden, heute die Muslime…"? Von den Gefahren falscher Analogien.," in: Botsch, Gideon, Olaf Glöckner, Christoph Kopke, and Michael Spieker (eds.). *Islamophobie und Antisemitismus: Ein umstrittener Vergleich*. Berlin/Boston: Walter de Gruyter, 2012, pp. 29–50.

Sebald, W.G. "Ein Kaddisch für Österreich—Über Joseph Roth," in: Sebald, W.G. *Unheimliche Heimat. Essays zur österreichischen Literatur*. Frankfurt am Main: Fischer Taschenbuch Verlag, 2012, pp. 104–17.

Seibel, Andrea, Hajo Schuhmacher, and Joachim Fahrun. "Mögen Sie keine Türken, Herr Sarrazin?," in: *Die Welt*. 29 Augus 2010: http://www.welt.de/politik/deutschland/article9255898/Moegen-Sie-keine-Tuerken-Herr-Sarrazin.html [March 2017].

——. "Thilo Sarrazin—'Ich bin kein Rassist'," in: *Berliner Morgenpost*. 28 October 2010: http://www.morgenpost.de/berlin-aktuell/article1385382/Thilo-Sarrazin-Ich-bin-kein-Rassist.html [March 2017].

Seiderer, Ute. *Flusspoeten und Ozeansucher. Konstruktionen von Kultur und Männlichkeit*. Würzburg: Verlag Königshausen und Neumann, 2009.

Şenocak, Zafer. *Deutschsein. Eine Aufklärungsschrift*. Hamburg-Bergedorf: Edition Körber Stiftung, 2011.

Seyhan, Azade. "From Istanbul to Berlin. Stations on the Road to a Transcultural/Translational Literature," in: *German Politics and Society*. 74 (23), 2005, pp. 152–170.

Sezgin, Hilal (ed.). *Manifest der Vielen. Deutschland erfindet sich neu*. Berlin, Blumenbar Verlag, 2011.

——. "Deutschland schafft mich ab," in: Sezgin, Hilal (ed.). *Manifest der Vielen. Deutschland erfindet sich neu*. Berlin, Blumenbar Verlag, 2011, p. 46.

Shafi, Monika. "Joint Ventures: Identity Politics and Travel in Novels by Emine Sevgi Özdamar and Zafer Şenocak," in: *Comparative Literature Studies*. 40 (2), 2003, pp. 193–214.

Shaya, Gregory. "The Flaneur, the Badaud, and the Making of a Mass Public in France, circa 1860–1910," in: *The American Historical Review*. 109 (1), 2004, pp. 41–77.

Sieg, Christian. "Von Alfred Döblin zu Terézia Mora: Stadt, Roman und Autorschaft im Zeitalter der Globalisierung," in: Amann, Wilhelm et al. (eds.). *Globalisierung und Gegenwartsliteratur. Konstellationen—Konzepte—Perspektiven.* Heidelberg: Synchron, 2010, pp.193–208.

Siemes, Christof. "Schwäne in goldenem Nebel," in: *Die Zeit*. 15, 6 April 2000: http://www.zeit.de/2000/15/200015.tutzingen_.xml/seite-2 [March 2017].

Simmel, Georg. "Die Großstädte und das Geistesleben," in: Theodor Petermann (ed.). *Die Grossstadt. Vorträge und Aufsätze zur Städteausstellung.* Dresden: Gehe-Stiftung, 1903, pp. 185–206.

——. "The Metropolis and Mental Life," in: Kurt H. Wolff (ed.). *The Sociology of Georg Simmel*. Translated by Kurt H. Wolff. New York/London: The Free Press, 1950/1964, pp. 409–424.

——. "Exkurs über den Fremden," in: Georg Simmel, *Soziologie. Untersuchungen über die Formen der Vergesellschaftung*. Berlin: Duncker & Humblot, 1908, pp. 509–12.

Skolnik, Jonathan. *Jewish Pasts, German Fictions*. Stanford: Stanford University Press, 2014.

Slavtcheva-Raiber, Anna. *Geschichte, Entwicklung und Sprachwerbetätigkeit der deutschen Schulen in Bulgarien im Zeitraum 1900–1939*. Mannheim, 2005. [Dissertation]

Slezkine, Yuri. *The Jewish Century*. Princeton/Oxford: Princeton University Press, 2004.

Sofka, James R. "Metternich's Theory of European Order: A Political Agenda for 'Perpetual Peace'," in: *The Review of Politics*. 60 (1), 1998, pp. 115–149.

Solçün, Sargut. "Literatur der türkischen Minderheit," in: Chiellino, Carmine (ed.). *Interkulturelle Literatur in Deutschland: Ein Handbuch*. Stuttgart: Metzler, 2000, pp. 138–144.

Sombart, Werner. *Die Juden und das Wirtschaftsleben*. Leipzig: Duncker & Humblot, 1911.

Sorkin, David. *The Transformation of German Jewry, 1780–1840*. New York: Oxford University Press, 1987.

——. "Emancipation and Assimilation. Two Concepts and their Application to German-Jewish History," in: *Leo Baeck Institute Yearbook*. 35, 1990, pp. 17–33.

Spector, Scott. "Beyond the Aesthetic Garden: Politics and Culture on the Margins of *Fin-de Siècle* Vienna," in: *Journal of the History of Ideas*. 59 (4), 1998, pp. 691–710.

——. "Forget assimilation: introducing subjectivity to German-Jewish history.," in: *Jewish History*. 20, 2006, pp. 349–361.

Spivak, Gayatri C. "Can the Subaltern Speak?," in: Nelson, Cary, and Lawrence Grossberg (eds.). *Marxism and the Interpretation of Culture*. Basingstoke: Macmillan Education, 1988, pp. 271–313.

Spohrer, Erika. "The Seeker-Consumer: Scientology and the Rhetoric of Consumerism," in: *Journal of Religion and Popular Culture*. 26 (1), 2014, pp.107–123.

Sprengel, Peter (ed.). *Berlin-Flaneure. Stadt-Lektüren in Roman und Feuilleton 1910–1930*. Berlin: Weidler Buchverlag, 1998.

Stanišić, Saša. "Three Myths of Immigrant Writing: A View from Germany," in: *Words Without Borders*. November 2008: http://wordswithoutborders.org/article/three-myths-of-immigrant-writing-a-view-from-germany#ixzz3YhoPp1VZ [March 2017].

Statistisches Bundesamt (Destatis). *Bevölkerung und Erwerbstätigkeit. Bevölkerung mit Migrationshintergrund. Ergebnisse des Mikrozensus 2015.* Statistisches Bundesamt (Destatis), 2017.
Statuten des löblichen militärischen Maria-Theresien-Ordens. Vienna: k.k. Hof- und Staatsdruckerey, 1811.
Stelzig, Eugene L. *The Romantic Subject in Autobiography. Rousseau & Goethe.* London/Charlottesville: University Press of Virginia, 2000.
Stemmler, Susanne (ed.). *Multikultur 2.0. Willkommen im Einwanderungsland Deutschland.* Göttingen: Wallstein, 2011.
Stoetzler, Marcel. *The State, the Nation, and the Jews. Liberalism and the Anti-Semitism Dispute in Bismarck's Germany.* Lincoln: University of Nebraska Press, 2008.
——. "Cultural difference in the national state: from trouser-selling Jews to unbridled multiculturalism," in: *Patterns of Prejudice.* 42 (3), 2008, pp. 245–279.
Strelka, Joseph P. (ed.). *Die Seele ... ist ein weites Land: Kritische Beiträge zum Werk Arthur Schnitzlers.* Bern: Peter Lang, 1996.
Suhr, Heidrun. "Ausländerliteratur: Minority Literature in the Federal Republic of Germany," in: *New German Critique.* 46, 1989, pp. 71–103.
Sundsbø, Astrid Ouahyb. *Grenzziehungen in der Stadt. Ethnische Kategorien und die Wahrnehmung und Bewertung von Wohnorten.* Wiesbaden: Springer, 2014.
Taylor, Charles. *Modern Social Imaginaries.* Durham and London: Duke University Press, 2004.
Teraoka, Arlene A. "Gastarbeiterliteratur: The Other speaks back.," in: *Cultural Critique.* 7, 1987, pp. 77–101.
Thompson, Bruce. "'Schlecht kommen wir beide dabei nicht weg!' Joseph Roth's satire on the Emperor Franz Joseph in his novel *Radetzkymarsch*," in: *Neophilologus.* 81, 1997, pp. 253–267.
Tibi, Bassam. *Europa ohne Identität. Die Krise der multikulturellen Gesellschaft.* München: Bertelsmann, 1998.
Todorova, Maria Nikolaeva. "Introduction: From Utopia to Propaganda and Back," in: Todorova, Maria Nikolaeva and Zsusza Gille (eds.). *Post-communist Nostalgia.* Oxford: Berghahn, 2002, pp. 1–16.
Tonkin, Kati. *Joseph Roth's March into History: From the Early Novels to 'Radetzkymarsch' and 'Die Kapuzinergruft'.* Rochester, New York: Camden House, 2008.
Treitschke, Heinrich von. "Unsere Aussichten," in: *Preußische Jahrbücher.* 44, 1879, pp. 559–576.
Turner, Victor. *The Ritual Process: Structure and Anti-Structure.* Chicago: Aldine Publishing, 1969.
Twist, Joseph. "'The Crossing of Love': The Inoperative Community and Romantic Love in Feridun Zaimoglu's 'Fünf klopfende Herzen, wenn die Liebe springt' and 'Hinterland," in: *German Life and Letters.* 67 (3), 2014, pp. 399–417.
Ulrich, Bernd, and Özlem Topçu. "Sind Muslime dümmer?," in: *Die Zeit.* 26 August, 2010: http://www.zeit.de/2010/35/Sarrazin/komplettansicht [March 2017].

Vaksberg, Tatiana, and Alexander Andreev. "Recalling the fate of Bulgaria's Turkish minority," in: *Deutsche Welle*. 24 December 2014: http://www.dw.com/en/recalling-the-fate-of-bulgarias-turkish-minority/a-18149416 [March 2017].
van Alphen, Ernst. "Configurations of Self. Modernism and Distraction," in: Eysteinsson, Astradur and Vivian Liska (eds.). *Modernism*. Amsterdam: John Benjamins Publishing Company, 2007, pp. 339–46.
van Rahden, Till. "Jews and the Ambivalences of Civil Society in Germany, 1800–1933: Assessment and Reassessment," in: *The Journal of Modern History*. 77 (4), 2005, pp.1024–1047.
Vannini, Phillip, and J. Patrick Williams (eds.). *Authenticity in Culture, Self, and Society*. London/New York: Routledge, 2009.
Verlaine, Paul. *Jadis et Naguère*. Paris: Léon Vanier, 1891.
Vertovec, Steven, and Susanne Wessendorf. *The Multiculturalism Backlash. European discourses, policies and practices*. New York: Routledge, 2010.
Vlasta, Sandra. *Contemporary Migration Literature in German and English: A Comparative Study*. Leiden/Boston: Brill/Rodopi, 2015.
Volkov, Shulamit. *Das jüdische Projekt der Moderne. Zehn Essays*. Munich: C.H. Beck, 2001.
——. *Die Juden in Deutschland 1780–1918*. München: Oldenbourg, 2000.
——. "Antisemitismus und Antifeminismus: Soziale Norm oder kultureller Code," in: Volkov, Shulamit (ed.). *Das jüdische Projekt der Moderne. Zehn Essays*. Munich: C.H. Beck, 2001, pp. 62–81.
——. "Die Erfindung einer Tradition. Zur Entstehung des modernen Judentums in Deutschland," in: Volkov, Shulamit. *Das jüdische Projekt der Moderne. Zehn Essays*. Munich: C.H. Beck, 2001, pp. 118–137.
——. "The Dynamics of Dissimilation: *Ostjuden* and German Jews," in: Reinharz, Jehuda, and Walter Schatzberg (eds.). *The Jewish Response to German Culture: From the Enlightenment to the Second World War*. Hanover: University Press of New England, 1985, pp. 195–211.
Voß, Torsten. *Körper, Uniformen und Offiziere. Soldatische Männlichkeiten in der Literatur von Grimmelshausen und J.M.R. Lenz bis Ernst Jünger und Hermann Broch*. Bielefeld: transcript Verlag, 2016.
——. "Kakanische Repräsentanten des melancholischen Untergangs. Offiziere, soldatische Zivilisten, Ikonen und maskulin aufgeladene Dingsymbole in Joseph Roths ‚Radetzkymarsch' (1932) und Alexander Lernet-Holenias ‚Die Standarte' (1934)," in: *Studia Austriaca* XXII. 2014, pp. 139–160.
Waldenfels, Bernhard. *Topographie des Fremden. Studien zur Phänomenologie des Fremden*. Frankfurt am Main: Suhrkamp, 1997.
Weber, Angela. *Im Spiegel der Migrationen. Transkulturelles Erzählen und Sprachpolitik bei Emine Sevgi Özdamar*. Bielefeld: transcript Verlag, 2009.
Weber, Beverly. "Cloth on her Head, Constitution in Hand. Germany's Headscarf Debates and the Cultural Politics of Difference," in: *German Politics and Society*. 22 (3), 2004, pp. 33–64.

Weigel, Sigrid. "Die Phantome der Kulturnation," in: Bartmann, Christoph, Carola Dürr, and Hans-Georg Knopp (eds.). *Wiedervorlage: Nationalkultur. Variationen über ein neuralgisches Thema.* Göttingen: Steidl Verlag, 2010, pp. 79–88.

———. "Flucht ins Erbe. Alle wollen die 'Kulturnation'—warum?," in: *Süddeutsche Zeitung.* 1 February 2008, s.p.

———. "Zur Weiblichkeit imaginärer Städte. Eine Forschungsskizze," in: Fuchs, Gotthard et al. (eds.). *Mythos Metropole.* Frankfurt am Main: Suhrkamp, 1995, pp. 35–45.

Weiss, Robert O. (ed.). *Aphorismen und Betrachtungen II: Der Geist im Wort und der Geist in der Tat.* Frankfurt am Main: Fischer Taschenbuch, 1993.

Welsch, Wolfgang. "Auf dem Weg zu transkulturellen Gesellschaften," in: Allolio-Näcke, Lars, Britta Kalscheuer, and Arne Manzeschke (eds.). *Differenzen anders denken. Bausteine zu einer Kulturtheorie der Transdifferenz.* Frankfurt am Main/New York, 2005, pp. 314–341.

Westwood, Salle, and John Williams (eds.). *Imagining Cities: Script, Sign, Memory.* New York: Routledge, 1997.

Wilde, Oscar. *De Profundis.* London: Methuen, 1915.

Willemsen, Roger. "Fahrtwind beim Umblättern," in: *Der Spiegel.* 52, 1992.

Williams, David. *Writing Postcommunism. Towards a Literature of the East European Ruins.* New York: Palgrave Macmillan, 2013.

Wirth-Nesher, Hana (ed.). *What is Jewish Literature?* Philadelphia: Jewish Publication Society, 1994.

Wistrich, Robert S. *The Jews of Vienna in the Age of Franz Joseph.* Oxford University Press, 1989.

Wolfenstein, Alfred. *Jüdisches Wesen und neue Dichtung.* Berlin, 1922.

Wörsching, Marscha. "Die rückwärtsgewandte Utopie. Sozialpsychologische Anmerkungen zu Joseph Roths Roman 'Radetzkymarsch'," in: Arnold, Heinz Ludwig (ed.). *Joseph Roth.* München: Edition Text u. Kritik, 1982, pp.136–146.

Wulf, Christoph. "Perfecting the Individual: Wilhelm von Humboldt's concept of anthropology, Bildung, and mimesis," in: *Educational Philosophy and Theory.* 35 (2), 2003, pp. 241–249.

Wulff, Christian. "Vielfalt schätzen, Zusammenhalt fördern. Rede zum 20. Jahrestag der Deutschen Einheit." 3 October, 2010: http://www.bundespraesident.de/SharedDocs/Reden/DE/Christian-Wulff/Reden/2010/10/20101003_Rede.html [March 2017].

Yates, W.E. *Schnitzler, Hofmannsthal and the Austrian Theatre.* London/New Haven, 1992.

Yeo, Siew Lian. "'Entweder oder': Dualism in Schnitzler's *Fräulein Else*," in: *Modern Austrian Literature.* 32.2, 1999, pp. 15–26.

Yildiz, Erol, and Birgit Mattausch-Yildiz. "Kultur der Urbanität. Stadt und Migration," in: *kulturrisse. Zeitschrift für radikaldemokratische Kulturpolitik.* February 2011, s.p.

Yildiz, Yasemin. *Beyond the Mother Tongue. The Postmonolingual Condition.* New York: Fordham University Press, 2011.

Zaimoglu, Feridun. *Abschaum—Die wahre Geschichte von Ertan Ongun.* Berlin: Rotbuch, 2003.

———. *Kanak Sprak. 24 Mißtöne vom Rande der Gesellschaft*. Berlin: Rotbuch, 1995/2004.
———. *Koppstoff. Kanaka Sprak vom Rande der Gesellschaft*. Berlin:Rotbuch, 2000.
———. *Liebesbrand*. Cologne: Kiepenheuer & Witsch, 2008/2010.
———. "Es tobt in Deutschland ein Kulturkampf," in: Sezgin, Hilal (ed.). *Manifest der Vielen, Deutschland erfindet sich neu*. Berlin, Blumenbar Verlag, 2011, pp. 11–15.
Zaimoglu, Feridun, and Julia Abel. "Migrationsliteratur ist ein toter Kadaver. Ein Gespräch," in: Arnold, Heinz Ludwig (ed.). *Text + Kritik. Zeitschrift für Literatur*. Sonderband Literatur und Migration. 9, 2006, pp. 159–166.
Ziolkowski, Saskia Elizabeth. "The Ends of an Empire: Pier Antonio Quarantotti Gambini's *Il cavallo Tripoli* and Joseph Roth's *Radetzkymarsch*," in: *Comparative Literature Studies*. 52, 2015, p. 349–378.
Žižek, Slavoj. *Violence*. London: Profile Books, 2008.
———, "Multiculturalism, Or, the Cultural Logic of Multinational Capitalism," in: *New Left Review*. 225, 1997, pp. 28–51.
Zweig, Arnold. *Das ostjüdische Antlitz*. Berlin: Welt-Verlag, 1920.
Zweig, Stefan. *Die Welt von Gestern. Erinnerungen eines Europäers*. Frankfurt am Main: S. Fischer Verlag, 1942/2012.
———. *The World of Yesterday*. Translated by Benjamin W. Huebsch and Helmut Ripperger. Plunkett Lake Press, 1943/2011.
———. "Der Roman 'Hiob' von Joseph Roth," in: Zweig, Stefan. *Begegnungen mit Büchern: Aufsätze und Einleitungen aus den Jahren 1902–1939*. Edited by Knut Beck. Frankfurt am Main: Fischer Taschenbuch Verlag, 1983.

www.ingramcontent.com/pod-product-compliance
Ingram Content Group UK Ltd.
Pitfield, Milton Keynes, MK11 3LW, UK
UKHW021847140426
5217IPUK00022B/1631